Oracle Press™

OCA Oracle Database 11g: SQL Fundamentals I

Exam Guide (Exam 1Z0-051)

ABOUT THE AUTHORS

John Watson (Oxford, UK) works for BPLC Management Consultants, teaching and consulting throughout Europe and Africa. He was with Oracle University for several years in South Africa, and before that worked for a number of companies, government departments, and NGOs in England and Europe. He is OCP qualified in both database and Application Server administration. John is the author of several books and numerous articles on technology and has 25 years of experience in IT.

Roopesh Ramklass (South Africa), OCP, is an independent Oracle specialist with over 10 years of experience in a wide variety of IT environments. These include software design and development, systems analysis, courseware development, and lecturing. He has worked for Oracle Support and taught at Oracle University in South Africa for several years. Roopesh is experienced in managing and executing IT development projects, including infrastructure systems provisioning, software development, and systems integration.

About the Technical Editor

Bruce Swart (South Africa) works for 2Cana Solutions and has over 14 years of experience in IT. Whilst maintaining a keen interest for teaching others, he has performed several roles including developer, analyst, team leader, administrator, project manager, consultant, and lecturer. He is OCP qualified in both database and developer roles. He has taught at Oracle University in South Africa for several years and has also spoken at numerous local Oracle User Group conferences. His passion is helping others achieve greatness.

Oracle Press™

OCA Oracle Database 11g: SQL Fundamentals 1

Exam Guide (Exam 1Z0-051)

John Watson
Roopesh Ramklass

New York   Chicago   San Francisco   Lisbon   London   Madrid
Mexico City   Milan   New Delhi   San Juan   Seoul   Singapore   Sydney   Toronto

The McGraw·Hill Companies

Library of Congress Cataloging-in-Publication Data

Watson, John.
   Oca oracle database 11g : sql fundamentals i exam guide (exam 1z0-051)/
John Watson, Roopesh Ramklass.
      p. cm.
   ISBN 978-0-07-159786-9 (alk. paper)
   1. Oracle (Computer file)—Examinations.   2. Electronic data
processing personnel—Certification—Study guides. I. Ramklass,
Roopesh. II. Title.
   QA76.3.W3566 2008
   005.75'65—dc22

                                                        2008018686

McGraw-Hill books are available at special quantity discounts to use as premiums and sales promotions, or for use in corporate training programs. To contact a special sales representative, please visit the Contact Us page at www.mhprofessional.com.

OCA Oracle Database 11g: SQL Fundamentals I Exam Guide (Exam 1Z0-051)

1 2 3 4 5 6 7 8 9 0   FGR FGR   0 1 9 8

ISBN: Book p/n 978-0-07-159788-3 and CD p/n 978-0-07-159789-0
of set 978-0-07-159786-9

MHID: Book p/n 0-07-159788-3 and CD p/n 0-07-159789-1
of set 0-07-159786-7

Sponsoring Editor Timothy Green	**Acquisitions Coordinator** Jenni Housh	**Indexer** Kevin Broccoli	**Illustration** International Typesetting and Composition
Editorial Supervisor Jody McKenzie	**Technical Editor** Bruce Swart	**Production Supervisor** George Anderson	**Art Director, Cover** Jeff Weeks
Project Manager Madhu Bhardwaj, International Typesetting and Composition	**Copy Editor** Sally Engelfried **Proofreader** Pam Simonic	**Composition** International Typesetting and Composition	**Cover Designer** Patti Lee

With thanks to Silvia for making life worth living.
—John

Ameetha, you have been wonderfully supportive and I want to
thank you for every moment that you share with me.
—Roopesh

CONTENTS AT A GLANCE

CONTENTS

7 Displaying Data from Multiple Tables 309

INTRODUCTION

There is an ever-increasing demand for staff with IT industry certification. The benefits to employers are significant—they can be certain that staff have a certain level of competence—and the benefits to the individuals, in terms of demand for their services, are equally great. Many employers are now requiring technical staff to have certifications, and many IT purchasers will not buy from firms that do not have certified staff. The Oracle certifications are among the most sought after. But apart from rewards in a business sense, knowing that you are among a relatively small pool of elite Oracle professionals and that you have proved your competence is a personal reward well worth attaining.

There are several Oracle certification *tracks*—this book is concerned with the Oracle Database Administration certification track, specifically for release 11g of the database. There are three levels of DBA certification: Certified Associate (OCA), Certified Professional (OCP), and Certified Master (OCM). The OCA qualification is based on two examinations, the first of which is covered in this book. The OCP qualification requires passing a third examination. These examinations can be taken at any Prometric Center and consist of 60 to 70 questions to be completed in 90 minutes. The OCM qualification requires completing a further two-day evaluation at an Oracle testing center, involving simulations of complex environments and use of advanced techniques.

The exam content is also likely to be the starting point if you intend to study for the Oracle PL/SQL and Oracle Forms Developer track, though (as of the time of writing) this is at release 10g with no announcement of an 11g release.

To prepare for the first OCA examination, you can attend an Oracle University instructor-led training course, you can study Oracle University online learning material, or you can read this book. In all cases, you should also refer to the Oracle Documentation Library for details on syntax. This book will be a valuable addition to other study methods, but it is also sufficient by itself. It has been designed with the examination objectives in mind, though it also includes a great deal of information that will be useful to you in the course of your work. For readers working in development, the subject matter of this book is also the starting point for studying Oracle Corporation's development tools: SQL, PL/SQL, and the Internet application development kits shipped with the Oracle Application Server.

However, it is not enough to buy the book, place it under your pillow, and assume that knowledge will permeate the brain by a process of osmosis: you must read it thoroughly, work through the exercises and sample questions, and experiment further with various commands. As you become more familiar with the Oracle environment, you will realize that there is one golden rule:

When in doubt, try it out.

In a multitude of cases, you will find that a simple test that takes a couple of minutes can save hours of speculation and poring through manuals. If anything is ever unclear, construct an example and see what happens. This book was developed using Windows and Linux, but to carry out the exercises and your further investigations you can use any platform that is supported for Oracle.

Your initiation into the magical world of Oracle database administration is about to begin. This is a subject you can study and enjoy for the rest of your life.

In This Book

This book is organized to serve as an in-depth review for the OCA Oracle Database 11g: SQL Fundamentals I Exam for Oracle professionals. Each chapter covers a major aspect of the exam; all the OCA official certification objectives are carefully covered in the book.

On the CD

The CD-ROM contains the entire contents of the book in electronic form, as well as a practice test that simulates the real Oracle Database 11g OCA certification test. For more information on the CD-ROM, please see the appendix.

Exam Readiness Checklist

At the end of this introduction, you will find an Exam Readiness Checklist. This table is the official exam objectives. The checklist also allows you to gauge your level of expertise on each objective at the outset of your studies. This should allow you to check your progress and make sure you spend the time you need on more difficult or unfamiliar sections. Each objective is exactly as Oracle Corporation presents it, including the chapter and page reference.

In Every Chapter

This book includes a set of chapter components that call your attention to important items, reinforce important points, and provide helpful exam-taking hints. Take a look at what you'll find in every chapter:

■ **Exam Watch** notes call attention to information about the exam, as well as potential pitfalls.

e x a m

w a t c h The redo log stream includes all changes: those applied to data segments and to undo segments, for both committed and uncommitted transactions.

■ **Exercises** are interspersed throughout the chapters, and they allow you to get the hands-on experience you need in order to pass the exams. They help you master skills that are likely to be an area of focus on the exam. Don't just read through the exercises; they are hands-on practice that you should be comfortable completing. Learning by doing is an effective way to increase your competency with a product.

on the
job

■ **On the Job** notes describe the issues that come up most often in real-world settings. They provide a valuable perspective on certification- and product-related topics. They point out common mistakes and address questions that have arisen from on-the-job discussions and experience.

■ **Inside the Exam** sections toward the end of each chapter are designed to anticipate what the exam will emphasize. These are pointers regarding key topics to focus on based on the authors' experiences of sitting through many production and beta examinations and having been on the Oracle internal group that validates examination questions.

■ The **Certification Summary** is a succinct review of the chapter and a restatement of salient points regarding the exam.

✓■ The **Two-Minute Drill** at the end of every chapter is a checklist of the main points of the chapter. You can use it for a quick, last-minute review before the test.

Q&A ■ The **Self Test** offers questions similar to those found on the certification exam. The answers to these questions, as well as explanations of the answers, can be found at the end of each chapter. By taking the Self Test after completing each chapter, you'll reinforce what you've learned from that chapter, while becoming familiar with the structure of the exam questions.

■ The **Lab Questions** at the end of the Self Test sections offer a unique and challenging question format that, in order to answer correctly, require the reader to understand multiple chapter concepts. These questions are more complex and more comprehensive than the other questions, as they test your ability to take all the knowledge you have gained from reading the chapter and apply it to complicated, real-world situations.

Some Pointers

Once you've finished reading this book, set aside some time to do a thorough review. You might want to return to the book several times and make use of all the methods it offers for reviewing the material before sitting the examination.

■ **Reread all the Two-Minute Drills or have someone quiz you.** You also can use the drills as a way to do a quick cram before the exam.

■ **Reread all the Exam Watch notes.** Remember that these notes are based on the OCA exam. They will draw your attention to what you should expect—and what you should be on the lookout for.

■ **Retake the Self Tests.** It is a good idea to take the Self Test right after you've read the chapter because the questions help reinforce what you've just learned, and then take them all again at the end. In the examination, the questions do not come conveniently grouped by subject: you will have to be prepared to jump from one topic to another.

■ **Complete the Exercises.** Did you do the chapter Exercises and the Lab Questions when you read each chapter? If not, do them! These exercises are designed to cover exam topics, and there's no better way to get to know this material than by practicing. Be sure you understand why you are performing each step in each exercise. If there is something you are not completely clear about, reread that section in the chapter.

Test Structure

The OCA examinations are multiple choice questions, but they are not necessarily questions where you must pick one answer. Some will ask for two or three answers, some will say something on the lines of "choose all correct answers." Most questions are text based, but some will have an *exhibit*, which is a diagram or perhaps a screen shot that illustrates the question.

Read all the questions very carefully. In some cases, when the question asks for one answer, you may think they are all wrong or that several are correct. Often, when you reread the question carefully, you will see what the examiners are looking for.

You will have an average of only a minute or two for each question. Go through them all, fast, answering the ones you know and marking the ones you don't know for review. Then go through the marked questions again. That will take up most of the time. If there are some questions you really don't know, guess the answer: there are no marks deducted for incorrect answers.

How to Prepare for the Exam

Study and practice! Go through each chapter of the book, doing all the exercises and trying out further experiments. Make use of other resources if anything is still not clear: the Oracle Documentation Library (a free download from Oracle Corporation's website) is essential reading. If you have the opportunity to attend an Oracle University course or have access to the Oracle University Self-paced Online courses, these may also be of value.

The example questions at the end of each chapter and on the CD are not copies of real OCA questions (because that would be fraudulent), but they are realistic examples of the types of question and the format of questions with which you will be faced. They cover all the examined material. The day before you sit the exam, it makes sense to go through them all, looking up any for which you do not know the answer.

This book is not intended to be just an exam crammer: it is intended to teach you how to develop applications with SQL. If you know how to do that, you will pass the exam. Do not memorize answers to questions—learn the techniques, principles, and syntax that will let you work out the answers to any question.

Exam 1Z0-051

1

Oracle Server Technologies and the Relational Paradigm

T he content of this chapter is not directly tested by the OCP examination, but it is vital to understanding the purpose of SQL and what it is meant to achieve. This is considered to be prerequisite knowledge that every student should have, beginning with an appreciation of how the Oracle server technologies fit together and the relative position of each product.

The Oracle server technologies product set is more than a database. There is also the Oracle Application Server and the Oracle Enterprise Manager. Taken together, these are the server technologies that make up the Grid. Grid computing is an emerging environment for managing the complete IT environment and providing resources to users on demand.

The relational paradigm for database information management was first formalized in the late '60s and has been continually refined since. A *paradigm* is a set of standards agreed upon by all those involved that specifies how problems should be understood and addressed. There are other paradigms within the data processing world. The Oracle database is an implementation of a Relational Database Management System (RDBMS) that conforms to the relational paradigm, but it then goes beyond it to include some aspects of other paradigms such as hierarchical and object-oriented models.

Structured Query Language (SQL, pronounced "sequel") is an international standard for managing data stored in relational databases. Oracle Database 11g offers an implementation of SQL that is generally compliant with the current standard, which is SQL-2003. Full details of the compliancy are in Appendix B of the SQL Language Reference, which is part of the Oracle Database Documentation Library. As a rule, compliancy can be assumed.

Throughout this book, two tools are used extensively for exercises: SQL*Plus and SQL Developer. These are tools that developers use every day in their work. The exercises and many of the examples are based on two demonstration sets of data, known as the HR and OE schemas. There are instructions on how to launch the tools and create the demonstration schemas, though you may need assistance from your local database administrator to get started.

This chapter consists of summarized descriptions of the Oracle Server Technologies; the concepts behind the relational paradigm and normalizing of data into relational structures; the SQL language; the client tools; and the demonstration schemas.

CERTIFICATION OBJECTIVE 1.01

Position the Server Technologies

There is a family of products that makes up the Oracle server technologies:

- The Oracle Database
- The Oracle Application Server
- The Oracle Enterprise Manager
- Various application development tools and languages

These products each have a position in the Oracle product set. The database is the repository for data and the engine that manages access to it. The Oracle Application Server runs software on behalf of end users: it generates the user interface in the form of windows displayed in users' browsers and submits calls for data retrieval and modification to the database for execution. The Oracle Enterprise Manager is a comprehensive administration tool for monitoring, managing, and tuning the Oracle processes and also (through plug-ins) third-party products. Lastly, there are tools and languages for developing applications; either applications that run on end users' machines in the client-server model, or applications that run centrally on application servers.

The combination of the server technologies and the development tools make up a platform for application development and delivery that enables the Grid. The Grid is an approach to the delivery of IT services that maximizes the cost efficiency of the whole environment by delivering computing power from a pool of available resources to wherever it is needed, on demand.

The Oracle Server Architecture

An Oracle database is a set of files on disk. It exists until these files are deliberately deleted. There are no practical limits to the size and number of these files, and therefore no practical limits to the size of a database. Access to the database is through the Oracle instance. The instance is a set of processes and memory structures: it exists on the CPU(s) and in the memory of the server node, and this existence is temporary. An instance can be started and stopped. Users of the database establish sessions against the instance, and the instance then manages all access to the database. It is absolutely impossible in the Oracle environment for any user to have direct contact with the database. An Oracle instance with an Oracle database makes up an Oracle server.

The processing model implemented by the Oracle server is that of client-server processing, often referred to as *two-tier*. In the client-server model, the generation of the user interface and much of the application logic is separated from the management of the data. For an application developed using SQL (as all relational database applications will be), this means that the client tier generates the SQL commands, and the server tier executes them. This is the basic client-server split, with (as a general rule) a local area network between the two sides. The network communications protocol used between the user process and the server process is Oracle's proprietary protocol, Oracle Net.

The client tier consists of two components: the users and the user processes. The server tier has three components: the server processes that execute the SQL, the instance, and the database itself. Each user interacts with a user process. Each user process interacts with a server process, usually across a local area network. The server processes interact with the instance, and the instance with the database. Figure 1-1 shows this relationship diagrammatically. A *session* is a user process in communication with a server process. There will usually be one user process per user and one server process per user process. The user and server processes that make up sessions are launched on demand by users and terminated when no longer required; this is the log-on and log-off cycle. The instance processes and memory structures are launched by the database administrator and persist until the administrator deliberately terminates them; this is the database start-up and shut-down cycle.

The user process can be any client-side software that is capable of connecting to an Oracle server process. Throughout this book, two user processes will be used extensively: SQL*Plus and SQL Developer. These are simple processes provided by Oracle for establishing sessions against an Oracle server and issuing ad hoc SQL.

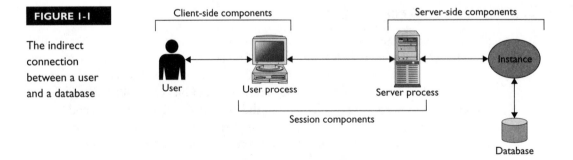

FIGURE 1-1

The indirect connection between a user and a database

A widely used alternative is TOAD (the Tool for Application Developers) from Quest Software, though this is licensed software and before using it one must always ensure that the license is legal. End-user applications will need to be written with something more sophisticated than these tools, something capable of managing windows, menus, proper onscreen dialogs, and so on. Such an application could be written with the Oracle Developer Suite products; with Microsoft Access linked to the Oracle ODBC drivers; with any third-generation language (such as C or Java) for which Oracle has provided a library of function calls that will let it interact with the server; or with any number of Oracle-compatible third-party tools. What the user process actually is does not matter to the Oracle server at all. When an end user fills in a form and clicks a Submit button, the user process will be generating an INSERT statement (detailed in Chapter 11) and sending it to a server process for execution against the instance and the database. As far as the server is concerned, the INSERT statement might just as well have been typed into SQL*Plus as what is known as ad hoc SQL.

Never forget that all communication with an Oracle server follows this client-server model. The separation of user code from server code dates back to the earliest releases of the database and is unavoidable. Even if the user process is running on the same machine as the server (as is the case if, for example, one is running a database on one's own laptop PC for development or training purposes), the client-server split is still enforced, and network protocols are still used for the communications between the two processes. Applications running in an application server environment (described in the next section) also follow the client-server model for their database access.

The simplest form of the database server is one instance connected to one database, but in a more complex environment one database can be opened by many instances. This is known as a RAC (Real Application Cluster). RAC can bring many potential benefits, which may include scalability, performance, and zero downtime. The ability to add dynamically more instances running on more nodes to a database is a major part of the database's contribution to the Grid.

The Oracle Application Server

With the emergence of the Web as the standard communications platform for delivering applications to end users has come the need for application servers. An application server replaces the client-side software traditionally installed on end-user terminals; it runs applications centrally, presenting them to users in windows displayed locally in web browsers. The applications make use of data stored in one or more database servers.

The Oracle Application Server is a platform for developing, deploying, and managing *web applications*. A web application can be defined as any application with which users communicate with HTTP. Web applications usually run in at least three tiers: a database tier manages access to the data, the client tier (often implemented as a web browser) handles the local window management for communications with the users, and an application tier in the middle executes the program logic that generates the user interface and the SQL calls to the database.

Web applications can be developed with a number of technologies, predominant among which is Java. Applications written in Java should conform to the J2EE (Java 2 Enterprise Edition) standard, which defines how such applications should be packaged and deployed. J2EE and related standards are controlled by Sun Microsystems and accepted by virtually all software developers. Oracle Application Server is a J2EE-compliant application server. Oracle's implementation of the standards allows for automatic load balancing and fault tolerance across multiple application servers on multiple machines though J2EE clustering. Clustering virtualizes the provision of the application service; users ask for an application that might be available from a number of locations, and the cluster works out from where any one session or request can best be serviced. If one location fails, others will take up the load, and more resources can be made available to an application as necessary. The ability to separate the request for a service from the location of its provision and to add or remove J2EE servers from a cluster dynamically is a major part of the Oracle Application Server's contribution to the Grid.

It is important to note that Oracle's commitment to international standards is very strong. Applications running in the Oracle Application Server environment can connect to any database for which there are Java-compliant drivers; it is not necessary to use an Oracle database. Applications developed with the Oracle Application Server toolkits can be deployed to a third-party J2EE-compliant application server.

The simplest processing model of web applications is three tier: a client tier that manages the user interface; a middle tier that generates the interface and issues SQL statements to the data tier; and a data tier that manages the data itself. In the Oracle environment, the client tier will be a browser (such as Mozilla or Microsoft Internet Explorer) that handles local window management, controls the keyboard, and tracks mouse movements. The middle tier will be an Oracle Application Server running the software (probably written in Java) that generates the windows sent to the client tier for display and the SQL statements sent to the data tier for execution. The data tier will be an Oracle server: an instance and a database. In this three-tier environment, there are two types of sessions: end-user sessions from the client tier to the middle tier, and database sessions from the middle tier to the data tier. The end-user sessions will be established with HTTP. The database sessions are client-server sessions consisting of a user process and a server process, as described in the previous section.

It is possible for an application to use a one-for-one mapping of end-user session to database session: each user, from their browser, will establish a session against the application server, and the application server will then establish a session against the database server on the user's behalf. However, this model has been proven to be very inefficient when compared to the *connection pooling* model. With connection pooling, the application server establishes a relatively small number of persistent database sessions and makes them available on demand (queuing requests if necessary) to a relatively large number of end-user sessions against the application server. Figure 1-2 illustrates the three-tier architecture using connection pooling.

From the point of view of the database, it makes no difference whether a SQL statement comes from a client-side process such as SQL*Plus or Microsoft Access or from a pooled session to an application server. In the former case, the user process all happens on one machine; in the latter, the user process has been divided into two tiers: an applications tier that generates the user interface and a client tier that displays it.

Oracle Enterprise Manager

The increasing size and complexity of IT installations makes management a challenging task. This is hardly surprising: no one ever said that managing a powerful environment should necessarily be simple. However, management tools can make the task easier and the management staff more productive.

FIGURE 1-2

The connection pooling model

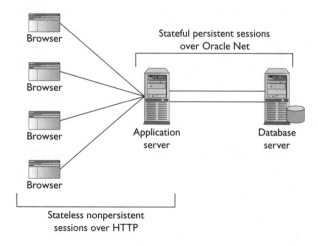

Oracle Enterprise Manager comes in three forms:

- Database Control
- Application Server Control
- Grid Control

Oracle Enterprise Manager Database Control is a graphical tool for managing one database, which may be a RAC clustered database. It consists of a Java process running on the database server machine. Administrators connect to Database Control from a browser, and Database Control then connects to the database server. Database Control has facilities for real-time management and monitoring, running scheduled jobs, and reporting alert conditions interactively and through e-mail.

Oracle Enterprise Manager Application Server Control is a graphical tool for managing one application server instance or a group of instances. The grouping technology is dependent on the version. Up to Oracle Application Server 10*g* release 2, multiple application servers were managed as a "farm," with a metadata repository (typically residing in an Oracle database) as the central management point. From release 3 onward, the technology is based on J2EE clustering, which is not proprietary to Oracle.

Oracle Enterprise Manager Grid Control globalizes the management environment. A management repository (residing in an Oracle database) and one or more management servers manage the complete environment: all the databases and application servers, wherever they may be. Grid Control can also manage the nodes, or machines, on which the servers run, as well as (through plug-ins) a wide range of third-party products. Each managed node runs an agent process, which is responsible for monitoring the managed target on the node: executing jobs against them and reporting status, activity levels, and alert conditions back to the management server(s).

Grid Control gives a holistic view of the environment and, if well configured, makes administration staff far more productive than they are without it. It becomes possible for one administrator to manage effectively hundreds of targets.

Grid Computing

Critical to the concept of Grid computing is *virtualization.* This means that at all levels there is a layer of abstraction between what is requested and what is provided. End users ask for an application service and let the Grid work out which clustered J2EE application server can best provide it. Application servers ask for a database service and let the Grid work out from which RAC node the data can best be served. Within the Grid there is a mapping of possible services to available service providers, and there are algorithms for assigning the workload and resources appropriately.

The result is that end users have neither the need nor the capacity to know from where their computing resources are actually being provided. The analogy often drawn is with delivery of domestic electricity: it is supplied on demand, and the home owner has no way of telling which power station is currently supplying him.

The Grid is not exclusive to Oracle. At the physical level, some operating system and hardware vendors are providing Grid-like capabilities. These include the ability to partition servers into virtual machines and dynamically add or remove CPU(s) and RAM from the virtual machines according to demand. This is conceptually similar to Oracle's approach of dynamically assigning application server and database server resources to logical services. There is no reason why the two approaches cannot be combined. Both are working toward the same goal and can work together. The result should be an environment where adequate resources are always available on demand, without facing the issues of excess capacity at some times and under-performance at others. It should also be possible to design a Grid environment with no single point of failure, thus achieving the goal of 100 percent uptime that is being demanded by many users.

The SQL application developer need not know how the Grid has been implemented. The SQL will be invoked from an application server and executed by an instance against a database: the Grid will take care of making sure that at any moment pools of application servers and instances sized appropriately for the current workload are available.

EXERCISE 1-1

Investigate Your Database and Application Environment

This is a paper-based exercise, with no specific solution.

Attempt to identify the user processes, application servers, and database servers used in your environment. Try to work out where the SQL is being generated and where it is being executed. Bear in mind that usually the user processes used by end users will be graphical and will frequently go through application servers; the database administration and development staff will often prefer to use client-server tools that connect to the database server directly.

Development Tools and Languages

The Oracle server technologies include various facilities for developing applications, some existing within the database, others external to it.

Within the database, it is possible to use three languages. The one that is unavoidable, and the subject of this book, is SQL. SQL is used for data access, but it cannot be used for developing complete applications. It has no real facilities for developing user interfaces, and it also lacks the procedural structures needed for manipulating rows individually. The other two languages available within the database fill these gaps. They are PL/SQL and Java. PL/SQL is a third-generation language (3GL) proprietary to Oracle. It has the usual procedural constructs (such as if-then-else and looping) and facilities for user interface design. In the PL/SQL code, one can embed calls to SQL. Thus, a PL/SQL application might use SQL to retrieve one or more rows from the database, then perform various actions based on their content, and then issue more SQL to write rows back to the database. Java offers a similar capability to embed SQL calls within the Java code. This is industry standard technology: any Java programmer should be able write code that will work with an Oracle database (or indeed with any other Java-compliant database.)

Other languages are available for developing client-server applications that run externally to the database. The most commonly used are C and Java, but it is possible to use most of the mainstream 3GLs. For all these languages, Oracle Corporation provides OCI (Oracle Call Interface) libraries that let code written in these languages establish sessions against an Oracle database and invoke SQL commands.

Many organizations will not want to use a 3GL to develop database applications. Oracle Corporation provides rapid application development tools as part of the Oracle Developer Suite, and there are many third-party products. These can make programmers far more productive than if they were working with a 3GL. Like the languages, all these application development tools end up doing the same thing: constructing SQL statements that are sent to the database server for execution.

on the
❶ o b   *All developers and administrators working in the Oracle environment must know PL/SQL. C and Java are not necessary, unless the project specifically uses them.*

CERTIFICATION OBJECTIVE 1.02

Understand Relational Structures

Critical to an understanding of SQL is an understanding of the relational paradigm and the ability to *normalize* data into relational structures. Normalization is the work of systems analysts, as they model business data into a form suitable for storing in relational tables. It is a science that can be studied for years, and there are many schools of thought that have developed their own methods and notations.

Rows and Tables

The relational paradigm models data as two-dimensional tables. A table consists of a number of rows, each consisting of a set of columns. Within a table, all the rows have the same column structure, though it is possible that in some rows some columns may have nothing in them. An example of a table would be a list of one's employees, each employee being represented by one row. The columns might be employee number, name, and a code for the department in which the employee works. Any employees not currently assigned to a department would have that column blank. Another table could represent the departments: one row per department, with columns for the department's code and the department's name.

A note on terminology: what Oracle refers to as a *table* may also be called a *relation* or an *entity*. Rows are sometimes called *records* or *tuples*, and *columns* may be called *attributes* or *fields*. The number of "rows in the table" is the "cardinality of the tuples."

Relational tables conform to certain rules that constrain and define the data. At the column level, each column must be of a certain data type, such as numeric, date-time, or character. The character data type is the most general, in that it can accept any type of data. At the row level, usually each row must have some uniquely identifying characteristic: this could be the value of one column, such as the employee number and department number in the preceding examples, which cannot be repeated in different rows. There may also be rules that define links between the tables, such as a rule that every employee must be assigned a department code that can be matched to a row in the departments table. Following are examples of the tabulated data definitions:

Departments table:

Column Name	Description	Data Type	Length
DEPTNO	Department number	Numeric	2
DNAME	Department name	Character	14

Employees table:

Column Name	Description	Data Type	Length
EMPNO	Employee number	Numeric	4
ENAME	Employee name	Character	10
DEPTNO	Department number	Numeric	2

The tables could contain these rows:
Departments:

DEPTNO	DNAME
10	ACCOUNTING
20	RESEARCH
30	SALES
40	OPERATIONS

Employees:

EMPNO	ENAME	DEPTNO
7369	SMITH	20
7499	ALLEN	30
7521	WARD	30
7566	JONES	20
7654	MARTIN	30
7698	BLAKE	30
7782	CLARK	10
7788	SCOTT	20

Looking at the tables, the two-dimensional structure is clear. Each row is of fixed length, each column is of fixed length (padded with spaces when necessary), and the rows are delimited with a new line. The rows have been stored in code order, but this is a matter of chance, not design: relational tables do not impose any particular ordering on their rows. Department number 10 has one employee, and department number 40 has none. Changes to data are usually very efficient with the relational model. New employees can be appended to the employees table, or they can be moved from one department to another simply by changing the DEPTNO value in their row.

Consider an alternative structure, where the data is stored according to the hierarchical paradigm. The hierarchical model was developed before the relational model, for technology reasons. In the early days of computing, storage devices lacked the capability for maintaining the many separate files that were needed for the many relational tables. Note that this problem is avoided in the Oracle database by abstracting the physical storage (files) from the logical storage (tables): there is no direct connection between tables and files and certainly not a one-to-one mapping. In effect, many tables can be stored in a very few files.

A hierarchical structure stores all related data in one unit. For example, the record for a department would include all that department's employees. The hierarchical paradigm can be very fast and very space efficient. One file access may be all that is needed to retrieve all the data needed to satisfy a query. The employees and departments listed previously could be stored hierarchically as follows:

| 10,ACCOUNTING,7782,CLARK |
| 20,RESEARCH,7369,SMITH,7566,JONES,7788,SCOTT |
| 30,SALES,7499,ALLEN,7521,WARD,7654,MARTIN,7698,BLAKE |
| 40,OPERATIONS |

In this example layout, the rows and columns are of variable length. Columns are delimited with a comma, rows with a new line. Data retrieval is typically very efficient if the query can navigate the hierarchy: if one knows an employee's department, the employee can be found quickly. If one doesn't, the retrieval may be slow. Changes to data can be a problem if the change necessitates movement. For example, to move employee 7566, JONES from RESEARCH to SALES would involve considerable effort on the part of the database because the move has to be implemented as a removal from one line and an insertion into another. Note that in this example, while it is possible to have a department with no employees (the OPERATIONS department) it is absolutely impossible to have an employee without a department: there is nowhere to put him or her. This is excellent if there is a business rule stating that all employees must be in a department but not so good if that is not the case.

The relational paradigm is highly efficient in many respects for many types of data, but it is not appropriate for all applications. As a general rule, a relational analysis should be the first approach taken when modeling a system. Only if it proves inappropriate should one resort to nonrelational structures. Applications where the relational model has proven highly effective include virtually all Online Transaction Processing (OLTP) systems and Decision Support Systems (DSS). The relational paradigm can be demanding in its hardware requirements and in the skill needed to develop applications around it, but if the data fits, it has proved to be the most versatile model. There can be, for example, problems caused by the need to maintain the indexes that maintain the links between tables and the space requirements of maintaining multiple copies of the indexed data in the indexes themselves and in the tables in which the columns reside. Nonetheless, relational design is in most circumstances the optimal model.

A number of software publishers have produced database management systems that conform (with varying degrees of accuracy) to the relational paradigm; Oracle is only one. IBM was perhaps the first company to commit major resources to it, but their product (which later developed into DB2) was not ported to non-IBM platforms for many years. Microsoft's SQL Server is another relational database that has been limited by the platforms on which it runs. Oracle databases, by contrast, have always been ported to every major platform from the first release. It may be this that gave Oracle the edge in the RDBMS market place.

A note on terminology: confusion can arise when discussing relational databases with people used to working with Microsoft products. SQL is a language and SQL Server is a database, but in the Microsoft world, the term SQL is often used to refer to either.

Data Normalization

The process of modeling data into relational tables is known as normalization and can be studied at university level for years. There are commonly said to be three levels of normalization: the first, second, and third normal forms. There are higher levels of normalization: fourth and fifth normal forms are well defined, but any normal data analyst (and certainly any normal human being) will not need to be concerned with them. It is possible for a SQL application to address un-normalized data, but this will usually be inefficient as that is not what the language is designed to do. In most cases, data stored in a relational database and accessed with SQL should be normalized to the third normal form.

SCENARIO & SOLUTION

Your organization is designing a new application. Who should be involved?	Everyone! The project team must involve business analysts (who model the business processes), systems analysts (who model the data), system designers (who decide how to implement the models), developers (you), database administrators, system administrators, and (most importantly) end users.
It is possible that relational structures may not be suitable for a particular application. How can this be determined, and what should be done next? Can Oracle help?	Attempt to normalize the data into two-dimensional tables, linked with one-to-many relationships. If this really cannot be done, consider other paradigms. Oracle may well be able to help. For instance, maps and other geographical data really don't work relationally. Neither does text data (such as word processing documents). But the Spatial and Text database options can be used for these purposes. There is also the possibility of using user-defined objects to store nontabular data.

on the job

There are often several possible normalized models for an application. It is important to use the most appropriate—if the systems analyst gets this wrong, the implications can be serious for performance, storage needs, and development effort.

As an example of normalization, consider an un-normalized table called BOOKS that stores details of books, authors, and publishers, using the ISBN number as the primary key. A *primary key* is the one attribute (or attributes) that can uniquely identify a record. These are two entries:

ISBN	Title	Authors	Publisher
12345	Oracle 11g OCP SQL Fundamentals 1 Exam Guide	John Watson, Roopesh Ramklass	McGraw-Hill, Spear Street, San Francisco, CA 94105
67890	Oracle 11g New Features Exam Guide	Sam Alapati	McGraw-Hill, Spear Street, San Francisco, CA 94105

Storing the data in this table gives rise to several anomalies. First, here is the insertion anomaly: it is impossible to enter details of authors who are not yet published, because there will be no ISBN number under which to store them. Second, a book cannot be deleted without losing the details of the publisher: a deletion anomaly. Third, if a publisher's address changes, it will be necessary to update the rows for every book he has published: an update anomaly. Furthermore, it will be very difficult to identify every book written by one author. The fact that a book may have several authors means that the "author" field must be multivalued, and a search will have to search all the values. Related to this is the problem of having to restructure the table of a book that comes along with more authors than the original design can handle. Also, the storage is very inefficient due to replication of address details across rows, and the possibility of error as this data is repeatedly entered is high. Normalization should solve all these issues.

The first normal form is to remove the repeating groups, in this case, the multiple authors: pull them out into a separate table called AUTHORS. The data structures will now look like the following.

Two rows in the BOOKS table:

ISBN	TITLE	PUBLISHER
12345	Oracle 11g OCP SQL Fundamentals 1 Exam Guide	McGraw-Hill, Spear Street, San Francisco, California
67890	Oracle 11g New Features Exam Guide	McGraw-Hill, Spear Street, San Francisco, California

And three rows in the AUTHOR table:

NAME	ISBN
John Watson	12345
Roopesh Ramklass	12345
Sam Alapati	67890

The one row in the BOOKS table is now linked to two rows in the AUTHORS table. This solves the insertion anomaly (there is no reason not to insert as many unpublished authors as necessary), the retrieval problem of identifying all the books by one author (one can search the AUTHORS table on just one name) and the problem of a fixed maximum number of authors for any one book (simply insert as many or as few AUTHORS as are needed).

This is the first normal form: no repeating groups.

The second normal form removes columns from the table that are not dependent on the primary key. In this example, that is the publisher's address details: these are dependent on the publisher, not the ISBN. The BOOKS table and a new PUBLISHERS table will then look like this:

BOOKS

ISBN	TITLE	PUBLISHER
12345	Oracle 11g OCP SQL Fundamentals 1 Exam Guide	McGraw-Hill
67890	Oracle 11g New Features Exam Guide	McGraw-Hill

PUBLISHERS

PUBLISHER	STREET	CITY	STATE
McGraw-Hill	Spear Street	San Francisco	California

All the books published by one publisher will now point to a single record in PUBLISHERS. This solves the problem of storing the address many times, and also solves the consequent update anomalies and the data consistency errors caused by inaccurate multiple entries.

Third normal form removes all columns that are interdependent. In the PUBLISHERS table, this means the address columns: the street exists in only one city, and the city can be in only one state; one column should do, not three. This could be achieved by adding an address code, pointing to a separate address table:

PUBLISHERS

PUBLISHER	ADDRESS CODE
McGraw-Hill	123

ADDRESSES

ADDRESS CODE	STREET	CITY	STATE
123	Spear Street	San Francisco	California

One characteristic of normalized data that should be emphasized now is the use of primary keys and foreign keys. A *primary key* is the unique identifier of a row in a table, either one column or a concatenation of several columns (known as a *composite* key). Every table should have a primary key defined. This is a requirement of the relational paradigm. Note that the Oracle database deviates from this standard: it is possible to define tables without a primary key—though it is usually not a good idea, and some other RDBMSs do not permit this.

A *foreign key* is a column (or a concatenation of several columns) that can be used to identify a related row in another table. A foreign key in one table will match a primary key in another table. This is the basis of the *many-to-one relationship*. A many-to-one relationship is a connection between two tables, where many rows in one table refer to a single row in another table. This is sometimes called a parent-child relationship: one parent can have many children. In the BOOKS example so far, the keys are as follows:

TABLE	KEYS
BOOKS	Primary key: ISBN Foreign key: Publisher
AUTHORS	Primary key: Name + ISBN Foreign key: ISBN
PUBLISHERS	Primary key: Publisher Foreign key: Address code
ADDRESSES	Primary key: Address code

These keys define relationships such as that one book can have several authors.

There are various standards for documenting normalized data structures, developed by different organizations as structured formal methods. Generally speaking, it really doesn't matter which method one uses as long as everyone reading the documents understands it. Part of the documentation will always include a listing of the attributes that make up each entity (also known as the columns that make up each table) and an entity-relationship diagram representing graphically the foreign to primary key connections. A widely used standard is as follows:

- Primary key columns identified with a hash (#)
- Foreign key columns identified with a back slash (\ )
- Mandatory columns (those that cannot be left empty) with an asterisk (*)
- Optional columns with a lowercase "o"

The BOOKS tables can now be described as follows:

Table BOOKS

#*	ISBN	Primary key, required
o	Title	Optional
*	Publisher	Foreign key, link to the PUBLISHERS table

Table AUTHORS

#*	Name	Together with the ISBN, the primary key
#\o	ISBN	Part of the primary key, and a foreign key to the BOOKS table. Optional, because some authors may not yet be published.

Table PUBLISHERS

#*	Publisher	Primary key
\o	Address code	Foreign key, link to the ADDRESSES table

Table ADDRESSES

#*	Address code	Primary key
o	Street	
o	City	
o	State	

The second necessary part of documenting the normalized data model is the *entity-relationship diagram*. This represents the connections between the tables graphically. There are different standards for these; Figure 1-3 shows the entity-relationship diagram for the BOOKS example using a very simple notation limited to showing the direction of the one-to-many relationships, using what are often called *crow's feet* to indicate which sides of the relationship are the many and the one. It can be seen that one BOOK can have multiple AUTHORS, one PUBLISHER can publish many books. Note that the diagram also states that both AUTHORS and PUBLISHERS have exactly one ADDRESS. More complex notations can be used to show whether the link is required or optional, information which will match that given in the table columns listed previously.

FIGURE 1-3

An entity-relationship diagram

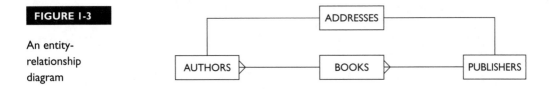

This is a very simple example of normalization, and is not in fact complete. If one author were to write several books, this would require multiple values in the ISBN column of the AUTHORS table. That would be a repeating group, which would have to be removed because repeating groups break the rule for first normal form. A major exercise with data normalization is ensuring that the structures can handle all possibilities.

A table in a real-world application may have hundreds of columns and dozens of foreign keys. The standards for notation vary across organizations—the example given is very basic. Entity-relationship diagrams for applications with hundreds or thousands of entities can be challenging to interpret.

EXERCISE 1-2

Perform an Extended Relational Analysis

This is a paper-based exercise, with no specific solution.

Consider the situation where one author can write many books, and one book can have many authors. This is a many-to-many relationship, which cannot be fit into the relational model. Sketch out data structures that demonstrate the problem, and develop another structure that would solve it. Following is a possible solution.

The un-normalized table of books with many authors could look like this:

BOOKS

| #* | Title |
| * | Authors |

There could be two rows in this table:

Title	Authors
11g SQL Fundamentals Exam Guide	John Watson, Roopesh Ramklass
10g DBA Exam Guide	John Watson, Damir Bersinic

And that of authors could look like this:

AUTHORS

| #* | Name |
| * | Books |

There could be three rows in this table:

Name	Books
John Watson	11g SQL Fundamentals Exam Guide, 10g DBA Exam Guide
Roopesh Ramklass	11g SQL Fundamentals Exam Guide
Damir Bersinic	10g DBA Exam Guide

This many-to-many relationship needs to be resolved into many-to-one relationships by taking the repeating groups out of the two tables and storing them in a separate books-per-author table. It will also become necessary to introduce some codes, such as ISBNs to identify books and social security numbers to identify authors. This is a possible normalized structure:

BOOKS

| #* | ISBN |
| o | Title |

AUTHORS

| #* | SSNO |
| o | Name |

BOOKAUTHORS

| #* | ISBN | Part of the primary key and a foreign key to BOOKS |
| #* | SSNO | Part of the primary key and a foreign key to AUTHORS |

The rows in these normalized tables would be as follows:

BOOKS

ISBN	Title
12345	11g SQL Fundamentals Exam Guide
67890	DBA Exam Guide

AUTHORS

SSNO	Name
11111	John Watson
22222	Damir Bersinic
33333	Roopesh Ramklass

BOOKAUTHORS

ISBN	SSNO
12345	11111
12345	22222
67890	11111
67890	33333

Figure 1-4 shows the entity-relationship diagram for the original un-normalized structure, followed by the normalized structure.

As a further exercise, consider the possibility that one publisher could have offices at several addresses, and one address could have offices for several companies. Authors will also have addresses, and this connection too needs to be defined. These enhancements can be added to the example worked through previously.

FIGURE 1-4

Un-normalized and normalized data models

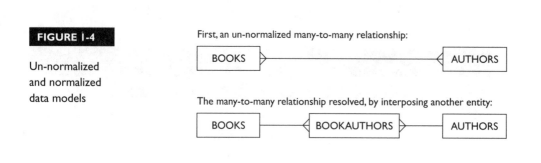

First, an un-normalized many-to-many relationship:

The many-to-many relationship resolved, by interposing another entity:

CERTIFICATION OBJECTIVE 1.03

Summarize the SQL Language

SQL is defined, developed, and controlled by international bodies. Oracle Corporation does not have to conform to the SQL standard but chooses to do so. The language itself can be thought as being very simple (there are only 16 commands), but in practice SQL coding can be phenomenally complicated. That is why a whole book is needed to cover the bare fundamentals.

SQL Standards

Structured Query Language (SQL) was first invented by an IBM research group in the '70s, but in fact Oracle Corporation (then trading as Relational Software, Inc.) claims to have beaten IBM to market by a few weeks with the first commercial implementation: Oracle 2, released in 1979. Since then the language has evolved enormously and is no longer driven by any one organization. SQL is now an international standard. It is managed by committees from ISO and ANSI. ISO is the Organisation Internationale de Normalisation, based in Geneva; ANSI is the American National Standards Institute, based in Washington, DC. The two bodies cooperate, and their SQL standards are identical.

Earlier releases of the Oracle database used an implementation of SQL that had some significant deviations from the standard. This was not because Oracle was being deliberately different: it was usually because Oracle implemented features that were ahead of the standard, and when the standard caught up, it used different syntax. An example is the outer join (detailed in Chapter 8), which Oracle implemented long before standard SQL; when standard SQL introduced an outer join, Oracle added support for the new join syntax while retaining support for its own proprietary syntax. Oracle Corporation ensures future compliance by inserting personnel onto the various ISO and ANSI committees and is now assisting with driving the SQL standard forward.

SQL Commands

These are the 16 SQL commands, separated into commonly used groups:

The Data Manipulation Language (DML) commands:

- SELECT
- INSERT
- UPDATE
- DELETE
- MERGE

The Data Definition Language (DDL) commands:

- CREATE
- ALTER
- DROP
- RENAME
- TRUNCATE
- COMMENT

The Data Control Language (DCL) commands:

- GRANT
- REVOKE

The Transaction Control Language (TCL) commands:

- COMMIT
- ROLLBACK
- SAVEPOINT

The first command, SELECT, is the main subject of Chapters 2 through 9. The remaining DML commands are covered in Chapter 10, along with the TCL commands. DDL is detailed in Chapters 11 and 12. DCL, which has to do with security, is only briefly mentioned: it falls more into the domain of the database administrator than the developers.

on the *Job*

According to all the docs, SELECT is a DML statement. In practice, no one includes it when they refer to DML—they talk about it as though it were a language in its own right (it almost is) and use DML to mean only the commands that change data.

A Set-oriented Language

Most 3GLs are procedural languages. Programmers working in procedural languages specify what to do with data, one row at a time. Programmers working in a set-oriented language say what they want to do to a group (a "set") of rows and let the database work out how to do it to however many rows are in the set.

Procedural languages are usually less efficient than set-oriented languages at managing data, as regards both development and execution. A procedural routine for looping through group of rows and updating them one by one will involve many lines of code, where SQL might do the whole operation with one command: programmers' productivity increases. During program execution, procedural code gives the database no options; it must run the code as it has been written. With SQL, the programmer states what he or she wants to do but not how to do it: the database has the freedom to work out how best to carry out the operation. This will usually give better results.

Where SQL fails to provide a complete solution is that it is purely a data access language. Most applications will need procedural constructs, such as flow control: conditional branching and iteration. They will also usually need screen control, user interface facilities, and variables. SQL has none of these. SQL is a set-oriented language capable of nothing other than data access. For application development, one will therefore need a procedural language that can invoke SQL calls. It is therefore necessary for SQL to work with a procedural language.

Consider an application that prompts a user for a name, retrieves all the people with that name from a table, prompts the user to choose one of them, and then deletes the chosen person. The procedural language will draw a screen and generate a prompt for a name. The user will enter the name. The procedural language will construct a SQL SELECT statement using the name and submit the statement through a database session to the database server for execution. The server will return a set of rows (all the people with that name) to the procedural language, which will format the set for display to the user and prompt him to choose one (or more) of them. The identifier for the chosen person (or people) will then be used to construct a SQL DELETE statement for the server to execute. If the identifier is a unique identifier (the primary key) then the set of rows to be deleted will be a set of just one row; if the identifier is nonunique, then the set selected for deletion would be larger. The procedural code will know nothing about the likely size of the sets retrieved or deleted.

Use the Client Tools

There are numerous tools that can be used to connect to an Oracle database. Two of the most basic are SQL*Plus and SQL Developer. These are provided by Oracle Corporation and are perfectly adequate for much of the work that a developer or a database administrator needs to do. The choice between them is partly a matter of personal preference, partly to do with the environment, and partly to do with functionality. SQL Developer undoubtedly offers far more functionality that SQL*Plus, but it is more demanding in that it needs a graphical terminal, whereas SQL*Plus can be used on character mode devices.

Oracle Corporation has a history of producing simple tools for interacting with a database that users disliked and which therefore fell into disuse. Most recently, these include the iSQL*Plus tool which was introduced with release 9i and dropped with release 11g. The tool that has lasted longest is SQL*Plus, and even though Oracle Corporation is promoting SQL Developer very strongly as a replacement, all people working in the Oracle environment will be well advised to become familiar with it.

on the
ð o b
Many experienced developers and database administrators (perhaps including the authors of this book) treat the newer tools with a certain degree of skepticism—though this may be nothing more than an indication that these people are somewhat old-fashioned. Throughout this book both tools will be used.

SQL*Plus

SQL*Plus is a client-server tool for connecting to a database and issuing ad hoc SQL commands. It can also be used for creating PL/SQL code and has facilities for formatting results. It is available on all platforms to which the database has been ported—the sections that follow give some detail on using SQL*Plus on Linux and Windows. There are no significant differences with using SQL*Plus on any other platform.

In terms of architecture, SQL*Plus is a user process written in C. It establishes a session against an instance and a database over the Oracle Net protocol. The platforms for the client and the server can be different. For example, there is no reason not to use SQL*Plus on a Windows PC to connect to a database running on a mainframe (or the other way round) provided that Oracle Net has been configured to make the connection.

SQL*Plus on Linux

The SQL*Plus executable file on a Linux installation is `sqlplus`. The location of this file will be installation specific but will typically be something like:

```
/u01/app/oracle/product/db_1/bin/sqlplus
```

Your Linux account should be set up appropriately to run SQL*Plus. There are some environment variables that will need to be set. These are

ORACLE_HOME
PATH
LD_LIBRARY_PATH

The ORACLE_HOME variable points to the *Oracle Home*. An Oracle Home is the Oracle software installation: the set of files and directories containing the executable code and some of the configuration files. The PATH must include the `bin` directory in the Oracle Home. The LD_LIBRARY_PATH should include the `lib` directory in the Oracle Home, but in practice you may get away without setting this. Figure 1-5 shows a Linux terminal window and some tests to see if the environment is correct.

In Figure 1-5, first the `echo` command checks whether the three variables have been set up correctly: there is an ORACLE_HOME, and the `bin` and `lib` directories in it have been set as the first element of the PATH and LD_LIBRARY_PATH variables. Then `which` confirms that the SQL*Plus executable file really is available,

```
db11g@jwlnx1:~
[db11g@jwlnx1 ~]$
[db11g@jwlnx1 ~]$ echo $ORACLE_HOME
/u01/app/db11g/product/11.1.0/db_1
[db11g@jwlnx1 ~]$ echo $LD_LIBRARY_PATH
/u01/app/db11g/product/11.1.0/db_1/lib:
[db11g@jwlnx1 ~]$ echo $PATH
/u01/app/db11g/product/11.1.0/db_1/bin:/usr/kerberos/bin:/usr/local/bin:/bin:/us
r/bin:/usr/X11R6/bin:/home/db11g/bin:.
[db11g@jwlnx1 ~]$
[db11g@jwlnx1 ~]$ which sqlplus
/u01/app/db11g/product/11.1.0/db_1/bin/sqlplus
[db11g@jwlnx1 ~]$
[db11g@jwlnx1 ~]$ sqlplus system/oracle@orcl

SQL*Plus: Release 11.1.0.6.0 - Production on Mon Oct 22 02:44:59 2007

Copyright (c) 1982, 2007, Oracle.  All rights reserved.


Connected to:
Oracle Database 11g Enterprise Edition Release 11.1.0.6.0 - Production
With the Partitioning, OLAP, Data Mining and Real Application Testing options

SQL>
```

in the PATH. Finally, SQL*Plus is launched with a username, a password, and a connect identifier passed to it on the command line. If the tests do not return acceptable results and SQL*Plus fails to launch, this should be discussed with your system administrator and your database administrator. Some common errors with the logon itself are described in the section "Creating and Testing a Database Connection" later in this chapter.

The format of the login string is the database username followed by a forward slash character as a delimiter, then a password followed by an @ symbol as a delimiter, and finally an Oracle Net connect identifier. In this example, the username is system, whose password is oracle, and the database is identified by orcl.

Following the logon, the next lines of text display the version of SQL*Plus being used, which is 11.1.0.6.0, the version of the database to which the connection has been made (which happens to be the same as the version of the SQL*Plus tool), and which options have been installed within the database. The last line is the prompt to the user, SQL> , at which point the user can enter any SQL*Plus or SQL command. If the login does not succeed with whatever username (probably not system) you have been allocated, this should be discussed with your database administrator.

SQL*Plus on Windows

Historically, there were always two versions of SQL*Plus for Microsoft Windows: the character version and the graphical version. The character version is the executable file sqlplus.exe, and the graphical version was sqlplusw.exe. With the current release the graphical version no longer exists, but many developers will prefer to use it and the versions shipped with earlier releases are perfectly good tools for working with an 11g database. There are no problems with mixing versions: an 11g SQL*Plus client can connect to a 10g database, and a 10g SQL*Plus client can connect to an 11g database. Following a default installation of either the Oracle database or just the Oracle client on Windows, SQL*Plus will be available as a shortcut on the Windows Start menu. The navigation path will be as follows:

1. Start
2. Programs
3. Oracle—OraDB11g_home1
4. Application Development
5. SQL Plus

Note that the third part of the navigation path may vary depending on the installation. The location of the executable file launched by the shortcut will, typically, be something like the following:

```
D:\oracle\app\product\11.1.0\db_2\BIN\sqlplus.exe
```

However, the exact path will be installation specific. Figure 1-6 shows a logon to a database with SQL*Plus, launched from the shortcut. The first line of text shows the version of SQL*Plus, which is the 11.1.0.4.0 beta release, and the time the program was launched. The third line of text is a logon prompt:

```
Enter user-name:
```

followed by the logon string entered manually, which was

```
system/oracle@orcl
```

A change some people like to make to the shortcut that launches SQL*Plus is to prevent it from immediately presenting a login prompt. To do this, add the NOLOG switch to the end of the command:

```
sqlplus /nolog
```

There is no reason not to launch SQL*Plus from an operating system prompt rather than from the Start menu shortcut: simply open a command window and run it. The program will immediately prompt for a logon, unless you invoke it with the NOLOG switch described above.

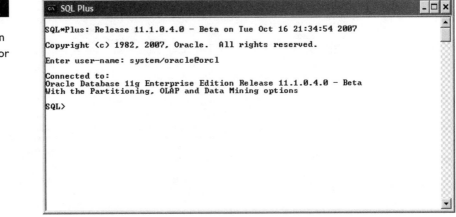

FIGURE 1-6

A database logon with SQL*Plus for Windows

The tests of the environment and the need to set the variables if they are not correct, previously described for a Linux installation, are not usually necessary on a Windows installation. This is because the variables are set in the Windows Registry by the Oracle Universal Installer when the software is installed. If SQL*Plus does not launch successfully, check the Registry variables. Figure 1-7 shows the relevant section of the Registry, viewed with the Windows `regedit.exe` Registry Editor utility. Within the Registry Editor, navigate to the key:

HKEY_LOCAL_MACHINE
SOFTWARE
ORACLE
KEY_OraDb11g_home1

The final element of this navigation path will have a different name if there have been several 11g installations on the machine.

Note the values of the Registry variables ORACLE_HOME and ORACLE_HOME_NAME. These will relate to location of the `sqlplus.exe` executable and the Start menu navigation path to reach the shortcut that will launch it.

Creating and Testing a Database Connection

SQL*Plus does not have any way of storing database connection details. Each time a user wishes to connect to a database, the user must tell SQL*Plus who they are and where the database is. There are variations depending on site-specific security

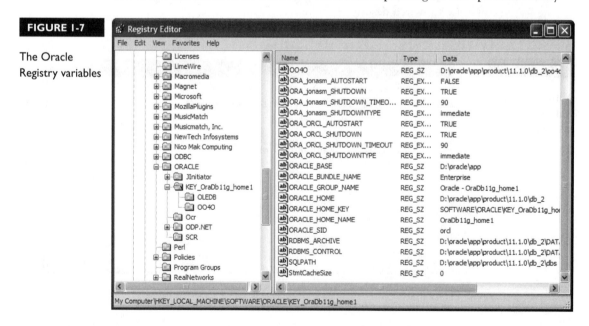

FIGURE 1-7

The Oracle Registry variables

facilities, but the most common means of identifying oneself to the database is by presenting a username and a password. There are two commonly used forms of connect identifier for identifying the database: either by giving an alias that is resolved into the full connect details, or by entering the full details.

From an operating system prompt, these commands will launch SQL*Plus and connect as database user SCOTT whose password is TIGER using each technique:

```
sqlplus scott/tiger@orcl
sqlplus scott/tiger@linsrv1.bplc.co.za:1521/orcl.bplc.com
```

The first example uses an alias, orcl, to identify the database. This must be *resolved* into the full connect details. This resolution can be done in a number of ways, but one way or another it must be accomplished. The usual techniques for this are to use a locally stored text file called the `tnsnames.ora` file, or to contact an LDAP directory such as Microsoft's Active Directory or Oracle's Oracle Internet Directory.

The second example provides all the connect details in line. The connect details needed are the hostname of the computer on which the database instance is running; the TCP port on which the Oracle Net database listener can be contacted; and the database service to which the user wishes the database listener to connect him. The first technique, where the user need only enter an alias, requires the database administrator to configure a name resolution mechanism; the second technique can only work if the user knows the details himself.

There are a number of circumstances that will cause a SQL*Plus connection attempt to fail. Figure 1-8 illustrates some of the more common problems.

FIGURE 1-8

Some common logon problems

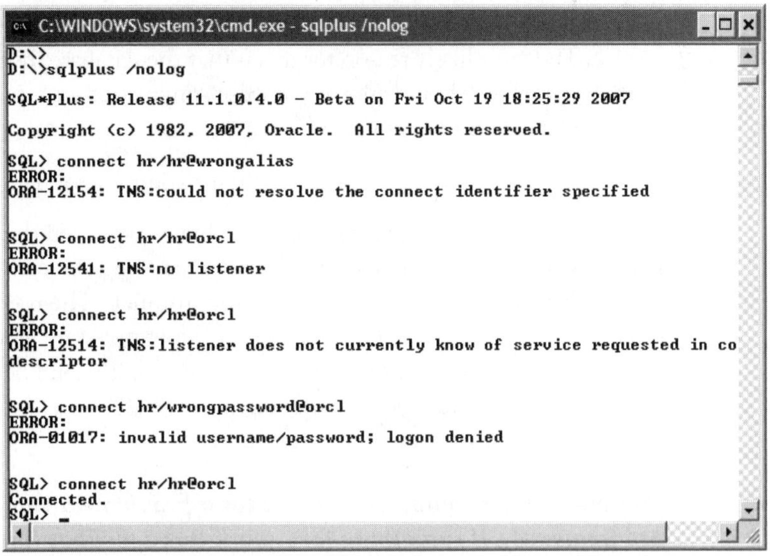

```
C:\WINDOWS\system32\cmd.exe - sqlplus /nolog

D:\>
D:\>sqlplus /nolog

SQL*Plus: Release 11.1.0.4.0 - Beta on Fri Oct 19 18:25:29 2007

Copyright (c) 1982, 2007, Oracle.  All rights reserved.

SQL> connect hr/hr@wrongalias
ERROR:
ORA-12154: TNS:could not resolve the connect identifier specified


SQL> connect hr/hr@orcl
ERROR:
ORA-12541: TNS:no listener


SQL> connect hr/hr@orcl
ERROR:
ORA-12514: TNS:listener does not currently know of service requested in co
descriptor


SQL> connect hr/wrongpassword@orcl
ERROR:
ORA-01017: invalid username/password; logon denied


SQL> connect hr/hr@orcl
Connected.
SQL> _
```

First, the user launches SQL*Plus from a Windows operating system prompt, using the NOLOG switch to prevent the immediate login prompt. No problem so far.

Second, from the SQL> prompt, the user issues a connection request, which fails with a well known error:

```
ORA-1254: TNS: could not resolve the connect identifier specified
```

This error is because the connect identifier given, wrongalias, cannot be resolved into database connection details by the TNS (Transparent Network Substrate—not an acronym particularly worth remembering) layer of Oracle Net. The name resolution method to be used and its configuration is a matter for the database administrator. In this case, the error is obvious: the user entered the wrong connect identifier.

The second connect attempt gives the correct identifier, orcl. This fails with

```
ORA-12541: TNS:no listener
```

This indicates that the connect identifier has resolved correctly into the address of a database listener, but that the listener is not actually running. Note that another possibility would be that the address resolution is faulty and is sending SQL*Plus to the wrong address. Following this error, the user should contact the database administrator and ask him or her to start the listener. Then try again.

The third connect request fails with

```
ORA-12514: TNS:listener does not currently know of service
requested in connect descriptor
```

This error is generated by the database listener. SQL*Plus has found the listener with no problems, but the listener cannot make the onward connection to the database service. The most likely reason for this is that the database instance has not been started, so the user should ask the database administrator to start it and then try again.

The fourth connect request fails with

```
ORA-01017: invalid username/password; logon denied
```

To receive this message, the user must have contacted the database. The user has got through all the possible network problems, the database instance is running, and the database itself has been opened by the instance. The user just has the password or username wrong. Note that the message does not state whether it is the password or the username that is wrong: if it were to do so, it would be giving out information to the effect that the other one was right.

Finally, the fifth connect attempt succeeds.

on the *Job* *The preceding example demonstrates a problem-solving technique you will use frequently. If something fails, work through what it is doing step by step. Read every error message.*

SQL Developer

SQL Developer is a tool for connecting to an Oracle database (or, in fact, some non-Oracle databases too) and issuing ad hoc SQL commands. It can also manage PL/SQL objects. Unlike SQL*Plus, it is a graphical tool with wizards for commonly needed actions. SQL Developer is written in Java and requires a Java Runtime Environment (JRE) to run.

Being written in Java, SQL Developer is available on all platforms that support the appropriate version of the JRE. There are no significant differences between platforms.

Installing and Launching SQL Developer

SQL Developer is not installed with the Oracle Universal Installer, which is used to install all other Oracle products. It does not exist in an Oracle Home but is a completely self contained product. The latest version can be downloaded from Oracle Corporation's website.

on the
Øob
An installation of the 11g database will include a copy of SQL Developer, but it will not be the current version. Even if you happen to have an installation of the database, you will usually want to install the current version of SQQ Developer as well.

To install SQL Developer, unzip the ZIP file. That's all. It does require JDK1.5, the Java Runtime Environment release 1.5, to be available: this comes from Sun Microsystems. But if JDK1.5 (or a later release) is not already available on the machine being used, there are downloadable versions of SQL Developer for Windows that include it. For platforms other than Windows, the JDK1.5 must be preinstalled. Download it from Sun Microsystem's website and install according to the platform-specific directions. To check that the JDK is available with the correct version, from an operating system prompt run the following command:

```
java -version
```

This should return something like the following:

```
java version "1.5.0_13"
Java(TM) 2 Runtime Environment, Standard Edition (build 1.5.0_13-b05)
Java HotSpot(TM) Client VM (build 1.5.0_13-b05, mixed mode, sharing)
```

If it does not, using `which java` may help identify the problem: the search path could be locating an incorrect version.

Once SQL Developer has been unzipped, change your current directory to the directory in which SQL Developer was unzipped and launch it. On Windows, the executable file is `sqldeveloper.exe`. On Linux, it is the `sqldeveloper.sh` shell script. Remember to check that the DISPLAY environment variable has been set to a suitable value (such as 127.0.0.1:0.0, if SQL Developer is being run on the system console) before running the shell script.

Any problems with installing the JRE and launching SQL Developer should be referred to your system administrator.

The SQL Developer User Interface

Figure 1-9 shows the SQL Developer User Interface after connecting to a database.

The general layout of the SQL Developer window is a left pane for navigation around objects, and a right pane to display and enter information.

In the figure, the left-hand pane shows that a connection has been made to a database. The connection is called orcl_sys. This name is just a label chosen when the connection was defined, but most developers will use some sort of naming convention—in this case, the name chosen is the database identifier, which is orcl, and the name of the user the connection was made as, which was sys. The branches beneath list all the possible object types that can be managed. Expanding the branches would list the objects themselves. The right-hand pane has an upper part prompting the user to enter a SQL statement and a lower part that will display the

FIGURE 1-9

The SQL Developer User Interface

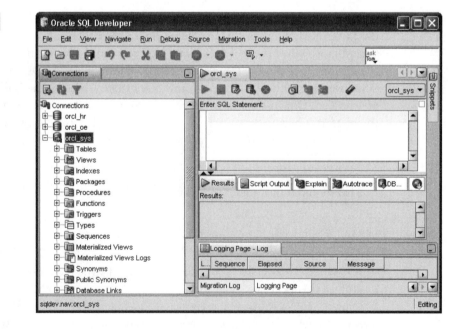

result of the statement. The layout of the panes and the tabs visible on them are highly customizable.

The menu buttons across the top menu bar give access to standard facilities:

- **File**   A normal Windows-like file menu, from which one can save work and exit from the tool.
- **Edit**   A normal Windows-like edit menu, from which one can undo, redo, copy, paste, find, and so on.
- **View**   The options for customizing the SQL Developer user interface.
- **Navigate**   Facilities for moving between panes and for moving around code that is being edited.
- **Run**   Forces execution of the SQL statements, SQL script, or PL/SQL block that is being worked on.
- **Debug**   Rather than running a whole block of code, steps through it line by line with breakpoints.
- **Source**   Options for use when writing SQL and PL/SQL code, such as keyword completion and automatic indenting.
- **Tools**   Links to external programs, including SQL*Plus.
- **Migrate**   Tools for converting applications designed for third-party databases (Microsoft Access, SQL Server, and MySQL) to the Oracle environment.
- **Help**   It's pretty good.

SQL Developer can be a very useful tool, and it is very customizable. Experiment with it, read the Help, and set up the user interface the way that works best for you.

Creating a Database Connection

Database connections can be created and saved for reuse. Figure 1-10 shows the window where connections can be defined. To reach this window, click the "+" symbol visible on the Connections tab shown previously in Figure 1-9.

The name for the connection is arbitrary. In this example, the name chosen is the name of the database connect identifier (orcl) suffixed with the username (hr) that will be embedded in the connection.

The username and password must both be supplied, but only the username will be saved unless the Save Password check box is selected. Saving a password means that future connections can be made without any password prompt. This is convenient but highly dangerous if there is any possibility that the computer you are working on is not secure. In effect, you are delegating the authentication to your local operating system: if you can log on to that, you can log on to the database.

Assuming that you are using SQL Developer to connect to an Oracle database rather than to third-party database, select the Oracle tab.

The Role drop-down box gives you the option to connect as *sysdba*. A sysdba connection is required before certain particularly serious operations (such as database startup and shutdown) can be carried out. It will never be needed for the exercises covered in this book.

The Connection Type radio buttons let you choose between three options:

- **Basic**   This prompts for the machine name of the database server, the port on which the database listener will accept connection requests, and the instance (the SID) or the service to which the connection will be made.

- **TNS**   If a name resolution method has been configured, then an alias for the database can be entered, rather than the full details needed by the Basic option.

- **Advanced**   This allows entry of a full JDBC (Java Database Connectivity) connect string. This is completely Oracle independent and could be used to connect to any database that conforms to the JDBC standard.

Selecting Basic requires the user to know how to connect to the database; selecting TNS requires some configuration to have been done on the client machine by the database administrator, in order that the alias can be resolved into the full connection details.

SCENARIO & SOLUTION	
If a connection fails what can you do? How should you try to fix the problem?	If a connection attempt fails, there should be some sort of error message. Read it! If it isn't immediately self explanatory, look it up in the Oracle documentation and on Metalink. Try to follow the flow of a connection: from the user process to the database listener to the instance to the database, and check each step.
If you can't fix the problem yourself, where can you go for help?	The documentation and Metalink will get you a long way. Most support groups will refuse to talk to you unless you can show that you have tried to solve the problem yourself. Then talk to your network administrators, system administrators, and database administrators. Often, a large part of solving the problem is finding out whose responsibility it is: be wary of people trying to avoid responsibility but don't dump problems on people inappropriately.

After you enter the details, the Test button will force SQL Developer to attempt a logon. If this returns an error, then either the connection details are wrong, or there is a problem on the server side. Typical server-side problems are that the database listener is not running, or that the database has not been started. Whatever the error is, it will be prefixed with an error number—some of the common errors were described in the preceding section, which described the use of SQL*Plus.

CERTIFICATION OBJECTIVE 1.05

Create the Demonstration Schemas

Throughout this book, there are hundreds of examples of running SQL code against tables of data. For the most part, the examples use tables in two demonstration schemas provided by Oracle: the HR schema, which is sample data that simulates a simple human resources application, and the OE schema, which simulates a more complicated order entry application.

These schemas can be created when the database is created; it is an option presented by the Database Configuration Assistant. If they do not exist, they can be created later by running some scripts that will exist in the database Oracle Home.

on the
Ⓙob
An earlier demonstration schema was SCOTT (password TIGER). This schema is simpler than HR or OE. Many people with long experience of Oracle will prefer to use this. The creation script is still supplied, it is utlsampl.sql.

Users and Schemas

First, two definitions. In Oracle parlance, a database *user* is a person who can log on to the database. A database *schema* is all the objects in the database owned by one user. The two terms can often be used interchangeably, as there is a one-to-one relationship between users and schemas. Note that while there is in fact a CREATE SCHEMA command, this does not actually create a schema—it is only a quick way of creating objects in a schema. A schema is initially created empty, when a user is created with the CREATE USER command.

Schemas are used for storing objects. These may be data objects such as tables or programmatic objects such as PL/SQL stored procedures. User logons are used to connect to the database and access these objects. By default, users have access to the objects in their own schema and to no others, but most applications change this. Typically, one schema may be used for storing data that is accessed by other users who have been given permission to use the objects, even though they do not own them. In practice, very few users will ever have objects in their own schema, or permission to create them: they will have access rights (which will be strictly controlled) only to objects in another schema. These objects will be used by all users who run the application whose data that schema stores. Conversely, the users who own the data-storing schemas may never in fact log on: the only purpose of their schemas is to contain data used by others.

It is impossible for a data object to exist independently of a schema. Or in other words, all tables must have an owner. The owner is the user in whose schema the table resides. The unique identifier for a table (or any other schema object) is the username, followed by the object name. It follows that it is not possible for two tables with the same name to exist in the same schema, but that two tables with the same name (though possibly different structures or contents) can exist in different schemas. If an object does not exist in one's own schema, to access it one must qualify its name with the name of the schema in which it resides. For example, HR.EMPLOYEES is the table called EMPLOYEES in user HR's schema. Only a user connected as HR could get to the table by referring to EMPLOYEES without a schema name qualifier.

The HR and OE Schemas

The HR demonstration schema consists of seven tables, linked by primary key to foreign key relationships. Figure 1-11 illustrates the relationships between the tables, as an entity relationship diagram.

FIGURE 1-11

The HR entity
relationship
diagram

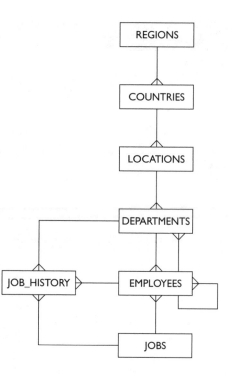

Two of the relationships shown in Figure 1-11 may not be immediately comprehensible. First, there is a many-to-one relationship from EMPLOYEES to EMPLOYEES. This is what is known as a *self-referencing foreign key*. This means that many employees can be connected to one employee, and it's based on the fact that many employees may have one manager, but the manager is also an employee. The relationship is implemented by the column manager_id being a foreign key to employee_id, which is the table's primary key.

The second relationship that may require explanation is between DEPARTMENTS and EMPLOYEES, which is bidirectional. The one department-to-many employees relationship simply states that there may be many staff members in each department, based on the EMPLOYEES dept_id column being a foreign key to the DEPARTMENTS primary key dept_id column. The one employee-to-many departments relationship shows that one employee could be the manager of several departments and is implemented by the manager_id column in DEPARTMENTS being a foreign key to the primary key employee_id column in EMPLOYEES.

Table 1-1 shows the columns of each table in the HR schema, using the notation described in the earlier section "Data Normalization" to indicate primary keys (#), foreign keys (\ ), and whether columns are optional (o) or mandatory (*).

TABLE 1-1	Table	Columns	
The tables and columns on the HR schema	REGIONS	#*	region_id
		o	region_name
	COUNTRIES	#*	country_id
		o	country_name
		\o	region_id
	LOCATIONS	#*	location_id
		o	street_address
		o	postal_code
		*	city
		o	state_province
		\o	country_id
	DEPARTMENTS	#*	department_id
		*	department_name
		\o	manager_id
		\o	location_id
	EMPLOYEES	#*	employee_id
		o	first_name
		*	last_name
		*	e-mail
		o	phone_number
		*	hire_date
		*	job_id
		o	salary
		o	commission_pct
		\o	manager_id
		\o	department_id
	JOBS	#*	job_id
		*	job_title
		o	min_salary
		o	max_salary

TABLE 1-1	Table	Columns	
The tables and columns on the HR schema (*cntd.*)	JOB_HISTORY	#*	employee_id
		#*	start_date
		*	end_date
		*	job_id
		\o	department_id

The tables are:

- REGIONS has rows for major geographical areas.
- COUNTRIES has rows for each country, which are optionally assigned to a region.
- LOCATIONS includes individual addresses, which are optionally assigned to a country.
- DEPARTMENTS has a row for each department, optionally assigned to a location and optionally with a manager (who must exist as an employee).
- EMPLOYEES has a row for every employee, each of whom must be assigned to a job and optionally to a department and to a manager. The managers must themselves be employees.
- JOBS lists all possible jobs in the organization. It is possible for many employees to have the same job.
- JOB_HISTORY lists previous jobs held by employees, uniquely identified by employee_id and start_date; it is not possible for an employee to hold two jobs concurrently. Each job history record will refer to one employee, who will have had one job at that time and may have been a member of one department.

This HR schema is used for most of the exercises and many of the examples embedded in the chapters of this book and does need to be available.

on the **Job**

There are rows in EMPLOYEES that do not have a matching parent row in DEPARTMENTS. This could be by design but might well be a design mistake that is possible because the DEPARTMENT_ID column in EMPLOYEES is not mandatory. There are similar possible errors in the REGIONS—COUNTRIES—LOCATIONS hierarchy, which really does not make a lot of sense.

The OE schema is considerably more complex than the HR schema. The table structures are much more complicated: they include columns defined as nested tables, user-defined data types, and XML data types. There are a number of optional exercises at the end of each chapter that are usually based on the OE schema. The objects referred to are described as they are used.

Demonstration Schema Creation

If the database you are using was created specifically for studying for the OCP SQL examination, the demonstration schemas should have been created already. They are an option presented by the Database Configuration Assistant when it creates a database. After database creation, the schemas may have to be unlocked and their passwords set; by default the accounts are locked, which means you cannot log on to them. These commands, which could be issued from SQL*Plus or SQL Developer, will make it possible to log on as users HR and OE using the passwords HR and OE:

```
alter user hr account unlock identified by hr;
alter user oe account unlock identified by oe;
```

These `alter user` commands can only be issued when connected to the database as a user with DBA privileges, such as the user SYSTEM.

If the schemas were not created at database creation time, they can be created later by running scripts installed into the Oracle Home of the database. These scripts will need to be run from SQL*Plus or SQL Developer as a user with SYSDBA privileges. The script will prompt for certain values as it runs. For example, on Linux, first launch SQL*Plus from an operating system prompt:

```
sqlplus / as sysdba
```

There are various options for this connection, but the preceding syntax will usually work if the database is running on the same machine where you are running SQL*Plus. Then invoke the script from the SQL> prompt:

```
SQL> @?/demo/schema/human_resources/hr_main.sql
```

The "?" character is a variable that SQL*Plus will expand into the path to the Oracle Home directory. The script will prompt for HR's password, default tablespace, and temporary tablespace; the SYS password; and a destination for a logfile of the script's running. Typical values for the default tablespace and temporary tablespace are USERS and TEMP, but these will have to have been created already. After completion, you will be connected to the database as the new HR user. To verify this, run this statements.

```
SQL> show user;
```

You will see that you are currently connected as HR; then run:

```
SQL> select table_name from user_tables;
```

You will see a list of the seven tables in the HR schema.

To create the OE schema, follow the same process, nominating the script:

```
?/demo/schema/order_entry/oe_main.sql
```

The process for creating the schemas on Windows is identical, except for the path delimiters—where most operating systems use forward slashes, Windows uses back slashes. So the path to the Windows HR creation script becomes:

```
@?\demo\schema\human_resources\hr_main.sql
```

Note that running these schema creation scripts will *drop* the schemas first if they already exist. Dropping a schema means removing every item in it and then removing the user. This should not be a problem, unless the schema has been used for some development work that needs to be kept. The drop is absolutely nonreversible, so any object in a dropped schema will be irretrievable lost.

If the demonstration creation schema scripts do not exist as just described, this will be because the Oracle Home installation has not been completed. Installing a database Oracle Home can be done from one CD, but there is a second CD (called the *companion* CD) that includes a number of components that are, strictly speaking, optional. These include the demonstration schemas. The companion CD should normally be installed; if this has not been done, this must be discussed with the database administrator.

on the
Job   *The demonstration schemas should not exist in production databases. It is not good, for security reasons, to have unnecessary schemas in a database that have well known usernames, capabilities, and (possibly) passwords.*

CERTIFICATION SUMMARY

SQL is a language for managing access to normalized data stored in relational databases. It is not an application development language, but is invoked by such languages when they need to access data. The Oracle server technologies provide a platform for developing and deploying such applications. The combination of the Oracle server technologies and SQL result in an environment conforming to the relational database paradigm that is an enabling technology for Grid computing.

Numerous client tools can be used to connect to an Oracle database. Two provided by Oracle Corporation are SQL*Plus and SQL Developer: SQL*Plus is installed as part of every Oracle client and Oracle database install, but SQL Developer can be installed as a separate product. Both tools can be used for preparing for the OCP examinations, and students should be familiar with both.

The demonstration schemas store example data that is used to illustrate the use of SQL, and also of more advanced Oracle development facilities.

✓ TWO-MINUTE DRILL

Position the Server Technologies

- ❑ The Oracle database stores and manages access to user data.
- ❑ The Oracle Application Server runs applications that connect users to the database.
- ❑ Oracle Enterprise Manager is a tool for managing databases, application servers, and, if desired, the entire computing environment.
- ❑ Languages built into the database for application development are SQL, PL/SQL, and Java.

Understand Relational Structures

- ❑ Data must be normalized into two-dimensional tables.
- ❑ Tables are linked through primary and foreign keys.
- ❑ Entity-relationship diagrams represent the tables graphically.

Summarize the SQL Language

- ❑ The DML commands are SELECT, INSERT, UPDATE, DELETE, and MERGE.
- ❑ The DDL commands are CREATE, ALTER, DROP, RENAME, TRUNCATE, and COMMENT.
- ❑ The DCL commands are GRANT and REVOKE.
- ❑ The TCL commands are COMMIT, ROLLBACK, and SAVEPOINT.

Use the Client Tools

- ❑ SQL*Plus is a command-line utility installed into the Oracle Home.
- ❑ SQL Developer is a graphical tool installed into its own directory.
- ❑ Both tools require a database connection, consisting of a username, a password, and a connect identifier.

Create the Demonstration Schemas

- ❑ The demonstration schemas are provided by Oracle to facilitate learning but must be created before they can be used.

SELF TEST

Position the Server Technologies

1. What components of the IT environment can Oracle Enterprise Manager Grid Control manage? (Choose the best answer.)
   A. Oracle databases
   B. Oracle application servers
   C. Third-party products
   D. The server machines
   E. All of the above

2. What languages can run within the database? (Choose all that apply.)
   A. SQL
   B. C
   C. PL/SQL
   D. Java
   E. Any other language linked to the OCI libraries

Understand Relational Structures

3. Data that is modeled into a form suitable for processing in a relational database may be described as being (Choose the best answer.)
   A. First normal form
   B. Third normal form
   C. Abnormal form
   D. Paranormal form

4. An entity-relationship diagram shows data modeled into (Choose the best answer.)
   A. Two-dimensional tables
   B. Multidimensional tables
   C. Hierarchical structures
   D. Object-oriented structures

Summarize the SQL Language

5. SQL is a set-oriented language. Which of these features is a consequence of this? (Choose the best answer.)
   A. Individual rows must have a unique identifier.
   B. Sets of users can be managed in groups.
   C. SQL statements can be placed within blocks of code in other languages, such as Java and PL/SQL.
   D. One statement can affect multiple rows.

6. Which of these constructs is not part of the SQL language? (Choose all that apply.)
   A. Iteration, based on DO..WHILE
   B. Iteration, based on FOR..NEXT
   C. Branching, based on IF..THEN..ELSE
   D. Transaction control, based on COMMIT
   E. Transaction control, based on ROLLBACK

Use the Client Tools

7. Which of these statements regarding SQL Developer are correct? (Choose two answers.)
   A. SQL Developer cannot connect to databases earlier than release 10g.
   B. SQL Developer can be installed outside an Oracle Home.
   C. SQL Developer can store passwords.
   D. SQL Developer relies on an LDAP directory for name resolution.

8. Which of the following are requirements for using SQL Developer? (Choose two correct answers.)
   A. A Java Runtime Environment
   B. The OCI libraries
   C. A name resolution method such as LDAP or a TNSNAMES.ORA file
   D. The SQL*Plus libraries
   E. A graphical terminal

Create the Demonstration Schemas

9. Where may the demonstration schemas be created? (Choose the best answer.)

    A. The demonstration schemas must be created in a demonstration database.

    B. The demonstration schemas cannot be created in a production database.

    C. The demonstration schemas can be created in any database.

    D. The demonstration schemas can be created in any database if the demonstration user is created first.

10. How can you move a schema from one user to another? (Choose the best answer.)

    A. Use the ALTER SCHEMA MOVE… command.

    B. You cannot move a schema from one user to another.

    C. A schema can only be moved if it is empty (or if all objects within it have been dropped).

    D. Attach the new user to the schema, then detach the old user from the schema.

LAB QUESTION

The OE schema includes these tables:

- CUSTOMERS
- INVENTORIES
- ORDERS
- ORDER_ITEMS
- PRODUCT_DESCRIPTIONS
- PRODUCT_INFORMATION
- WAREHOUSES

A CUSTOMER can place many ORDERS, and an order can have many ORDER_ITEMS. Each item will be of one product, described by its PRODUCT_INFORMATION, and each product may have several PRODUCT_DESCRIPTIONS, in different languages. There are a number of WAREHOUSES, each of which can store many products; one product may be stored in many warehouses. An INVENTORIES entry relates products to warehouses, showing how much of each product is in each warehouse.

Sketch out this schema as an entity-relationship diagram, showing the many-to-one connections between the tables and ensuring that there are no many-to-many connections.

SELF TEST ANSWERS

Position the Server Technologies

1. ☑ **E.** Grid Control can manage the complete environment (according to Oracle Corporation).
☒ **A, B, C, D.** All of these can be managed by Grid Control.

2. ☑ **A, C, D.** SQL, PL/SQL, and Java can all run in the database.
☒ **B, E.** C cannot run inside the database, and OCI is used by external processes to connect to the database; it does not run within it.

Understand Relational Structures

3. ☑ **B.** Third normal form is the usual form aimed for by systems analysts when they normalize data into relational structures.
☒ **A, C, D.** A is wrong because first normal form is only the first stage of data normalization. C and D would be more suitable to the X-Files than to a database.

4. ☑ **A.** The relational model uses two-dimensional tables.
☒ **B, C, D.** B is wrong because two dimensions is the limit for relational structures. C and D are wrong because they refer to nonrelational structures (though there are facilities within the Oracle database for simulating them).

Summarize the SQL Language

5. ☑ **D.** In a set-oriented language, one command can affect many rows (a set), whereas a procedural language processes rows one by one.
☒ **A, B, C.** A is wrong because while rows should have a unique a identifier in a well designed application, this is not actually a requirement. B is wrong because users cannot be grouped in the Oracle environment. C is wrong because (even though the statement is correct) it is not relevant to the question.

6. ☑ **A, B, C.** These are all procedural constructions, which are not part of a set-oriented language. They are all used in PL/SQL.
☒ **D, E.** These are SQL's transaction control statements.

Use the Client Tools

7. ☑ **B, C.** B is correct because SQL Developer can be installed in its own directory. C is correct because passwords can be saved as part of a connection definition (though this may not be a good idea).
☒ **A, D.** A is wrong because the Oracle Net protocol lets SQL Developer connect to a number of versions of the database. D is wrong because LDAP is only one of several techniques for name resolution.

8. ☑ **A, E.** A is correct because SQL Developer is written in Java and therefore requires a Java Runtime Environment. E is correct because SQL Developer needs a graphics terminal to display windows.

 ☒ **B, C, D.** B is wrong because SQL Developer uses JDBC to connect to databases, not OCI. C is wrong because, while SQL Developer can use LDAP or a TNSNAMES.ORA file, it can also use and store the basic connection details. D is wrong because SQL Developer is a completely independent product.

Create the Demonstration Schemas

9. ☑ **C.** The demonstration schemas can be created in any database, either at database creation time or by running scripts later.

 ☒ **A, B, D.** A and B are wrong because, while they may be good practice, they are not a technical requirement. D is wrong because it fails to understand that a schema can only be (and always is) created with a user.

10. ☑ **B.** A schema and a user are inseparable.

 ☒ **A, C, D.** A is wrong because there is no such command. C and D are wrong because they assume the impossible: that you can separate a user from his or her schema.

LAB ANSWER

Figure 1-12 shows a solution.

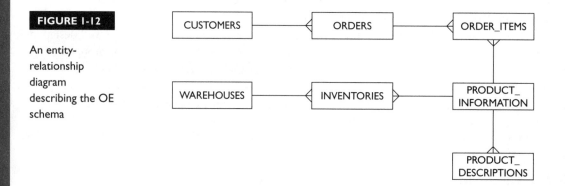

FIGURE 1-12

An entity-relationship diagram describing the OE schema

2

Data Retrieval Using the SQL SELECT Statement

CERTIFICATION OBJECTIVES

This chapter explores the concepts of extracting or retrieving data stored in relational tables using the SELECT statement. The statement is introduced in its basic form and is progressively built on to extend its core functionality. As you learn the rules governing this statement, an important point to remember is that the SELECT statement never alters information stored in the database. Instead, it provides a read-only method of extracting information. When you ask a question using SQL SELECT, you are guaranteed to extract results, even from the difficult questions.

CERTIFICATION OBJECTIVE 2.01

List the Capabilities of SQL SELECT Statements

Knowing how to retrieve data in a set format using a query language is the first step toward understanding the capabilities of SELECT statements. Describing the relations involved provides a tangible link between the theory of how data is stored in tables and the practical visualization of the structure of these tables. These topics form an important precursor to the discussion of the capabilities of the SELECT statement. The three primary areas explored are as follows:

- Introducing the SQL SELECT statement
- The DESCRIBE table command
- Capabilities of the SELECT statement

Introducing the SQL SELECT Statement

The SELECT statement from Structured Query Language (SQL) has to be the single most powerful nonspoken language construct. The SELECT statement is an elegant, flexible, and highly extensible mechanism created to retrieve information from a database table. A database would serve little purpose if it could not be queried to answer all sorts of interesting questions. For example, you may have a database that contains personal financial records like your bank statements, your utility bills, and your salary statements. You could easily ask the database for a date-ordered list of your electrical utility bills for the last six months or query your bank statement for a list of payments made to a certain account over the same period. The beauty of the SELECT statement is encapsulated in its simple English-like format that allows questions to be asked of the database in a natural manner.

Tables, also known as relations, consist of *rows* of information divided by *columns*. Consider two of the sample tables introduced in the previous chapter: the EMPLOYEES table and the DEPARTMENTS table. This sample dataset is based on the Human Resources (HR) information for some fictitious organization. In Oracle terminology, each table belongs to a schema (owner): in this case the HR schema. The EMPLOYEES table stores rows or records of information. These contain several attributes (columns) that describe each employee in this organization. The DEPARTMENTS table contains descriptive information about each department within this organization, stored as rows of data divided into columns.

Assuming a connection to a database containing the sample HR schema is available, then using either SQL*Plus or SQL Developer you can establish a user session. Once connected to the database, you are ready to begin your tour of SQL.

The **DESCRIBE** Table Command

To get the answers one seeks, one must ask the correct questions. An understanding of the terms of reference, which in this case, are relational tables, is essential for the formulation of the correct questions. A structural description of a table is useful to establish what questions can be asked of it. The Oracle server stores information about all tables in a special set of relational tables called the *data dictionary*, in order to manage them. The data dictionary is quite similar to a regular language dictionary. It stores definitions of database objects in a centralized, ordered, and structured format.

A clear distinction must be drawn between storing the definition and the contents of a table. The definition of a table includes information like table name, table owner, details about the columns that comprise it, and its physical storage size on disk. This information is also referred to as *metadata*. The contents of a table are stored in rows and are referred to as *data*.

The structural metadata of a table may be obtained by querying the database for the list of columns that comprise it using the *DESCRIBE* command. The general form of the syntax for this command is intuitively:

DESC[RIBE] <SCHEMA>.*tablename*

This command shall be systematically unpacked. The DESCRIBE keyword can be shortened to DESC. All tables belong to a schema or owner. If you are describing a table that belongs to the schema to which you have connected, the <SCHEMA> portion of the command may be omitted. Figure 2-1 shows how the EMPLOYEES table is described from SQL*Plus after connecting to the database as the HR user with the DESCRIBE EMPLOYEES command and how the DEPARTMENTS table

FIGURE 2-1

Describing
EMPLOYEES,
DEPARTMENTS,
and DUAL tables

```
Command Prompt - SQLPLUS HR                                              _ □ ✕

SQL> DESCRIBE EMPLOYEES;
 Name                                        Null?      Type
 ─────────────────────────────────────────────────────────────────────────

 EMPLOYEE_ID                                 NOT NULL   NUMBER(6)
 FIRST_NAME                                             VARCHAR2(20)
 LAST_NAME                                   NOT NULL   VARCHAR2(25)
 EMAIL                                       NOT NULL   VARCHAR2(25)
 PHONE_NUMBER                                           VARCHAR2(20)
 HIRE_DATE                                   NOT NULL   DATE
 JOB_ID                                      NOT NULL   VARCHAR2(10)
 SALARY                                                 NUMBER(8,2)
 COMMISSION_PCT                                         NUMBER(2,2)
 MANAGER_ID                                             NUMBER(6)
 DEPARTMENT_ID                                          NUMBER(4)

SQL> DESC HR.DEPARTMENTS
 Name                                        Null?      Type
 ─────────────────────────────────────────────────────────────────────────

 DEPARTMENT_ID                               NOT NULL   NUMBER(4)
 DEPARTMENT_NAME                             NOT NULL   VARCHAR2(30)
 MANAGER_ID                                             NUMBER(6)
 LOCATION_ID                                            NUMBER(4)

SQL> DESC SYS.DUAL
 Name                                        Null?      Type
 ─────────────────────────────────────────────────────────────────────────

 DUMMY                                                  VARCHAR2(1)
```

is described using the shorthand notation: DESC HR.DEPARTMENTS. The HR.
notational prefix could be omitted since the DEPARTMENTS table belongs to the
HR schema. The HR schema (and every other schema) has access to a special table
called *DUAL*, which belongs to the SYS schema. This table can be structurally
described with the command: DESCRIBE SYS.DUAL.

Describing tables yields interesting and useful results. You know which columns
of a table can be selected since their names are exposed. You also know the nature
of the data contained in these columns since the column data type is exposed.
Column data types are discussed in detail in Chapter 11. For the current discussion,
it is sufficient to regard the different data type columns as detailed in this section.

Numeric columns are often specified as *NUMBER(p,s)*, where the first parameter
is *precision* and the second is *scale*. In Figure 2-1, the SALARY column of the
EMPLOYEES table has a data type of: NUMBER(8,2). This means that the values
stored in this column can have at most 8 digits. Of these 8 digits, 2 must be to the right
of the decimal point. A SALARY value of 999999.99 is acceptable, but a SALARY
value of 9999999.9 is not, even though both these numbers contain 8 digits.

VARCHAR2(length) data type columns store variable length alphanumeric
character data, where *length* determines the maximum number of characters a column
can contain. The FIRST_NAME column of the EMPLOYEES table has data type
VARCHAR2(20), which means it can store employees' names of up to 20 characters.
Note that if this column contains no data or its content is less than 20 characters,

it will not necessarily use the same space as it would use to store a name that is 20 characters long. The *CHAR(size)* column data type specifies fixed-length columns where row space is preallocated to contain a fixed number of characters regardless of its contents. CHAR is much less commonly used than VARCHAR2. Unless the length of the data is predictable and constant, the CHAR data type utilizes storage inefficiently, padding any unused components with spaces.

DATE and *TIMESTAMP* column data types store date and time information. DATE stores a moment in time with precision including day, month, year, hours, minutes, and seconds. TIMESTAMP(f) stores the same information as DATE but is also capable of storing fractional seconds.

on the
(j)ob

A variety of data types is available for use as column data types. Many have a specialized purpose like Binary Large Objects (BLOBs), used for storing binary data like music or video data. The vast majority of tables, however, use the primitive column data types of NUMBER, VARCHAR2, and DATE. The TIMESTAMP data type has become widely used since its introduction in Oracle 9i. Becoming familiar and interacting with these generic primitive data types prepares you for dealing with a significant range of database-related queries.

Mandatory columns, which are forced to store data for each row, are exposed by the *"Null?"* column output from the DESCRIBE command having the value: *NOT NULL*. You are guaranteed that any column of data which is restricted by the NOT NULL constraint when the table is created must contain some data. It is important to note that NULL has special meaning for the Oracle server. NULL refers to an absence of data. Blank spaces do not count as NULL since they are present in the row and have some length even though they are not visible.

EXERCISE 2-1

Describing the Human Resources Schema

The HR schema contains seven tables representing a data model of a fictitious Human Resources department. The EMPLOYEES table, which stores details of the staff, and the DEPARTMENTS table, which contains the details of the departments in the organization, have been described. In this step-by-step exercise, a connection is made using SQL Developer as the HR user and the remaining five sample tables are described. They are the JOBS table, which keeps track of the different job types available in the organization, and the JOB_HISTORY table, which keeps track of the job details of employees who changed jobs but remained in the organization. To understand the data model further, the LOCATIONS, COUNTRIES, and

REGIONS tables, which keep track of the geographical information pertaining to departments in the organization, will be described.

1. Launch SQL Developer and choose New from the File menu. Choose Database Connection. If this is the first time you are connecting to the database from SQL Developer, you are required to create a connection. Provide a descriptive connection name and input HR as the username. The remaining connection details should be obtained from your database administrator. Once the connection is saved, choose the Connect button.

2. Navigate to the SQL Editor, which is the section titled Enter SQL Statement.

3. Type in the command: DESCRIBE JOBS. Terminating this command with a semicolon is optional.

4. Execute the DESCRIBE command, either by pressing the F5 key or by clicking the solid green triangular arrow icon located on the toolbar above the SQL Editor.

5. The JOBS table description appears in the Results frame as shown in the following illustration.

6. Steps 3 to 5 can be repeated to describe the remaining JOB_HISTORY, LOCATIONS, COUNTRIES, and REGIONS tables.

7. SQL Developer provides an alternative to the DESCRIBE command when it comes to obtaining the structural information of tables.

8. Navigate to the LOCATIONS table using the Tree navigator located on the left frame underneath the connection name.

9. SQL Developer describes the table automatically on the right side of the tool as shown in the following illustration.

Capabilities of the SELECT Statement

Relational database tables are built on a strong mathematical foundation called *relational theory*. In this theory, relations, or tables, are operated on by a formal language called *relational algebra*. SQL is a commercial interpretation of the relational algebraic constructs. Three concepts from relational theory encompass the capability of the SELECT statement: projection, selection, and joining.

Projection refers to the restriction of attributes (columns) selected from a relation or table. When requesting information from a table, you can ask to view all the columns. For example, in the HR.DEPARTMENTS table, you can retrieve all rows and all columns with a simple SELECT statement. This query will return DEPARTMENT_ID, DEPARTMENT_NAME, MANAGER_ID, and LOCATION_ID information for every department record stored in the table. What if you wanted a list containing only the DEPARTMENT_NAME and MANAGER_ID columns? Well, you would request just those two columns from the table. This restriction of columns is called *projection*.

Selection refers to the restriction of the tuples or rows selected from a relation (table). It is often not desirable to retrieve every row from a table. Tables may contain many rows and, instead of asking for all of them, selection provides a means to restrict the rows returned. Perhaps you have been asked to identify only the employees who belong to department 30. With *selection* it is possible to limit the results set to those rows of data which have a DEPARTMENT_ID value of 30.

Joining, as a relational concept, refers to the interaction of tables with each other in a query. Third normal form, as discussed in Chapter1, presented the notion of separating different types of data into autonomous tables to avoid duplication and maintenance anomalies and to associate related data using primary and foreign key relationships. These relationships provide the mechanism to join tables with each other. Joining is discussed extensively in Chapter7.

Assume there is a need to retrieve the e-mail addresses for all employees who work in the Sales department. The EMAIL column belongs to the EMPLOYEES table, while the DEPARTMENT_NAME column belongs to the DEPARTMENTS table. *Projection* and *selection* from the DEPARTMENTS table may be used to obtain the DEPARTMENT_ID value that corresponds to the Sales department. The matching rows in the EMPLOYEES table may be *joined* to the DEPARTMENTS table based on this common DEPARTMENT_ID value. The EMAIL column may then be *projected* from this set of results.

The SQL SELECT statement is mathematically governed by these three tenets. An unlimited combination of projections, selections, and joins provides the language to extract the relational data required.

Execute a Basic SELECT Statement

The practical capabilities of the SELECT statement are realized in its execution. The key to executing any query language statement is a thorough understanding of its syntax and the rules governing its usage. This topic is discussed first. It is followed by a discussion of the execution of a basic query before expressions and operators, which exponentially increase the utility of data stored in relational tables, are introduced. Next, the concept of a null value is demystified, as its pitfalls are exposed. These topics will be covered in the following four sections:

- Syntax of the primitive SELECT statement
- Rules are meant to be followed
- SQL expressions and operators
- NULL is nothing

Syntax of the Primitive SELECT Statement

In its most primitive form, the SELECT statement supports the projection of columns and the creation of arithmetic, character, and date expressions. It also facilitates the elimination of duplicate values from the results set. The basic SELECT statement syntax is as follows:

SELECT * | {[DISTINCT] *column* | *expression* [*alias*],...}
FROM *table*;

The special keywords or reserved words of the SELECT statement syntax appear in uppercase. When using the commands, however, the case of the reserved words in your query statement does not matter. The reserved words cannot be used as column names or other database object names. SELECT, DISTINCT, and FROM are three keyword elements. A SELECT statement always comprises two or more clauses. The two mandatory clauses are the SELECT clause and the FROM clause. The pipe symbol | is used to denote OR. So you can read the first form of the above SELECT statement as:

SELECT *
FROM *table*;

In this format, the asterisk symbol (*) is used to denote all columns. SELECT * is a succinct way of asking the Oracle server to return all possible columns. It is used as a shorthand, time-saving symbol instead of typing in SELECT *column1, column2, column3, column4,...,columnX*, to select all the columns. The FROM clause specifies which table to query to fetch the columns requested in the SELECT clause.

You can issue the following SQL command to retrieve all the columns and all the rows from the REGIONS table in the HR schema:

```
SELECT * FROM REGIONS;
```

As shown in Figure 2-2, when this command is executed in SQL*Plus, it returns all the rows of data and all the columns belonging to this table. Use of the asterisk in a SELECT statement is sometimes referred to as a "blind" query because the exact columns to be fetched are not specified.

The second form of the basic SELECT statement has the same FROM clause as the first form, but the SELECT clause is different:

SELECT {[DISTINCT] *column* | *expression* [*alias*],...}
FROM *table*;

This SELECT clause can be simplified into two formats:

SELECT *column1 (possibly other columns or expressions)* [alias optional]
OR
SELECT DISTINCT *column1 (possibly other columns or expressions)* [alias optional]

FIGURE 2-2	
Projecting all columns from the REGIONS table	

```
SQL> SELECT * FROM REGIONS;

 REGION_ID REGION_NAME
---------- --------------------------
         1 Europe
         2 Americas
         3 Asia
         4 Middle East and Africa

SQL> SELECT REGION_NAME
  2  FROM REGIONS;

REGION_NAME
--------------------------
Europe
Americas
Asia
Middle East and Africa

SQL>
```

An *alias* is an alternative name for referencing a column or expression. Aliases are typically used for displaying output in a user-friendly manner. They also serve as shorthand when referring to columns or expressions to reduce typing. Aliases will be discussed in detail later in this chapter. By explicitly listing only the relevant columns in the SELECT clause you, in effect, *project* the exact subset of the results you wish to retrieve. The following statement will return just the REGION_NAME column subset of the REGIONS table as shown in Figure 2-2:

```
SELECT REGION_NAME
FROM REGIONS;
```

You may be asked to obtain all the job roles in the organization that employees have historically fulfilled. For this you can issue the command: SELECT * FROM JOB_HISTORY. However, in addition, the SELECT * construct returns the EMPLOYEE_ID, START_DATE, and END_DATE columns. The uncluttered results set containing only JOB_ID and DEPARTMENT_ID columns can be obtained with the following statement executed in SQL*Plus, as shown in Figure 2-3.

Using the DISTINCT keyword allows duplicate rows to be eliminated from the results set. In numerous situations a unique set of rows is required. It is important to note that the criterion employed by the Oracle server in determining whether a

FIGURE 2-3

Projecting specific columns from the JOB_HISTORY table

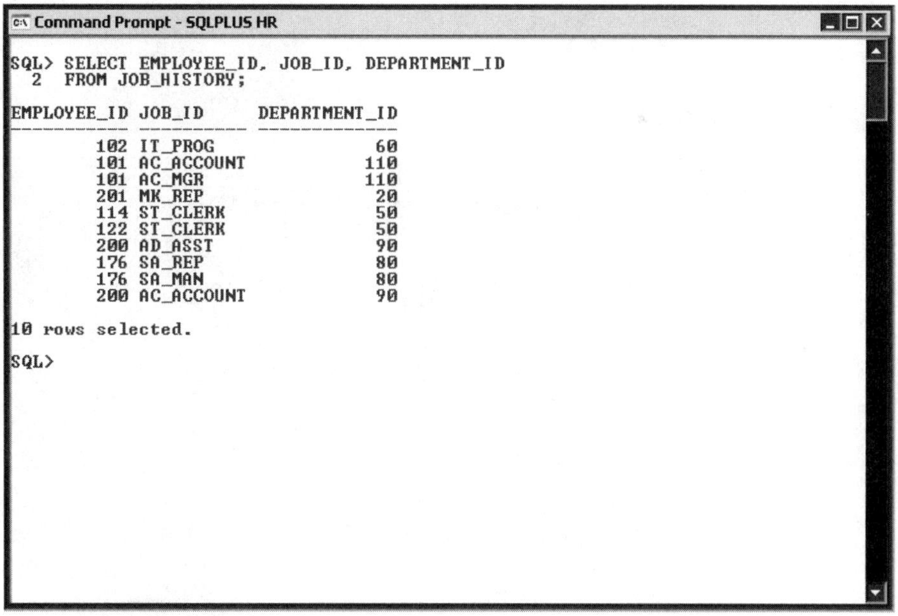

row is unique or distinct depends entirely on what is specified after the DISTINCT keyword in the SELECT clause. Selecting distinct JOB_ID values from the JOB_HISTORY table will return the eight distinct job types as shown in Figure 2-4.

Compare this output to Figure 2-3, where ten rows are returned. Can you see that there are two occurrences of the AC_ACCOUNT and ST_CLERK JOB_ID values? These are the two duplicate rows that have been eliminated by looking for distinct JOB_ID values. Selecting the distinct DEPARTMENT_ID column from the JOB_HISTORY table returns only six rows, as Figure 2-5 demonstrates. DEPARTMENT_ID values 50, 80, 90, and 110 each occur twice in the JOB_HISTORY table, and thus four rows have been eliminated by searching for distinct DEPARTMENT_ID values.

An important feature of the DISTINCT keyword is the elimination of duplicate values from *combinations* of columns. There are ten rows in the JOB_HISTORY table. Eight rows contain distinct JOB_ID values. Six rows contain distinct DEPARTMENT_ID values. Can you guess how many rows contain distinct combinations of JOB_ID and DEPARTMENT_ID values? As Figure 2-6 reveals,

FIGURE 2-4	
Selecting unique JOB_IDs from the JOB_HISTORY table	

FIGURE 2-5

Selecting unique
DEPARTMENT_
IDs from the
JOB_HISTORY
table

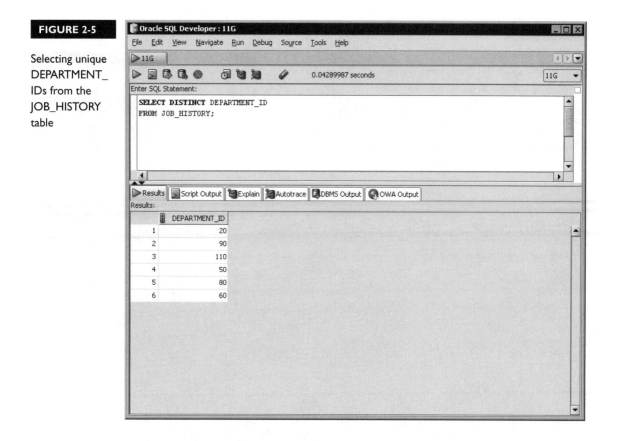

there are nine rows returned in the results set that contain distinct JOB_ID and
DEPARTMENT_ID combinations, with one row from Figure 2-3 having being
eliminated. This is, of course, the row that contains a JOB_ID value of ST_CLERK
and a DEPARTMENT_ID value of 50.

on the *The ability to project specific columns from a table is very useful. Coupled*
ob *with the ability to remove duplicate values or combinations of values*
empowers you to assist with basic user reporting requirements. In many
application databases, tables can sometimes store duplicate data. End user
reporting frequently requires this data to be presented as a manageable set
of unique records. This is something you now have the ability to do. Be careful,
though, when using blind queries to select data from large tables. Executing a
SELECT * FROM HUGE_TABLE; *statement may cause performance issues if*
the table contains millions of rows of data.

FIGURE 2-6   Unique JOB_ID, DEPARTMENT_ID combinations from JOB_HISTORY

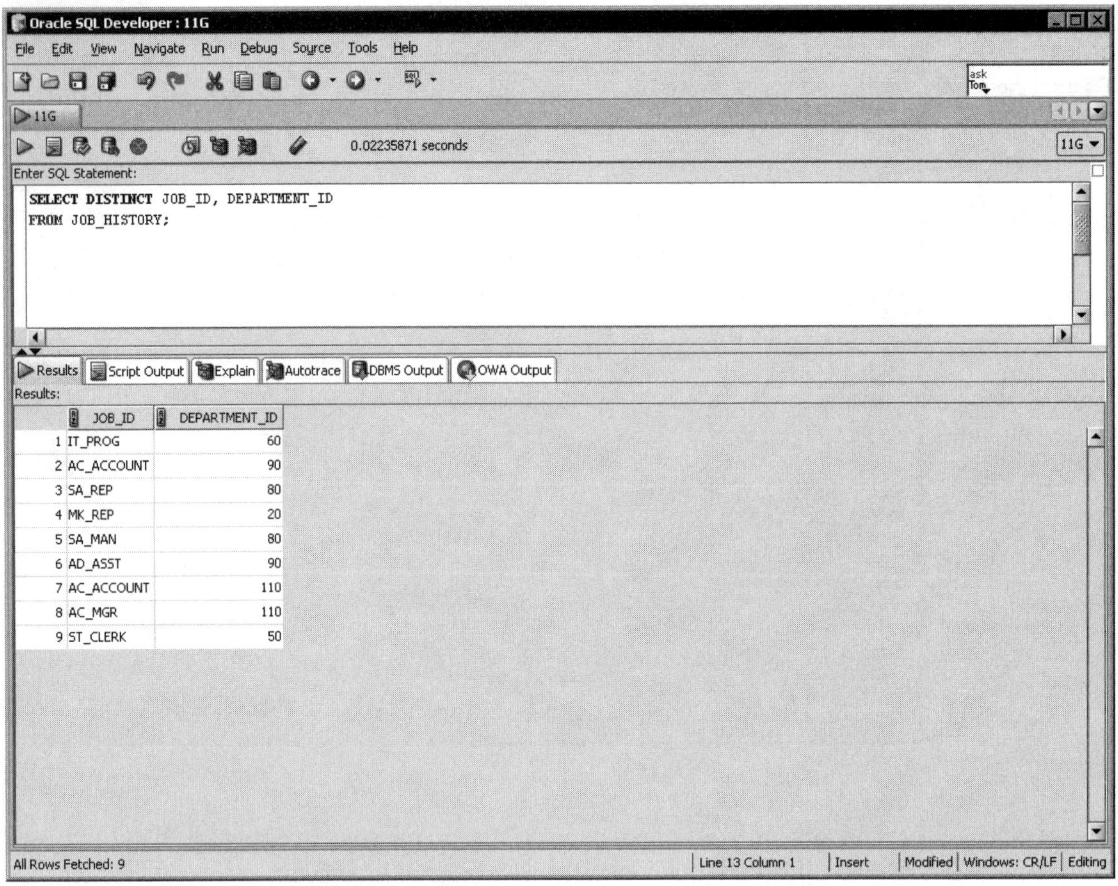

Rules Are Meant to be Followed

SQL is a fairly strict language in terms of syntax rules, but it remains simple and flexible enough to support a variety of programming styles. This section discusses some of the basic rules governing SQL statements.

Uppercase or Lowercase

It is a matter of personal taste about the case in which SQL statements are submitted to the database. The examples used thus far have been written in uppercase. Many developers, including the authors of this book, prefer to write their SQL statements in lowercase. There is also a common misconception that SQL reserved words need to be specified in uppercase. Again, this is up to you. Adhering to a consistent and standardized format is advised. The following three statements are syntactically equivalent:

```
SELECT * FROM LOCATIONS;
Select * from locations;
select * from locations;
```

There is one caveat regarding case sensitivity. When interacting with literal values, case does matter. Consider the JOB_ID column from the JOB_HISTORY table. This column contains rows of data which happen to be stored in the database in uppercase; for example, SA_REP and ST_CLERK. When requesting that the results set be restricted by a literal column, the case is critical. The Oracle server treats the request for all the rows in the JOB_HISTORY table that contain a value of St_Clerk in the JOB_ID column differently from the request for all rows which have a value of ST_CLERK in JOB_ID column.

Metadata about different database objects is stored by default in uppercase in the data dictionary. If you query a database dictionary table to return a list of tables owned by the HR schema, it is likely that the table names returned are stored in uppercase. This does not mean that a table cannot be created with a lowercase name; it can be. It is just more common and the default behavior of the Oracle server to create and store tables, columns, and other database object metadata in uppercase in the database dictionary.

e x a m

ⓦ a t c h *SQL statements may be submitted to the database in either lowercase or uppercase. You must pay careful attention to case when interacting with character literal data and aliases. Asking for a column called JOB_ID or job_id returns the same column, but asking for rows where the JOB_ID value is PRESIDENT is different from asking for rows where the JOB_ID value is President. Character literal data should always be treated in a case-sensitive manner.*

Statement Terminators

Semicolons are generally used as SQL statement terminators. SQL*Plus always requires a statement terminator, and usually a semicolon is used. A single SQL statement or even groups of associated statements are often saved as script files for future use. Individual statements in SQL scripts are commonly terminated by a line break (or carriage return) and a forward slash on the next line, instead of a semicolon. You can create a SELECT statement, terminate it with a line break, include a forward slash to execute the statement, and save it in a script file. The script file can then be called from within SQL*Plus. Note that SQL Developer does not require a statement terminator if only a single statement is present, but it will not object if one is used. It is good practice to always terminate your SQL statements with a semicolon. Several examples of SQL*Plus statements follow:

```
select country_name, country_id, location_id from countries;
select city, location_id,
       state_province, country_id
from locations
/
```

The first example of code demonstrates two important rules. First, the statement is terminated by a semicolon. Second, the entire statement is written on one line. It is entirely acceptable for a SQL statement to either be written on one line or to span multiple lines as long as no words in the statement span multiple lines. The second sample of code demonstrates a statement that spans three lines that is terminated by a new line and executed with a forward slash.

Indentation, Readability, and Good Practice

Consider the following query:

```
select city, location_id,
       state_province, country_id
from locations
/
```

This example highlights the benefits of indenting your SQL statement to enhance the readability of your code. The Oracle server does not object if the entire statement is written on one line without indentation. It is good practice to separate different clauses of the SELECT statement onto different lines. When an expression in a clause is particularly complex, it is often better to separate that term of the statement onto a new line. When developing SQL to meet your reporting needs, the process is often iterative. The SQL interpreter is far more useful during development if complex expressions are isolated on separate lines, since errors are usually thrown in the format of: "ERROR at line X:" This makes the debugging process much simpler.

SCENARIO & SOLUTION

You want to construct and execute queries against tables stored in an Oracle database. Are you confined to using SQL*Plus or SQL Developer?	No. Oracle provides SQL*Plus and SQL Developer as free tools to create and execute queries. There are numerous tools available from Oracle (for example, Discoverer, Forms, and JDeveloper) and other third-party vendors that provide an interface to the tables stored in an Oracle database.
To explore your database environment further, you would like a list of tables, owned by your current schema, available for you to query. How do you interrogate the database dictionary to provide this metadata?	The data dictionary is a set of tables and views of other tables that can be queried via SQL. The statement SELECT TABLE_NAME from USER_TABLES; queries the database dictionary for a list of table names that belong to the current user.
When querying the JOBS table for every row containing just the JOB_ID and MAX_SALARY columns, is a projection, selection, or join being performed?	A projection is performed since the columns in the JOBS table have been restricted to the JOB_ID and MAX_SALARY columns.

EXERCISE 2-2

Answering Our First Questions with SQL

In this step-by-step exercise, a connection is made using SQL*Plus as the HR user to answer two questions using the SELECT statement.

Question 1: How many unique departments have employees currently working in them?

1. Start SQL*Plus and connect to the HR schema.

2. You may initially be tempted to find the answer in the DEPARTMENTS table. A careful examination reveals that the question asks for information about employees. This information is contained in the EMPLOYEES table.

3. The word "unique" should guide you to use the DISTINCT keyword.

4. Combining steps 2 and 3, you can construct the following SQL statement:

```
select distinct department_id
from employees;
```

5. As shown in the following illustration, this query returns 12 rows. Notice that the third row is empty. This is a null value in the DEPARTMENT_ID column.

```
Command Prompt - SQLPLUS HR                                    _ □ X
SQL> SELECT DISTINCT DEPARTMENT_ID
  2  FROM EMPLOYEES;

DEPARTMENT_ID
-------------
          100
           30

           20
           70
           90
          110
           50
           40
           80
           10
           60

12 rows selected.

SQL>
```

6. The answer to the first question is therefore: Eleven unique departments have employees working in them, but at least one employee has not been assigned to a department.

Question 2: How many countries are there in the Europe region?

1. This question comprises two parts. Consider the REGIONS table, which contains four regions each uniquely identified by a REGION_ID value, and the COUNTRIES table, which has a REGION_ID column indicating which region a country belongs to.

2. The first query needs to identify the REGION_ID of the Europe region. This is accomplished by the SQL statement:

```
select * from regions;
```

3. The following illustration shows that the Europe region has a REGION_ID value of 1:

```
Command Prompt - SQLPLUS HR                                    _□X
SQL> SELECT *
  2  FROM REGIONS;

 REGION_ID REGION_NAME
---------- --------------------------------
         1 Europe
         2 Americas
         3 Asia
         4 Middle East and Africa

SQL> _
```

4. To identify which countries have 1 as their REGION_ID, you need to execute the following SQL query

   ```
   select region_id, country_name from countries;
   ```

5. Manually counting the country rows with a REGION_ID of 1 in the following illustration helps answer the second question:

```
Command Prompt - SQLPLUS HR                                    _□X
SQL> SELECT REGION_ID, COUNTRY_NAME
  2  FROM COUNTRIES;

 REGION_ID COUNTRY_NAME
---------- ----------------------------------------
         2 Argentina
         3 Australia
         1 Belgium
         2 Brazil
         2 Canada
         1 Switzerland
         3 China
         1 Germany
         1 Denmark
         4 Egypt
         1 France
         3 HongKong
         4 Israel
         3 India
         1 Italy
         3 Japan
         4 Kuwait
         2 Mexico
         4 Nigeria
         1 Netherlands
         3 Singapore
         1 United Kingdom
         2 United States of America
         4 Zambia
         4 Zimbabwe

25 rows selected.
```

6. The answer to the second question is therefore: There are eight countries in the Europe region as far as the HR data model is concerned.

SQL Expressions and Operators

The general form of the SELECT statement introduced the notion that columns and expressions are selectable. An expression is usually made up of an operation being performed on one or more column values. The operators that can act upon column values to form an expression depend on the data type of the column. They are the four cardinal arithmetic operators (addition, subtraction, multiplication, and division) for numeric columns; the concatenation operator for character or string columns; and the addition and subtraction operators for date and timestamp columns. As in regular arithmetic, there is a predefined order of evaluation (operator precedence) when more than one operator occurs in an expression. Round brackets have the highest precedence. Division and multiplication operations are next in the hierarchy and are evaluated before addition and subtraction, which have lowest precedence. These precedence levels are shown in Table 2-1.

Operations with the same level of precedence are evaluated from left to right. Round brackets may therefore be used to enforce nondefault operator precedence. Using brackets generously when constructing complex expressions is good practice and is encouraged. It leads to readable code that is less prone to error. Expressions open up a large number of useful data manipulation possibilities.

Arithmetic Operators

Consider the example of the JOB_HISTORY table, which stores the start date and end date of an employee's term in a previous job role. It may be useful for tax or pension purposes, for example, to calculate how long an employee worked in that role. This information can be obtained using an arithmetic expression. There are a few interesting elements of both the SQL statement and the results returned from Figure 2-7 that warrant further discussion.

Five elements have been specified in the SELECT clause. The first four are regular columns of the JOB_HISTORY table namely: EMPLOYEE_ID, JOB_ID, START_DATE, and END_DATE. The latter two terms provide the source information required to calculate the number of days that an employee filled a particular position. Consider employee number 176 on the ninth row of output. This employee started as a Sales

TABLE 2-1	Precedence Level	Operator Symbol	Operation
Precedence of Arithmetic Operators	Highest	( )	Brackets or parentheses
	Medium	/	Division
	Medium	*	Multiplication
	Lowest	−	Subtraction
	Lowest	+	Addition

FIGURE 2-7   Arithmetic expression to calculate number of days worked

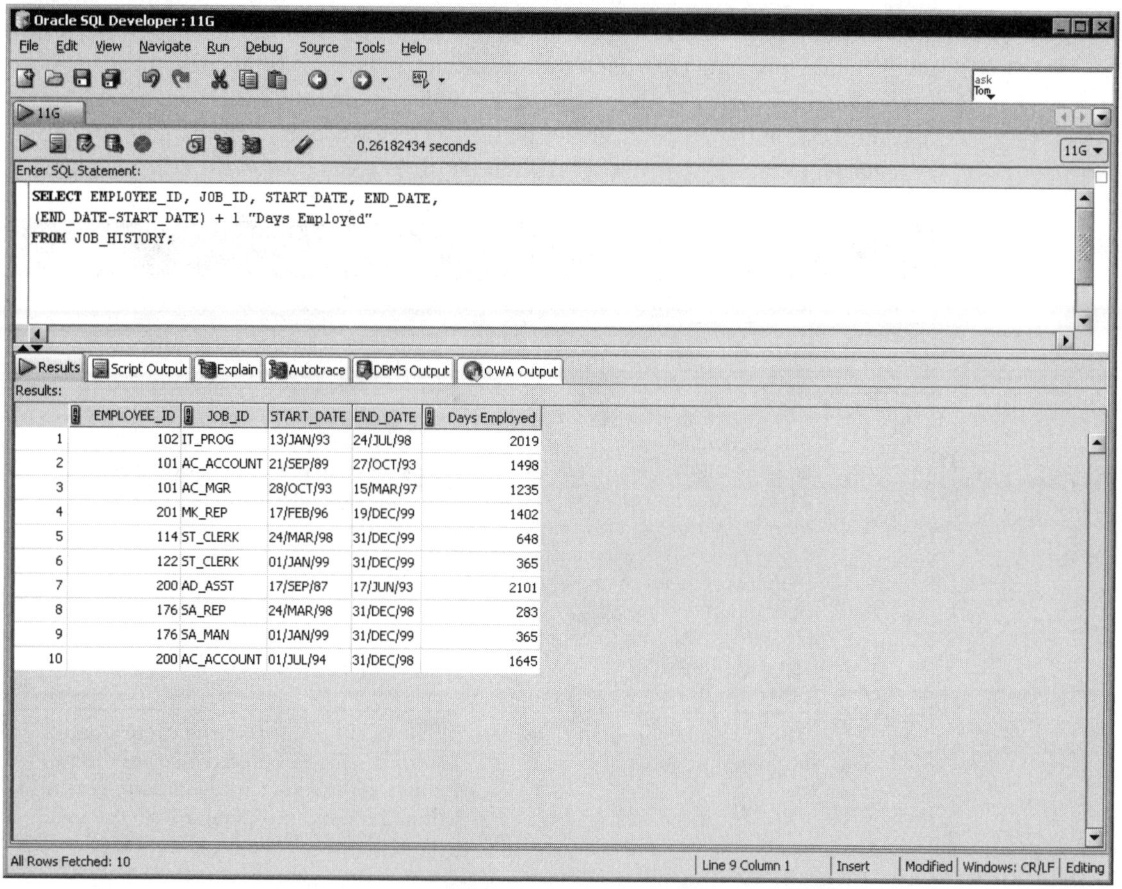

Manager on January 1, 1999 and ended employment on December 31, 1999. Therefore, this employee worked for exactly one year, which, in 1999, consisted of 365 days.

The number of days for which an employee was employed can be calculated by using the fifth element in the SELECT clause, which is an expression. This expression demonstrates that arithmetic performed on columns containing date information returns numeric values which represent a certain number of days.

To enforce operator precedence of the subtraction operation, the subexpression *end_date-start_date* is enclosed in round brackets. One day was added to compensate for the arithmetic loss of a day arising from the subtraction operation. Suppose an employee started work on January 1 and quit later that day. One day must be added to the formula, otherwise the subexpression *end_date-start_date* would incorrectly return zero days worked.

A hypothetical formula for predicting the probability of a meteor shower in a particular geographic region has been devised. The two expressions listed in Figure 2-8 are identical except for the Meteor Shower Probability % expression. However, as the results in the following table demonstrate, a different calculation is being made by each expression. Notice that the two expressions differ very slightly. Expression 2 has a pair of parentheses at the very end, enclosing $(10 - 5)$. Consider how the expressions are evaluated for the Asia region where REGION_ID is 3 as shown in the following table:

Step	Expression 1	Expression 2
1.	*region_id* * 100/5 + 20 / 10 − 5	*region_id* * 100/5 + 20 / (10 − 5)
2.	Substitute *region_id* with value: 3 * 100 /5 + 20 / 10 − 5	Substitute *region_id* with value: 3 * 100 / 5 + 20 / (10 − 5)
3.	The operators with the highest precedence are the two division and one multiplication operators. These must be evaluated first. If more than one operator with the same level of precedence is present in an expression, then these will be evaluated from left to right. Therefore, the first subexpression to be evaluated is: 3*100: **300** / 5 + 20 / 10 − 5	The operator with the highest precedence is the pair of parentheses and these must be evaluated first. Therefore, the first subexpression to be evaluated is: $(10 - 5)$: 3*100/5 + 20/5
4.	The next subexpression to be evaluated is: 300/5: **60** + 20/10 − 5	The next operators in the expression with the highest precedence are the two division and one multiplication operators. If more than one operator with the same level of precedence is present in an expression, then these will be evaluated from left to right. Therefore, the next subexpression to be evaluated is: 3*100: **300**/5 + 20/5
5.	The next subexpression to be evaluated is: 20/10: 60 + **2** − 5	The next subexpression to be evaluated is: 300/5: **60** + 20/5
6.	The remaining operators are one addition and one subtraction operator which share the same level of precedence. These will therefore be evaluated from left to right. The next subexpression to be evaluated is: 60+2: **62** − 5=**57**	The next subexpression to be evaluated is: 20/5: 60 + **4** = **64**

FIGURE 2-8 Use of the concatenation and arithmetic operators

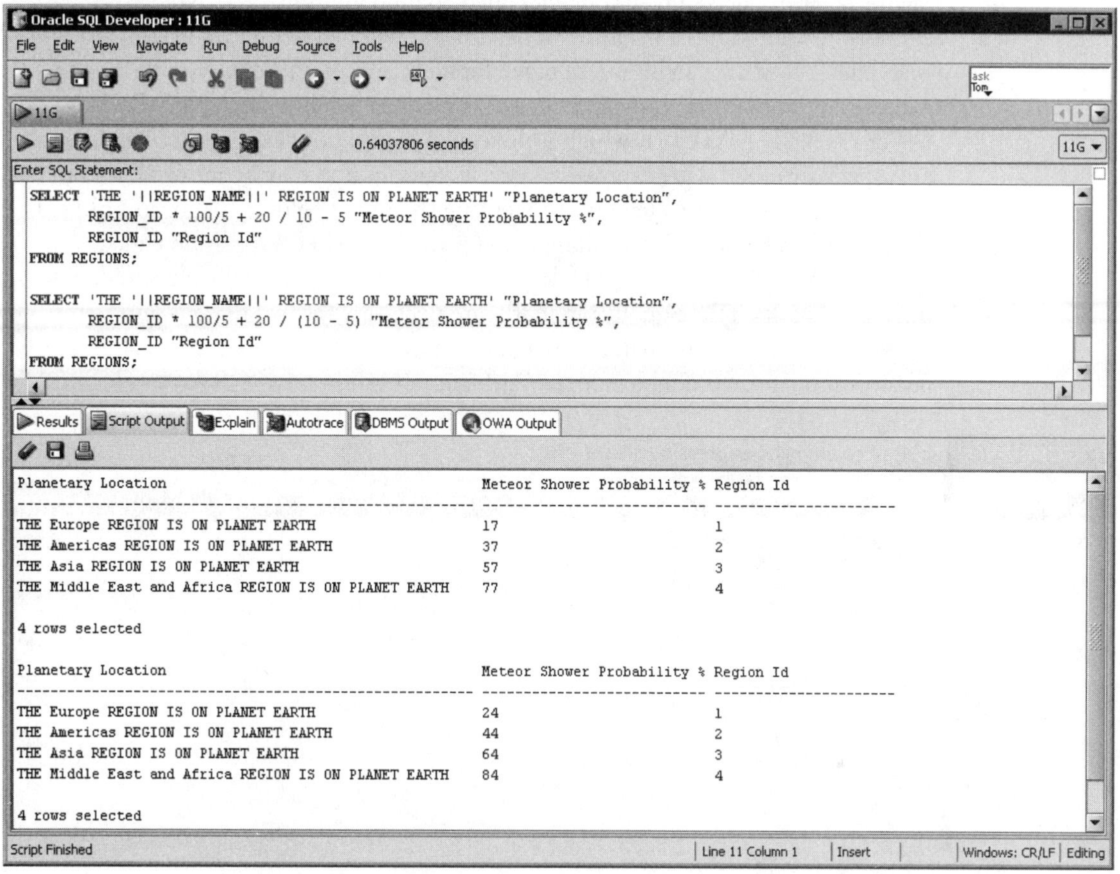
Oracle SQL Developer : 11G
File Edit View Navigate Run Debug Source Tools Help
11G
0.64037806 seconds
Enter SQL Statement:
SELECT 'THE '||REGION_NAME||' REGION IS ON PLANET EARTH' "Planetary Location",
REGION_ID * 100/5 + 20 / 10 - 5 "Meteor Shower Probability %",
REGION_ID "Region Id"
FROM REGIONS;
SELECT 'THE '||REGION_NAME||' REGION IS ON PLANET EARTH' "Planetary Location",
REGION_ID * 100/5 + 20 / (10 - 5) "Meteor Shower Probability %",
REGION_ID "Region Id"
FROM REGIONS;
Results
Script Output
Explain
Autotrace
DBMS Output
OWA Output
Planetary Location Meteor Shower Probability % Region Id
THE Europe REGION IS ON PLANET EARTH 17 1
THE Americas REGION IS ON PLANET EARTH 37 2
THE Asia REGION IS ON PLANET EARTH 57 3
THE Middle East and Africa REGION IS ON PLANET EARTH 77 4
4 rows selected
Planetary Location Meteor Shower Probability % Region Id
THE Europe REGION IS ON PLANET EARTH 24 1
THE Americas REGION IS ON PLANET EARTH 44 2
THE Asia REGION IS ON PLANET EARTH 64 3
THE Middle East and Africa REGION IS ON PLANET EARTH 84 4
4 rows selected
Script Finished
Line 11 Column 1
Insert
Windows: CR/LF
Editing

on the job

Expressions offer endless possibilities and are one of the fundamental constructs in SELECT statements. As you practice SQL on your test database environment, you may encounter two infamous Oracle errors: "ORA-00923: FROM keyword not found where expected" and "ORA-00942: table or view does not exist". These are indicative of spelling or punctuation errors, such as missing enclosing quotes around character literals. Do not be perturbed by these messages. Remember, you cannot cause damage to the database if all you are doing is selecting data. It is a read-only operation and the worst you can do is execute a nonperformant query.

Expression and Column Aliasing

Figure 2-7 introduced a new concept called column aliasing. Notice how the expression column has a meaningful heading named Days Employed. This heading is an alias. An *alias* is an alternate name for a column or an expression. If this expression did not make use of an alias, the column heading would be: (END_DATE-START_DATE)+1, which is unattractive and not very descriptive. Aliases are especially useful with expressions or calculations and may be implemented in several ways. There are a few rules governing the use of column aliases in SELECT statements. In Figure 2-7, the alias given for the calculated expression called "Days Employed" was specified by leaving a space and entering the alias in double quotation marks. These quotation marks are necessary for two reasons. First, this alias is made up of more than one word. Second, case preservation of an alias is only possible if the alias is double quoted. As Figure 2-9 shows, an "ORA-00923: FROM

FIGURE 2-9	Use of column and expression aliases

keyword not found where expected" error is returned when a multiworded alias is not double quoted.

The ORA-00923 error is not randomly generated by the server. The Oracle interpreter tries to process the statement and finds a problem with it. As it processes this particular statement, it finds a problem with line 2. An asterisk symbol is inserted at the starting point of the problem: the word Employed. Line 2 was processed and the expression was aliased with the word Days. The space after Days indicates to the Oracle interpreter that, since there is no additional comma to indicate another term belonging to the SELECT clause, it is complete. Therefore, it expects to find the FROM clause next. Instead it finds the word Employed and yields this error. Error messages from the Oracle server are informative and you should read them carefully to resolve problems. This error is avoided by enclosing an alias that contains a space or other special characters, such as # and $, in double quotation marks as shown around the alias "Days Employed" in Figure 2-7.

The second example in Figure 2-9 illustrates another interesting characteristic of column aliasing. Double quotation marks have once again been dispensed with and an underscore character is substituted for the space between the words to avoid an error being returned. The Oracle interpreter processes the statement, finds no problem, and executes it. Notice that although the alias was specified as Date_ Employed, with only the title letters of the alias being capitalized, the expression heading was returned as DATE_EMPLOYED: all letters were automatically converted to uppercase. Thus, to preserve the case of the alias, it must be enclosed in double quotation marks.

The aliases encountered so far have been specified by leaving a space after a column or expression and inserting the alias. SQL offers a more formalized way of inserting aliases. The AS keyword is inserted between the column or expression and the alias. Figure 2-10 illustrates the mixed use of the different types of column aliasing. Both the EMPLOYEE_ID and JOB_ID columns are aliased using the AS keyword, while the "Days Employed" expression is aliased using a space. The AS keyword is optional since it is also possible to use a space before specifying an alias, as discussed earlier. Use of the AS keyword does, however, improve the readability of SQL statements, and the authors believe it is a good SQL coding habit to form.

Character and String Concatenation Operator

The double pipe symbols || represent the character *concatenation* operator. This operator is used to join character expressions or columns together to create a larger character expression. Columns of a table may be linked to each other or to strings of literal characters to create one resultant character expression.

FIGURE 2-10

Use of the AS
keyword to
specify column
aliases

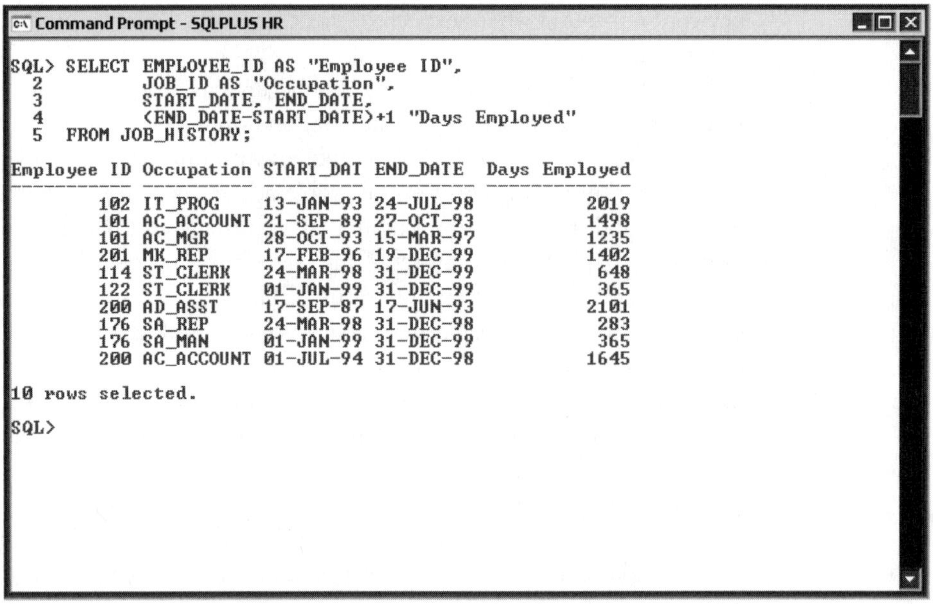

```
c:\ Command Prompt - SQLPLUS HR                                    _ □ X

SQL> SELECT EMPLOYEE_ID AS "Employee ID",
  2         JOB_ID AS "Occupation",
  3         START_DATE, END_DATE,
  4         (END_DATE-START_DATE)+1 "Days Employed"
  5  FROM JOB_HISTORY;

Employee ID Occupation START_DAT END_DATE  Days Employed
----------- ---------- --------- --------- -------------
        102 IT_PROG    13-JAN-93 24-JUL-98          2019
        101 AC_ACCOUNT 21-SEP-89 27-OCT-93          1498
        101 AC_MGR     28-OCT-93 15-MAR-97          1235
        201 MK_REP     17-FEB-96 19-DEC-99          1402
        114 ST_CLERK   24-MAR-98 31-DEC-99           648
        122 ST_CLERK   01-JAN-99 31-DEC-99           365
        200 AD_ASST    17-SEP-87 17-JUN-93          2101
        176 SA_REP     24-MAR-98 31-DEC-98           283
        176 SA_MAN     01-JAN-99 31-DEC-99           365
        200 AC_ACCOUNT 01-JUL-94 31-DEC-98          1645

10 rows selected.

SQL>
```

Figure 2-8 shows that the concatenation operator is flexible enough to be used multiple times and almost anywhere in a character expression. Here, the character literal "The" is concatenated to the data contents of the REGION_NAME column. This new string of characters is further concatenated to the character literal "region is on Planet Earth," and the whole expression is aliased with the friendly column heading "Planetary Location." Notice how each row in the results set is constructed by the systematic application of the expression to every row value from the table.

Consider the first data row from the "Planetary Location" expression column. It returns "The Europe region is on Planet Earth." A legible sentence for the rows of data has been created by concatenating literal strings of characters and spaces to either side of each row's REGION_NAME column value. The REGION_ID column has been aliased to show that regular columns as well as expressions may be aliased. Further, column headings are by default displayed in uppercase but can be overridden using an alias like "Region Id." The data types of the columns being queried determine how SQL*Plus and SQL Developer present their default data outputs. If the data type is numeric then the column data is formatted to be right aligned. If the data type is character or date, then the column data is formatted to be left aligned.

Literals and the DUAL Table

Literal values in expressions are a common occurrence. These values refer to numeric, character, or date and time values found in SELECT clauses that do not originate from any database object. Concatenating character literals to existing column data can be useful, as introduced in Figure 2-8. What about processing literals that have nothing to do with existing column data? To ensure relational consistency, Oracle offers a clever solution to the problem of using the database to evaluate expressions that have nothing to do with any tables or columns. To get the database to evaluate an expression, a syntactically legal SELECT statement must be submitted. What if you wanted to know the sum of two numbers or two numeric literals? These questions can only be answered by interacting with the database in a relational manner. Oracle solves the problem of relational interaction with the database operating on literal expressions by offering a special table called DUAL. Recall the DUAL table described in Figure 2-1. It contains one column called DUMMY of character data type. You can execute the query: SELECT * FROM DUAL, and the data value "X" is returned as the contents of the DUMMY column. The DUAL table allows literal expressions to be selected from it for processing and returns the expression results in its single row. It is exceptionally useful since it enables a variety of different processing requests to be made from the database. You may want to know how many seconds there are in a year. Figure 2-11 demonstrates an arithmetic expression executed against the DUAL table. Testing complex expressions during development, by querying the dual table, is an effective method to evaluate whether these expressions are working correctly. Literal expressions can be queried from any table, but remember that the expression will be processed for every row in the table.

```
select 'literal'||'processing using the REGIONS table'
from regions;
```

The preceding statement will return four lines in the results set, since there are four rows of data in the REGIONS table.

Two Single Quotes or the Alternative Quote Operator

The literal character strings concatenated so far have been singular words prepended and appended to column expressions. These character literals are specified using single quotation marks. For example:

```
select 'I am a character literal string'
```

FIGURE 2-11   Using the DUAL table

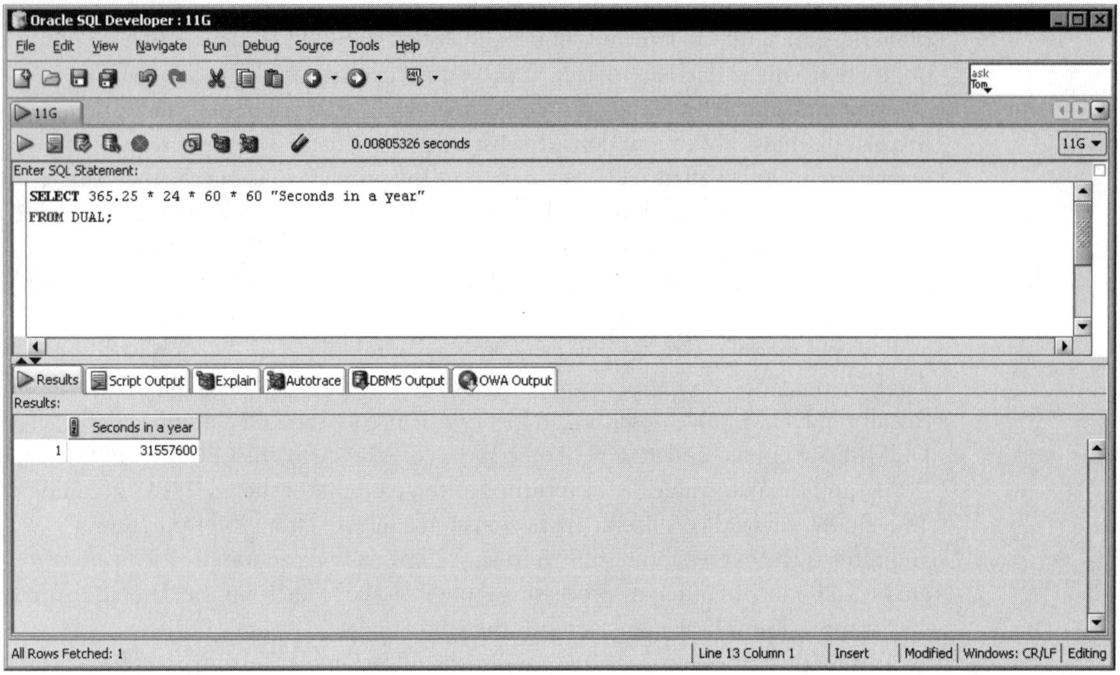

What about character literals that contain single quotation marks? Plurals pose a particular problem for character literal processing. Consider the following statement:

```
select 'Plural's have one quote too many' from dual;
```

As the example in Figure 2-12 shows, executing this statement causes an ORA-00923 Oracle error to be generated. It might seem like an odd error, but upon closer examination, the Oracle interpreter successfully processes the SELECT statement until position 16, at which point it expects a "FROM" clause. Position 1 to position 16 is:

```
select 'Plural's
```

FIGURE 2-12

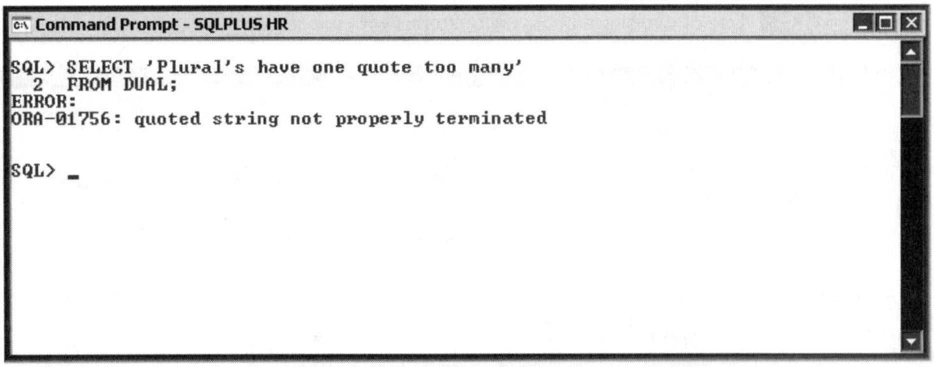

Error while
dealing with
literals with
implicit quotes

```
Command Prompt - SQLPLUS HR                                    _ □ X
SQL> SELECT 'Plural's have one quote too many'
  2   FROM DUAL;
ERROR:
ORA-01756: quoted string not properly terminated

SQL> _
```

The Oracle server processes this segment to mean that the character literal 'Plural' is aliased as column "s". At this point, the interpreter expects a "FROM" clause, but instead finds the word "have." It then generates an error.

So, how are words that contain single quotation marks dealt with? There are essentially two mechanisms available. The most popular of these is to add an additional single quotation mark next to each naturally occurring single quotation mark in the character string. Figure 2-13 demonstrates how the previous error is avoided by replacing the character literal `'Plural's` with the literal `'Plural''s`.

The second example in Figure 2-13 shows that using two single quotes to handle each naturally occurring single quote in a character literal can become messy and error prone as the number of affected literals increases. Oracle offers a neat way to deal with this type of character literal in the form of the alternative quote (q) operator. Notice that the problem is that Oracle chose the single quote characters as the special pair of symbols that enclose or wrap any other character literal. These character-enclosing symbols could have been anything other than single quotation marks.

Bearing this in mind, consider the alternative quote (q) operator. The q operator enables you to choose from a set of possible pairs of wrapping symbols for character literals as alternatives to the single quote symbols. The options are any single-byte

FIGURE 2-13   Use of two single quotes with literals with implicit quotes

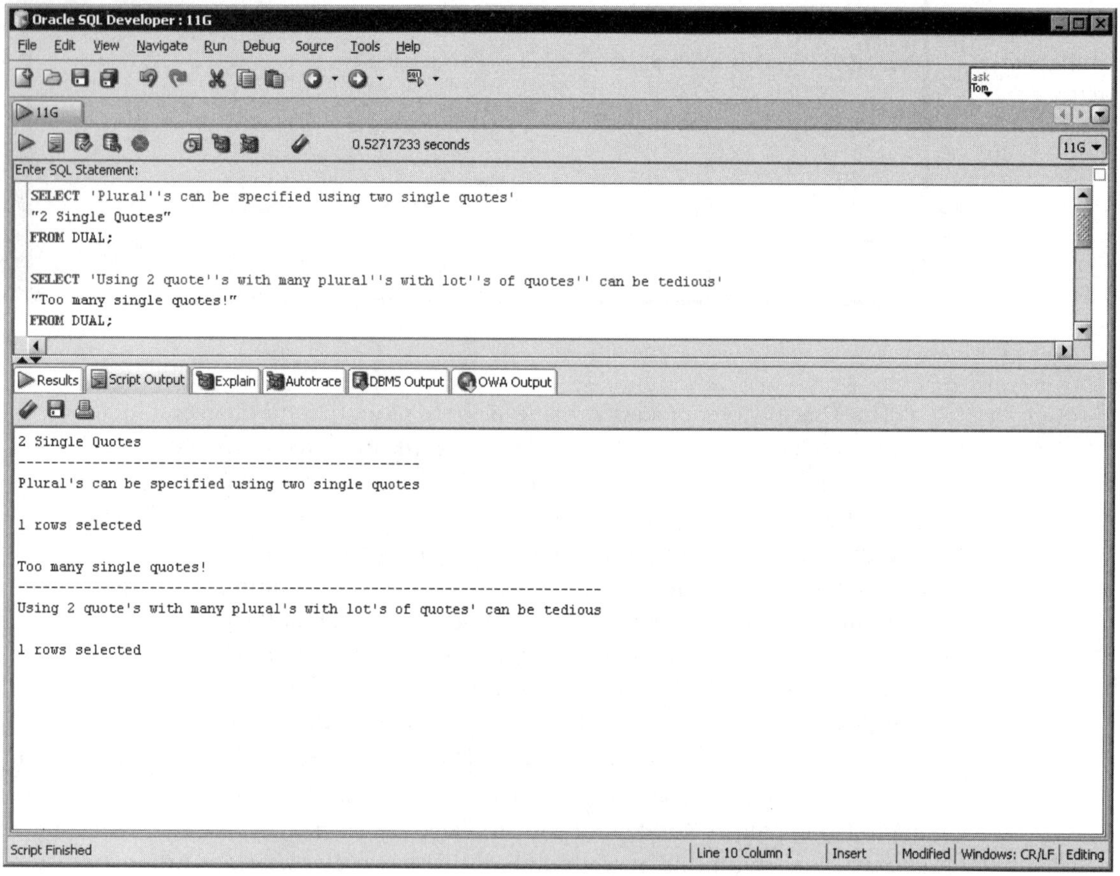

or multibyte character or the four brackets: (round brackets), {curly braces}, [square brackets], or <angle brackets>. Using the q operator, the character delimiter can effectively be changed from a single quotation mark to any other character, as shown in Figure 2-14.

The syntax of the alternative quote operator is as follows:

q'*delimiter*'character literal which may include the single quotes *delimiter*' where *delimiter* can be any character or bracket. The first and second examples in Figure 2-14 show the use of angle and square brackets as character delimiters, while the third example demonstrates how an uppercase "X" has been used as the special character delimiter symbol through the alternative quote operator.

FIGURE 2-14   The alternate quote (q) operator

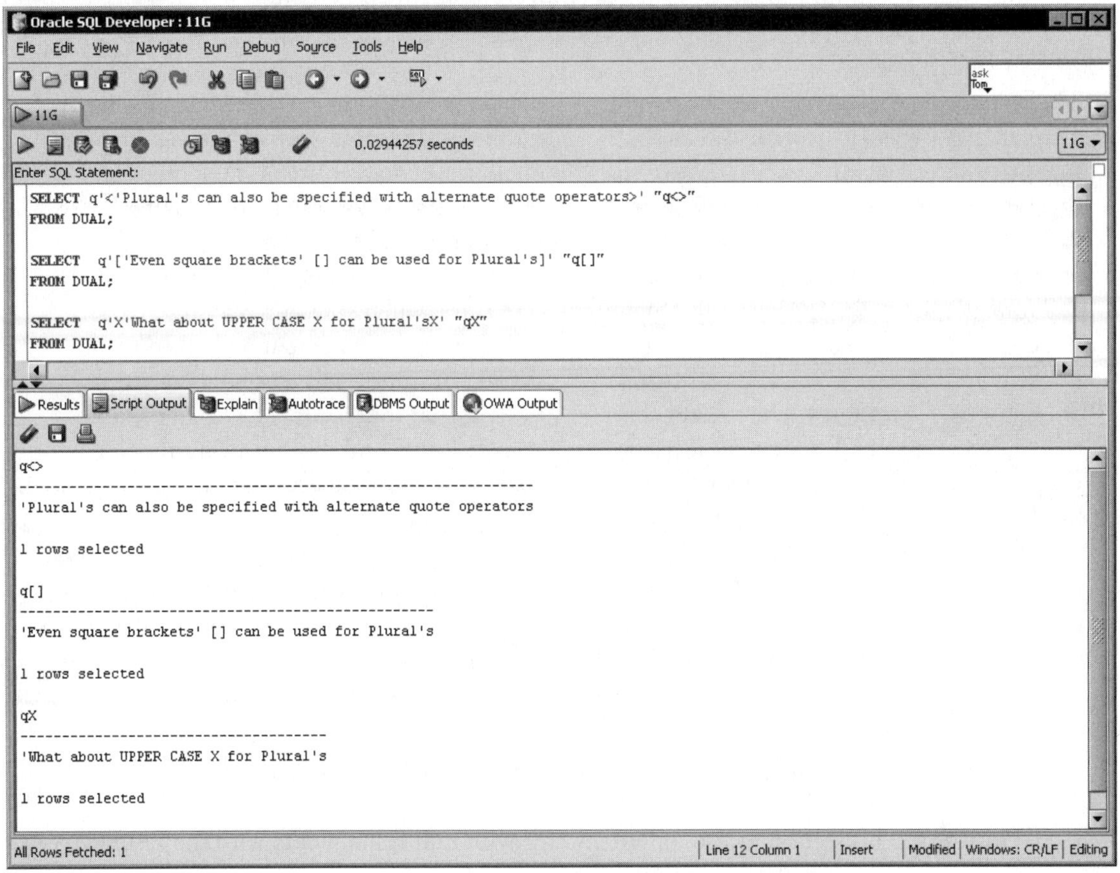

NULL Is Nothing

The concept of a null value was introduced in the earlier discussion of the DESCRIBE command. Both the number zero and a blank space are different from null since they occupy space. *Null* refers to an absence of data. A row that contains a null value lacks data for that column. Null is formally defined as a value that is unavailable, unassigned, unknown, or inapplicable. In other words, the rules of engaging with null values need careful examination. Failure to heed the special treatment that null values require will almost certainly lead to an error, or worse, an inaccurate answer.

Null values may be a tricky concept to come to grips with. The problem stems from the absence of null on a number line. It is not a real, tangible value that can be related to the physical world. Null is a placeholder in a nonmandatory column until

INSIDE THE EXAM

There are two certification objectives in this chapter. The capabilities of the SELECT statement introduce the three fundamental theoretical concepts of projection, selection, and joining. Practical examples that illustrate selection include building the SELECT clause and using the DISTINCT keyword to limit the rows returned. Projection is demonstrated in examples where columns and expressions are restricted for retrieval. The second objective of executing a SQL statement measures your understanding of the basic form of the SELECT statement. The exam measures two aspects. First, syntax is measured: you are required to spot syntax errors. SQL syntax errors are raised when the Oracle interpreter does not understand a statement. These errors could take the form of statements missing terminators such as a missing semicolon, not enclosing character literals in appropriate quote operators, or statements making use of invalid reserved words.

Second, the meaning of a statement is measured. You will be presented with a syntactically legitimate statement and asked to choose between accurate and inaccurate descriptions of that statement. The exam measures knowledge around the certification objectives using multiple choice format questions. Your understanding of column aliasing, arithmetic and concatenation operators, character literal quoting, the alternative quote operator, SQL statement syntax, and basic column data types will be tested.

some real data is stored in its place. Until then, beware of conducting arithmetic with null columns.

This section focuses on interacting with null column data with the SELECT statement and its impact on expressions.

Not Null and Nullable Columns

Tables store rows of data that are divided into one or more columns. These columns have names and data types associated with them. Some of them are constrained by database rules to be mandatory columns. It is compulsory for some data to be stored in the NOT NULL columns in each row. When columns of a table, however, are not compelled by the database constraints to hold data for a row, these columns run the risk of being empty.

In Figure 2-15, the EMPLOYEES table is described, and a few columns are selected from it. There are five NOT NULL columns and six NULLABLE columns. *Nullable* is a term sometimes used to describe a column that is allowed to store null values. One of the nullable columns is the COMMISSION_PCT column.

FIGURE 2-15   Null values in the Commission_Pct column

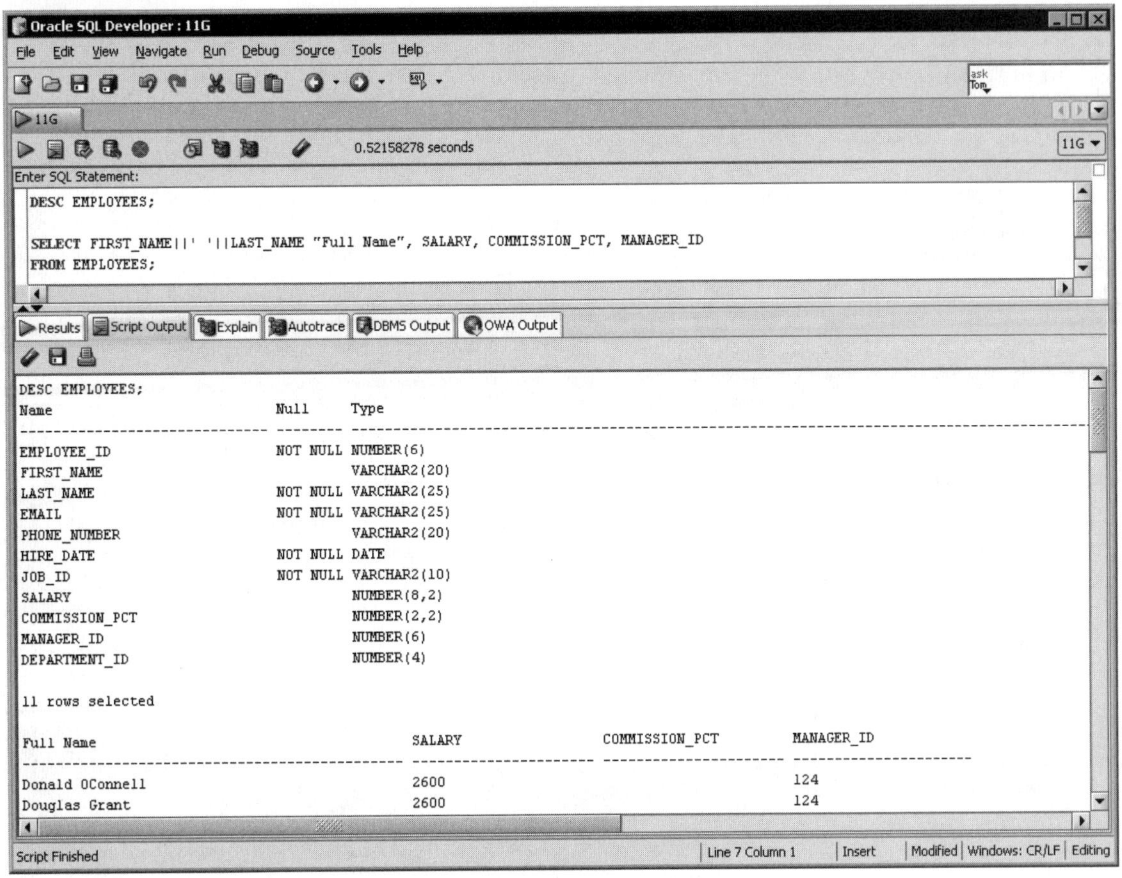

Figure 2-15 shows the first two rows of data from the EMPLOYEES table. This is sufficient to illustrate that both these employee records have null values in their COMMISSION_PCT columns.

SQL Developer makes it simple to observe null values in columns, as displayed in Figure 2-16. Here, the word (null) is output when a null value is encountered, as with the COMMISSION_PCT column. SQL Developer supports customizing this default description of null column data.

The column aliased as "Null Arithmetic" is an expression made up of COMMISSION_PCT + EMPLOYEE_ID + 10. Instead of returning a numeric value, this column returns null. There is an important reason for this:

Any arithmetic calculation with a NULL value always returns NULL.

FIGURE 2-16   Null arithmetic always returns a null value.

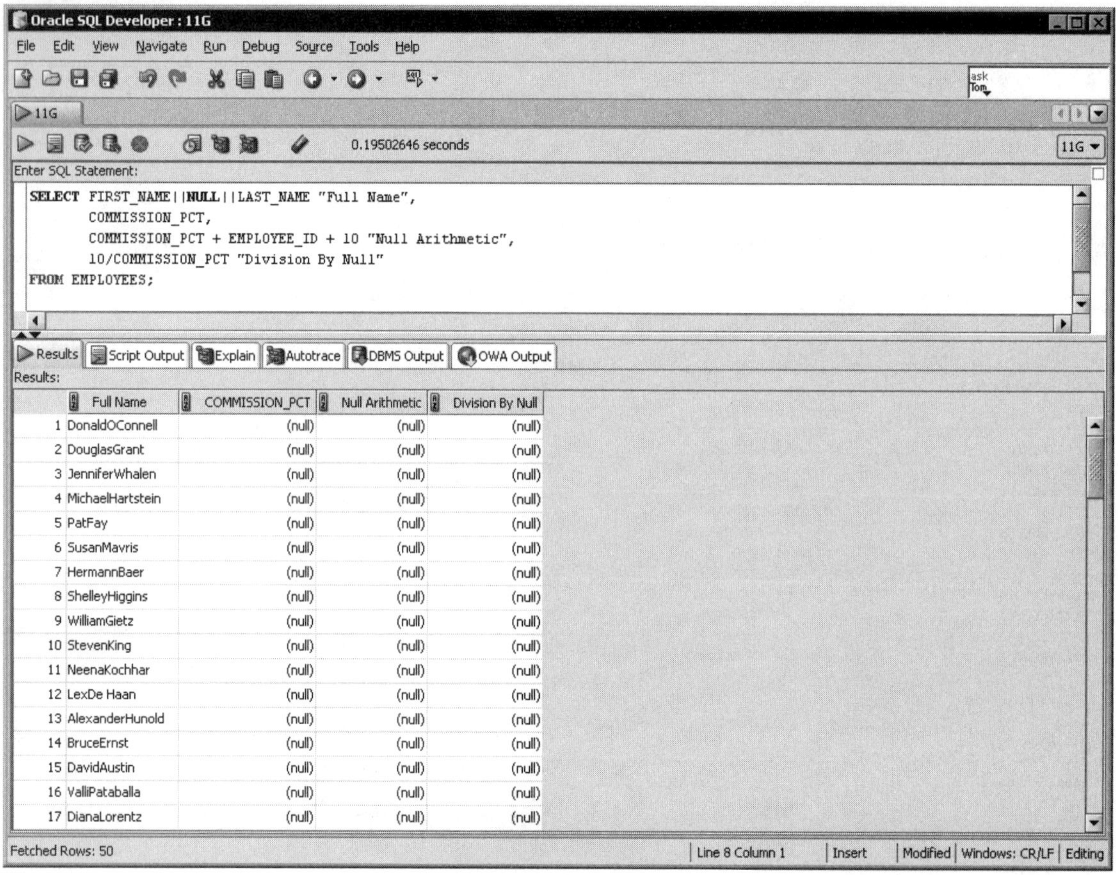

Oracle offers a mechanism for interacting arithmetically with NULL values using the general functions discussed in Chapter 5. As the column expression aliased as "Division by Null" illustrates, even division by a null value results in null, unlike division by zero, which results in an error. Finally, notice the impact of the null keyword when used with the character concatenation operator. Null is concatenated between the FIRST_NAME and LAST_NAME columns, yet it has no impact. The character concatenation operators ignore null, whilst the arithmetic operations involving null values always result in null.

Foreign Keys and Nullable Columns

Data model design sometimes leads to problematic situations when tables are related to each other via a primary and foreign key relationship, but the column that the foreign key is based on is nullable.

The DEPARTMENTS table has, as its primary key, the DEPARTMENT_ID column. The EMPLOYEES table has a DEPARTMENT_ID column that is constrained by its foreign key relationship to the DEPARTMENT_ID column in the DEPARTMENTS table. This means that no record in the EMPLOYEES table is allowed to have in its DEPARTMENT_ID column a value that is not in the DEPARTMENTS table. This referential integrity forms the basis for third normal form and is critical to overall database integrity.

But what about NULL values? Can the DEPARTMENT_ID column in the DEPARTMENTS table contain nulls? The answer is *no*. Oracle insists that any column that is a primary key is implicitly constrained to be mandatory. But what about implicit constraints on foreign key columns? This is a quandary for Oracle, since in order to remain flexible and cater to the widest audience, it cannot insist that columns related through referential integrity constraints must be mandatory. Further, not all situations demand this functionality.

SCENARIO & SOLUTION

You are constructing an arithmetic expression that calculates taxable income based on an employee's SALARY and COMMISSION_PCT columns, both of which are nullable. Is it possible to convert the null values in either column to zero to always return a numeric taxable income?	Yes, but not with the information you have covered so far. Null values require special handling. In Chapter 5, we discuss the NVL function, which provides a mechanism to convert null values into more arithmetic-friendly data values.
An alias provides a mechanism to rename a column or an expression. Under what conditions should you enclose an alias in double quotes?	If an alias contains more than one word or if the case of an alias must be preserved, then it should be enclosed in double quotation marks. Failure to double quote a multiworded alias will raise an Oracle error. Failure to double quote a single-word alias will result in the alias being returned in uppercase.
When working with character literal values that include single quotation marks, how should you specify these literals in the SELECT clause without raising an error?	There are two mechanisms available. The more common approach is to replace each naturally occurring single quote with two single quotes. The other approach is to make use of the alternate quote operator to specify an alternate pair of characters with which to enclose character literals.

The DEPARTMENT_ID column in the EMPLOYEES table is actually nullable. Therefore, the risk exists that there are records with null DEPARTMENT_ID values present in this table. In fact, there are such records in the EMPLOYEES table. The HR data model allows employees, correctly or not, to belong to no department. When performing relational joins between tables, it is entirely possible to miss or exclude certain records that contain nulls in the join column. Chapter 7 explores ways to deal with this challenge.

EXERCISE 2-3

Experimenting with Expressions and the DUAL Table

In this step-by-step exercise a connection is made using SQL Developer as the HR user. Use expressions and operators to answer three questions related to the SELECT statement:

Question 1: It was demonstrated earlier how the number of days for which staff were employed in a job could be calculated. For how many years were staff employed while fulfilling these job roles and what were their EMPLOYEE_ID, JOB_ID, START_DATE, and END_DATE values? Alias the expression column in your query with the alias Years Employed. Assume that a year consists of 365.25 days.

1. Start SQL Developer and connect to the HR schema.

2. The projection of columns required includes EMPLOYEE_ID, JOB_ID, START_DATE, END_DATE, and an expression called Years Employed from the JOB_HISTORY table.

3. The expression can be calculated by dividing one plus the difference between END_DATE and START_DATE by 365.25 days, as shown next:

```
select employee_id, job_id, start_date, end_date,
((end_date-start_date) + 1)/365.25 "Years Employed"
from job_history;
```

4. Executing the preceding SELECT statement yields the results displayed in the following illustration:

Question 2: Query the JOBS table and return a single expression of the form The Job Id for the <job_title's> job is: <job_id>. Take note that the job_title should have an apostrophe and an "s" appended to it to read more naturally. A sample of this output for the organization president is: "The Job Id for the President's job is: AD_PRES." Alias this column expression as "Job Description" using the AS keyword.

1. There are multiple solutions to this problem. The approach chosen here is to handle the naturally occurring single quotation marks with an additional single quote.

2. A single expression aliased as Job Description is required and may be constructed by dissecting the requirement into the literal *The Job Id for the* being concatenated to the JOB_TITLE column. This string is then concatenated to the literal *"'s job is:*," which is further concatenated to the JOB_ID column. An additional single quotation mark is added to yield the SELECT statement that follows:

```
select 'The Job Id for the '||job_title||'''s job is: '||job_id
AS "Job Description"
from jobs;
```

3. The results of this SQL query are shown in the following illustration:

```
Command Prompt - SQLPLUS HR

SQL> SELECT 'The Job Id for the '||JOB_TITLE||'''s job is: '||JOB_ID
  2  AS "Job Description"
  3  FROM JOBS;

Job Description
-----------------------------------------------------------------------
The Job Id for the President's job is: AD_PRES
The Job Id for the Administration Vice President's job is: AD_VP
The Job Id for the Administration Assistant's job is: AD_ASST
The Job Id for the Finance Manager's job is: FI_MGR
The Job Id for the Accountant's job is: FI_ACCOUNT
The Job Id for the Accounting Manager's job is: AC_MGR
The Job Id for the Public Accountant's job is: AC_ACCOUNT
The Job Id for the Sales Manager's job is: SA_MAN
The Job Id for the Sales Representative's job is: SA_REP
The Job Id for the Purchasing Manager's job is: PU_MAN
The Job Id for the Purchasing Clerk's job is: PU_CLERK
The Job Id for the Stock Manager's job is: ST_MAN
The Job Id for the Stock Clerk's job is: ST_CLERK
The Job Id for the Shipping Clerk's job is: SH_CLERK
The Job Id for the Programmer's job is: IT_PROG
The Job Id for the Marketing Manager's job is: MK_MAN
The Job Id for the Marketing Representative's job is: MK_REP
The Job Id for the Human Resources Representative's job is: HR_REP
The Job Id for the Public Relations Representative's job is: PR_REP

19 rows selected.

SQL>
```

Question 3: Using the DUAL table, calculate the area of a circle with radius 6000 units, with pi being approximately 22/7. Use the formula: Area = pi × radius × radius. Alias the result as "Area."

1. Working with the DUAL table may initially seem curious. You get used to it as its functionality becomes more apparent. This question involves selecting a literal arithmetic expression from the DUAL table to yield a single row calculated answer that is not based on the column values in any table.

2. The expression may be calculated using the following SQL statement; note the use of brackets for precedence.

```
select (22/7) * (6000 * 6000) Area
from dual
```

3. The results returned show the approximate area of the circle as 113142857.14 square units.

CERTIFICATION SUMMARY

The SELECT statement construct forms the basis for the majority of interactions that occur with an Oracle database. These interactions may take the form of queries issued from SQL Developer or SQL*Plus or any number of Oracle and other third-party client tools. At their core, these tools translate requests for information into SELECT statements, which are then executed by the database.

The structure of a table has been described. Rows of data have been retrieved and the set-oriented format of the results was revealed. The results were refined by projection. In other words, your queries can include only the columns you are interested in retrieving and exclude the remaining columns in a table.

SELECT syntax rules are basic and flexible, and language errors should be rare due to its English-like grammar. Statement termination using semicolons, regard for character literal case-sensitivity, and awareness of null values should assist with avoiding errors.

Expressions expose a vista of data manipulation possibilities through the interaction of arithmetic and character operators with column or literal data, or a combination of the two.

The general form of the SELECT statement was explored and the foundation for the expansion of this statement was constructed.

The Self Test exercises are made up of two components. The first component is comprised of questions that give you an idea about what you may be asked during the exam. The second component enables you to practice the language skills discussed in this chapter in a lab format. The solutions to both categories of questions are discussed in detail in the solutions section.

✓ TWO-MINUTE DRILL

List the Capabilities of SQL SELECT Statements

❑ The three fundamental operations that SELECT statements are capable of are projection, selection, and joining.

❑ Projection refers to the restriction of columns selected from a table. Using projection, you retrieve only the columns of interest and not every possible column.

❑ Selection refers to the extraction of rows from a table. Selection includes the further restriction of the extracted rows based on various criteria or conditions. This allows you to retrieve only the rows that are of interest and not every row in the table.

❑ Joining involves linking two or more tables based on common attributes. Joining allows data to be stored in third normal form in discrete tables, instead of in one large table.

❑ An unlimited combination of projections, selections, and joins provides the language to extract the relational data required.

❑ A structural definition of a table can be obtained using the DESCRIBE command.

❑ Columns in tables store different types of data using various data types, the most common of which are NUMBER, VARCHAR2, DATE, and TIMESTAMP.

❑ The data type NUMBER(x,y) implies that numeric information stored in this column can have at most x digits, but at least y of these digits must appear on the right hand side of the decimal point.

❑ The DESCRIBE command lists the names, data types, and nullable status of all columns in a table.

❑ Mandatory columns are also referred to as NOT NULL columns

Execute a Basic SELECT Statement

❑ The syntax of the primitive SELECT clause is as follows:
SELECT * | {[DISTINCT] column | expression [alias],...}

❑ The SELECT statement is also referred to as a SELECT query and comprises at least two clauses, namely the SELECT clause and the FROM clause.

❑ The SELECT clause determines the *projection* of columns. In other words, the SELECT clause specifies which columns are included in the results returned.

❑ The asterisk (*) operator is used as a wildcard symbol to indicate all columns. So, the statement SELECT * FROM ACCOUNTS returns all the columns available in the ACCOUNTS table.

❑ The FROM clause specifies the source table or tables from which items are selected.

❑ The DISTINCT keyword preceding items in the SELECT clause causes duplicate combinations of these items to be excluded from the returned results set.

❑ SQL statements should be terminated with a semicolon. As an alternative, a new line can be added after a statement and a forward slash can be used to execute the statement.

❑ SQL statements can be written and executed in lowercase or uppercase. Be careful when interacting with character literals since these are case-sensitive.

❑ Arithmetic operators and the string concatenation operator acting on column and literal data form the basis of SQL expressions.

❑ Expressions and regular columns may be aliased using the AS keyword or by leaving a space between the column or expression and the alias.

❑ If an alias contains multiple words or the case of the alias is important, it must be enclosed in double quotation marks.

❑ Naturally occurring single quotes in a character literal can be selected by making use of either an additional single quote per naturally occurring quote or the alternative quote operator.

❑ The DUAL table is a single column and single row table that is often used to evaluate expressions that do not refer to specific columns or tables.

❑ Columns which are not governed by a NOT NULL constraint have the potential to store null values and are sometimes referred to as nullable columns.

❑ NULL values are not the same as a blank space or zero. NULL values refer to an absence of data. Null is defined as a value that is unavailable, unassigned, unknown, or inapplicable.

❑ Caution must be exercised when working with null values since arithmetic with a null value always yields a null result.

SELF TEST

The following questions will help you measure your understanding of the material presented in this chapter. Read all the choices carefully because there might be more than one correct answer. Choose all the correct answers for each question.

The following test is typical of the questions and format of the OCP 11g examination for the topic "Retrieving Data using the SQL SELECT Statement." These questions often make use of the Human Resources schema.

List the Capabilities of SQL SELECT Statements

1. Which query creates a projection of the DEPARTMENT_NAME and LOCATION_ID columns from the DEPARTMENTS table? (Choose the best answer.)

   A. SELECT DISTINCT DEPARTMENT_NAME, LOCATION_ID
      FROM DEPARTMENTS;

   B. SELECT DEPARTMENT_NAME, LOCATION_ID
      FROM DEPARTMENTS;

   C. SELECT DEPT_NAME, LOC_ID
      FROM DEPT;

   D. SELECT DEPARTMENT_NAME AS "LOCATION_ID"
      FROM DEPARTMENTS;

2. After describing the EMPLOYEES table, you discover that the SALARY column has a data type of NUMBER(8,2). Which SALARY value(s) will not be permitted in this column? (Choose all that apply.)

   A. SALARY=12345678

   B. SALARY=123456.78

   C. SALARY=12345.678

   D. SALARY=123456

   E. SALARY=12.34

3. After describing the JOB_HISTORY table, you discover that the START_DATE and END_DATE columns have a data type of DATE. Consider the expression END_DATE-START_DATE. (Choose two correct statements.)

   A. A value of DATE data type is returned.

   B. A value of type NUMBER is returned.

   C. A value of type VARCHAR2 is returned.

D. The expression is invalid since arithmetic cannot be performed on columns with DATE data types.

E. The expression represents the days between the END_DATE and START_DATE less one day.

4. The DEPARTMENTS table contains a DEPARTMENT_NAME column with data type VARCHAR2(30). (Choose two true statements about this column.)

A. This column can store character data up to a maximum of 30 characters.

B. This column must store character data that is at least 30 characters long.

C. The VARCHAR2 data type is replaced by the CHAR data type.

D. This column can store data in a column with data type VARCHAR2(50) provided that the contents are at most 30 characters long.

Execute a Basic SELECT Statement

5. Which statement reports on unique JOB_ID values from the EMPLOYEES table? (Choose all that apply.)

A. SELECT JOB_ID FROM EMPLOYEES;

B. SELECT UNIQUE JOB_ID FROM EMPLOYEES;

C. SELECT DISTINCT JOB_ID, EMPLOYEE_ID FROM EMPLOYEES;

D. SELECT DISTINCT JOB_ID FROM EMPLOYEES;

6. Choose the two illegal statements. The two correct statements produce identical results. The two illegal statements will cause an error to be raised:

A. SELECT DEPARTMENT_ID || ' represents the ' || DEPARTMENT_NAME ||' Department' as "Department Info" FROM DEPARTMENTS;

B. SELECT DEPARTMENT_ID || ' represents the || DEPARTMENT_NAME ||' Department' as "Department Info" FROM DEPARTMENTS;

C. select department_id || ' represents the ' || department_name || ' Department' "Department Info" from departments;

D. SELECT DEPARTMENT_ID represents the DEPARTMENT_NAME Department as "Department Info" FROM DEPARTMENTS;

7. Which expressions do not return NULL values? (Choose all that apply.)
   A. select ((10 + 20) * 50) + null from dual;
   B. select 'this is a ' || null || 'test with nulls' from dual;
   C. select null/0 from dual;
   D. select null || 'test' || null as "Test" from dual;

8. Choose the correct syntax to return all columns and rows of data from the EMPLOYEES table.
   A. select all from employees;
   B. select employee_id, first_name, last_name, first_name, department_id
      from employees;
   C. select % from employees;
   D. select * from employees;
   E. select *.* from employees;

9. The following character literal expression is selected from the DUAL table:
   SELECT 'Coda''s favorite fetch toy is his orange ring' FROM DUAL;
   (Choose the result that is returned.)
   A. An error would be returned due to the presence of two adjacent quotes
   B. Coda's favorite fetch toy is his orange ring
   C. Coda''s favorite fetch toy is his orange ring
   D. 'Coda''s favorite fetch toy is his orange ring'

10. There are four rows of data in the REGIONS table. Consider the following SQL statement:
    SELECT '6 * 6' "Area" FROM REGIONS;
    How many rows of results are returned and what value is returned by the Area column?
    (Choose the best answer.)
    A. 1 row returned, Area column contains value 36
    B. 4 rows returned, Area column contains value 36 for all 4 rows
    C. 1 row returned, Area column contains value 6 * 6
    D. 4 rows returned, Area column contains value 6 * 6 for all 4 rows
    E. A syntax error is returned.

LAB QUESTION

In this chapter you worked through examples in the Human Resources schema. Oracle provides a number of example schemas for you to experiment with and to learn different concepts from. For the practical exercises, you will be using the Order Entry, or OE, schema. The solutions for these exercises will be provided later using SQL Developer. Using SQL Developer or SQL*Plus, connect to the OE schema and complete the following tasks.

1. Obtain structural information for the PRODUCT_INFORMATION and ORDERS tables.

2. Select the unique SALES_REP_ID values from the ORDERS table. How many different sales representatives have been assigned to orders in the ORDERS table?

3. Create a results set based on the ORDERS table that includes the ORDER_ID, ORDER_DATE, and ORDER_TOTAL columns. Notice how the ORDER_DATE output is formatted differently from the START_DATE and END_DATE columns in the HR.JOB_ID table.

4. The PRODUCT_INFORMATION table stores data regarding the products available for sale in a fictitious IT hardware store. Produce a set of results that will be useful for a sales person. Extract product information in the format <PRODUCT_NAME> with code: <PRODUCT_ID> has status of: <PRODUCT_STATUS>. Alias the expression as "Product." The results should provide the LIST_PRICE, the MIN_PRICE, the difference between LIST_PRICE, and MIN_PRICE aliased as "Max Actual Savings," along with an additional expression that takes the difference between LIST_PRICE and MIN_PRICE and divides it by the LIST_PRICE and then multiplies the total by 100. This last expression should be aliased as "Max Discount %."

5. Calculate the surface area of the Earth using the DUAL table. Alias this expression as "Earth's Area." The formula for calculating the area of a sphere is: $4\pi r^2$. Assume, for this example, that the earth is a simple sphere with a radius of 3,958.759 miles and that π is 22/7.

SELF TEST ANSWERS

List the Capabilities of SQL SELECT Statements

1. ☑ **B.** A projection is an intentional restriction of the columns returned from a table.
   ☒ **A** is eliminated since the question has nothing to do with duplicates, distinctiveness, or uniqueness of data. **C** incorrectly selects nonexistent columns called DEPT_NAME and LOC_ID from a nonexistent table called DEPT. **D** returns just one of the requested columns: DEPARTMENT_NAME. Instead of additionally projecting the LOCATION_ID column from the DEPARTMENTS table, it attempts to alias the DEPARTMENT_NAME column as LOCATION_ID.

2. ☑ **A and C.** Columns with NUMBER(8,2) data type can store, at most, eight digits; of which, at most, two of those digits are to the right of the decimal point. Although **A** and **C** are the correct answers, note that since the question is phrased in the negative, these values are NOT allowed to be stored in such a column. **A** is not allowed because it contains eight whole number digits, but the data type is constrained to store six whole number digits and two fractional digits. **C** is not allowed since it has three fractional digits and the data type allows a maximum of two fractional digits.
   ☒ **B, D,** and **E** can legitimately be stored in this data type and, therefore, are the incorrect answers to this question. **D** shows that numbers with no fractional part are legitimate values for this column, as long as the number of digits in the whole number portion does not exceed six digits.

3. ☑ **B and E.** The result of arithmetic between two date values represents a certain number of days.
   ☒ **A, C,** and **D** are incorrect. It is a common mistake to expect the result of arithmetic between two date values to be a date as well, so **A** may seem plausible, but it is false.

4. ☑ **A and D.** The scale of the VARCHAR2 data type, specified in brackets, determines its maximum capacity for storing character data as mentioned by **A**. If a data value that is at most 30 characters long is stored in any data type, it can also be stored in this column as stated by **D**.
   ☒ **B** is incorrect because it is possible to store character data of any length up to 30 characters in this column. **C** is false, since the CHAR data type exists in parallel with the VARCHAR2 data type.

Execute a Basic SELECT Statement

5. ☑ **D.** Unique JOB_ID values are projected from the EMPLOYEES table by applying the DISTINCT keyword to just the JOB_ID column.
   ☒ **A, B,** and **C** are eliminated since **A** returns an unrestricted list of JOB_ID values including duplicates; **B** makes use of the UNIQUE keyword in the incorrect context; and **C** selects the

distinct combination of JOB_ID and EMPLOYEE_ID values. This has the effect of returning all the rows from the EMPLOYEES table since the EMPLOYEE_ID column contains unique values for each employee record. Additionally, **C** returns two columns, which is not what was originally requested.

6. ☑ **B** and **D** represent the two illegal statements that will return syntax errors if they are executed. This is a tricky question because it asks for the illegal statements and not the legal statements. **B** is illegal because it is missing a single quote enclosing the character literal "represents the." **D** is illegal because it does not make use of single quotes to enclose its character literals.
☒ **A** and **C** are the legal statements and, therefore, in the context of the question, are the incorrect answers. **A** and **C** appear to be different since the case of the SQL statements are different and **A** uses the alias keyword AS, whereas **C** just leaves a space between the expression and the alias. Yet both **A** and **C** produce identical results.

7. ☑ **B** and **D** do not return null values since character expressions are not affected in the same way by null values as arithmetic expressions. **B** and **D** ignore the presence of null values in their expressions and return the remaining character literals.
☒ **A** and **C** return null values because any arithmetic expression that involves a null will return a null.

8. ☑ **D.** An asterisk is the SQL operator that implies that all columns must be selected from a table.
☒ **A, B, C,** and **E** are incorrect. **A** uses the ALL reserved word but is missing any column specification and will, therefore, generate an error. **B** selects some columns but not all columns and, therefore, does not answer the question. **C** and **E** make use of illegal selection operators.

9. ☑ **B.** The key to identifying the correct result lies in understanding the role of the single quotation marks. The entire literal is enclosed by a pair of quotes to avoid the generation of an error. The two adjacent quotes are necessary to delimit the single quote that appears in literal **B**.
☒ **A, C,** and **D** are incorrect. **A** is eliminated since no error is returned. **C** inaccurately returns two adjacent quotes in the literal expression and **D** returns a literal with all the quotes still present. The Oracle server removes the quotes used as character delimiters after processing the literal.

10. ☑ **D.** The literal expression '6 * 6' is selected once for each row of data in the REGIONS table.
☒ **A, B, C,** and **E** are incorrect. **A** returns one row instead of four and calculates the product 6 * 6. The enclosing quote operators render 6 * 6 a character literal and not a numeric literal that can be calculated. **B** correctly returns four rows but incorrectly evaluates the character literal as a numeric literal. **C** incorrectly returns one row instead of four and **E** is incorrect, because the given SQL statement can be executed.

LAB ANSWER

The assumption is made that an Oracle database is available for you to practice on. The database administrator (DBA) in your organization may assist you with installing and setting this up. In order for any client tool such as SQL*Plus or SQL Developer to connect to the database, a listener process should be running and the database must be opened. Additionally, you may have to request that the HR and OE schema accounts be unlocked and that the passwords be reset. If these sample schemas are not present, it is a simple matter to get the DBA to run the scripts, which are installed when the database is installed, to create them. Connect to the OE schema using either SQL*Plus or SQL Developer.

I. The DESCRIBE command gives us the structural description of a table. The following illustration shows these two tables being described:

2. The request for unique values usually involves using the DISTINCT keyword as part of your SELECT statement. The two components of the statement involve the SELECT clause and the FROM clause. You were asked for unique SALES_REP_ID values FROM the ORDERS table. It is simple to translate this request into the following SELECT statement:

```
select distinct sales_rep_id
from orders;
```

From the results in the illustration, you can answer the original question: There are nine different sales representatives responsible for orders listed in the ORDERS table, but there is one order that contains null values in their SALES_REP_ID fields.

3. When asked to create a results set, it translates to SELECT one or more columns from a table. In this case, your SELECT clause is constructed from the three columns requested. There is no request for unique values, so there is no need to consider the DISTINCT keyword. The FROM clause need only include the ORDERS table to build the following SELECT statement:

```
select order_id, order_date, order_total
from orders;
```

Consider the output in the following illustration, specifically the ORDER_DATE column. This column contains the day, month, year, hours, minutes, seconds, and fractional seconds up to six decimal places or accurate up to a millionth of a second. The description of the ORDERS table exposes ORDER_DATE as a TIMESTAMP(6) with LOCAL TIMEZONE column. This means that the data in this column can be stored with fractional precision up to six decimal places and that the data is time zone-aware. Basically, data may be worked on by people in different time zones. So Oracle provides a data type that normalizes the local time to the database time zone to avoid confusion. Compared to the START_DATE and END_DATE columns in the HR.JOB_ID table, the ORDER_DATE column data type is far more sophisticated. Essentially, though, both these data types store date and time information but to differing degrees of precision.

```
Oracle SQL Developer : OE_11G                                        _ □ X

File   Edit   View   Navigate   Run   Debug   Source   Tools   Help

▷ OE_11G                                                            ◁ ▷ ▼

▷ ▤ ▤ ▤ ●    ▤ ▤ ▤   ✎        0.15949737 seconds              OE_11G ▼
Enter SQL Statement:
  SELECT ORDER_ID, ORDER_DATE, ORDER_TOTAL
  FROM ORDERS;

▷ Results   Script Output   Explain   Autotrace   DBMS Output   OWA Output
Results:
```

	ORDER_ID	ORDER_DATE	ORDER_TOTAL
1	2458	16/AUG/99 21:34:12.234359000	78279.6
2	2397	19/NOV/99 22:41:54.696211000	42283.2
3	2454	02/OCT/99 23:49:34.678340000	6653.4
4	2354	15/JUL/00 00:18:23.234567000	46257
5	2358	09/JAN/00 01:03:12.654278000	7826
6	2381	15/MAY/00 02:59:08.843679000	23034.6
7	2440	01/SEP/99 03:53:06.008765000	70576.9
8	2357	09/JAN/98 04:19:44.123456000	59872.4
9	2394	11/FEB/00 05:22:35.564789000	21863
10	2435	03/SEP/99 05:22:53.134567000	62303
11	2455	20/SEP/99 17:34:11.456789000	14087.5
12	2379	16/MAY/99 08:22:24.234567000	17848.2
13	2396	02/FEB/98 09:34:56.345678000	34930
14	2406	29/JUN/99 10:41:20.098765000	2854.2
15	2434	13/SEP/99 11:49:30.647893000	268651.8
16	2436	02/SEP/99 12:18:04.378034000	6394.8
17	2446	27/JUL/99 13:03:08.302945000	103679.3

4. The SELECT clause to answer this question should contain an expression aliased as "Product" made up of concatenations of character literals with the PRODUCT_NAME, PRODUCT_ID, and PRODUCT_STATUS columns. Additionally, the SELECT clause must contain the LIST_PRICE and MIN_PRICE columns and two further arithmetic expressions aliased as "Max Actual Savings" and "Max Discount %." The FROM clause need only include the PRODUCT_INFORMATION table. Proceed by constructing each of the three expressions in turn and put them all together. The "Product" expression could be derived with the following SELECT statement:

```
select product_name||' with code: '||product_id'||' has status of:'||order_
status AS Product
```

The "Max Actual Savings" expression could be derived with the following SELECT statement:

```
select list_price - min_price AS "Max Actual Savings"
```

The "Max Discount %" expression takes the calculation for "Max Actual Savings", divides this amount by the LIST_PRICE, and multiplies it by 100. It could be derived with the following SELECT statement:

```
Select ((list_price-min_price)/list_price) * 100 AS "Max Discount %"
```

These three expressions, along with the two regular columns, form the SELECT clause executed against the PRODUCT_INFORMATION table as shown next:

5. The versatile DUAL table clearly forms the FROM clause. The SELECT clause is more interesting, since no actual columns are being selected, just an arithmetic expression. A possible SELECT statement to derive this calculation could be:

```
select (4 * (22/7) * (3958.759 * 3958.759)) AS "Earth's Area"
from dual;
```

This calculation approximates that planet Earth's surface area is 197016572.595304 square miles.

3
Restricting and Sorting Data

L imiting the columns retrieved by a SELECT statement is known as *projection* and was introduced in Chapter 2. Restricting the rows returned is known as *selection*. This chapter discusses the *WHERE* clause, which is an enhancement to the selection functionality of the SELECT statement. The *WHERE* clause specifies one or more conditions that the Oracle server evaluates to restrict the rows returned by the statement. A further language enhancement is introduced by the ORDER BY clause, which provides data sorting capabilities. Ampersand substitution introduces a way to reuse the same statement to execute different queries by substituting query elements at runtime. This area of runtime binding in SQL statements is thoroughly explored.

CERTIFICATION OBJECTIVE 3.01

Limit the Rows Retrieved by a Query

One of the cornerstone principles in relational theory is selection. Selection is actualized using the WHERE clause of the SELECT statement. Conditions that restrict the dataset returned take many forms and operate on columns as well as expressions. Only those rows in a table that conform to these conditions are returned. Conditions restrict rows using comparison operators in conjunction with columns and literal values. Boolean operators provide a mechanism to specify multiple conditions to restrict the rows returned. Boolean, conditional, concatenation, and arithmetic operators are discussed to establish their order of precedence when they are encountered in a SELECT statement. The following four areas are investigated:

- The WHERE clause
- Comparison operators
- Boolean operators
- Precedence rules

The WHERE clause

The *WHERE* clause extends the SELECT statement by providing the language to restrict rows returned based on one or more conditions. Querying a table with just the SELECT and FROM clauses results in every row of data stored in the table being returned. Using the DISTINCT keyword, duplicate values are excluded, and the resultant rows are restricted to some degree. What if very specific information is required from a table, for example, only the data where a column contains a specific value? How would you retrieve the countries that belong to the Europe region from the COUNTRIES table? What about retrieving just those employees who work as sales representatives? These questions are answered using the WHERE clause to specify exactly which rows must be returned. The format of the SQL SELECT statement which includes the WHERE clause is:

SELECT * | {[DISTINCT] *column* | *expression* [*alias*],…}
FROM *table*
[WHERE *condition(s)*];

The SELECT and FROM clauses were examined in Chapter 2. The WHERE clause always follows the FROM clause. The square brackets indicate that the WHERE clause is optional. One or more conditions may be simultaneously applied to restrict the result set. A condition is specified by comparing two terms using a conditional operator. These terms may be column values, literals, or expressions. The *equality* operator is most commonly used to restrict result sets. Two examples of WHERE clauses are shown next:

```
select country_name
from countries
where region_id=3;

select last_name, first_name from employees
where job_id='SA_REP';
```

The first example projects the COUNTRY_NAME column from the COUNTRIES table. Instead of selecting every row, the WHERE clause restricts the rows returned to only those which contain a 3 in the REGION_ID column. The second example projects two columns, LAST_NAME and FIRST_NAME from the EMPLOYEES table. The rows returned are restricted to those which contain the value SA_REP in their JOB_ID columns.

Numeric-Based Conditions

Conditions must be formulated appropriately for different column data types. The conditions restricting rows based on numeric columns can be specified in several different ways. Consider the SALARY column in the EMPLOYEES table. This column has a data type of NUMBER(8,2). Figure 3-1 shows two different ways in which the SALARY column has been restricted. The first and second examples

FIGURE 3-1

Two ways to
select numeric
values in a
WHERE clause

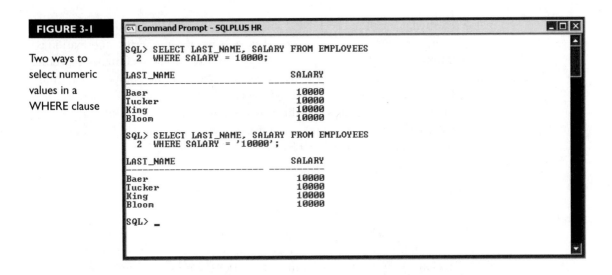

retrieve the LAST_NAME and SALARY values of the employees who earn $ 10,000.
Notice the difference in the WHERE clauses of the following queries. The first query
specifies the number 10000, while the second encloses the number within single
quotes like a character literal. Both formats are acceptable to Oracle since an implicit
data type conversion is performed when necessary.

```
select last_name, salary from employees
where salary = 10000;
```

```
select last_name, salary from employees
where salary = '10000';
```

A numeric column can be compared to another numeric column in the same row
to construct a WHERE clause condition, as the following query demonstrates:

```
select last_name, salary from employees
where salary = department_id;
```

The first example in Figure 3-2 shows how the WHERE clause is too restrictive
and results in no rows being selected. This is because the range of SALARY values
is 2100 to 999999.99, and the range of DEPARTMENT_ID values is 10 to 110.
Since there is no overlap in the range of DEPARTMENT_ID and SALARY values,
there are no rows that satisfy this condition and therefore nothing is returned. The
example also illustrates how a WHERE clause condition compares one numeric
column to another.

FIGURE 3-2

Using the
WHERE clause
with numeric
expressions

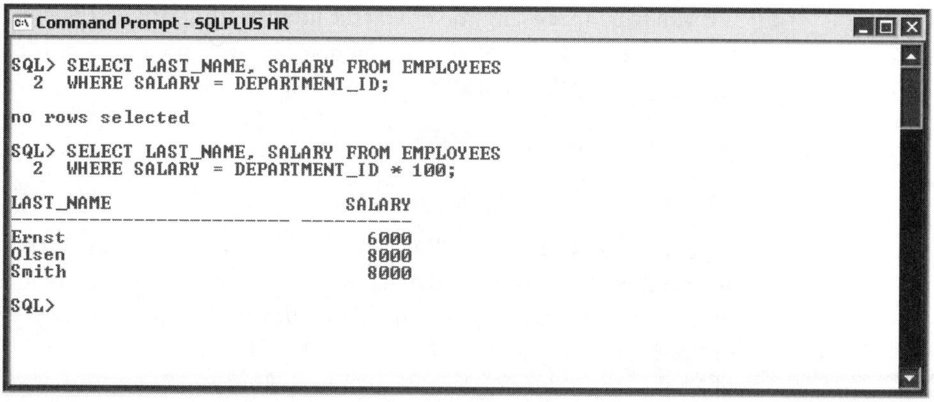

```
Command Prompt - SQLPLUS HR                              _ □ ×
SQL> SELECT LAST_NAME, SALARY FROM EMPLOYEES
  2  WHERE SALARY = DEPARTMENT_ID;

no rows selected

SQL> SELECT LAST_NAME, SALARY FROM EMPLOYEES
  2  WHERE SALARY = DEPARTMENT_ID * 100;

LAST_NAME                        SALARY
------------------------         -----------
Ernst                              6000
Olsen                              8000
Smith                              8000

SQL>
```

The second example in Figure 3-2 demonstrates extending the WHERE clause condition to compare a numeric column, SALARY, to the numeric expression: DEPARTMENT_ID*100. For each row, the value in the SALARY column is compared to the product of the DEPARTMENT_ID value and 100. The WHERE clause also permits expressions on either side of the comparison operator. You could issue the following statement to yield identical results:

```
select last_name, salary from employees
where salary/10 = department_id*10;
```

As in regular algebra, the expression (SALARY = DEPARTMENT_ID * 100) is equivalent to (SALARY/10 = DEPARTMENT_ID * 10). The notable feature about this example is that the terms on either side of the comparison operator are expressions.

Character-Based Conditions

Conditions determining which rows are selected based on character data, are specified by enclosing character literals in the conditional clause, within single quotes. The JOB_ID column in the EMPLOYEES table has a data type of VARCHAR2(10). Suppose you wanted a report consisting of the LAST_NAME values of those employees currently employed as sales representatives. The JOB_ID value for a sales representative is SA_REP. The following statement produces such a report.

```
select last_name
from employees
where job_id='SA_REP';
```

If you tried specifying the character literal without the quotes, an Oracle error would be raised. Remember that character literal data is case sensitive, so the following WHERE clauses are not equivalent.

```
Clause 1: where job_id=SA_REP
Clause 2: where job_id='Sa_Rep'
Clause 3: where job_id='sa_rep'
```

Clause 1 generates an "ORA-00904: "SA_REP": invalid identifier" error since the literal SA_REP is not wrapped in single quotes. Clause 2 and Clause 3 are syntactically correct but not equivalent. Further, neither of these clauses yields any data since there are no rows in the EMPLOYEES table which have JOB_ID column values that are either Sa_Rep or sa_rep, as shown in Figure 3-3.

Character-based conditions are not limited to comparing column values with literals. They may also be specified using other character columns and expressions. The LAST_NAME and FIRST_NAME columns are both specified as VARCHAR2(25) data typed columns. Consider the query:

```
select employee_id, job_id
from employees
where last_name=first_name;
```

Both the LAST_NAME and FIRST_NAME columns appear on either side of the equality operator in the WHERE clause. No literal values are present; therefore no

---

FIGURE 3-3	
Using the WHERE clause with character data	

```
SQL> SELECT LAST_NAME
  2    FROM EMPLOYEES
  3    WHERE JOB_ID=SA_REP;
WHERE JOB_ID=SA_REP
             *
ERROR at line 3:
ORA-00904: "SA_REP": invalid identifier

SQL> SELECT LAST_NAME
  2    FROM EMPLOYEES
  3    WHERE JOB_ID='Sa_Rep';

no rows selected

SQL> SELECT LAST_NAME
  2    FROM EMPLOYEES
  3    WHERE JOB_ID='sa_rep';

no rows selected

SQL>
```

single quote characters are necessary to delimit them. This condition stipulates that only rows which contain the same data value (an exact case-sensitive match) in the LAST_NAME and FIRST_NAME columns will be returned. This condition is too restrictive and, as Figure 3-4 shows, no rows are returned.

Character-based expressions form either one or both parts of a condition separated by a conditional operator. These expressions can be formed by concatenating literal values with one or more character columns. The following four clauses demonstrate some of the options for character-based conditions:

```
Clause 1: where 'A '||last_name||first_name = 'A King'
Clause 2: where first_name||' '||last_name = last_name||' '||first_name
Clause 3: where 'SA_REP'||'King' = job_id||last_name
Clause 4: where job_id||last_name ='SA_REP'||'King'
```

FIGURE 3-4

Character
column-based
WHERE clause

Clause 1 concatenates the string literal "A" to the LAST_NAME and FIRST_
NAME columns. This expression is compared to the literal "A King," and any
row that fulfils this condition is returned. Clause 2 demonstrates that character
expressions may be placed on both sides of the conditional operator. Clause 3
illustrates that literal expressions may also be placed on the left of the conditional
operator. It is logically equivalent to clause 4, which has swapped the operands in
clause 3 around. Both clauses 3 and 4 result in the same row of data being returned,
as shown in Figure 3-5.

Date-Based Conditions

DATE columns are useful when storing date and time information. Date literals
must be enclosed in single quotation marks just like character data; otherwise an
error is raised. When used in conditional WHERE clauses, DATE columns are

FIGURE 3-5	
Equivalence of conditional expressions	

compared to other DATE columns or to date literals. The literals are automatically converted into DATE values based on the default date format, which is DD-MON-RR. If a literal occurs in an expression involving a DATE column, it is automatically converted into a date value using the default format mask. DD represents days, MON represents the first three letters of a month, and RR represents a Year 2000–compliant year (that is, if RR is between 50 and 99, then the Oracle server returns the previous century, else it returns the current century). The full four-digit year, YYYY, can also be specified. Consider the following four SQL statements:

```
Statement 1:
select employee_id from job_history
where start_date = end_date;

Statement 2:
select employee_id from job_history
where start_date = '01-JAN-2001';

Statement 3:
select employee_id from job_history
where start_date = '01-JAN-01';

Statement 4:
select employee_id from job_history
where start_date = '01-JAN-99';
```

The first statement tests equality between two DATE columns. Rows that contain the same values in their START_DATE and END_DATE columns will be returned. Note, however, that DATE values are only equal to each other if there is an exact match between all their components including day, month, year, hours, minutes, and seconds. Chapter 4 discusses the details of storing DATE values. Until then, don't worry about the hours, minutes, and seconds components.

In the WHERE clause of the second statement, the START_DATE column is compared to the character literal: '01-JAN-2001'. The entire four-digit year component (YYYY) has been specified. This is acceptable to the Oracle server, and all rows in the JOB_HISTORY table with START_DATE column values equal to the first of January 2001 will be returned.

The third statement is equivalent to the second since the literal '01-JAN-01' is converted to the date value 01-JAN-2001. This is due to the RR component being less than 50, so the current (twenty-first) century, 20, is prefixed to the year RR component to provide a century value. All rows in the JOB_HISTORY table with START_DATE column values = 01-JAN-2001 will be returned.

The century component for the literal '01-JAN-99' becomes the previous (twentieth) century, 19, yields a date value of 01-JAN-1999 for the fourth statement, since the RR component, 99, is greater than 50. Rows in the JOB_HISTORY table with START_DATE column values = 01-JAN-1999 will be returned.

Arithmetic using the addition and subtraction operators is supported in expressions involving DATE values. An expression like: END_DATE – START_DATE returns a numeric value representing the number of days between START_DATE and END_DATE. An expression like: START_DATE + 30 returns a DATE value that is 30 days later than START_DATE. So the following expression is legitimate, as shown in Figure 3-6:

```
select employee_id from job_history
where start_date + 30 = '31-JAN-99';
```

This query returns rows from the JOB_HISTORY table containing a START_DATE value equal to 30 days before 31-JAN-1999. Therefore, only rows with a value of 01-JAN-1999 in the START_DATE column will be retrieved.

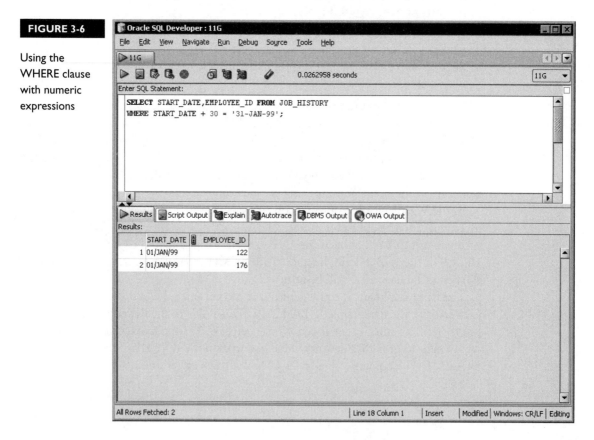

FIGURE 3-6

Using the WHERE clause with numeric expressions

Comparison Operators

The *equality* operator is used extensively to illustrate the concept of restricting rows using a WHERE clause. There are several alternative operators that may also be used. The *inequality* operators like "less than" or "greater than or equal to" may be used to return rows conforming to inequality conditions. The *BETWEEN* operator facilitates range-based comparison to test whether a column value lies between two values. The *IN* operator tests set membership, so a row is returned if the column value tested in the condition is a member of a set of literals. The pattern matching comparison operator *LIKE* is extremely powerful, allowing components of character column data to be matched to literals conforming to a specific pattern. The last comparison operator discussed in this section is the *IS NULL* operator, which returns rows where the column value contains a null value. These operators may be used in any combination in the WHERE clause and will be discussed next.

Equality and Inequality

Limiting the rows returned by a query involves specifying a suitable WHERE clause. If the clause is too restrictive, then few or no rows are returned. If the conditional clause is too broadly specified, then more rows than are required are returned. Exploring the different available operators should equip you with the language to request exactly those rows you are interested in. Testing for *equality* in a condition is both natural and intuitive. Such a condition is formed using the "is equal to" (=) operator. A row is returned if the equality condition is true for that row. Consider the following query:

```
select last_name, salary
from employees
where job_id='SA_REP';
```

The JOB_ID column of every row in the EMPLOYEES table is tested for equality with the character literal SA_REP. For character information to be equal, there must be an exact case-sensitive match. When such a match is encountered, the values for the projected columns, LAST_NAME and SALARY, are returned for that row, as shown in Figure 3-7. Note that although the conditional clause is based on the JOB_ID column, it is not necessary for this column to be projected by the query.

Inequality-based conditions enhance the WHERE clause specification. Range and pattern matching comparisons are possible using inequality and equality operators, but it is often preferable to use the BETWEEN and LIKE operators for these comparisons. The inequality operators are described in Table 3-1.

Inequality operators allow range-based queries to be fulfilled. You may be required to provide a set of results where a column value is *greater than* another value.

FIGURE 3-7	
Conditions based on the equality operator	

Operator	Description
<	Less than
>	Greater than
<=	Less than or equal to
>=	Greater than or equal to
<>	Not equal to
!=	Not equal to

TABLE 3-1

Inequality Operators

For example, the following query may be issued to obtain a list of LAST_NAME and SALARY values for employees who earn more that $5000:

```
select last_name, salary from employees
where salary > 5000;
```

Similarly, to obtain a list of employees who earn less than $3000, the following query may be submitted:

```
select last_name, salary from employees
where salary < 3000;
```

The *composite inequality operators* (made up of more than one symbol) are utilized in the following four clauses:

```
Clause 1: where salary <= 3000;
Clause 2: where salary >= 5000;
Clause 3: where salary <> department_id;
Clause 4: where salary != 4000+department_id;
```

Clause 1 returns those rows which contain a SALARY value that is less than or equal to 3000. Clause 2 obtains data where the SALARY value is greater than or equal to 5000, whilst clauses 3 and 4 demonstrate the two forms of the "not equal to" operators. Clause 3 returns the rows which have SALARY column values that are not equal to the DEPARTMENT_ID values. The alternate "not equal to" operator in clause 4 illustrates that columns, literals, and expressions may all be compared using inequality operators. Clause 4 returns those rows which contain a SALARY value that is not equal to the sum of the DEPARTMENT_ID for that row and 4000.

Numeric inequality is naturally intuitive. The comparison of character and date terms, however, is more complex. Testing character inequality is interesting since the strings being compared on either side of the inequality operator are converted to a numeric representation of its characters. Based on the database character set and NLS (National Language Support) settings, each character string is assigned a numeric value. These numeric values form the basis for the evaluation of the inequality comparison. Consider the following statement:

```
select last_name from employees
where last_name < 'King';
```

The character literal 'King' is converted to a numeric representation. Assuming a US7ASCII database character set with AMERICAN NLS settings, the literal 'King' is converted into a sum of its ordinal character values: K + i + n + g = (75+105+110+103=393). For each row in the EMPLOYEES table, the LAST_NAME column is similarly converted to a numeric value. If this value is less than 393, then the row is selected. The same process for comparing numeric data using the inequality operators applies to character data. The only difference is that character data is converted implicitly by the Oracle server to a numeric value based on certain database settings.

Inequality comparisons operating on date values follow a similar process to character data. The Oracle server stores dates in an internal numeric format, and these values are compared within the conditions. The second of June of a certain year occurs earlier than the third of June of the same year. Therefore, the numeric value of the date 02-JUN-2008 is less than the numeric value of the date 03-JUN-2008. Consider the following query:

```
select last_name from employees
where hire_date < '01-JAN-2000';
```

This query retrieves each employee record containing a HIRE_DATE value that is earlier than '01-JAN-2000'. Rows with employee HIRE_DATE=31-DEC-1999 will be returned, while rows with employee HIRE_DATE values later than the first of January 2000 will not be returned, as shown in Figure 3-8.

on the ***Job***

The WHERE clause is a fundamental extension to the SELECT statement and forms part of most queries. Although many comparison operators exist, the majority of conditions are based on comparing two terms using both the equality and the inequality operators.

Range Comparison with the BETWEEN Operator

The BETWEEN operator tests whether a column or expression value falls within a range of two boundary values. The item must be at least the same as the lower boundary value, or at most the same as the higher boundary value, or fall within the range, for the condition to be true.

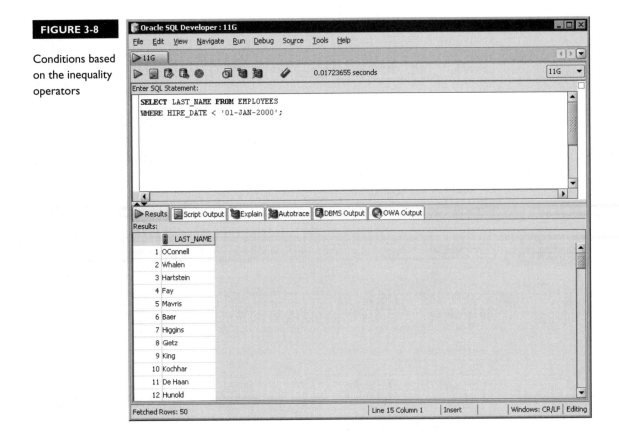

FIGURE 3-8

Conditions based on the inequality operators

Suppose you want the last names of employees who earn a salary in the range of $3400 and $4000. A possible solution using the BETWEEN operator is as follows:

```
select last_name from employees
where salary between 3400 and 4000;
```

This operator allows the WHERE condition to read in a natural English manner. The last names of all the employees earning from $3400 to $4000 will be returned. *Boolean* operators like AND, OR, and NOT are discussed later in this chapter, but they are introduced here to enhance the description of the BETWEEN operator. The AND operator is used to specify multiple WHERE conditions, all of which must be satisfied for a row to be returned. Using the AND operator, the BETWEEN operator is equivalent to two conditions using the "greater than or equal to" and "less than or equal to" operators, respectively. The preceding SQL statement is equivalent to the following statement, as shown in Figure 3-9.

```
select last_name from employees
where salary >= 3400
and salary <= 4000;
```

The SALARY value for a row is tested first if it is greater than or equal to 3400 and second if it is less than or equal to 4000. If both conditions are satisfied, the LAST_NAME value from the row forms part of the results set. If only one or neither of the conditions is satisfied, the row is not selected.

Conditions specified with the BETWEEN operator can therefore be equivalently denoted using two inequality-based conditions, but it is shorter and simpler to

FIGURE 3-9

The BETWEEN
operator

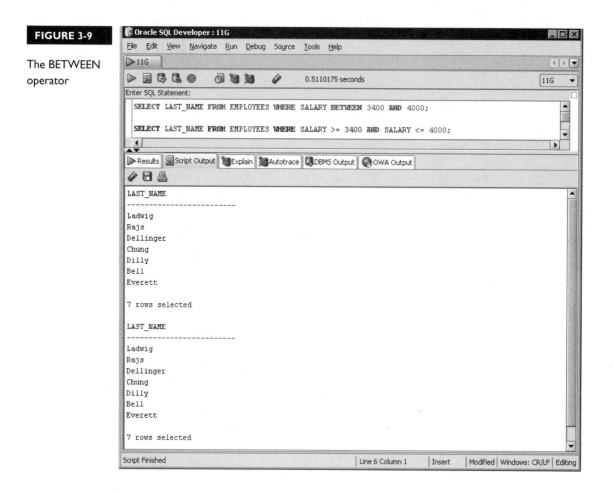

specify the range condition using the BETWEEN operator. The implication of this equivalence is that the mechanism utilized to evaluate numeric, character, and date operands by the inequality operators is the same for the BETWEEN operator. The following query tests whether the HIRE_DATE column value is later than 24-JUL-1994 but earlier than 07-JUN-1996:

```
select first_name, hire_date from employees
where hire_date between '24-JUL-1994' and '07-JUN-1996';
```

You are not restricted to specifying literal values as the operands to the BETWEEN operator, since these may be column values and expressions such as the following:

```
select first_name, hire_date from employees
where '24-JUL-1994' between hire_date+30 and '07-JUN-1996';
```

For a row to be returned by this query, the date literal 24-JUL-1994 must fall between the row's HIRE_DATE column value plus 30 days and the date literal 07-JUN-1996.

Set Comparison with the IN Operator

The *IN* operator tests whether an item is a member of a set of literal values. The set is specified by a comma separating the literals and enclosing them in round brackets. If the literals are character or date values, then these must be delimited using single quotes. You may include as many literals in the set as you wish. Consider the following example:

```
select last_name from employees
where salary in (1000,4000,6000);
```

The SALARY value in each row is compared for equality to the literals specified in the set. If the SALARY value equals 1000, 4000, or 6000, the LAST_NAME value for that row is returned. The Boolean OR operator, discussed later in this chapter, is used to specify multiple WHERE conditions, at least one of which must be satisfied for a row to be returned. The *IN* operator is therefore equivalent to a series of OR conditions. The preceding SQL statement may be written using multiple OR condition clauses, for example:

```
select last_name from employees
where salary = 1000
OR salary = 4000
OR salary = 6000;
```

This statement will return an employee's LAST_NAME if at least one of the WHERE clause conditions is true; it has the same meaning as the previous statement that uses the IN operator, as shown in Figure 3-10.

Testing set membership using the *IN* operator is more succinct than using multiple OR conditions, especially as the number of members in the set increases. The following two statements demonstrate use of the *IN* operator with DATE and CHARACTER data.

```
select last_name from employees
where last_name in ('King','Garbharran','Ramklass');

select last_name from employees
where hire_date in ('01-JAN-1998','01-DEC-1999');
```

Pattern Comparison with the LIKE Operator

To review, the BETWEEN operator provides a concise way to specify range-based conditions, and the IN operator provides an optimal method to test set membership. Now we introduce the *LIKE* operator, which is designed exclusively for character data and provides a powerful mechanism for searching for letters or words.

LIKE is accompanied by two wildcard characters: the percentage symbol (%) and the underscore character (_). The percentage symbol is used to specify zero or more wildcard characters, while the underscore character specifies one wildcard character. A wildcard may represent any character.

FIGURE 3-10	
The IN operator	

```
Command Prompt - SQLPLUS HR

SQL> SELECT LAST_NAME FROM EMPLOYEES
  2  WHERE SALARY IN (1000,4000,6000);

LAST_NAME
------------------------------
Fay
Ernst
Bell

SQL> SELECT LAST_NAME FROM EMPLOYEES
  2  WHERE SALARY = 1000
  3  OR SALARY = 4000
  4  OR SALARY = 6000;

LAST_NAME
------------------------------
Fay
Ernst
Bell

SQL>
```

You may be requested to provide a list of employees whose first names begin with the letter "A." The following query can be used to provide this set of results:

```
select first_name from employees
where first_name like 'A%';
```

The character literal that the FIRST_NAME column is compared to is enclosed in single quotes like a regular character literal. In addition, it has a percentage symbol, which has a special meaning in the context of the LIKE operator. The percentage symbol substitutes zero or more characters appended to the letter A. Employee records with FIRST_NAME values beginning with the letter A are returned.

The wildcard characters can appear at the beginning, middle or at the end of the character literal. They can even appear alone as in:

```
where first_name like '%';
```

In this case, every row containing a FIRST_NAME value that is not null will be returned. Wildcard symbols are not mandatory when using the LIKE operator. In such cases, LIKE behaves as an equality operator testing for exact character matches; so the following two WHERE clauses are equivalent:

```
where last_name like 'King';
where last_name = 'King';
```

The underscore wildcard symbol substitutes exactly one other character in a literal. Consider searching for employees whose last names are four letters long, begin with a "K," have an unknown second letter, and end with an ng. You may issue the following statement:

```
where last_name like 'K_ng';
```

Depending on the dataset, you may retrieve employees named King, Kong, and Kung. An alternate way to perform pattern matching is to use an interminable series of OR conditions, but to achieve the preceding results without using the LIKE operator is prohibitively complex. For example, it may be achieved with the following series of OR conditions:

```
where last_name = 'Kang'
OR last_name ='Kbng'
OR last_name ='Kcng'
...
OR last_name ='Kzng'
```

This example is incomplete, since it is not feasible to list every possible character that could be substituted. This example demonstrates the sheer effort required to substitute a single character without using the LIKE operator and the underscore wildcard symbol. For an unknown number (zero or more) of character substitutions, the possibilities are exponentially larger than for single-character substitution. It is not practically possible to perform character pattern matching without the use of the LIKE operator and the wildcard symbols.

As Figure 3-11 shows, the two wildcard symbols can be used independently, together, or even multiple times in a single WHERE condition. The first query retrieves those records where COUNTRY_NAME begins with the letter "I" followed by zero or more characters, one of which must be a lowercase "a."

The second query retrieves those countries whose names contain the letter "i" as its fifth character. The length of the COUNTRY_NAME values and the letter they begin with are unimportant. The four underscore wildcard symbols preceding the lowercase "i" in the WHERE clause represent exactly four characters (which could be any characters). The fifth letter must be an "i," and the percentage symbol

FIGURE 3-11	
The wildcard symbols of the LIKE operator	

specifies that the COUNTRY_NAME can have zero or more characters from the sixth character onward.

What about the scenario when you are searching for a literal that contains a percentage or underscore character? Oracle provides a way to temporarily disable their special meaning and regard them as regular characters using the *ESCAPE* identifier. The JOBS table contains JOB_ID values that are literally specified with an underscore character, such as SA_MAN, AD_VP, MK_REP, and SA_REP. Assume there is, in addition, a row in the JOBS table with a JOB_ID of SA%MAN. Notice there is no underscore character in this JOB_ID. How can values be retrieved from the JOBS table if you are looking for JOB_ID values beginning with the characters SA_? Consider the following SQL statement:

```
select * from jobs
where job_id like 'SA_%';
```

This query will return the rows SA_REP, SA_MAN, and SA%MAN. The requirement in this example is not met since an additional row, SA%MAN, not conforming to the criterion that it begins with the characters SA_, is also returned, as the first example in Figure 3-12 shows.

A naturally occurring underscore character may be escaped (or treated as a regular nonspecial symbol) using the ESCAPE identifier in conjunction with an ESCAPE character. The second example in Figure 3-12 shows the SQL statement that retrieves the JOBS table records with JOB_ID values equal to SA_MAN and SA_REP and which conforms to the original requirement:

```
select job_id from jobs
where job_id like 'SA\_%' escape '\';
```

FIGURE 3-12

The ESCAPE identifier and the LIKE operator

```
Command Prompt - SQLPLUS HR

SQL> SELECT * FROM JOBS
  2  WHERE JOB_ID LIKE 'SA_%';

JOB_ID     JOB_TITLE                           MIN_SALARY MAX_SALARY
SA_MAN     Sales Manager                            10000      20000
SA_REP     Sales Representative                      6000      12000

SQL> SELECT JOB_ID FROM JOBS
  2  WHERE JOB_ID LIKE 'SA\_%' ESCAPE '\';

JOB_ID
SA_MAN
SA_REP

SQL> SELECT JOB_ID FROM JOBS
  2  WHERE JOB_ID LIKE 'SA$_%' ESCAPE '$';

JOB_ID
SA_MAN
SA_REP

SQL>
```

The ESCAPE identifier instructs the Oracle server to treat any character found after the backslash character as a regular nonspecial symbol with no wildcard meaning. In the preceding WHERE clause, any JOB_ID values that begin with the three characters "SA_" will be returned. Traditionally, the ESCAPE character is the backslash symbol, but it does not have to be. The following statement is equivalent to the previous one but uses a dollar symbol as the ESCAPE character instead.

```
select job_id from jobs
where job_id like 'SA$_%' escape '$';
```

The percentage symbol may be similarly escaped when it occurs naturally as character data. Suppose, there is a requirement to retrieve the row with the hypothetical JOB_ID: SA%MAN introduced earlier. Querying the JOBS table for JOB_ID values such as SA%MAN using the following code results in the records SA_MAN and SA%MAN being returned.

```
select job_id from jobs
where job_id like 'SA%MAN';
```

The Oracle server interprets the percentage symbol in the WHERE clause as a wildcard symbol when used with the LIKE operator. To obtain the row with JOB_ID: SA%MAN using the LIKE operator, the percentage symbol may be escaped using the following statement:

```
select job_id from jobs
where job_id like 'SA\%MAN' ESCAPE '\';
```

The backslash is defined as the ESCAPE character that instructs the Oracle server to ignore the wildcard properties of the symbol occurring immediately after the backslash. In this way, both wildcard symbols can be used as either specialized or regular characters in different segments of the same character string.

EXERCISE 3-1

Using the LIKE Operator

Retrieve a list of DEPARTMENT_NAME values that end with the three letters "ing" from the DEPARTMENTS table.

1. Start SQL*Plus and connect to the HR schema.
2. The SELECT clause is
   SELECT DEPARTMENT_NAME

3. The FROM clause is
   FROM DEPARTMENTS

4. The WHERE clause must perform a comparison between the DEPARTMENT_ NAME column values and a pattern of characters beginning with zero or more characters but ending with three specific characters, "ing."

5. The operator enabling character pattern matching is the LIKE operator. The pattern the DEPARTMENT_NAME column must conform to is '%ing'. The percentage wildcard symbol indicates that zero or more characters may precede the "ing" string of characters.

6. Thus, the WHERE clause is
   WHERE DEPARTMENT_NAME LIKE '%ing'

7. Executing this statement returns the set of results matching this pattern as shown in the following illustration:

Null Comparison with the IS NULL Operator

NULL values inevitably find their way into database tables. It is often required that only those records that contain a NULL value in a specific column are sought. The *IS NULL* operator selects only the rows where a specific column value is NULL. Testing column values for equality to NULL is performed using the *IS NULL* operator instead of the "is equal to" operator (=).

Consider the following query that fetches the LAST_NAME column from the EMPLOYEES table for those rows which have NULL values stored in the COMMISSION_PCT column:

```
select last_name from employees
where commission_pct is null;
```

This WHERE clause reads naturally and retrieves only the records which contain NULL COMMISSION_PCT values. As Figure 3-13 shows, the query using the "is equal to" operator does not return any rows, while the query using the IS NULL operator does.

Boolean Operators

Data is restricted using a WHERE clause with a single condition. *Boolean* or *logical* operators enable multiple conditions to be specified in the WHERE clause of the SELECT statement. This facilitates a more refined data extraction capability. Consider isolating those employee records with FIRST_NAME values that begin with the letter "J" and who earn a COMMISSION_PCT greater than 10 percent. First, the data in the EMPLOYEES table must be restricted to FIRST_NAME values like "J%", and second, the COMMISSION_PCT values for the records must be tested to ascertain if they are larger than 10 percent. These two separate conditions may be associated using the Boolean *AND* operator and are applied consecutively in a WHERE clause. A result set conforming to any or all conditions or to the negation of one or more conditions may be specified using Boolean operators.

The AND Operator

The *AND* operator merges conditions into one larger condition to which a row must conform to be included in the results set. Boolean operators are defined using *truth tables*. Table 3-2, the AND operator truth table, summarizes its functionality.

If two conditions specified in a WHERE clause are joined with an AND operator, then a row is tested consecutively for conformance to both conditions before being retrieved. If it conforms to neither or only one of the conditions, the row is excluded since the result is FALSE. If the row contains a NULL value that causes one of the conditions to evaluate to NULL, then that row is excluded. A row will only be

FIGURE 3-13

Using the IS
NULL operator

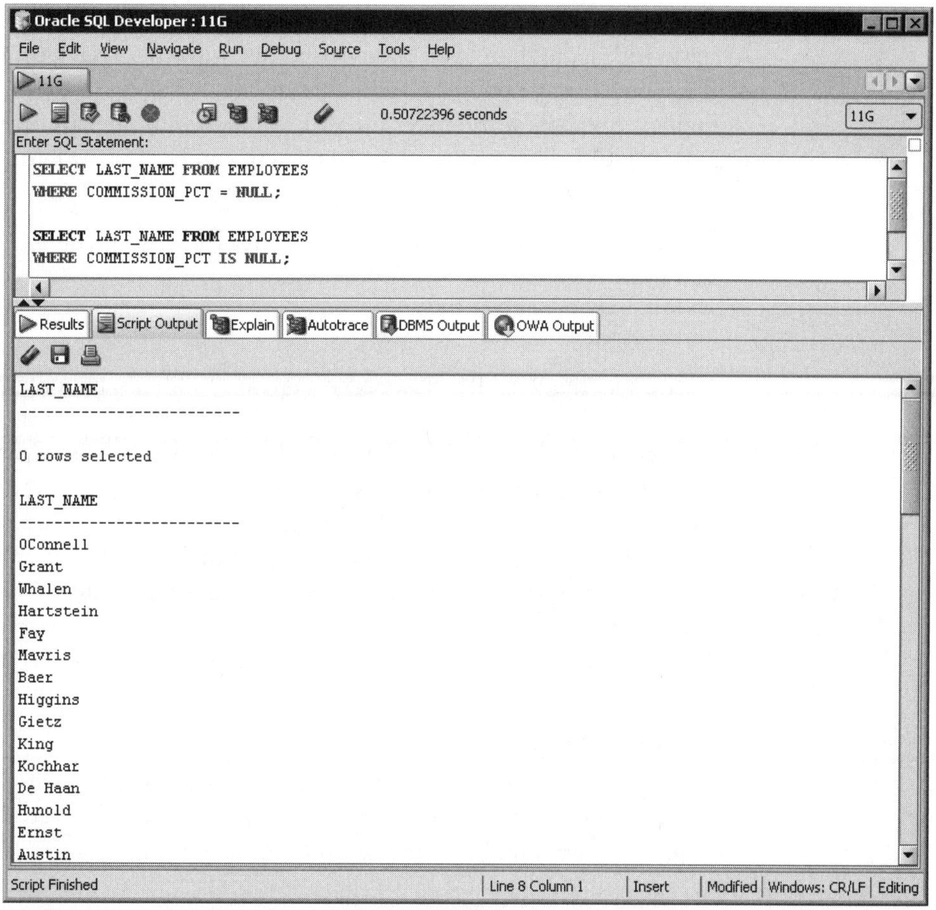

TABLE 3-2	**Condition X**	**Condition Y**	**Result**
AND Operator Truth Table	FALSE	FALSE	FALSE
	TRUE	FALSE	FALSE
	FALSE	TRUE	FALSE
	TRUE	TRUE	TRUE
	TRUE	NULL	NULL
	NULL	TRUE	NULL
	FALSE	NULL	FALSE
	NULL	FALSE	FALSE
	NULL	NULL	NULL

returned if every condition joined with an AND operator evaluates to TRUE. In a scenario with more than two conditions joined with the AND operator, only data conforming to every condition will be returned.

Employee records with FIRST_NAME values beginning with the letter "J" and COMMISSION_PCT greater than 10 percent can be retrieved using the following query:

```
select first_name, last_name, commission_pct, hire_date
from employees
where first_name like 'J%'
and commission_pct > 0.1;
```

Notice that the WHERE clause now has two conditions, but only one WHERE keyword. The AND operator separates the two conditions. To specify further mandatory conditions, simply add them and ensure that they are separated by additional AND operators. You can specify as many conditions as you wish. Remember, though, the more AND conditions specified, the more restrictive the query becomes. Figure 3-14 shows the preceding query followed by two additional restrictions. The HIRE_DATE value must be larger than 01-JUN-1996, and the LAST_NAME must contain the letter "o." The first query returns four rows. Notice that the additional AND conditions in the second query are satisfied by only two rows.

The OR Operator

The OR operator separates multiple conditions, at least one of which must be satisfied by the row selected to warrant inclusion in the results set. Table 3-3, the OR operator truth table, summarizes its functionality.

TABLE 3-3	Condition X	Condition Y	Result
OR Operator Truth Table	FALSE	FALSE	FALSE
	TRUE	FALSE	TRUE
	FALSE	TRUE	TRUE
	TRUE	TRUE	TRUE
	TRUE	NULL	TRUE
	NULL	TRUE	TRUE
	FALSE	NULL	NULL
	NULL	FALSE	NULL
	NULL	NULL	NULL

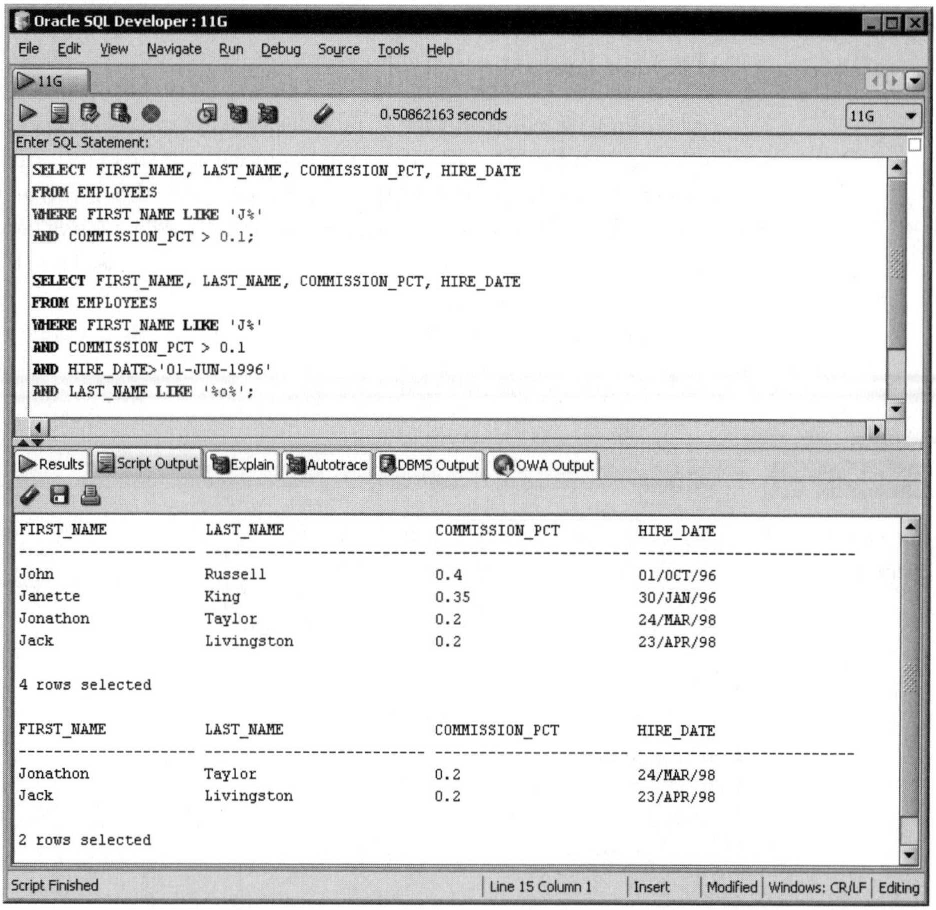

FIGURE 3-14

Using the AND
operator

```
Oracle SQL Developer : 11G                                          _ □ ✕

File   Edit   View   Navigate   Run   Debug   Source   Tools   Help

▶ 11G                                                              ◀ ▶ ▼

▶ 🔲 📑 📑 ●    🔳 📄 📄    🖊         0.50862163 seconds        11G   ▼

Enter SQL Statement:

SELECT FIRST_NAME, LAST_NAME, COMMISSION_PCT, HIRE_DATE
FROM EMPLOYEES
WHERE FIRST_NAME LIKE 'J%'
AND COMMISSION_PCT > 0.1;

SELECT FIRST_NAME, LAST_NAME, COMMISSION_PCT, HIRE_DATE
FROM EMPLOYEES
WHERE FIRST_NAME LIKE 'J%'
AND COMMISSION_PCT > 0.1
AND HIRE_DATE>'01-JUN-1996'
AND LAST_NAME LIKE '%o%';


▶ Results | 📄 Script Output | 📄 Explain | 📄 Autotrace | 📄 DBMS Output | 🌐 OWA Output

🖊 🔲 📄

FIRST_NAME            LAST_NAME                COMMISSION_PCT          HIRE_DATE
-------------------   ----------------------   ---------------------   ------------------------
John                  Russell                  0.4                     01/OCT/96
Janette               King                     0.35                    30/JAN/96
Jonathon              Taylor                   0.2                     24/MAR/98
Jack                  Livingston               0.2                     23/APR/98

4 rows selected

FIRST_NAME            LAST_NAME                COMMISSION_PCT          HIRE_DATE
-------------------   ----------------------   ---------------------   ------------------------
Jonathon              Taylor                   0.2                     24/MAR/98
Jack                  Livingston               0.2                     23/APR/98

2 rows selected

Script Finished                        Line 15 Column 1    Insert    Modified  Windows: CR/LF  Editing
```

If two conditions specified in a WHERE clause are joined with an OR operator
then a row is tested consecutively for conformance to either or both conditions
before being retrieved. Conforming to just one of the OR conditions is sufficient
for the record to be returned. If it conforms to none of the conditions, the row is
excluded since the result is FALSE. A row will only be returned if at least one of the
conditions associated with an OR operator evaluates to TRUE.

Retrieving employee records having FIRST_NAME values beginning with
the letter B or those with a COMMISSION_PCT greater than 35 percent can be
written as:

```
select first_name, last_name, commission_pct, hire_date
from employees
where first_name like 'B%'
or commission_pct > 0.35;
```

Notice that the two conditions are separated by the OR keyword. All employee records with FIRST_NAME values beginning with an uppercase "B" will be returned regardless of their COMMISSION_PCT values, even if they are NULL. All those records having COMMISSION_PCT values greater that 35 percent, regardless of what letter their FIRST_NAME values begin with, are also returned.

Further OR conditions may be specified by separating them with an OR operator. The more OR conditions you specify, the less restrictive your query becomes. Figure 3-15 shows the preceding query with two additional OR conditions. The HIRE_DATE value must be larger than 01-JAN-2000 or the LAST_NAME must begin with the letter "B." The first query returns fewer rows than the second query since more rows meet the less restrictive conditions in the second query than in the first.

FIGURE 3-15

Using the OR operator

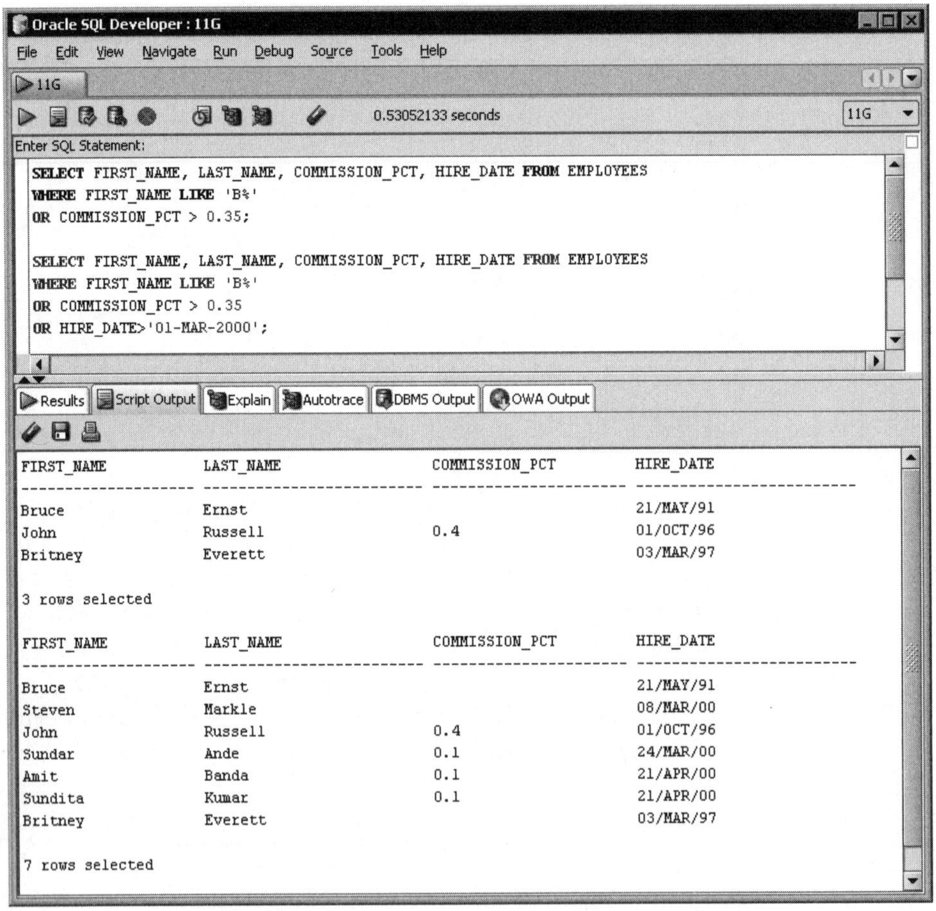

SCENARIO & SOLUTION

You have a complex query with multiple conditions. Is there a restriction on the number of conditions you can specify in the WHERE clause? Is there a limit to the number of comparison operators you can use in a single query?	No. You may specify any number of conditions in the WHERE clause separated by the Boolean operators. There is no limit when using the comparison operators, and they may be specified multiple times if necessary in a single query.
You have been tasked to locate rows in the EMPLOYEES table where the SALARY values contain the numbers 8 and 0 adjacent to each other. The SALARY column has a NUMBER data type. Is it possible to use the LIKE comparison operator with numeric data?	Yes. Oracle automatically casts the data into the required data type, if possible. In this case, the numeric SALARY values are momentarily "changed" into character data allowing the use of the LIKE operator to locate matching patterns. The following query locates the required rows: SELECT * FROM EMPLOYEES WHERE SALARY LIKE '%80%';"
By restricting the rows returned from the JOBS table to those which contain the value SA_REP in the JOB_ID column, is a projection, selection or join performed?	A selection is performed since rows are restricted.

The NOT Operator

The *NOT* operator negates conditional operators. A selected row must conform to the logical opposite of the condition in order to be included in the results set. Table 3-4, the NOT operator truth table, summarizes its functionality.

Conditional operators may be negated by the NOT operator as shown by the WHERE clauses listed in Table 3-5.

As the examples in Table 3-5 suggest, the NOT operator can be very useful. It is important to understand that the NOT operator negates the comparison operator in a condition, whether it's an equality, inequality, range based, pattern matching, set membership, or null testing operator.

TABLE 3-4	Condition X	NOT Condition X
The NOT Operator Truth Table	FALSE	TRUE
	TRUE	FALSE
	NULL	NULL

TABLE 3-5	Positive	Negative
Conditions Negated by the NOT Operator	where last_name='King'	where NOT (last_name='King')
	where first_name LIKE 'R%'	where first_name NOT LIKE 'R%'
	where department_id IN (10,20,30)	where department_id NOT IN (10,20,30)
	where salary BETWEEN 1 and 3000	where salary NOT BETWEEN 1 and 3000
	where commission_pct IS NULL	where commission_pct IS NOT NULL

Retrieving employee records with FIRST_NAME values that do NOT begin with the letter "B" or those that do NOT comply with a COMMISSION_PCT greater than 35 percent can be written as:

```
select first_name, last_name, commission_pct, hire_date
from employees
where first_name not like 'B%'
or not (commission_pct > 0.35);
```

Notice that the two conditions are still separated by the OR operator and the NOT operator has just been added to them.

on the Job *AND and OR are Boolean operators that enable multiple WHERE clause conditions to be specified in a single query. All conditions separated by an AND operator must evaluate to true after testing a row's values to prevent it from being excluded from the final results set. However, only one of the conditions separated by an OR operator must evaluate to true to avoid its exclusion from the final results set. If five conditions, A, B, C, D, and E, occur in a WHERE clause as WHERE A and B or C or D and E, then a row will be returned if both conditions A and B are fulfilled, or only condition C is met, or only condition D is met, or both conditions D and E are fulfilled.*

Precedence Rules

Arithmetic, character, comparison, and Boolean expressions were examined in the context of the WHERE clause. But how do these operators interact with each other? Arithmetic operators subscribe to a precedence hierarchy. Bracketed expressions are evaluated before multiplication and division operators, which are evaluated before subtraction and addition operators. Similarly, there is a precedence hierarchy for the previously mentioned operators as shown in Table 3-6.

Operators at the same level of precedence are evaluated from left to right if they are encountered together in an expression. When the NOT operator modifies the

	Precedence Level	Operator Symbol	Operation
TABLE 3-6	1	( )	Parentheses or brackets
Operator Precedence Hierarchy	2	/,*	Division and multiplication
	3	+,−	Addition and subtraction
	4	| |	Concatenation
	5	=,<,>,<=,>=	Equality and inequality comparison
	6	[NOT] LIKE, IS [NOT] NULL, [NOT] IN	Pattern, null, and set comparison
	7	[NOT] BETWEEN	Range comparison
	8	!=,<>	Not equal to
	9	NOT	NOT logical condition
	10	AND	AND logical condition
	11	OR	OR logical condition

LIKE, IS NULL, and IN comparison operators, their precedence level remains the same as the positive form of these operators.

Consider the following SELECT statement that demonstrates the interaction of various different operators:

```
select last_name,salary,department_id,job_id,commission_pct
from employees
where last_name like '%a%' and salary > department_id * 200
or
job_id in ('MK_REP','MK_MAN') and commission_pct is not null
```

The LAST_NAME, SALARY, DEPARTMENT_ID, JOB_ID, and COMMISSION_PCT columns are projected from the EMPLOYEES table based on two discrete conditions. The first condition retrieves the records containing the character "a" in the LAST_NAME field AND with a SALARY value greater than 200 times the DEPARTMENT_ID value. The product of DEPARTMENT_ID and 200 is processed before the inequality operator since the precedence of multiplication is higher than inequality comparison.

The second condition fetches those rows with JOB_ID values of either MK_MAN or MK_REP in which COMMISSION_PCT values are not null. For a row to be returned by this query, either the first OR second conditions need to be fulfilled. Figure 3-16 illustrates three queries. Query 1 returns four rows. Query 2 is based on the first condition just discussed and returns four rows. Query 3 is based on the second condition and returns zero rows.

FIGURE 3-16

Operator
precedence in the
WHERE clause

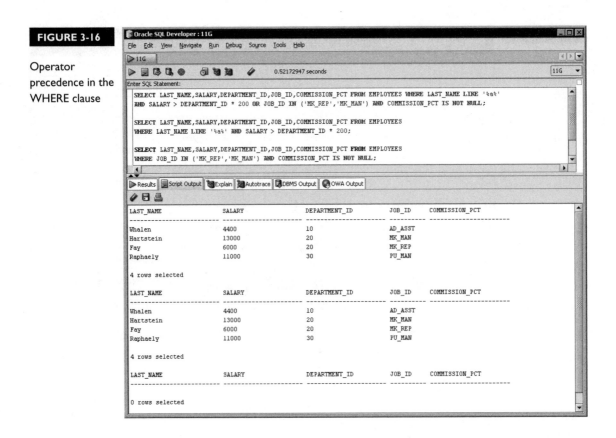

Changing the order of the conditions in the WHERE clause changes its meaning
due to the different precedence of the operators. Consider the following code sample:

```
select last_name,salary,department_id,job_id,commission_pct
from employees
where last_name like '%a%' and salary > department_id * 100 and
commission_pct is not null
or
job_id = 'MK_MAN'
```

There are two composite conditions in this query. The first condition retrieves
the records with the character "a" in the LAST_NAME field AND a SALARY
value greater than 100 times the DEPARTMENT_ID value AND where the
COMMISSION_PCT value is not null. The second condition fetches those rows
with JOB_ID values of MK_MAN. A row is returned by this query, if it conforms to
either condition one OR condition two, but not necessarily to both.

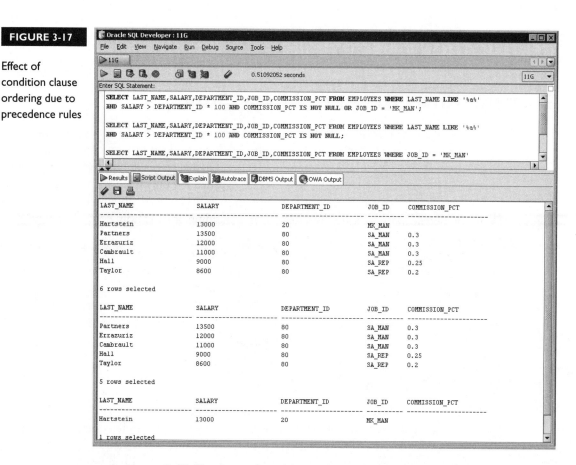

FIGURE 3-17

Effect of
condition clause
ordering due to
precedence rules

As Figure 3-17 illustrates, this query returns six rows. It further shows the division
of the query into two queries based on its two composite conditions. The first
condition results in five rows being returned while the second results in the retrieval
of just one row with a JOB_ID value of MK_MAN.

exam

ⓦatch

*Boolean operators OR
and AND allow multiple WHERE clause
conditions to be specified. The Boolean
NOT operator negates a conditional
operator and may be used several times
within the same condition. The equality,
inequality, BETWEEN, IN, and LIKE*

*comparison operators test two terms within
a single condition. Only one comparison
operator is used per conditional clause.
The distinction between Boolean and
comparison operators is important and
forms the basis for many questions related
to this chapter in the exam.*

CERTIFICATION OBJECTIVE 3.02

Sort the Rows Retrieved by a Query

Regular language dictionaries sort words in alphabetical order. Pages printed in a book are sorted numerically in ascending order from beginning to end. The practical implementations of selection and projection have been covered thus far. The usability of the retrieved datasets may be significantly enhanced with a mechanism to order or sort the information. Information may be sorted alphabetically, numerically, from earliest to latest, or in ascending or descending order. Further, the data may be sorted by one or more columns, including columns that are not listed in the SELECT clause. Sorting is performed once the results of a SELECT statement have been fetched. The sorting parameters do not influence the records returned by a query, just the presentation of the results. Exactly the same rows are returned by a statement including a sort clause as are returned by a statement excluding a sort clause. Only the ordering of the output may differ. Sorting the results of a query is accomplished using the ORDER BY clause.

The ORDER BY Clause

When tables are created, they are initially empty and contain no rows. As rows are inserted, updated, and deleted by one or more users or application systems, the original ordering of the stored rows is lost. The Oracle server cannot and does not guarantee that rows are stored sequentially. This is not a problem since a mechanism to sort the retrieved dataset is available in the form of the *ORDER BY* clause.

This clause is responsible for transforming the output of a query into more practical, user-friendly sorted data. The ORDER BY clause is always the last clause in a SELECT statement. As the full syntax of the SELECT statement is progressively exposed, you will observe new clauses added but none of them will be positioned after the ORDER BY clause. The format of the ORDER BY clause in the context of the SQL SELECT statement is as follows:

```
SELECT * | {[DISTINCT] column | expression [alias],...}
FROM table
[WHERE condition(s)]
[ORDER BY {col(s) | expr | numeric_pos} [ASC | DESC] [NULLS FIRST | LAST]];
```

Ascending and Descending Sorting

Ascending sort order is natural for most types of data and is therefore the default sort order used whenever the ORDER BY clause is specified. An ascending sort order for numbers is lowest to highest, while it is earliest to latest for dates and alphabetically for characters. The first form of the ORDER BY clause shows that results of a query may be sorted by one or more columns or expressions:

ORDER BY *col(s)* | *expr;*

Suppose that a report is requested that must contain an employee's LAST_NAME, HIRE_DATE, and SALARY information, sorted alphabetically by the LAST_NAME column for all sales representatives and marketing managers. This report could be extracted with the following SELECT statement:

```
select last_name, hire_date, salary
from employees
where job_id in ('SA_REP','MK_MAN')
order by last_name;
```

The data selected may be ordered by any of the columns from the tables in the FROM clause, including those that do not appear in the SELECT list. The results from the preceding query may be sorted by the COMMISSION_PCT column, as shown in Figure 3-18.

The second example in Figure 3-18 shows that by appending the keyword *DESC* to the ORDER BY clause, the rows are returned sorted in descending order based on the COMMISSION_PCT column. The third example demonstrates the optional *NULLS LAST* keywords, which specify that if the sort column contains null values, then these rows are to be listed last after sorting the remaining rows based on their NOT NULL values. To specify that rows with null values in the sort column should be displayed first, append the *NULLS FIRST* keywords to the ORDER BY clause.

The following example sorts a dataset based on an expression. This expression calculates an employee's value to a company based on their HIRE_DATE and SALARY values. This formula takes the HIRE_DATE value and subtracts a specified number of days to return an earlier date. The number of days subtracted is calculated by dividing the SALARY value by 10. The expression is aliased as EMP_VALUE as follows:

```
select last_name, salary, hire_date, hire_date-(salary/10) emp_value
from employees
where job_id in ('SA_REP','MK_MAN')
order by emp_value;
```

FIGURE 3-18

Sorting data using the ORDER BY clause

```
Command Prompt - SQLPLUS HR                                                    _ □ X

SQL> SELECT LAST_NAME, SALARY, COMMISSION_PCT FROM EMPLOYEES
  2  WHERE JOB_ID IN ('SA_MAN','MK_MAN') ORDER BY COMMISSION_PCT;

LAST_NAME                       SALARY COMMISSION_PCT
------------------------ ------------- --------------
Zlotkey                          10500             .2
Partners                         13500             .3
Cambrault                        11000             .3
Errazuriz                        12000             .3
Russell                          14000             .4
Hartstein                        13000

6 rows selected.

SQL> SELECT LAST_NAME, SALARY, COMMISSION_PCT FROM EMPLOYEES
  2  WHERE JOB_ID IN ('SA_MAN','MK_MAN') ORDER BY COMMISSION_PCT DESC;

LAST_NAME                       SALARY COMMISSION_PCT
------------------------ ------------- --------------
Hartstein                        13000
Russell                          14000             .4
Partners                         13500             .3
Errazuriz                        12000             .3
Cambrault                        11000             .3
Zlotkey                          10500             .2

6 rows selected.

SQL> SELECT LAST_NAME, SALARY, COMMISSION_PCT FROM EMPLOYEES
  2  WHERE JOB_ID IN ('SA_MAN','MK_MAN') ORDER BY COMMISSION_PCT DESC NULLS LAST
;

LAST_NAME                       SALARY COMMISSION_PCT
------------------------ ------------- --------------
Russell                          14000             .4
Partners                         13500             .3
Cambrault                        11000             .3
Errazuriz                        12000             .3
Zlotkey                          10500             .2
Hartstein                        13000

6 rows selected.

SQL>
```

The EMP_VALUE expression is initialized with the HIRE_DATE value and is offset further into the past based on the SALARY field. The earliest EMP_VALUE date appears first in the result set output since the ORDER BY clause specifies that the results will be sorted by the expression alias. Note that the results could be sorted by the explicit expression and the alias could be omitted as in ORDER BY HIRE_DATE-(SALARY/10), but using aliases renders the query easier to read.

Several implicit default options are selected when you use the ORDER BY clause. The most important of these is that unless DESC is specified, the sort order is assumed to be ascending. If null values occur in the sort column, the default sort order is assumed to be NULLS LAST for ascending sorts and NULLS FIRST for descending sorts. If no ORDER BY clause is specified, the same query executed at different times may return the same set of results in different row order, so no assumptions should be made regarding the default row order.

Positional Sorting

Oracle offers an alternate and shorter way to specify the sort column or expression. Instead of specifying the column name, the position of the column as it occurs in the SELECT list is appended to the ORDER BY clause. Consider the following example:

```
select last_name, hire_date, salary
from employees
where job_id in ('SA_REP','MK_MAN')
order by 2;
```

The ORDER BY clause specifies the numeric literal two. This is equivalent to specifying ORDER BY HIRE_DATE, since the HIRE_DATE column is the second column selected in the SELECT clause.

Positional sorting applies only to columns in the SELECT list that have a numeric position associated with them. Modifying the preceding query to sort the results by the JOB_ID column is not possible using positional sorting since this column does not occur in the SELECT list.

Composite Sorting

Results of a query may be sorted by more than one column using *composite sorting*. Two or more columns may be specified (either literally or positionally) as the composite sort key by commas separating them in the ORDER BY clause. Consider the requirement to fetch the JOB_ID, LAST_NAME, SALARY, and HIRE_DATE values from the EMPLOYEES table. The further requirements are that the results must be sorted in reverse alphabetical order by JOB_ID first, then in ascending alphabetical order by LAST_NAME, and finally in numerically descending order based on the SALARY column. The following SELECT statement fulfils these requirements:

```
select job_id, last_name, salary, hire_date
from employees
where job_id in ('SA_REP','MK_MAN')
order by job_id desc, last_name, 3 desc;
```

Each column involved in the sort is listed left to right in order of importance separated by commas in the ORDER BY clause, including the modifier DESC, which occurs twice in this clause. This example also demonstrates mixing literal and positional column specifications. As Figure 3-19 shows, there are several rows with the same JOB_ID value, for example, SA_REP. For these rows, the data is sorted alphabetically by the secondary sort key, which is the LAST_NAME column.

FIGURE 3-19

Composite
sorting using
the ORDER BY
clause

```
Command Prompt - SQLPLUS HR                                          _ □ ✗

SQL> SELECT JOB_ID, LAST_NAME, SALARY, HIRE_DATE
  2  FROM EMPLOYEES
  3  WHERE JOB_ID IN ('SA_REP','MK_MAN')
  4  ORDER BY JOB_ID DESC, LAST_NAME, 3 DESC;

JOB_ID     LAST_NAME                        SALARY HIRE_DATE
---------- ------------------------- ------------- ----------
SA_REP     Abel                              11000 11-MAY-96
SA_REP     Ande                               6400 24-MAR-00
SA_REP     Banda                              6200 21-APR-00
SA_REP     Bates                              7300 24-MAR-99
SA_REP     Bernstein                          9500 24-MAR-97
SA_REP     Bloom                             10000 23-MAR-98
SA_REP     Cambrault                          7500 09-DEC-98
SA_REP     Doran                              7500 15-DEC-97
SA_REP     Fox                                9600 24-JAN-98
SA_REP     Grant                              7000 24-MAY-99
SA_REP     Greene                             9500 19-MAR-99
SA_REP     Hall                               9000 20-AUG-97
SA_REP     Hutton                             8800 19-MAR-97
SA_REP     Johnson                            6200 04-JAN-00
SA_REP     King                              10000 30-JAN-96
SA_REP     Kumar                              6100 21-APR-00
SA_REP     Lee                                6800 23-FEB-00
SA_REP     Livingston                         8400 23-APR-98
SA_REP     Marvins                            7200 24-JAN-00
SA_REP     McEwen                             9000 01-AUG-96
SA_REP     Olsen                              8000 30-MAR-98
SA_REP     Ozer                              11500 11-MAR-97
SA_REP     Sewall                             7000 03-NOV-98
SA_REP     Smith                              8000 10-MAR-97
SA_REP     Smith                              7400 23-FEB-99
SA_REP     Sully                              9500 04-MAR-96
SA_REP     Taylor                             8600 24-MAR-98
SA_REP     Tucker                            10000 30-JAN-97
SA_REP     Tuvault                            7000 23-NOV-99
SA_REP     Vishney                           10500 11-NOV-97
MK_MAN     Hartstein                         13000 17-FEB-96

31 rows selected.

SQL>
```

For the rows with the same JOB_ID and same LAST_NAME column values such as
SA_REP and Smith, these rows are sorted in numeric descending order by the third
sort column, SALARY.

ⓦatch   *The concept of sorting data
is usually thoroughly tested. The syntax of
the ORDER BY clause is straightforward,
but multiple sort terms like expressions,
columns, and positional specifiers, coupled
with descending sort orders for some*
*terms and ascending sort orders for others,
provide a powerful data sorting mechanism
that comes with a corresponding increase
in complexity. This complexity is often
tested, so ensure that you have a solid
understanding of the ORDER BY clause.*

EXERCISE 3-2

Sorting Data Using the ORDER BY Clause

The JOBS table contains descriptions of different types of jobs an employee in the organization may occupy. It contains the JOB_ID, JOB_TITLE, MIN_SALARY, and MAX_SALARY columns. You are required to write a query that extracts the JOB_TITLE, MIN_SALARY, and MAX_SALARY columns, as well as an expression called VARIANCE, which is the difference between the MAX_SALARY and MIN_SALARY values, for each row. The results must include only JOB_TITLE values that contain either the word "President" or "Manager." Sort the list in descending order based on the VARIANCE expression. If more than one row has the same VARIANCE value, then, in addition, sort these rows by JOB_TITLE in reverse alphabetic order.

1. Start SQL Developer and connect to the HR schema.

2. The SELECT clause is
   SELECT JOB_TITLE, MIN_SALARY, MAX_SALARY, (MAX_SALARY – MIN_SALARY) VARIANCE

3. The FROM clause is
   FROM JOBS

4. The WHERE conditions must allow only those rows whose JOB_TITLE column contains either the string "President" OR the string "Manager."

5. The WHERE clause is
   WHERE JOB_TITLE LIKE '%President%' OR JOB_TITLE LIKE '%Manager%'

6. Sorting is accomplished with the ORDER BY clause. Composite sorting is required using both the VARIANCE expression and the JOB_TITLE column in descending order.

7. The ORDER BY clause is
   ORDER BY VARIANCE DESC, JOB_TITLE DESC.
   You may alternately specify the explicit expression in the ORDER BY clause instead of the expression alias.

8. Executing the statement returns a set of results matching this pattern as shown in the following illustration.

CERTIFICATION OBJECTIVE 3.03

Ampersand Substitution

As queries are developed and perfected, they may be saved for future use. Sometimes, queries differ very slightly, and it is desirable to have a more generic form of the query that has a variable or placeholder defined that can be substituted at runtime.

Oracle offers this functionality in the form of *ampersand substitution*. Every element of the SELECT statement may be substituted, and the reduction of queries to their core elements to facilitate reuse can save you hours of tedious and repetitive work. The following areas are examined in this section:

- Substitution variables
- The DEFINE and VERIFY commands

Substitution Variables

The key to understanding substitution variables is to regard them as placeholders. A SQL query is composed of two or more clauses. Each clause can be divided into subclauses, which are in turn made up of character text. Any text, subclause or clause element, or even the entire SQL query is a candidate for substitution. Consider the SELECT statement in its general form:

SELECT * | {[DISTINCT] *column* | *expression* [*alias*],...}
FROM *table*
[WHERE *condition(s)*]
[ORDER BY {*col(s)* | *expr* | *numeric_pos*} [ASC | DESC] [NULLS FIRST | LAST]];

Using substitution, you insert values into the italicized elements, choosing which optional keywords to use in your queries. When the LAST_NAME column in the EMPLOYEES table is required, the query is constructed using the general form of the SELECT statement and substituting the column name: LAST_NAME in place of the word *column* in the SELECT clause and the table name; EMPLOYEES in place of the word *table* in the FROM clause.

Single Ampersand Substitution

The most basic and popular form of substitution of elements in a SQL statement is *single ampersand substitution*. The ampersand character (&) is the symbol chosen to designate a substitution variable in a statement and precedes the variable name with no spaces between them. When the statement is executed, the Oracle server processes the statement, notices a substitution variable, and attempts to resolve this variable's value in one of two ways. First, it checks whether the variable is *defined* in the user session. (The *DEFINE* command is discussed later in this chapter.) If the variable is not defined, the user process prompts for a value that will be substituted in place of the variable. Once a value is submitted, the statement is complete and is executed by the Oracle server. The *ampersand substitution* variable is resolved at execution time and is sometimes known as *runtime binding* or *runtime substitution*.

A common requirement in the sample HR department may be to retrieve the same information for different employees at different times. Perhaps you are required to look up contact information like PHONE_NUMBER data given either LAST_NAME or EMPLOYEE_ID values. This generic request can be written as follows:

```
select employee_id, last_name, phone_number
from employees
where last_name = &LASTNAME
or employee_id = &EMPNO;
```

As Figure 3-20 shows, when running this query, Oracle server prompts you to input a value for the variable called LASTNAME. You enter an employee's last name, if you know it, for example, 'King'. If you don't know the last name but know the employee ID number, you can type in any value and press the ENTER key to submit the value. Oracle then prompts you to enter a value for the EMPNO variable. After typing in a value, for example, 0, and hitting ENTER, there are no remaining substitution variables for Oracle to resolve and the following statement is executed:

```
select employee_id, last_name, phone_number
from employees
where last_name = 'King'
or employee_id = 0;
```

Variables can be assigned any alphanumeric name that is a valid identifier name. The literal you substitute when prompted for a variable must be an appropriate data type for that context; otherwise, an ORA-00904: invalid identifier error is returned. If the variable is meant to substitute a character or date value, the literal needs to be enclosed in single quotes. A useful technique is to enclose the *ampersand substitution* variable in single quotes when dealing with character and date values. In this way,

FIGURE 3-20

Single ampersand
substitution

```
SQL> SELECT EMPLOYEE_ID, LAST_NAME, PHONE_NUMBER
  2  FROM EMPLOYEES
  3  WHERE LAST_NAME = &LASTNAME
  4  OR EMPLOYEE_ID = &EMPNO;
Enter value for lastname: 'King'
old   3: WHERE LAST_NAME = &LASTNAME
new   3: WHERE LAST_NAME = 'King'
Enter value for empno: 0
old   4: OR EMPLOYEE_ID = &EMPNO
new   4: OR EMPLOYEE_ID = 0

EMPLOYEE_ID LAST_NAME                      PHONE_NUMBER
----------- ------------------------------ --------------------
        100 King                           515.123.4567
        156 King                           011.44.1345.429268

SQL>
```

the user is required to submit a literal value without worrying about enclosing it in quotes. The following statement rewrites the previous one but encloses the LASTNAME variable in quotes:

```
select employee_id, last_name, phone_number, email
from employees
where last_name = '&LASTNAME'
or employee_id = &EMPNO;
```

When prompted for a value to substitute for the LASTNAME variable, you may for example, submit the value King without any single quotes, as these are already present and when the *runtime substitution* is performed, the first WHERE clause condition will resolve to: WHERE LAST_NAME = 'King'.

Double Ampersand Substitution

There are occasions when a substitution variable is referenced multiple times in the same query. In such situations, the Oracle server will prompt you to enter a value for every occurrence of the single ampersand substitution variable. For complex scripts this can be very inefficient and tedious. The following statement retrieves the FIRST_NAME and LAST_NAME columns from the EMPLOYEES table for those rows that contain the same set of characters in both these fields:

```
select first_name, last_name
from employees
where last_name like '%&SEARCH%'
and first_name like '%&SEARCH%';
```

The two conditions are identical but apply to different columns. When this statement is executed, you are first prompted to enter a substitution value for the SEARCH variable used in the comparison with the LAST_NAME column. Thereafter, you are prompted to enter a substitution value for the SEARCH variable used in the comparison with the FIRST_NAME column. This poses two problems. First, it is inefficient to enter the same value twice, but second and more importantly, typographical errors may confound the query since Oracle does not verify that the same literal value is entered each time substitution variables with the same name are used. In this example, the logical assumption is that the contents of the variables substituted should be the same, but the fact that the variables have the same name has no meaning to the Oracle server and it makes no such assumption. The first example in Figure 3-21 shows the results of running the preceding query and submitting two distinct values for the SEARCH substitution variable. In this particular example, the results are incorrect since the requirement was to retrieve FIRST_NAME and LAST_NAME pairs which contained the identical string of characters.

FIGURE 3-21

Double
ampersand
substitution

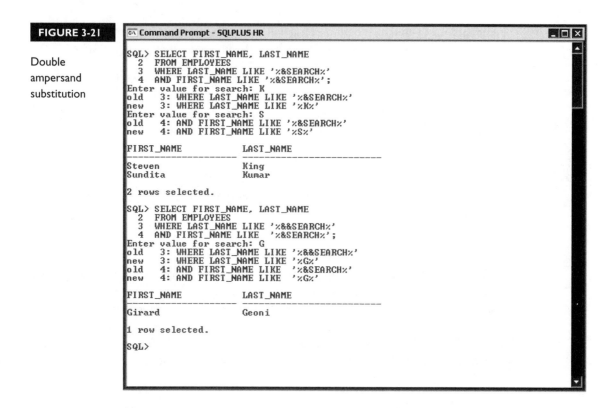

```
SQL> SELECT FIRST_NAME, LAST_NAME
  2    FROM EMPLOYEES
  3    WHERE LAST_NAME LIKE '%&SEARCH%'
  4    AND FIRST_NAME LIKE '%&SEARCH%';
Enter value for search: K
old   3: WHERE LAST_NAME LIKE '%&SEARCH%'
new   3: WHERE LAST_NAME LIKE '%K%'
Enter value for search: S
old   4: AND FIRST_NAME LIKE '%&SEARCH%'
new   4: AND FIRST_NAME LIKE '%S%'

FIRST_NAME              LAST_NAME
----------------------  -----------------------------
Steven                  King
Sundita                 Kumar

2 rows selected.

SQL> SELECT FIRST_NAME, LAST_NAME
  2    FROM EMPLOYEES
  3    WHERE LAST_NAME LIKE '%&&SEARCH%'
  4    AND FIRST_NAME LIKE  '%&SEARCH%';
Enter value for search: G
old   3: WHERE LAST_NAME LIKE '%&&SEARCH%'
new   3: WHERE LAST_NAME LIKE '%G%'
old   4: AND FIRST_NAME LIKE  '%&SEARCH%'
new   4: AND FIRST_NAME LIKE  '%G%'

FIRST_NAME              LAST_NAME
----------------------  -----------------------------
Girard                  Geoni

1 row selected.

SQL>
```

In situations when a substitution variable is referenced multiple times in the same query and your intention is that the variable must have the same value at each occurrence in the statement, it is preferable to make use of *double ampersand substitution*. This involves prefixing the first occurrence of the substitution variable that occurs multiple times in a query, with two ampersand symbols instead of one. When the Oracle server encounters a *double ampersand substitution* variable, a session value is defined for that variable and you are not prompted to enter a value to be substituted for this variable in subsequent references.

The second example in Figure 3-21 demonstrates how the SEARCH variable is preceded by two ampersands in the condition with the FIRST_NAME column and thereafter is prefixed by one ampersand in the condition with the LAST_NAME column. When executed, you are prompted to enter a value to be substituted for the SEARCH variable only once for the condition with the FIRST_NAME column. This value is then automatically resolved from the session value of the variable in subsequent references to it, as in the condition with the LAST_NAME column. To undefine the SEARCH variable, you need to use the *UNDEFINE* command described later in this chapter.

on the
job

Whether you work as a developer, database administrator, or business end user, all SQL queries you encounter may be broadly classified as either ad hoc or repeated queries. Ad hoc queries are usually one-off statements written during some data investigation exercise that are unlikely to be reused. The repeated queries are those that are run frequently or periodically, which are usually saved as script files and run with little to no modification whenever required. Reuse prevents costly redevelopment time and allows these consistent queries to potentially benefit from Oracle's native automatic tuning features geared toward improving query performance.

Substituting Column Names

Literal elements of the WHERE clause have been the focus of the discussion on substitution thus far, but virtually any element of a SQL statement is a candidate for substitution. In the following statement, the FIRST_NAME and JOB_ID columns are static and will always be retrieved, but the third column selected is variable and specified as a substitution variable named: COL. The result set is further sorted by this variable column in the ORDER BY clause:

```
select first_name, job_id, &&col
from employees
where job_id in ('MK_MAN','SA_MAN')
order by &col;
```

As Figure 3-22 demonstrates, at runtime, you are prompted to provide a value for the double ampersand variable called COL. You could, for example, enter the column named SALARY and submit your input. The statement that executes performs the substitution and retrieves the FIRST_NAME, JOB_ID, and SALARY columns from the EMPLOYEES table sorted by SALARY.

Unlike character and date literals, column name references do not require single quotes both when explicitly specified and when substituted via ampersand substitution.

Substituting Expressions and Text

Almost any element of a SQL statement may be substituted at runtime. The constraint is that Oracle requires at least the first word to be static. In the case of the SELECT statement, at the very minimum, the SELECT keyword is required and the remainder of the statement may be substituted as follows:

```
select &rest_of_statement;
```

```
Command Prompt - SQLPLUS HR                                        _ □ ×
SQL> SELECT FIRST_NAME, JOB_ID, &&COL
  2   FROM EMPLOYEES
  3   WHERE JOB_ID IN ('MK_MAN','SA_MAN')
  4   ORDER BY &COL;
Enter value for col: SALARY
old   1: SELECT FIRST_NAME, JOB_ID, &&COL
new   1: SELECT FIRST_NAME, JOB_ID, SALARY
old   4: ORDER BY &COL
new   4: ORDER BY SALARY

FIRST_NAME              JOB_ID          SALARY
--------------------    --------        ----------
Eleni                   SA_MAN           10500
Gerald                  SA_MAN           11000
Alberto                 SA_MAN           12000
Michael                 MK_MAN           13000
Karen                   SA_MAN           13500
John                    SA_MAN           14000

6 rows selected.

SQL> _
```

When executed, you are prompted to submit a value for the variable called:
REST_OF_STATEMENT, which could be any legitimate query, such as
DEPARTMENT_NAME from DEPARMENTS. If you submit this text as input for
the variable, the query that is run will be resolved to the following statement:

```
select department_name from departments;
```

Consider the general form of the SQL statement rewritten using ampersand
substitution, as shown next:

```
select &SELECT_CLAUSE
from &FROM_CLAUSE
where &WHERE_CLAUSE
order by &ORDER_BY_CLAUSE;
```

The usefulness of this statement is arguable, but it does illustrate the concept
of substitution effectively. As Figure 3-23 shows, the preceding statement allows
any query discussed so far to be submitted at runtime. The first execution queries
the REGIONS table, while the second execution queries the COUNTRIES table.
Useful candidates for ampersand substitution are statements that are run multiple
times and differ slightly from each other.

FIGURE 3-23

Substituting
expressions and
text

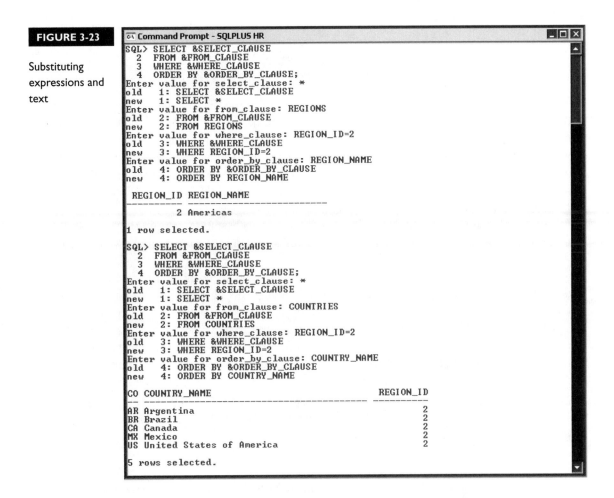

```
Command Prompt - SQLPLUS HR                                    _ □ X
SQL> SELECT &SELECT_CLAUSE
  2    FROM &FROM_CLAUSE
  3    WHERE &WHERE_CLAUSE
  4    ORDER BY &ORDER_BY_CLAUSE;
Enter value for select_clause: *
old    1: SELECT &SELECT_CLAUSE
new    1: SELECT *
Enter value for from_clause: REGIONS
old    2: FROM &FROM_CLAUSE
new    2: FROM REGIONS
Enter value for where_clause: REGION_ID=2
old    3: WHERE &WHERE_CLAUSE
new    3: WHERE REGION_ID=2
Enter value for order_by_clause: REGION_NAME
old    4: ORDER BY &ORDER_BY_CLAUSE
new    4: ORDER BY REGION_NAME

 REGION_ID REGION_NAME
---------- --------------------------
         2 Americas

1 row selected.

SQL> SELECT &SELECT_CLAUSE
  2    FROM &FROM_CLAUSE
  3    WHERE &WHERE_CLAUSE
  4    ORDER BY &ORDER_BY_CLAUSE;
Enter value for select_clause: *
old    1: SELECT &SELECT_CLAUSE
new    1: SELECT *
Enter value for from_clause: COUNTRIES
old    2: FROM &FROM_CLAUSE
new    2: FROM COUNTRIES
Enter value for where_clause: REGION_ID=2
old    3: WHERE &WHERE_CLAUSE
new    3: WHERE REGION_ID=2
Enter value for order_by_clause: COUNTRY_NAME
old    4: ORDER BY &ORDER_BY_CLAUSE
new    4: ORDER BY COUNTRY_NAME

CO COUNTRY_NAME                              REGION_ID
-- ---------------------------------------- ---------
AR Argentina                                        2
BR Brazil                                           2
CA Canada                                           2
MX Mexico                                           2
US United States of America                         2

5 rows selected.
```

Define and Verify

Double ampersand substitution is used to avoid repetitive input when the same variable occurs multiple times in a statement. When a double ampersand substitution occurs, the variable is stored as a session variable. As the statement executes, all further occurrences of the variable are automatically resolved using the stored session variable. Any subsequent executions of the statement within the same session automatically resolve the substitution variables from stored session values. This is not always desirable and indeed limits the usefulness of substitution variables. Oracle does, however, provide a mechanism to *UNDEFINE* these session variables.

INSIDE THE EXAM

There are three certification objectives in this chapter. Limiting the rows retrieved by a query introduced the WHERE clause, which practically demonstrates the concept of selection. The conditions that limit the rows returned are based on comparisons using the BETWEEN, IN, LIKE, Equality, and Inequality operators. Your thorough understanding of these comparison operators and their behavior with character, numeric, and date data types will be examined, along with how they are different from the Boolean NOT, AND, and OR operators.

Using the ORDER BY clause to sort results retrieved is optional and extremely useful. Exam questions that test the concepts of traditional, positional, and composite sorting, along with how NULL values can be handled, are common. When multiple sort terms are present in the ORDER BY clause, it is acceptable to specify ascending sort orders for some and descending sort orders for others. It is a common mistake to forget that Oracle provides this mixed sorting feature as well for the specification of the NULLS FIRST | LAST modifier.

Your understanding of substitution using single and double ampersands as well as the DEFINE and UNDEFINE commands will be tested. You may be given a statement that includes a double ampersand substitution variable that is subsequently referenced multiple times in the statement, along with a single ampersand substitution variable; you will be expected to understand the differences in their behavior. Your understanding of column name, expression, and text substitution will also be measured.

The *VERIFY* command is specific to SQL*Plus and controls whether or not substituted elements are echoed on the user's screen prior to executing a SQL statement that uses substitution variables. These commands are discussed in the next sections.

The DEFINE and UNDEFINE Commands

Session level variables are implicitly created when they are initially referenced in SQL statements using double ampersand substitution. They persist or remain available for the duration of the session or until they are explicitly undefined. A session ends when the user exits their client tool like SQL*Plus or when the user process is terminated abnormally.

The problem with persistent session variables is they tend to detract from the generic nature of statements that use ampersand substitution variables. Fortunately, these session variables can be removed with the UNDEFINE command. Within a script or at the command line of SQL*Plus or SQL Developer, the syntax for undefining session variables is as follows:

UNDEFINE *variable*;

Consider a simple generic example that selects a static and variable column from the EMPLOYEES table and sorts the output based on the variable column. The static column could be the LAST_NAME column.

```
select last_name, &&COLNAME
from employees
where department_id=30
order by &COLNAME;
```

The first time this statement executes, you are prompted to input a value for the variable called COLNAME. Let's assume you enter SALARY. This value is substituted and the statement executes. A subsequent execution of this statement within the same session does not prompt for any COLNAME values since it is already defined as SALARY in the context of this session and can only be undefined with the UNDEFINE COLNAME command, as shown in Figure 3-24. Once the variable has been undefined, the next execution of the statement prompts the user for a value for the COLNAME variable.

The DEFINE command serves two purposes. It can be used to retrieve a list of all the variables currently defined in your SQL session; it can also be used to explicitly define a value for a variable referenced as a substitution variable by one or more statements during the lifetime of that session. The syntax for the two variants of the DEFINE command are as follows:

DEFINE;
DEFINE *variable=value*;

As Figure 3-25 demonstrates, a variable called EMPNAME is defined explicitly to have the value 'King'. The stand-alone DEFINE command in SQL*Plus then returns a number of session variables prefixed with an underscore character as well as other familiar variables, including EMPNAME and double ampersand substitution variables implicitly defined earlier. Two different but simplistic query examples are executed, and the explicitly defined substitution variable EMPNAME is referenced by both queries. Finally, the variable is UNDEFINED.

FIGURE 3-24

The UNDEFINE
command

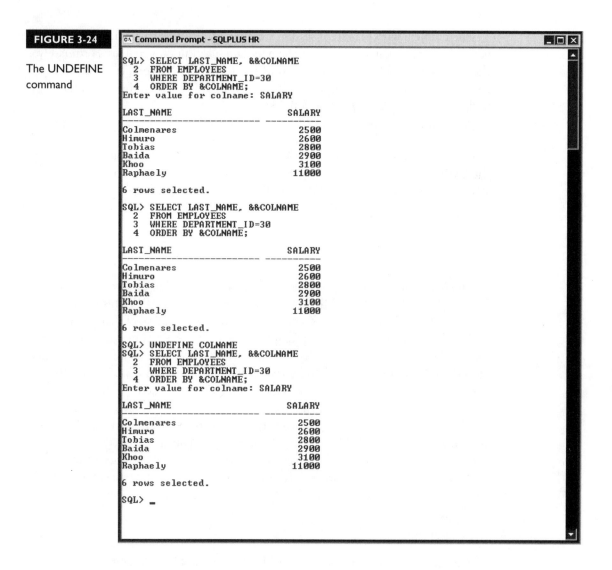

```
Command Prompt - SQLPLUS HR                                    _ □ X
SQL> SELECT LAST_NAME, &&COLNAME
  2    FROM EMPLOYEES
  3    WHERE DEPARTMENT_ID=30
  4    ORDER BY &COLNAME;
Enter value for colname: SALARY

LAST_NAME                    SALARY
------------------------  ----------
Colmenares                     2500
Himuro                         2600
Tobias                         2800
Baida                          2900
Khoo                           3100
Raphaely                      11000

6 rows selected.

SQL> SELECT LAST_NAME, &&COLNAME
  2    FROM EMPLOYEES
  3    WHERE DEPARTMENT_ID=30
  4    ORDER BY &COLNAME;

LAST_NAME                    SALARY
------------------------  ----------
Colmenares                     2500
Himuro                         2600
Tobias                         2800
Baida                          2900
Khoo                           3100
Raphaely                      11000

6 rows selected.

SQL> UNDEFINE COLNAME
SQL> SELECT LAST_NAME, &&COLNAME
  2    FROM EMPLOYEES
  3    WHERE DEPARTMENT_ID=30
  4    ORDER BY &COLNAME;
Enter value for colname: SALARY

LAST_NAME                    SALARY
------------------------  ----------
Colmenares                     2500
Himuro                         2600
Tobias                         2800
Baida                          2900
Khoo                           3100
Raphaely                      11000

6 rows selected.

SQL> _
```

The capacity of the SQL client tool to support session-persistent variables may
be switched off and on as required using the *SET* command. The SET command is
not a SQL language command, but rather a SQL environment control command. By
specifying SET DEFINE OFF, the client tool (for example, SQL*Plus) does not save
session variables or attach special meaning to the ampersand symbol. This allows
the ampersand symbol to be used as an ordinary literal character if necessary. The
SET DEFINE ON | OFF command therefore determines whether or not ampersand
substitution is available in your session.

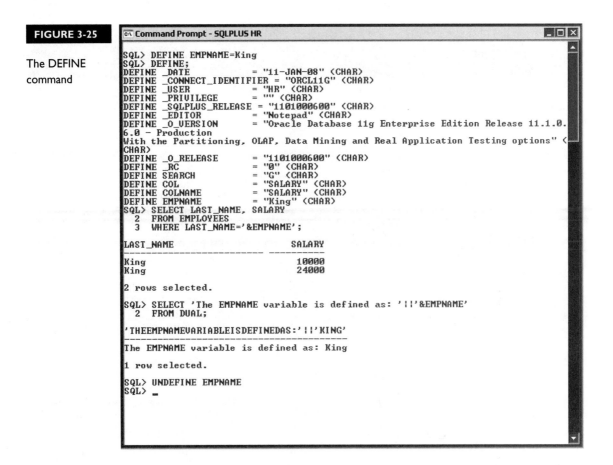

FIGURE 3-25

The DEFINE
command

The following example uses the ampersand symbol as a literal value. When executed, you are prompted to submit a value for bind variable SID.

```
select 'Coda & Sid' from dual;
```

By turning off the ampersand substitution functionality as follows, this query may be executed without prompts:

```
SET DEFINE OFF
select 'Coda & Sid' from dual;
SET DEFINE ON
```

Once the statement executes, the SET DEFINE ON command may be used to switch the substitution functionality back on. If DEFINE is SET OFF and the context that an ampersand is used in a statement cannot be resolved literally, Oracle returns an error.

SCENARIO & SOLUTION

The SELECT list of a query contains a single column. Is it possible to sort the results retrieved by this query by another column?	Yes. Unless positional sorting is used, the ORDER BY clause is independent of the SELECT clause in a statement.
Ampersand substitution variables support reusability of repetitively executed SQL statements. If a substituted value is to be used multiple times at different parts of the same statement, is it possible to be prompted to submit a substitution value just once and for that value to automatically be substituted during subsequent references to the same variable?	Yes. The two methods that may be used are double ampersand substitution or the DEFINE command. Both methods result in the user providing input for a specific substitution variable once. This value remains bound to the variable for the duration of the session unless it is explicitly UNDEFINED.
You have been tasked to retrieve the LAST_NAME and DEPARTMENT_ID values for all rows in the EMPLOYEES table. The output must be sorted by the nullable DEPARTMENT_ID column, and all rows with NULL DEPARTMENT_ID values must be listed last. Is it possible to provide the results as requested?	Yes. The ORDER BY clause provides for sorting by columns that potentially contain NULL values by permitting the modifiers NULLS FIRST or NULLS LAST to be specified. The following query locates the required rows: SELECT LAST_NAME, DEPARTMENT_ID FROM EMPLOYEES ORDER BY DEPARTMENT_ID NULLS LAST;

The VERIFY Command

As discussed earlier, two categories of commands are available when dealing with the Oracle server: SQL language commands and the SQL client control commands. The SELECT statement is an example of a language command, whilst the SET command controls the SQL client environment. There are many different language and control commands available, but the control commands pertinent to substitution are DEFINE and *VERIFY*.

The VERIFY command controls whether the substitution variable submitted is displayed onscreen so you can *verify* that the correct substitution has occurred. A message is displayed showing the *old* clause followed by the *new* clause containing the substituted value. The VERIFY command is switched ON and OFF with the command SET VERIFY ON | OFF. As Figure 3-26 shows, VERIFY is first switched OFF, a query that uses ampersand substitution is executed, and you are prompted to input a value. The value is then substituted, the statement runs, and its results are displayed.

VERIFY is then switched ON, the same query is executed, and you are prompted to input a value. Once the value is input and before the statement commences execution, Oracle displays the clause containing the reference to the substitution variable as the *old* clause with its line number and, immediately below this, the *new* clause displays the statement containing the substituted value.

FIGURE 3-26

The VERIFY command

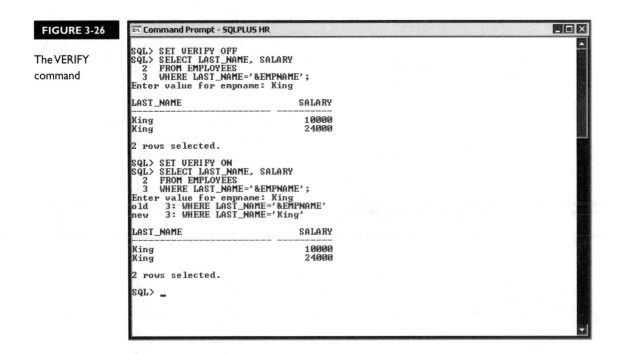

```
Command Prompt - SQLPLUS HR

SQL> SET VERIFY OFF
SQL> SELECT LAST_NAME, SALARY
  2    FROM EMPLOYEES
  3    WHERE LAST_NAME='&EMPNAME';
Enter value for empname: King

LAST_NAME                      SALARY
------------------------- -----------
King                            10000
King                            24000

2 rows selected.

SQL> SET VERIFY ON
SQL> SELECT LAST_NAME, SALARY
  2    FROM EMPLOYEES
  3    WHERE LAST_NAME='&EMPNAME';
Enter value for empname: King
old   3:  WHERE LAST_NAME='&EMPNAME'
new   3:  WHERE LAST_NAME='King'

LAST_NAME                      SALARY
------------------------- -----------
King                            10000
King                            24000

2 rows selected.

SQL> _
```

EXERCISE 3-3

Using Ampersand Substitution

A common calculation performed by the Human Resources department relates to the calculation of taxes levied upon an employee. Although, this is done for all employees, there are always a few staff members who dispute the tax deducted from their income. The tax deducted per employee is calculated by obtaining the annual salary for the employee and multiplying this by the current tax rate, which may vary from year to year. You are required to write a reusable query using the current tax rate and the EMPLOYEE_ID number as inputs and return the EMPLOYEE_ID, FIRST_NAME, SALARY, ANNUAL SALARY (SALARY * 12), TAX_RATE, and TAX (TAX_RATE * ANNUAL SALARY) information.

1. Start SQL*Plus and connect to the HR schema.

2. The select list must include the four specified columns as well as two expressions. The first expression aliased as ANNUAL SALARY is a simple calculation, while the second expression aliased as TAX depends on the TAX_RATE. Since the TAX RATE may vary, this value must be substituted at runtime.

3. The SELECT clause is
SELECT &&EMPLOYEE_ID, FIRST_NAME, SALARY, SALARY * 12 AS "ANNUAL SALARY", &&TAX_RATE, (&TAX_RATE * (SALARY * 12)) AS "TAX"

4. The double ampersand preceding EMPLOYEE_ID and TAX_RATE in the SELECT clause stipulates to Oracle that when the statement is executed the user must be prompted to submit a value for each substitution variable that will be used wherever they are subsequently referenced as &EMPLOYEE_ID and &TAX_RATE, respectively.

5. The FROM clause is
FROM EMPLOYEES

6. The WHERE clause must allow only the row whose EMPLOYEE_ID value is specified at runtime.

7. The WHERE clause is
WHERE EMPLOYEE_ID = &EMPLOYEE_ID

8. Executing this statement returns the set of results shown in the following illustration.

```
Command Prompt - SQLPLUS HR                                           _ □ X

SQL> SELECT &&EMPLOYEE_ID, FIRST_NAME, SALARY,
  2    SALARY * 12 AS "ANNUAL SALARY",
  3    &&TAX_RATE, (&TAX_RATE * (SALARY * 12)) AS "TAX"
  4    FROM EMPLOYEES
  5    WHERE EMPLOYEE_ID = &EMPLOYEE_ID;
Enter value for employee_id: 101
old   1: SELECT &&EMPLOYEE_ID, FIRST_NAME, SALARY,
new   1: SELECT 101, FIRST_NAME, SALARY,
Enter value for tax_rate: 10
old   3: &&TAX_RATE, (&TAX_RATE * (SALARY * 12)) AS "TAX"
new   3: 10, (10 * (SALARY * 12)) AS "TAX"
old   5: WHERE EMPLOYEE_ID = &EMPLOYEE_ID
new   5: WHERE EMPLOYEE_ID = 101

       101 FIRST_NAME               SALARY ANNUAL SALARY          10        TAX
    ---------- -------------------- -------- ------------- ---------- ----------
       101 Neena                     17000        204000          10    2040000

1 row selected.

SQL> _
```

CERTIFICATION SUMMARY

The *WHERE* clause provides the language that enables *selection* in SELECT statements. The criteria for including or excluding rows take the form of conditions. Using comparison operators, two terms are compared with each other and the condition is evaluated as being true or false for each row. These terms may be column values, literals, or expressions. If the Boolean sum of the results of each condition evaluates to true for a particular row, then that row is retrieved. Conditional operators allow terms to be compared to each other in a variety of ways including equality, inequality, range based, set membership, and character pattern matching comparison.

Once a set of data is isolated by your query, the *ORDER BY* clause facilitates sorting the retrieved rows based on numeric, date or character columns or expressions. Results may be sorted using combinations of columns or expressions or both. Data is sorted in ascending order by default.

Generic, reusable statements may be constructed using ampersand substitution variables which prompt for runtime values during execution. Session-persistent substitution variables may be defined and are extremely convenient in situations where many substitutions of the same variable occur in a statement or script.

The simple SELECT statement has been expanded to include a WHERE, and ORDER BY clause. These basic building blocks offer a practical and useful language that can be applied while you build your knowledge of SQL.

✓ TWO-MINUTE DRILL

Limit the Rows Retrieved by a Query

❑ The WHERE clause extends the SELECT statement by providing the language that enables selection.

❑ One or more conditions constitute a WHERE clause. These conditions specify rules to which the data in a row must conform to be eligible for selection.

❑ For each row tested in a condition, there are terms on the left and right of a comparison operator. Terms in a condition can be column values, literals, or expressions.

❑ Comparison operators may test two terms in many ways. Equality or inequality tests are very common, but range, set, and pattern comparisons are also available.

❑ Range comparison is performed using the BETWEEN operator, which tests whether a term falls between given start and end boundary values.

❑ Set membership is tested using the IN operator. A condition based on a set comparison evaluates to true if the left-side term is listed in the single-quoted, comma-delimited set on the right-side.

❑ The LIKE operator enables literal character patterns to be matched with other literals, column values, or evaluated expressions. The percentage symbol (%) behaves as a wildcard that matches zero or more characters. The underscore symbol (_) behaves as a single character wildcard that matches exactly one other character.

❑ Boolean operators include the AND, OR, and NOT operators. The AND and OR operators enable multiple conditional clauses to be specified. These are sometimes referred to as multiple WHERE clauses.

❑ The NOT operator negates the comparison operator involved in a condition.

Sort the Rows Retrieved by a Query

❑ Results are sorted using the ORDER BY clause. Rows retrieved may be ordered according to one or more columns by specifying either the column names or their numeric position in the SELECT clause.

❑ The sorted output may be arranged in descending or ascending order using the DESC or ASC modifiers after the sort terms in the ORDER BY clause.

Ampersand Substitution

❑ Ampersand substitution facilitates SQL statement reuse by providing a means to substitute elements of a statement at runtime. The same SQL statement may therefore be run multiple times with different input parameters.

❑ Single ampersand substitution requires user input for every occurrence of the substitution variable in the statement. Double ampersand substitution requires user input only once per occurrence of a substitution variable, since it defines a session-persistent variable with the given input value.

❑ Session-persistent variables may be set explicitly using the DEFINE command. The UNDEFINE command may be used to unset both implicitly (double ampersand substitution) and explicitly defined session variables.

❑ The VERIFY environmental setting controls whether SQL*Plus displays the old and new versions of statement lines which contain substitution variables.

SELF TEST

The following questions will help you measure your understanding of the material presented in this chapter. Read all the choices carefully because there may be more than one correct answer. Choose all the correct answers for each question.

Limit the Rows Retrieved by a Query

1. Which two clauses of the SELECT statement facilitate selection and projection?
   A. SELECT, FROM
   B. ORDER BY, WHERE
   C. SELECT, WHERE
   D. SELECT, ORDER BY

2. Choose the query that extracts the LAST_NAME, JOB_ID, and SALARY values from the EMPLOYEES table for records having JOB_ID values of either SA_REP or MK_MAN and having SALARY values in the range of $1000 to $4000. The SELECT and FROM clauses are SELECT LAST_NAME, JOB_ID, SALARY FROM EMPLOYEES:
   A. WHERE JOB_ID IN ('SA_REP','MK_MAN')
      AND SALARY > 1000 AND SALARY < 4000;
   B. WHERE JOB_ID IN ('SA_REP','MK_MAN')
      AND SALARY BETWEEN 1000 AND 4000;
   C. WHERE JOB_ID LIKE 'SA_REP%' AND 'MK_MAN%'
      AND SALARY > 1000 AND SALARY < 4000;
   D. WHERE JOB_ID = 'SA_REP'
      AND SALARY BETWEEN 1000 AND 4000
      OR JOB_ID='MK_MAN';

3. Which of the following WHERE clauses contains an error? The SELECT and FROM clauses are SELECT * FROM EMPLOYEES:
   A. WHERE HIRE_DATE IN ('02-JUN-2004');
   B. WHERE SALARY IN ('1000','4000','2000');
   C. WHERE JOB_ID IN (SA_REP,MK_MAN);
   D. WHERE COMMISSION_PCT BETWEEN 0.1 AND 0.5;

4. Choose the WHERE clause that extracts the DEPARTMENT_NAME values containing the character literal "er" from the DEPARTMENTS table. The SELECT and FROM clauses are SELECT DEPARTMENT_NAME FROM DEPARTMENTS:

    A. WHERE DEPARTMENT_NAME IN ('%e%r');
    B. WHERE DEPARTMENT_NAME LIKE '%er%';
    C. WHERE DEPARTMENT_NAME BETWEEN 'e' AND 'r';
    D. WHERE DEPARTMENT_NAME CONTAINS 'e%r';

5. Which two of the following conditions are equivalent to each other?

    A. WHERE COMMISSION_PCT IS NULL
    B. WHERE COMMISSION_PCT = NULL
    C. WHERE COMMISSION_PCT IN (NULL)
    D. WHERE NOT(COMMISSION_PCT IS NOT NULL)

6. Which three of the following conditions are equivalent to each other?

    A. WHERE SALARY <=5000 AND SALARY >=2000
    B. WHERE SALARY IN (2000,3000,4000,5000)
    C. WHERE SALARY BETWEEN 2000 AND 5000
    D. WHERE SALARY > 1999 AND SALARY < 5001
    E. WHERE SALARY >=2000 AND <=5000

Sort the Rows Retrieved by a Query

7. Choose one false statement about the ORDER BY clause.

    A. When using the ORDER BY clause, it always appears as the last clause in a SELECT statement.
    B. The ORDER BY clause may appear in a SELECT statement that does not contain a WHERE clause.
    C. The ORDER BY clause specifies one or more terms by which the retrieved rows are sorted. These terms can only be column names.
    D. Positional sorting is accomplished by specifying the numeric position of a column as it appears in the SELECT list, in the ORDER BY clause.

8. The following query retrieves the LAST_NAME, SALARY, and COMMISSION_PCT values for employees whose LAST_NAME begins with the letter R. Based on the following query, choose the ORDER BY clause that first sorts the results by the COMMISSION_PCT column, listing highest commission earners first, and then sorts the results in ascending order by the SALARY column. Any records with NULL COMMISSION_PCT must appear last:

SELECT LAST_NAME, SALARY, COMMISSION_PCT
FROM EMPLOYEES
WHERE LAST_NAME LIKE 'R%'

A. ORDER BY COMMISSION_PCT DESC, 2;

B. ORDER BY 3 DESC, 2 ASC NULLS LAST;

C. ORDER BY 3 DESC NULLS LAST, 2 ASC;

D. ORDER BY COMMISSION_PCT DESC, SALARY ASC;

Ampersand Substitution

9. The DEFINE command explicitly declares a session-persistent substitution variable with a specific value. How is this variable referenced in an SQL statement? Consider an expression that calculates tax on an employee's SALARY based on the current tax rate. For the following session-persistent substitution variable, which statement correctly references the TAX_RATE variable?

DEFINE TAX_RATE=0.14

A. SELECT SALARY * :TAX_RATE TAX FROM EMPLOYEES;

B. SELECT SALARY * &TAX_RATE TAX FROM EMPLOYEES;

C. SELECT SALARY * :&&TAX TAX FROM EMPLOYEES;

D. SELECT SALARY * TAX_RATE TAX FROM EMPLOYEES;

10. When using ampersand substitution variables in the following query, how many times will you be prompted to input a value for the variable called JOB the first time this query is executed?

SELECT FIRST_NAME, '&JOB'
FROM EMPLOYEES
WHERE JOB_ID LIKE '%'||&JOB||'%'
AND '&&JOB' BETWEEN 'A' AND 'Z';

A. 0

B. 1

C. 2

D. 3

LAB QUESTION

Using SQL Developer or SQL*Plus, connect to the OE schema and complete the following tasks.

A customer requires a hard disk drive and a graphics card for her personal computer. She is willing to spend between $500 and $800 on the disk drive but is unsure about the cost of a graphics card. Her only requirement is that the resolution supported by the graphics card should be either 1024×768 or 1280×1024. As the sales representative, you have been tasked to write one query that searches the PRODUCT_INFORMATION table where the PRODUCT_NAME value begins with HD (hard disk) or GP (graphics processor) and their list prices. Remember the hard disk list prices must be between $500 and $800 and the graphics processors need to support either 1024×768 or 1280×1024. Sort the results in descending LIST_PRICE order.

SELF TEST ANSWERS

Limit the Rows Retrieved by a Query

1. ☑ **C.** The SELECT clause facilitates projection by specifying the list of columns to be projected from a table, whilst the WHERE clause facilitates selection by limiting the rows retrieved based on its conditions.

   ☒ **A**, **B**, and **D** are incorrect because the FROM clause specifies the source of the rows being projected and the ORDER BY clause is used for sorting the selected rows.

2. ☑ **B.** The IN operator efficiently tests whether the JOB_ID for a particular row is either SA_REP or MK_MAN, whilst the BETWEEN operator efficiently measures whether an employee's SALARY value falls within the required range.

   ☒ **A** and **C** exclude employees who earn a salary of $1000 or $4000, since these SALARY values are excluded by the inequality operators. **C** also selects JOB_ID values like SA_REP% and MK_MAN%, potentially selecting incorrect JOB_ID values. **D** is half right. The first half returns the rows with JOB_ID equal to SA_REP having SALARY values between $1000 and $4000. However, the second part (the OR clause), correctly tests for JOB_ID equal to MK_MAN but ignores the SALARY condition.

3. ☑ **C.** The character literals being compared to the JOB_ID column by the IN operator must be enclosed by single quotation marks.

   ☒ **A**, **B**, and **D** are syntactically correct. Notice that **B** does not require quotes around the numeric literals. Having them, however, does not cause an error.

4. ☑ **B.** The LIKE operator tests the DEPARTMENT_NAME column of each row for values that contain the characters "er". The percentage symbols before and after the character literal indicate that any characters enclosing the "er" literal are permissible.

   ☒ **A** and **C** are syntactically correct. **A** uses the IN operator, which is used to test set membership. **C** tests whether the alphabetic value of the DEPARTMENT_NAME column is between the letter "e" and the letter "r." Finally, **D** uses the word "contains," which cannot be used in this context.

5. ☑ **A** and **D.** The IS NULL operator correctly evaluates the COMMISSION_PCT column for NULL values. **D** uses the NOT operator to negate the already negative version of the IS NULL operator, IS NOT NULL. Two negatives return a positive, and therefore **A** and **D** are equivalent.

   ☒ **B** and **C** are incorrect since NULL values cannot be tested by the equality operator or the IN operator.

6. ☑ **A, C,** and **D.** Each of these conditions tests for SALARY values in the range of $2000 to $5000.
☒ **B** and **E** are incorrect. **B** excludes values like $2500 from its set, and **E** is illegal since it is missing the SALARY column name reference after the AND operator.

Sort the Rows Retrieved by a Query

7. ☑ **C.** The terms specified in an ORDER BY clause can include column names, positional sorting, numeric values, and expressions.
☒ **A, B,** and **D** are true.

8. ☑ **C.** Positional sorting is performed, and the third term in the SELECT list, COMMISSION_PCT, is sorted first in descending order, and any NULL COMMISSION_PCT values are listed last. The second term in the SELECT list, SALARY, is sorted next in ascending order.
☒ **A, B,** and **D** are incorrect. **A** does not specify what to do with NULL COMMISSION_PCT values, and the default behavior during a descending sort is to list NULLS FIRST. **B** applies the NULLS LAST modifier to the SALARY column instead of the COMMISSION_PCT column, and **D** ignores NULLS completely.

Ampersand Substitution

9. ☑ **B.** A session-persistent substitution variable may be referenced using an ampersand symbol from within any SQL statement executed in that session.
☒ **A, C,** and **D** are incorrect. **A** and **D** attempt to reference the substitution variable using a colon prefix to its name and the variable name on its own. These are invalid references to substitution variables in SQL. **C** references a variable called TAX and not the variable TAX_RATE.

10. ☑ **D.** The first time this statement is executed, two single ampersand substitution variables are encountered before the third double ampersand substitution variable. If the first reference on line one of the query contained a double ampersand substitution, you would only be prompted to input a value once.
☒ **A, B,** and **C** are incorrect since you are prompted thrice to input a value for the JOB substitution variable. In subsequent executions of this statement in the same session you will not be prompted to input a value for this variable.

LAB ANSWER

Using SQL Developer or SQL*Plus, connect to the OE schema and complete the following tasks.

You are required to query the PRODUCT_INFORMATION table in the OE schema for the PRODUCT_NAME and LIST_PRICE columns. The rows selected must conform to either of two conditions. The first condition is that the PRODUCT_NAME must begin with the characters 'HD' and their LIST_PRICE must fall in the range between $500 and $800. Alternately, the row can conform to the second condition that the PRODUCT_NAME must begin with the characters 'GP' and contain the characters '1024'. Finally, the results must be sorted in descending LIST_PRICE order.

1. Start SQL Developer and connect to the OE schema.

2. The SELECT clause is
   SELECT PRODUCT_NAME, LIST_PRICE

3. The FROM clause is
   FROM PRODUCT_INFORMATION

4. The first condition is
   PRODUCT_NAME LIKE 'HD%' AND LIST_PRICE BETWEEN 500 AND 800

5. The second condition is
   PRODUCT_NAME LIKE 'GP%1024%'

6. Since either the first or second condition must be fulfilled by a row in order to be retrieved, these two conditions must be separated with the Boolean OR operator.

7. The WHERE clause is
   WHERE (PRODUCT_NAME LIKE 'HD%' AND LIST_PRICE BETWEEN 500 AND 800) OR (PRODUCT_NAME LIKE 'GP%1024%')

8. The ORDER BY clause is
   ORDER BY LIST_PRICE DESC

9. Executing this statement returns the set of results matching this pattern as shown in the illustration:

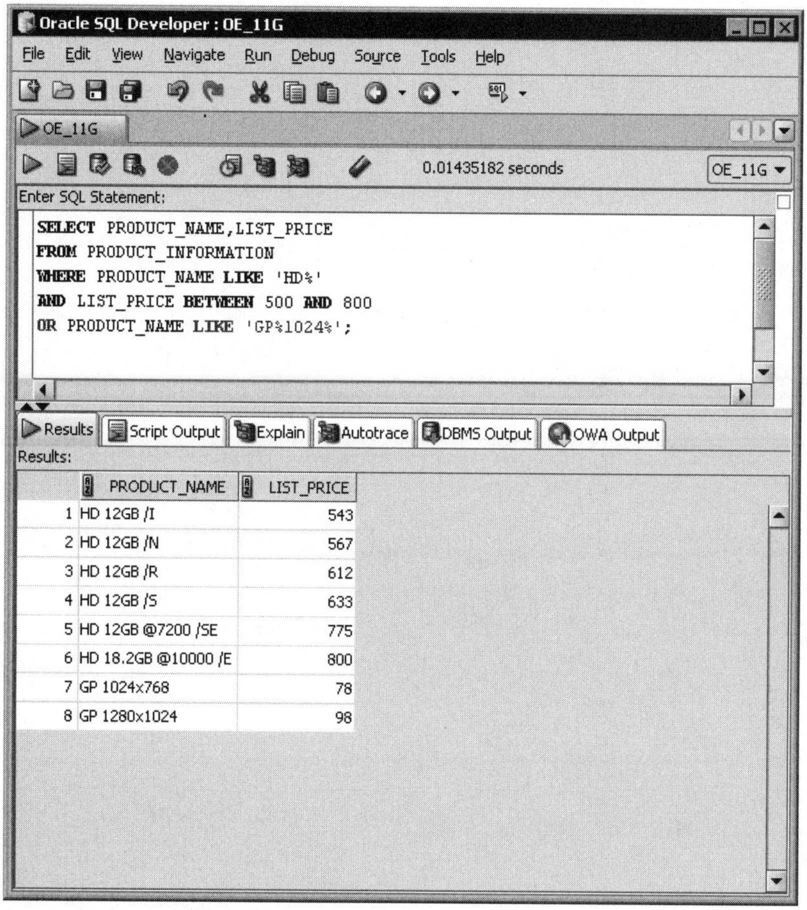
Oracle SQL Developer : OE_11G
File Edit View Navigate Run Debug Source Tools Help
OE_11G
0.01435182 seconds
OE_11G
Enter SQL Statement:
SELECT PRODUCT_NAME,LIST_PRICE
FROM PRODUCT_INFORMATION
WHERE PRODUCT_NAME LIKE 'HD%'
AND LIST_PRICE BETWEEN 500 AND 800
OR PRODUCT_NAME LIKE 'GP%1024%';
Results Script Output Explain Autotrace DBMS Output OWA Output
Results:
PRODUCT_NAME LIST_PRICE
1 HD 12GB /I 543
2 HD 12GB /N 567
3 HD 12GB /R 612
4 HD 12GB /S 633
5 HD 12GB @7200 /SE 775
6 HD 18.2GB @10000 /E 800
7 GP 1024x768 78
8 GP 1280x1024 98

4
Single-Row Functions

*F*unctions are a wonderful extension to SQL and provide a first glimpse of the procedural capabilities Oracle supports. Procedural languages allow a rich degree of programming that yields an almost unlimited range of data manipulation possibilities. Oracle server implements a proprietary procedural language called PL/SQL, or procedural SQL. A range of named programmatic objects may be constructed using PL/SQL. These include procedures, functions, and packages. Although writing PL/SQL is relatively straightforward, a thorough understanding of SQL is a prerequisite and the focus of this guide. The functions discussed in this chapter are confined to PL/SQL programs packaged and supplied by Oracle as built-in features.

CERTIFICATION OBJECTIVE 4.01

Describe Various Types of Functions Available in SQL

SQL functions are broadly divided into those that calculate and return a value for every row in a data set and those that return a single aggregated value for all rows. The following two areas are explored:

- Defining a function
- Types of functions

Defining a Function

A *function* is a program written to optionally accept input parameters, perform an operation, or return a single value. A function returns only one value per execution.

Three important components form the basis of defining a function. The first is the input parameter list. It specifies zero or more arguments that may be passed to a function as input for processing. These arguments or parameters may be of differing data types, and some are mandatory while others may be optional. The second component is the data type of its resultant value. Upon execution, only one value is returned by the function. The third encapsulates the details of the processing performed by the function and contains the program code that optionally manipulates the input parameters, performs calculations and operations, and generates a return value.

A function is often described as a *black box* that takes an input, performs a calculation, and returns a value as illustrated by the following equation. Instead of focusing on their implementation details, you are encouraged to concentrate on the features that built-in functions provide.

F(x, y, z, …) = result;

Functions may be *nested* within other functions, such as F1(x, y, F2(a, b), z), where F2, which takes two input parameters, a and b, and forms the third of four parameters submitted to F1. Functions can operate on any available data types, the most popular being character, date, and numeric data. These operands may be columns or expressions.

As an example, consider a function that calculates a person's age. The AGE function takes one date input parameter, which is the person's birthday. The result returned by the AGE function is a number representing a person's age. The *black box* calculation involves obtaining the difference in years between the current date and the birthday input parameter.

Operating on Character Data

Character data or strings are versatile since they facilitate the storage of almost any type of data. Functions that operate on character data are broadly classified as *case conversion* and *character manipulation* functions. The following string built-in functions are examined in detail later in this chapter, but a brief description is provided here.

LOWER, UPPER, and INITCAP are the case conversion functions that convert a given character column, literal, or expression into lowercase, uppercase, or initial case, respectively:

```
lower('SQL') = sql
upper('sql') = SQL
initcap('sql') = Sql
```

The character manipulation functions are exceptionally powerful and include the LENGTH, CONCAT, SUBSTR, INSTR, LPAD, RPAD, TRIM, and REPLACE functions.

The LENGTH(*string*) function uses a character string as an input parameter and returns a numeric value representing the number of characters present in that string:

```
length('A short string') = 14
```

The CONCAT(*string 1, string 2*) function takes two strings and concatenates or joins them in the same way that the concatenation operator || does:

```
concat('SQL is',' easy to learn.') = SQL is easy to learn.
```

The SUBSTR(*string, start position, number of characters*) function accepts three parameters and returns a string consisting of the number of characters extracted from the source string, beginning at the specified start position:

```
substr('http://www.domain.com',12,6) = domain
```

The INSTR(source string, search item, [start position],[*nth* occurrence of search item]) function returns a number that represents the position in the source string, beginning from the given start position, where the *nth* occurrence of the search item begins:

```
instr('http://www.domain.com','.',1,2) = 18
```

The LPAD(*string, length after padding, padding string*) and RPAD(*string, length after padding, padding string*) functions add a padding string of characters to the left or right of a string until it reaches the specified length after padding.

The TRIM function literally trims off leading or trailing (or both) character strings from a given source string:

```
rpad('#PASSWORD#',11,'#') = #PASSWORD##
lpad('#PASSWORD#',11,'#') = ##PASSWORD#
trim('#' from '#PASSWORD#') = PASSWORD
```

The REPLACE(*string, search item, replacement item*) function locates the search item in a given string and replaces it with the replacement item, returning a string with replaced values:

```
replace('#PASSWORD#','WORD','PORT') = #PASSPORT#
```

Operating on Numeric Data

Many numeric built-in functions are available. Some calculate square roots, perform exponentiation, and convert numbers into hexadecimal format. There are too many to mention, and many popular mathematical, scientific, and financial calculations have been exposed as built-in functions by Oracle.

Three common numeric functions, examined later in this chapter, are ROUND, TRUNC, and MOD. ROUND(*number, decimal precision*) facilitates rounding off a number to the lowest or highest value given a decimal precision format:

```
round(42.39,1) = 42.4
```

The TRUNC(*number, decimal precision*) function drops off or truncates the number given a decimal precision value:

```
trunc(42.39,1) = 42.3
```

The MOD(*dividend, divisor*) returns the remainder of a division operation:

```
mod(42,10) = 2
```

Operating on Date Information

Working with date values may be challenging. Performing date arithmetic that accommodates leap years and variable month lengths can be frustrating and error prone. Oracle addresses this challenge by providing native support for date arithmetic and several built-in date functions such as MONTHS_BETWEEN, ADD_MONTHS, LAST_DAY, NEXT_DAY, SYSDATE, ROUND, and TRUNC.

The MONTHS_BETWEEN(*date 1, date 2*) function returns the number of months between two dates, while the ADD_MONTHS(*date 1, number of months*) returns the date resulting from adding a specified number of months to a date:

```
months_between('01-FEB-2008','01-JAN-2008') = 1
add_months('01-JAN-2008',1) = 01-FEB-2008
```

The LAST_DAY(*date 1*) function returns the last day of the month that the specified date falls into, while the NEXT_DAY(*date 1, day of the week*) returns the date on which the next specified day of the week falls after the given date:

```
last_day('01-FEB-2008') = 29-FEB-2008
next_day('01-FEB-2008','Friday') = 08-FEB-2008
```

The SYSDATE function takes no parameters and returns a date value that represents the current server date and time. ROUND(*date, date precision format*) and TRUNC(*date, date precision format*) round and truncate a given date value to the nearest date precision format like day, month, or year:

```
sysdate = 17-DEC-2007
round(sysdate,'month') = 01-JAN-2008
trunc(sysdate,'month') = 01-DEC-2007
```

on the **Job**

Single-row functions are used in almost every query issued by analysts, developers, and administrators. When searching for character data, the TRIM function is frequently used to eliminate extra spaces that occur in character fields. The case conversion functions are used to standardize the column data. This facilitates more accurate and efficient searching since the case in which character data is captured is often inconsistent.

Types of Functions

Two broad types of functions operating on single and multiple rows, respectively, are discussed next. This distinction is vital to understanding the larger context in which functions are used. Oracle continuously strives to ensure that its commercial interpretation of SQL conforms to international standards. This facilitates ease of systems and skills migration across vendors and suppliers of RDBMS software. Oracle's implementation of SQL is compliant with the ANSI:1999 (American National Standards Institute) standard for SQL. More recently, it claimed partial compliance to the SQL:2003 standard endorsed by both ISO (International Organization for Standardization) and ANSI. SQL functions have been standardized, and Oracle has documented those that are fully or partially compliant to the SQL:2003 standard.

Single-Row Functions

There are several categories of *single-row* functions including character, numeric, date, conversion, and general. The focus of this chapter is on the character, numeric, and date single-row functions. These are functions that operate on one row of a dataset at a time. If a query selects 10 rows, the function is executed 10 times, once per row with the values from that row as input to the function.

As Figure 4-1 shows, two columns of the REGIONS table have been selected along with an expression using the LENGTH function with the REGION_NAME column.

The length of the REGION_NAME column is calculated for each row, proving that the function has executed four separate times, returning one result per row.

Single-row functions manipulate the data items in a row to extract and format them for display purposes. The input values to a single-row function can be user-specified constants or literals, column data, variables, or expressions optionally supplied by other nested single-row functions. The nesting of single-row functions is a commonly used technique. Functions can return a value with a different data type from its input parameters. As Figure 4-1 demonstrates, the LENGTH function accepts one character input parameter and returns a numeric output.

Conversion functions like TO_CHAR, TO_NUMBER, and TO_DATE are discussed in Chapter 5. They change the data type of column data or expressions allowing other functions to operate on them. The *general* functions are also discussed in Chapter 5. They simplify working with NULL values and facilitate conditional logic within a SELECT statement. These include the NVL, NVL2, NULLIF, COALESCE, CASE, and DECODE functions.

Apart from their inclusion in the SELECT list of a SQL query, single-row functions may be used in the WHERE and ORDER BY clauses. Assume there is a requirement to list rows from the REGIONS table where the length of the REGION_NAME column data is at least five characters long. There is a further

FIGURE 4-1

FIGURE 4-1   A single-row function

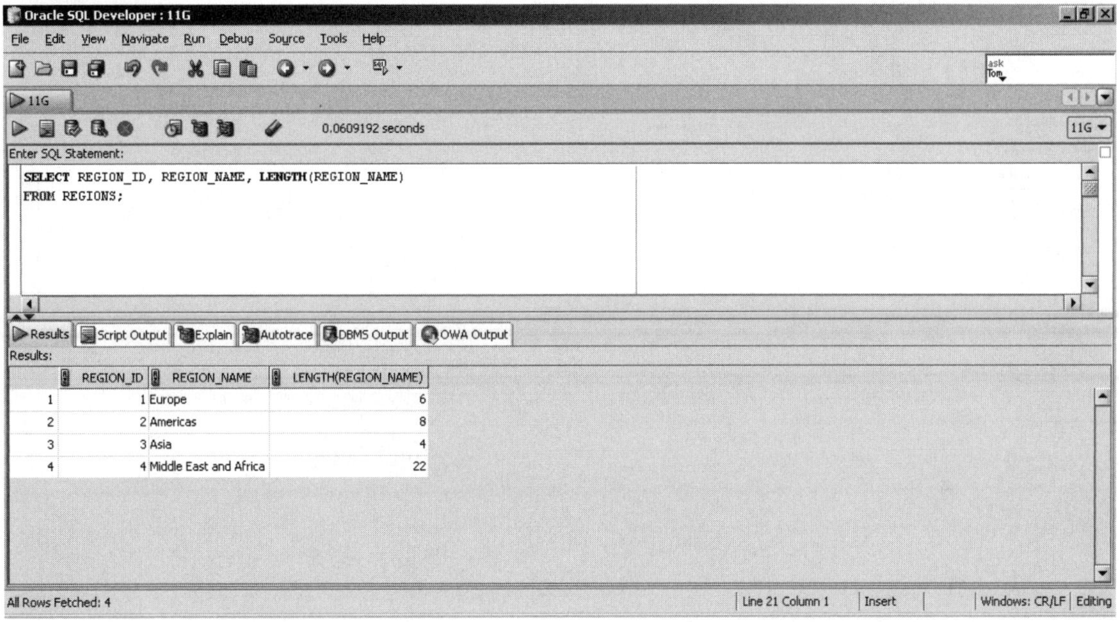

need for this list to be sorted in alphabetic order based on the value of the last character in the REGION_NAME column. The WHERE clause is shown here:

```
where length(region_name) > 4
```

To obtain the last character in a string, the SUBSTR function is used with the REGION_NAME column as the source string. The length of the REGION_NAME is used as the start position, producing the following ORDER BY clause:

```
order by substr(region_name, length(region_name),1)
```

As Figure 4-2 shows, only three of the four regions are returned, and the list is sorted in alphabetic order based on the last character in the REGION_NAME column for each row.

Multiple-Row Functions

As the name suggests, this category of functions operates on more than one row at a time. Typical uses of *multiple-row* functions include calculating the sum or average of the numeric column values or counting the total number of records in sets. These are sometimes known as *aggregation* or *group* functions and are explored in Chapter 7.

FIGURE 4-2   Functions in SELECT, WHERE, and ORDER BY clauses

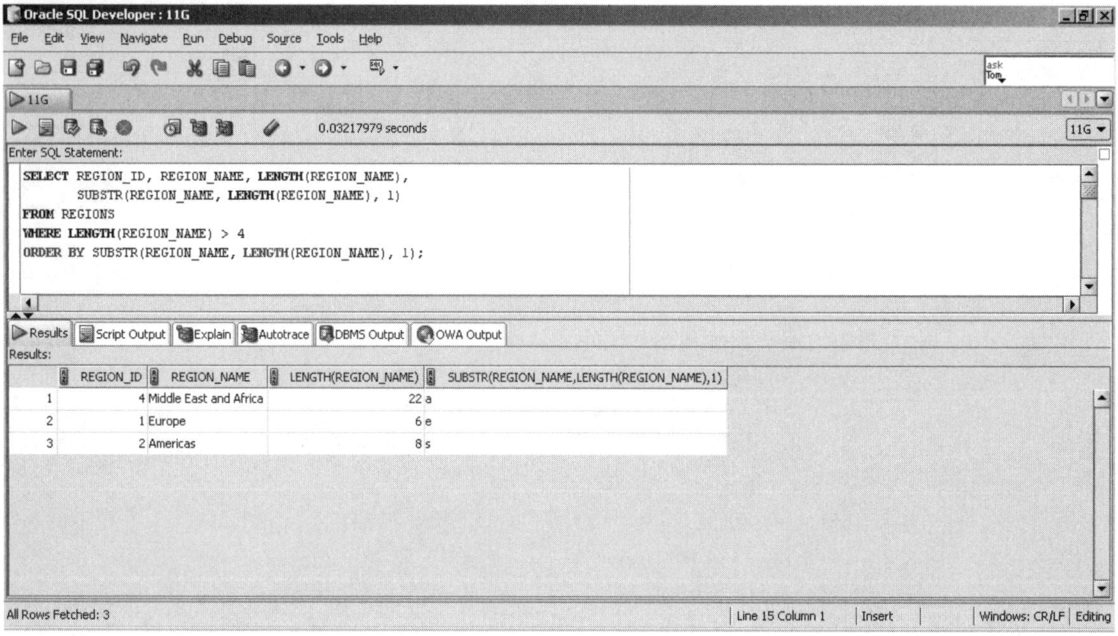

```
Oracle SQL Developer : 11G                                                    _ 8 X
File  Edit  View  Navigate  Run  Debug  Source  Tools  Help

11G

0.03217979 seconds                                                      11G

Enter SQL Statement:
SELECT REGION_ID, REGION_NAME, LENGTH(REGION_NAME),
    SUBSTR(REGION_NAME, LENGTH(REGION_NAME), 1)
FROM REGIONS
WHERE LENGTH(REGION_NAME) > 4
ORDER BY SUBSTR(REGION_NAME, LENGTH(REGION_NAME), 1);
```

Results | Script Output | Explain | Autotrace | DBMS Output | OWA Output

Results:

	REGION_ID	REGION_NAME	LENGTH(REGION_NAME)	SUBSTR(REGION_NAME,LENGTH(REGION_NAME),1)
1	4	Middle East and Africa	22	a
2	1	Europe	6	e
3	2	Americas	8	s

All Rows Fetched: 3   Line 15 Column 1   Insert   Windows: CR/LF Editing

e x a m

ⓦatch   *Single-row functions are
executed for each row in the selected
data set. This concept is implicitly tested
via practical examples in the exam.
Functions always return only one value of a
predetermined data type. They may accept
zero or more parameters of differing data
types. The single-row character functions*
*like LENGTH, SUBSTR, and INSTR are
frequently used together, and a thorough
understanding of these is required.
Remember that input parameters that can
be implicitly converted to the data types
required by functions are acceptable to
Oracle.*

Use Character, Number, and Date Functions in SELECT Statements

This section conducts a detailed investigation of the single-row functions introduced earlier. A structured approach will be taken that includes function descriptions, syntax rules, parameter descriptions, and usage examples. The character case conversion functions are examined, followed by the character manipulation functions. Next, the numeric functions are examined, and the section concludes with a discussion of the date functions.

Using Character Case Conversion Functions

Character data may be saved in tables from numerous sources, including application interfaces and batch programs. It is not safe to assume that character data has been committed in a consistent manner. The character *case conversion* functions serve two important purposes. They may be used first, to modify the appearance of a character data item for display purposes and second, to render them consistent for comparison operations. It is simpler to search for a string using a consistent case format instead of testing every permutation of uppercase and lowercase characters that could match the string. It is important to remember that these functions do not alter the data stored in tables. They still form part of the read-only SQL query.

The character functions discussed next expect string parameters. These may be any string literal, character column value, or expression resulting in a character value. If it is a numeric or a date value, it is implicitly converted into a string.

The LOWER Function

The LOWER function converts a string of characters into their lowercase equivalents. It does not add extra characters or shorten the length of the initial string. Uppercase characters are converted into their lowercase equivalents. Numeric, punctuation, or special characters are ignored.

The LOWER function can take only one parameter. Its syntax is LOWER(s). The following queries illustrate the usage of this function:

```
Query 1: select lower(100) from dual
Query 2: select lower(100+100) from dual
Query 3: select lower('The SUM '||'100+100'||' =  200') from dual
```

Queries 1 and 2 return the strings 100 and 200, respectively. The parameter to the LOWER function in query 3 is a character expression and the string returned by the function is "The sum 100 + 100 = 200."

```
Query 4: select lower(SYSDATE) from dual
Query 5: select lower(SYSDATE+2) from dual
```

Assume that the current system date is: 17-DEC-2007. Queries 4 and 5 return the strings 17-dec-2007 and 19-dec-2007, respectively. The date expressions are evaluated and implicitly converted into character data before the LOWER function is executed.

As Figure 4-3 shows, the LOWER function is used in the WHERE clause to locate the records with the lowercase letters "u" and "r" adjacent to each other in the LAST_NAME field.

Consider writing an alternative query to return the same results without using the LOWER function. It could be done as follows:

```
select first_name, last_name
from employees
where last_name like '%ur%'
```

FIGURE 4-3   The LOWER function

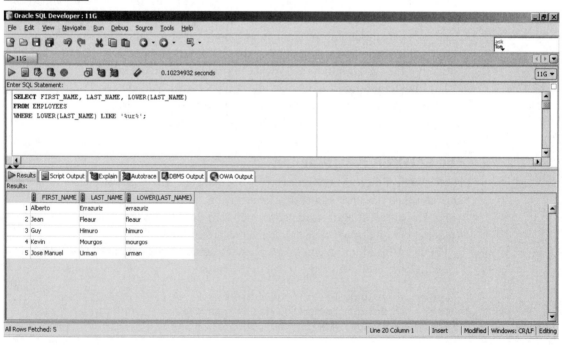

```
or last_name like '%UR%'
or last_name like '%uR%'
or last_name like '%Ur%'
```

This query works but is cumbersome, and the number of OR clauses required increases exponentially as the length of the search string increases.

The UPPER Function

The UPPER function is the logical opposite of the LOWER function and converts a string of characters into their uppercase equivalents. It does not add extra characters or shorten the length of the initial string. All lowercase characters are converted into their uppercase equivalents. Numeric, punctuation, or special characters are ignored.

The UPPER function takes only one parameter. Its syntax is UPPER(*s*). The following queries illustrate the usage of this function:

```
Query 1: select upper(1+2.14) from dual
Query 2: select upper(SYSDATE) from dual
```

Query 1 returns the string 3.14. The parameter to the UPPER function in query 2 is SYSDATE, which returns the current system date. Since this value is returned in uppercase by default, no case conversion is performed.

The UPPER function is used in Figure 4-4 to extract the rows from the COUNTRIES table where the COUNTRY_NAME values contain the letters "U," "S," and "A" in that order. The letters "U," "S," and "A" do not have to be adjacent to each other.

Writing an alternative query to return the same results without using the UPPER or LOWER functions could be done using a query with eight conditions:

```
SELECT * FROM COUNTRIES
WHERE country_name like '%u%s%a%' or country_name like '%u%s%A%'
or country_name like '%u%S%a%'    or country_name like '%u%S%A%'
or country_name like '%U%s%a%'    or country_name like '%U%s%A%'
or country_name like '%U%S%a%'    or country_name like '%U%S%A%'
```

This query works but is cumbersome. The number of OR clauses required increases exponentially as the length of the search string increases.

The INITCAP Function

The INITCAP function converts a string of characters into capitalized case. It is often used for data presentation purposes. The first letters of each word in the string are converted to their uppercase equivalents, while the remaining letters of each word are converted to their lowercase equivalents. A word is usually a string of adjacent characters separated by a space or underscore, but other characters such as

FIGURE 4-4 The UPPER function

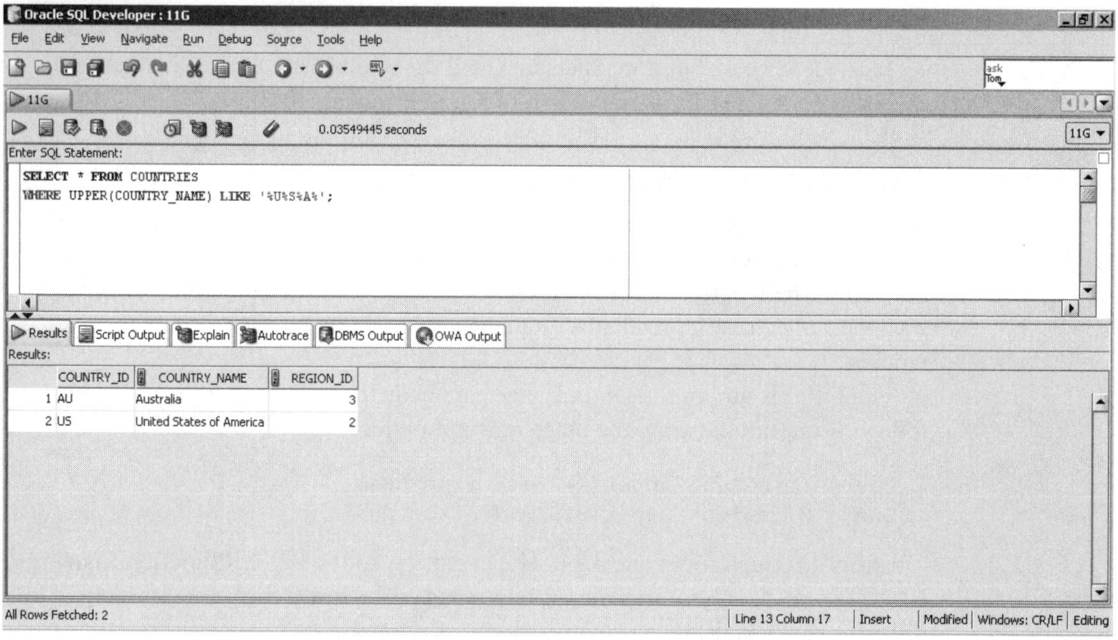

the percentage symbol, exclamation mark, or dollar sign are valid word separators. Punctuation or special characters are regarded as valid word separators.

The INITCAP function can take only one parameter. Its syntax is INITCAP(s). The following queries illustrate the usage of this function:

```
Query 1: select initcap(21/7) from dual
Query 2: select initcap(SYSDATE) from dual
Query 3: select initcap('init cap or init_cap or init%cap') from dual
```

Query 1 returns the quotient 3 as a string. Query 2 returns the character string value of the current system date, with the month portion changed from uppercase to initial case. Assuming that the current system date is 17-DEC-2007, query 2 therefore returns 17-Dec-2007. Query 3 returns Init Cap Or Init_Cap Or Init%Cap.

The queries in Figure 4-5 select the LAST_NAME and JOB_ID values from the EMPLOYEES table for those employees with LAST_NAME values starting with the letter "H." The first query applies the INITCAP function to the entire SELECT clause. The second query shows how the INITCAP function is applied separately to each character component. Both queries yield identical results.

FIGURE 4-5   The INITCAP function

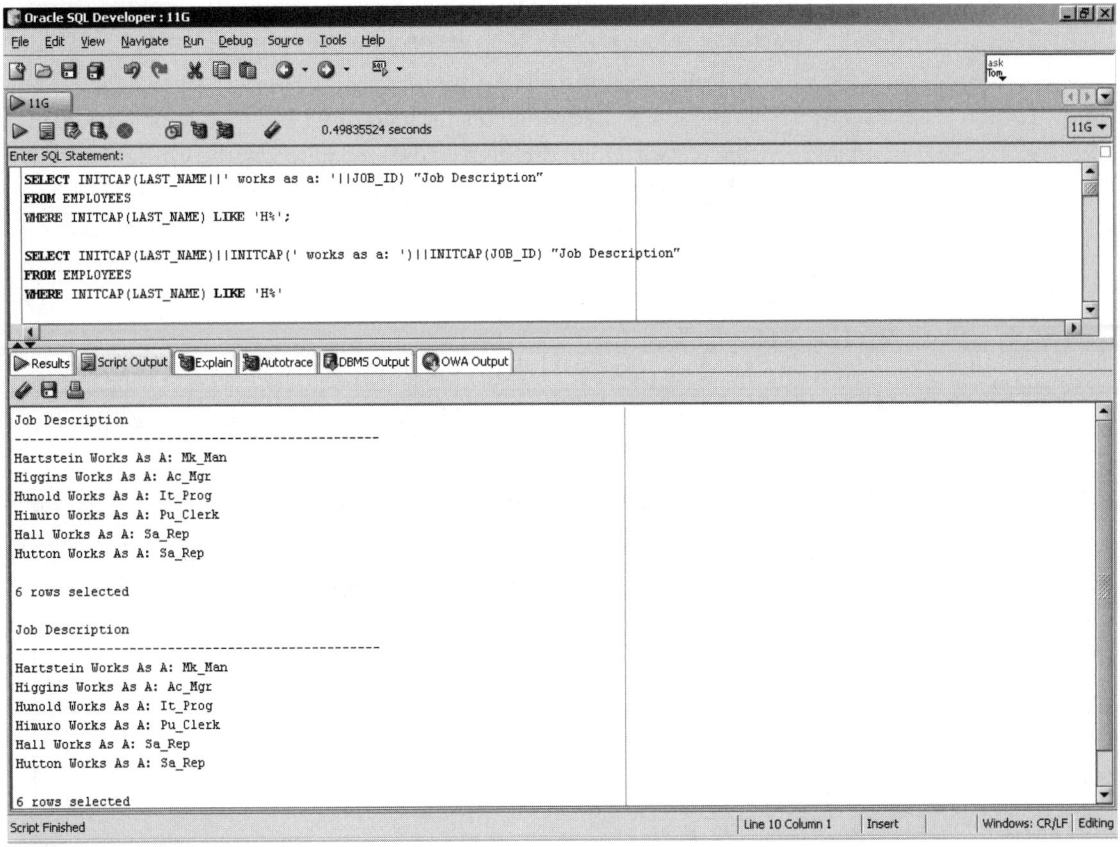

EXERCISE 4-1

Using the Case Conversion Functions

Retrieve a list of all FIRST_NAME and LAST_NAME values from the EMPLOYEES table where FIRST_NAME contains the character string "li."

1. Start SQL Developer and connect to the HR schema.

2. The SELECT clause is
   SELECT FIRST_NAME, LAST_NAME

3. The FROM clause is
   FROM EMPLOYEES

4. The WHERE clause must compare the FIRST_NAME column values with a pattern of characters containing all possible case combinations of the string "li." Therefore, if the FIRST_NAME contains the character strings "LI," "Li," "lI," or "li," that row must be retrieved.

5. The LIKE operator is used for character matching, and four combinations can be extracted with four WHERE clauses separated by the OR keyword. However, the case conversion functions can simplify the condition. If the LOWER function is used on the FIRST_NAME column, the comparison can be done with one WHERE clause condition. The UPPER or INITCAP functions could also be used.

6. The WHERE clause is
   WHERE LOWER(FIRST_NAME) LIKE '%li%'

7. Executing this statement returns employees' names containing the characters "li" as shown in this illustration:

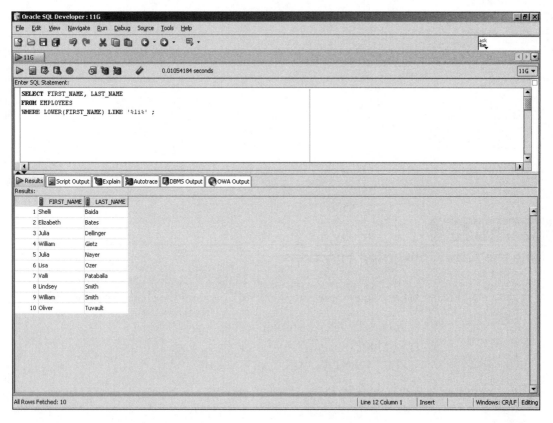

Using Character Manipulations Functions

Some of the most powerful features to emerge from Oracle are the *character manipulation* functions. Their usefulness in data manipulation is almost without peer, and many seasoned technical professionals whip together a quick script to massage data items with SQL *character manipulation* functions. Nesting these functions is common. The concatenation operator (||) is generally used instead of the CONCAT function. The LENGTH, INSTR, SUBSTR, and REPLACE functions often find themselves in each other's company as do RPAD, LPAD, and TRIM.

The CONCAT Function

The CONCAT function joins two character literals, columns, or expressions to yield one larger character expression. Numeric and date literals are implicitly cast as characters when they occur as parameters to the CONCAT function. Numeric or date expressions are evaluated before being converted to strings ready to be concatenated.

The CONCAT function takes two parameters. Its syntax is CONCAT(*s1, s2*), where *s1* and *s2* represent string literals, character column values, or expressions resulting in character values. The following queries illustrate the usage of this function:

```
Query 1: select concat(1+2.14,' approximates pi') from dual
Query 2: select concat('Today is:',SYSDATE) from dual
```

Query 1 returns the string "3.14 approximates pi." The numeric expression is evaluated to return the number 3.14. This number is automatically changed into the character string "3.14," which is concatenated to the character literal in the second parameter. The second parameter to the CONCAT function in query 2 is SYSDATE, which returns the current system date. This value is implicitly converted to a string to which the literal in the first parameter is concatenated. If the system date is 17-DEC-2007, query 2 returns the string "Today is 17-DEC-2007."

Consider using the CONCAT function to join three terms to return one character string. Since CONCAT takes only two parameters, it is only possible to join two terms with one instance of this function. The solution is to nest the CONCAT function within another CONCAT function, as shown here:

```
select concat('Outer1 ', concat('Inner1',' Inner2')) from dual;
```

The first CONCAT function has two parameters: the first is the literal "Outer1," while the second is a nested CONCAT function. The second CONCAT function takes two parameters: the first is the literal "Inner1," while the second is the literal "Inner2." This query results in the following string: Outer1 Inner1 Inner2. Nested functions are described in detail in Chapter 5.

The CONCAT function was used in Figure 4-6 to extract the rows from the EMPLOYEES table where the DEPARTMENT_ID=100. The objective was to produce a single string literal output from the CONCAT function of the format FIRST_NAME LAST_NAME earns SALARY.

This simple task was transformed into a complex four-level-deep nested set of function calls. As the second example in Figure 4-6 demonstrates, the concatenation operator performs the equivalent task in a simpler manner.

The LENGTH Function

The LENGTH function returns the number of characters that constitute a character string. This includes character literals, columns, or expressions. Numeric and date literals are automatically cast as characters when they occur as parameters to

---

FIGURE 4-6   The CONCAT function

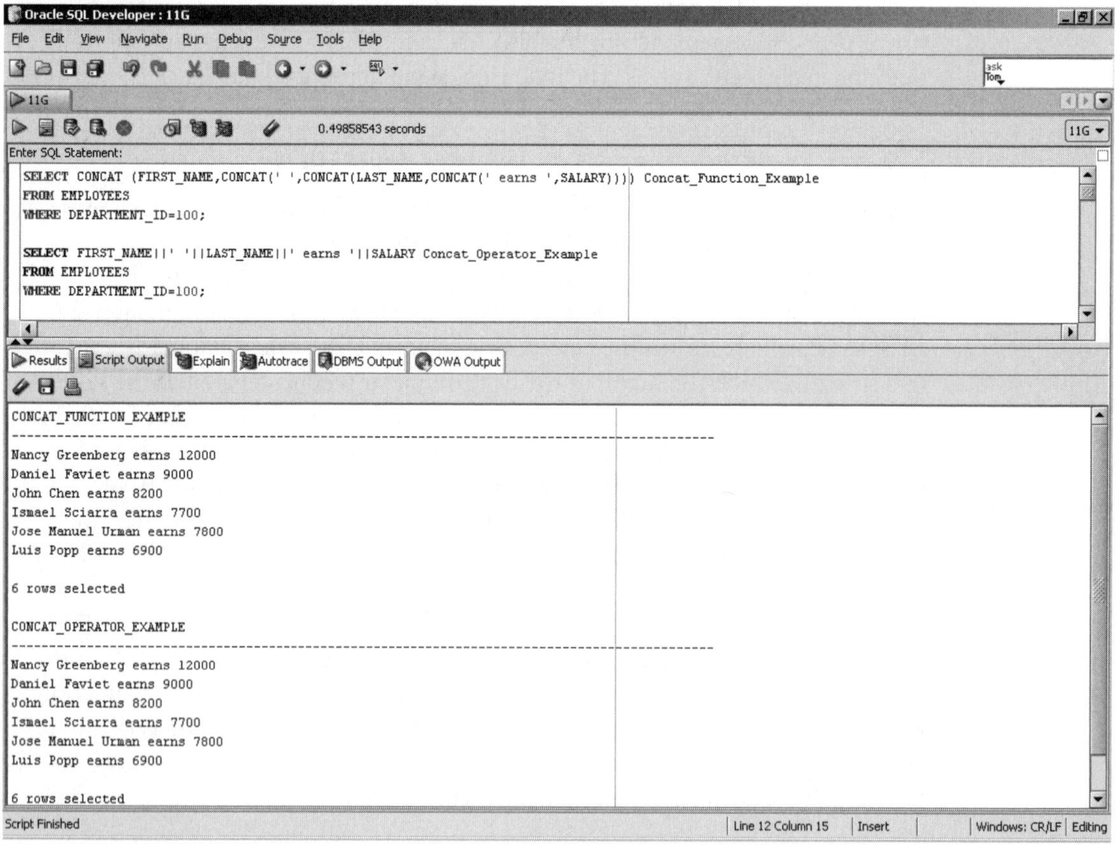

the LENGTH function. Numeric or date expressions are evaluated before being converted to strings ready to be measured. Blank spaces, tabs, and special characters are all counted by the LENGTH function.

The LENGTH function takes only one parameter. Its syntax is LENGTH(*s*), where *s* represents any string literal, character column value, or expression resulting in a character value. The following queries illustrate the usage of this function:

```
Query 1: select length(1+2.14||' approximates pi') from dual
Query 2: select length(SYSDATE) from dual
```

Query 1 returns the number 20. The numeric expression is evaluated to return the number 3.14. This number is cast as the character string "3.14," which is then concatenated to the character literal "approximates pi." The resultant character string contains 20 characters. Query 2 first evaluates the SYSDATE function, which returns the current system date. This value is automatically converted to a character string whose length is then determined. Assuming that the system date returned is 17-DEC-07, query 2 returns value 9.

The LENGTH function is used in Figure 4-7 to extract the COUNTRY_NAME value with length greater than ten characters from the COUNTRIES table.

FIGURE 4-7 The LENGTH function

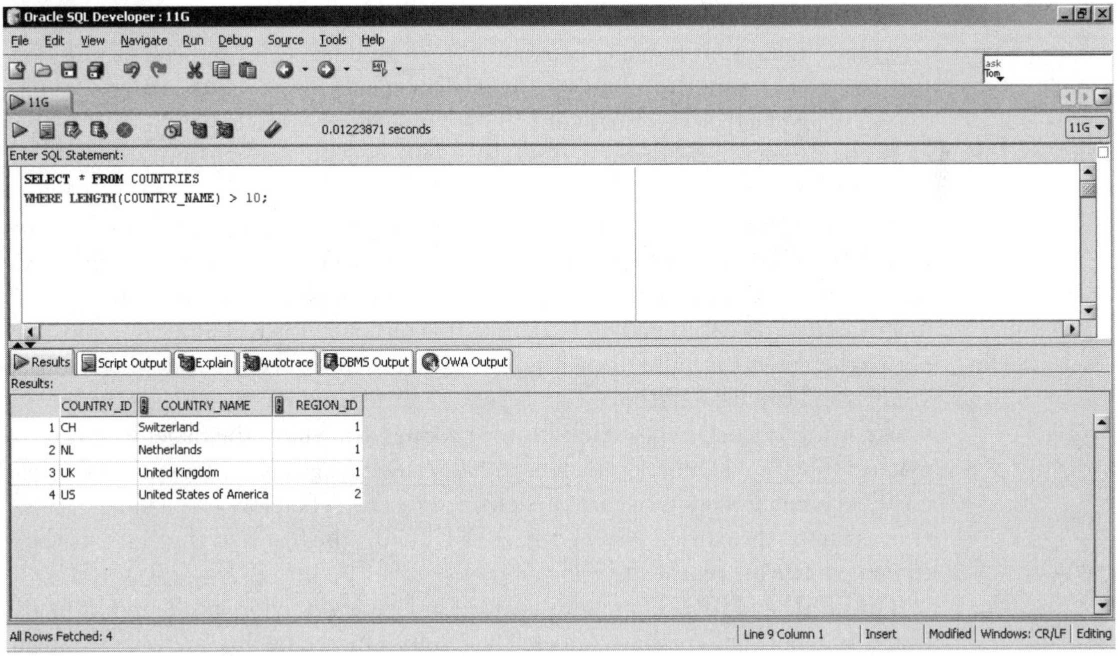

The LPAD and RPAD Functions

The LPAD and RPAD functions, also known as left pad and right pad functions, return a string padded with a specified number of characters to the left or right of the source string respectively. The character strings used for padding include character literals, column values, or expressions. Numeric and date literals are implicitly cast as characters when they occur as parameters to the LPAD or RPAD functions. Numeric or date expressions are evaluated before being converted to strings destined for padding. Blank spaces, tabs, and special characters may be used as padding characters.

The LPAD and RPAD functions take three parameters. Their syntaxes are LPAD(s, n, p) and RPAD(s, n, p), where s represents the source string, n represents the final length of the string returned, and p specifies the character string to be used as padding. If LPAD is used, the padding characters p are added to the left of the source string s until it reaches length n. If RPAD is used, the padding characters p are added to the right of the source string s until it reaches length n. Note that if the parameter n is smaller than or equal to the length of the source string s, then no padding occurs and only the first n characters of s are returned.

The following queries illustrate the usage of this function:

```
Query 1: select lpad(1000+200.55,14,'*') from dual
Query 2: select rpad(1000+200.55,14,'*') from dual
Query 3: select lpad(SYSDATE,14,'$#') from dual
Query 4: select rpad(SYSDATE,4,'$#') from dual
```

Query 1 returns a 14-character string: *******1200.55. The numeric expression is evaluated to return the number 1200.55. This number is cast as the string "1200.55" of length seven (including the decimal point). To achieve the final length of 14 characters, 7 asterisks are left padded to the string. Query 2 returns the string "1200.55*******."

The LPAD function in query 3 has a target string length of 14 characters. Assume that SYSDATE returns a 9-character date value: 17-DEC-07. This date is converted into a string, and the padding string is systematically applied to reach the target length. It returns: $#$#$17-DEC-07. Note that although the padding string consists of two characters ($#), the string was not applied evenly since there are three dollar symbols and two hash symbols. This is because LPAD and RPAD will pad the source string as much as possible with the padding string until the target length is reached. The RPAD function in query 4 has a target length of 4 characters, but the SYSDATE function alone returns a 9-character value. Therefore no padding occurs and, assuming the current system date is 17-DEC-07, the first four characters of the converted date are returned: 17-D.

The LPAD and RPAD functions are used in Figure 4-8 to format the results in a neater and more presentable manner. The results returned by this query are identical

FIGURE 4-8	The LPAD and RPAD functions

to those in Figure 4-6 but have been rendered more user friendly using the LPAD and RPAD functions.

The TRIM Function

The TRIM function removes characters from the beginning or end of character literals, columns or expressions to yield one potentially shorter character item. Numeric and date literals are automatically cast as characters when they occur as parameters to the TRIM function. Numeric or date expressions are evaluated first before being converted to strings ready to be trimmed.

The TRIM function takes a parameter made up of an optional and a mandatory component. Its syntax is TRIM([*trailing* | *leading* | *both*] *trimstring* from *s*). The string to be trimmed (*s*) is mandatory. The following points list the rules governing the use of this function:

- TRIM(*s*) removes spaces from both sides of the input string.
- TRIM(*trailing trimstring* from *s*) removes all occurrences of *trimstring* from the end of the string *s* if it is present.

- TRIM(*leading trimstring* from *s*) removes all occurrences of *trimstring* from the beginning of the string *s* if it is present.
- TRIM(*both trimstring* from *s*) removes all occurrences of *trimstring* from the beginning and end of the string *s* if it is present.

The following queries illustrate the usage of this function:

```
Query 1: select trim(trailing 'e' from 1+2.14||' is pie') from dual
Query 2: select trim(both '*' from '******Hidden*******') from dual
Query 3: select trim(1 from sysdate) from dual
```

Query 1 evaluates the numeric expression to return the number 3.14. This number is then cast as the character string "3.14," which is then concatenated to the character literal to construct the string "3.14 is pie." The TRIM function then removes any occurrences of the character "e" from the end of the string to return "3.14 approximates pi." Query 2 peels away all occurrences of the asterisk trim character from the beginning and end of the character literal and returns the string "Hidden." Note that although one trim character is specified, multiple occurrences will be trimmed if they are consecutively present. Query 3 has two interesting aspects. The trim character is not enclosed in quotes and is implicitly converted to a character. The SYSDATE function returns the current system date, which is assumed to be 17-DEC-07. Since no keyword is specified for trailing, leading, or both trim directions, the default of both applies. Therefore all occurrences of character 1 at the beginning or ending of the date string are trimmed resulting in 7-DEC-07 being returned.

The TRIM function used in Figure 4-9 does not appear to do anything but closer examination reveals a common practical use for it. As discussed earlier, data is frequently entered into application database tables through a variety of sources. It may happen that spaces are accidentally entered and saved in character fields unintentionally. The contrived trim string in the WHERE clause simulates the LAST_NAME field padded with spaces. This could hinder searching for employees with LAST_NAME values of Smith. Trimming the space padded LAST_NAME field enables accurate searching and eliminates the risk of unintended spaces that may be present in character data. Remember that when no parameters other than the string *s* are specified to the TRIM function then its default behavior is to trim(both ' ' from *s*).

FIGURE 4-9   The TRIM function

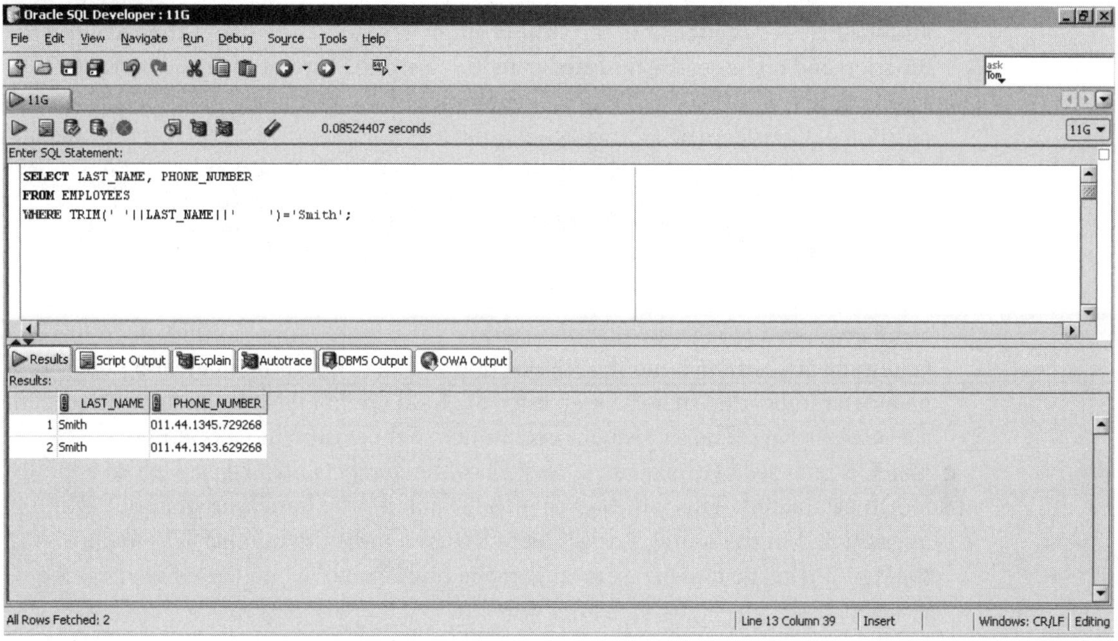

The INSTR Function (In-string)

The INSTR function locates the position of a search string within a given string. It returns the numeric position at which the *nth* occurrence of the search string begins, relative to a specified start position. If the search string is not present the INSTR function returns zero.

Numeric and date literals are implicitly cast as characters when they occur as parameters to the INSTR function. Numeric or date expressions are first evaluated before being converted to strings ready to be searched.

The INSTR function takes four parameters made up of two optional and two mandatory arguments. The syntax is INSTR(*source string, search string, [search start position], [nth occurrence]*). The default value for the *search start position* is 1 or the beginning of the *source string*. The default value for the *nth* occurrence is 1 or the first occurrence. The following queries illustrate the INSTR function with numeric and date expressions:

```
Query 1: select instr(3+0.14,'.') from dual
Query 2: select instr(sysdate, 'DEC') from dual
```

Query 1 evaluates the numeric expression to return the number 3.14. This number is implicitly cast as the string 3.14. The period character is searched for and the first occurrence of it occurs at position 2. Query 2 evaluates the SYSDATE function and converts the returned date into a string. Assume that the current system date is 17-DEC-07. The first occurrence of the characters DEC occurs at position 4. Consider the following queries with character data illustrating the default values and the third and fourth parameters of the INSTR function:

```
Query 3: select instr('1#3#5#7#9#','#') from dual
Query 4: select instr('1#3#5#7#9#','#',5) from dual
Query 5: select instr('1#3#5#7#9#','#',3,4) from dual
```

Query 3 searches for the first occurrence of the hash symbol in the source string beginning at position 1 and returns position 2. Query 4 has the number 5 as its third parameter indicating that the search for the hash symbol must begin at position 5 in the source string. The subsequent occurrence of the hash symbol is at position 6, which is returned by the query. Query 5 has the numbers 3 and 4 as its third and fourth parameters. This indicates that the search for the hash symbol must begin at position 3 in the source string. Query 5 then returns the number 10, which is the position of the fourth occurrence of the hash symbol when the search begins at position 3.

The INSTR function used in Figure 4-10 returns records from the DEPARTMENTS table where the DEPARTMENT_NAME values have the character n as their third character.

on the
Ůob
The INSTR function is often used in combination with the SUBSTR function in utility programs designed to extract encoded data from electronic data streams.

The SUBSTR Function (Substring)

The SUBSTR function extracts and returns a segment from a given source string. It extracts a substring of a specified length from the source string beginning at a given position. If the start position is larger than the length of the source string, null is returned. If the number of characters to extract from a given start position is greater than the length of the source string, the segment returned is the substring from the start position to the end of the string.

Numeric and date literals are automatically cast as characters when they occur as parameters to the SUBSTR function. Numeric and date expressions are evaluated before being converted to strings ready to be searched.

FIGURE 4-10   The INSTR function

The SUBSTR function takes three parameters, with the first two being mandatory. Its syntax is SUBSTR(*source string, start position, [number of characters to extract]*). The default number of characters to extract is equal to the number of characters from the *start position* to the end of the *source string*. The following queries illustrate the SUBSTR function with numeric and date expressions:

```
Query 1: select substr(10000-3,3,2) from dual
Query 2: select substr(sysdate,4,3) from dual
```

Query 1 evaluates the numeric expression to return the number 9997. This number is automatically changed into the character string 9997. The search for the substring begins at position 3 and the two characters from that position onward are extracted, yielding the substring 97. Query 2 evaluates the SYSDATE function and converts the date returned into a character string. Assume that the current system date is 17-DEC-07. The search for the substring begins at position 4 and the three characters from that position onward are extracted, yielding the substring DEC.

Consider the following queries with character data illustrating the default behavior of the optional parameter of the SUBSTR function:

```
Query 3: select substr('1#3#5#7#9#',5) from dual
Query 4: select substr('1#3#5#7#9#',5,6) from dual
Query 5: select substr('1#3#5#7#9#',-3,2) from dual
```

Query 3 extracts the substring beginning at position 5. Since the third parameter is not specified, the default extraction length is equal to number of characters from and including the start position to the end of the source string, which is 6. Therefore query 3 is equivalent to query 4 and the substring returned by both queries is 5#7#9#. Query five has the number –3 as its start position. The negative start position parameter instructs Oracle to commence searching 3 characters from the end of the string. Therefore start position is three characters from the end of the string, which is position 8. The third parameter is 2, which results in the substring #9 being returned.

The SUBSTR function used in Figure 4-11 returns records from the EMPLOYEES table, where the first two characters in the JOB_ID values are AD. This function has been further used in the SELECT list to extract the initial character from the FIRST_NAME field of each employee in the result set.

FIGURE 4-11   The SUBSTR function

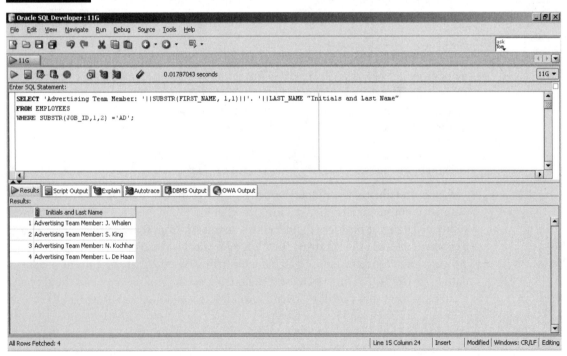

SCENARIO & SOLUTION

You would like to search for a character string stored in the database. The case in which it is stored is unknown and there are potentially leading and trailing spaces surrounding the string. Can such a search be performed?	Yes. The simplest solution is to first TRIM the leading and trailing spaces from the column and then convert the column data using a case conversion function like LOWER, UPPER, or INITCAP to simplify the number of comparisons required in the WHERE clause condition.
You have been asked to extract the last three characters from the LAST_NAME column in the EMPLOYEES table. Can such a query be performed without using the LENGTH function?	Yes. The SUBSTR(*source string, start position, number of characters*) function takes three parameters. If the start position is set to –3, and the number of characters parameter is set to three or is omitted, the last three characters of the LAST_NAME column data is retrieved. The following query may be used: SELECT SUBSTR(LAST_NAME,–3) FROM EMPLOYEES;
You would like to extract a consistent 10-character string based on the SALARY column in the EMPLOYEES table. If the SALARY value is less than 10 characters long, zeros must be added to the left of the value to yield a 10-character string. Is this possible?	Yes. The LPAD function may be used as follows: SELECT LPAD(SALARY,10,0) FROM EMPLOYEES;

The REPLACE Function

The REPLACE function replaces all occurrences of a search item in a source string with a replacement term and returns the modified source string. If the length of the replacement term is different from that of the search item, then the lengths of the returned and source strings will be different. If the search string is not found, the source string is returned unchanged. Numeric and date literals and expressions are evaluated before being implicitly cast as characters when they occur as parameters to the REPLACE function.

The REPLACE function takes three parameters, with the first two being mandatory. Its syntax is REPLACE(*source string, search item,* [*replacement term*]). If the *replacement term* parameter is omitted, each occurrence of the *search item* is removed from the *source string*. In other words, the *search item* is replaced by an empty string. The following queries illustrate the REPLACE function with numeric and date expressions:

```
Query 1: select replace(10000-3,'9','85') from dual
Query 2: select replace(sysdate, 'DEC','NOV') from dual
```

Query 1 evaluates the numeric expression to return the number 9997, which is cast as the character string "9997." The search string is the character "9," which occurs three times in the source. Each search character is substituted with the replacement string "85," yielding the string "8585857." Query 2 evaluates the SYSDATE function and converts the date returned into a character string. Assume that the current system date is 17-DEC-07. The search string "DEC" occurs once in the source string and is replaced with the characters "NOV," yielding the result 17-NOV-07. Note that this is a character string and not a date value. Consider the following queries with character data, which illustrate the default behavior of the optional parameter of the REPLACE function:

```
Query 3: select replace('1#3#5#7#9#','#','->') from dual
Query 4: select replace('1#3#5#7#9#','#') from dual
```

The hash symbol in query 3 is specified as the search character and the replacement string is specified as ->. The hash symbol occurs five times in the source, and the resultant string is: 1->3->5->7->9->. Query 4 does not specify a replacement string. The default behavior is therefore to replace the search string with an empty string which, in effect, removes the search character completely from the source, resulting in the string "13579" being returned.

The REPLACE function used in Figure 4-12 returns records from the EMPLOYEES table where the JOB_ID values are SA_MAN, but it modifies the SALARY column by replacing each 0 with 000 and aliasing the new expression as Dream Salary.

EXERCISE 4-2

Using the Case Manipulation Functions

Envelope printing restricts the addressee field to 16 characters. Ideally, the addressee field contains employees' FIRST_NAME and LAST_NAME values separated by a single space. When the combined length of an employee's FIRST_NAME and LAST_NAME exceeds 15 characters, the addressee field should contain their formal name. An employee's formal name is made up of the first letter of their FIRST_NAME and the first 14 characters of their LAST_NAME.

You are required to retrieve a list of FIRST_NAME and LAST_NAME values and formal names for employees where the combined length of FIRST_NAME and LAST_NAME exceeds 15 characters.

1. Start SQL*Plus and connect to the HR schema.

FIGURE 4-12   The REPLACE function

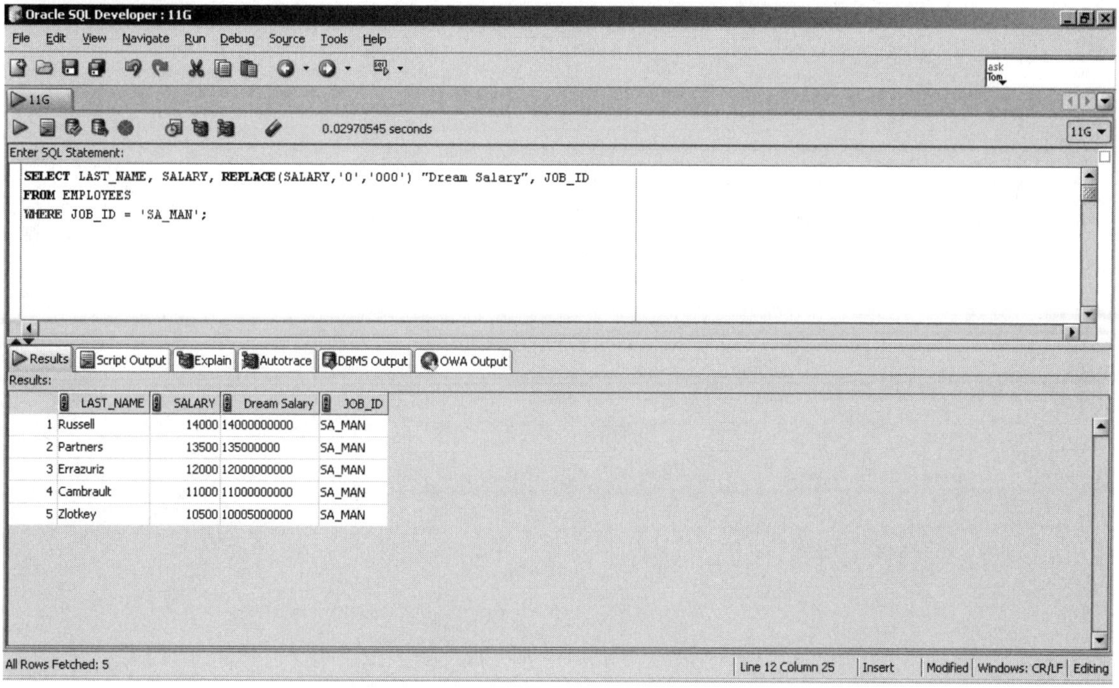

```
Oracle SQL Developer : 11G                                                          _ | 8 | X
File  Edit  View  Navigate  Run  Debug  Source  Tools  Help
[toolbar icons]                                                              ask
                                                                             Tom
11G                                                                          ◄ | ► | ▼
▶  🔲 🔳 🔲 ●   📇 📇 📇   ✏   0.02970545 seconds                              11G ▼
Enter SQL Statement:
SELECT LAST_NAME, SALARY, REPLACE(SALARY,'0','000') "Dream Salary", JOB_ID
FROM EMPLOYEES
WHERE JOB_ID = 'SA_MAN';



◄
▶Results  Script Output  Explain  Autotrace  DBMS Output  OWA Output
Results:
     LAST_NAME    SALARY   Dream Salary    JOB_ID
  1  Russell      14000   14000000000      SA_MAN
  2  Partners     13500   135000000        SA_MAN
  3  Errazuriz    12000   12000000000      SA_MAN
  4  Cambrault    11000   11000000000      SA_MAN
  5  Zlotkey      10500   10005000000      SA_MAN



All Rows Fetched: 5                        Line 12 Column 25  Insert  Modified  Windows: CR/LF  Editing
```

2. The formal name is constructed by concatenating the first character in the FIRST_NAME field with a space and the first 14 characters of the LAST_NAME field to return a string that is 16 characters long. The SUBSTR function is used to extract the initial and surname portions.

3. The SELECT clause is
   SELECT FIRST_NAME, LAST_NAME, SUBSTR(FIRST_NAME,1,1)||' '||SUBSTR(LAST_NAME,1,14) FORMAL_NAME

4. The FROM clause is
   FROM EMPLOYEES

5. The WHERE clause must limit the records returned to only those where the combined lengths of their FIRST_NAME and LAST_NAME exceeds 15 characters.

6. The WHERE clause is
   WHERE LENGTH(FIRST_NAME) + LENGTH(LAST_NAME) > 15

7. Executing this statement returns the following set of results:

Using Numeric Functions

There is a range of built-in *numeric functions* provided by Oracle that rivals the mathematical toolboxes of popular spreadsheet software packages. A significant differentiator between numeric and other functions is that they accept and return only numeric data. Oracle provides numeric functions for solving trigonometric, exponentiation, and logarithmic problems, amongst others. This guide focuses on three *numeric single-row functions*: ROUND, TRUNC, and MOD, discussed next.

The Numeric ROUND Function

The ROUND function performs a rounding operation on a numeric value based on the decimal precision specified. The value returned is either rounded up or down based on the numeric value of the significant digit at the specified decimal precision position. If the specified decimal precision is *n*, the digit significant to the rounding is found ($n + 1$) places to the RIGHT of the decimal point. If it is negative, the digit significant to the rounding is found n places to the LEFT of the decimal point. If the numeric value of the significant digit is greater than or equal to 5, a "round up" occurs, else a "round down" occurs.

The ROUND function takes two parameters. Its syntax is ROUND(*source number, decimal precision*). The *source number* parameter represents any numeric literal, column, or expression. The *decimal precision* parameter specifies the degree of rounding and is optional. If the *decimal precision* parameter is absent, the default degree of rounding is zero, which means the source is rounded to the nearest whole number.

Consider the decimal degrees listed in Table 4-1 for the number 1234.5678. The negative decimal precision values are located to the left of the decimal point while the positive values are found to the right.

If the decimal precision parameter is one, then the source number is rounded to the nearest tenth. If it is two, then the source is rounded to the nearest hundredth, and so on. The following queries illustrate the usage of this function:

```
Query 1: select round(1601.916718,1) from dual
Query 2: select round(1601.916718,2) from dual
Query 3: select round(1601.916718,-3) from dual
Query 4: select round(1601.916718) from dual
```

Query 1 has a decimal precision parameter (n) of 1, which implies that the source number is rounded to the nearest tenth. Since the hundredths ($n + 1$) digit is 1 (less than 5), no rounding occurs and the number returned is 1601.9. The decimal precision parameter in query 2 is 2, so the source number is rounded to the nearest hundredth. Since the thousandths unit is 6 (greater than 5), rounding up occurs and the number returned is 1601.92. The decimal precision parameter of the query 3 is –3. Since it is negative, the digit significant for rounding is found 3 places to the left of

TABLE 4-1	Decimal Precision	Significant Rounding Digit	Decimal Position
Decimal Precision Descriptions	-4	1	Thousands ($n \times 1000$)
	-3	2	Hundreds ($n \times 100$)
	-2	3	Tens ($n \times 10$)
	-1	4	Units ($n \times 1$)
	1	5	Tenths ($n \div 10$)
	2	6	Hundredths ($n \div 100$)
	3	7	Thousandths ($n \div 1000$)

the decimal point, at the hundreds digit, which is 6. Since the hundreds unit is 6, rounding up occurs and the number returned is 2000. Query 4 has dispensed with the decimal precision parameter. This implies that rounding is done to the nearest whole number. Since the tenth unit is 9, the number is rounded up and 1602 is returned.

The example shown in Figure 4-13 selects employees working as sales managers and computes a loyalty bonus based on the number of days employed rounded to the nearest whole number. The ROUND function is used to round the fractional part of the difference between the current system date and the HIRE_DATE for each sales manager.

The Numeric TRUNC Function (Truncate)

The TRUNC function performs a truncation operation on a numeric value based on the decimal precision specified. A numeric truncation is different from rounding because the resulting value drops the numbers at the decimal precision specified and does not attempt to round up or down if the decimal precision is positive. However, if the decimal precision specified (n) is negative, the input value is zeroed down from the nth decimal position.

FIGURE 4-13   The numeric ROUND function

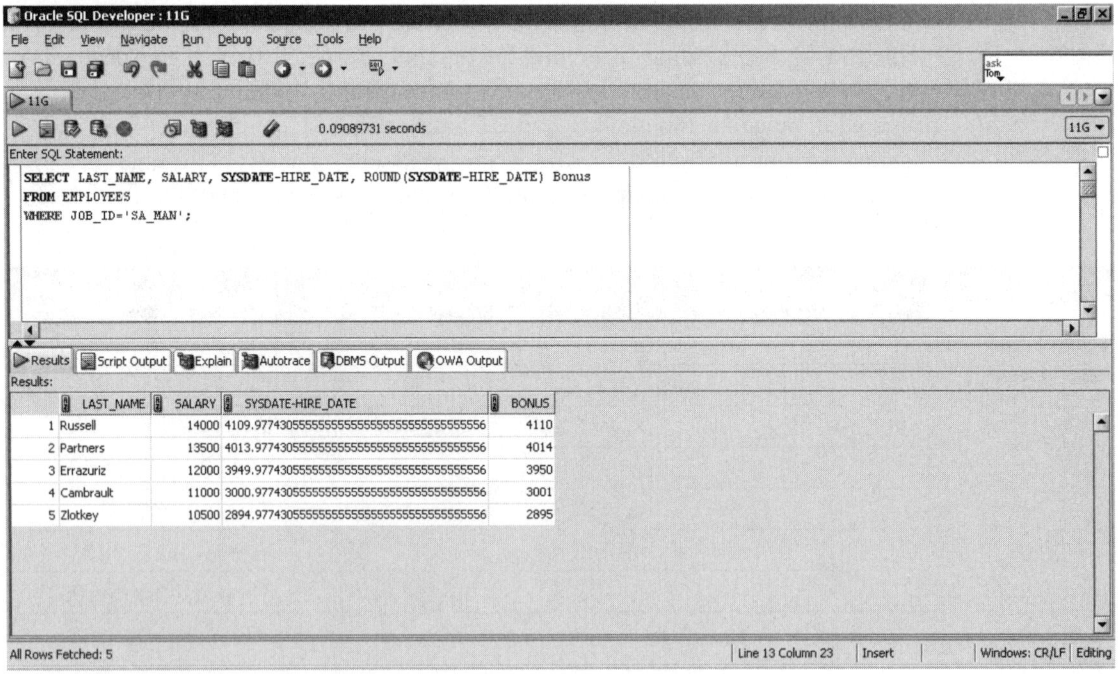

The TRUNC function takes two parameters. Its syntax is TRUNC (*source number, decimal precision*). *Source number* represents any numeric literal, column, or expression. *Decimal precision* specifies the degree of truncation and is optional. If the *decimal precision* parameter is absent, the default degree of rounding is zero, which means the *source number* is truncated to the nearest whole number.

If the *decimal precision* parameter is 1, then the *source number* is truncated at its tenths unit. If it is 2, it is truncated at its hundredths unit, and so on. The following queries illustrate the usage of this function:

```
Query 1: select trunc(1601.916718,1) from dual
Query 2: select trunc(1601.916718,2) from dual
Query 3: select trunc(1601.916718,-3) from dual
Query 4: select trunc(1601.916718) from dual
```

Query 1 has a *decimal precision* parameter of 1, which implies that the *source number* is truncated at its tenths unit and the number returned is 1601.9. The *decimal precision* parameter (n) in query 2 is 2, so the *source number* is truncated at its hundredths unit and the number returned is 1601.91. Note that this result would be different if a rounding operation was performed since the digit in position ($n + 1$) is 6 (greater than 5). Query 3 specifies a negative number (-3) as its decimal precision. Three places to the left of the decimal point implies that the truncation happens at the hundreds digit as shown earlier in Table 4-1. Therefore, the *source number* is zeroed down from its hundreds digit (6) and the number returned is 1000. Finally, query 4 does not have a *decimal precision* parameter implying that truncation is done at the whole number degree of precision. The number returned is 1601.

The finance department has qualified for a top departmental award for which the company decided to reward its finance staff by adjusting their salaries. Since the fractional salary adjustment results in numbers with three decimal places, the TRUNC function is used to truncate the proposed salary increase to a whole number, as shown in Figure 4-14.

The MOD Function (Modulus)

The MOD function returns the numeric remainder of a division operation. Two numbers, the dividend (number being divided) and the divisor (number to divide by) are provided, and a division operation is performed. If the divisor is a factor of the dividend, MOD returns zero since there is no remainder. If the divisor is zero, no division by zero error is returned and the MOD function returns a zero instead. If the divisor is larger than the dividend, then the MOD function returns the dividend as its result. This is because it divides zero times into the divisor, leaving the remainder equal to the dividend.

FIGURE 4-14 The numeric TRUNC function

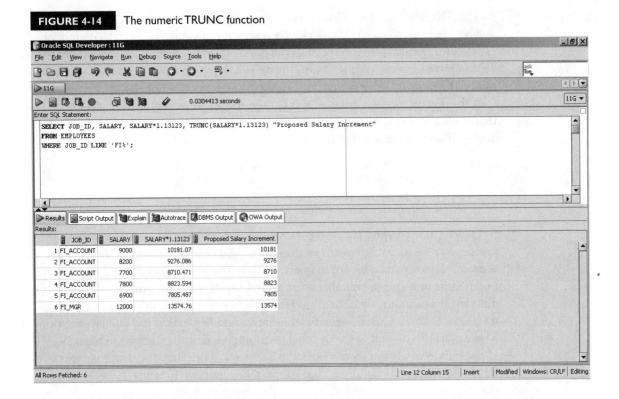

The MOD function takes two parameters. Its syntax is MOD(*dividend, divisor*). The *dividend* and *divisor* parameters represent a numeric literal, column, or expression, which may be negative or positive. The following queries illustrate the usage of this function:

```
Query 1: select mod(6,2) from dual
Query 2: select mod(5,3) from dual
Query 3: select mod(7,35) from dual
Query 4: select mod(5.2,3) from dual
```

Query 1 divides 6 by 2 perfectly, yielding 0 as the remainder. Query 2 divides 5 by 3, yielding 1 with remainder 2. Query 3 attempts to divide 7 by 35. Since the *divisor* is larger than the *dividend*, the number 7 is returned as the modulus value. Query 4 has an improper fraction as the *dividend*. Dividing 5.2 by 3 yields 1 with remainder 2.2.

on the
ⓘ o b

Any even number divided by 2 naturally has no remainder, but odd numbers divided by 2 always have a remainder of 1. Therefore, the MOD function is often used distinguish between even and odd numbers.

The EMPLOYEE_ID column in the EMPLOYEES table stores a unique sequential number for each record beginning with employee number 100. The first 12 employees must be allocated to one of four teams in a round-robin manner for a particular task. Figure 4-15 shows how this is accomplished using the MOD function.

The 12 employees' records are isolated with a BETWEEN operator in the WHERE clause. The MOD function is applied to the division of the EMPLOYEE_ID column values by the numeric literal 4. As Figure 4-15 shows, the MOD function allocates the numbers 0 to 3 to each row in a round-robin manner.

FIGURE 4-15   The MOD function

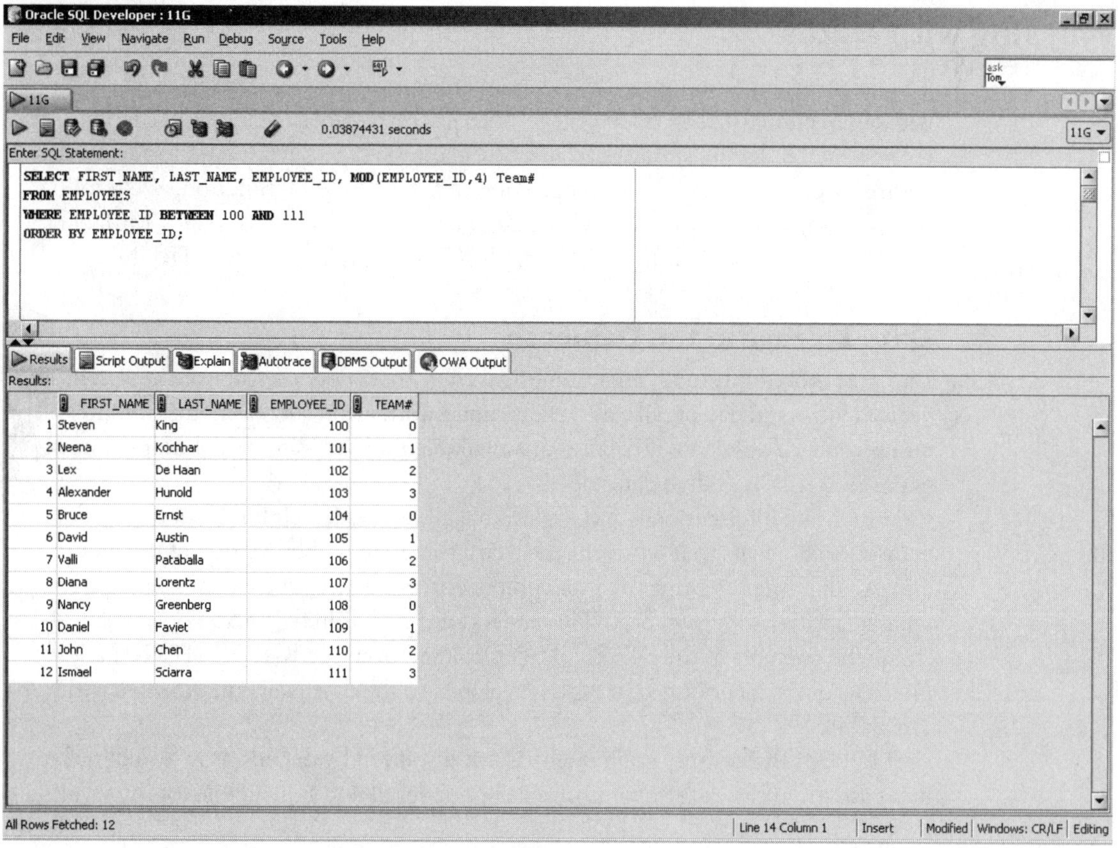

The default values assumed by the optional parameters of functions are not always intuitive but are often tested. For example, calling the SUBSTR function with just the first two parameters results in the function extracting a substring from a start position to the end of the given source string. The optional parameter for both the numeric and date TRUNC and ROUND functions is the degree of precision. For example, calling the numeric TRUNC function without specifying degree of truncation results in the number being truncated to the nearest whole number. It is useful to be familiar with the default values assumed by optional parameters for these functions.

Working with Dates

The *date* built-in functions provide a convenient way to solve date-related problems without needing to keep track of leap years or the number of days in particular months. We'll discuss storage of dates by Oracle and the default date format masks before we conduct a detailed examination of the SYSDATE function. We'll follow by discussing date arithmetic and the *date manipulation functions*: ADD_MONTHS, MONTHS_BETWEEN, LAST_DAY, NEXT_DAY, ROUND, and TRUNC.

Date Storage in the Database

Dates are stored internally in a numeric format that supports the storage of century, year, month, and day details, as well as time information such as hours, minutes, and seconds. These date attributes are available for every literal, column value, or expression that is of date data type.

When date information is accessed from a table, the default format of the results comprises two digits that represent the day, a three-letter abbreviation of the month, and two digits representing the year component. By default, these components are separated with hyphens in SQL*Plus and forward slashes in SQL Developer. Figure 4-16 shows the contents of the START_DATE column from the JOB_HISTORY table. Note the query is performed in SQL Developer, so the date elements are separated by forward slashes.

Although the century component is not displayed by default, it is stored in the database when the date value is inserted or updated and is available for retrieval.

FIGURE 4-16   Default date storage in the database

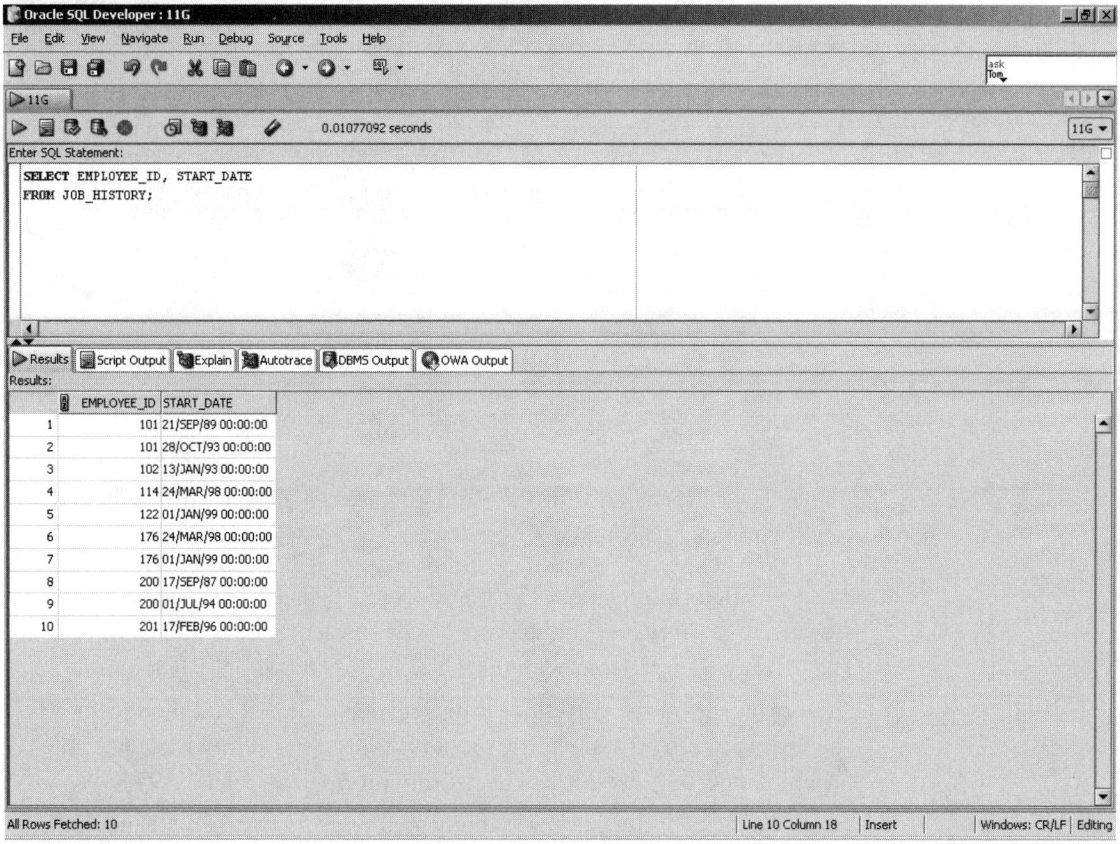

The format in which a date is displayed is referred to as its format mask. There are several formatting codes or date format masks available, as shown in Table 4-2.

The language to format date items using the full range of date format masks is discussed in Chapter 5. The DD-MON-RR format mask is the default for display and input. When inserting or updating date information, the century component is obtained from the SYSDATE function if it is not supplied. The RR date format mask differs from the YY format mask since it is may be used to specify different centuries based on the current and specified years. The century component assigned

204 Chapter 4: Single-Row Functions

TABLE 4-2	Format Mask	Format Description
Date Format Masks	DD	Day of the month
	MON	Month of the year
	YY	Two-digit year
	YYYY	Four-digit year including century
	RR	Two-digit year (Year 2000–compliant)
	CC	Two-digit century
	HH	Hours with AM and PM
	HH24	Twenty-four-hour time
	MI	Minutes
	SS	Seconds

to a date with its year specified with the RR date format may be better understood by considering the following principles:

■ If the two digits of the current year and specified year lie between 0 and 49, the current century is returned. Suppose the present date is 02-JUN-2007. The century returned for the date 24-JUL-04 in DD-MON-RR format is 20.

■ If the two digits of the current year lie between 0 and 49 and the specified year falls between 50 and 99, the previous century is returned. Suppose the current date is 02-JUN-2007. The century returned for 24-JUL-94 is 19.

■ If the two digits of the current and specified years lie between 50 and 99, the current century is returned by default. Suppose the current date is 02-JUN-1975. The century returned for 24-JUL-94 is 19.

■ If the two digits of the current year lie between 50 and 99 and the specified year falls between 0 and 49, the next century is returned. Suppose the current date is 02-JUN-1975. The century returned for 24-JUL-07 is 20.

The SYSDATE Function

The SYSDATE function takes no parameters and returns the current system date and time according to the database server. By default the SYSDATE function returns the DD-MON-RR components of the current system date. It is important to remember that SYSDATE does not return the date and time as specified by your local system clock. If the database server is located in a different time zone from a client querying the database, the date and time returned will differ from the local operating system clock on the client machine. The query to retrieve the database server date is as follows:

```
select sysdate from dual
```

Date Arithmetic

Arithmetic with date columns and expressions were briefly discussed in Chapter 2. The following equations illustrate an important principle regarding *date arithmetic*:

$$Date1 - Date2 = Num1$$
$$Date1 - Num1 = Date2$$
$$Date1 = Date2 + Num1$$

A date can be subtracted from another date. The difference between two date items represents the number of days between them. Any number, including fractions, may be added to or subtracted from a date item. In this context the number represents a number of days. The sum or difference between a number and a date item always returns a date item. This principle implies that adding, multiplying, or dividing two date items is not permitted.

To illustrate the time component of the SYSDATE function as it pertains to date arithmetic, the SQL Developer environment has been temporarily modified to display time information as well as date information.

on the job

To modify the SQL Developer environment to display time information for date columns, by default, navigate to Tools | Preferences | Database | NLS Parameters | Date Format. Change the default display mask (DD/MON/RR) to (DD/MON/RR HH24:MI:SS).

A conversion function, which will be discussed in detail in Chapter 5, is introduced here to aid this example. Figure 4-17 demonstrates how the TO_DATE conversion function is used to convert the date literal 02-JUN-2008 with time component 12.10pm into a date data type.

The first query in the figure is dissected as follows: two days prior to the second of June, 12.10pm is the thirty-first of May, 12.10pm, which is the date and time returned by expression 1. Adding 0.5 days or 12 hours to 02/JUN/08 12:10pm, as expression 2 demonstrates, results in the date 03/JUN/08 and the time 00.10 being returned. Expression 3 adds 6/24 or six hours, resulting in the date 02/JUN/08, 18.10 being returned.

FIGURE 4-17   The SYSDATE function and date arithmetic

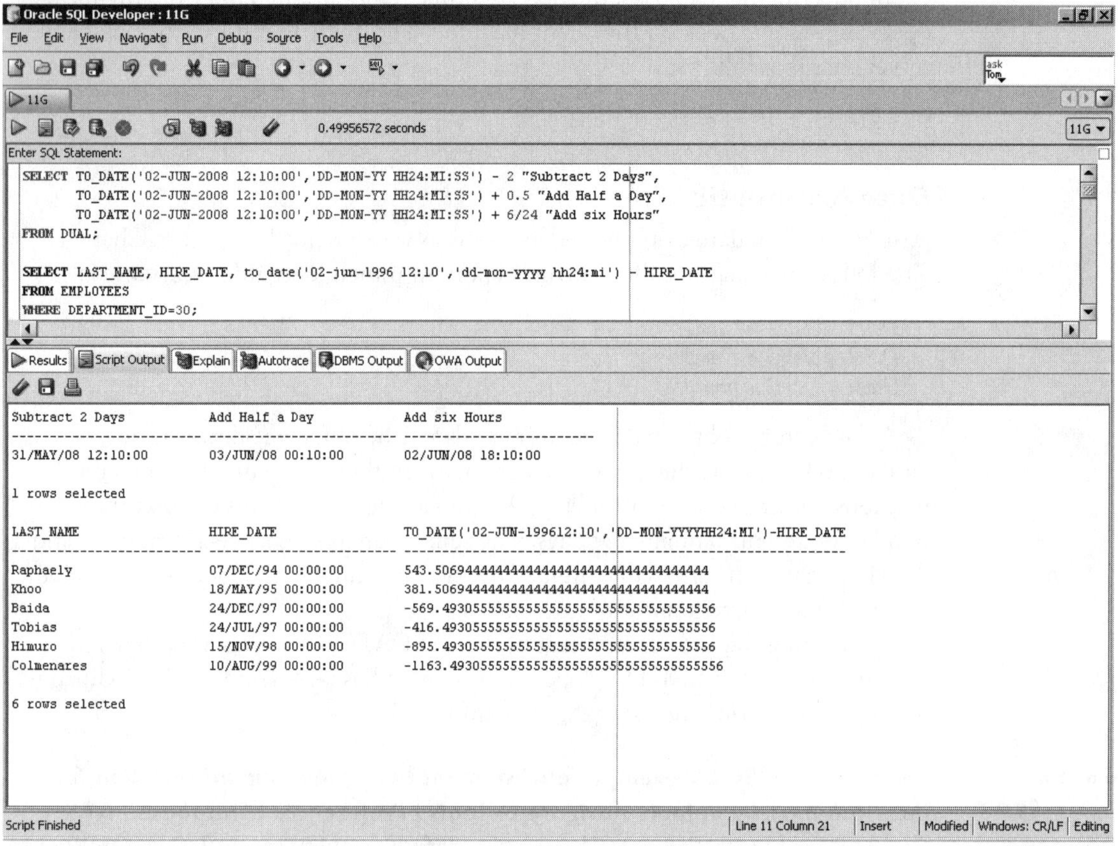

The HIREDATE column for employees with DEPARTMENT_ID values of 30 is subtracted from the date item 02/JUN/96 12:10pm in the figure's second query. The number of days between these two dates is returned for each row. Notice that when the HIREDATE column value occurs later than 02/JUN/96, a negative number is returned.

Using Date Functions

The *date manipulation* functions provide a reliable and accurate means of working with date items. These functions provide such ease and flexibility for date manipulation that many integration specialists, database administrators, and other developers make frequent use of them.

The MONTHS_BETWEEN Function

The MONTHS_BETWEEN function returns a numeric value representing the number of months between two date values. Date literals in the format DD-MON-RR or DD-MON-YYYY are automatically cast as date items when they occur as parameters to the MONTHS_BETWEEN function.

The MONTHS_BETWEEN function takes two mandatory parameters. Its syntax is MONTHS_BETWEEN(*start date, end date*). The function computes the difference in months between *start date* and *end date*. If the *end date* occurs before the *start date*, a negative number is returned. The difference between the two date parameters may consist of a whole number and a fractional component. The whole number represents the number of months between the two dates. The fractional component represents the days and time remaining after the integer difference between years and months is calculated and is based on a 31-day month. A whole number with no fractional part is returned if the day components of the dates being compared are either the same or the last day of their respective months.

The following queries illustrate the MONTHS_BETWEEN function:

```
Query 1: select sysdate, sysdate+31, sysdate+62, sysdate+91,
months_between(sysdate+91, sysdate) from dual
Query 2: select months_between('29-mar-2008','28-feb-2008')  from dual
Query 3: select months_between('29-mar-2008','28-feb-2008') * 31 from dual
Query 4: select months_between(to_date('29-feb-2008'),
to_date('28-feb-2008 12:00:00','dd-mon-yyyy hh24:mi:ss'))* 31 from dual;
```

Assume that the current date is 29-DEC-2007.

The first expression in query 1 returns the number 1, as the month between 29-DEC-2007 is 29-JAN-2008 (31 days later). The second expression similarly returns 2 months between 29-DEC-2007 and 29-FEB-2008 (62 days later). Since February 2008 has 29 days, 91 days must be added to 29-DEC-2007 to get 29-MAR-2008, and the MONTHS_BETWEEN (29-MAR-2008, 29-DEC-2007) function returns exactly three months in the third expression in query 1.

Query 2 implicitly converts the date literals into date items of the format DD-MON-YYYY. Since no time information is provided, Oracle assumes the time to be midnight on both days, or 00:00:00. The MONTHS_BETWEEN function returns approximately 1.03225806. The whole number component indicates that there is one month between these two dates. Closer examination of the fractional component interestingly reveals that there is exactly one month between 28-MAR-2008 and 28-FEB-2008. The fractional component must therefore represent the one-day difference. It would include differences in hours, minutes, and seconds as well, but for this example, the time components are identical. Multiplying 0.03225806 by 31 returns 1, since the fractional component returned by MONTHS_BETWEEN is based on a 31-day month.

Similarly, query 3 returns the whole number 32. Query 4 demonstrates how the time component is factored into the computation by the MONTHS_BETWEEN function, which returns approximately 0.016129. There is a 12-hour difference between the start and end date parameters, so zero months between them is correct. Multiplying the fractional part by 31 yields 0.5 days, which corresponds to the 12-hour difference.

The MONTHS_BETWEEN function used in Figure 4-18 returns records from the JOB_HISTORY table. The months between the dates an employee started in a particular job and ended that job are computed, and the results are sorted in descending order.

The ADD_MONTHS Function

The ADD_MONTHS function returns a date item calculated by adding a specified number of months to a given date value. Date literals in the format DD-MON-RR or DD-MON-YYYY are automatically cast as date items when they occur as parameters to the ADD_MONTHS function.

The ADD_MONTHS function takes two mandatory parameters. Its syntax is ADD_MONTHS (*start date, number of months*). The function computes the target date after adding the specified number of months to the *start date*. The number of months may be negative, resulting in a target date earlier than the start date being returned. The *number of months* may be fractional, but the fractional component is ignored and the integer component is used.

FIGURE 4-18	The MONTHS_BETWEEN function

```
SELECT EMPLOYEE_ID, END_DATE, START_DATE, MONTHS_BETWEEN(END_DATE, START_DATE) DURATION
FROM JOB_HISTORY
ORDER BY DURATION DESC;
```

	EMPLOYEE_ID	END_DATE	START_DATE	DURATION
1	200	17/JUN/93 00:00:00	17/SEP/87 00:00:00	69
2	102	24/JUL/98 00:00:00	13/JAN/93 00:00:00	66.3548387096774193548387096774193548387
3	200	31/DEC/98 00:00:00	01/JUL/94 00:00:00	53.9677419354838709677419354838709677419
4	101	27/OCT/93 00:00:00	21/SEP/89 00:00:00	49.1935483870967741935483870967741935483 9
5	201	19/DEC/99 00:00:00	17/FEB/96 00:00:00	46.0645161290322580645161290322580645161 3
6	101	15/MAR/97 00:00:00	28/OCT/93 00:00:00	40.5806451612903225806451612903225806451 6
7	114	31/DEC/99 00:00:00	24/MAR/98 00:00:00	21.2258064516129032258064516129032258064 5
8	176	31/DEC/99 00:00:00	01/JAN/99 00:00:00	11.9677419354838709677419354838709677419 4
9	122	31/DEC/99 00:00:00	01/JAN/99 00:00:00	11.9677419354838709677419354838709677419 4
10	176	31/DEC/98 00:00:00	24/MAR/98 00:00:00	9.2258064516129032258064516129032258064 5

The three queries in Figure 4-19 illustrate the behavior of the ADD_MONTHS function.

The first query in the figure returns 07-MAY-2009 since the day component remains the same if possible and the month is incremented by one. The second query has two interesting dimensions. The parameter specifying the number of months to add contains a fractional component, which is ignored. Therefore, it is equivalent to ADD_MONTHS ('31-dec-2008',2). Adding two months to the date 31-DEC-2008 should return the date 31-FEB-2009, but there is no such date, so the last day of the month, 28-FEB-2009, is returned. Since the number of months added in the third query is –12, the date 07-APR-2008 is returned, which is 12 months prior to the start date.

FIGURE 4-19   The ADD_MONTHS function

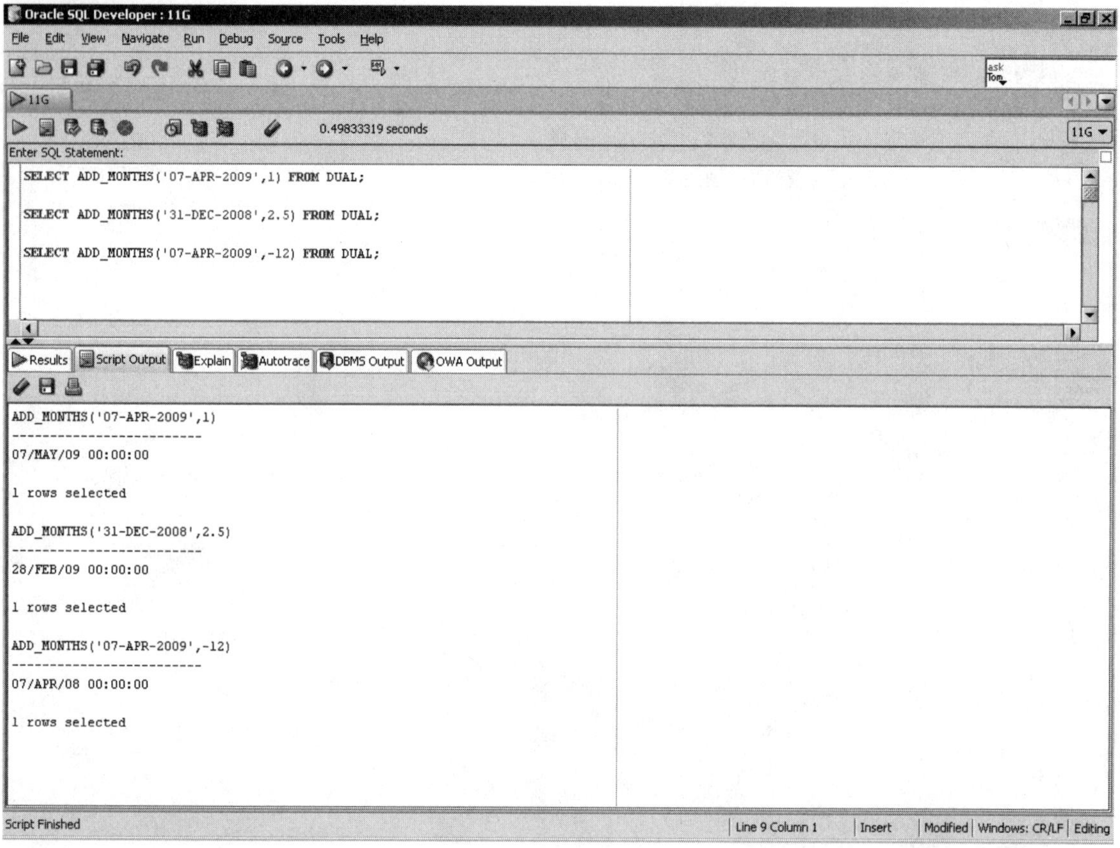

EXERCISE 4-3

Using the Date Functions

You are required to obtain a list of EMPLOYEE_ID, LAST_NAME, and HIRE_
DATE values for the employees who have worked more than 100 months between
the date they were hired and 01-JAN-2000.

1. Start SQL Developer and connect to the HR schema.
2. The SELECT clause is
   SELECT EMPLOYEE_ID, LAST_NAME, HIRE_DATE
3. The FROM clause is
   FROM EMPLOYEES

4. The WHERE clause must compare the months between the given date literal and the HIRE_DATE value with the numeric literal 100.

5. The MONTHS_BETWEEN function may be used in the WHERE clause.

6. The WHERE clause is
WHERE MONTHS_BETWEEN('01-JAN-2000', HIRE_DATE) > 100

7. Executing this statement returns the set of results shown in the following illustration:

The **NEXT_DAY** Function

The NEXT_DAY function returns the date when the next occurrence of a specified day of the week occurs. Literals that may be implicitly cast as date items are acceptable when they occur as parameters to the NEXT_DAY function.

The NEXT_DAY function takes two mandatory parameters. Its syntax is NEXT_DAY (*start date, day of the week*). The function computes the date on which the *day of the week* parameter next occurs after the *start date*. The *day of the week* parameter may be either a character value or an integer value. The acceptable values are determined by the NLS_DATE_LANGUAGE database parameter but the default values are at least the first three characters of the day name or integer values, where 1 represents Sunday, 2 represents Monday, and so on. The character values representing the days of the week may be specified in any case. The short name may be longer than three characters, for example, Sunday may be referenced as sun, sund, sunda or Sunday.

The three queries in Figure 4-20 illustrate the behavior of the NEXT_DAY function.

01-JAN-2009 is a Thursday. Therefore, the next time a Tuesday occurs will be five days later on 06-JAN-2009, which is what the first query in the figure retrieves. The second query specifies the character literal WEDNE, which is interpreted as Wednesday.

FIGURE 4-20   The NEXT_DAY function

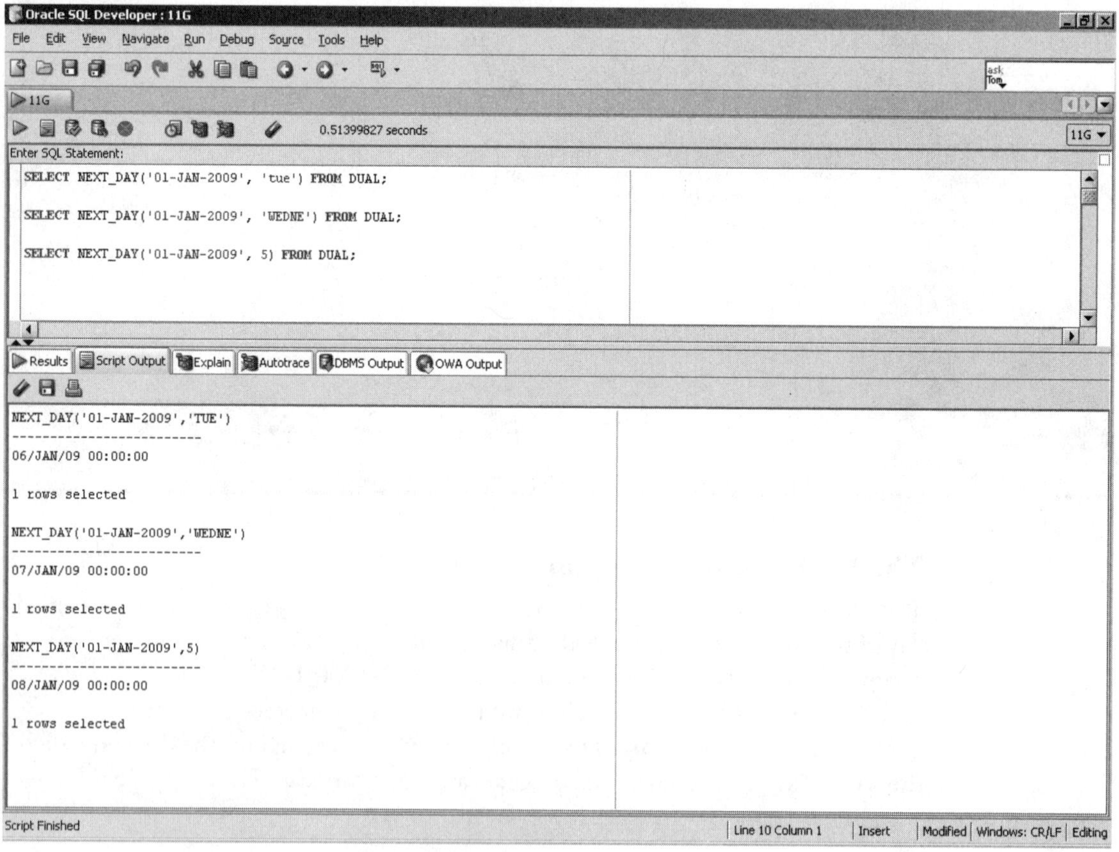

SCENARIO & SOLUTION

You wish to retrieve the duration of employment in days for each employee. Is it possible to perform such a calculation?	Yes. The SYSDATE function may be used to obtain the current system date. The following query computes the duration by subtracting the HIRE_DATE column from the value returned by the SYSDATE function: SELECT SYSDATE-HIRE_DATE FROM EMPLOYEES;
You are tasked with identifying the date the end of year staff bonus will be paid. Bonuses are usually paid on the last Friday in December. Can the bonus date be computed using the NEXT_DAY function?	Yes. If the NEXT_DAY function is called with the start date parameter set to the last day in December and the search day set to Friday, then the first Friday in January is returned. Subtracting seven days from this date yields the date of the last Friday in December. Consider the following query for the year 2009: SELECT NEXT_DAY('31-DEC-2009', 'Friday') -7 FROM DUAL;
Employees working in the IT department have moved to new offices and, although the last four digits of their phone numbers are the same, the set of the three digits 423 is changed to 623. A typical phone number of an IT staff member is 590-423-4567. You are required to provide a list of employees' names with their old and new phone numbers. Can this list be provided?	Yes. The REPLACE function is used. To replace every 4 with a 6 will change digits that should not be changed as well, so the string to be replaced must be uniquely specified. The following query provides the list: SELECT FIRST_NAME, LAST_NAME, REPLACE(PHONE_NUMBER, '.423.','.623.') FROM EMPLOYEES WHERE DEPARTMENT_ID=60

The next Wednesday after 01-JAN-2009 is 07-JAN-2009. The third query uses the integer form to specify the fifth day of the week. Assuming the default values where Sunday is represented by the number 1, the fifth day is Thursday. The next time another Thursday occurs after 01-JAN-2009 is 08-JAN-2009.

The LAST_DAY Function

The LAST_DAY function returns the date of the last day in the month a specified day belongs to. Literals that may be implicitly cast as date items are acceptable when they occur as parameters to the LAST_DAY function.

The LAST_DAY function takes one mandatory parameter. Its syntax is LAST_DAY(*start date*). The function extracts the month that the *start date* parameter belongs to and calculates the date of the last day of that month. The two queries in Figure 4-21 illustrate the behavior of the LAST_DAY function.

FIGURE 4-21 The LAST_DAY function

```
Oracle SQL Developer : 11G                                                              _ |8|X|
File  Edit  View  Navigate  Run  Debug  Source  Tools  Help
[icons]                                                                            ask
                                                                                  Tom
> 11G                                                                               < > ▼
> [icons]                    [icons]    /    0.49857929 seconds                    11G ▼
Enter SQL Statement:
  SELECT LAST_DAY('01-JAN-2009')                                                      ▲
  FROM DUAL;

  SELECT LAST_NAME, HIRE_DATE, LAST_DAY(HIRE_DATE),
        LAST_DAY(HIRE_DATE)-HIRE_DATE "Days worked in first month"
  FROM EMPLOYEES
  WHERE JOB_ID='IT_PROG';
                                                                                     ▼
 ◄|                                                                               ►|
> Results | Script Output | Explain | Autotrace | DBMS Output | OWA Output
 [icons]

LAST_DAY('01-JAN-2009')
-------------------------
31/JAN/09 00:00:00

1 rows selected

LAST_NAME            HIRE_DATE             LAST_DAY(HIRE_DATE)   Days worked in first month
-------------------- --------------------  --------------------  --------------------------
Hunold               03/JAN/90 00:00:00     31/JAN/90 00:00:00   28
Ernst                21/MAY/91 00:00:00     31/MAY/91 00:00:00   10
Austin               25/JUN/97 00:00:00     30/JUN/97 00:00:00   5
Pataballa            05/FEB/98 00:00:00     28/FEB/98 00:00:00   23
Lorentz              07/FEB/99 00:00:00     28/FEB/99 00:00:00   21

5 rows selected




Script Finished                                    Line 11 Column 1 | Insert | Modified | Windows: CR/LF | Editing
```

The last day in the month of January 2009 is 31-JAN-2009, which is returned by the LAST_DAY('01-JAN-2009') function call in the first query in the figure. The second query extracts the employees with JOB_ID values of IT_PROG. The number of days worked by these employees in their first month of employment is calculated by subtracting the HIRE_DATE values from the LAST_DAY of that month.

The Date ROUND Function

The date ROUND function performs a rounding operation on a value based on a specified date precision format. The value returned is either rounded up or down to the nearest date precision format.

INSIDE THE EXAM

There are two certification objectives in this chapter. Various types of SQL functions are described and the concept of a function is defined. A distinction is made between single-row functions, which execute once for each row in a dataset, and multiple-row functions, which execute once for all the rows in a dataset. Single-row functions may be used in the SELECT, WHERE, and ORDER BY clauses of the SELECT statement.

The second objective relates to the use of character, numeric, and date functions in queries. The exam tests your understanding of these functions by providing practical examples of their usage. You may be asked to predict the results returned or to identify errors inherent in the syntax of these examples.

Functions can take zero or more input parameters, some of which may be mandatory

while others are optional. Mandatory parameters are listed first, and optional parameters are always last. Common errors relate to confusion about the meaning of positions of parameters in functions. A character function like INSTR takes four parameters, with the first two being mandatory. The first is the source string; the second is the search string, while the third and fourth are not always intuitive and may be easily forgotten or mixed up. Be sure to remember the meaning of parameters in different positions. Another mistake related to parameters relates to confusion about the default values used by Oracle when optional parameters are not specified. You may be expected to predict the results returned from function calls that do not have all their optional parameters specified.

The date ROUND function takes one mandatory and one optional parameter. Its syntax is ROUND(*source date*, *[date precision format]*). The *source date* parameter represents any value that can be implicitly converted into a date item. The *date precision format* parameter specifies the degree of rounding and is optional. If it is absent, the default degree of rounding is *day*. This means the *source date* is rounded to the nearest day. The *date precision formats* include *century* (CC), *year* (YYYY), *quarter* (Q), *month* (MM), *week* (W), *day* (DD), *hour* (HH), and *minute* (MI). Many of these formats are discussed in Chapter 5.

Rounding up to *century* is equivalent to adding one to the current century. Rounding up to the next month occurs if the *day* component is greater than 16, else rounding down to the beginning of the current month occurs. If the month falls between one and six, then rounding to *year* returns the date at the beginning of the current year, else it returns the date at the beginning of the following year. Figure 4-22 shows four items in the SELECT list, each rounding a date literal to a different degree of precision.

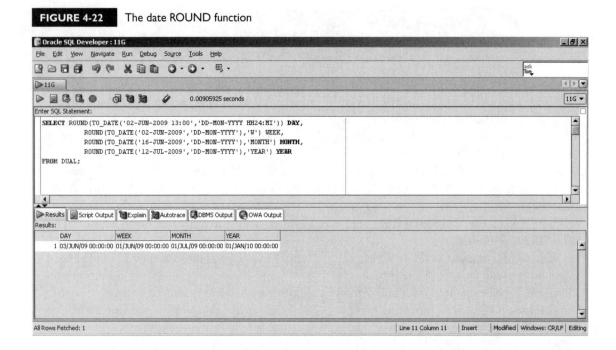

FIGURE 4-22   The date ROUND function

The first item rounds the date to the nearest day. Since the time is 13:00, which is after 12:00, the date is rounded to midnight on the following day, or 03-JUN-2009 00:00. The second item rounds the date to the same day of the week as the first day of the month and returns 01-JUN-2009. The third item rounds the date to the beginning of the following month, since the day component is 16 and returns 01-JUL-2009. The fourth item is rounded up to the date at the beginning of the following year since the month component is 7, and 01-JAN-2010 is returned.

The Date TRUNC Function

The date TRUNC function performs a truncation operation on a date value based on a specified date precision format.

The date TRUNC function takes one mandatory and one optional parameter. Its syntax is TRUNC(*source date*, [*date precision format*]). The *source date* parameter represents any value that can be implicitly converted into a date item. The *date precision format* parameter specifies the degree of truncation and is optional. If it is absent, the default degree of truncation is *day*. This means that any time component

FIGURE 4-23 The date TRUNC function

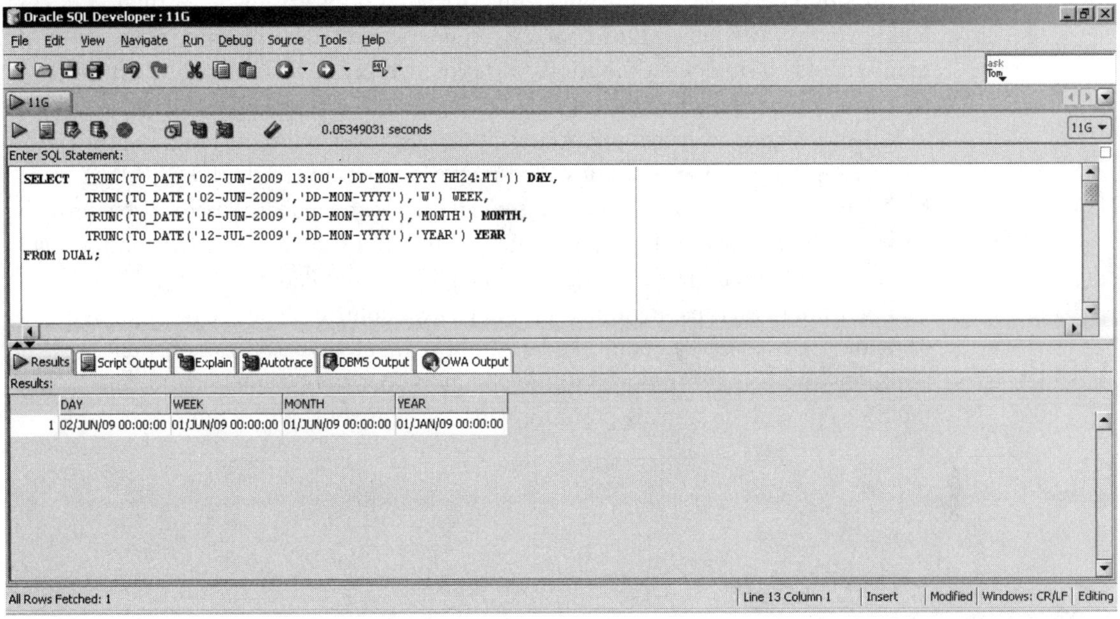

of the *source date* is set to midnight or 00:00:00 (00 hours, 00 minutes and 00 seconds). Truncating at the month level sets the date of the *source date* to the first day of the month. Truncating at the year level returns the date at the beginning of the current year. Figure 4-23 shows four items in the SELECT list, each truncating a date literal to a different degree of precision.

The first item sets the time component of 13:00 to 00:00 and returns the current day. The second item truncates the date to the same day of the week as the first day of the month and returns 01-JUN-2009. The third item truncates the date to the beginning of the current month and returns 01-JUN-2009. The fourth item is truncated to the date at the beginning of the current year and returns 01-JAN-2009.

CERTIFICATION SUMMARY

Single-row functions exponentially enhance the data manipulation possibilities offered by SQL statements. These functions execute once for each row of data selected. They may be used in SELECT, WHERE, and ORDER BY clauses in a SELECT statement.

The black box nature of the built-in PL/SQL functions was discussed and a distinction between multiple and single-row functions was made. A high-level overview describing how character, numeric, and date information may be manipulated by single-row functions was provided before systematically exploring several key functions in detail.

Character-case conversion functions were described before introducing the character manipulation functions. The numeric functions ROUND, TRUNC, and MOD were discussed, but these represent the tip of the iceberg since Oracle provides a vast toolbox of mathematical and numeric functions. Date arithmetic and storage was briefly explored before taking a detailed look at the date functions.

There are numerous single-row functions available, and you are not required to memorize their every detail. Understanding the broad categories of single-row functions and being introduced to the common character, numeric, and date functions provides a starting point for your discovery of their usefulness.

✓ TWO-MINUTE DRILL

Describe Various Types of Functions Available in SQL

❑ Functions accept zero or more input parameters but always return one result of a predetermined data type.

❑ Single-row functions execute once for each row selected, while multiple-row functions execute once for the entire set of rows queried.

❑ Character functions are either case-conversion or character-manipulation functions.

Use Character, Number, and Date Functions in SELECT Statements

❑ The INITCAP function accepts a string of characters and returns each word in title case.

❑ The function that computes the number of characters in a string including spaces and special characters is the LENGTH function.

❑ The INSTR function returns the positional location of the *nth* occurrence of a specified string of characters in a source string.

❑ The SUBSTR function extracts and returns a segment from a given source string.

❑ The REPLACE function substitutes each occurrence of a search item in the source string with a replacement term and returns the modified source string.

❑ A modulus operation returns the remainder of a division operation and is available via the MOD function.

❑ The numeric ROUND function rounds numbers either up or down to the specified degree of precision.

❑ The SYSDATE function is traditionally executed against the DUAL table and returns current date and time of the database server.

❑ Date types store century, year, month, day, hour, minutes, and seconds information.

❑ The difference between two date items is always a number that represents the number of days between these two items.

❑ Any number, including fractions, may be added to or subtracted from a date item and in this context the number represents a specified number of days.

❑ The MONTHS_BETWEEN function computes the number of months between two given date parameters and is based on a 31-day month.

❑ The LAST_DAY function is used to obtain the last day in a month given any valid date item.

SELF TEST

The following questions will help you measure your understanding of the material presented in this chapter. Read all the choices carefully because there might be more than one correct answer. Choose all the correct answers for each question.

Describe Various Types of Functions Available in SQL

1. Which statements regarding single-row functions are true? (Choose all that apply.)
- **A.** They may return more than one result.
- **B.** They execute once for each record processed.
- **C.** They may have zero or more input parameters.
- **D.** They must have at least one mandatory parameter.

2. Which of these are single-row character-case conversion functions? (Choose all that apply.)
- **A.** LOWER
- **B.** SMALLER
- **C.** INITCASE
- **D.** INITCAP

Use Character, Number, and Date Functions in SELECT Statements

3. What value is returned after executing the following statement:
SELECT LENGTH('How_long_is_a_piece_of_string?') FROM DUAL; (Choose the best answer.)
- **A.** 29
- **B.** 30
- **C.** 24
- **D.** None of the above

4. What value is returned after executing the following statement:
SELECT SUBSTR('How_long_is_a_piece_of_string?', 5,4) FROM DUAL; (Choose the best answer.)
- **A.** long
- **B.** _long
- **C.** string?
- **D.** None of the above

5. What value is returned after executing the following statement?
   SELECT INSTR('How_long_is_a_piece_of_string?','_',5,3) FROM DUAL; (Choose the best answer.)

   A. 4

   B. 14

   C. 12

   D. None of the above

6. What value is returned after executing the following statement?
   SELECT REPLACE('How_long_is_a_piece_of_string?','_','') FROM DUAL; (Choose the best answer.)

   A. How long is a piece of string?

   B. How_long_is_a_piece_of_string?

   C. Howlongisapieceofstring?

   D. None of the above

7. What value is returned after executing the following statement?
   SELECT MOD(14,3) FROM DUAL; (Choose the best answer.)

   A. 3

   B. 42

   C. 2

   D. None of the above

8. Assuming SYSDATE=07-JUN-1996 12:05pm, what value is returned after executing the following statement?
   SELECT ADD_MONTHS(SYSDATE,-1) FROM DUAL; (Choose the best answer.)

   A. 07-MAY-1996 12:05pm

   B. 06-JUN-1996 12:05pm

   C. 07-JUL-1996 12:05pm

   D. None of the above

9. What value is returned after executing the following statement? Take note that 01-JAN-2009 occurs on a Thursday. (Choose the best answer.)
   SELECT NEXT_DAY('01-JAN-2009','wed') FROM DUAL;

   A. 07-JAN-2009

   B. 31-JAN-2009

   C. Wednesday

   D. None of the above

10. Assuming SYSDATE=30-DEC-2007, what value is returned after executing the following statement?
SELECT TRUNC(SYSDATE,'YEAR') FROM DUAL; (Choose the best answer.)

A. 31-DEC-2007

B. 01-JAN-2008

C. 01-JAN-2007

D. None of the above

LAB QUESTION

Using SQL Developer or SQL*Plus, connect to the OE schema and complete the following tasks.

Several quotations were requested for prices on color printers. The supplier information is not available from the usual source, but you know that the supplier identification number is embedded in the CATALOG_URL column from the PRODUCT_INFORMATION table. You are required to retrieve the PRODUCT_NAME and CATALOG_URL values and to extract the supplier number from the CATALOG_URL column for all products which have both the words COLOR and PRINTER in the PRODUCT_DESCRIPTION column stored in any case.

SELF TEST ANSWERS

Describe Various Types of Functions Available in SQL

1. ☑ **B** and **C.** Single-row functions execute once for every record selected in a dataset and may either take no input parameters, like SYSDATE, or many input parameters.
    ☒ **A** and **D** are incorrect because a function by definition returns only one result and there are many functions with no parameters.

2. ☑ **A** and **D.** The LOWER function converts the case of the input string parameter to its lowercase equivalent, while INITCAP converts the given input parameter to title case.
    ☒ **B** and **C** are not valid function names.

Use Character, Number, and Date Functions in SELECT Statements

3. ☑ **B.** The LENGTH function computes the number of characters in a given input string including spaces, tabs, punctuation mark, and other nonprintable special characters.
    ☒ **A, C,** and **D** are incorrect.

4. ☑ **A.** The SUBSTR function extracts a four-character substring from the given input string starting with and including the fifth character. The characters at positions 1 to 4 are How_. Starting with the character at position 5, the next four characters form the word "long."
    ☒ **B, C,** and **D** are incorrect because **B** is a five-character substring beginning at position 4, while ring?, which is also five characters long, starts five characters from the end of the given string.

5. ☑ **B.** The INSTR function returns the position that the *nth* occurrence of the search string may be found after starting the search from a given start position. The search string is the underscore character, and the third occurrence of this character starting from position 5 in the source string occurs at position 14.
    ☒ **A, C,** and **D** are incorrect since position 4 is the first occurrence of the search string and position 12 is the third occurrence if the search began at position 1.

6. ☑ **C.** All occurrences of the underscore character are replaced by an empty string, which removes them from the string.
    ☒ **A, B,** and **D** are incorrect. **A** is incorrect because the underscore characters are not replaced by spaces, and **B** does not change the source string.

7. ☑ **C.** When 14 is divided by 3, the answer is 4 with remainder 2.
    ☒ **A, B,** and **D** are incorrect.

8. ☑ **A.** The minus one parameter indicates to the ADD_MONTHS function that the date to be returned must be one month prior to the given date.

☒ **B, C,** and **D** are incorrect. **B** is one day and not one month prior to the given date. **C** is one month after the given date.

9. ☑ **A.** Since the first of January 2009 falls on a Thursday, the date of the following Wednesday is six days later.

☒ **B, C,** and **D** are incorrect. **B** returns the last day of the month in which the given date falls, and **C** returns a character string instead of a date.

10. ☑ **C.** The date TRUNC function does not perform rounding and since the degree of truncation is YEAR, the day and month components of the given date are ignored and the first day of the year it belongs to is returned.

☒ **A, B,** and **D** are incorrect. **A** returns the last day in the month in which the given date occurs, and **B** returns a result achieved by rounding instead of truncation.

LAB ANSWER

Using SQL Developer or SQL*Plus, connect to the OE schema, complete the following tasks.

1. Start SQL Developer and connect to the OE schema.

2. A typical CATALOG_URL entry looks as follows: www.supp-102094.com/cat/hw/p1797.html. The supplier identification number is consistently six characters long and starts from the seventeenth character of the CATALOG_URL value. The SUBSTR function is used to extract this value.

3. The SELECT clause is therefore
SELECT PRODUCT_NAME, CATALOG_URL, SUBSTR(CATALOG_URL, 17, 6) SUPPLIER

4. The FROM clause is
FROM PRODUCT_INFORMATION

5. The records retrieved must be limited to those containing both the words COLOR and PRINTER. These words may occur in any order and may be present in uppercase or lowercase or mixed case. Any of the case conversion functions may be used to deal with case issues, but because the two words can occur in any order, two conditions are necessary. The UPPER function will be used for case conversion for comparison.

6. The first condition is
UPPER(PRODUCT_DESCRIPTION) LIKE '%COLOR%'

7. The second condition is
   UPPER(PRODUCT_DESCRIPTION) LIKE '%PRINTER%'

8. The WHERE clause is
   WHERE UPPER(PRODUCT_DESCRIPTION) LIKE '%COLOR%' AND
   UPPER(PRODUCT_DESCRIPTION) LIKE '%PRINTER%'

9. Executing the statement returns the set of results matching this pattern as shown in the
   following illustration:

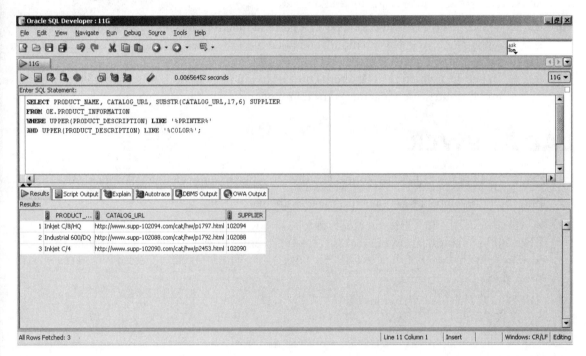

5

Using Conversion Functions and Conditional Expressions

CERTIFICATION OBJECTIVES

Functions that operate on numeric, date, and character information were discussed in Chapter 4, and familiarity with that content is assumed in this chapter. Sometimes data is not available in the exact format a function is defined to accept, resulting in a data type mismatch. To avoid mismatch errors, Oracle implicitly converts compatible data types. Implicit conversion is discussed before introducing explicit conversion functions, which are used for reliable data type conversions.

The concept of nesting functions is defined and a category of general functions aimed at simplifying interactions with NULL values is introduced. These include the NVL, NVL2, NULLIF, and COALESCE functions.

Conditional logic, or the ability to display different results depending on data values, is exposed by the conditional functions CASE and DECODE. These functions provide *if-then-else* logic in the context of a SQL query.

CERTIFICATION OBJECTIVE 5.01

Describe Various Types of Conversion Functions Available in SQL

SQL conversion *functions* are single row functions designed to alter the nature of the data type of a column value, expression or literal. *TO_CHAR*, *TO_NUMBER* and *TO_DATE* are the three most widely used conversion functions and are discussed in detail. The TO_CHAR function converts numeric and date information into characters, while TO_NUMBER and TO_DATE convert character data into numbers and dates, respectively. The concepts of implicit and explicit data type conversion are discussed in the next section.

Conversion Functions

Oracle allows columns to be defined with ANSI, DB2, and SQL/DS data types. These are converted internally to Oracle data types. This approach allows applications written for other database systems to be migrated to Oracle with ease.

Table definitions are obtained using the DESCRIBE command discussed in Chapter 2. Each column has an associated data type that constrains the nature of the data it can store. A NUMBER column cannot store character information. A DATE column cannot store random characters or numbers. However, the character equivalents of both number and date information can be stored in a VARCHAR2 field.

If a function that accepts a character input parameter finds a number instead, Oracle automatically converts it into its character equivalent. If a function that accepts a number or a date parameter encounters a character value, there are specific conditions under which automatic data type conversion occurs. DATE and NUMBER data types are very strict compared to VARCHAR2 and CHAR.

Although implicit data type conversions are available, it is more reliable to explicitly convert values from one data type to another using single-row conversion functions. Converting character information to NUMBER and DATE relies on format masks, which are discussed later in this section.

on the *When numeric values are supplied as input to functions expecting character* **Job** *parameters, implicit data type conversion ensures that they are treated as character values. Similarly, character strings consisting of numeric digits are implicitly converted into numeric values if possible when a data type mismatch occurs. But be wary of implicit conversions. There are some cases when it does not work as expected, as in the following WHERE clause. Consider limiting data from a table T based on a character column C, which contains the string '100'. The condition clause WHERE C='100' works as you might expect, but the condition WHERE C=100 returns an invalid number error.*

Implicit Data Type Conversion

Values that do not share identical data types with function parameters are *implicitly converted* to the required format if possible. VARCHAR2 and CHAR data types are collectively referred to as character types. Character fields are flexible and allow the storage of almost any type of information. Therefore, DATE and NUMBER values can easily be converted to their character equivalents. These conversions are known as *number to character* and *date to character* conversions. Consider the following queries:

```
Query 1: select length(1234567890) from dual
Query 2: select length(SYSDATE) from dual
```

Both queries use the LENGTH function, which takes a character string parameter. The number 1234567890 in query 1 is implicitly converted into a character string, '1234567890', before being evaluated by the LENGTH function, which returns the number 10. Query 2 first evaluates the SYSDATE function, which is assumed to be 07-APR-38. This date is implicitly converted into the character string '07-APR-38', and the LENGTH function returns the number 9.

It is uncommon for character data to be implicitly converted into numeric data types since the only condition under which this occurs is if the character data represents a valid number. The character string '11' will be implicitly converted to a number, but '11.123.456' will not be, as the following queries demonstrate:

```
Query 3: select mod('11',2) from dual
Query 4: select mod('11.123',2) from dual
Query 5: select mod('11.123.456',2) from dual
Query 6: select mod('$11',2) from dual
```

Queries 3 and 4 implicitly convert the character strings '11' and '11.123' into the numbers 11 and 11.123, respectively, before the MOD function evaluates them and returns the results 1 and 1.123. Query 5 returns the error "ORA-1722: invalid number," when Oracle tries to perform an implicit *character to number* conversion. It fails because the string '11.123.456' is not a valid number. Query 6 also fails with the invalid number error, since the dollar symbol cannot be implicitly converted into a number.

Implicit *character to date* conversions are possible when the character string conforms to the following date patterns: [D | DD] *separator1* [MON | MONTH] *separator2* [R | RR | YY | YYYY]. D and DD represent a single and 2-digit day of the month. MON is a 3-character abbreviation, while MONTH is the full name for a month. R and RR represent a single and 2-digit year. YY and YYYY represent a 2- and 4-digit year, respectively. The *separator1* and *separator2* elements may be most punctuation marks, spaces, and tabs. Table 5-1 demonstrates implicit character to date conversion, listing several function calls and the results SQL Developer returns.

TABLE 5-1	Function Call	Format	Results
Examples of Implicit Character to Date Conversion	add_months('24-JAN-09',1)	DD-MON-RR	24/FEB/09
	add_months('1 \january/8',1)	D\MONTH/R	01/FEB/08
	months_between('13*jan*8', '13/feb/2008')	DD*MON*R, DD/MON/YYYY	−1
	add_months('01$jan/08',1)	DD$MON/RR	01/FEB/08
	add_months('13!jana08',1)	JANA is an invalid month	ORA-1841: (full) year must be between −4713 and +9999 and not be 0
	add_months('24-JAN-09 18:45',1)	DD-MON-RR HH24:MI	ORA-1830: date format picture ends before converting entire input string

Explicit Data Type Conversion

Oracle offers many functions to convert items from one data type to another, known as *explicit* data type conversion functions. These return a value guaranteed to be the type required and offer a safe and reliable method of converting data items.

NUMBER and DATE items can be converted explicitly into character items using the TO_CHAR function. A character string can be explicitly changed into a NUMBER using the TO_NUMBER function. The TO_DATE function is used to convert character strings into DATE items. Oracle's format masks enable a wide range of control over *character to number* and *character to date* conversions.

exam
ⓦatch

The explicit conversion functions are critical to manipulating date, character, and numeric information. Questions on this topic test your understanding of commonly used format models or masks. Practical usage questions typically take the form, "What is returned when the TO_DATE, TO_CHAR, and

TO_NUMBER functions are applied to the following data values and format masks?" These are often nested within broader functions, and it is common to be asked to predict the result of a function call such as TO_CHAR(TO_DATE('01-JAN-00', 'DD-MON-RR),'Day').

CERTIFICATION OBJECTIVE 5.02

Use the TO_CHAR, TO_NUMBER, and TO_DATE Conversion Functions

This certification objective contains a systematic description of the TO_NUMBER, TO_DATE, and TO_CHAR functions, with examples. The discussion of TO_CHAR is divided into the conversion of two types of items to characters: DATE and NUMBER. This separation is warranted by the availability of different format masks for controlling conversion to character values. These conversion functions exist alongside many others but tend to be the most widely used. This section focuses on the practicalities of using the conversion functions.

Using the Conversion Functions

Many situations demand the use of conversion functions. They may range from formatting DATE fields in a report to ensuring that numeric digits extracted from character fields are correctly converted into numbers before applying them in an arithmetic expression.

Table 5-2 illustrates the syntax of the single-row explicit data type conversion functions.

Optional national language support parameters (nls_parameters) are useful for specifying the language and format in which the names of date and numeric elements are returned. These parameters are usually absent, and the default values for elements such as day or month names and abbreviations are used. As Figure 5-1 shows, there is a publicly available view called NLS_SESSION_PARAMETERS that contains the NLS parameters for your current session. The default NLS_CURRENCY value is the dollar symbol, but this can be changed at the user session level. For example, to change the currency to the 3-character-long string GBP, the following command may be issued:

```
ALTER SESSION set NLS_CURRENCY='GBP';
```

Converting Numbers to Characters Using the TO_CHAR Function

The TO_CHAR function returns an item of data type VARCHAR2. When applied to items of type NUMBER, several formatting options are available. The syntax is as follows:

TO_CHAR(*number1*, *[format]*, *[nls_parameter]*),

The *number1* parameter is mandatory and must be a value that either is or can be implicitly converted into a number. The optional *format* parameter may be used to specify numeric formatting information like width, currency symbol, the position of a decimal point, and group (or thousands) separators and must be enclosed in single

TABLE 5-2	TO_NUMBER(*char1*, [format mask], [nls_parameters]) = *num1*	TO_CHAR(*num1*, [format mask], [nls_parameters]) = *char1*
Syntax of Explicit Data Type Conversion Functions	TO_DATE(*char1*, [format mask], [nls_parameters]) = *date1*	TO_CHAR(*date1*, [format mask], [nls_parameters]) = *char1*

FIGURE 5-1   National Language Support (NLS) session parameters

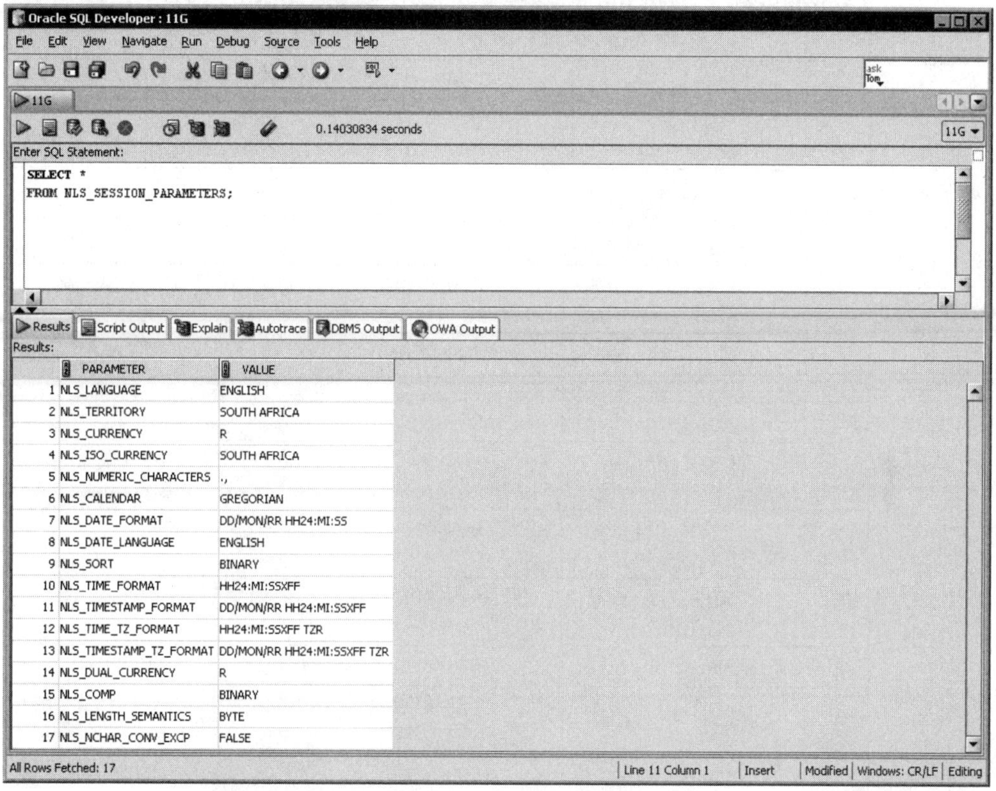

quotation marks. There are other formatting options for numbers being converted into characters, some of which are listed in Table 5-3. Consider the following two queries:

```
Query 1: select to_char(00001)||' is a special number' from dual;
Query 2: select to_char(00001,'0999999')||' is a special number'
from dual;
```

Query 1 evaluates the number 00001, removes the leading zeros, converts the number 1 into the character '1' and returns the character string '1 is a special number'. Query 2 applies the numeric format mask '0999999' to the number 00001, converting it into the character string '0000001'. After concatenation to the character literals, the string returned is '0000001 is a special number'. The zero and 6 nines in the format mask indicate to the TO_CHAR function that leading zeros must be displayed and that the display width must be set to seven characters. Therefore, the string returned by the TO_CHAR function contains seven characters.

	Format Element	Description of Element	Format	Number	Character Result
TABLE 5-3	9	Numeric width	9999	12	12
Numeric Format Masks	0	Displays leading zeros	09999	0012	00012
	.	Position of decimal point	09999.999	030.40	00030.400
	D	Decimal separator position (period is default)	09999D999	030.40	00030.400
	,	Position of comma symbol	09999,999	03040	00003,040
	G	Group separator position (comma is default)	09999G999	03040	00003,040
	$	Dollar sign	$099999	03040	$003040
	L	Local currency	L099999	03040	GBP003040 if nls_currency is set to GBP
	MI	Position of minus sign for negatives	99999MI	−3040	3040−
	PR	Wrap negatives in parentheses	99999PR	−3040	<3040>
	EEEE	Scientific notation	99.99999EEEE	121.976	1.21976E+02
	U	nls_dual_currency	U099999	03040	CAD003040 if nls_dual_currency is set to CAD
	V	Multiplies by 10n times (n is the number of nines after V)	9999V99	3040	304000
	S	+ or − sign is prefixed	S999999	3040	+3040

The query in Figure 5-2 retrieves the JOB_TITLE and MAX_SALARY columns from the JOBS table for the rows with the word "president" in the JOB_TITLE column. MAX_SALARY has further been formatted to have a dollar currency symbol, a comma thousands separator, and a decimal point. When a format mask is smaller than the number being converted, as illustrated in the fourth item in the SELECT list, a string of hash symbols is returned instead. When a format mask contains fewer fractional components than the number, it is first rounded to the number of decimal places in the format mask before being converted.

FIGURE 5-2   TO_CHAR function with numbers

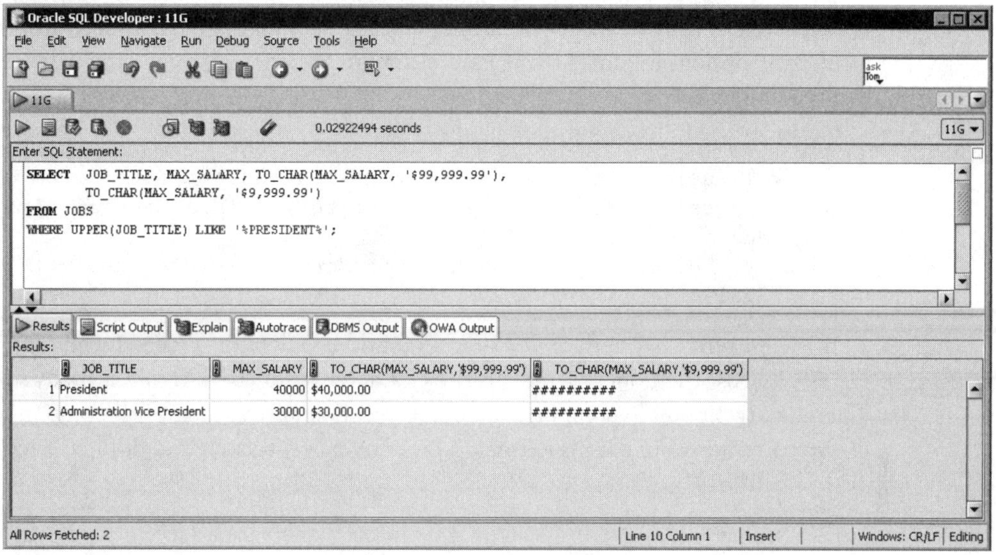

```
Oracle SQL Developer : 11G                                                    _ □ ×
File  Edit  View  Navigate  Run  Debug  Source  Tools  Help

[toolbar icons]                                                          ask
                                                                        Tom

▷11G                                                                    ◀ ▶ ▼

▷ [toolbar icons]        [icons]        0.02922494 seconds              11G ▼
Enter SQL Statement:
  SELECT  JOB_TITLE, MAX_SALARY, TO_CHAR(MAX_SALARY, '$99,999.99'),
        TO_CHAR(MAX_SALARY, '$9,999.99')
  FROM  JOBS
  WHERE UPPER(JOB_TITLE) LIKE '%PRESIDENT%';



◀                                                                           ▶
▷ Results  Script Output  Explain  Autotrace  DBMS Output  OWA Output
Results:
    JOB_TITLE            MAX_SALARY  TO_CHAR(MAX_SALARY,'$99,999.99')  TO_CHAR(MAX_SALARY,'$9,999.99')
  1 President                 40000  $40,000.00                        ##########
  2 Administration Vice President  30000  $30,000.00                   ##########



All Rows Fetched: 2                          Line 10 Column 1  Insert      Windows: CR/LF  Editing
```

on the Job   *Converting numbers into characters is a reliable way to ensure that functions and general SQL syntax, which expects character input, do not return errors when numbers are encountered. Converting numbers into character strings is common when numeric data must be formatted for reporting purposes. The format masks that support currency, thousands separators, and decimal point separators are frequently used when presenting financial data.*

Converting Dates to Characters Using the TO_CHAR Function

You can take advantage of a variety of format models to convert DATE items into almost any character representation of a date using TO_CHAR. Its syntax is as follows:

TO_CHAR(*date1*, [*format*], [*nls_parameter*]),

Only the *date1* parameter is mandatory and must take the form of a value that can be implicitly converted to a date. The optional *format* parameter is case sensitive and must be enclosed in single quotes. The format mask specifies which date elements are extracted and whether the element should be described by a long or an abbreviated name. The names of days and months are automatically padded with spaces. These may be removed using a modifier to the format mask called the fill mode (*fm*) operator. By prefixing the format model with the letters fm, Oracle is instructed to trim all spaces from the names of days and months. There are many formatting options for dates being converted into characters, some of which are listed in Table 5-4.

Consider the following three queries:

```
Query 1: select to_char(sysdate)||' is today''s date' from dual;
Query 2: select to_char(sysdate,'Month')||'is a special time'
from dual;
Query 3: select to_char(sysdate,'fmMonth')||'is a special time'
from dual;
```

If the current system date is 03/JAN/09 and the default display format is DD/MON/RR, then query 1 returns the character string '03/JAN/09 is today's date'. There are two notable components in query 2. First, only the month component of the current system date is extracted for conversion to a character type. Second,

TABLE 5-4	Format Element	Description	Result
Date Format Masks for Days, Months, and Years	Y	Last digit of year	5
	YY	Last two digits of year	75
	YYY	Last three digits of year	975
	YYYY	Four-digit year	1975
	RR	Two-digit year (see Chapter 3 for details)	75
	YEAR	Case-sensitive English spelling of year	NINETEEN SEVENTY-FIVE
	MM	Two-digit month	06
	MON	Three-letter abbreviation of month	JUN
	MONTH	Case-sensitive English spelling of month	JUNE
	D	Day of the week	2
	DD	Two-digit day of month	02
	DDD	Day of the year	153
	DY	Three-letter abbreviation of day	MON
	DAY	Case-sensitive English spelling of day	MONDAY

since the format mask is case sensitive and 'Month' appears in title case, the string returned is 'January is a special time'. There is no need to add a space in front of the literal 'is a special time' since the TO_CHAR function automatically pads the name of the month with a space. If the format mask in query 2 was 'MONTH', the string returned would be 'JANUARY is a special time'. The *fm* modifier is applied to query 3, and the resultant string is 'January is a special time'. Note there is no space between January and the literal 'is a special time'. In Table 5-4, assume the elements are operating on the date 02-JUN-1975 and the current year is 2009.

The date format elements pertaining to weeks, quarters, centuries, and other less commonly used format masks are listed in Table 5-5. The result column is obtained by evaluating the TO_CHAR function using the date 24-SEP-1000 BC, with the format mask from the format element column in the table.

The time component of a date time data type is extracted using the format models in Table 5-6. The result is obtained by evaluating the TO_CHAR function using the date including its time component 27-JUN-2010 21:35:13, with the format mask in the format element column in Table 5-6.

TABLE 5-5	**Format Element**	**Description**	**Result**
Less Commonly Used Date Format Masks	W	Week of month	4
	WW	Week of year	39
	Q	Quarter of year	3
	CC	Century	10
	S preceding CC, YYYY, or YEAR	If date is BC, a minus is prefixed to result	–10, –1000 or –ONE THOUSAND
	IYYY,IYY,IY,I	ISO dates of four, three, two, and one digit, respectively	1000, 000, 00, 0
	BC, AD, B.C. and A.D.	BC or AD and period spaced B.C. or A.D.	BC
	J	Julian day—days since 31 December 4713 BC	1356075
	IW	ISO standard week (1 to 53)	39
	RM	Roman numeral month	IX

TABLE 5-6	Format Element	Description	Result
	AM, PM, A.M. and P.M.	Meridian indicators	PM
Date Format Mask for Time Components	HH, HH12 and HH24	Hour of day, 1–12 hours, and 0–23 hours	09, 09, 21
	MI	Minute (0–59)	35
	SS	Second (0–59)	13
	SSSSS	Seconds past midnight (0–86399)	77713

Several other elements that may be used in date time format models are summarized in Table 5-7. Punctuation marks are used to separate format elements. Three types of suffixes exist to format components of date time elements. Furthermore, character literals may be included in a date format model if they are enclosed in double quotation marks. The results in Table 5-7 are obtained by applying the TO_CHAR function using the date 12/SEP/08 14:31 with the format masks listed in the description and format mask column.

The JOB_HISTORY table keeps track of jobs occupied by employees in the company. The query in Figure 5-3 retrieves a descriptive sentence about the quitting date for each employee based on their END_DATE, EMPLOYEE_ID, and JOB_ID fields. A character expression is concatenated to a TO_CHAR function call with a format model of: 'fmDay "the "ddth "of" Month YYYY'. The fm modifier is used to trim blank spaces that trail the names of the shorter days and shorter months. The two character literals enclosed in double quotation marks are the words: "the" and "of". The 'th' format model is applied to the 'dd' date element to create an ordinal

TABLE 5-7	Format Element	Description and Format Mask	Result
	-/.,?#!	Punctuation marks: 'MM.YY'	09.08
Miscellaneous Date Format Masks	"any character literal"	Character literals: '"Week" W "of" Month'	Week 2 of September
	TH	Positional or ordinal text: 'DDth "of" Month'	12TH of September
	SP	Spelled out number: 'MmSP Month Yyyysp'	Nine September Two Thousand Eight
	THSP or SPTH	Spelled out positional or ordinal number: 'hh24SpTh'	Fourteenth

FIGURE 5-3   TO_CHAR function with dates

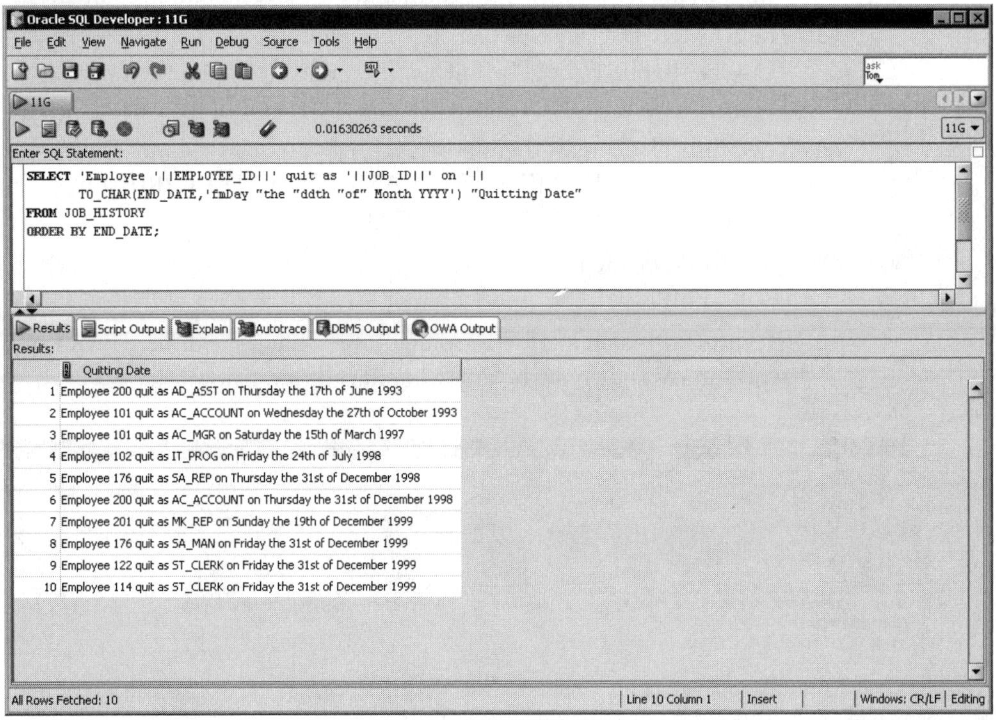

day such as the 17th or 31st. The 'Month' format model displays the full name of the month element of the END_DATE column in title case. Finally, the YYYY format mask retrieves the 4-digit year component.

EXERCISE 5-1

Converting Dates into Characters Using the TO_CHAR Function

You are required to retrieve a list of FIRST_NAME and LAST_NAME values and an expression based on the HIRE_DATE column for employees hired on a Saturday. The expression must be aliased as START_DATE and a HIRE_DATE value of 17-FEB-1996 must return the following string:

Saturday, the 17th of February, One Thousand Nine Hundred Ninety-Six.

1. Start SQL Developer and connect to the HR schema.

2. The WHERE clause is
WHERE TO_CHAR(HIRE_DATE,'fmDay') = 'Saturday'

The *fm* modifier is necessary to remove trailing blanks since a comparison with a character literal is performed and an exact match is required.

3. The START_DATE expression is
   TO_CHAR(HIRE_DATE, 'fmDay, "the "ddth "of" Month, Yyyysp.')
   The year format mask results in it being spelled out in title case.

4. The SELECT clause is therefore
   SELECT FIRST_NAME, LAST_NAME, TO_CHAR(HIRE_DATE, 'fmDay, "the "ddth "of" Month, Yyyysp.') START_DATE

5. The FROM clause is
   FROM EMPLOYEES

6. Executing this statement returns employees' names and the START_DATE expression as shown in the following illustration below:

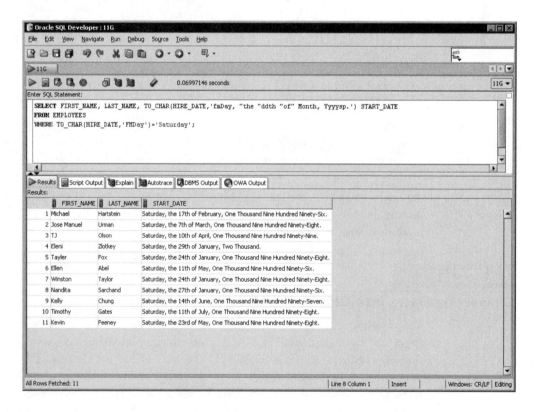

Converting Characters to Dates Using the TO_DATE Function

The TO_DATE function returns an item of type DATE. Character strings converted to dates may contain all or just a subset of the date time elements comprising a DATE. When strings with only a subset of the date time elements are converted, Oracle provides default values to construct a complete date. Components of character strings are associated with different date time elements using a format model or mask. The syntax is as follows:

TO_DATE(*string1*, *[format]*, *[nls_parameter]*),

Only the *string1* parameter is mandatory and if no format mask is supplied, *string1* must take the form of a value that can be implicitly converted into a date. The optional *format* parameter is almost always used and is specified in single quotation marks. The format masks are identical to those listed in Tables 5-4, 5-5, and 5-6. The TO_DATE function has an *fx* modifier which is similar to *fm* used with the TO_CHAR function. *fx* specifies an exact match for *string1* and the format mask. When the *fx* modifier is specified, character items that do not exactly match the format mask yield an error. Consider the following five queries:

```
Query 1: select to_date('25-DEC-2010') from dual;
Query 2: select to_date('25-DEC') from dual;
Query 3: select to_date('25-DEC', 'DD-MON') from dual;
Query 4: select to_date('25-DEC-2010 18:03:45', 'DD-MON-YYYY
HH24:MI:SS') from dual;
Query 5: select to_date('25-DEC-10', 'fxDD-MON-YYYY') from dual;
```

Query 1 evaluates the string 25-DEC-2010 and has sufficient information to implicitly convert it into a DATE item with a default mask of DD-MON-YYYY. The hyphen separator could be substituted with another punctuation character. Since no time components are provided, the time for this converted date is set to midnight or 00:00:00. Query 2 cannot implicitly convert the string into a date because there is insufficient information and an "ORA-01840: input value is not long enough for date format" error is returned. By supplying a format mask DD-MON to the string 25-DEC in query 3, Oracle can match the number 25 to DD and the abbreviated month name DEC to the MON component. Year and time components are absent, so the current year returned by the SYSDATE function is used and the time is set to midnight. If the current year is 2009, query 3 returns the date 25/DEC/09 00:00:00. Query 4 performs a complete conversion of a string with all the date time elements present, and no default values are supplied by Oracle. Query 5 uses the *fx* modifier in its format mask. Since the year component of the string is 10 and the corresponding format mask is YYYY, the *fx* modifier results in an "ORA-01862: the numeric value does not match the length of the format item" error being returned.

FIGURE 5-4   The TO_DATE function

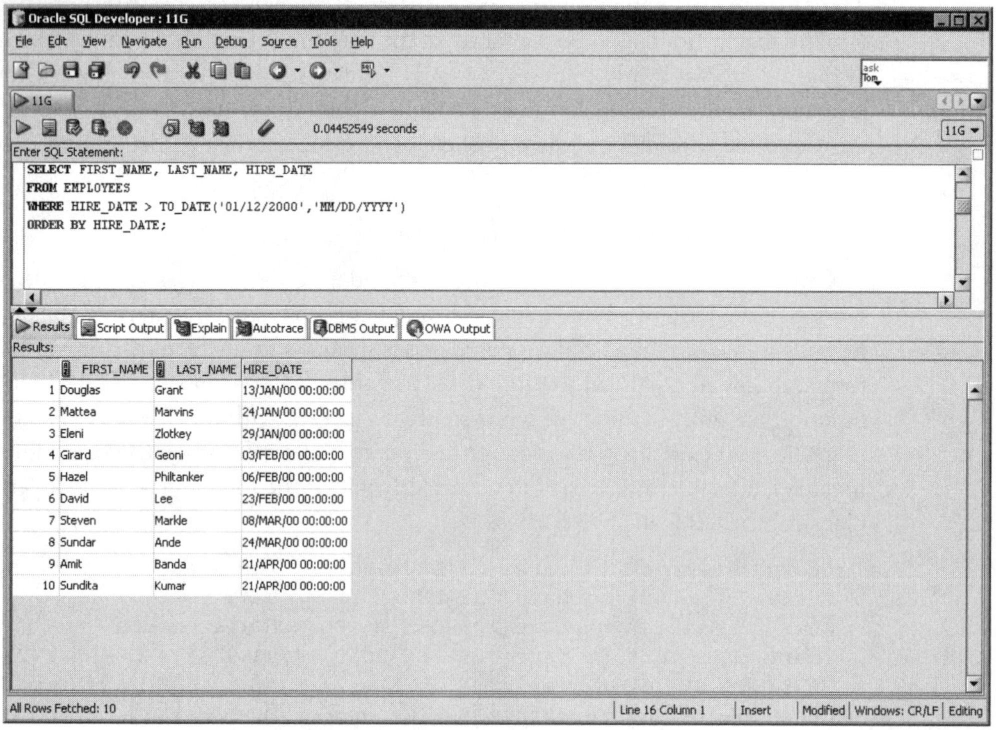

The TO_DATE function is used in the WHERE clause in Figure 5-4 to limit the rows returned for those employees hired after 12 January 2000. The format mask matches 01 to MM, 12 to DD and 2000 to YYYY.

Converting Characters to Numbers Using the TO_NUMBER Function

The TO_NUMBER function returns an item of type NUMBER. Character strings converted into numbers must be suitably formatted so that any nonnumeric components are translated or stripped away with an appropriate format mask. The syntax is as follows:

TO_NUMBER(*string1*, *[format]*, *[nls_parameter]*),

SCENARIO & SOLUTION

Your task is to extract the day and month portion of a date column and compare it with the corresponding components of the current system date. Can such a comparison be performed?	Yes. The TO_CHAR function used on a date item with a format mask like 'DD-MON' causes the day and month component to be isolated. This value can be compared with the current system date using the following expression: TO_CHAR(SYSDATE, 'DD-MON')
A report of profit and loss is required with the results displayed as follows: if the amount is negative, it must be enclosed in angle brackets. The amount must be displayed with a leading dollar sign. Can results be retrieved in the specified format?	Yes. The numeric amount must be converted into a character string using the TO_CHAR function with a format mask that encloses it in angle brackets if it is negative and precedes it with a dollar sign. The following function call retrieves the results in the required format: TO_CHAR(AMOUNT, '$999999PR')
You are asked to input past employee data into the JOB_HISTORY table from a paper-based source, but the start date information is only available as the year the employee started. Can this value be converted into the first of January of the year?	Yes. Consider the conversion function call TO_DATE('2000','YYYY') for an employee who started in the year 2000. If this date is extracted as follows, the character string 01/01/2000 is returned TO_CHAR(TO_DATE('2000','YYYY'), 'MM/DD/YYYY')

Only the *string1* parameter is mandatory and if no *format* mask is supplied, it must be a value that can be implicitly converted into a number. The optional *format* parameter is specified in single quotation marks. The format masks are identical to those listed in Table 5-3. Consider the following two queries:

```
Query 1: select to_number('$1,000.55') from dual;
Query 2: select to_number('$1,000.55','$999,999.99') from dual;
```

Query 1 cannot perform an implicit conversion to a number because of the dollar sign, comma, and period and returns the error, "ORA-1722: invalid number." Query 2 matches the dollar symbol, comma, and period from the string to the format mask and, although the numeric width is larger than the string width, the number 1000.55 is returned.

Figure 5-5 shows how the SUBSTR function was first used to extract the last eight characters from the PHONE_NUMBER character column. The TO_NUMBER

FIGURE 5-5

FIGURE 5-5 The TO_NUMBER function

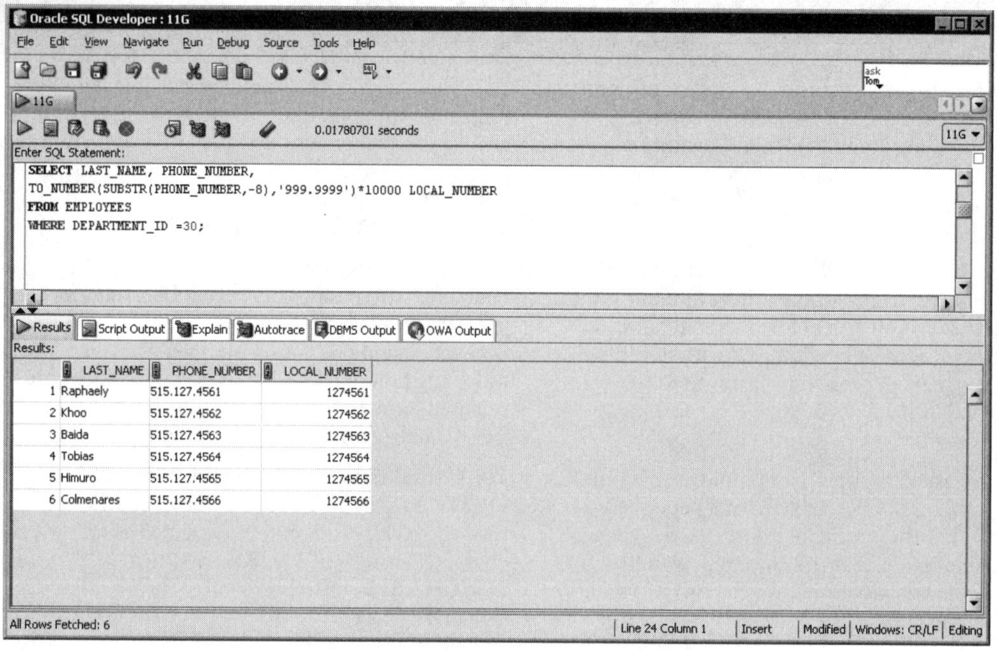

function was then used to convert these eight characters, including a decimal point, into a number which was multiplied by 10000, for employees belonging to DEPARTMENT_ID 30.

e x a m

ⓦatch

Read the exam questions very carefully. The TO_NUMBER function converts character items into numbers. If you convert a number using a shorter format mask, an error is returned. If you convert a number based on a longer format mask, the original number is returned. Be careful not to confuse TO_NUMBER conversions with TO_CHAR. For example, TO_NUMBER(123.56,'999.9') returns an error, while TO_CHAR(123.56,'999.9') returns 123.6.

Apply Conditional Expressions in a SELECT Statement

Nested functions were introduced in Chapter 4, but a formal discussion of this concept is provided in this section. Two new categories of functions are also introduced. These include the *general functions*, which provide the language for dealing effectively with NULL values, and the *conditional functions*, which support conditional logic in expressions. This certification objective covers the following areas:

- Nested functions
- General functions
- Conditional functions

Nested Functions

Nested functions use the output from one function as the input to another. Functions always return exactly one result. Therefore, you can reliably consider a function call in the same way as you would a literal value, when providing input parameters to a function. Single row functions can be nested to any level of depth. The general form of a function is as follows:

Function1(*parameter 1, parameter2,…*) = *result1*

Substituting function calls as parameters to other functions may lead to an expression such as the following:

F1(*param1.1,* F2(*param2.1, param2.2,* F3(*param3.1*)), *param1.3*)

Nested functions are first evaluated before their return values are used as parametric input to other functions. They are evaluated from the innermost to outermost levels. The preceding expression is evaluated as follows:

1. F3(*param3.1*) is evaluated and its return value provides the third parameter to function F2 and may be called: *param2.3.*
2. F2(*param2.1,param2.2,param2.3*) is evaluated and its return value provides the second parameter to function F1 and is *param1.2.*

3. F1(*param1.1*, *param1.2*, *param1.3*) is evaluated and the result is returned to the calling program.

Function F3 is said to be nested three levels deep in this example. Consider the following query:

```
select length(to_char(to_date('28/10/09', 'DD/MM/RR'),'fmMonth'))from dual;
```

There are three functions in the SELECT list which, from inner to outer levels, are TO_DATE, TO_CHAR and *LENGTH*. The query is evaluated as follows:

1. The innermost function is evaluated first. TO_DATE('28/10/09','DD/MM/RR') converts the character string 28/10/09 into the DATE value 28-OCT-2009. The RR format mask is used for the year portion. Therefore, the century component returned is the current century (the twenty-first), since the year component is between 0 and 49.

2. The second innermost function is evaluated next. TO_CHAR('28-OCT-2009', 'fmMonth') converts the given date based on the Month format mask and returns the character string October. The *fm* modifier trims trailing blank spaces from the name of the month.

3. Finally, the LENGTH('October') function is evaluated and the query returns the number 7.

SCENARIO & SOLUTION

Are nested functions evaluated from the outermost level to the innermost level?	No. Nested functions are resolved from the innermost nested level moving outward.
Must all functions in a nested expression return the same data type?	No. The data types of the parameters of nested functions may be different from each other. It is important to ensure that the correct data types are always supplied to functions to avoid errors.
Is there a simpler way to display the SALARY information from the EMPLOYEES table in the form $13,000 without using the following statement? SELECT '$' || SUBSTR(SALARY,1, MOD(LENGTH(SALARY),3)) || ',', ' || SUBSTR(SALARY, MOD (LENGTH(SALARY),3)+1)	Yes. A simple and elegant solution is to use the TO_CHAR function with the '$99G999' format mask SELECT TO_CHAR(SALARY, '$99G999') FROM EMPLOYEES;

General Functions

General functions simplify working with columns that potentially contain null values. These functions accept input parameters of all data types. The services they offer are primarily relevant to null values.

The functions examined in the next sections include the *NVL* function, which provides an alternative value to use if a null is encountered. The *NVL2* function performs a conditional evaluation of its first parameter and returns a value if a null is encountered and an alternative if the parameter is not null. The *NULLIF* function compares two terms and returns a null result if they are equal, otherwise it returns the first term. The *COALESCE* function accepts an unlimited number of parameters and returns the first nonnull parameter else it returns null.

The NVL Function

The NVL function evaluates whether a column or expression of any data type is null or not. If the term is null, an alternative not null value is returned; otherwise, the initial term is returned.

The NVL function takes two mandatory parameters. Its syntax is **NVL(*original, ifnull*)**, where *original* represents the term being tested and *ifnull* is the result returned if the *original* term evaluates to null. The data types of the *original* and *ifnull* parameters must always be compatible. They must either be of the same type, or it must be possible to implicitly convert *ifnull* to the type of the *original* parameter. The NVL function returns a value with the same data type as the *original* parameter. Consider the following three queries:

```
Query 1: select nvl(1234) from dual;
Query 2: select nvl(null,1234) from dual;
Query 3: select nvl(substr('abc',4),'No substring exists') from
dual;
```

Since the NVL function takes two mandatory parameters, query 1 returns the error, "ORA-00909: invalid number of arguments." Query 2 returns 1234 after the null keyword is tested and found to be null. Query 3 involves a nested SUBSTR function that attempts to extract the fourth character from a 3-character string. The inner function returns null, leaving the NVL(null,'No substring exists') function to execute, which then returns the string 'No substring exists'.

Figure 5-6 shows two almost identical queries. Both queries select rows where the LAST_NAME begins with the letter E. The LAST_NAME, SALARY, and COMMISSION_PCT columns are also selected. The difference between the queries is in the calculated expression aliased as MONTHLY_COMMISSION. Due to the NVL

FIGURE 5-6 The NVL function

```
Oracle SQL Developer : 11G                                                    _ □ ×
File  Edit  View  Navigate  Run  Debug  Source  Tools  Help

 ▷ 11G

 ▷  ■                                   0.5070225 seconds                      11G ▼
Enter SQL Statement:
  SELECT LAST_NAME, SALARY, COMMISSION_PCT, (NVL(COMMISSION_PCT,0)*SALARY + 1000) MONTHLY_COMMISSION
  FROM EMPLOYEES
  WHERE LAST_NAME LIKE 'E%';

  SELECT LAST_NAME, SALARY, COMMISSION_PCT, (COMMISSION_PCT*SALARY + 1000) MONTHLY_COMMISSION
  FROM EMPLOYEES
  WHERE LAST_NAME LIKE 'E%';

 ▷ Results  Script Output  Explain  Autotrace  DBMS Output  OWA Output

LAST_NAME                SALARY              COMMISSION_PCT          MONTHLY_COMMISSION
------------------------ ------------------- ----------------------- -----------------------
Ernst                    6000                                        1000
Errazuriz                12000               0.3                     4600
Everett                  3900                                        1000

3 rows selected

LAST_NAME                SALARY              COMMISSION_PCT          MONTHLY_COMMISSION
------------------------ ------------------- ----------------------- -----------------------
Ernst                    6000
Errazuriz                12000               0.3                     4600
Everett                  3900

3 rows selected


Script Finished                                  Line 11 Column 1   Insert        Windows: CR/LF  Editing
```

function in the first query, numeric results are returned. The second query returns some null values and one numeric item even though 1000 is added to each row.

It is tempting to dive in and construct a complex expression comprising many nested function calls, but this approach evolves with practice and experience. Conceptualize a solution to a query and break it down into the component function calls. The DUAL table is useful for ad hoc logical testing and debugging of separate function calls. Do not be afraid to execute queries as many times as you wish to perfect the components before assembling them into progressively larger components. Test and debug these until the final expression is formed.

The NVL2 Function

The NVL2 function provides an enhancement to NVL but serves a very similar purpose. It evaluates whether a column or expression of any data type is null or not.

If the first term is not null, the second parameter is returned, else the third parameter is returned. Recall that the NVL function is different since it returns the original term if it is not null.

The NVL2 function takes three mandatory parameters. Its syntax is NVL2(*original*, *ifnotnull*, *ifnull*), where *original* represents the term being tested. *Ifnotnull* is returned if *original* is not null, and *ifnull* is returned if *original* is null. The data types of the *ifnotnull* and *ifnull* parameters must be compatible, and they cannot be of type LONG. They must either be of the same type, or it must be possible to convert *ifnull* to the type of the *ifnotnull* parameter. The data type returned by the NVL2 function is the same as that of the *ifnotnull* parameter. Consider the following three queries:

```
Query 1: select nvl2(1234,1,'a string') from dual;
Query 2: select nvl2(null,1234,5678) from dual;
Query 3: select nvl2(substr('abc',2),'Not bc','No substring') from dual;
```

The *ifnotnull* term in query 1 is a number and the *ifnull* parameter is 'a string'. Since there is a data type incompatibility between them, an "ORA-01722: invalid number" error is returned. Query 2 returns the *ifnull* parameter, which is 5678. Query 3 extracts the characters "bc" using the SUBSTR function and the NVL2('bc',Not bc','No Substring') function is evaluated. The *ifnotnull* parameter, the string 'Not bc', is returned.

Figure 5-7 shows how the NVL2 function is used to provide descriptive text classifying employees with LAST_NAME values beginning with "F" into commission and noncommission earners based on the nullable COMMISSION_PCT column.

The NULLIF Function

The NULLIF function tests two terms for equality. If they are equal the function returns a null, else it returns the first of the two terms tested.

The NULLIF function takes two mandatory parameters of any data type. The syntax is NULLIF(*ifunequal*, *comparison_term*), where the parameters *ifunequal* and *comparison_term* are compared. If they are identical, then NULL is returned. If they differ, the *ifunequal* parameter is returned. Consider the following three queries:

```
Query 1: select nullif(1234,1234) from dual;
Query 2: select nullif(1234,123+1) from dual;
Query 3: select nullif('24-JUL-2009','24-JUL-09') from dual;
```

Query 1 returns a null value since the parameters are identical. The arithmetic equation in query 2 is not implicitly evaluated, and the NULLIF function finds

FIGURE 5-7   The NVL2 function

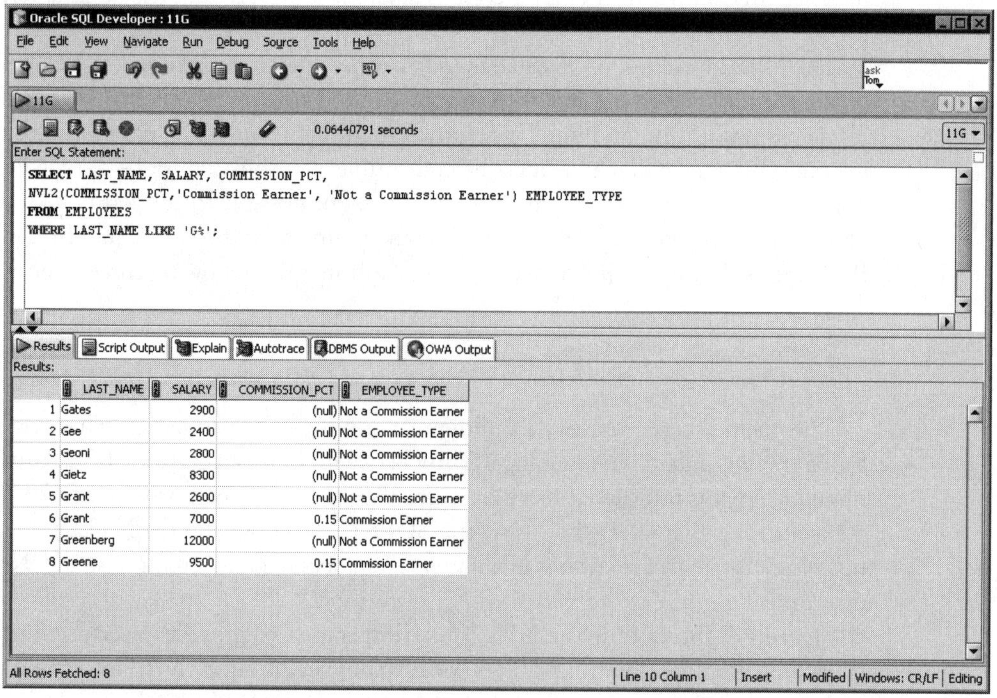

1234 different from 123+1, so it returns the *ifunequal* parameter, which is 1234. The character literals in query 3 are not implicitly converted to DATE items and are compared as two character strings by the NULLIF function. Since the strings are of different lengths, the *ifunequal* parameter 24-JUL-2009 is returned.

Figure 5-8 shows how NULLIF is nested as a parameter to the NVL2 function. The NULLIF function itself has the SUBSTR and UPPER character functions embedded in the expression used as its *ifunequal* parameter. The EMAIL column is compared with an expression, formed by concatenating the first character of the FIRST_NAME to the uppercase equivalent of the LAST_NAME column, for employees with 4-character-long first names. When these terms are equal, NULLIF returns a null, else it returns the evaluated *ifunequal* parameter. This is used as a parameter to NVL2. The NVL2 function provides descriptive text classifying rows as matching the pattern or not.

FIGURE 5-8   The NULLIF function

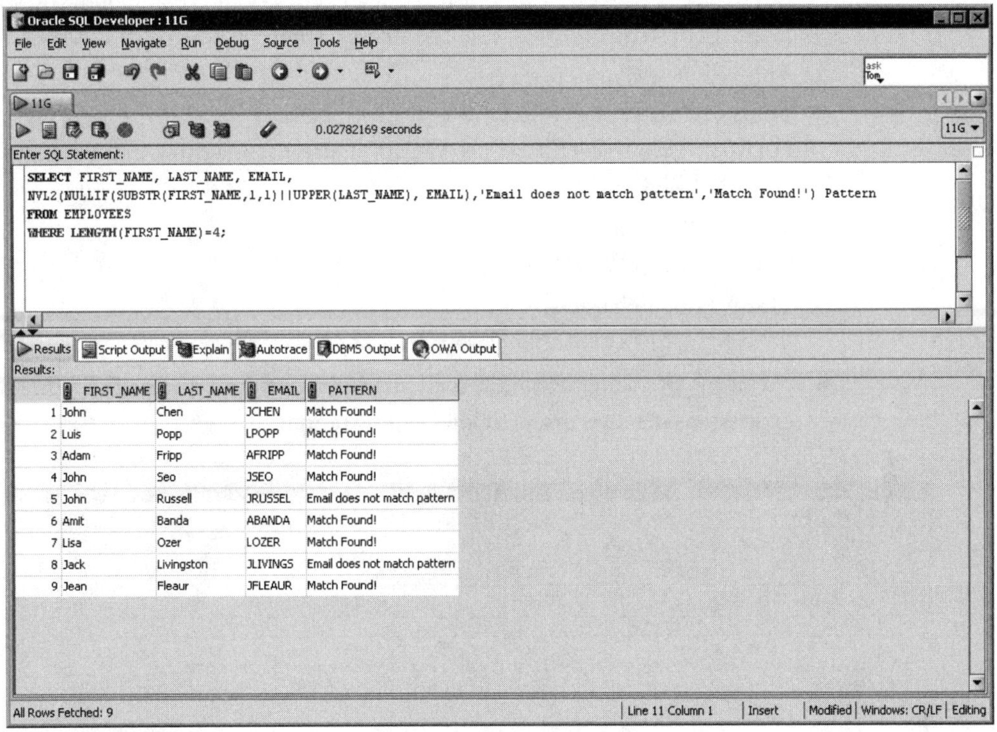

EXERCISE 5-2
=========

Using NULLIF and NVL2 for Simple Conditional Logic

You are required to return a set of rows from the EMPLOYEES table with
DEPARTMENT_ID values of 100. The set must also contain FIRST_NAME
and LAST_NAME values and an expression aliased as NAME_LENGTHS. This
expression must return the string 'Different Length' if the length of the FIRST_NAME
differs from that of the LAST_NAME, else the string 'Same Length' must be returned.

1. Start SQL Developer and connect to the HR schema.

2. The NAME_LENGTHS expression may be calculated in several ways. The
   solution provided uses the NULLIF function to test whether the LENGTH
   values returned for the FIRST_NAME and LAST_NAME columns are

the same. If they are, NULL is returned, else the LENGTH of the LAST_NAME is returned. If the outer function (NVL2) gets a NULL parameter, the string 'Same Length' is returned, else the string 'Different Length' is returned.

3. The SELECT clause is therefore
SELECT FIRST_NAME, LAST_NAME, NVL2(NULLIF(LENGTH(LAST_NAME), LENGTH(FIRST_NAME)), 'Different Length', 'Same Length') NAME_LENGTHS

4. The FROM clause is
FROM EMPLOYEES

5. The WHERE clause is
WHERE DEPARTMENT_ID=100

6. Executing this statement returns employees' names and the NAME_LENGTHS expression as shown in the following illustration:

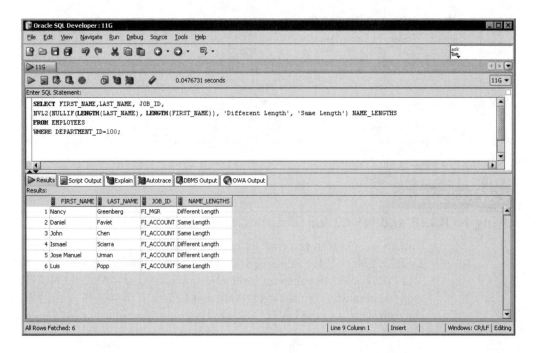

The COALESCE Function

The COALESCE function returns the first nonnull value from its parameter list. If all its parameters are null, then null is returned.

The COALESCE function takes two mandatory parameters and any number of optional parameters. The syntax is COALESCE(*expr1, expr2,…,exprn*), where *expr1* is returned if it is not null, else *expr2* if it is not null, and so on. COALESCE is a general form of the NVL function, as the following two equations illustrate:

COALESCE(expr1,expr2) = NVL(expr1,expr2)
COALESCE(expr1,expr2,expr3) = NVL(expr1,NVL(expr2,expr3))

The data type COALESCE returns if a not null value is found is the same as that of the first not null parameter. To avoid an "ORA-00932: inconsistent data types" error, all not null parameters must have data types compatible with the first not null parameter. Consider the following three queries:

```
Query 1: select coalesce(null, null, null, 'a string') from dual;
Query 2: select coalesce(null, null, null) from dual;
Query 3: select coalesce(substr('abc',4),'Not bc','No substring') from dual;
```

Query 1 returns the fourth parameter: a string, since this is the first not null parameter encountered. Query 2 returns null because all its parameters are null. Query 3 evaluates its first parameter, which is a nested SUBSTR function, and finds it to be null. The second parameter is not null so the string 'Not bc' is returned.

The STATE_PROVINCE, POSTAL_CODE, and CITY information was retrieved from the LOCATIONS table for the rows with COUNTRY_ID values of UK, IT, or JP. As Figure 5-9 shows, the COALESCE function returns the STATE_PROVINCE value for a row if it is not null. If it is null the POSTAL_CODE value is returned. If that is null, the CITY field is returned, else the result is null.

FIGURE 5-9   The COALESCE function

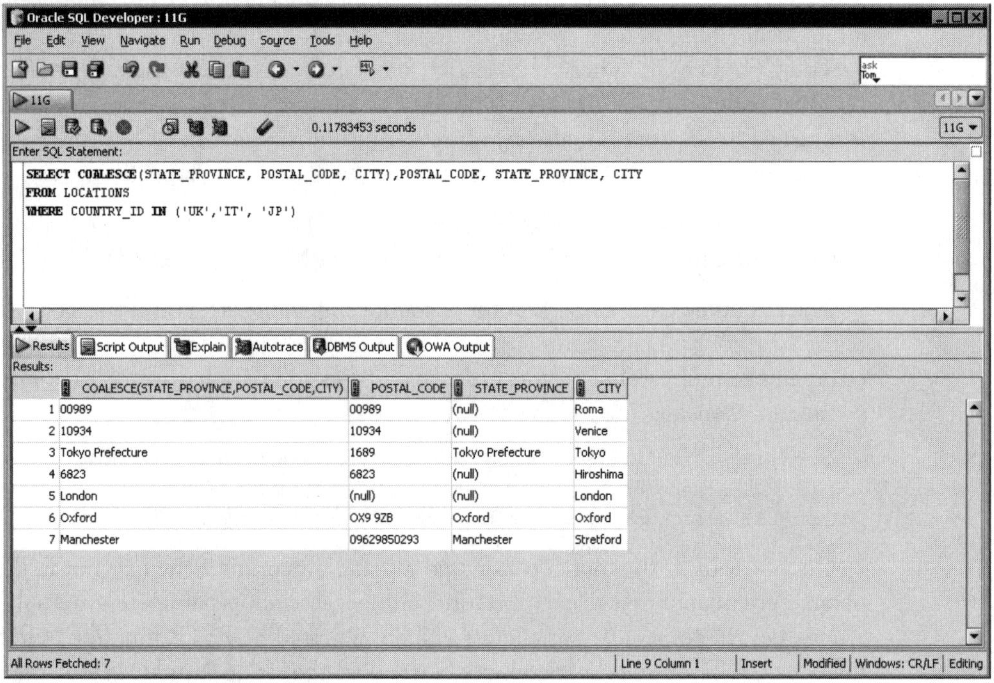

Conditional Functions

Conditional logic, also known as *if-then-else* logic, refers to choosing a path of execution based on data values meeting certain conditions. *Conditional functions*, like DECODE and the CASE expression, return different values based on evaluating comparison conditions. These conditions are specified as parameters to the DECODE function and the CASE expression. The DECODE function is specific to Oracle, while the CASE expression is ANSI SQL compliant. An example of *if-then-else* logic is: if the country value is Brazil or Australia, then return Southern Hemisphere, else return Northern Hemisphere.

The DECODE Function

Although its name sounds mysterious, this function is straightforward. The DECODE function implements *if-then-else* conditional logic by testing its first two terms for equality and returns the third if they are equal and optionally returns another term if they are not.

The DECODE function takes at least three mandatory parameters, but can take many more. The syntax of the function is DECODE(*expr1*,*comp1*, *iftrue1*, *[comp2*,*iftrue2…[compN*,*iftrueN]], [iffalse]*). These parameters are evaluated as shown in the following pseudocode example:

```
If expr1 = comp1 then return iftrue1
     else if expr1 = comp2 then return iftrue2
        . . .
        . . .
          else if expr1 = compN then return iftrueN
     else return null | iffalse;
```

Expr1 is compared to *comp1*. If they are equal, then *iftrue1* is returned. If *expr1* is not equal to *comp1*, then what happens next depends on whether the optional parameters *comp2* and *iftrue2* are present. If they are, then *expr1* is compared to *comp2*. If they are equal, then *iftrue2* is returned. If not, what happens next depends on whether further *compn,iftruen* pairs exist, and the cycle continues until no comparison terms remain. If no matches have been found and if the *iffalse* parameter is defined, then *iffalse* is returned. If the *iffalse* parameter does not exist and no matches are found, a null value is returned.

All parameters to the DECODE function may be expressions. The return data type is the same as that of the first matching comparison item. The expression *expr1* is implicitly converted to the data type of the first comparison parameter *comp1*. As the other comparison parameters *comp2…compn* are evaluated, they too are implicitly converted to the same data type as *comp1*. *Decode* considers two nulls to be equivalent, so if *expr1* is null and *comp3* is the first null comparison parameter encountered, then the corresponding result parameter *iftrue3* is returned. Consider the following three queries:

```
Query 1: select decode(1234,123,'123 is a match') from dual;
Query 2: select decode(1234,123,'123 is a match','No match') from dual;
Query 3: select decode('search','comp1','true1', 'comp2','true2',
     'search','true3', substr('2search',2,6)),'true4', 'false') from dual;
```

Query 1 compares the number 1234 with the first comparison term 123. Since they are not equal, the first result term cannot be returned. Further, as there is no default *iffalse* parameter defined, a null is returned. Query 2 is identical to the first except that an *iffalse* parameter is defined. Therefore, since 1234 is not equal to 123, the string 'No match' is returned. Query 3 searches through the comparison parameters for a match. The character terms 'comp1' and 'comp2' are not equal to search, so the results true1 and true2 are not returned. A match is found in the third comparison term 'comp3' (parameter 6), which contains the string search. Therefore, the third result term *iftrue3* (parameter 7) containing the string 'true3' is returned. Note that since a match has been found, no further searching takes place. So, although the fourth comparison term (parameter 8) is also a match to *expr1*, this expression is never evaluated, because a match was found in an earlier comparison term.

Distinct occurrences of the COUNTRY_ID column values in the LOCATIONS table have been classified into either Northern or Southern Hemisphere countries using a DECODE function. Figure 5-10 shows how the COUNTRY_ID column is the expression for which a match is sought. *If* the COUNTRY_ID value is BR (Brazil) or AU (Australia), *then* the function returns the string Southern Hemisphere, *else* Northern Hemisphere is returned.

FIGURE 5-10   The DECODE function

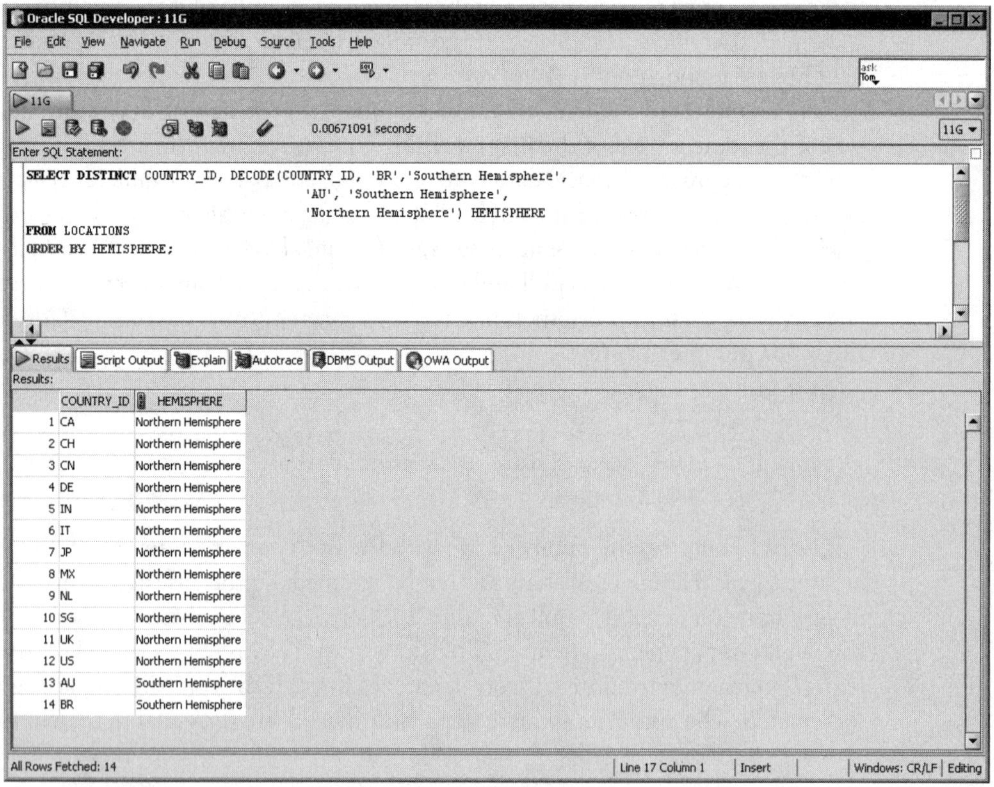

INSIDE THE EXAM

The certification objectives in this chapter are primarily measured with practical examples that require you to predict the results returned by an expression. Explicit conversion functions with their many format masks are tested. The TO_CHAR function; *fm* modifier; and the *sp*, *th*, and *spth* format models are commonly examined. Use of the TO_CHAR function to convert numbers into characters is tested, and emphasis is often placed on the format masks that determine numeric width, dollar symbol, group separator, and decimal separator formats.

Many questions consist of expressions with nested functions, and it is vital for you to know how to interpret and trace them. The innermost to outermost sequence of evaluation of nested functions is important and must be remembered.

The general functions NVL, NVL2, NULLIF, and COALESCE all pertain to working with NULL. Since null values are prevalent in many databases, a thorough understanding of all these functions, particularly NVL and NVL2, is required.

The DECODE function and CASE expression are sometimes perceived as complex and difficult to understand. They are, however, two of the simplest and most useful functions guaranteed to be examined. Pay attention to the positional meaning of the parameters when using the DECODE function. The simple and searched CASE expression differs from the functions discussed earlier. This is due to the CASE…END block, which encloses one or more WHEN…OTHER pairs and optionally an ELSE statement. Practice with this expression and you will quickly learn its readable and standardized structure.

The CASE Expression

Virtually all third and fourth generation programming languages implement a *case* statement. Like the DECODE function, the CASE expression facilitates *if-then-else* conditional logic. There are two variants of the CASE expression. The *simple CASE expression* lists the conditional search item once, and equality to the search item is tested by each comparison expression. The *searched CASE expression* lists a separate condition for each comparison expression.

The CASE expression takes at least three mandatory parameters but can take many more. Its syntax depends on whether a simple or a searched CASE expression is used. The syntax for the simple CASE expression is as follows:

```
CASE search_expr
  WHEN comparison_expr1 THEN iftrue1
  [WHEN comparison_expr2 THEN iftrue2
  ...
      WHEN comparison_exprN THEN iftrueN
  ELSE iffalse]
END
```

The simple CASE expression is enclosed within a CASE...END block and consists of at least one WHEN...THEN statement. In its simplest form, with one WHEN...THEN statement, the *search_expr* is compared with the *comparison_expr1*. If they are equal, then the result *iftrue1* is returned. If not, a null value is returned unless an ELSE component is defined, in which case, the default *iffalse* value is returned. When more than one WHEN...THEN statement exists in the CASE expression, searching for a matching comparison expression continues until a match is found.

The search, comparison, and result parameters can be column values, expressions, or literals but must all be of the same data type. Consider the following query:

```
select
  case substr(1234,1,3)
    when '134' then '1234 is a match'
    when '1235' then '1235 is a match'
    when concat('1','23') then concat('1','23')||' is a match'
    else 'no match'
  end
from dual;
```

The search expression derived from the SUBSTR(1234,1,3) is the character string 123. The first WHEN...THEN statement compares the string 134 with 123. Since they are not equal, the result expression is not evaluated. The second WHEN...THEN statement compares the string 1235 with 123 and again, they are not equal. The third WHEN...THEN statement compares the results derived from the CONCAT('1','23') expression, which is 123, to the search expression. Since they are identical, the third results expression '123 is a match', is returned.

The LAST_NAME and HIRE_DATE columns for employees with DEPARTMENT_ID values of 10 or 60 are retrieved along with two numeric expressions and one CASE expression, as shown in Figure 5-11.

Assume that SYSDATE is 01-JAN-2008. The numeric expression aliased as YEARS returns a truncated value obtained by dividing the months of service by 12.

FIGURE 5-11   The CASE expression

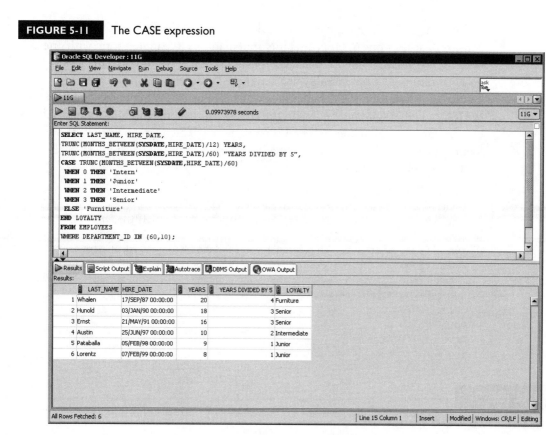

Five categories of loyalty classification based on years of service are defined by truncating the quotient obtained by dividing the months of service by 60. This forms the search expression in the CASE statement. None of the rows in the dataset match the comparison expression in the first WHEN...THEN statement, but as Figure 5-11 shows, five rows met the remaining WHEN...THEN statements and one row is caught by the ELSE statement.

The syntax for the searched CASE expression is as follows:

CASE
 WHEN *condition1* THEN *iftrue1*
 [WHEN *condition2* THEN *iftrue2*
 ...
   WHEN *conditionN* THEN *iftrueN*
  ELSE *iffalse*]
END

The searched CASE expression is enclosed within a CASE…END block and consists of at least one WHEN…THEN statement. In its simplest form with one WHEN…THEN statement, *condition1* is evaluated; if it is true, then the result *iftrue1* is returned. If not, a null value is returned unless an ELSE component is defined, in which case the default *iffalse* value is returned. When more than one WHEN…THEN statement exists in the CASE expression, searching for a matching comparison expression continues until one is found. The query to retrieve the identical set of results to those obtained in Figure 5-11, using a searched CASE expression is listed next:

```
select last_name, hire_date,
trunc(months_between(sysdate,hire_date)/12) years,
trunc(months_between(sysdate,hire_date)/60) "Years divided by 5",
case
 when trunc(months_between(sysdate,hire_date)/60) < 1 then 'Intern'
 when trunc(months_between(sysdate,hire_date)/60) < 2 then 'Junior'
 when trunc(months_between(sysdate,hire_date)/60) < 3 then 'Intermediate'
 when trunc(months_between(sysdate,hire_date)/60) < 4 then 'Senior'
 else 'Furniture'
end Loyalty
from employees
where department_id in (60,10);
```

EXERCISE 5-3

Using the DECODE Function

You are requested to query the LOCATIONS table for rows with the value US in the COUNTRY_ID column. An expression aliased as LOCATION_INFO is required to evaluate the STATE_PROVINCE column values and returns different information as per the following table. Sort the output based on the LOCATION_INFO expression.

If STATE_PROVINCE is	The value returned is
Washington	The string 'Headquarters'
Texas	The string 'Oil Wells'
California	The CITY column value
New Jersey	The STREET_ADDRESS column value

1. Start SQL Developer and connect to the HR schema.
2. The LOCATION_ID expression may be calculated in several different ways. This includes using a CASE expression or a DECODE function. The solution below uses DECODE.

3. The SELECT clause is
   SELECT DECODE(STATE_PROVINCE, 'Washington', 'Headquarters', 'Texas', 'Oil Wells', 'California', CITY, 'New Jersey', STREET_ADDRESS) LOCATION_INFO

   Notice the mixture of character literals and columns specified as parameters to the DECODE function.

4. The FROM clause is
   FROM EMPLOYEES

5. The WHERE clause is
   WHERE COUNTRY_ID='US'

6. The ORDER BY clause is
   ORDER BY LOCATION_INFO

7. The result of executing this statement is shown in the following illustration:

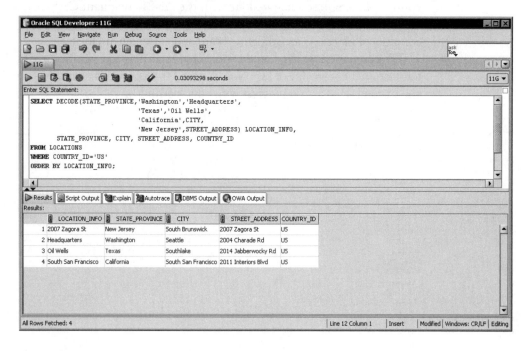

CERTIFICATION SUMMARY

This chapter builds on the single row functions introduced previously. The concepts of implicit and explicit data type conversion are explained along with the reliability risks associated with implicit conversions.

Date to character and *number to character* conversions are described using the TO_CHAR function. A variety of format models or masks are available. The TO_NUMBER function performs *character to number* conversions, while the TO_DATE function performs *character to date* data type conversions.

Nested functions and their evaluation is one of the most valuable lessons in this chapter. Understanding this fundamental concept is crucial. The general functions NVL, NVL2, NULLIF, and COALESCE are designed to simplify working with null values and provide basic conditional logic functionality.

DECODE is an Oracle-specific function that supports *if-then-else* logic in the context of an SQL statement along with the ANSI-compliant CASE expression. The two variants are the simple CASE and searched CASE expressions. These conditional functions are straightforward and extremely useful.

The conversion, general, and conditional functions add significantly to the foundational knowledge of SQL you acquired from previous chapters and will hold you in good stead as you progress with your learning.

✓ TWO-MINUTE DRILL

Describe Various Types of Conversion Functions Available in SQL

- ❑ When values do not match the defined parameters of functions, Oracle attempts to convert them into the required data types. This is known as implicit conversion.
- ❑ Explicit conversion occurs when a function like TO_CHAR is invoked to change the data type of a value.
- ❑ The TO_CHAR function performs date to character and number to character data type conversions.
- ❑ Character items are explicitly transformed into date values using the TO_DATE conversion function.
- ❑ Character items are changed into number values using the TO_NUMBER conversion function.

Use the TO_CHAR, TO_NUMBER, and TO_DATE Conversion Functions

- ❑ The TO_CHAR function returns an item of type VARCHAR2.
- ❑ Format models or masks prescribe patterns that character strings must match to facilitate accurate and consistent conversion into number or date items.
- ❑ When the TO_CHAR function performs number to character conversions, the format mask can specify currency, numeric width, position of decimal operator, thousands separator, and many other formatting codes.
- ❑ The format masks available when TO_CHAR is used to convert character items to date include day, week, month, quarter, year, and century.
- ❑ Format masks must always be specified enclosed in single quotes.
- ❑ When performing date to character conversion, the format mask specifies which date elements are extracted and whether the element should be described by a long or abbreviated name.
- ❑ Character terms, like month and day names, extracted from dates with the TO_CHAR function are automatically padded with spaces that may be trimmed by prefixing the format mask with the *fm* modifier.

❑ The TO_DATE function has an *fx* modifier that specifies an exact match for the character string to be converted and the date format mask.

Apply Conditional Expressions in a SELECT Statement

❑ Nesting functions use the output from one function as the input to another.

❑ The NVL function either returns the original item unchanged or an alternative item if the initial term is null.

❑ The NVL2 function returns a new *if-null* item if the original item is null or an alternative *if-not-null* item if the original term is not null.

❑ The NULLIF function tests two terms for equality. If they are equal, the function returns null, else it returns the first of the two terms tested.

❑ The COALESCE function returns the first nonnull value from its parameter list. If all its parameters are null, then a null value is returned.

❑ The DECODE function implements *if-then-else* conditional logic by testing two terms for equality and returning the third term if they are equal or, optionally, some other term if they are not.

❑ There are two variants of the CASE expression used to facilitate *if-then-else* conditional logic: the simple CASE and searched CASE expressions.

SELF TEST

The following questions will measure your understanding of the material presented in this chapter. Read all the choices carefully because there may be more than one correct answer. Choose all the correct answers for each question.

Describe Various Types of Conversion Functions Available in SQL

1. What type of conversion is performed by the following statement?
   SELECT LENGTH(3.14285) FROM DUAL;
   (Choose the best answer.)
   A. Explicit conversion
   B. Implicit conversion
   C. TO_NUMBER function conversion
   D. None of the above

2. Choose any incorrect statements regarding conversion functions. (Choose all that apply.)
   A. TO_CHAR may convert date items to character items.
   B. TO_DATE may convert character items to date items.
   C. TO_CHAR may convert numbers to character items.
   D. TO_DATE may convert date items to character items.

Use the TO_CHAR, TO_NUMBER, and TO_DATE Conversion Functions

3. What value is returned after executing the following statement?
   SELECT TO_NUMBER(1234.49, '999999.9') FROM DUAL;
   (Choose the best answer.)
   A. 1234.49
   B. 001234.5
   C. 1234.5
   D. None of the above

4. What value is returned after executing the following statement?
   SELECT TO_CHAR(1234.49, '999999.9') FROM DUAL;
   (Choose the best answer.)
   A. 1234.49
   B. 001234.5
   C. 1234.5
   D. None of the above

5. If SYSDATE returns 12-JUL-2009, what is returned by the following statement?
   SELECT TO_CHAR(SYSDATE, 'fmMONTH, YEAR') FROM DUAL;
   (Choose the best answer.)

   A. JUL, 2009
   B. JULY, TWO THOUSAND NINE
   C. JUL-09
   D. None of the above

6. If SYSDATE returns 12-JUL-2009, what is returned by the following statement?
   SELECT TO_CHAR(SYSDATE, 'fmDDth MONTH') FROM DUAL;
   (Choose the best answer.)

   A. 12TH JULY
   B. 12th July
   C. TWELFTH JULY
   D. None of the above

Apply Conditional Expressions in a SELECT Statement

7. If SYSDATE returns 12-JUL-2009, what is returned by the following statement?
   SELECT TO_CHAR(TO_DATE(TO_CHAR(SYSDATE,'DD'),'DD'),'YEAR') FROM DUAL;
   (Choose the best answer.)

   A. 2009
   B. TWO THOUSAND NINE
   C. 12-JUL-2009
   D. None of the above

8. What value is returned after executing the following statement?
   SELECT NVL2(NULLIF('CODA','SID'),'SPANIEL','TERRIER') FROM DUAL;
   (Choose the best answer.)

   A. SPANIEL
   B. TERRIER
   C. NULL
   D. None of the above

9. What value is returned after executing the following statement?
SELECT NVL(SUBSTR('AM I NULL',10),'YES I AM') FROM DUAL;
(Choose the best answer.)

A. NO

B. NULL

C. YES I AM

D. None of the above

10. If SYSDATE returns 12-JUL-2009, what is returned by the following statement?
SELECT DECODE(TO_CHAR(SYSDATE,'MM'),'02','TAX DUE','PARTY') FROM DUAL;
(Choose the best answer.)

A. TAX DUE

B. PARTY

C. 02

D. None of the above

LAB QUESTION

Using SQL Developer or SQL*Plus, connect to the OE schema and complete the following tasks.

As part of a new marketing initiative, you are asked to prepare a list of customer birthdays that occur between two days ago and seven days from now. The list should retrieve rows from the CUSTOMERS table which include the CUST_FIRST_NAME, CUST_LAST_NAME, CUST_EMAIL, and DATE_OF_BIRTH columns in ascending order based on the day and month components of the DATE_OF_BIRTH value. An additional expression aliased as BIRTHDAY is required to return a descriptive message based on the following table. There are several approaches to solving this question. Your approach may differ from the solution described here.

BIRTHDAY	CHARACTER STRING
Two days ago	Day before yesterday
One day ago	Yesterday
Today	Today
Tomorrow	Tomorrow
Two days in the future	Day after tomorrow
Within seven days from today	Later this week

SELF TEST ANSWERS

Describe Various Types of Conversion Functions Available in SQL

1. ☑ **B.** The number 3.14285 is given as a parameter to the LENGTH function. There is a data type mismatch, but Oracle implicitly converts the parameter to the character string '3.14285', allowing the function to operate correctly.

   ☒ **A, C,** and **D** are incorrect. Explicit conversion occurs when a function like TO_CHAR is executed. **C** is the correct length of the string '3.14285', but this is not asked for in the question.

2. ☑ **D.** Dates are only converted into character strings using TO_CHAR and not the TO_DATE function.

   ☒ **A, B,** and **C** are correct statements.

Use the TO_CHAR, TO_NUMBER, and TO_DATE Conversion Functions

3. ☑ **D.** An "ORA-1722: invalid number" error is returned because the statement is trying to convert a number using an incompatible format mask. If the expression was TO_NUMBER(1234.49, '999999.99'), the number 1234.49 would be returned.

   ☒ **A, B,** and **D** are incorrect.

4. ☑ **C.** For the number 1234.49 to match the character format mask with one decimal place, the number is first rounded to 1234.5 before TO_CHAR converts it into the string '1234.5'.

   ☒ **A, B,** and **D** are incorrect. **A** cannot be returned because the format mask only allows one character after the decimal point. **B** would be returned if the format mask was '009999.9'.

5. ☑ **B.** The MONTH and YEAR components of the format mask separated by a comma and a space indicate that TO_CHAR must extract the spelled out month and year values in uppercase separated by a comma and a space. The *fm* modifier removes extra blanks from the spelled out components.

   ☒ **A, C,** and **D** are incorrect. If the format mask was 'MON, YYYY' or 'MON-YY', **A** and **C**, respectively, would be returned.

6. ☑ **A.** The DD component returns the day of the month in uppercase. Since it is a number, it does not matter, unless the 'th' mask is applied, in which case that component is specified in uppercase. MONTH returns the month spelled out in uppercase.

   ☒ **B, C,** and **D** are incorrect. **B** would be returned if the format mask was 'fmddth Month', and **C** would be returned if the format mask was 'fmDDspth MONTH'.

Apply Conditional Expressions in a SELECT Statement

7. ☑ **B.** The innermost nested function is TO_CHAR(SYSDATE,'DD'), which extracts the day component of SYSDATE and returns the character 12. The next function executed is TO_DATE('12','DD') where the character 12 is cast as the day component. When such an incomplete date is provided, Oracle substitutes values from the SYSDATE function; since SYSDATE is 12-JUL-2009, this is the date used. The outermost function executed in TO_CHAR('12-JUL-2009','YEAR') returns the year spelled out as TWO THOUSAND NINE.
☒ **A, C,** and **D** are incorrect.

8. ☑ **A.** The NULLIF function compares its two parameters and, since they are different, the first parameter is returned. The NVL2('CODA', 'SPANIEL','TERRIER') function call returns SPANIEL since its first parameter is not null.
☒ **B, C,** and **D** are incorrect.

9. ☑ **C.** The character literal 'AM I NULL' is nine characters long. Therefore, trying to obtain a substring beginning at the tenth character returns a null. The outer function then becomes NVL(NULL,'YES I AM'), resulting in the string 'YES I AM' being returned.
☒ **A, B,** and **D** are incorrect.

10. ☑ **B.** The innermost function TO_CHAR(SYSDATE, 'MM') results in the character string '07' being returned. The outer function is DECODE('07','02','TAX DUE','PARTY'). Since '07' is not equal to '02', the else component 'PARTY' is returned.
☒ **A, C,** and **D** are incorrect. **A** would only be returned if the month component extracted from SYSDATE was '02'.

LAB ANSWER

Using SQL Developer or SQL*Plus, connect to the OE schema and complete the following tasks.

1. Start SQL Developer and connect to the OE schema.
2. The dataset must be restricted to rows from the CUSTOMERS table where DATE_OF_BIRTH values first have the same month as the current month, and second, the day component of the DATE_OF_BIRTH is between two days ago and seven days from now. There are therefore two conditions that make up the WHERE clause.

3. The first condition of the WHERE clause is

```
TO_CHAR(DATE_OF_BIRTH,'MON')=TO_CHAR(SYSDATE,'MON')
```

4. The second condition is

```
TO_NUMBER(TO_CHAR(DATE_OF_BIRTH,'DD')) - TO_NUMBER(TO_CHAR(SYSDATE,'DD')) BETWEEN -2 AND 7
```

5. The BIRTHDAY expression may be calculated in several ways. Based on the preceding WHERE clause, you are assured that the dataset is limited to the correct set of rows. The SELECT clause has to retrieve and manipulate the records for appropriate display. The CASE expression provides functionality for conditional logic and is well suited to this situation.

6. The case tested is based on the day component of the DATE_OF_BIRTH minus the day component returned by the SYSDATE function. For example, if the difference is –2, then the string 'Day before yesterday' is returned. The different CASE conditions are tested is a similar manner. The ELSE component catches any rows not matching the CASE conditions and returns the string 'Later in the week'.

7. The SELECT clause is therefore

```
SELECT CUST_FIRST_NAME, CUST_LAST_NAME, CUST_EMAIL, DATE_OF_BIRTH,
CASE TO_NUMBER(TO_CHAR(DATE_OF_BIRTH,'DD')) - TO_NUMBER(TO_CHAR(SYSDATE,'DD'))
 WHEN -2 THEN 'Day before yesterday'
 WHEN -1 THEN 'Yesterday'
 WHEN 0  THEN 'Today'
 WHEN 1  THEN 'Tomorrow'
 WHEN 2  THEN 'Day after tomorrow'
 ELSE 'Later this week'
END BIRTHDAY
```

8. The FROM clause is

```
FROM CUSTOMERS
```

9. The ORDER BY clause is

```
ORDER BY TO_CHAR(DATE_OF_BIRTH,'MMDD')
```

10. Executing this statement returns the set of results matching this pattern as shown in the following illustration for SYSDATE=08-JAN-2008:

6

Reporting Aggregated Data Using the Group Functions

S ingle-row functions, explored in Chapters 4 and 5, return a single value for each row in a set of results. *Group* or *aggregate* functions operate on multiple rows. They are used to count the number of rows or to find the average of specific column values in a dataset. Many statistical operations, such as calculating standard deviation, medians, and averages, depend on executing functions against grouped data and not just single rows.

Group functions are examined in two stages. First, their purpose and syntax is discussed. Second, a detailed analysis of the AVG, SUM, MIN, MAX, and COUNT functions is conducted. The concept of grouping or segregating data based on one or more column values is explored before introducing the GROUP BY clause.

The WHERE clause restricts rows in a dataset before grouping, while the HAVING clause restricts them after grouping. This chapter concludes with a discussion of the HAVING clause.

CERTIFICATION OBJECTIVE 6.01

Describe the Group Functions

SQL *group functions* are defined and the different variants are discussed. The syntax of selected group functions is explained, their data types are discussed, and the DISTINCT keyword's effect on them is explored. This discussion is divided into two main areas:

- Definition of group functions
- Types and syntax of group functions

Definition of Group Functions

Group functions operate on aggregated data and return a single result per group. These groups usually consist of zero or more rows of data. Single-row functions are defined with the formula: $F(x, y, z, \ldots)$ = result, where x,y,z... are input parameters. The function F executes on one row of the data set at a time and returns a result for each row. Group functions may be defined using the following formula:

$F(g1, g2, g3, \ldots, gn)$ = result1, result2, result2,..., resultn;

The group function executes once for each cluster of rows and returns a single result per group. These groups may be entire tables or portions of tables associated using a common value or attribute. If all the rows in tables are presented as one group to the group function then one result is returned. One or more group functions may appear in the SELECT list as follows:

```
SELECT group_function(column or expression),…
FROM table [WHERE …] [ORDER BY…]
```

Consider the EMPLOYEES table. There are 107 rows in this table. Groups may be created based on the common values that rows share. For example, the rows that share the same DEPARTMENT_ID value may be clustered together. Thereafter, group functions are executed separately against each unique group.

As Figure 6-1 shows, there are 12 distinct DEPARTMENT_ID values in the EMPLOYEES table including a null value. The rows are distributed into 12 groups based on common DEPARTMENT_ID values. The COUNT function executes 12 times, once for each group. Notice that the distinct groups do not contain the same number of rows.

on the
job

Group functions aggregate a number of values from multiple rows into a single result. They are widely used for reporting purposes and are also known as summary or aggregate functions. Useful aggregated data such as sum totals, averages, and counts often form the basis of more sophisticated statistical calculations. It is useful to have a good understanding of the data stored in your application tables to maximize the quality of your aggregate reporting.

Types and Syntax of Group Functions

A brief description of the most commonly used group functions is provided next. Many are examined in detail later in this chapter.

The COUNT function counts the number of rows in a group. Its syntax is as follows:

COUNT({* | [DISTINCT | ALL] *expr*}) ;

This syntax may be deconstructed into the following forms:

1. COUNT(*)
2. COUNT(DISTINCT *expr*)
3. COUNT(ALL *expr*)
4. COUNT(*expr*)

When COUNT(*) is invoked, all rows in the group, including those with nulls or duplicate values are counted. When COUNT(DISTINCT *expr*) is executed, only unique occurrences of *expr* are counted for each group. The ALL keyword is part of the default syntax, so COUNT(ALL *expr*) and COUNT(*expr*) are equivalent. These count the number of nonnull occurrences of *expr* in each group. The data type of *expr* may be

FIGURE 6-1

Group functions operating on 12 groups

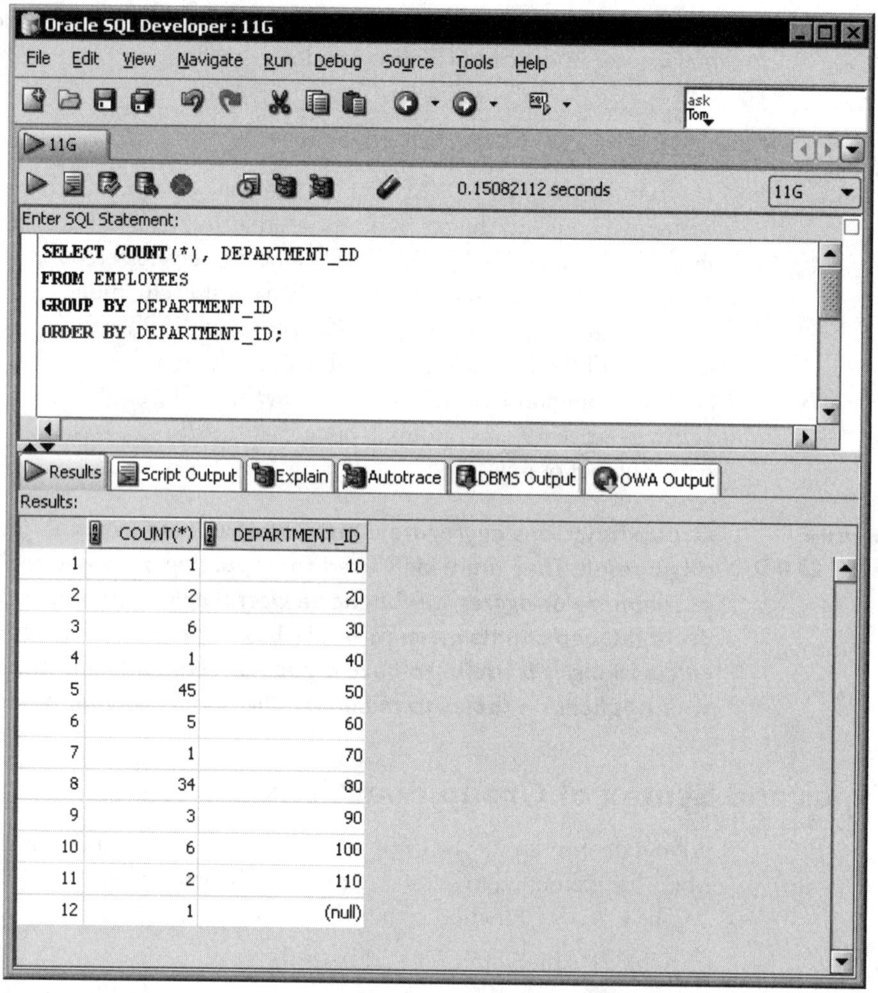

NUMBER, DATE, CHAR, or VARCHAR2. If *expr* is a null, it is ignored unless it is managed using a general function like NVL, NVL2, or COALESCE.

The AVG function calculates the average value of a numeric column or expression in a group. Its syntax is as follows:

AVG([DISTINCT | ALL] *expr*) ;

This syntax may be deconstructed into the following forms:

1. AVG(DISTINCT *expr*)
2. AVG(ALL *expr*)
3. AVG(*expr*)

When AVG(DISTINCT *expr*) is invoked, the distinct values of *expr* are summed and divided by the number of unique occurrences of *expr*. AVG(ALL *expr*) and AVG(*expr*) add the nonnull values of *expr* for each row and divide the sum by the number of nonnull rows in the group. The data type of the *expr* parameter is NUMBER.

The *SUM* function returns the aggregated total of the nonnull numeric expression values in a group. It has the following syntax:

SUM([DISTINCT | ALL] *expr*) ;

This syntax may be deconstructed into the following forms:

1. SUM(DISTINCT *expr*)
2. SUM(ALL *expr*)
3. SUM(*expr*)

SUM(DISTINCT *expr*) provides a total by adding all the unique values returned after *expr* is evaluated for each row in the group. SUM(*expr*) and SUM(ALL *expr*) provide a total by adding *expr* for each row in the group. Null values are ignored. The data type of *expr* is NUMBER.

The *MAX* and *MIN* functions return the maximum (largest) and minimum (smallest) *expr* value in a group. Their syntax is as follows:

MAX([DISTINCT | ALL] *expr*); MIN([DISTINCT | ALL] *expr*)

This syntax may be deconstructed into the following forms:

1. MAX(DISTINCT *expr*); MIN(DISTINCT *expr*)
2. MAX(ALL *expr*); MIN(ALL *expr*)
3. MAX(*expr*); MIN(*expr*);

MAX(*expr*), MAX(ALL *expr*) and MAX(DISTINCT *expr*) examine the values for *expr* in a group of rows and return the largest value. Null values are ignored. MIN(*expr*), MIN(ALL *expr*) and MIN(DISTINCT *expr*) examine the values for *expr* in a group of rows and return the smallest value. The data type of the *expr* parameter may be NUMBER, DATE, CHAR or VARCHAR2.

The *STDDEV* and *VARIANCE* functions are two of many statistical group functions Oracle provides. VARIANCE has the following syntax:

VARIANCE([DISTINCT | ALL] *expr*);

This syntax may be deconstructed into the following forms:

1. VARIANCE(DISTINCT *expr*)
2. VARIANCE(ALL *expr*)
3. VARIANCE(*expr*)

STDDEV has the following syntax:

STDDEV([DISTINCT | ALL] *expr*);

This syntax may be deconstructed into the following forms:

1. STDDEV(DISTINCT *expr*)
2. STDDEV(ALL *expr*)
3. STDDEV(*expr*)

Statistical variance refers to the variability of scores in a sample or set of data. VARIANCE(DISTINCT *expr*) returns the variability of unique nonnull data in a group. VARIANCE(*expr*) and VARIANCE(ALL *expr*) return the variability of nonnull data in the group.

STDDEV calculates statistical standard deviation, which is the degree of deviation from the mean value in a group. It is derived by finding the square root of the variance. STDDEV(DISTINCT *expr*) returns the standard deviation of unique nonnull data in a group. STDDEV(*expr*) and STDDEV(ALL *expr*) return the standard deviation of nonnull data in the group. The data type of the *expr* parameter is NUMBER.

exam
ⓦatch

There are two fundamental rules to remember when studying group functions. First, they always operate on a single group of rows at a time. The group may be one of many groups a dataset has been segmented into or it may be an entire table. The group function executes once per group. Second, rows with nulls occurring in group columns or expressions are ignored, unless a general function like NVL, NVL2, or COALESCE is provided to handle them.

Consider the following example. If the average value for COMMISSION_PCT is retrieved from the EMPLOYEES table, only the nonnull values are considered. The expression AVG(COMMISSION_PCT) adds the 35 nonnull COMMISSION_PCT values and divides the total by 35. The average based on all 107 rows may be computed using the expression AVG(NVL(COMMISSION_PCT,0)).

CERTIFICATION OBJECTIVE 6.02

Identify the Available Group Functions

The different variants of *group functions* and their syntax were just discussed. This section provides examples demonstrating the application of these functions. The interactions of *group functions* with null values and the DISTINCT keyword are discussed, and the concept of nesting group functions is also considered. The available *group functions* are identified and explored under the following headings:

- Using the group functions
- Nesting group functions

Using the Group Functions

The practical application of *group functions* is demonstrated using AVG, SUM, MIN, MAX, and COUNT. These group functions all return numeric results. Additionally, the MIN and MAX functions may return character and date results. These five functions operate on nonnull values but, unlike the others, the COUNT(*) function call also counts rows with null values. The DISTINCT keyword is used to constrain the rows submitted to the group functions.

Analysts frequently wish to know the aggregated total or average value of a column or an expression. This is simple to achieve using most spreadsheet packages. Using the SQL group functions for reporting provides two advantages over using a spreadsheet for analysis. First, they offer a convenient platform for performing calculations using real-time live data. Second, they allow for easy analysis of every value in a dataset or of specific groups of values.

The COUNT Function

The execution of COUNT on a column or an expression returns an integer value that represents the number of rows in the group. The COUNT function has the following syntax:

COUNT({* | [DISTINCT | ALL] *expr*});

There is one parameter that can be either *, which represents all columns including null values, or a specific column or expression. It may be preceded by the DISTINCT or ALL keywords. Consider the following queries:

```
Query 1: select count(*) from employees
Query 2: select count(commission_pct) from employees
```

```
Query 3: select count(distinct commission_pct) from employees
Query 4: select count(hire_date), count(manager_id) from employees
```

Query 1 counts the rows in the EMPLOYEES table and returns the integer 107. Query 2 counts the rows with nonnull COMMISSION_PCT values and returns 35. Query 3 considers the 35 nonnull rows, determines the number of unique values, and returns 7. Query 4 demonstrates two features. First, multiple group functions may be used in the same SELECT list and second, the COUNT function is used on both a DATE column and a NUMBER column. The integers 107 and 106 are returned since there are 107 nonnull HIRE_DATE values and 106 nonnull MANAGER_ID values in the group.

Three adjacent expressions using the COUNT function are shown in Figure 6-2. This query illustrates that there are 107 employee records in the EMPLOYEES table. Further, these 107 employees are allocated to 12 departments, including null departments, and work in 19 unique jobs.

The SUM Function

The aggregated total of a column or an expression is computed with the SUM function. Its syntax is as follows:

SUM([DISTINCT | ALL] *expr*);

One numeric parameter, optionally preceded by the DISTINCT or ALL keywords, is provided to the SUM function, which returns a numeric value. Consider the following queries:

```
Query 1: select sum(2) from employees
Query 2: select sum(salary) from employees
Query 3: select sum(distinct salary) from employees
Query 4: select sum(commission_pct) from employees
```

FIGURE 6-2	
The COUNT function	

```
SQL> SELECT COUNT(*),
  2         COUNT(DISTINCT NUL<DEPARTMENT_ID,0>),
  3         COUNT(DISTINCT NUL<JOB_ID,0>)
  4  FROM EMPLOYEES;

  COUNT(*) COUNT(DISTINCTNUL<DEPARTMENT_ID,0>) COUNT(DISTINCTNUL<JOB_ID,0>)
---------- ----------------------------------- ----------------------------
       107                                  12                           19

SQL> _
```

There are 107 rows in the EMPLOYEES table. Query 1 adds the number 2 across 107 rows and returns 214. Query 2 takes the SALARY column value for every row in the group, which in this case is the entire table, and returns the total salary amount of 691400. Query 3 returns a total of 397900 since many employees get paid the same salary and the DISTINCT keyword only adds unique values in the column to the total. Query 4 returns 7.8 after adding the nonnull values.

Figure 6-3 shows two queries. The first calculates the number of days between the current system date and the value in the HIRE_DATE column. The date arithmetic is performed for every row. The number returned is added using one SUM function call. The result is divided by 365.25 to give the total number of years worked by all current employees. The second query shows that the SUM function returns an "ORA-00932: inconsistent datatypes" error if it is provided with a nonnumeric argument.

The AVG Function

The *average* value of a column or expression divides the sum by the number of nonnull rows in the group. The AVG function has the following syntax:

AVG([DISTINCT | ALL] *expr*);

One numeric parameter, preceded by the DISTINCT or ALL keywords, is provided to the AVG function, which returns a numeric value. Consider the following queries:

```
Query 1: select avg(2) from employees
Query 2: select avg(salary) from employees
Query 3: select avg(distinct salary) from employees
Query 4: select avg(commission_pct) from employees
```

FIGURE 6-3	
The SUM function	

```
Command Prompt - SQLPLUS HR
SQL> SELECT SUM(SYSDATE-HIRE_DATE)/365.25 "Total Years worked by all"
  2    FROM EMPLOYEES;

Total Years worked by all
-------------------------
               1128.93987

SQL> SELECT SUM(HIRE_DATE)
  2    FROM EMPLOYEES;
SELECT SUM(HIRE_DATE)
           *
ERROR at line 1:
ORA-00932: inconsistent datatypes: expected NUMBER got DATE

SQL>
```

There are 107 rows in the EMPLOYEES table. Query 1 adds the number 2 across 107 rows and divides the total by the number of rows to return the number 2. Numeric literals submitted to the AVG function are returned unchanged. Query 2 adds the SALARY value for each row to obtain the total salary amount of 691400. This is divided by the 107 rows with nonnull SALARY values to return the average 6461.68224. You may expect query 3 to return a smaller result than query 2, but it does not. There are 57 unique salary values, which when added, yields a total of 397900. Dividing 397900 by 57 returns 6980.70175 as the average of the distinct salary values. Query 4 may produce unanticipated results if not properly understood. Adding the nonnull values, including duplicates, produces a total of 7.8. There are 35 employee records with nonnull COMMISSION_PCT values. Dividing 7.8 by 35 yields an average COMMISSION_PCT of 0.222857143.

Figure 6-4 shows two queries. The first lists the LAST_NAME and JOB_ID columns with an expression that calculates the total number of years worked by programmers in the organization. The second uses the AVG function to calculate the average number of years for which current programmers have been employed.

The MAX and MIN Functions

The MAX and MIN functions operate on NUMBER, DATE, CHAR, and VARCHAR2 data types. They return a value of the same data type as their input arguments, which are either the largest or smallest items in the group. When applied to DATE items, MAX returns the latest date and MIN returns the earliest one.

FIGURE 6-4	
The AVG function	

```
Command Prompt - SQLPLUS HR

SQL> SELECT LAST_NAME, JOB_ID, (SYSDATE-HIRE_DATE)/365.25 "Years worked"
  2  FROM EMPLOYEES
  3  WHERE JOB_ID='IT_PROG';

LAST_NAME                JOB_ID       Years worked
------------------------ ------------ ------------
Hunold                   IT_PROG        18.0269951
Ernst                    IT_PROG        16.6498561
Austin                   IT_PROG        10.5526624
Pataballa                IT_PROG        9.93664597
Lorentz                  IT_PROG        8.93185474

SQL> SELECT AVG((SYSDATE-HIRE_DATE)/365.25) "Avg years worked by IT staff"
  2  FROM EMPLOYEES
  3  WHERE JOB_ID='IT_PROG';

Avg years worked by IT staff
----------------------------
                  12.8196033

SQL> _
```

Character strings are converted to numeric representations of their constituent characters based on the NLS settings in the database. When the MIN function is applied to a group of character strings, the word that appears first alphabetically is returned, while MAX returns the word that would appear last. The MAX and MIN functions have the following syntax:

MAX([DISTINCT | ALL] *expr*); MIN([DISTINCT | ALL] *expr*)

They take one parameter preceded by the DISTINCT or ALL keywords. Consider the following queries:

```
Query 1: select min(commission_pct), max(commission_pct) from
employees
Query 2: select min(start_date),max(end_date) from job_history
Query 3: select min(job_id),max(job_id) from employees
```

Query 1 returns the numeric values 0.1 and 0.4 for the minimum and maximum COMMISSION_PCT values in the EMPLOYEES table. Note that null values for COMMISSION_PCT are ignored. Query 2 evaluates a DATE column and indicates that the earliest START_DATE in the JOB_HISTORY table is 17-SEP-1987 and the latest END_DATE is 31-DEC-1999. Query 3 returns AC_ACCOUNT and ST_MAN as the JOB_ID values appearing first and last alphabetically in the EMPLOYEES table.

The first query shown in Figure 6-5 uses the MAX and MIN functions to obtain information about employees with JOB_ID values of SA_REP. The results indicate that the sales representatives working for the shortest and longest durations were

FIGURE 6-5	
The MIN and MAX functions	

```
SQL> SELECT MIN(HIRE_DATE), MIN(SALARY), MAX(HIRE_DATE), MAX(SALARY)
  2  FROM EMPLOYEES
  3  WHERE JOB_ID = 'SA_REP';

MIN(HIRE_ MIN(SALARY) MAX(HIRE_ MAX(SALARY)
--------- ----------- --------- -----------
30-JAN-96        6100 21-APR-00       11500

SQL> SELECT LAST_NAME, HIRE_DATE, SALARY
  2  FROM EMPLOYEES
  3  WHERE JOB_ID   = 'SA_REP'
  4  AND SALARY IN (6100,11500)
  5  OR HIRE_DATE IN ('30-JAN-1996','21-APR-2000');

LAST_NAME                 HIRE_DATE    SALARY
------------------------- --------- ---------
King                      30-JAN-96     10000
Banda                     21-APR-00      6200
Ozer                      11-MAR-97     11500
Kumar                     21-APR-00      6100

SQL> _
```

hired on 21-APR-2000 and 30-JAN-1996, respectively. Furthermore, the sales representatives earning the largest and smallest salaries earn 11500 and 6100, respectively. The second query fetches the LAST_NAME values for the sales representatives to whom the minimum and maximum HIRE_DATE and SALARY values apply.

EXERCISE 6-1

Using the Group Functions

The COUNTRIES table stores a list of COUNTRY_NAME values. You are required to calculate the average length of all the country names. Any fractional components must be rounded to the nearest whole number.

1. Start SQL*Plus and connect to the HR schema.

2. The length of the country name value for each row is calculated using the LENGTH function. The average length may be determined using the AVG function. It may be rounded to the nearest whole number using the ROUND function.

3. The SELECT clause using alias AVERAGE_COUNTRY_NAME_LENGTH is
SELECT ROUND(AVG(LENGTH(COUNTRY_NAME)))
AVERAGE_COUNTRY_NAME_LENGTH

4. The FROM clause is
FROM COUNTRIES

5. Executing this statement returns a single row representing the average length of all the country names in the COUNTRIES table, as shown in the following illustration:

```
Command Prompt - SQLPLUS HR
SQL> SELECT ROUND(AVG(LENGTH(COUNTRY_NAME))) AVERAGE_COUNTRY_NAME_LENGTH
  2  FROM COUNTRIES
  3  /

AVERAGE_COUNTRY_NAME_LENGTH
---------------------------
                          8

SQL>
```

SCENARIO & SOLUTION

You would like to retrieve the earliest date from a column that stores DATE information. Can a group function be utilized to retrieve this value?	Yes. The MIN function operates on numeric, date, and character data. When the MIN function is executed against a DATE column, the earliest date value is returned.
Summary statistics are required by senior management. This includes details like number of employees, total staff salary cost, lowest salary, and highest salary values. Can such a report be drawn using one query?	Yes. There is no restriction to the number of group functions listed in the SELECT clause. The requested report can be drawn using the following query: SELECT COUNT(*) Num_Employees, SUM(SALARY) Tot_Salary_Cost, MIN(SALARY) Lowest Salary, MAX(SALARY) Maximum Salary FROM EMPLOYEES;
You are asked to list the number of unique jobs performed by employees in the organization. Counting the JOB_ID records will give you all the jobs. Is it possible to count the unique jobs?	Yes. The DISTINCT keyword may be used with the aggregate functions. To count unique JOB_ID values in the EMPLOYEES table, you can issue the query: SELECT COUNT(DISTINCT JOB_ID) FROM EMPLOYEES;

Nested Group Functions

Recall that single-row functions may be nested or embedded to any level of depth. *Group functions may only be nested two levels deep*. Three formats using group functions are shown here:

G1(*group_item*) = result
G1(G2(*group_item*) = result
G1(G2(G3(*group_item*))) is NOT allowed.

Group functions are represented by the letter G followed by a number. The first simple form contains no nested functions. Examples include the SUM(*group_item*) or AVG(*group_item*) functions that return a single result per group. The second form supports two nested group functions, like SUM(AVG(*group_item*)). In this case, a GROUP BY clause is mandatory since the average value of the *group_item* per group is calculated before being aggregated by the SUM function.

The third form is disallowed by Oracle. Consider an expression that nests three group functions. If the MAX function is applied to the previous example, the expression MAX(SUM(AVG(*group_item*))) is formed. The two inner group functions return a *single value* representing the sum of a set of average values. This expression becomes MAX(*single value*). A group function cannot be applied to a single value.

Figure 6-6 demonstrates two queries. Both restrict the rows returned to those with
DEPARTMENT_ID values of null, 40, and 80. These are then partitioned by their
DEPARTMENT_ID values into three groups. The first query calculates the sum of
the COMMISSION_PCT values for each group and returns the values 0.15, null,
and 7.65. Query 2 contains the nested group functions, which may be evaluated as
follows: AVG(SUM(COMMISSION_PCT)) = (0.15 + 7.65) /2 = 3.9.

FIGURE 6-6

Nested group
functions

exam
watch

Single-row functions may be nested to any level, but group functions may be nested to, at most, two levels deep. The nested function call COUNT(SUM(AVG(X))) returns the error, "ORA-00935: group function is nested too deeply." It is acceptable to *nest single-row functions within group functions. Consider the following query: SELECT SUM(AVG(LENGTH(LAST_NAME))) FROM EMPLOYEES GROUP BY DEPARTMENT_ID. It calculates the sum of the average length of LAST_NAME values per department.*

CERTIFICATION OBJECTIVE 6.03

Group Data Using the GROUP BY Clause

The *group functions* discussed earlier use groups of rows comprising the entire table. This section explores partitioning a set of data into groups using the GROUP BY clause. Group functions may be applied to these subsets or clusters of rows. The syntax of group functions and the GROUP BY clause are discussed in the following areas:

- Creating groups of data
- The GROUP BY clause
- Grouping by multiple columns

Creating Groups of Data

A table has at least one column and zero or more rows of data. In many tables this data requires analysis to transform it into useful information. It is a common reporting requirement to calculate statistics from a set of data divided into groups using different attributes. Previous examples using group functions operated against all the rows in a table. The entire table was treated as one large group.

Groups of data within a set are created by associating rows with common properties or attributes with each other. Thereafter, group functions can execute against each of these groups. Groups of data include entire rows and not specific columns.

Consider the EMPLOYEES table. It comprises 11 columns and 107 rows. You could create groups of rows that share a common DEPARTMENT_ID value. The SUM function may then be used to create salary totals per department. Another possible set of groups may share common JOB_ID column values. The AVG group function may then be used to identify the average salary paid to employees in different jobs.

A group is defined as a subset of the entire dataset sharing one or more common attributes. These attributes are typically column values but may also be expressions. The number of groups created depends on the distinct values present in the common attribute.

As Figure 6-7 shows, there are 12 unique DEPARTMENT_ID values in the EMPLOYEES table. If rows are grouped using common DEPARTMENT_ID values, there will be 12 groups. If a group function is executed against these groups, there will be 12 values returned, as it will execute once for each group.

on the

i̇ o b

Grouping data and using summary functions are widely utilized for reporting purposes. It is valuable to practice the segmentation of a set of data into different groupings. Oracle provides the analytical language to deconstruct datasets into groups, divide these into further subgroups, and so on. Aggregate grouping functions can then be executed against these groups and subgroups.

The GROUP BY Clause

The SELECT statement is enhanced by the addition of the GROUP BY clause. This clause facilitates the creation of groups. It appears after the WHERE clause but before the ORDER BY clause, as follows:

SELECT *column* | *expression* | *group_function(column* | *expression* [*alias*]),…}
FROM *table*
[WHERE *condition(s)*]
[GROUP BY {*col(s)* | *expr*}]
[ORDER BY {*col(s)* | *expr* | *numeric_pos*} [ASC | DESC] [NULLS FIRST | LAST]];

The column or expression specified in the GROUP BY clause is also known as the *grouping attribute* and is the component that rows are grouped by. The dataset is segmented based on the grouping attribute. Consider the following query:

```
select max(salary), count(*)
from employees
group by department_id
order by department_id
```

FIGURE 6-7

Unique
DEPARTMENT_
ID values in the
EMPLOYEES table

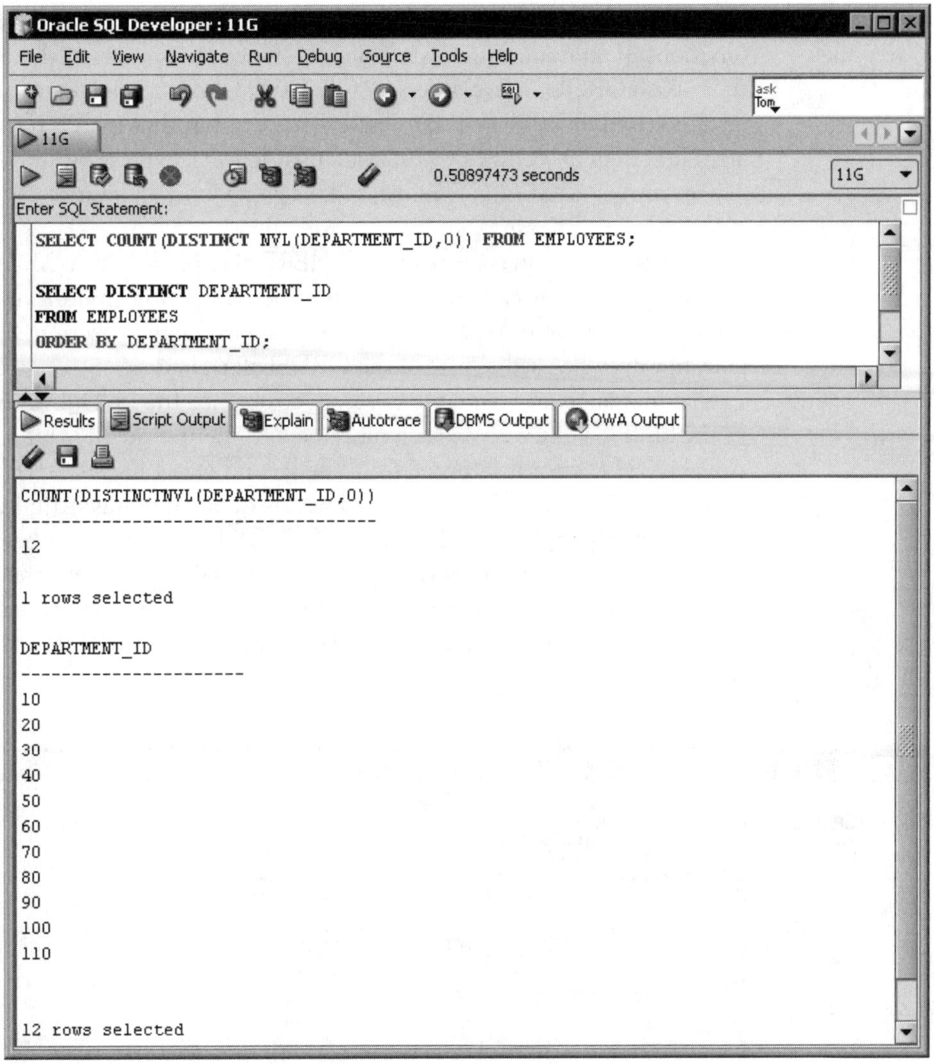

```
Oracle SQL Developer : 11G                                           _ □ ×

File   Edit   View   Navigate   Run   Debug   Source   Tools   Help

                                                              ask
                                                              Tom

▷ 11G                                                          ◀ ▷ ▼

▷ ▤ ▨ ▨ ●    ▨ ▨ ▨    ✎    0.50897473 seconds        11G    ▼

Enter SQL Statement:

 SELECT COUNT(DISTINCT NVL(DEPARTMENT_ID,0)) FROM EMPLOYEES;

 SELECT DISTINCT DEPARTMENT_ID
 FROM EMPLOYEES
 ORDER BY DEPARTMENT_ID;

▷ Results  ▤ Script Output  ▨ Explain  ▨ Autotrace  ▨ DBMS Output  ▨ OWA Output

✎ ▤ ▨

COUNT(DISTINCTNVL(DEPARTMENT_ID,0))
-----------------------------------
12

1 rows selected


DEPARTMENT_ID
---------------------
10
20
30
40
50
60
70
80
90
100
110

12 rows selected
```

The grouping attribute in this example is the DEPARTMENT_ID column. The
dataset, on which the group functions in the SELECT list must operate, is divided
into 12 groups, one for each department. For each group (department), the maximum
salary value and the number of rows are returned. Since the results are sorted by
DEPARTMENT_ID, the third row in the set of results contains the values 11000 and 6.
This indicates that 6 employees have a DEPARTMENT_ID value of 30. Of these 6,
the highest earner has a SALARY value of 11000. This query demonstrates that the
grouping attribute does not have to be included in the SELECT list.

It is common to see the grouping attribute in the SELECT list alongside grouping functions. If an item, which is not a group function, appears in the SELECT list and there is no GROUP BY clause, an "ORA-00937: not a single-group group function" error is raised. If a GROUP BY clause is present but that item is not a grouping attribute, then an "ORA-00979: not a GROUP BY expression" error is returned.

Any item in the SELECT list that is not a group function must be a grouping attribute of the GROUP BY clause.

If a group function is placed in a WHERE clause, an "ORA-00934: group function is not allowed here" error is returned. Imposing group-level conditions is achieved using the HAVING clause discussed in the next section. Group functions may, however, be used as part of the ORDER BY clause.

The first query in Figure 6-8 raises an error since the END_DATE column is in the SELECT list with a group function and there is no GROUP BY clause. An "ORA-00979" error is returned from the second query since the START_DATE item is listed in the SELECT clause, but it is not a grouping attribute.

The third query divides the JOB_HISTORY rows into groups based on the 4-digit year component from the END_DATE column. Four groups are created using this grouping attribute. These represent different years when employees ended their jobs. The COUNT shows the number of employees who quit their jobs during each

FIGURE 6-8	
The GROUP BY clause	

```
Command Prompt - SQLPLUS HR/HR

SQL> SELECT   END_DATE ,COUNT(*)
  2  FROM JOB_HISTORY;
SELECT   END_DATE ,COUNT(*)
          *
ERROR at line 1:
ORA-00937: not a single-group group function


SQL> SELECT   END_DATE, START_DATE, COUNT(*)
  2  FROM JOB_HISTORY
  3  GROUP BY END_DATE;
SELECT   END_DATE, START_DATE, COUNT(*)
                   *
ERROR at line 1:
ORA-00979: not a GROUP BY expression


SQL> SELECT   TO_CHAR(END_DATE,'YYYY') "Year" ,
  2           COUNT(*) "Number of Employees"
  3  FROM JOB_HISTORY
  4  GROUP BY TO_CHAR(END_DATE,'YYYY')
  5  ORDER BY COUNT(*) DESC;

Year Number of Employees
---- ------------------
1999                  4
1998                  3
1993                  2
1997                  1
```

of these years. The results are listed in descending order based on the "Number of Employees" expression. Note that the COUNT group function is present in the ORDER BY clause.

Grouping by Multiple Columns

A powerful extension to the GROUP BY clause uses multiple grouping attributes. Oracle permits datasets to be partitioned into groups and allows these groups to be further divided into subgroups using a different grouping attribute. Consider the following two queries:

```
Query 1: select department_id, sum(commission_pct) from employees
where commission_pct is not null group by department_id
Query 2: select department_id, job_id, sum(commission_pct) from
employees
where commission_pct is not null group by department_id, job_id
```

Query 1 restricts the rows returned from the EMPLOYEES table to the 35 rows with nonnull COMMISSION_PCT values. These rows are then divided into two groups: 80 and NULL based on the DEPARTMENT_ID grouping attribute. The result set contains two rows, which return the sum of the COMMISSION_PCT values for each group.

Query 2 is similar to the first one except it has an additional item: JOB_ID in both the SELECT and GROUP BY clauses. This second grouping attribute decomposes the two groups based on DEPARTMENT_ID into the constituent JOB_ID components belonging to the rows in each group. The distinct JOB_ID values for rows with DEPARTMENT_ID=80 are SA_REP and SA_MAN. The distinct JOB_ID value for rows with null DEPARTMENT_ID is SA_REP. Therefore, query 2 returns two groupings, one which consists of two subgroups, and the other with only one, as shown in Figure 6-9.

FIGURE 6-9

The GROUP
BY clause with
multiple columns

```
ⓒ Command Prompt - SQLPLUS HR                                        _ □ ✕
SQL> SELECT DEPARTMENT_ID, SUM<COMMISSION_PCT>
  2  FROM EMPLOYEES
  3  WHERE COMMISSION_PCT IS NOT NULL
  4  GROUP BY DEPARTMENT_ID;

DEPARTMENT_ID SUM<COMMISSION_PCT>
------------- -------------------
                              .15
           80                7.65
SQL> SELECT DEPARTMENT_ID, JOB_ID, SUM<COMMISSION_PCT>
  2  FROM EMPLOYEES
  3  WHERE COMMISSION_PCT IS NOT NULL
  4  GROUP BY DEPARTMENT_ID, JOB_ID;

DEPARTMENT_ID JOB_ID      SUM<COMMISSION_PCT>
------------- ----------  -------------------
           80 SA_REP                     6.15
           80 SA_MAN                      1.5
              SA_REP                      .15

SQL> _
```

EXERCISE 6-2

Grouping Data Based on Multiple Columns

Analysis of staff turnover is a common reporting requirement. You are required to create a report containing the number of employees who left their jobs, grouped by the year in which they left. The jobs they performed are also required. The results must be sorted in descending order based on the number of employees in each group. The report must list the year, the JOB_ID, and the number of employees who left a particular job in that year.

1. Start SQL Developer and connect to the HR schema.

2. The JOB_HISTORY table contains the END_DATE and JOB_ID columns, which constitute the source data for this report.

3. The year component is extracted using the TO_CHAR function. The number of employees who quit a particular job in each year is obtained using the COUNT(*) function.

4. The SELECT clause is
   TO_CHAR(END_DATE,'YYYY') "Quitting Year", JOB_ID, COUNT(*) "Number of Employees"

5. The FROM clause is
   FROM EMPLOYEES

6. There is no WHERE clause.

7. Since the report requires employees to be listed by year and JOB_ID, these two items must appear in the GROUP BY clause, which is
GROUP BY TO_CHAR(END_DATE,'YYYY'), JOB_ID

8. The sorting is performed with
ORDER BY COUNT(*) DESC

9. Executing this statement returns the staff turnover report requested as shown in the following illustration:

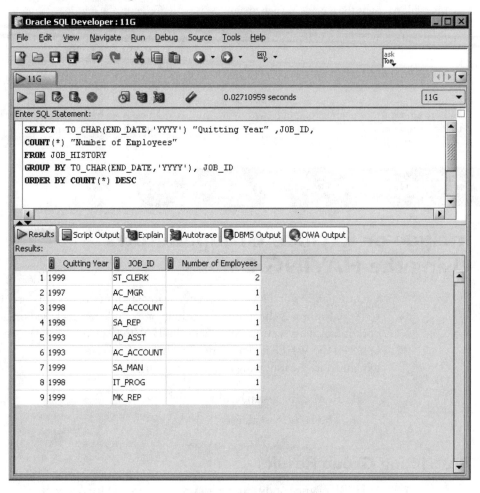

SCENARIO & SOLUTION	
You wish to print name badges for the staff who work as sales representatives. Can the length of the shortest and longest LAST_NAME values be determined for these employees?	Yes. The MAX and MIN functions applied to the LAST_NAME field will determine the shortest and longest names as shown in the following query: SELECT MIN(LENGTH(LAST_NAME)), MAX(LENGTH(LAST_NAME)) FROM EMPLOYEES WHERE JOB_ID='SA_REP';
Is it possible to count the records in each group, first by dividing the employee records by year of employment, then by job, and finally by salary?	Yes. Grouping by multiple columns is a powerful option allowing fine-grained analysis as shown in the following query: SELECT COUNT(*), TO_CHAR(HIRE_DATE, 'YYYY'), JOB_ID, SALARY FROM EMPLOYEES GROUP BY TO_CHAR(HIRE_DATE,'YYYY') , JOB_ID, SALARY
Is there a limit to the number of groups within groups that can be formed?	No. There is no limit to the number of groups and subgroups that can be formed.

CERTIFICATION OBJECTIVE 6.04

Include or Exclude Grouped Rows Using the HAVING Clause

Creating groups of data and applying aggregate functions is very useful. A refinement to these features is the ability to include or exclude results based on group-level conditions. This section introduces the *HAVING* clause. A clear distinction is made between the WHERE clause and the HAVING clause. The HAVING clause is explained in the following areas:

- Restricting group results
- The HAVING clause

Restricting Group Results

WHERE clause conditions restrict rows returned by a query. Rows are included based on whether they fulfill the conditions listed and are sometimes known as *row-level results*. Clustering rows using the GROUP BY clause and applying an aggregate function to these groups returns results often referred to as *group-level results*. The HAVING clause provides the language to restrict group-level results.

The following query limits the rows retrieved from the JOB_HISTORY table by specifying a WHERE condition based on the DEPARTMENT_ID column values.

```
select department_id
from job_history
where department_id in (50,60,80,110);
```

This query returns seven rows. If the WHERE clause was absent, all ten rows would be retrieved. Suppose you want to know how many employees were previously employed in each of these departments. There are seven rows that can be manually grouped and counted. However, if there are a large number of rows, an aggregate function like COUNT may be used, as shown in the following query:

```
select department_id, count(*)
from job_history
where department_id in (50,60,80,110)
group by department_id;
```

This query is very similar to the previous statement. The aggregate function COUNT was added to the SELECT list, and a GROUP BY DEPARTMENT_ID clause was also added. Four rows with their aggregate row count are returned and it is clear that the original seven rows restricted by the WHERE clause were clustered into four groups based on common DEPARTMENT_ID values, as shown in the following table:

DEPARTMENT_ID	COUNT(*)
50	2
60	1
80	2
110	2

Suppose you wanted to refine this list to include only those departments with more than one employee. The HAVING clause limits or restricts the group-level rows as required.

This query must perform the following steps:

1. Consider the entire row-level dataset.

2. Limit the dataset based on any WHERE clause conditions.

3. Segment the data into one or more groups using the grouping attributes specified in the GROUP BY clause.

4. Apply any aggregate functions to create a new group-level dataset. Each row may be regarded as an aggregation of its source row-level data based on the groups created.

5. Limit or restrict the group-level data with a HAVING clause condition. Only group-level results matching these conditions are returned.

on the Job *Choosing the appropriate context to use a WHERE or a HAVING clause depends on whether physical or group-level rows are to be restricted. Rows containing data stored in columns are sometimes called actual or physical rows. When actual (physical) rows are restricted, one or more conditions are imposed using a WHERE clause. When these rows are grouped together, one or more aggregate functions may be applied, yielding one or more group-level rows. These are not physical rows, but temporary aggregations of data. Group-level rows are restricted using conditions imposed by a HAVING clause.*

The HAVING Clause

The general form of the SELECT statement is further enhanced by the addition of the HAVING clause and becomes:

SELECT *column* | *expression* | *group_function(column* | *expression* [*alias*]),…}
FROM *table*
[WHERE *condition(s)*]
[GROUP BY {*col(s)* | *expr*}]
[HAVING *group_condition(s)*]
[ORDER BY {*col(s)* | *expr* | *numeric_pos*} [ASC | DESC] [NULLS FIRST | LAST]];

An important difference between the HAVING clause and the other SELECT statement clauses is that it may only be specified if a GROUP BY clause is present. This dependency is sensible since group-level rows must exist before they can be restricted. The HAVING clause can occur before the GROUP BY clause in the SELECT statement. However, it is more common to place the HAVING clause after the GROUP BY clause. All grouping is performed and group functions are executed prior to evaluating the HAVING clause.

The following query shows how the HAVING clause is used to restrict an aggregated dataset. Records from the JOB_HISTORY table are divided into four groups. The rows that meet the HAVING clause condition (contributing more than one row to the group row count) are returned:

```
select department_id, count(*)
from job_history
where department_id in (50,60,80,110)
group by department_id
having count(*)>1
```

Three rows with DEPARTMENT_ID values of 50, 80, and 110, each with a
COUNT(*) value of 2, are returned.

Figure 6-10 shows three queries. Query 1 divides the 107 records from the
EMPLOYEES table into 19 groups based on common JOB_ID values. The average
salary for each JOB_ID group and the aggregate row count is computed. Query
2 refines the results by conditionally excluding those aggregated rows where the

FIGURE 6-10	

The HAVING
clause

```
SQL> SELECT JOB_ID, AVG(SALARY), COUNT(*) FROM EMPLOYEES
  2   GROUP BY JOB_ID;

JOB_ID      AVG(SALARY)    COUNT(*)
----------  -----------    --------
AC_MGR           12000            1
AC_ACCOUNT        8300            1
IT_PROG           5760            5
ST_MAN            7280            5
AD_ASST           4400            1
PU_MAN           11000            1
SH_CLERK          3215           20
AD_VP            17000            2
FI_ACCOUNT        7920            5
MK_MAN           13000            1
PR_REP           10000            1
FI_MGR           12000            1
PU_CLERK          2780            5
SA_MAN           12200            5
MK_REP            6000            1
AD_PRES          24000            1
SA_REP            8350           30
HR_REP            6500            1
ST_CLERK          2785           20

19 rows selected.

SQL> SELECT JOB_ID, AVG(SALARY), COUNT(*) FROM EMPLOYEES
  2   GROUP BY JOB_ID
  3   HAVING AVG(SALARY) > 10000;

JOB_ID      AVG(SALARY)    COUNT(*)
----------  -----------    --------
AC_MGR           12000            1
PU_MAN           11000            1
AD_VP            17000            2
MK_MAN           13000            1
FI_MGR           12000            1
SA_MAN           12200            5
AD_PRES          24000            1

7 rows selected.

SQL> SELECT JOB_ID, AVG(SALARY), COUNT(*) FROM EMPLOYEES
  2   GROUP BY JOB_ID
  3   HAVING AVG(SALARY) > 10000
  4   AND COUNT(*) >1;

JOB_ID      AVG(SALARY)    COUNT(*)
----------  -----------    --------
AD_VP            17000            2
SA_MAN           12200            5
```

average salary is less than or equal to 10000, using a HAVING clause. Query 3 demonstrates that the Boolean operators may be used to specify multiple HAVING clause conditions.

e x a m

w a t c h   *The HAVING clause may only be specified when a GROUP BY clause is present. A GROUP BY clause can be specified without a HAVING clause. Multiple conditions may be imposed by a* *HAVING clause using the Boolean AND, OR, and NOT operators. The HAVING clause conditions restrict group-level data and must contain a group function or an expression that uses one.*

EXERCISE 6-3

Using the HAVING Clause

The company is planning a recruitment drive and wants to identify the days of the week on which 20 or more staff members were hired. Your report must list the days and the number of employees hired on each of them.

1. Start SQL*Plus and connect to the HR schema.
2. EMPLOYEES records must be divided into groups based on the day component of the HIRE_DATE column. The number of employees per group may be obtained using the COUNT function.
3. The SELECT clause is
SELECT TO_CHAR(HIRE_DATE,'DAY'), COUNT(*)
4. No WHERE clause is required since all the physical rows of the EMPLOYEES table are considered.
5. The GROUP BY clause is
GROUP BY TO_CHAR(HIRE_DATE,'DAY')
This GROUP BY clause potentially creates seven group-level rows, one for each day of the week.
6. The COUNT function in the SELECT clause then lists the number of staff members employed on each day. The HAVING clause must be used to restrict these seven rows to only those where the count is greater than or equal to 20.

7. The HAVING clause is
   HAVING COUNT(*) >= 20

8. The FROM clause is
   FROM EMPLOYEES

9. Executing this statement returns the days of the week on which 20 or more employees were hired as shown in the following illustration:

```
Command Prompt - SQLPLUS HR                                       _ □ X

SQL> SELECT TO_CHAR(HIRE_DATE,'DAY') HIRE_DAY, COUNT(*)
  2  FROM EMPLOYEES
  3  GROUP BY TO_CHAR(HIRE_DATE,'DAY')
  4  HAVING COUNT(*)>=20
  5  /

HIRE_DAY    COUNT(*)
---------- ----------
TUESDAY           20
WEDNESDAY         21

SQL> _
```

INSIDE THE EXAM

The certification objectives in this chapter are examined using practical examples and scenarios that require you to predict the results returned from SQL queries. These queries focus on dividing datasets into groups using one or more grouping attributes.

Understand the limitations of nesting group functions. Remember that group functions must exist in the SELECT clause if there is a GROUP BY clause. The HAVING clause may occur before the GROUP BY clause but is usually followed by it. An error is returned if the HAVING clause is used without a GROUP BY clause. Recall that the HAVING clause may contain multiple conditions, but each one must contain a group function.

Knowing how to interpret and trace nested group and single-row functions is vital, as many questions contain expressions with nested functions. The innermost to outermost order of evaluation of nested group and single functions is identical and must be remembered.

There are many built-in group functions available, but the exams will test your understanding of the COUNT, SUM, AVG, MAX, and MIN functions. Ensure that you have a thorough understanding of these functions and how they interact with the DISTINCT keyword and NULL values.

CERTIFICATION SUMMARY

Multiple row functions and the concept of dividing data into groups are described in this chapter. There is a multitude of group or aggregate functions available. The key functions for creating sum totals; calculating averages, minimums, or maximums; and obtaining a record count are explored in detail.

The differences between nesting group functions and single-row functions are investigated, and the limitations of the former are explained. Creating groups using common grouping attributes is concretized with the introduction of the GROUP BY clause to the SELECT statement. Row-level data is limited by conditions specified in the WHERE clause. The restriction of group-level data using the HAVING clause is also discussed.

✓ TWO-MINUTE DRILL

Describe the Group Functions

❏ Group functions are also known as multiple row, aggregate, or summary functions. They execute once for each group of data and aggregate the data from multiple rows into a single result for each group.

❏ Groups may be entire tables or portions of a table grouped together by a common grouping attribute.

Identify the Available Group Functions

❏ The COUNT of a function returns an integer value representing the number of rows in a group.

❏ The SUM function returns an aggregated total of all the nonnull numeric expression values in a group.

❏ The AVG function divides the sum of a column or expression by the number of nonnull rows in a group.

❏ The MAX and MIN functions operate on NUMBER, DATE, CHAR, and VARCHAR2 data types. They return a value that is either the largest or smallest item in the group.

❏ Group functions may only be nested two levels deep.

Group Data Using the GROUP BY Clause

❏ The GROUP BY clause specifies the grouping attribute rows must have in common for them to be clustered together.

❏ The GROUP BY clause facilitates the creation of groups within a selected set of data and appears after the WHERE clause but before the ORDER BY clause.

❏ Any item on the SELECT list that is not a group function must be a grouping attribute.

❏ Group functions may not be placed in a WHERE clause.

❏ Datasets may be partitioned into groups and further divided into subgroups based on multiple grouping attributes.

Include or Exclude Grouped Rows Using the HAVING Clause

❑ Clustering rows using a common grouping attribute with the GROUP BY clause and applying an aggregate function to each of these groups returns *group-level results*.

❑ The HAVING clause provides the language to limit the group-level results returned.

❑ The HAVING clause may only be specified if there is a GROUP BY clause present.

❑ All grouping is performed and group functions are executed prior to evaluating the HAVING clause.

SELF TEST

The following questions will help you measure your understanding of the material presented in this chapter. Read all the choices carefully because there may be more than one correct answer. Choose all the correct answers for each question.

Describe the Group Functions

1. What result is returned by the following statement?
SELECT COUNT(*) FROM DUAL; (Choose the best answer.)

    A. NULL

    B. 0

    C. 1

    D. None of the above

2. Choose one correct statement regarding group functions.

    A. Group functions may only be used when a GROUP BY clause is present.

    B. Group functions can operate on multiple rows at a time.

    C. Group functions only operate on a single row at a time.

    D. Group functions can execute multiple times within a single group.

Identify the Available Group Functions

3. What value is returned after executing the following statement?
SELECT SUM(SALARY) FROM EMPLOYEES;
Assume there are 10 employee records and each contains a SALARY value of 100, except for 1, which has a null value in the SALARY field. (Choose the best answer.)

    A. 900

    B. 1000

    C. NULL

    D. None of the above

4. Which values are returned after executing the following statement?
SELECT COUNT(*), COUNT(SALARY) FROM EMPLOYEES;
Assume there are 10 employee records and each contains a SALARY value of 100, except for 1, which has a null value in their SALARY field. (Choose all that apply.)

    A. 10 and 10

    B. 10 and NULL

    C. 10 and 9

    D. None of the above

5. What value is returned after executing the following statement?
SELECT AVG(NVL(SALARY,100)) FROM EMPLOYEES;
Assume there are ten employee records and each contains a SALARY value of 100, except for one employee, who has a null value in the SALARY field. (Choose the best answer.)
A. NULL
B. 90
C. 100
D. None of the above

Group Data Using the GROUP BY Clause

6. What value is returned after executing the following statement?
SELECT SUM((AVG(LENGTH(NVL(SALARY,0)))))
FROM EMPLOYEES
GROUP BY SALARY;
Assume there are ten employee records and each contains a SALARY value of 100, except for one, which has a null value in the SALARY field. (Choose the best answer.)
A. An error is returned
B. 3
C. 4
D. None of the above

7. How many records are returned by the following query?
SELECT SUM(SALARY), DEPARTMENT_ID FROM EMPLOYEES
GROUP BY DEPARTMENT_ID;
Assume there are 11 nonnull and 1 null unique DEPARTMENT_ID values. All records have a nonnull SALARY value. (Choose the best answer.)
A. 12
B. 11
C. NULL
D. None of the above

8. What values are returned after executing the following statement?
SELECT JOB_ID, MAX_SALARY FROM JOBS GROUP BY MAX_SALARY;
Assume that the JOBS table has ten records with the same JOB_ID value of DBA and the same MAX_SALARY value of 100. (Choose the best answer.)
A. One row of output with the values DBA, 100
B. Ten rows of output with the values DBA, 100
C. An error is returned
D. None of the above

Include or Exclude Grouped Rows Using the **HAVING** Clause

9. How many rows of data are returned after executing the following statement?
SELECT DEPT_ID, SUM(NVL(SALARY,100)) FROM EMP
GROUP BY DEPT_ID HAVING SUM(SALARY) > 400;
Assume the EMP table has ten rows and each contains a SALARY value of 100, except for one,
which has a null value in the SALARY field. The first and second five rows have DEPT_ID
values of 10 and 20, respectively. (Choose the best answer.)

    A. Two rows

    B. One row

    C. Zero rows

    D. None of the above

10. How many rows of data are returned after executing the following statement?
SELECT DEPT_ID, SUM(SALARY) FROM EMP GROUP BY DEPT_ID HAVING
SUM(NVL(SALARY,100)) > 400;
Assume the EMP table has ten rows and each contains a SALARY value of 100, except for one,
which has a null value in the SALARY field. The first and second five rows have DEPT_ID
values of 10 and 20, respectively. (Choose the best answer.)

    A. Two rows

    B. One row

    C. Zero rows

    D. None of the above

LAB QUESTION

Using SQL Developer or SQL*Plus, connect to the OE schema and complete the following tasks.

The PRODUCT_INFORMATION table lists items that are orderable and others that are
planned, obsolete, or under development. You are required to prepare a report that groups the nonorderable products by their PRODUCT_STATUS and shows the number of products in each group
and the sum of the LIST_PRICE of the products per group. Further, only the group-level rows, where
the sum of the LIST_PRICE is greater than 4000, must be displayed. A product is nonorderable if the
PRODUCT_STATUS value is not equal to the string 'orderable'. There are several approaches to
solving this question. Your approach may differ from the solution proposed.

SELF TEST ANSWERS

Describe the Group Functions

1. ☑ **C.** The DUAL table has one row and one column. The COUNT(*) function returns the number of rows in a table or group.
   ☒ **A, B,** and **D** are incorrect.

2. ☑ **B.** By definition, group functions can operate on multiple rows at a time, unlike single-row functions.
   ☒ **A, C,** and **D** are incorrect statements. A group function may be used without a GROUP BY clause. In this case, the entire dataset is operated on as a group. The COUNT function is often executed against an entire table, which behaves as one group. **D** is incorrect. Once a dataset has been partitioned into different groups, any group functions execute once per group.

Identify the Available Group Functions

3. ☑ **A.** The SUM aggregate function ignores null values and adds nonnull values. Since nine rows contain the SALARY value 100, 900 is returned.
   ☒ **B, C,** and **D** are incorrect. **B** would be returned if SUM(NVL(SALARY,100)) was executed. **C** is a tempting choice since regular arithmetic with NULL values returns a NULL result. However, the aggregate functions, except for COUNT(*), ignore NULL values.

4. ☑ **C.** COUNT(*) considers all rows including those with NULL values. COUNT(SALARY) only considers the nonnull rows.
   ☒ **A, B,** and **D** are incorrect.

5. ☑ **C.** The NVL function converts the one NULL value into 100. Thereafter, the average function adds the SALARY values and obtains 1000. Dividing this by the number of records returns 100.
   ☒ **A, B,** and **D** are incorrect. **B** would be returned if AVG(NVL(SALARY,0)) was selected. It is interesting to note that if AVG(SALARY) was selected, 100 would have also been returned, since the AVG function would sum the nonnull values and divide the total by the number of rows with nonnull SALARY values. So AVG(SALARY) would be calculated as: 900/9=100.

Group Data Using the GROUP BY Clause

6. ☑ **C.** The dataset is segmented based on the SALARY column. This creates two groups: one with SALARY values of 100 and the other with a null SALARY value. The average length of SALARY value 100 is 3 for the rows in the first group. The NULL salary value is first converted

into the number 0 by the NVL function, and the average length of SALARY is 1. The SUM function operates across the two groups adding the values 3 and 1 returning 4.

☒   **A, B,** and **D** are incorrect. **A** seems plausible since group functions may not be nested more than two levels deep. Although there are four functions, only two are group functions while the others are single-row functions evaluated before the group functions. **B** would be returned if the expression SUM(AVG(LENGTH(SALARY))) was selected.

7.   ☑   **A.** There are 12 distinct DEPARTMENT_ID values. Since this is the grouping attribute, 12 groups are created, including 1 with a null DEPARTMENT_ID value. Therefore 12 rows are returned.

☒   **B, C,** and **D** are incorrect.

Include or Exclude Grouped Rows Using the HAVING Clause

8.   ☑   **C.** For a GROUP BY clause to be used, a group function must appear in the SELECT list.

☒   **A, B,** and **D** are incorrect since the statement is syntactically inaccurate and is disallowed by Oracle. Do not mistake the column named MAX_SALARY for the MAX(SALARY) function.

9.   ☑   **B.** Two groups are created based on their common DEPT_ID values. The group with DEPT_ID values of ten consists of five rows with SALARY values of 100 in each of them. Therefore, the SUM(SALARY) function returns 500 for this group, and it satisfies the HAVING SUM(SALARY) > 400 clause. The group with DEPT_ID values of 20 has four rows with SALARY values of 100 and one row with a NULL SALARY. SUM(SALARY) only returns 400 and this group does not satisfy the HAVING clause.

☒   **A, C,** and **D** are incorrect. Beware of the SUM(NVL(SALARY,100)) expression in the SELECT clause. This expression selects the format of the output. It does not restrict or limit the dataset in anyway.

10.   ☑   **A.** Two groups are created based on their common DEPT_ID values. The group with DEPT_ID values of 10 consists of five rows with SALARY values of 100 in each of them. Therefore the SUM(NVL(SALARY,100)) function returns 500 for this group and it satisfies the HAVING SUM(SALARY) > 400 clause. The group with DEPT_ID values of 20 has four rows with SALARY values of 100 and one row with a null SALARY. SUM(NVL(SALARY,100)) returns 500 and this group satisfies the HAVING clause. Therefore two rows are returned.

☒   **B, C,** and **D** are incorrect. Although the SELECT clause contains SUM(SALARY), which returns 500 and 400 for the two groups, the HAVING clause contains the SUM(NVL(SALARY,100)) expression, which specifies the inclusion or exclusion criteria for a group-level row.

LAB ANSWER

Using SQL Developer or SQL*Plus, connect to the OE schema and complete the following tasks.

There are several approaches to solving this question. Your approach may differ from the solution proposed here.

1. Start SQL Developer and connect to the OE schema.

2. The dataset must be restricted to rows from the PRODUCT_INFORMATION table where the PRODUCT_STATUS is not equal to the string 'orderable'. Since this character literal may have been input in mixed case, a case conversion function like UPPER can be used.

3. The WHERE clause is
   ```
   WHERE UPPER(PRODUCT_STATUS) <> 'ORDERABLE'
   ```

4. Since the dataset must be segmented into groups based on the PRODUCT_STATUS column, the GROUP BY statement is
   ```
   GROUP BY PRODUCT_STATUS
   ```

5. The dataset is now partitioned into different groups based on their PRODUCT_STATUS values. Therefore, the COUNT(*) function may be used to obtain the number of products in each group. The SUM(LIST_PRICE) aggregate function can be used to calculate the sum of the LIST_PRICE values for all the rows in each group.

6. The SELECT clause is therefore
   ```
   SELECT COUNT(*), SUM(LIST_PRICE), PRODUCT_STATUS
   ```

7. The HAVING clause which restricts group-level rows is therefore
   ```
   HAVING SUM(LIST_PRICE) > 4000
   ```

8. The FROM clause is
   ```
   FROM PRODUCT_INFORMATION
   ```

9. Executing this statement returns the report required as shown in the following illustration.

7

Displaying Data from Multiple Tables

CERTIFICATION OBJECTIVES

The three pillars of relational theory are selection, projection, and joining. This chapter focuses on the practical implementation of *joining*. Rows from different tables are associated with each other using *joins*. Support for joining has implications for the way data is stored in database tables. Many data models such as third normal form or star schemas have emerged to exploit this feature.

Tables may be joined in several ways. The most common technique is called an *equijoin*. A row is associated with one or more rows in another table based on the *equality* of column values or expressions. Tables may also be joined using a *nonequijoin*. In this case, a row is associated with one or more rows in another table if its column values fall into a range determined by inequality operators.

A less common technique is to associate rows with other rows in the same table. This association is based on columns with logical and usually hierarchical relationships with each other. This is called a *self-join*. Rows with null or differing entries in common *join columns* are excluded when equijoins and nonequijoins are performed. An *outer join* is available to fetch these *one-legged* or *orphaned* rows if necessary.

A *cross join* or *Cartesian product* is formed when every row from one table is joined to all rows in another. This join is often the result of missing or inadequate join conditions but is occasionally intentional.

CERTIFICATION OBJECTIVE 7.01

Write SELECT Statements to Access Data from More Than One Table Using Equijoins and Nonequijoins

This certification objective receives extensive coverage in this chapter. It is crucial to learning the concepts and language for performing joins. Different types of joins are introduced in their primitive forms outlining the broad categories that are available. An in-depth discussion of the various join clauses is then conducted. The modern ANSI-compliant and traditional Oracle syntaxes are discussed, but emphasis is placed on the modern syntax. This section concludes with a discussion of nonequijoins and additional join conditions. Joining is described by focusing on the following eight areas:

- Types of joins
- Joining tables using SQL:1999 syntax
- Qualifying ambiguous column names
- The NATURAL JOIN clause
- The natural JOIN USING clause
- The natural JOIN ON clause
- N-way joins and additional join conditions
- Nonequijoins

Types of Joins

Two basic joins are the *equijoin* and the *nonequijoin*. Equijoins are more frequently used. Joins may be performed between multiple tables, but much of the following discussion will use two hypothetical tables to illustrate the concepts and language of joins. The first table is called the *source* and the second is called the *target*. Rows in the source and target tables comprise one or more columns. As an example, assume that the *source* and *target* are the COUNTRIES and REGIONS tables from the HR schema, respectively.

The COUNTRIES table contains three columns named COUNTRY_ID, COUNTRY_NAME, and REGION_ID. The REGIONS table is comprised of two columns named REGION_ID and REGION_NAME. The data in these two tables is related to each other based on the common REGION_ID column. Consider the following queries:

```
Query 1: select * from countries where country_id='CA';
Query 2: select region_name from regions where region_id='2';
```

The name of the region to which a country belongs may be determined by obtaining its REGION_ID value. This value is used to join it with the row in the REGIONS table with the same REGION_ID. Query 1 retrieves the column values associated with the row from the COUNTRIES table where the COUNTRY_ID='CA'. The REGION_ID value of this row is 2. Query 2 fetches the Americas REGION_NAME from the REGIONS table for the row with REGION_ID=2. Equijoining facilitates the retrieval of column values from multiple tables using a single query.

The source and target tables can be swapped, so the REGIONS table could be the source and the COUNTRIES table could be the target. Consider the following two queries:

```
Query 1: select * from regions where region_name='Americas';
Query 2: select country_name from countries where region_id='2';
```

Query 1 fetches one row with a REGION_ID value of 2. Joining in this reversed manner allows the following question to be asked: What countries belong to the Americas region? The answers from the second query are five COUNTRY_NAME values: Argentina, Brazil, Canada, Mexico, and the United States of America. These results may be obtained from a single query that joins the tables together. The language to perform equijoins, nonequijoins, outer joins, and cross joins is introduced next, along with a discussion of the traditional Oracle join syntax.

Natural Joins

The natural join is implemented using three possible *join clauses* that use the following keywords in different combinations: *NATURAL JOIN, USING*, and *ON*.

When the source and target tables share identically named columns, it is possible to perform a natural join between them without specifying a join column. This is sometimes referred to as a *pure natural join*. In this scenario, columns with the same names in the source and target tables are automatically associated with each other. Rows with matching column values in both tables are retrieved. The REGIONS and COUNTRIES table both share the REGION_ID column. They may be naturally joined without specifying join columns, as shown in the first two queries in Figure 7-1.

The NATURAL JOIN keywords instruct Oracle to identify columns with identical names between the source and target tables. Thereafter, a join is implicitly performed between them. In the first query, the REGION_ID column is identified as the only commonly named column in both tables. REGIONS is the source table and appears after the FROM clause. The target table is therefore COUNTRIES. For each row in the REGIONS table, a match for the REGION_ID value is sought from all the rows in the COUNTRIES table. An interim result set is constructed containing rows matching the join condition. This set is then restricted by the WHERE clause. In this case, because the COUNTRY_NAME value must be Canada, REGION_ NAME of Americas is returned.

The second query shows a natural join where COUNTRIES is the source table. The REGION_ID value for each row in the COUNTRIES table is identified and a search for a matching row in the REGIONS table is initiated. If matches are found, the interim results are limited by any WHERE conditions. The COUNTRY_NAME from rows with Americas as their REGION_NAME are returned.

FIGURE 7-1

Natural joins

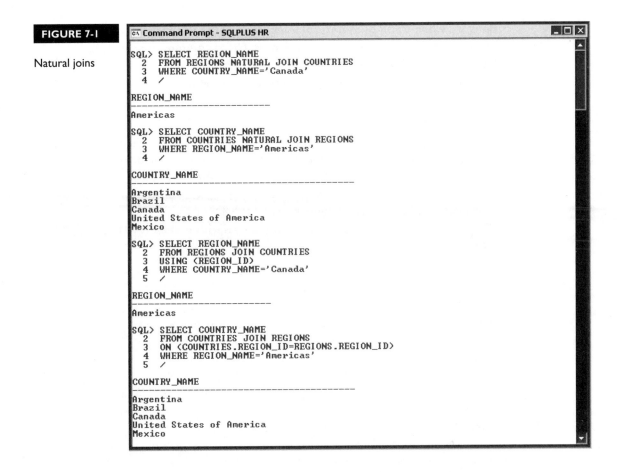

Sometimes more control must be exercised regarding which columns to use for joins. When there are identical column names in the source and target tables you want to exclude as join columns, the *JOIN...USING* format may be used. Remember that Oracle does not impose any rules stating that columns with the same name in two discrete tables must have a relationship with each other. The third query explicitly specifies that the REGIONS table be joined to the COUNTRIES table based on common values in their REGION_ID columns. This syntax allows natural joins to be formed on specific columns instead of on all commonly named columns.

The fourth query demonstrates the JOIN...ON format of the natural join, which allows join columns to be explicitly stated. This format does not depend on the columns in the source and target tables having identical names. This form is more general and is the most widely used natural join format.

Be wary when using pure natural joins since database designers may assign the same name to key or unique columns. These columns may have names like ID or SEQ_NO. If a pure natural join is attempted between such tables, ambiguous and unexpected results may be returned.

Outer Joins

Not all tables share a perfect relationship, where every record in the source table can be matched to at least one row in the target table. It is occasionally required that rows with nonmatching join column values also be retrieved by a query. This may seem to defeat the purpose of joins but has some practical benefits.

Suppose the EMPLOYEES and DEPARTMENTS tables are joined with common DEPARTMENT_ID values. EMPLOYEES records with null DEPARTMENT_ID values are excluded along with values absent from the DEPARTMENTS table. An *outer join* fetches these rows.

Cross Joins

A *cross join* or *Cartesian product* derives its names from mathematics, where it is also referred to as a cross product between two sets or matrices. This join creates one row of output for every combination of source and target table rows.

If the source and target tables have three and four rows, respectively, a cross join between them results in ($3 \times 4 = 12$) rows being returned. Consider the row counts retrieved from the queries in Figure 7-2.

The first two row counts are performed on the COUNTRIES and REGIONS tables yielding 25 and 4 rows respectively. The third query counts the number of rows returned from a cross join of these tables and yields 100. Query 4 would return 100 records if the WHERE clause was absent. Each of the four rows in the REGIONS table is joined to the one row from the COUNTRIES table. Each row returned contains every column from both tables.

Oracle Join Syntax

A proprietary Oracle join syntax has evolved that is stable and understood by millions of users. This traditional syntax is supported by Oracle and is present in software systems across the world. You will no doubt encounter the traditional Oracle join syntax that is now making way for the standardized ANSI-compliant syntax discussed in this chapter.

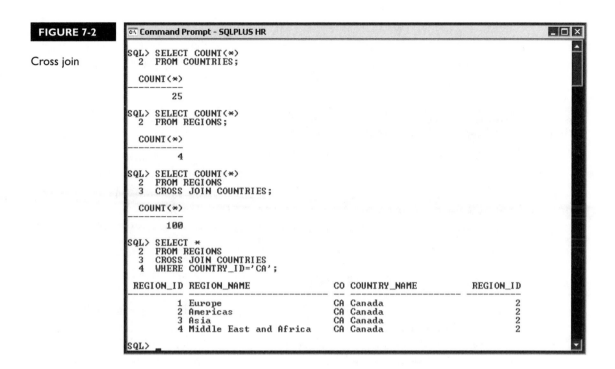

The traditional Oracle join syntax supports natural joining, outer joins, and Cartesian joins, as shown in the following queries:

```
Query 1: select regions.region_name, countries.country_name
from regions, countries
where regions.region_id=countries.region_id;
Query 2: select last_name, department_name
from employees, departments
where employees.department_id (+) = departments.department_id;
Query 3: select * from regions,countries;
```

Query 1 performs a natural join by specifying the join as a condition in the WHERE clause. This is the most significant difference between the traditional and ANSI SQL join syntaxes. Take note of the column aliasing using the TABLE .COLUMN_NAME notation to disambiguate the identical column names. This notation is discussed in detail later in this chapter. Query 2 specifies the join between the source and target tables as a WHERE condition. There is a plus symbol enclosed in brackets (+) to the *left* of the equal sign that indicates to Oracle that a *right outer join* must be performed. This query returns employees' LAST_NAME and their matching DEPARTMENT_NAME values. In addition, the outer join retrieves DEPARTMENT_NAME from the rows with DEPARTMENT_ID values not currently assigned to any employee records. Query 3 performs a Cartesian or cross join by excluding the join condition.

Joining Tables Using SQL:1999 Syntax

Prior to Oracle 9*i*, the traditional join syntax was the only language available to join tables. Since then, Oracle has introduced a new language that is compliant to the ANSI SQL:1999 standards. It offers no performance benefits over the traditional syntax. Natural, outer, and cross joins may be written using both SQL:1999 and traditional Oracle SQL.

The general form of the SELECT statement using ANSI SQL:1999 syntax is as follows:

```
SELECT table1.column, table2.column
FROM table1
[NATURAL JOIN table2] |
[JOIN table2 USING (column_name)] |
[JOIN table2 ON (table1.column_name = table2.column_name)] |
[LEFT | RIGHT | FULL OUTER JOIN table2
ON (table1.column_name = table2.column_name)] |
[CROSS JOIN table2];
```

This is dissected and examples are explained in the following sections. The general form of the traditional Oracle-proprietary syntax relevant to joins is as follows:

```
SELECT table1.column, table2.column
FROM table1, table2
[WHERE (table1.column_name = table2.column_name)] |
[WHERE (table1.column_name(+)= table2.column_name)] |
[WHERE (table1.column_name)= table2.column_name) (+)] ;
```

If no joins or fewer than N-1 joins are specified in the WHERE clause conditions, where N refers to the number of tables in the query, then a Cartesian or cross join is performed. If an adequate number of join conditions is specified, then the first optional conditional clause specifies a natural join, while the second two optional clauses specify the syntax for right and left outer joins.

Qualifying Ambiguous Column Names

Columns with the same names may occur in tables involved in a join. The columns named DEPARTMENT_ID and MANAGER_ID are found in both the EMPLOYEES and DEPARTMENTS tables. The REGION_ID column is present in both the REGIONS and COUNTRIES tables. Listing such columns in a query becomes problematic when Oracle cannot resolve their origin. Columns with unique names across the tables involved in a join cause no ambiguity, and Oracle can easily resolve their source table.

The problem of ambiguous column names is addressed with dot notation. A column may be prefixed by its table name and a dot or period symbol to designate its origin. This differentiates it from a column with the same name in another table. Dot notation may be used in queries involving any number of tables. Referencing some columns using dot notation does not imply that all columns must be referenced in this way.

Dot notation is enhanced with table aliases. A *table alias* provides an alternate, usually shorter name for a table. A column may be referenced as *TABLE_NAME .COLUMN_NAME* or *TABLE_ALIAS.COLUMN_NAME*. Consider the query shown in Figure 7-3.

The EMPLOYEES table is aliased with the short name EMP while the DEPARTMENTS table is not. The SELECT clause references the EMPLOYEE_ID and MANAGER_ID columns as EMP.EMPLOYEE_ID and EMP.MANAGER_ID. The MANAGER_ID column from the DEPARTMENTS table is referred to as DEPARTMENTS.MANAGER_ID. Qualifying the EMPLOYEE_ID column using dot notation is unnecessary because there is only one column with this name between the two tables. Therefore, there is no ambiguity.

The MANAGER_ID column must be qualified to avoid ambiguity because it is featured in both tables. Since the JOIN…USING format is applied, only DEPARTMENT_ID is used as the join column. If a NATURAL JOIN was employed, both the DEPARTMENT_ID and MANAGER_ID columns would be used. If the MANAGER_ID column was not qualified, an "ORA-00918:column ambiguously defined" error would be returned. If DEPARTMENT_ID was aliased, an "ORA-25154:column part of USING clause cannot have qualifier" error would be raised.

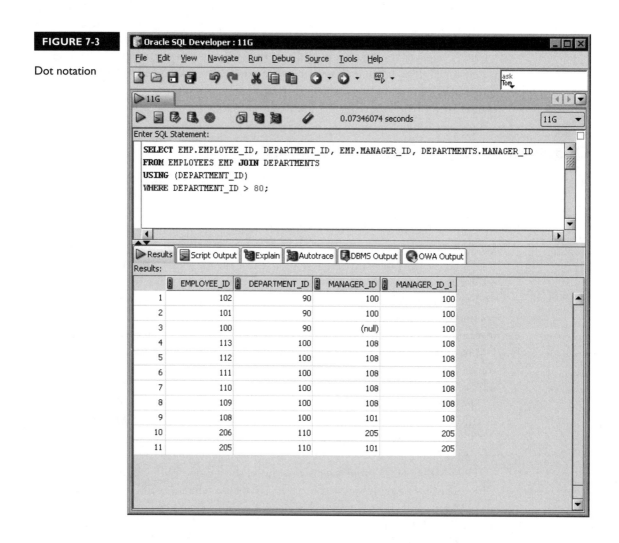

FIGURE 7-3

Dot notation

SQL Developer provides the heading MANAGER_ID to the first reference made in the SELECT clause. The string "_1" is automatically appended to the second reference, creating the heading MANAGER_ID_1.

on the job

Qualifying column references with dot notation to indicate a column's table of origin has a performance benefit. Time is saved because Oracle is directed instantaneously to the appropriate table and does not have to resolve the table name.

The **NATURAL JOIN** Clause

The general syntax for the NATURAL JOIN clause is as follows:

SELECT *table1*.*column*, *table2*.*column*
FROM *table1*
NATURAL JOIN *table2*;

The pure natural join identifies the columns with common names in *table1* and *table2* and implicitly joins the tables using all these columns. The columns in the SELECT clause may be qualified using dot notation unless they are one of the join columns. Consider the following queries:

```
Query 1: select * from locations natural join countries;
Query 2: select * from locations, countries
where locations.country_id = countries.country_id;
Query 3: select * from jobs natural join countries;
Query 4: select * from jobs, countries;
```

The natural join identifies columns with common names between the two tables. In query 1, COUNTRY_ID occurs in both tables and becomes the join column. Query 2 is written using traditional Oracle syntax and retrieves the same rows as query 1. Unless you are familiar with the columns in the source and target tables, natural joins must be used with caution, as join conditions are automatically formed between all columns with shared names.

Query 3 performs a natural join between the JOBS and COUNTRIES tables. There are no columns with identical names, resulting in a Cartesian product. Query 4 is equivalent to query 3, and a Cartesian join is performed using traditional Oracle syntax.

The natural join is simple but prone to a fundamental weakness. It suffers the risk that two columns with the same name might have no relationship and may not even have compatible data types. In Figure 7-4, the COUNTRIES, REGIONS, and SALE_REGIONS tables are described. The SALES_REGIONS table was constructed to illustrate the following important point: Although it has REGION_ ID in common with the COUNTRIES table, it cannot be naturally joined to it because their data types are incompatible. The data types of the COUNTRIES. REGION_ID and SALES_REGIONS.REGION_ID columns are NUMBER and VARCHAR2, respectively. The character data cannot be implicitly converted into numeric data and an "ORA-01722: invalid number" error is raised. The REGIONS .REGION_ID column is of type NUMBER and its data is related to the data in the COUNTRIES table. Therefore, the natural join between the REGIONS and COUNTRIES table works perfectly.

FIGURE 7-4	
The natural join	

```
🗔 Command Prompt - SQLPLUS HR                                              _□ ×

SQL> DESC COUNTRIES
 Name                                          Null?     Type
 ---------------------------------             ------    --------------

 COUNTRY_ID                                    NOT NULL  CHAR(2)
 COUNTRY_NAME                                            VARCHAR2(40)
 REGION_ID                                               NUMBER
SQL> DESC REGIONS
 Name                                          Null?     Type
 ---------------------------------             ------    --------------

 REGION_ID                                     NOT NULL  NUMBER
 REGION_NAME                                             VARCHAR2(25)
SQL> DESC SALES_REGIONS
 Name                                          Null?     Type
 ---------------------------------             ------    --------------

 REGION_ID                                               VARCHAR2(10)
 REGION_NAME                                             VARCHAR2(25)
SQL> SELECT * FROM REGIONS NATURAL JOIN COUNTRIES WHERE COUNTRY_ID='US';

 REGION_ID REGION_NAME                  CO COUNTRY_NAME
 --------- ---------------------------  -- -------------------------

         2 Americas                     US United States of America
SQL> SELECT * FROM SALES_REGIONS NATURAL JOIN COUNTRIES WHERE COUNTRY_ID='US';
SELECT * FROM SALES_REGIONS NATURAL JOIN COUNTRIES WHERE COUNTRY_ID='US'
*
ERROR at line 1:
ORA-01722: invalid number


SQL> SELECT * FROM SALES_REGIONS;

REGION_ID  REGION_NAME
---------  ---------------------------
MEA        Middle East and Africa
AMERICAS   North and South America
APAC       Asia Pacific
EU         European Union

SQL> _
```

EXERCISE 7-1

Using the NATURAL JOIN

The JOB_HISTORY table shares three identically named columns with the EMPLOYEES table: EMPLOYEE_ID, JOB_ID, and DEPARTMENT_ID. You are required to describe the tables and fetch the EMPLOYEE_ID, JOB_ID, DEPARTMENT_ID, LAST_NAME, HIRE_DATE, and END_DATE values for all rows retrieved using a pure natural join. Alias the EMPLOYEES table as EMP and the JOB_HISTORY table as JH and use dot notation where possible.

   1. Start SQL*Plus and connect to the HR schema.

   2. The tables are described using the commands DESC EMPLOYEES and DESC JOB_HISTORY, and the columns with identical names and their data types may be examined.

3. The FROM clause is
   FROM JOB_HISTORY JH

4. The JOIN clause is
   NATURAL JOIN EMPLOYEES EMP

5. The SELECT clause is
   SELECT EMP.LAST_NAME, EMP.HIRE_DATE, JH.END_DATE

6. Executing this statement returns a single row with the same EMPLOYEE_ID, JOB_ID, and DEPARTMENT_ID values in both tables and is shown in the following illustration:

```
Command Prompt - SQLPLUS HR

SQL> DESC EMPLOYEES
 Name                                      Null?    Type
 ------------------------------------      -------- ----------------

 EMPLOYEE_ID                               NOT NULL NUMBER(6)
 FIRST_NAME                                         VARCHAR2(20)
 LAST_NAME                                 NOT NULL VARCHAR2(25)
 EMAIL                                     NOT NULL VARCHAR2(25)
 PHONE_NUMBER                                       VARCHAR2(20)
 HIRE_DATE                                 NOT NULL DATE
 JOB_ID                                    NOT NULL VARCHAR2(10)
 SALARY                                             NUMBER(8,2)
 COMMISSION_PCT                                     NUMBER(2,2)
 MANAGER_ID                                         NUMBER(6)
 DEPARTMENT_ID                                      NUMBER(4)

SQL> DESC JOB_HISTORY
 Name                                      Null?    Type
 ------------------------------------      -------- ----------------

 EMPLOYEE_ID                               NOT NULL NUMBER(6)
 START_DATE                                NOT NULL DATE
 END_DATE                                  NOT NULL DATE
 JOB_ID                                    NOT NULL VARCHAR2(10)
 DEPARTMENT_ID                                      NUMBER(4)

SQL> SELECT EMPLOYEE_ID, JOB_ID, DEPARTMENT_ID,
  2         EMP.LAST_NAME, EMP.HIRE_DATE, JH.END_DATE
  3  FROM JOB_HISTORY JH
  4  NATURAL JOIN EMPLOYEES EMP;

EMPLOYEE_ID JOB_ID     DEPARTMENT_ID LAST_NAME           HIRE_DATE END_DATE
----------- ---------- ------------- ------------------- --------- ---------
        176 SA_REP                80 Taylor              24-MAR-98 31-DEC-98

SQL>
```

The Natural JOIN USING Clause

The format of the syntax for the natural JOIN USING clause is as follows:

SELECT *table1.column*, *table2.column*
FROM *table1*
JOIN *table2* USING (*join_column1*, *join_column2*…);

While the pure natural join contains the NATURAL keyword in its syntax, the JOIN...USING syntax does not. An error is raised if the keywords NATURAL and USING occur in the same join clause. The JOIN...USING clause allows one or more equijoin columns to be explicitly specified in brackets after the USING keyword. This avoids the shortcomings associated with the pure natural join. Many situations demand that tables be joined only on certain columns, and this format caters to this requirement. Consider the following queries:

```
Query 1: select * from locations join countries using (country_id);
Query 2: select * from locations, countries
where locations.country_id = countries.country_id;
Query 3: select * from jobs join countries using ;
```

Query 1 specifies that the LOCATIONS and COUNTRIES tables must be joined on common COUNTRY_ID column values. All columns from these tables are retrieved for the rows with matching join column values. Query 2 shows a traditionally specified query that retrieves the same rows as query 1. Query 3 illustrates that a Cartesian join cannot be accidentally specified with the JOIN...USING syntax since only columns with shared names are permitted after the USING keyword. The join columns cannot be qualified using table names or aliases when they are referenced. Since this join syntax potentially excludes some columns with identical names from the join clause, these must be qualified if they are referenced to avoid ambiguity.

As Figure 7-5 shows, the JOB_HISTORY and EMPLOYEES tables were joined based on the presence of equal values in their JOB_ID and EMPLOYEE_ID columns. Rows conforming to this join condition are retrieved. These tables share three identically named columns. The JOIN...USING syntax allows the specification of only two of these as join columns. Notice that although the third identically named column is DEPARTMENT_ID, it is qualified with a table alias to avoid ambiguity. However, the join columns in the SELECT clause cannot be qualified with table aliases.

The Natural JOIN ON Clause

The format of the syntax for the natural JOIN ON clause is as follows:

SELECT *table1*.*column*, *table2*.*column*
FROM *table1*
JOIN *table2* ON (*table1*.*column_name* = *table2*.*column_name*);

FIGURE 7-5

Natural join using
the JOIN...
USING clause

FIGURE 7-5 Natural join using the JOIN...USING clause

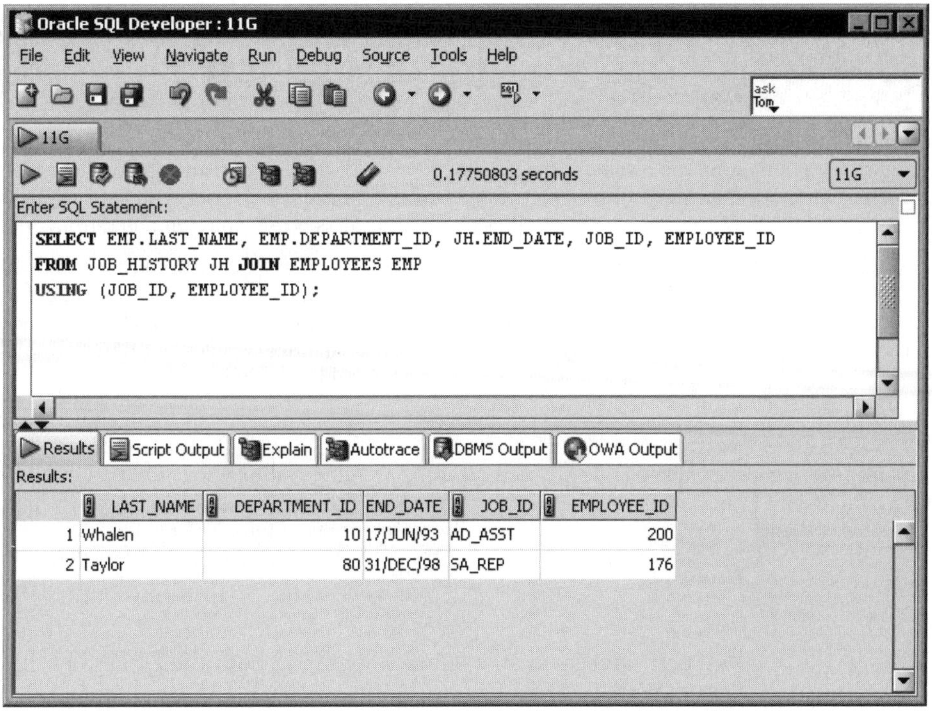

The pure natural join and the JOIN...USING clauses depend on join columns with identical column names. The JOIN...ON clause allows the explicit specification of join columns, regardless of their column names. This is the most flexible and widely used form of the join clauses. The ON and NATURAL keywords cannot appear together in a join clause. The equijoin columns are fully qualified as *table1.column1 = table2.column2* and are optionally specified in brackets after the ON keyword. The following queries illustrate the JOIN...ON clause:

```
Query 1: select * from departments d
join employees e on (e.employee_id=d.department_id);
Query 2: select * from employees e, departments d
where e.employee_id=d.department_id;
```

SCENARIO & SOLUTION

You are required to retrieve information from multiple tables, group the results, and apply an aggregate function to them. Can a group function be used against data from multiple table sources?	Yes. Joining multiple tables ultimately yields a set of data comprising one or more rows and columns. Once the dataset is created, aggregate functions treat it as if the data originated from one source.
When joining two tables, there is a risk that between them they contain common column names. Does Oracle know which tables to fetch data from if such columns are present in the SELECT list?	No. Oracle does not know from which tables such columns originate, and an error is raised. Ambiguous column references can be avoided using qualifiers. Qualifiers employ dot notation to clarify a column's table of origin.
The NATURAL JOIN clause is used to join rows from two tables based on columns with common names sharing identical values. Is it possible to join two tables based on some of the shared columns and not all of them?	Yes. The clause recommended to naturally join two tables based on one or more of the columns with identical names is JOIN…USING. A pair of brackets follows the USING clause in which the unqualified join columns are specified.

Query 1 retrieves all column values from both the DEPARTMENTS and EMPLOYEES tables for the rows that meet an equijoin condition. This condition is fulfilled by EMPLOYEE_ID values matching DEPARTMENT_ID values in the DEPARTMENTS table. The traditional Oracle syntax in query 2 returns the same results as query 1. Notice the similarities between the traditional join condition specified in the WHERE clause and the join condition specified after the ON keyword.

The START_DATE column in the JOB_HISTORY table is joined to the HIRE_DATE column in the EMPLOYEES table in Figure 7-6. This equijoin retrieves the details of employees who worked for the organization and changed jobs.

EXERCISE 7-2

Using the **NATURAL JOIN...ON** Clause

Each record in the DEPARTMENTS table has a MANAGER_ID column matching an EMPLOYEE_ID value in the EMPLOYEES table. You are required to produce a report with one column aliased as Managers. Each row must contain a sentence of the format FIRST_NAME LAST_NAME is manager of the DEPARTMENT_NAME

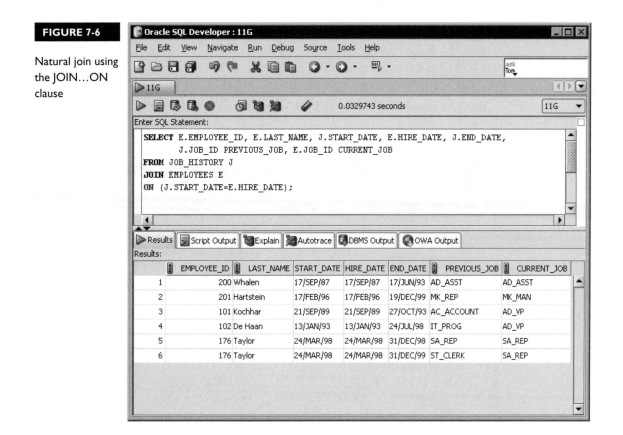

FIGURE 7-6

Natural join using the JOIN...ON clause

department. Alias the EMPLOYEES table as E and the DEPARTMENTS table as D and use dot notation where possible.

1. Start SQL Developer and connect to the HR schema.
2. The Managers column may be constructed by concatenating the required items and separating them with spaces.
3. The SELECT clause is
   SELECT E.FIRST_NAME||' '||E.LAST_NAME||' is manager of the '||
   D.DEPARTMENT_NAME||' department.' "Managers"

4. The FROM clause is
   FROM EMPLOYEES E

5. The JOIN...ON clause is
   JOIN DEPARTMENTS D
   ON (E. EMPLOYEE_ID=D.MANAGER_ID).

6. Executing this statement returns 11 rows describing the managers of each department as shown in the following illustration:

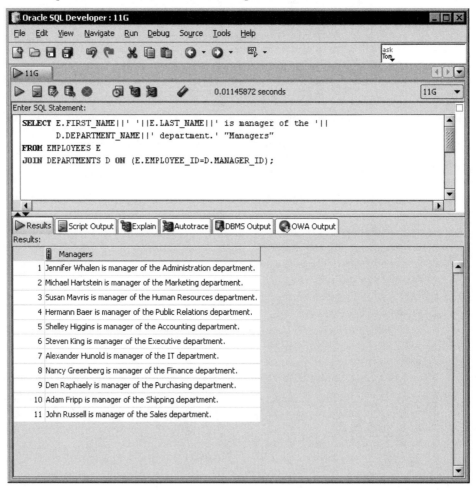

N-Way Joins and Additional Join Conditions

The joins just discussed were demonstrated using two tables. There is no restriction on the number of tables that may be related using joins. Third normal form consists of a set of tables connected through a series of primary and foreign key relationships. Traversing these relationships using joins enables consistent and reliable retrieval of data. When multiple joins exist in a statement, they are evaluated from left to right. Consider the following query using pure natural joins:

```
select r.region_name, c.country_name, l.city, d.department_name
from departments d natural join locations l
natural join countries c natural join regions r
```

The join between DEPARTMENTS and LOCATIONS creates an interim result set consisting of 27 rows. These tables provide the DEPARTMENT_NAME and CITY columns. This set is naturally joined to the COUNTRIES table. Since the interim set does not contain the COUNTRY_ID column, a Cartesian join is performed. The 27 interim rows are joined to the 25 rows in the COUNTRIES table, yielding a new interim results set with 675 (27×25) rows and three columns: DEPARTMENT_NAME, CITY, and COUNTRY_NAME. This set is naturally joined to the REGIONS table. Once again, a Cartesian join occurs because the REGION_ID column is absent from the interim set. The final result set contains 2700 (675×4) rows and four columns. Using pure natural joins with multiple tables is error prone and not recommended.

The JOIN…USING and JOIN…ON syntaxes are better suited for joining multiple tables. The following query joins four tables using the pure natural join syntax:

```
select region_id, country_id, c.country_name, l.city, d.department_name
from departments d natural join locations l
natural join countries c natural join regions r
```

This query correctly yields 27 rows in the final results set since the required join columns are listed in the SELECT clause. The following query demonstrates how the JOIN…ON clause is used to fetch the same 27 rows. A join condition can reference only columns in its scope. In the following example, the join from DEPARTMENTS to LOCATIONS may not reference columns in the COUNTRIES or REGIONS tables, but the join between COUNTRIES and REGIONS may reference any column from the four tables involved in the query.

```
select r.region_name, c.country_name, l.city, d.department_name
from departments d
join locations l on (l.location_id=d.location_id)
join countries c on (c.country_id=l.country_id)
join regions r on (r.region_id=c.region_id)
```

The JOIN…USING clause can also be used to join these four tables as follows:

```
select r.region_name, c.country_name, l.city, d.department_name
from departments d
join locations l using (location_id)
join countries c using (country_id)
join regions r using (region_id)
```

The WHERE clause is used to specify conditions that restrict the results set of a query whether it contains joins or not. The JOIN…ON clause is also used to specify conditions that limit the results set created by the join. Consider the following two queries:

```
Query 1: select d.department_name from departments d
join locations l on (l.LOCATION_ID=d.LOCATION_ID)
where d.department_name like 'P%'
```

```
Query 2: select d.department_name from departments d
join locations l on
(l.LOCATION_ID=d.LOCATION_ID and d.department_name like 'P%')
```

Query 1 uses a WHERE clause to restrict the 27 rows created by equijoining the DEPARTMENTS and LOCATIONS tables based on their LOCATION_ID values to the three that contain DEPARTMENT_ID values beginning with the letter P. Query 2 implements the condition within the brackets of the ON subclause and returns the same three rows.

Five tables are joined in Figure 7-7, resulting in a list describing the top earning employees and geographical information about their departments.

FIGURE 7-7		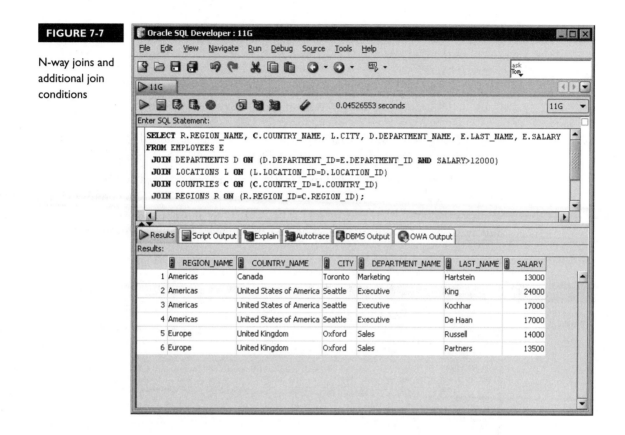
N-way joins and additional join conditions		

Nonequijoins

Nonequijoins match column values from different tables based on an inequality expression. The value of the join column in each row in the source table is compared to the corresponding values in the target table. A match is found if the expression used in the join, based on an inequality operator, evaluates to true. When such a join is constructed, a nonequijoin is performed.

A nonequijoin is specified using the JOIN…ON syntax, but the join condition contains an inequality operator instead of an equal sign.

The format of the syntax for a nonequijoin clause is as follows:

SELECT *table1.column, table2.column*
FROM *table1*
[JOIN *table2* ON (*table1.column_name < table2.column_name*)] |
[JOIN *table2* ON (*table1.column_name > table2.column_name*)] |
[JOIN *table2* ON (*table1.column_name <= table2.column_name*)] |
[JOIN *table2* ON (*table1.column_name >= table2.column_name*)] |
[JOIN *table2* ON (*table1.column* BETWEEN *table2.col1* AND *table2.col2*)] |

Consider the first 15 rows returned by the query in Figure 7-8. The EMPLOYEES
table is nonequijoined to the JOBS table based on the inequality join condition
(2*E.SALARY < J.MAX_SALARY). The JOBS table stores the salary range for
different jobs in the organization. The SALARY value for each employee record is

<table>
<tr><td>FIGURE 7-8</td></tr>
<tr><td>Nonequijoins</td></tr>
</table>

FIGURE 7-8   Nonequijoins

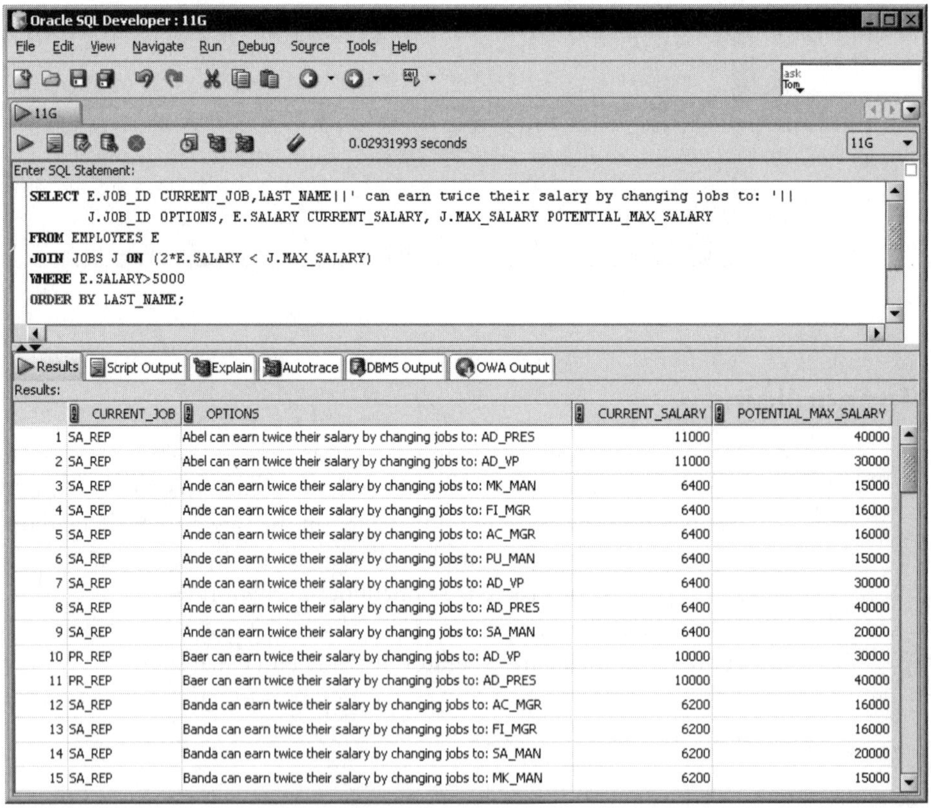

doubled and compared with all MAX_SALARY values in the JOBS table. If the join condition evaluates to true, the row is returned.

The first two rows display the employee with a LAST_NAME of Abel who currently has a JOB_ID value of SA_REP and earns a SALARY of 11000. These are the only two rows in the JOBS table that satisfy the inequality join condition (2*E.SALARY < J.MAX_SALARY) for this employee record.

on the **job**   *Nonequijoins are not commonly used. The BETWEEN range operator often appears with nonequijoin conditions. It is simpler to use one BETWEEN operator in a condition than two nonequijoin conditions based on the less than or equal to (<=) and the greater than or equal to (>=) operators.*

CERTIFICATION OBJECTIVE 7.02

Join a Table to Itself Using a Self-Join

Storing hierarchical data in a single relational table is accomplished by allocating at least two columns per row. One column stores an identifier of the row's parent record and the second stores the row's identifier. Associating rows with each other based on a hierarchical relationship requires Oracle to join a table to itself. This *self-join* technique is discussed in the next section.

Joining a Table to Itself Using the JOIN...ON Clause

Suppose there is a need to store a family tree in a relational table. There are several approaches one could take. One option is to use a table called FAMILY with columns named ID, NAME, MOTHER_ID, and FATHER_ID, where each row stores a person's name, unique ID number, and the ID values for their parents.

When two tables are joined, each row from the source table is subjected to the join condition with rows from the target table. If the condition evaluates to true, then the joined row, consisting of columns from both tables, is returned.

When the join columns originate from the same table, a self-join is required. Conceptually, the source table is duplicated to create the target table. The self-join works like a regular join between these tables. Note that, internally, Oracle does not duplicate the table and this description is merely provided to explain the concept of self-joining. Consider the following four queries:

```
Query 1: select id, name, father_id from family;
Query 2: select name from family where id=&father_id;
Query 3: select f1.name Dad, f2.name Child
from family f1 join family f2 on (f1.id=f2.father_id)
```

To identify a person's father in the FAMILY table, you could use query 1 to get that person's ID, NAME, and FATHER_ID value. In query 2, the FATHER_ID value obtained from the first query can be substituted to obtain the father's NAME value. Notice that both queries 1 and 2 source information from the FAMILY table.

Query 3 performs a self-join with the JOIN…ON clause by aliasing the FAMILY table as f1 and f2. Oracle treats these as different tables even though they point to the same physical table. The first occurrence of the FAMILY table, aliased as f1, is designated as the source table, while the second occurrence, aliased as f2, is assigned as the target table. The join condition in the ON clause is of the format *source.child_ id=target.parent_id*. Figure 7-9 shows a sample of FAMILY data and demonstrates a three-way self-join to the same table.

EXERCISE 7-3

Performing a Self-Join

There is a hierarchical relationship between employees and their managers. For each row in the EMPLOYEES table the MANAGER_ID column stores the EMPLOYEE_ID of every employee's manager. Using a self-join on the EMPLOYEES table, you are required to retrieve the employee's LAST_NAME, EMPLOYEE_ID, manager's LAST_NAME, and employee's DEPARTMENT_ID for the rows with DEPARMENT_ID values of 10, 20, or 30. Alias the EMPLOYEES table as E and the second instance of the EMPLOYEES table as M. Sort the results based on the DEPARTMENT_ID column.

1. Start SQL Developer and connect to the HR schema.
2. The SELECT clause is
   SELECT E.LAST_NAME EMPLOYEE, E.EMPLOYEE_ID, E.MANAGER_ID, M.LAST_NAME MANAGER, E.DEPARTMENT_ID.
3. The FROM clause with source table and alias is
   FROM EMPLOYEES E.

FIGURE 7-9

Self-join

```
C:\ Command Prompt - SQLPLUS HR                                    _ □ ×
SQL> SELECT * FROM FAMILY;

        ID NAME         MOTHER_ID  FATHER_ID
_____ _____   _____  _____
        15 Niresh               2          1
        16 Fats
        17 Kiara               16         15
        17 Amira               16         15
        19 Tanishka             6          4
         1 Harry
         2 Sabita
         3 Reg                  2          1
         4 Dee                  2          1
         5 Mona                 2          1
         6 Vee
         7 Ish                  6          4
         8 Yash                 6          4
         9 Roopesh              2          1
        10 Ameetha             14         13
        11 Coda                10          9
        12 Sid                 10          9
        13 Hari
        14 Indra

19 rows selected.

SQL> SELECT F1.NAME Mum, F3.NAME Dad, F2.NAME Child
  2  FROM FAMILY F1
  3  JOIN FAMILY F2 ON (F2.MOTHER_ID=F1.ID)
  4  JOIN FAMILY F3 ON (F2.FATHER_ID=F3.ID);

MUM          DAD          CHILD
_____   _____   _____
Fats         Niresh       Kiara
Fats         Niresh       Amira
Sabita       Harry        Niresh
Sabita       Harry        Reg
Sabita       Harry        Dee
Sabita       Harry        Mona
Sabita       Harry        Roopesh
Vee          Dee          Tanishka
Vee          Dee          Ish
Vee          Dee          Yash
Ameetha      Roopesh      Coda
Ameetha      Roopesh      Sid
Indra        Hari         Ameetha

13 rows selected.

SQL>
```

4. The JOIN...ON clause with aliased target table is
   JOIN EMPLOYEES M ON (E.MANAGER_ID=M.EMPLOYEE_ID).

5. The WHERE clause is
   WHERE E.DEPARTMENT_ID IN (10,20,30).

6. The ORDER BY clause is
   ORDER BY E.DEPARTMENT_ID.

7. Executing this statement returns nine rows describing the managers of each employee in these departments as shown in the following illustration:

CERTIFICATION OBJECTIVE 7.03

View Data That Does Not Meet a Join Condition by Using Outer Joins

Equijoins match rows between two tables based on the equality of the column data stored in each table. Nonequijoins rely on matching rows between tables based on a join condition containing an inequality expression. Target table rows with no matching join column in the source table are usually not required. When they are required, however, an *outer join* is used to fetch them. Several variations of outer joins may be used depending on whether join column data is missing from the source or target tables or both. These outer join techniques are described in the following topics:

- Inner versus outer joins
- Left outer joins
- Right outer joins
- Full outer joins

Inner versus Outer Joins

When equijoins and nonequijoins are performed, rows from the source and target tables are matched using a join condition formulated with equality and inequality operators, respectively. These are referred to as *inner joins*. An *outer join* is performed when rows, which are not retrieved by an inner join, are returned.

Two tables sometimes share a *master-detail* or *parent-child* relationship. In the sample HR schema there are several pairs of tables with such a relationship. One pair is the DEPARTMENTS and EMPLOYEES tables. The DEPARTMENTS table stores a master list of DEPARTMENT_NAME and DEPARTMENT_ID values. Each EMPLOYEES record has a DEPARTMENT_ID column constrained to be either a value that exists in the DEPARTMENTS table or null. This leads to one of the following three scenarios. The fourth scenario could occur if the constraint between the tables was removed.

1. An employee row has a DEPARTMENT_ID value that matches a row in the DEPARTMENTS table.
2. An employee row has a null value in its DEPARTMENT_ID column.
3. There are rows in the DEPARTMENTS table with DEPARTMENT_ID values that are not stored in any employee records.
4. An employee row has a DEPARTMENT_ID value that is not featured in the DEPARTMENTS table.

The first scenario describes a natural inner join between the two tables. The second and third scenarios cause many problems. Joining the EMPLOYEES and DEPARTMENTS tables results in employee rows being excluded. An outer join can be used to include these orphaned rows in the results set. The fourth scenario should rarely occur in a well designed database, because foreign key constraints would prevent the insertion of child records with no parent values. Since this row will be excluded by an inner join, it may be retrieved using an outer join.

A left outer join between the source and target tables returns the results of an inner join as well as rows from the source table excluded by that inner join. A right outer join between the source and target tables returns the results of an inner join as well as rows from the target table excluded by that inner join. If a join returns the results of an inner join as well as rows from both the source and target tables excluded by that inner join, then a full outer join has been performed.

Left Outer Joins

The format of the syntax for the LEFT OUTER JOIN clause is as follow:

SELECT *table1.column, table2.column*
FROM *table1*
LEFT OUTER JOIN *table2*
ON (*table1.column = table2.column*);

A left outer join performs an inner join of *table1* and *table2* based on the condition specified after the ON keyword. Any rows from the table on the *left* of the JOIN keyword excluded for not fulfilling the join condition are also returned. Consider the following two queries:

```
Query 1: select e.employee_id, e.department_id EMP_DEPT_ID,
d.department_id DEPT_DEPT_ID, d.department_name
from departments d left outer join employees e
on (d.DEPARTMENT_ID=e.DEPARTMENT_ID)
where d.department_name like 'P%'
Query 2: select e.employee_id, e.department_id EMP_DEPT_ID,
d.department_id DEPT_DEPT_ID, d.department_name
from departments d join employees e
on (d.DEPARTMENT_ID=e.DEPARTMENT_ID)
where d.department_name like 'P%'
```

Queries 1 and 2 are identical except for the join clauses, which have the keywords LEFT OUTER JOIN and JOIN, respectively. Query 2 performs an inner join and seven rows are returned. These rows share identical DEPARTMENT_ID values in both tables. Query 1 returns the same seven rows and one additional row. This extra row is obtained from the table to the left of the JOIN keyword, which is the DEPARTMENTS table. It is the row containing details of the Payroll department. The inner join does not include this row since no employees are currently assigned to the department.

A left outer join is shown in Figure 7-10. The inner join produces 27 rows with matching LOCATION_ID values in both tables. There are 43 rows in total, which implies that 16 rows were retrieved from the LOCATIONS table, which is on the

FIGURE 7-10

Left outer join

```
Command Prompt - SQLPLUS HR                                           _ □ X
SQL> SELECT CITY, L.LOCATION_ID "L.LOCATION_ID", D.LOCATION_ID "D.LOCATION_ID"
  2    FROM LOCATIONS L LEFT OUTER JOIN DEPARTMENTS D
  3    ON (L.LOCATION_ID=D.LOCATION_ID);

CITY                         L.LOCATION_ID D.LOCATION_ID
---------------------------- ------------- -------------
Roma                                  1000
Venice                                1100
Tokyo                                 1200
Hiroshima                             1300
Southlake                             1400          1400
South San Francisco                   1500          1500
South Brunswick                       1600
Seattle                               1700          1700
Seattle                               1700          1700
Seattle                               1700          1700
Seattle                               1700          1700
Seattle                               1700          1700
Seattle                               1700          1700
Seattle                               1700          1700
Seattle                               1700          1700
Seattle                               1700          1700
Seattle                               1700          1700
Seattle                               1700          1700
Seattle                               1700          1700
Seattle                               1700          1700
Seattle                               1700          1700
Seattle                               1700          1700
Seattle                               1700          1700
Seattle                               1700          1700
Seattle                               1700          1700
Seattle                               1700          1700
Toronto                               1800          1800
Whitehorse                            1900
Beijing                               2000
Bombay                                2100
Sydney                                2200
Singapore                             2300
London                                2400          2400
Oxford                                2500          2500
Stretford                             2600
Munich                                2700          2700
Sao Paulo                             2800
Geneva                                2900
Bern                                  3000
Utrecht                               3100
Mexico City                           3200

43 rows selected.
```

left of the JOIN keyword. None of the rows from the DEPARTMENTS table contain any of these 16 LOCATION_ID values.

Right Outer Joins

The format of the syntax for the RIGHT OUTER JOIN clause is as follows:

SELECT *table1.column, table2.column*
FROM *table1*
RIGHT OUTER JOIN *table2*
ON (*table1.column = table2.column*);

A right outer join performs an inner join of *table1* and *table2* based on the join condition specified after the ON keyword. Rows from the table to the *right* of the JOIN keyword, excluded by the join condition, are also returned. Consider the following query:

```
select e.last_name, d.department_name from departments d
right outer join employees e
on (e.department_id=d.department_id)
where e.last_name like 'G%';
```

The inner join produces seven rows containing details for the employees with LAST_NAME values that begin with G. The EMPLOYEES table is to the *right* of the JOIN keyword. Any employee records which do not conform to the join condition are included, provided they conform to the WHERE clause condition. In addition, the right outer join fetches one EMPLOYEE record with a LAST_NAME of Grant. This record currently has a null DEPARTMENT_ID value. The inner join excludes the record since no DEPARTMENT_ID is assigned to this employee.

A right outer join between the JOB_HISTORY and EMPLOYEES tables is shown in Figure 7-11. The EMPLOYEES table is on the right of the JOIN keyword. The DISTINCT keyword eliminates duplicate combinations of JOB_ID values from the tables. The results show the jobs that employees have historically left. The jobs that no employees have left are also returned.

Full Outer Joins

The format of the syntax for the FULL OUTER JOIN clause is as follows:

```
SELECT table1.column, table2.column
FROM table1
FULL OUTER JOIN table2
ON (table1.column = table2.column);
```

FIGURE 7-11

Right outer join

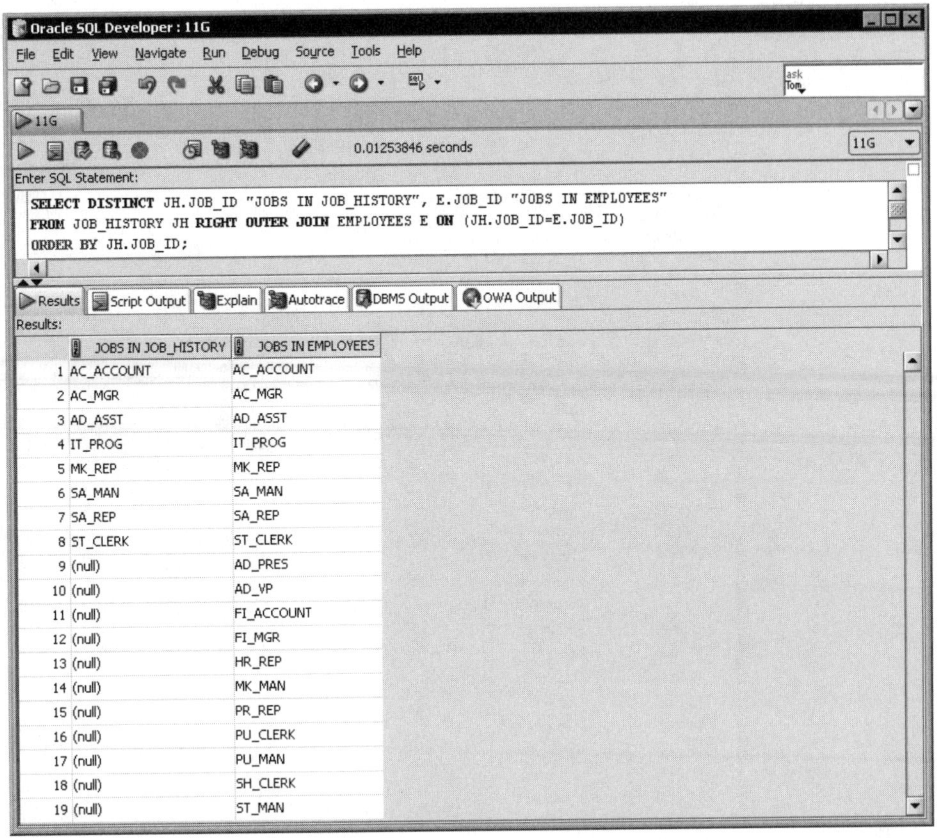

```
Oracle SQL Developer : 11G                                              _ □ ×
File  Edit  View  Navigate  Run  Debug  Source  Tools  Help

11G

                                    0.01253846 seconds                  11G

Enter SQL Statement:
SELECT DISTINCT JH.JOB_ID "JOBS IN JOB_HISTORY", E.JOB_ID "JOBS IN EMPLOYEES"
FROM JOB_HISTORY JH RIGHT OUTER JOIN EMPLOYEES E ON (JH.JOB_ID=E.JOB_ID)
ORDER BY JH.JOB_ID;
```

Results | Script Output | Explain | Autotrace | DBMS Output | OWA Output

Results:

	JOBS IN JOB_HISTORY	JOBS IN EMPLOYEES
1	AC_ACCOUNT	AC_ACCOUNT
2	AC_MGR	AC_MGR
3	AD_ASST	AD_ASST
4	IT_PROG	IT_PROG
5	MK_REP	MK_REP
6	SA_MAN	SA_MAN
7	SA_REP	SA_REP
8	ST_CLERK	ST_CLERK
9	(null)	AD_PRES
10	(null)	AD_VP
11	(null)	FI_ACCOUNT
12	(null)	FI_MGR
13	(null)	HR_REP
14	(null)	MK_MAN
15	(null)	PR_REP
16	(null)	PU_CLERK
17	(null)	PU_MAN
18	(null)	SH_CLERK
19	(null)	ST_MAN

A *full outer join* returns the combined results of a left and right outer join. An inner join of *table1* and *table2* is performed before rows excluded by the join condition from both tables are merged into the results set.

The traditional Oracle join syntax does not support a full outer join, which is typically performed by combining the results from a left and right outer join using the UNION set operator described in Chapter 9. Consider the full outer join shown in Figure 7-12. The WHERE clause restricting the results to rows with NULL DEPARTMENT_ID values shows the orphan rows in both tables. There is one record in the EMPLOYEES table which has no DEPARTMENT_ID values, and there are 16 departments to which no employees belong.

FIGURE 7-12

Full outer join

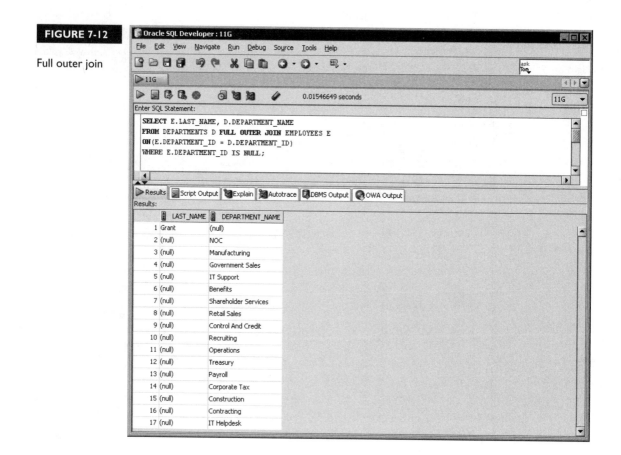

EXERCISE 7-4

Performing an Outer-Join

The DEPARTMENTS table contains details of all departments in the organization.
You are required to retrieve the DEPARTMENT_NAME and DEPARTMENT_ID
values for those departments to which no employees are currently assigned.

1. Start SQL*Plus and connect to the HR schema.
2. The SELECT clause is
   SELECT D.DEPARTMENT_NAME, D.DEPARTMENT_ID.

SCENARIO & SOLUTION

The data in two tables you wish to join is related but does not share any identically named columns. Is it possible to join tables using columns that do not share the same name?	Yes. The JOIN...ON clause is provided for this purpose. It provides a flexible and generic solution to joining tables based on nonidentical column names.
You wish to divide staff into four groups named after the four regions in the REGIONS table. Is it possible to obtain a list of EMPLOYEE_ID, LAST_NAME, and REGION_NAME values for each employee by joining the EMPLOYEE_ID and REGION_ID columns in a round-robin manner?	Yes. The REGION_ID value ranges from 1 to 4. Adding 1 to the remainder of EMPLOYEE_ID divided by 4 creates a value in the range 1 to 4. The round-robin assignment of employees may be done as follows: SELECT LAST_NAME, EMPLOYEE_ID, REGION_NAME, FROM EMPLOYEES JOIN REGIONS ON (MOD(EMPLOYEE_ID,4)+1= REGION_ID)
You are required to retrieve a list of DEPARTMENT_NAME and LAST_NAME values for all departments, including those that currently have no employees assigned to them. In such cases the string 'No Employees' should be displayed as the LAST_NAME column value. Can this be done using joins?	Yes. Depending on which side of the JOIN keyword the DEPARTMENTS table is placed, a left or right outer join may be used, since this is the table from where the orphan rows originate. The following query satisfies the request: SELECT DEPARTMENT_NAME, NVL(LAST_NAME,'No Employees') FROM EMPLOYEES RIGHT OUTER JOIN DEPARTMENTS USING (DEPARTMENT_ID)

3. The FROM clause with source table and alias is
   FROM DEPARTMENTS D.

4. The LEFT OUTER JOIN clause with aliased target table is
   LEFT OUTER JOIN EMPLOYEES E ON
   E.DEPARTMENT_ID=D.DEPARTMENT_ID.

5. The WHERE clause is
   WHERE E.DEPARTMENT_ID IS NULL.

6. Executing this statement returns sixteen rows describing the departments to which no employees are currently assigned as shown in the following illustration:

```
SQL Plus                                                              _ □ ×
SQL> SELECT DEPARTMENT_NAME, D.DEPARTMENT_ID
  2  FROM DEPARTMENTS D
  3  LEFT OUTER JOIN EMPLOYEES E
  4  ON E.DEPARTMENT_ID = D.DEPARTMENT_ID
  5  WHERE E.DEPARTMENT_ID IS NULL;

DEPARTMENT_NAME                      DEPARTMENT_ID
------------------------------       -------------
Treasury                                       120
Corporate Tax                                  130
Control And Credit                             140
Shareholder Services                           150
Benefits                                       160
Manufacturing                                  170
Construction                                   180
Contracting                                    190
Operations                                     200
IT Support                                     210
NOC                                            220
IT Helpdesk                                    230
Government Sales                               240
Retail Sales                                   250
Recruiting                                     260
Payroll                                        270

16 rows selected.
```

CERTIFICATION OBJECTIVE 7.04

Generate a Cartesian Product of Two or More Tables

A Cartesian product of two tables may be conceptualized as joining each row of the source table with every row in the target table. The number of rows in the result set created by a Cartesian product is equal to the number of rows in the source table multiplied by the number of rows in the target table. Cartesian products may be formed intentionally using the ANSI SQL:1999 cross join syntax. This technique is described in the next section.

Creating Cartesian Products Using Cross Joins

Cartesian product is a mathematical term. It refers to the set of data created by merging the rows from two or more tables together. Cross join is the syntax used to create a Cartesian product by joining multiple tables. Both terms are often used synonymously. The format of the syntax for the CROSS JOIN clause is as follows:

SELECT *table1*.column, *table2*.column
FROM *table1*
CROSS JOIN *table2*;

It is important to observe that no *join condition* is specified using the ON or USING keywords. A Cartesian product freely associates the rows from *table1* with every row in *table2*. Conditions that limit the results are permitted in the form of WHERE clause restrictions. If *table1* and *table2* contain *x* and *y* number of rows, respectively, the Cartesian product will contain *x* times *y* number of rows. The results from a *cross join* may be used to identify orphan rows or generate a large data set for use in application testing. Consider the following queries:

```
Query 1: select * from jobs cross join job_history;
Query 2: select * from jobs j cross join job_history jh
where j.job_id='AD_PRES';
```

Query 1 takes the 19 rows and 4 columns from the JOBS table and the 10 rows and 5 columns from the JOB_HISTORY table and generates one large set of 190 records with 9 columns. SQL*Plus presents any identically named columns as headings. SQL Developer appends an underscore and number to each shared column name and uses it as the heading. The JOB_ID column is common to both the JOBS and JOB_HISTORY tables. The headings in SQL Developer are labeled JOB_ID and JOB_ID_1, respectively. Query 2 generates the same Cartesian product as the first, but the 190 rows are constrained by the WHERE clause condition and only 10 rows are returned.

Figure 7-13 shows a cross join between the REGIONS and COUNTRIES tables. There are 4 rows in REGIONS and 25 rows in COUNTRIES. Since the WHERE clause limits the REGIONS table to 2 of 4 rows, the Cartesian product produces 50 (25 × 2) records. The results are sorted alphabetically, first on the REGION_NAME and then on the COUNTRY_NAME. The first record has the pair of values, Asia and Argentina. When the REGION_NAME changes, the first record has the pair of values, Africa and Argentina. Notice that the COUNTRY_NAME values are repeated for every REGION_NAME.

FIGURE 7-13

The cross join

```
Command Prompt - SQLPLUS HR                                    _□×
SQL> SELECT R.REGION_NAME,C.COUNTRY_NAME FROM REGIONS R CROSS JOIN COUNTRIES C
  2  WHERE R.REGION_ID IN (3,4) ORDER BY REGION_NAME, COUNTRY_NAME;

REGION_NAME                     COUNTRY_NAME
------------------------------  ------------------------------
Asia                            Argentina
Asia                            Australia
Asia                            Belgium
Asia                            Brazil
Asia                            Canada
Asia                            China
Asia                            Denmark
Asia                            Egypt
Asia                            France
Asia                            Germany
Asia                            HongKong
Asia                            India
Asia                            Israel
Asia                            Italy
Asia                            Japan
Asia                            Kuwait
Asia                            Mexico
Asia                            Netherlands
Asia                            Nigeria
Asia                            Singapore
Asia                            Switzerland
Asia                            United Kingdom
Asia                            United States of America
Asia                            Zambia
Asia                            Zimbabwe
Middle East and Africa          Argentina
Middle East and Africa          Australia
Middle East and Africa          Belgium
Middle East and Africa          Brazil
Middle East and Africa          Canada
Middle East and Africa          China
Middle East and Africa          Denmark
Middle East and Africa          Egypt
Middle East and Africa          France
Middle East and Africa          Germany
Middle East and Africa          HongKong
Middle East and Africa          India
Middle East and Africa          Israel
Middle East and Africa          Italy
Middle East and Africa          Japan
Middle East and Africa          Kuwait
Middle East and Africa          Mexico
Middle East and Africa          Netherlands
Middle East and Africa          Nigeria
Middle East and Africa          Singapore
Middle East and Africa          Switzerland
Middle East and Africa          United Kingdom
Middle East and Africa          United States of America
Middle East and Africa          Zambia
Middle East and Africa          Zimbabwe

50 rows selected.
```

EXERCISE 7-5

Performing a Cross-Join

You are required to obtain the number of rows in the EMPLOYEES and
DEPARTMENTS table as well as the number of records that would be created

by a Cartesian product of these two tables. Confirm your results by explicitly counting and multiplying the number of rows present in each of these tables.

1. Start SQL*Plus and connect to the HR schema.

2. The SELECT clause to find the number of rows in the Cartesian product is SELECT COUNT(*).

3. The FROM clause is FROM EMPLOYEES.

4. The Cartesian product is performed using CROSS JOIN DEPARTMENTS.

5. Explicit counts of the rows present in the source tables are performed using
SELECT COUNT(*) FROM EMPLOYEES;
SELECT COUNT(*) FROM DEPARTMENTS;

6. Explicit multiplication of the values resulting from the previous queries may be performed by querying the DUAL table.

7. Executing these statements reveals that there are 107 records in the EMPLOYEES table, 27 records in the DEPARTMENTS table, and 2889 records in the Cartesian product of these two data sets as shown in the following illustration:

INSIDE THE EXAM

Joining is a fundamental relational principle. The certification objectives in this chapter are examined using practical scenarios in which two tables are joined. You are required to predict the number of rows returned by a join query or to assess whether it is syntactically correct or not. The natural join clauses include NATURAL JOIN, JOIN…USING, and JOIN…ON.

Remember the following simple rules. The keywords NATURAL, USING, and ON are mutually exclusive. They may not be used together in the same join clause. The pure NATURAL join takes no join conditions. The JOIN…USING clause requires unqualified column references in join conditions, which must appear in brackets after the USING keyword.

Self-joins are often used for searching through hierarchical data stored in separate columns in the same table. It is an uncommon join and little emphasis is placed on testing your knowledge of self-joins in the exam. Outer joins, however, form a significant part of the exam content. Ensure that you have a solid understanding of LEFT, RIGHT, and FULL OUTER joins.

Cartesian products may be created inadvertently or intentionally using the CROSS JOIN clause. A mistake frequently made in the early stages of learning about joins is to specify fewer join conditions than are necessary when joining multiple tables. This leads to accidental Cartesian joins and is sometimes tested in the exams. Remember that when joining N tables, at least N-1 join conditions are required to avoid a Cartesian join.

CERTIFICATION SUMMARY

Data stored in separate tables may be associated with each other using various types of joins. Joins allow data to be stored in a relational manner. This prevents the need for multiple copies of the same data across multiple tables.

Equijoins and nonequijoins are referred to as inner joins. They associate rows from multiple tables that conform to join conditions and are specified using either equality or inequality operators. Rows that do not conform to these join conditions, which are ordinarily excluded by inner joins, may be retrieved with outer joins. Left, right, and full outer joins facilitate the retrieval of orphan rows.

The ANSI SQL:1999-compliant join syntax is discussed in detail, and three forms of the natural join are explored. Each form has a purpose, and the advantages and risks associated with them are considered.

Joins associate columns from multiple tables that may share the same name. Dot notation uses a method of qualifying columns to disambiguate them. It is accompanied by table aliasing, which is not strictly essential but helps a great deal when formulating joins between tables with lengthy names.

The retrieval of hierarchical data stored in a single table using self-joins is considered. N-way joins allow more than two tables to be joined, and this generalized option is discussed. Finally, cross joins and the unique challenges associated with them are examined.

Joining is one of the fundamental pillars of relational theory and is critical to your successful exploitation of the full potential that SQL offers.

TWO-MINUTE DRILL

Write SELECT Statements to Access Data from More Than One Table Using Equijoins and Nonequijoins

❑ *Equijoining* occurs when one query fetches column values from multiple tables in which the rows fulfill an *equality-based join condition*.

❑ A *pure natural* join is performed using the *NATURAL JOIN* syntax when the source and target tables are implicitly equijoined using all identically named columns.

❑ The *JOIN…USING* syntax allows a *natural join* to be formed on specific columns with shared names.

❑ Dot notation refers to qualifying a column by prefixing it with its table name and a dot or period symbol. This designates the table a column originates from and differentiates it from identically named columns from other tables.

❑ The *JOIN…ON* clause allows the explicit specification of *join columns* regardless of their column names. This provides a flexible joining format.

❑ The *ON*, *USING*, and *NATURAL* keywords are mutually exclusive and therefore cannot appear together in a join clause.

❑ A *nonequijoin* is performed when the values in the *join columns* fulfill the *join condition* based on an inequality expression.

Join a Table to Itself Using a Self-Join

❑ A *self-join* is required when the join columns originate from the same table. Conceptually, the source table is duplicated and a target table is created. The *self-join* then works as a regular join between two discrete tables.

❑ Storing hierarchical data in a relational table requires a minimum of two columns per row. One column stores an identifier of the row's parent record and the second stores the row's identifier.

View Data That Does Not Meet a Join Condition Using Outer Joins

❑ When equijoins and nonequijoins are performed, rows from the source and target tables are matched. These are referred to as *inner joins*.

❑ An *outer join* is performed when rows, which are not retrieved by an *inner join*, are included for retrieval.

❑ A *left outer join* between the source and target tables returns the results of an inner join and the missing rows it excluded from the *source* table.

❑ A *right outer join* between the source and target tables returns the results of an inner join and the missing rows it excluded from the *target* table.

❑ A *full outer join* returns the combined results of a *left outer join* and *right outer join*.

Generate a Cartesian Product of Two or More Tables

❑ A Cartesian product is sometimes called a cross join. It is a mathematical term that refers to the set of data created by merging the rows from two or more tables.

❑ The count of the rows returned from a Cartesian product is equal to the number of rows in the source table multiplied by the number of rows in the target table.

❑ Joins that specify fewer than N-1 join conditions when joining N tables, or that specify invalid join conditions, inadvertently create Cartesian products.

SELF TEST

The following questions will help you measure your understanding of the material presented in this chapter. Read all the choices carefully because there may be more than one correct answer. Choose all the correct answers for each question.

Write SELECT Statements to Access Data from More Than One Table Using Equijoins and Nonequijoins

1. The EMPLOYEES and DEPARTMENTS tables have two identically named columns: DEPARTMENT_ID and MANAGER_ID. Which of these statements joins these tables based only on common DEPARTMENT_ID values? (Choose all that apply.)

   A. SELECT * FROM EMPLOYEES NATURAL JOIN DEPARTMENTS;

   B. SELECT * FROM EMPLOYEES E NATURAL JOIN DEPARTMENTS D ON E.DEPARTMENT_ID=D.DEPARTMENT_ID;

   C. SELECT * FROM EMPLOYEES NATURAL JOIN DEPARTMENTS USING (DEPARTMENT_ID);

   D. None of the above

2. The EMPLOYEES and DEPARTMENTS tables have two identically named columns: DEPARTMENT_ID and MANAGER_ID. Which statements join these tables based on both column values? (Choose all that apply.)

   A. SELECT * FROM EMPLOYEES NATURAL JOIN DEPARTMENTS;

   B. SELECT * FROM EMPLOYEES JOIN DEPARTMENTS USING (DEPARTMENT_ID,MANAGER_ID);

   C. SELECT * FROM EMPLOYEES E JOIN DEPARTMENTS D ON E.DEPARTMENT_ID=D.DEPARTMENT_ID AND E.MANAGER_ID=D.MANAGER_ID;

   D. None of the above

3. Which join is performed by the following query?
   SELECT E.JOB_ID,J.JOB_ID FROM EMPLOYEES E
   JOIN JOBS J ON (E.SALARY < J.MAX_SALARY); (Choose the best answer.)

   A. Equijoin

   B. Nonequijoin

   C. Cross join

   D. Outer join

4. Which of the following statements are syntactically correct? (Choose all that apply.)

   A. SELECT * FROM EMPLOYEES E JOIN DEPARTMENTS D USING (DEPARTMENT_ID);

   B. SELECT * FROM EMPLOYEES JOIN DEPARTMENTS D USING (D.DEPARTMENT_ID);

    C. SELECT D.DEPARTMENT_ID FROM EMPLOYEES JOIN DEPARTMENTS D USING (DEPARTMENT_ID);

    D. None of the above

5. Which of the following statements are syntactically correct? (Choose all that apply.)

    A. SELECT E.EMPLOYEE_ID, J.JOB_ID PREVIOUS_JOB, E.JOB_ID CURRENT_JOB FROM JOB_HISTORY J CROSS JOIN EMPLOYEES E ON (J.START_DATE=E.HIRE_DATE);

    B. SELECT E.EMPLOYEE_ID, J.JOB_ID PREVIOUS_JOB, E.JOB_ID CURRENT_JOB FROM JOB_HISTORY J JOIN EMPLOYEES E ON (J.START_DATE=E.HIRE_DATE);

    C. SELECT E.EMPLOYEE_ID, J.JOB_ID PREVIOUS_JOB, E.JOB_ID CURRENT_JOB FROM JOB_HISTORY J OUTER JOIN EMPLOYEES E ON (J.START_DATE=E. HIRE_DATE);

    D. None of the above

6. Choose one correct statement regarding the following query:
SELECT * FROM EMPLOYEES E
JOIN DEPARTMENTS D ON (D.DEPARTMENT_ID=E.DEPARTMENT_ID) JOIN
LOCATIONS L ON (L.LOCATION_ID =D.LOCATION_ID);

    A. Joining three tables is not permitted.

    B. A Cartesian product is generated.

    C. The JOIN…ON clause may be used for joins between multiple tables.

    D. None of the above

Join a Table to Itself Using a Self-Join

7. How many rows are returned after executing the following statement?
SELECT * FROM REGIONS R1 JOIN REGIONS R2 ON (R1.REGION_ID=LENGTH(R2. REGION_NAME)/2);
The REGIONS table contains the following row data. (Choose the best answer.)

REGION_ID	REGION_NAME
1	Europe
2	Americas
3	Asia
4	Middle East and Africa

    A. 2

    B. 3

    C. 4

    D. None of the above

View Data That Does Not Meet a Join Condition Using Outer Joins

8. Choose one correct statement regarding the following query.
SELECT C.COUNTRY_ID
FROM LOCATIONS L RIGHT OUTER JOIN COUNTRIES C
ON (L.COUNTRY_ID=C.COUNTRY_ID) WHERE L.COUNTRY_ID is NULL

    A. No rows in the LOCATIONS table have the COUNTRY_ID values returned.

    B. No rows in the COUNTRIES table have the COUNTRY_ID values returned.

    C. The rows returned represent the COUNTRY_ID values for all the rows in the LOCATIONS table.

    D. None of the above

9. Which of the following statements are syntactically correct? (Choose all that apply.)

    A. SELECT JH.JOB_ID FROM JOB_HISTORY JH RIGHT OUTER JOIN JOBS J ON JH.JOB_ID=J.JOB_ID

    B. SELECT JOB_ID FROM JOB_HISTORY JH RIGHT OUTER JOIN JOBS J ON (JH.JOB_ID=J.JOB_ID)

    C. SELECT JOB_HISTORY.JOB_ID FROM JOB_HISTORY OUTER JOIN JOBS ON JOB_HISTORY.JOB_ID=JOBS.JOB_ID

    D. None of the above

Generate a Cartesian Product of Two or More Tables

10. If the REGIONS table, which contains 4 rows, is cross joined to the COUNTRIES table, which contains 25 rows, how many rows appear in the final results set? (Choose the best answer.)

    A. 100 rows

    B. 4 rows

    C. 25 rows

    D. None of the above

LAB QUESTION

Using SQL Developer or SQL*Plus, connect to the OE schema and complete the following tasks.

    You are required to produce a report of customers who purchased products with list prices of more than $1000. The report must contain customer first and last names and the product names and their list prices. Customer information is stored in the CUSTOMERS table, which has the CUSTOMER_ID column as its primary key. The product name and list price details are stored in the PRODUCT_INFORMATION table with the PRODUCT_ID column as its primary key. Two other related tables may assist in generating the required report: the ORDERS table, which stores the CUSTOMER_ID and ORDER_ID information, and the ORDER_ITEMS table, which stores the PRODUCT_ID values associated with each ORDER_ID.

There are several approaches to solving this question. Your approach may differ from the solution listed.

SELF TEST ANSWERS

Write SELECT Statements to Access Data from More Than One Table Using Equijoins and Nonequijoins

1. ☑ **D.** The queries in **B** and **C** incorrectly contain the NATURAL keyword. If this is removed, they will join the DEPARTMENTS and EMPLOYEES tables based on the DEPARTMENT_ID column.

   ☒ **A, B,** and **C** are incorrect. **A** performs a pure natural join that implicitly joins the two tables on all columns with identical names which, in this case, are DEPARTMENT_ID and MANAGER_ID.

2. ☑ **A, B,** and **C.** These clauses demonstrate different techniques to join the tables on both the DEPARTMENT_ID and MANAGER_ID columns.

   ☒ **D** is incorrect.

3. ☑ **B.** The join condition is an expression based on the *less than* inequality operator. Therefore, this join is a nonequijoin.

   ☒ **A, C,** and **D** are incorrect. **A** would be correct if the operator in the join condition expression was an equality operator. The CROSS JOIN keywords or the absence of a join condition would result in **C** being true. **D** would be true if one of the OUTER JOIN clause was used instead of the JOIN...ON clause.

4. ☑ **A.** This statement demonstrates the correct usage of the JOIN...USING clause.

   ☒ **B, C,** and **D** are incorrect. **B** is incorrect since only nonqualified column names are allowed in the brackets after the USING keyword. **C** is incorrect because the column in brackets after the USING keyword cannot be referenced with a qualifier in the SELECT clause.

5. ☑ **B** demonstrates the correct usage of the JOIN...ON clause.

   ☒ **A, C,** and **D** are incorrect. **A** is incorrect since the CROSS JOIN clause cannot contain the ON keyword. **C** is incorrect since the OUTER JOIN keywords must be preceded by the LEFT, RIGHT, or FULL keyword.

6. ☑ **C.** The JOIN...ON clause and the other join clauses may all be used for joins between multiple tables. The JOIN...ON and JOIN...USING clauses are better suited for N-way table joins.

   ☒ **A, B,** and **D** are incorrect. **A** is false since you may join as many tables as you wish. A Cartesian product is not created since there are two join conditions and three tables.

Join a Table to Itself Using a Self-Join

7. ☑ **B.** Three rows are returned. For the row with a REGION_ID value of 2, the REGION_NAME is Asia and half the length of the REGION_NAME is also 2. Therefore this row is returned.

The same logic results in the rows with REGION_ID values of three and four and REGION_NAME values of Europe and Americas being returned.

☒ **A, C,** and **D** are incorrect.

View Data That Does Not Meet a Join Condition Using Outer Joins

8. ☑ **A.** The right outer join fetches the COUNTRIES rows that the inner join between the LOCATIONS and COUNTRIES tables have excluded. The WHERE clause then restricts the results by eliminating the inner join results. This leaves the rows from the COUNTRIES table with which no records from the LOCATIONS table records are associated.

☒ **B, C,** and **D** are incorrect.

9. ☑ **A.** This statement demonstrates the correct use of the RIGHT OUTER JOIN...ON clause.

☒ **B, C,** and **D** are incorrect. The JOB_ID column in the SELECT clause in **B** is not qualified and is therefore ambiguous since the table from which this column comes is not specified. **C** uses an OUTER JOIN without the keywords LEFT, RIGHT, or FULL.

Generate a Cartesian Product of Two or More Tables

10. ☑ **A.** The cross join associates every four rows from the REGIONS table 25 times with the rows from the COUNTRIES table yielding a result set that contains 100 rows.

☒ **B, C,** and **D** are incorrect.

LAB ANSWER

Using SQL Developer or SQL*Plus, connect to the OE schema, and complete the following tasks. There are several approaches to solving this question. Your approach may differ from the following solution listed.

1. Start SQL Developer and connect to the OE schema.

2. The SELECT list consists of four columns from two tables, which will be associated with each other using several joins. The SELECT clause is
`SELECT CUST_FIRST_NAME, CUST_LAST_NAME, PRODUCT_NAME, LIST_PRICE.`

3. The FROM clause is
`FROM CUSTOMERS.`

4. The WHERE clause is
`WHERE LIST_PRICE > 1000.`

5. The JOIN clauses are interesting since the PRODUCT_INFORMATION and CUSTOMERS tables not directly related. They are related through two other tables.

6. The ORDERS table must first be joined to the CUSTOMERS table based on common CUSTOMER_ID values. The first join clause following the FROM CUSTOMERS clause is
   `JOIN ORDERS USING (CUSTOMER_ID)`.

7. This set must then be joined to the ORDER_ITEMS table based on common ORDER_ID values since the ORDER_ITEMS table can ultimately link to the PRODUCT_INFORMATION table. The second join clause is
   `JOIN ORDER_ITEMS USING (ORDER_ID)`.

8. The missing link to join to the PRODUCT_INFORMATION table based on common PRODUCT_ID column values is now available. The third join clause is
   `JOIN PRODUCT_INFORMATION USING (PRODUCT_ID)`.

9. Executing this statement returns the report required as shown in the following illustration:

8

Using Subqueries to Solve Problems

T he previous six chapters have dealt with the SELECT statement in considerable detail, but in every case the SELECT statement has been a single, self-contained command. This chapter is the first of two that show how two or more SELECT commands can be combined into one statement. The first technique (covered in this chapter) is the use of *subqueries*. A subquery is a SELECT statement whose output is used as input to another SELECT statement (or indeed to a DML statement, as done in Chapter 10). The second technique is the use of set operators, where the results of several SELECT commands are combined into a single result set.

CERTIFICATION OBJECTIVE 8.01

Define Subqueries

A subquery is a query that is nested inside a SELECT, INSERT, UPDATE, or DELETE statement or inside another subquery. A subquery can return a set of rows or just one row to its parent query. A *scalar* subquery is a query that returns exactly one value: a single row, with a single column. Scalar subqueries can be used in most places in a SQL statement where you could use an expression or a literal value.

The places in a query where a subquery may be used are as follows:

- In the SELECT list used for column projection
- In the FROM clause
- In the WHERE clause
- In the HAVING clause

e x a m

ⓦatch   *Subqueries can be nested to an unlimited depth in a FROM clause but to "only" 255 levels in a WHERE clause. They can be used in the SELECT list and in the FROM, WHERE, and HAVING clauses of a query.*

A subquery is often referred to as an *inner* query, and the statement within which it occurs is then called the *outer* query. There is nothing wrong with this terminology, except that it may imply that you can only have two levels, inner and outer. In fact, the Oracle implementation of subqueries does not impose any practical limits on the level of nesting: the depth of nesting permitted in the FROM clause of a statement is unlimited, and that in the WHERE clause is up to 255.

A subquery can have any of the usual clauses for selection and projection. The following are required clauses:

- A SELECT list
- A FROM clause

The following are optional clauses:

- WHERE
- GROUP BY
- HAVING

The subquery (or subqueries) within a statement must be executed before the parent query that calls it, in order that the results of the subquery can be passed to the parent.

EXERCISE 8-1

Types of Subqueries

In this exercise, you will write code that demonstrates the places where subqueries can be used. Use either SQL*Plus or SQL Developer. All the queries should be run when connected to the HR schema.

1. Log on to your database as user HR.

2. Write a query that uses subqueries in the column projection list. The query will report on the current numbers of departments and staff:

```
select sysdate Today,
(select count(*) from departments) Dept_count,
(select count(*) from employees) Emp_count
from dual;
```

3. Write a query to identify all the employees who are managers. This will require using a subquery in the WHERE clause to select all the employees whose EMPLOYEE_ID appears as a MANAGER_ID:

```
select last_name from employees where
(employee_id in (select manager_id from employees));
```

4. Write a query to identify the highest salary paid in each country. This will require using a subquery in the FROM clause:

```
select max(salary),country_id from
        (select salary,department_id,location_id,country_id from
        employees natural join departments natural join locations)
group by country_id;
```

CERTIFICATION OBJECTIVE 8.02

Describe the Types of Problems That the Subqueries Can Solve

There are many situations where you will need the result of one query as the input for another.

Use of a Subquery Result Set for Comparison Purposes

Which employees have a salary that is less than the average salary? This could be answered by two statements, or by a single statement with a subquery. The following example uses two statements:

```
select avg(salary) from employees;
select last_name from employees where salary < result_of_previous_query ;
```

Alternatively, this example uses one statement with a subquery:

```
select last_name from employees
where salary < (select avg(salary)from employees);
```

In this example, the subquery is used to substitute a value into the WHERE clause of the parent query: it is returning a single value, used for comparison with the rows retrieved by the parent query.

The subquery could return a set of rows. For example, you could use the following to find all departments that do actually have one or more employees assigned to them:

```
select department_name from departments where department_id in
(select distinct(department_id) from employees);
```

In the preceding example, the subquery is used as an alternative to a join. The same result could have been achieved with the following:

```
select department_name from departments inner join employees
on employees.department_id = departments.department_id
group by department_name;
```

If the subquery is going to return more than one row, then the comparison operator must be able to accept multiple values. These operators are IN, NOT IN, ANY, and ALL. If the comparison operator is EQUAL, GREATER THAN, or LESS THAN (which each can only accept one value), the parent query will fail.

on the
(Ì) o b   ***Using NOT IN is fraught with problems because of the way SQL handles NULLs. As a general rule, do not use NOT IN unless you are certain that the result set will not include a NULL.***

Star Transformation

An extension of the use of subqueries as an alternative to a join is to enable the *star transformation* often needed in data warehouse applications. Consider a large table recording sales. Each sale is marked as being of a particular product to a particular buyer through a particular channel. These attributes are identified by codes, used as foreign keys to dimension tables with rows that describe each product, buyer, and channel. To identify all sales of books to buyers in Germany through Internet orders, one could run a query like this:

```
select … from sales s, products p, buyers b, channels c
where s.prod_code=p.prod_code
and s.buy_code=b.buy_code
and s.chan_code=c.chan_code
and p.product='Books'
and b.country='Germany'
and c.channel='Internet';
```

This query uses the WHERE clause to join the tables and then to filter the results. The following is an alternative query that will yield the same result:

```
select … from sales
where prod_code in (select prod_code from products where product='Books')
and buy_code in (select buy_code from buyers where country='Germany')
and chan_code in (select chan_code from channels where channel='Internet);
```

The rewrite of the first statement to the second is the star transformation. Apart from being an inherently more elegant structure (most SQL developers with any sense of aesthetics will agree with that), there are technical reasons why the database may be able to execute it more efficiently than the original query. Also, star queries are easier to maintain; it is very simple to add more dimensions to the query or to replace the single literals ('Books,' 'Germany,' and 'Internet') with lists of values.

on the
Ọ o b

There is an instance initialization parameter, STAR_TRANSFORMATION_ ENABLED, which (if set to true) will permit the Oracle query optimizer to re-write code into star queries.

Generate a Table from Which to SELECT

Subqueries can also be used in the FROM clause, where they are sometimes referred to as *inline views*. Consider another problem based on the HR schema: employees are assigned to a department, and departments have a location. Each location is in a country. How can you find the average salary of staff in a country, even though they work for different departments? Like this:

```
select avg(salary),country_id from
    (select salary,department_id,location_id,country_id from
        employees natural join departments natural join locations)
group by country_id;
```

The subquery constructs a table with every employee's salary and the country in which his department is based. The parent query then addresses this table, averaging the SALARY and grouping by COUNTRY_ID.

Generate Values for Projection

The third place a subquery can go is in the SELECT list of a query. How can you identify the highest salary and the highest commission rate and thus what the maximum commission paid would be if the highest salaried employee also had the highest commission rate? Like this, with two subqueries:

```
select
(select max(salary) from employees) *
(select max(commission_pct) from employees)
/ 100
from dual;
```

In this usage, the SELECT list used to project columns is being populated with the results of the subqueries. A subquery used in this manner must be scalar, or the parent query will fail with an error.

Generate Rows to be Passed to a DML Statement

DML statements are covered in detail in Chapter 10. For now, consider these examples:

```
insert into sales_hist select * from sales where date > sysdate-1;
update employees set salary = (select avg(salary) from employees);
delete from departments
where department_id not in (select department_id from employees);
```

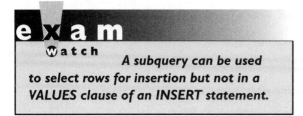

A subquery can be used to select rows for insertion but not in a VALUES clause of an INSERT statement.

The first example uses a subquery to identify a set of rows in one table that will be inserted into another. The second example uses a subquery to calculate the average salary of all employees and passes this value (a scalar quantity) to an update statement. The third example uses a subquery to retrieve all DEPARTMENT_IDs that are in use and passes the list to a DELETE command, which will remove all departments that are not in use.

Note that it is not legal to use a subquery in the VALUES clause of an insert statement; this is fine:

```
insert into dates select sysdate from dual;
```

But this is not:

```
insert into dates (date_col) values (select sysdate fom dual);
```

EXERCISE 8-2

More Complex Subqueries

In this exercise, you will write some more complicated subqueries. Use either SQL*Plus or SQL Developer. All the queries should be run when connected to the HR schema.

1. Log on to your database as user HR.
2. Write a query that will identify all employees who work in departments located in the United Kingdom. This will require three levels of nested subqueries:

```
select last_name from employees where department_id in
    (select department_id from departments
    where location_id in
        (select location_id from locations
```

```
                              where country_id =
                                  (select country_id from countries
                                  where country_name='United Kingdom')
                              )
                    );
```

3. Check that the result from step 2 is correct by running the subqueries independently. First, find the COUNTRY_ID for the United Kingdom:

```
select country_id from countries where country_name='United Kingdom';
```

The result will be UK. Then find the corresponding locations:

```
select location_id from locations where country_id = 'UK';
```

The LOCATION_IDs returned will be 2400, 2500, and 2600. Then find the DEPARTMENT_IDs of department in these locations:

```
select department_id from departments where location_id in (2400,2500,2600);
```

The result will be two departments, 40 and 80. Finally, find the relevant employees:

```
select last_name from employees where department_id in (40,80);
```

4. Write a query to identify all the employees who earn more than the average and who work in any of the IT departments. This will require two subqueries, not nested:

```
select last_name from employees
where department_id in
(select department_id from departments where department_name like 'IT%')
and salary > (select avg(salary) from employees);
```

CERTIFICATION OBJECTIVE 8.03

List the Types of Subqueries

There are three broad divisions of subquery:

- Single-row subqueries
- Multiple-row subqueries
- Correlated subqueries

Single- and Multiple-Row Subqueries

The *single-row* subquery returns one row. A special case is the scalar subquery, which returns a single row with one column. Scalar subqueries are acceptable (and often very useful) in virtually any situation where you could use a literal value, a constant, or an expression. *Multiple-row* subqueries return sets of rows. These queries are commonly used to generate result sets that will be passed to a DML or SELECT statement for further processing. Both single-row and multiple-row subqueries will be evaluated once, before the parent query is run.

Single- and multiple-row subqueries can be used in the WHERE and HAVING clauses of the parent query, but there are restrictions on the legal comparison operators. If the comparison operator is any of the ones in the following table, the subquery must be a single-row subquery:

Symbol	Meaning
=	equal
>	greater than
>=	greater than or equal
<	less than
<=	less than or equal
<>	not equal
!=	not equal

If any of the operators in the preceding table are used with a subquery that returns more than one row, the query will fail. The operators in the following table can use multiple-row subqueries:

Symbol	Meaning
IN	equal to any member in a list
NOT IN	not equal to any member in a list
ANY	returns rows that match any value on a list
ALL	returns rows that match all the values in a list

Correlated Subqueries

A *correlated subquery* has a more complex method of execution than single- and multiple-row subqueries and is potentially much more powerful. If a subquery references columns in the parent query, then its result will be dependent on the parent query. This makes it impossible to evaluate the subquery before evaluating the parent query. Consider this statement, which lists all employees who earn less than the average salary:

```
select last_name from employees
where salary < (select avg(salary) from employees);
```

The single-row subquery need only be executed once, and its result substituted into the parent query. But now consider a query that will list all employees whose salary is less than the average salary of their department. In this case, the subquery must be run for each employee to determine the average salary for her department; it is necessary to pass the employee's department code to the subquery. This can be done as follows:

```
select p.last_name, p.department_id from employees p
where p.salary < (select avg(s.salary) from employees s
where s.department_id=p.department_id);
```

In this example, the subquery references a column, `p.department_id`, from the select list of the parent query. This is the signal that, rather than evaluating the subquery once, it must be evaluated for every row in the parent query. To execute the query, Oracle will look at every row in EMPLOYEES and, as it does so, run the subquery using the DEPARTMENT_ID of the current employee row.

The flow of execution is as follows:

1. Start at the first row of the EMPLOYEES table.
2. Read the DEPARTMENT_ID and SALARY of the current row.
3. Run the subquery using the DEPARTMENT_ID from step 2.

4. Compare the result of step 3 with the SALARY from step 2, and return the row if the SALARY is less than the result.

5. Advance to the next row in the EMPLOYEES table.

6. Repeat from step 2.

A single-row or multiple-row subquery is evaluated once, before evaluating the outer query; a correlated subquery must be evaluated once for every row in the outer query. A correlated subquery can be single- or multiple-row, if the comparison operator is appropriate.

on the

Job *Correlated subqueries can be a very inefficient construct, due to the need for repeated execution of the subquery. Always try to find an alternative approach.*

EXERCISE 8-3

Investigate the Different Types of Subqueries

In this exercise, you will demonstrate problems that can occur with different types of subqueries. Use either SQL*Plus or SQL Developer. All the queries should be run when connected to the HR schema: it is assumed that the EMPLOYEES table has the standard sets of rows.

1. Log on to your database as user HR.

2. Write a query to determine who earns more than Mr. Tobias:

```
select last_name from employees where
salary > (select salary from employees where last_name='Tobias')
order by last_name;
```

This will return 86 names, in alphabetical order.

3. Write a query to determine who earns more than Mr. Taylor:

```
select last_name from employees where
salary > (select salary from employees where last_name='Taylor')
order by last_name;
```

This will fail with the error "ORA-01427: single-row subquery returns more than one row." The following illustration shows the last few lines of the output from step 2 followed by step 3 and the error, executed with SQL*Plus.

```
C:\WINDOWS\system32\cmd.exe - sqlplus hr/hr
Sully
Taylor
Taylor
Tucker
Tuvault
Urman
Uishney
Uollman
Walsh
Weiss
Whalen
Zlotkey

86 rows selected.

SQL> select last_name from employees where
  2   salary > (select salary from employees where last_name='Taylor')
  3   order by last_name;
salary > (select salary from employees where last_name='Taylor')
         *
ERROR at line 2:
ORA-01427: single-row subquery returns more than one row

SQL> _
```

4. Determine why the query in step 2 succeeded but failed in step 3. The answer lies in the state of the data:

```
select count(last_name) from employees where last_name='Tobias';
select count(last_name) from employees where last_name='Taylor';
```

The use of the "greater than" operator in the queries for steps 2 and 3 requires a single-row subquery, but the subquery used may return any number of rows, depending on the search predicate used.

5. Fix the code in steps 2 and 3 so that the statements will succeed no matter what LAST_NAME is used. There are two possible solutions: one uses a different comparison operator that can handle a multiple-row subquery; the other uses a subquery that will always be single-row.

The first solution:

```
select last_name from employees where
salary > all (select salary from employees where last_name='Taylor')
order by last_name;
```

The second solution:

```
select last_name from employees where
salary > (select max(salary) from employees where last_name='Taylor')
order by last_name;
```

SCENARIO & SOLUTION

How can you best design subqueries such that they will not fail with "ORA-01427: single-row subquery returns more than one row" errors?	There are two common techniques: use an aggregation so that if you do get multiple rows they will be reduced to one, or use one of the IN, ANY, or ALL operators so that it won't matter if multiple rows are returned. But these are both hacker's solutions; the real answer is always to use the primary key when identifying the row to be returned, not a nonunique key.
Sometimes there is a choice between using a subquery or using some other technique: the star transformation is a case in point. Which is better?	It depends on the circumstances. It is not uncommon for the different techniques to cause a different execution method within the database. Depending on how the instance, the database, and the data structures within it are configured, one may be much more efficient than another. Whenever such a choice arises, the statements should be subjected to a tuning analysis. Your DBA will be able to advise on this.

CERTIFICATION OBJECTIVE 8.04

Write Single-Row and Multiple-Row Subqueries

Following are examples of single- and multiple-row subqueries. They are based on the HR demonstration schema.

How would you figure out which employees have a manager who works for a department based in the United Kingdom? This is a possible solution, using multiple-row subqueries:

```
select last_name from employees
where manager_id in
(select employee_id from employees where department_id in
(select department_id from departments where location_id in
(select location_id from locations where country_id='UK')));
```

In the preceding example, subqueries are nested three levels deep. Note that the subqueries use the IN operator because it is possible that the queries could return several rows.

You have been asked to find the job with the highest average salary. This can be done with a single-row subquery:

```
select job_title from jobs natural join employees group by job_title
having avg(salary) =
(select max(avg(salary)) from employees group by job_id);
```

The subquery returns a single value: the average salary of the department with the highest average salary. It is safe to use the equality operator for this subquery because the MAX function guarantees that only one row will be returned.

The ANY and ALL operators are supported syntax, but their function can be duplicated with other more commonly used operators combined with aggregations. For example, these two statements, which retrieve all employees whose salary is above that of anyone in department 80, will return identical result sets:

```
select last_name from employees where salary > all
(select salary from employees where department_id=80);
select last_name from employees where salary >
(select max(salary) from employees where department_id=80);
```

The following table summarizes the equivalents for ANY and ALL:

Operator	Meaning
< ANY	less than the highest
> ANY	more than the lowest
= ANY	equivalent to IN
> ALL	more than the highest
< ALL	less than the lowest

EXERCISE 8-4

Write a Query That Is Reliable and User Friendly

In this exercise, develop a multi-row subquery that will prompt for user input. Use either SQL*Plus or SQL Developer. All the queries should be run when connected to the HR schema; it is assumed that the tables have the standard sets of rows.

 1. Log on to your database as user HR.

 2. Design a query that will prompt for a department name and list the last name of every employee in that department:

```
select last_name from employees where department_id =
(select department_id from departments
where department_name = '&Department_name');
```

3. Run the query in step 2 three times, when prompted supplying these values:

first time, Executive

second time, executive

third time, Executiv

The following illustration shows the result, using SQL*Plus:

4. Note the results from step 3. The first run succeeded because the value entered was an exact match, but the other failed. Adjust the query to make it more user friendly, so that it can handle minor variations in case or spelling:

```
select last_name from employees where department_id =
(select department_id from departments
where upper(department_name) like upper('%&Department_name%'));
```

5. Run the query in step 4 three times, using the same values as used in step 3. This time, the query will execute successfully.

6. Run the query in step 4 again, and this time enter the value Pu. The query will fail, with an "ORA-01427: single-row subquery returns more than one row" error, because the attempt to make it more user-friendly means that the subquery is no longer guaranteed to be a single-row subquery. The string Pu matches two departments.

7. Adjust the query to make it resilient against the ORA-01427 error, and adjust the output to prevent any possible confusion:

```
select last_name,department_name from employees join departments
on employees.department_id = departments.department_id
where departments.department_id in
(select department_id from departments
where upper(department_name) like upper('%&Department_name%'));
```

The following illustration shows this final step: code that is approaching the ideal of being both bullet proof and user friendly:

```
C:\WINDOWS\system32\cmd.exe - sqlplus hr/hr

SQL> select last_name,department_name from employees join departments
  2  on employees.department_id = departments.department_id
  3  where departments.department_id in
  4  (select department_id from departments
  5  where upper(department_name) like upper('%&Department_name%'));
Enter value for department_name: Pu
old   5: where upper(department_name) like upper('%&Department_name%'))
new   5: where upper(department_name) like upper('%Pu%'))
Raphaely                 Purchasing
Khoo                     Purchasing
Baida                    Purchasing
Tobias                   Purchasing
Himuro                   Purchasing
Colmenares               Purchasing
Baer                     Public Relations

7 rows selected.

SQL>
```

INSIDE THE EXAM

Use of Subqueries

Subqueries come in three general forms: single-row, multiple-row, and correlated. A special case of the single-row subquery is the scalar subquery, a subquery that returns exactly one value. This is a single-row single-column subquery. For the first SQL OCP exam, detailed knowledge is expected only of scalar subqueries and single-column multiple-row subqueries. Correlated subqueries and multiple column subqueries are unlikely to be examined at this level, but a general knowledge of them may be tested.

When using subqueries in a WHERE clause, you must be aware of which operators will succeed with single-row subqueries and which will succeed with multiple-row subqueries.

CERTIFICATION SUMMARY

A subquery is a query embedded within another SQL statement. This statement can be another query or a DML statement. Subqueries can be nested within each other with no practical limits.

Subqueries can be used to generate values for the select list of a query to generate an inline view to be used in the FROM clause, in the WHERE clause, and in the HAVING clause. When used in the WHERE or HAVING clauses, single-row subqueries can be used with these comparison operators: =, >, >=, <, <=, <>; multiple-row subqueries can be used with these comparison operators: IN, NOT IN, ANY, ALL.

✓ TWO-MINUTE DRILL

Define Subqueries

❑ A subquery is a select statement embedded within another SQL statement.

❑ Subqueries can be nested within each other.

❑ With the exception of the correlated subquery, subqueries are executed before the outer query within which they are embedded.

Describe the Types of Problems That the Subqueries Can Solve

❑ Selecting rows from a table with a condition that depends on the data within the table can be implemented with a subquery.

❑ Complex joins can sometimes be replaced with subqueries.

❑ Subqueries can add values to the outer query's output that are not available in the tables the outer query addresses.

List the Types of Subqueries

❑ Multiple-row subqueries can return several rows, possibly with several columns.

❑ Single-row subqueries return one row, possibly with several columns.

❑ A scalar subquery returns a single value; it is a single-row, single-column subquery.

❑ A correlated subquery is executed once for every row in the outer query.

Write Single-Row and Multiple-Row Subqueries

❑ Single-row subqueries should be used with single-row comparison operators.

❑ Multiple-row subqueries should be used with multiple-row comparison operators.

❑ The ALL and ANY operators can be alternatives to use of aggregations.

SELF TEST

Define Subqueries

1. Consider this generic description of a SELECT statement:

   SELECT *select_list*
   FROM *table*
   WHERE *condition*
   GROUP BY *expression_1*
   HAVING *expression_2*
   ORDER BY *expression_3* ;

   Where could subqueries be used? (Choose all correct answers.)

   A. *select_list*
   B. *table*
   C. *condition*
   D. *expression_1*
   E. *expression_2*
   F. *expression_3*

2. A query can have a subquery embedded within it. Under what circumstances could there be more than one subquery? (Choose the best answer.)

   A. The outer query can include an inner query. It is not possible to have another query within the inner query.
   B. It is possible to embed a single-row subquery inside a multiple-row subquery, but not the other way around.
   C. The outer query can have multiple inner queries, but they must not be embedded within each other.
   D. Subqueries can be embedded within each other with no practical limitations on depth.

3. Consider this statement:

   ```
   select employee_id, last_name from employees where
   salary > (select avg(salary) from employees);
   ```

   When will the subquery be executed? (Choose the best answer.)

   A. It will be executed before the outer query.
   B. It will be executed after the outer query.

    C. It will be executed concurrently with the outer query.

    D. It will be executed once for every row in the EMPLOYEES table.

4. Consider this statement:

```
select o.employee_id, o.last_name from employees o where
o.salary > (select avg(i.salary) from employees i
where i.department_id=o.department_id);
```

When will the subquery be executed? (Choose the best answer.)

    A. It will be executed before the outer query.

    B. It will be executed after the outer query.

    C. It will be executed concurrently with the outer query.

    D. It will be executed once for every row in the EMPLOYEES table.

Describe the Types of Problems That the Subqueries Can Solve

5. Consider the following statement:

```
select last_name from employees join departments
on employees.department_id = departments.department_id
where department_name='Executive';
```

and this statement:

```
select last_name from employees where department_id in
(select department_id from departments where department_name='Executive');
```

What can be said about the two statements? (Choose two correct answers.)

    A. The two statements should generate the same result.

    B. The two statements could generate different results.

    C. The first statement will always run successfully; the second statement will error if there are two departments with DEPARTMENT_NAME 'Executive.'

    D. Both statements will always run successfully, even if there are two departments with DEPARTMENT_NAME 'Executive.'

List the Types of Subqueries

6. What are the distinguishing characteristics of a scalar subquery? (Choose two correct answers.)

    A. A scalar subquery returns one row.

    B. A scalar subquery returns one column.

   C. A scalar subquery cannot be used in the SELECT LIST of the parent query.

   D. A scalar subquery cannot be used as a correlated subquery.

7. Which comparison operator cannot be used with multiple-row subqueries? (Choose the best answer.)

   A. ALL

   B. ANY

   C. IN

   D. NOT IN

   E. All the above can be used.

Write Single-Row and Multiple-Row Subqueries

8. Consider this statement:

```
select last_name, (select count(*) from departments) from employees
where salary = (select salary from employees);
```

What is wrong with it? (Choose the best answer.)

   A. Nothing is wrong—the statement should run without error.

   B. The statement will fail because the subquery in the SELECT list references a table that is not listed in the FROM clause.

   C. The statement will fail if the second query returns more than one row.

   D. The statement will run but is extremely inefficient because of the need to run the second subquery once for every row in EMPLOYEES.

9. Which of the following statements are equivalent? (Choose two answers.)

   A. select employee_id from employees where salary < all (select salary from employees where department_id=10);

   B. select employee_id from employees where salary < (select min(salary) from employees where department_id=10);

   C. select employee_id from employees where salary not >= any (select salary from employees where department_id=10);

   D. select employee_id from employees e join departments d on e.department_id= d.department_id where e.salary < (select min(salary) from employees) and d.department_id=10;

10. Consider this statement, which is intended to prompt for an employee's name and then find all employees who have the same job as the first employee:

```
select last_name,employee_id from employees where job_id =
(select job_id from employees where last_name = '&Name');
```

What would happen if a value were given for &Name that did not match with any row in EMPLOYEES? (Choose the best answer.)

A. The statement would fail with an error.

B. The statement would return every row in the table.

C. The statement would return no rows.

D. The statement would return all rows where JOB_ID is NULL.

LAB QUESTION

Exercise 8-3 included this query that attempted to find all employees whose salary is higher than that of a nominated employee:

```
select last_name from employees where
salary > (select salary from employees where last_name='Taylor')
order by last_name;
```

The query runs successfully if last_name is unique. Two variations were given that will run without error no matter what value is provided.

The first solution was as follows:

```
select last_name from employees where
salary > all (select salary from employees where last_name='Taylor')
order by last_name;
```

The second solution was as follows:

```
select last_name from employees where
salary > (select max(salary) from employees where last_name='Taylor')
order by last_name;
```

There are other queries that will run successfully; construct two other solutions, one using the ANY comparison operator, the other using the MIN aggregation function. Now that you have four solutions, do they all give the same result?

All these "solutions" are in fact just ways of avoiding error. They do not necessarily give the result the user wants, and they may not be consistent. What change needs to be made to give a consistent, unambiguous, result?

SELF TEST ANSWERS

Define Subqueries

1. ☑ **A, B, C, D, E.** Subqueries can be used at all these points.
☒ **F.** A subquery cannot be used in the ORDER BY clause of a query.

2. ☑ **D.** Subquery nesting can be done to many levels.
☒ **A, B,** and **C. A** and **C** are wrong because subqueries can be nested. **B** is wrong because the number of rows returned is not relevant to nesting subqueries, only to the operators being used.

3. ☑ **A.** The result set of the inner query is needed before the outer query can run.
☒ **B, C,** and **D. B** and **C** are not possible because the result of the subquery is needed before the parent query can start. **D** is wrong because the subquery is only run once.

4. ☑ **D.** This is a correlated subquery, which must be run for every row in the table.
☒ **A, B,** and **C.** The result of the inner query is dependent on a value from the outer query; it must therefore be run once for every row.

Describe the Types of Problems That the Subqueries Can Solve

5. ☑ **A, D.** The two statements will deliver the same result, and neither will fail if the name is duplicated.
☒ **B, C. B** is wrong because the statements are functionally identical, though syntactically different. **C** is wrong because the comparison operator used, IN, can handle a multiple-row subquery.

List the Types of Subqueries

6. ☑ **A, B.** A scalar subquery can be defined as a query that returns a single value.
☒ **C, D. C** is wrong because a scalar subquery is the only subquery that can be used in the SELECT LIST. **D** is wrong because scalar subqueries can be correlated.

7. ☑ **E.** ALL, ANY, IN, and NOT IN are the multiple-row comparison operators.
☒ **A, B, C, D.** All of these can be used.

Write Single-Row and Multiple-Row Subqueries

8. ☑ **C.** The equality operator requires a single-row subquery, and the second subquery could return several rows.
☒ **A, B, D. A** is wrong because the statement will fail in all circumstances except the unlikely case where there is zero or one employees. **B** is wrong because this is not a problem; there need be no relationship between the source of data for the inner and outer queries. **D** is wrong because the subquery will only run once; it is not a correlated subquery.

9. ☑ **A** and **B** are identical.

☒ **C** is logically the same as **A** and **B** but syntactically is not possible; it will give an error. **D** will always return no rows, because it asks for all employees who have a salary lower than all employees. This is not an error but can never return any rows. The filter on DEPARTMENTS is not relevant.

10. ☑ **C.** If a subquery returns NULL, then the comparison will also return NULL, meaning that no rows will be retrieved.

☒ **A, B, D. A** is wrong because this would not cause an error. **B** is wrong because a comparison with NULL will return nothing, not everything. **D** is wrong because a comparison with NULL can never return anything, not even other NULLs.

LAB ANSWER

The following are two possible solutions using ANY and MIN:

```
select last_name from employees where
salary > any (select salary from employees where last_name='Taylor')
order by last_name;

select last_name from employees where
salary not < (select min(salary) from employees where last_name='Taylor')
order by last_name;
```

These are just as valid as the solutions presented earlier that used ALL and MAX, but they do not give the same result. There is no way to say that these are better or worse than the earlier solutions. The problem is that the subquery is based on a column that is not the primary key. It would not be unreasonable to say that all these solutions are wrong, and the original query is the best; it gives a result that is unambiguously correct if the LAST_NAME is unique, and if LAST_NAME is not unique, it throws an error rather than giving a questionable answer. The real answer is that the query should be based on EMPLOYEE_ID, not LAST_NAME.

9

Using the Set Operators

A

ny SQL query can be described mathematically (*relational algebra* is the term used for this), but the use of set operators is what recalls school mathematics to many programmers. As your math curriculum may not have included set theory, following is a short summary.

All SELECT statements return a set of rows. The set operators take as their input the results of two or more SELECT statements and from these generate a single result set. This is known as a *compound query*. Oracle provides three set operators: UNION, INTERSECT, and MINUS. UNION can be qualified with ALL. There is a significant deviation from the ISO standard for SQL here, in that ISO SQL uses EXCEPT where Oracle uses MINUS, but the functionality is identical. The difference can be important when porting applications (or skills) developed for a third-party database to the Oracle environment.

CERTIFICATION OBJECTIVE 9.01

Describe the Set Operators

The set operators used in compound queries are as follows:

- **UNION**   Returns the combined rows from two queries, sorting them and removing duplicates.
- **UNION ALL**   Returns the combined rows from two queries without sorting or removing duplicates.
- **INTERSECT**   Returns only the rows that occur in both queries' result sets, sorting them and removing duplicates.
- **MINUS**   Returns only the rows in the first result set that do not appear in the second result set, sorting them and removing duplicates.

These commands are equivalent to the standard operators used in mathematics set theory, often depicted graphically as Venn diagrams.

Sets and Venn Diagrams

Consider groupings of living creatures, classified as follows:

- **Creatures with two legs**   Humans, parrots, bats
- **Creatures that can fly**   Parrots, bats, bees
- **Creatures with fur**   Bears, bats

Each classification is known as a *set*, and each member of the set is an *element*. The *union* of the three sets is humans, parrots, bats, bees, and bears. This is all the elements in all the sets, without the duplications. The *intersection* of the sets is all elements that are common to all three sets, again removing the duplicates. In this simple example, the intersection has just one element: bats. The intersection of the two-legged set and the flying set has two elements: parrots and bats. The *minus* of the sets is the elements of one set without the elements of another, so the two-legged creatures set, minus the flying creatures set, minus the furry creatures set, results in a single element: humans.

These sets can be represented graphically as the Venn diagram shown in Figure 9-1. (Venn diagrams are named after John Venn, who formalized the theory at Cambridge University in the nineteenth century.)

The circle in the top left of the figure represents the set of two-legged creatures; the circle top right is creatures that can fly; the bottom circle is furry animals. The unions, intersections, and minuses of the sets are immediately apparent by observing the elements in the various parts of the circles that do or do not overlap. The diagram

FIGURE 9-1

A Venn diagram, showing three sets and the universal set

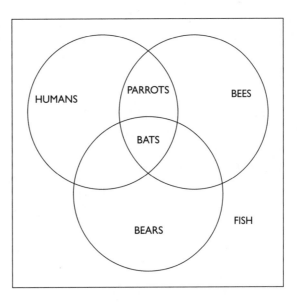

in the figure also includes the universal set, represented by the rectangle. The universal set is all elements that exist but are not members of the defined sets. In this case, the universal set would be defined as all living creatures that evolved without developing fur, two legs, or the ability to fly (such as fish).

That's enough school maths; now proceed to the implementation within SQL.

Set Operator General Principles

All set operators make compound queries by combining the result sets from two or more queries. If a SELECT statement includes more than one set operator (and therefore more than two queries), they will be applied in the order the programmer specifies: top to bottom and left to right. Although pending enhancements to ISO SQL will give INTERSECT a higher priority than the others, there is currently no priority of one operator over another. To override this precedence, based on the order in which the operators appear, you can use parentheses: operators within brackets will be evaluated before passing the results to operators outside the brackets.

on the **Job** *Given the pending change in operator priority, it may be good practice always to use parentheses. This will ensure that the code's function won't change when run against a later version of the database.*

Each query in a compound query will project its own list of selected columns. These lists must have the same number of elements, be nominated in the same sequence, and be of broadly similar data type. They do not have to have the same names (or column aliases), nor do they need to come from the same tables (or subqueries). If the column names (or aliases) are different, the result set of the compound query will have columns named as they were in the first query.

exam **watch** *The columns in the queries that make up a compound query can have different names, but the output result set will use the names of the columns in the first query.*

While the selected column lists do not have to be exactly the same data type, they must be from the same data type group. For example, the columns selected by one query could be of data types DATE and NUMBER, and those from the second query could be TIMESTAMP and INTEGER. The result set of the compound query will have columns with the higher level of precision: in this case, they would be TIMESTAMP and NUMBER. Other than

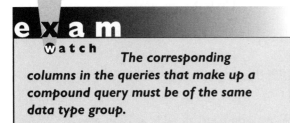

The corresponding columns in the queries that make up a compound query must be of the same data type group.

accepting data types from the same group, the set operators will not do any implicit type casting. If the second query retrieved columns of type VARCHAR2, the compound query would throw an error even if the string variables could be resolved to legitimate date and numeric values.

UNION, MINUS, and INTERSECT will always combine the results sets of the input queries, then sort the results to remove duplicate rows. The sorting is based on all the columns, from left to right. If all the columns in two rows have the same value, then only the first row is returned in the compound result set. A side effect of this is that the output of a compound query will be sorted. If the sort order (which is ascending, based on the order in which the columns happen to appear in the select lists) is not the order you want, it is possible to put a single ORDER BY clause at the end of the compound query. It is not possible to use ORDER BY in any of the queries that make up the whole compound query, as this would disrupt the sorting that is necessary to remove duplicates.

A compound query will by default return rows sorted across all the columns, from left to right. The only exception is UNION ALL, where the rows will not be sorted. The only place where an ORDER BY clause is permitted is at the end of the compound query.

UNION ALL is the exception to the sorting-no-duplicates rule: the result sets of the two input queries will be concatenated to form the result of the compound query. But you still can't use ORDER BY in the individual queries; it can only appear at the end of the compound query where it will be applied to the complete result set.

EXERCISE 9-1

Describe the Set Operators

In this exercise, you will see the effect of the set operators. Either SQL*Plus or SQL Developer can be used.

1. Connect to your database as user HR.

2. Run this query:

```
select region_name from regions;
```

Note the result, in particular the order of the rows. If the table is as originally created, there will be four rows returned. The order will be Europe, America, Asia, Middle East.

3. Query the Regions table twice, using UNION:

```
select region_name from regions union select region_name from
regions;
```

The rows returned will be as for step 1 but sorted alphabetically.

4. This time, use UNION ALL:

```
select region_name from regions union all select region_name
from regions;
```

There will be double the number of rows, and they will not be sorted.

5. An intersection will retrieve rows common to two queries:

```
select region_name from regions intersect select region_name
from regions;
```

All four rows are common, and the result is sorted.

6. A MINUS will remove common rows:

```
select region_name from regions minus select region_name from
regions;
```

The second query will remove all the rows in the first query. Result: no rows left.

Use a Set Operator to Combine Multiple Queries into a Single Query

Compound queries are two or more queries, linked with one or more set operators. The end result is a single result set.

The examples that follow are based on two tables, OLD_DEPT and NEW_DEPT. The table OLD_DEPT is intended to represent a table created with an earlier version of Oracle, when the only data type available for representing date and time data was DATE, the only option for numeric data was NUMBER, and character data was fixed-length CHAR. The table NEW_DEPT uses the more closely defined INTEGER numeric data type (which Oracle implements as a NUMBER of up to 38 significant digits but no decimal places), the more space-efficient VARCHAR2 for character data, and the TIMESTAMP data type, which can by default store date and time values with six decimals of precision on the seconds. There are two rows in each table.

The UNION ALL Operator

A UNION ALL takes two result sets and concatenates them together into a single result set. The result sets come from two queries that must select the same number of columns, and the corresponding columns of the two queries (in the order in which they are specified) must be of the same data type group. The columns do not have to have the same names.

Figure 9-2 demonstrates a UNION ALL operation from two tables. The UNION ALL of the two tables converts all the values to the higher level of precision: the dates are returned as timestamps (the less precise DATEs padded with zeros), the character data is the more efficient VARCHAR2 with the length of the longer input column, and the numbers (though this is not obvious due to the nature of the data) will accept decimals. The order of the rows is the rows from the first table, in whatever order they happen to be stored, followed by the rows from the second table in whatever order they happen to be stored.

The UNION Operator

A UNION performs a UNION ALL and then sorts the result across all the columns and removes duplicates. The first query in Figure 9-3 returns all four rows because there are no duplicates. However, the rows are now in order. It may appear that the first two rows are not in order because of the values in DATED, but they are: the DNAME

FIGURE 9-2	
A UNION ALL with data type conversions	

in the table OLD_DEPTS is 20 bytes long (padded with spaces), whereas the DNAME in NEW_DEPTS, where it is a VARCHAR2, is only as long as the name itself. The spaces give the row from OLD_DEPT a higher sort value, even though the date value is less.

The second query in Figure 9-3 removes any leading or trailing spaces from the DNAME columns and chops off the time elements from DATED and STARTED. Two of the rows thus become identical, and so only one appears in the output.

Because of the sort, the order of the queries in a UNION compound query makes no difference to the order of the rows returned.

o n t h e

J o b   *If you know that there can be no duplicates between two tables, then always use UNION ALL. It saves the database from doing a lot of sorting. Your DBA will not be pleased with you if you use UNION unnecessarily.*

The INTERSECT Operator

The intersection of two sets is the rows that are common to both sets, as shown in Figure 9-4.

The first query shown in Figure 9-4 returns no rows, because every row in the two tables is different. Next, applying functions to eliminate some of the differences returns the one common row. In this case, only one row is returned; had there been several common rows, they would be in order. The order in which the queries appear in the compound query has no effect on this.

FIGURE 9-3

UNION compound queries

FIGURE 9-4

INTERSECT and
MINUS

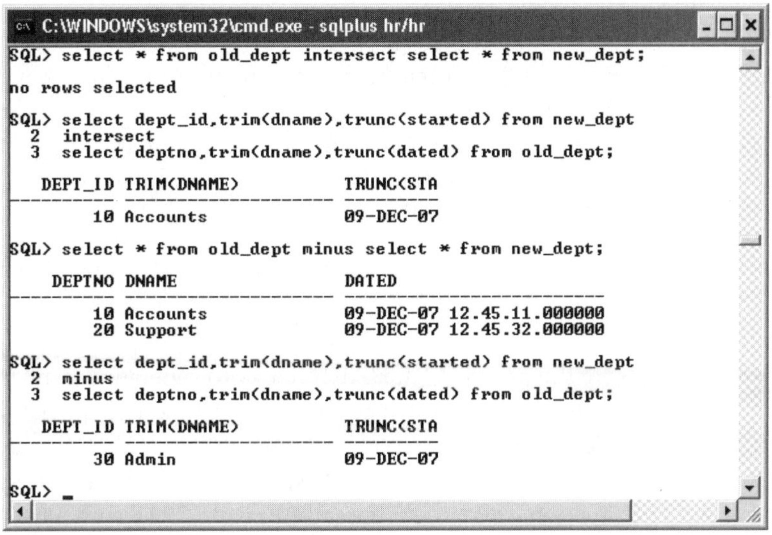

```
C:\WINDOWS\system32\cmd.exe - sqlplus hr/hr                    - □ ×
SQL> select * from old_dept intersect select * from new_dept;

no rows selected

SQL> select dept_id,trim(dname),trunc(started) from new_dept
  2  intersect
  3  select deptno,trim(dname),trunc(dated) from old_dept;

   DEPT_ID TRIM(DNAME)           TRUNC(STA
---------- -------------------- ---------
        10 Accounts              09-DEC-07

SQL> select * from old_dept minus select * from new_dept;

    DEPTNO DNAME                DATED
---------- -------------------- ---------
        10 Accounts              09-DEC-07 12.45.11.000000
        20 Support               09-DEC-07 12.45.32.000000

SQL> select dept_id,trim(dname),trunc(started) from new_dept
  2  minus
  3  select deptno,trim(dname),trunc(dated) from old_dept;

   DEPT_ID TRIM(DNAME)           TRUNC(STA
---------- -------------------- ---------
        30 Admin                 09-DEC-07

SQL> _
```

The MINUS Operator

A MINUS runs both queries, sorts the results, and returns only the rows from the first result set that do not appear in the second result set.

The third query in Figure 9-4 returns all the rows in OLD_DEPT because there are no matching rows in NEW_DEPT. The last query forces some commonality, causing one of the rows to removed. Because of the sort, the rows will be in order irrespective of the order in which the queries appear in the compound query.

INSIDE THE EXAM

Using the Set Operators

A compound query is one query made up of several queries, but they are not subqueries. A subquery generates a result set that is used by another query; the queries in a compound query run independently, and a separate stage of execution combines the result sets.

This combining operation is accomplished by sorting the result sets and merging them together. There is an exception to this: UNION ALL does no processing after running the two queries; it simply lists the results of each.

More Complex Examples

If two queries do not return the same number of columns, it may still be possible to run them in a compound query by generating additional columns with NULL values. For example, consider a classification system for animals: all animals have a name and a weight, but the birds have a wingspan whereas the cats have a tail length. A query to list all the birds and cats might be:

```
select name,tail_length,to_char(null) from cats
union all
select name,to_char(null),wing_span from birds;
```

Note the use of TO_CHAR(NULL) to generate the missing values.

A compound query can consist of more than two queries, in which case operator precedence can be controlled with parentheses. Without parentheses, the set operators will be applied in the sequence in which they are specified. Consider the situation where there is a table PERMSTAFF with a listing of all permanent staff members and a table CONSULTANTS with a listing of consultant staff. There is also a table BLACKLIST of people blacklisted for one reason or another. The following query will list all the permanent and consulting staff in a certain geographical, removing those on the blacklist:

```
select name from permstaff where location = 'Germany'
union all
select name from consultants where work_area = 'Western Europe'
minus
select name from blacklist;
```

Note the use of UNION ALL, because is assumed that no one will be in both the PERMSTAFF and the CONSULTANTS tables; a UNION would force an unnecessary sort. The order of precedence for set operators is the order specified by the programmer, so the MINUS operation will compare the BLACKLIST with the result of the UNION ALL. The result will be all staff (permanent and consulting) who do not appear on the blacklist. If the blacklisting could be applied only to consulting staff and not to permanent staff, there would be two possibilities. First, the queries could be listed in a different order:

```
select name from consultants where work_area = 'Western Europe'
minus
select name from blacklist
union all
select name from permstaff where location = 'Germany';
```

This would return consultants who are not blacklisted and then append all permanent staff. Alternatively, parentheses could control the precedence explicitly:

```
select name from permstaff where location = 'Germany'
union all
(select name from consultants where work_area = 'Western Europe'
minus
select name from blacklist);
```

This query will list all permanent staff and then append all consultant staff who are not blacklisted.

These two queries will return the same rows, but the order will be different because the UNION ALL operations list the PERMSTAFF and CONSULTANTS tables in a different sequence. To ensure that the queries return identical result sets, there would need to be an ORDER BY clause at the foot of the compound queries.

on the
◑ o b

The two preceding queries will return the same rows, but the second version could be considered better code because the parentheses make it more self-documenting. Furthermore, relying on implicit precedence based on the order of the queries works at the moment, but future releases of SQL may include set operator precedence.

SCENARIO & SOLUTION	
How can you present several tables with similar data as one table?	This is a common problem, often caused by bad systems analysis or perhaps by attempts to integrate systems together. Compound queries are often the answer. By using type casting functions to force columns to the same data type and TO_CHAR(NULL) to generate missing columns, you can present the data as though it were from one table.
Are there performance issues with compound queries?	Perhaps. With the exception of UNION ALL, compound queries have to sort data, across the full width of the rows. This may be expensive in both memory and CPU. Also, if the two queries both address the same table, there will be two passes through the data as each query is run independently; if the same result could be achieved with one (though probably more complicated) query, this would usually be a faster solution. Compound queries are a powerful tool but should be used with caution.

Using the Set Operators

In this exercise, you will run more complex compound queries.

1. Connect to your database as user HR.

2. Run this query to count the employees in three departments:

```
select department_id, count(1) from employees
where department_id in (20,30,40)
group by department_id;
```

3. Obtain the same result with a compound query:

```
select 20,count(1) from employees where department_id=20
union all
select 30,count(1) from employees where department_id=30
union all
select 40,count(1) from employees where department_id=40;
```

4. Find out if any managers manage staff in both departments 20 and 30, and exclude any managers with staff in department 40:

```
select manager_id from employees where department_id=20
intersect
select manager_id from employees where department_id=30
minus
select manager_id from employees where department_id=40;
```

5. Use a compound query to report salaries subtotaled by department, by manager, and the overall total:

```
select department_id,to_number(null),sum(salary) from employees
group by department_id
union
select to_number(null),manager_id,sum(salary) from employees
group by manager_id
union all
select to_number(null),to_number(null),sum(salary) from
employees;
```

Control the Order of Rows Returned

By default, the output of a UNION ALL compound query is not sorted at all: the rows will be returned in groups in the order of which query was listed first and within the groups in the order that they happen to be stored. The output of any other set operator will be sorted in ascending order of all the columns, starting with the first column named.

It is not syntactically possible to use an ORDER BY clause in the individual queries that make up a compound query. This is because the execution of most compound queries has to sort the rows, which would conflict with the ORDER BY. It might seem theoretically possible that a UNION ALL (which does not sort the rows) could take an ORDER BY for each query, but the Oracle implementation of UNION ALL does not permit this.

There is no problem with placing an ORDER BY clause at the end of the compound query, however. This will sort the entire output of the compound query. The default sorting of rows is based on all the columns in the sequence they appear. A specified ORDER BY clause has no restrictions: it can be based on any columns (and functions applied to columns) in any order. For example:

```
SQL> select deptno,trim(dname) name from old_dept
  2  union
  3  select dept_id,dname from new_dept
  4  order by name;
    DEPTNO NAME
---------- --------------------
        10 Accounts
        30 Admin
        20 Support
```

Note that the column names in the ORDER BY clause must be the name(s) (or, in this case, the alias) of the columns in the first query of the compound query.

Control the Order of Rows Returned

In this exercise, you will tidy up the result of the final step in Exercise 2. This step produced a listing of salaries totaled by department and then by manager, but the results were not very well formatted.

1. Connect to your database as user HR.

2. Generate better column headings for the query:

```
select department_id dept,to_number(null) mgr,sum(salary)
from employees
group by department_id
union all
select to_number(null),manager_id,sum(salary) from employees
group by manager_id
union all
select to_number(null),to_number(null),sum(salary) from
employees;
```

3. Attempt to sort the results of the queries that subtotal by using UNION instead of UNION ALL:

```
select department_id dept,to_number(null) mgr,sum(salary)
from employees
group by department_id
union
select to_number(null),manager_id,sum(salary) from employees
group by manager_id
union all
select to_number(null),to_number(null),sum(salary) from
employees;
```

This would be fine, except that the subtotals for staff without a department or a manager are placed at the bottom of the output above the grand total, not within the sections for departments and managers.

4. Generate a value to replace the NULLs for department and manager codes and for the overall total:

```
select 20,count(1) from employees where department_id=20
union all
select 30,count(1) from employees where department_id=30
union all
select 40,count(1) from employees where department_id=40;
```

5. Find out if any managers manage staff in both departments 20 and 30, and exclude any managers with staff in department 40:

```
select manager_id from employees where department_id=20
intersect
select manager_id from employees where department_id=30
minus
select manager_id from employees where department_id=40;
```

6. Use a compound query to report salaries subtotaled by department, by manager, and the overall total:

```
select department_id dept,to_number(null) mgr,sum(salary)
from employees
group by department_id
union
select to_number(null),manager_id,sum(salary) from employees
group by manager_id
union all
select to_number(null),to_number(null),sum(salary) from
employees;
```

CERTIFICATION SUMMARY

The set operators combine the result sets from two or more queries into one result set. A query that uses a set operator is a compound query. The set operators are UNION, UNION ALL, INTERSECT, and MINUS. They have equal precedence, and if more than one is included in a compound query they will be executed in the order in which they occur—though this can be controlled by using parentheses. All the set operators except for UNION ALL rely on sorting to merge result sets and remove duplicate rows.

The queries in a compound query must return the same number of columns. The corresponding columns in each query must be of compatible data types. The queries can use features of the SELECT statement with the exception of ORDER BY; it is, however, permissible to place a single ORDER BY clause at the end of the compound query.

✓ TWO-MINUTE DRILL

Describe the Set Operators

❑ UNION ALL concatenates the results of two queries.

❑ UNION sorts the results of two queries and removes duplicates.

❑ INTERSECT returns only the rows common to the result of two queries.

❑ MINUS returns the rows from the first query that do not exist in the second query.

Use a Set Operator to Combine Multiple Queries into a Single Query

❑ The queries in the compound query must return the same number of columns.

❑ The corresponding columns must be of compatible data type.

❑ The set operators have equal precedence and will be applied in the order they are specified.

Control the Order of Rows Returned

❑ It is not possible to use ORDER BY in the individual queries that make a compound query.

❑ An ORDER BY clause can be appended to the end of a compound query.

❑ The rows returned by a UNION ALL will be in the order they occur in the two source queries.

❑ The rows returned by a UNION will be sorted across all their columns, left to right.

SELF TEST

Describe the Set Operators

1. Which of these set operators will not sort the rows? (Choose the best answer.)

    A. INTERSECT

    B. MINUS

    C. UNION

    D. UNION ALL

2. Which of these operators will remove duplicate rows from the final result? (Choose all that apply.)

    A. INTERSECT

    B. MINUS

    C. UNION

    D. UNION ALL

Use a Set Operator to Combine Multiple Queries into a Single Query

3. If a compound query contains both a MINUS and an INTERSECT operator, which will be applied first? (Choose the best answer.)

    A. The INTERSECT, because INTERSECT has higher precedence than MINUS.

    B. The MINUS, because MINUS has a higher precedence than INTERSECT.

    C. The precedence is determined by the order in which they are specified.

    D. It is not possible for a compound query to include both MINUS and INTERSECT.

4. There are four rows in the REGIONS table. Consider the following statements and choose how many rows will be returned for each: 0, 4, 8, or 16.

    A. `select * from regions union select * from regions`

    B. `select * from regions union all select * from regions`

    C. `select * from regions minus select * from regions`

    D. `select * from regions intersect select * from regions`

5. Consider this compound query:

```
select empno, hired from emp
union all
select emp_id,hired,fired from ex_emp;
```

The columns EMP.EMPNO and EX_EMP.EMP_ID are integer; the column EMP.HIRED is timestamp; the columns EX_EMP.HIRED and EX_EMP.FIRED are date. Why will the statement fail? (Choose the best answer.)

A. Because the columns EMPNO and EMP_ID have different names

B. Because the columns EMP.HIRED and EX_EMP.HIRED are different data types

C. Because there are two columns in the first query and three columns in the second query

D. For all the reasons above

E. The query will succeed.

Control the Order of Rows Returned

6. Which line of this statement will cause it to fail? (Choose the best answer.)

A. `select ename, hired from current_staff`

B. `order by ename`

C. `minus`

D. `select ename, hired from current staff`

E. `where deptno=10`

F. `order by ename;`

7. Study this statement:

`select ename from emp union all select ename from ex_emp;`

In what order will the rows be returned? (Choose the best answer.)

A. The rows from each table will be grouped and within each group will be sorted on ENAME.

B. The rows from each table will be grouped but not sorted.

C. The rows will not be grouped but will all be sorted on ENAME.

D. The rows will be neither grouped nor sorted.

LAB QUESTION

Working in the HR schema, design some queries that will generate reports using the set operators. The reports required are as follows:

1. Employees have their current job (identified by JOB_ID) recorded in their EMPLOYEES row. Jobs they have held previously (but not their current job) are recorded in JOB_HISTORY. Which employees have never changed jobs? The listing should include the employees' EMPLOYEE_ID and LAST_NAME.

2. Which employees were recruited into one job, then changed to a different job, but are now back in a job they held before? Again, you will need to construct a query that compares EMPLOYEES with JOB_HISTORY. The report should show the employees' names and the job titles. Job titles are stored in the table JOBS.

3. What jobs has any one employee held? This will be the JOB_ID for the employee's current job (in EMPLOYEES) and all previous jobs (in JOB_HISTORY). If the employee has held a job more than once, there is no need to list it more than once. Use a replacement variable to prompt for the EMPLOYEE_ID and display the job title(s). Employees 101 and 200 will be suitable employees for testing.

SELF TEST ANSWERS

Describe the Set Operators

1. ☑ **D.** UNION ALL returns rows in the order that they are delivered by the two queries from which the compound query is made up.
   ☒ **A, B, C.** INTERSECT, MINUS, and UNION all use sorting as part of their execution.

2. ☑ **A, B, C.** INTERSECT, MINUS, and UNION all remove duplicate rows.
   ☒ **D.** UNION ALL returns all rows, duplicates included.

Use a Set Operator to Combine Multiple Queries into a Single Query

3. ☑ **C.** All set operators have equal precedence, so the precedence is determined by the sequence in which they occur.
   ☒ **A, B, D.** A and B are wrong because set operators have equal precedence—though this may change in future releases. D is wrong because many set operators can be used in one compound query.

4. ☑ **A = 4; B = 8; C = 0; D = 4**
   ☒ Note that 16 is not used; that would be the result of a Cartesian product query.

5. ☑ **C.** Every query in a compound query must return the same number of columns.
   ☒ **A, B, D, E.** A is wrong because the columns can have different names. B is wrong because the two columns are of the same data type group, which is all that was required. It therefore follows that D and E are also wrong.

Control the Order of Rows Returned

6. ☑ **B.** You cannot use ORDER BY for one query of a compound query; you may only place a single ORDER BY clause at the end.
   ☒ **A, C, D, E, F.** All these lines are legal.

7. ☑ **B.** The rows from each query will be together, but there will be no sorting.
   ☒ **A, C, D.** A is not possible with any syntax. C is wrong because that would be the result of a UNION, not a UNION ALL. D is wrong because UNION ALL will return the rows from each query grouped together.

LAB ANSWER

I. To identify all employees who have not changed job, query the EMPLOYEES table and remove all those who have a row in JOB_HISTORY:

```
select employee_id, last_name from employees
minus
select employee_id,last_name from
job_history join employees using (employee_id);
```

2. All employees who have changed job at least once will have a row in JOB_HISTORY; for those who are now back in a job they have held before, the JOB_ID in EMPLOYEES will be the same as the JOB_ID in one of their rows in JOB_HISTORY:

```
select last_name,job_title from employees join jobs using(job_id)
intersect
select last_name,job_title from job_history h
join jobs j on (h.job_id=j.job_id)
join employees e on (h.employee_id=e.employee_id);
```

3. This compound query will prompt for an EMPLOYEE_ID and then list the employee's current job and previous jobs,

```
select job_title from jobs join employees using (job_id)
where employee_id=&&Who
union
select job_title from jobs join job_history using (job_id)
where employee_id=&&Who;
```

Figure 9-5 shows the query and its result in SQL Developer, after giving 101 as the EMPLOYEE_ID.

FIGURE 9-5

A compound
query and the
result

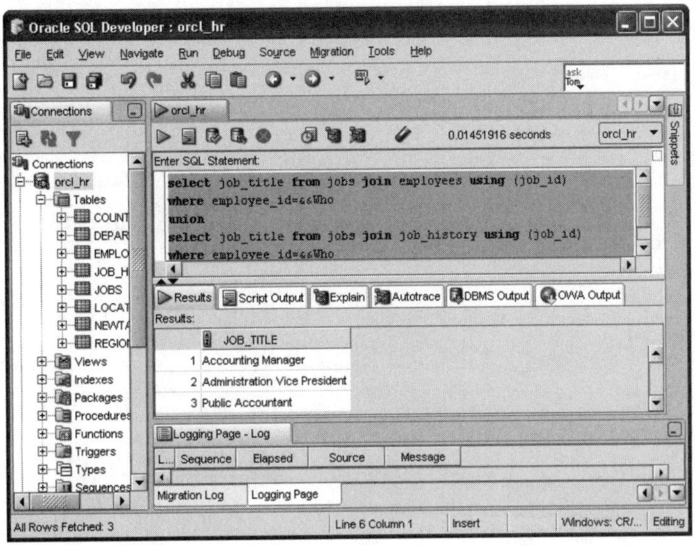

10

Manipulating Data

T his chapter is all about the commands that change data. Syntactically, the DML commands are much simpler than the SELECT command that has been studied so far. However, there is a large amount of relational database theory that comes along with DML. As well as understanding the commands that make the changes, it is essential to understand the theory of transaction management, which is part of the relational database paradigm. The transaction management mechanisms provided by the Oracle database guarantee conformance to the relational standards for transactions: they implement what is commonly referred to as the ACID (atomicity, consistency, isolation, and durability) test.

Following detail on the DML commands, this chapter includes a full treatment of the necessary theory: transactional integrity, record locking, and read consistency.

CERTIFICATION OBJECTIVE 10.01

Describe Each Data Manipulation Language (DML) Statement

Strictly speaking, there are five DML commands:

- SELECT
- INSERT
- UPDATE
- DELETE
- MERGE

In practice, most database professionals never include SELECT as part of DML. It is considered to be a separate language in its own right, which is not unreasonable when you consider that it has taken the eight preceding chapters to describe it. The MERGE command is often dropped as well, not because it isn't clearly a data manipulation command but because it doesn't do anything that cannot be done with other commands. MERGE can be thought of as a shortcut for executing either an INSERT or an UPDATE or a DELETE, depending on some condition. A command often considered with DML is TRUNCATE. This is actually a DDL (Data Definition Language) command, but as the effect for end users is the same as a DELETE (though its implementation is totally different), it does fit with DML. So, the following commands are described in the next sections, with syntax and examples:

- INSERT
- UPDATE
- DELETE
- TRUNCATE

In addition, we will discuss, for completeness:

- MERGE

These are the commands that manipulate data.

INSERT

Oracle stores data in the form of rows in tables. Tables are *populated* with rows (just as a country is *populated* with people) in several ways, but the most common method is with the INSERT statement. SQL is a set-oriented language, so any one command can affect one row or a set of rows. It follows that one INSERT statement can insert an individual row into one table or many rows into many tables. The basic versions of the statement do insert just one row, but more complex variations can, with one command, insert multiple rows into multiple tables.

on the **Job**

There are much faster techniques than INSERT for populating a table with large numbers of rows. These are the SQL*Loader utility, which can upload data from files produced by an external feeder system, and Datapump, which can transfer data in bulk from one Oracle database to another—either via disk files or through a network link.

Tables have rules defined that control the rows that may be inserted. These rules are *constraints*. A constraint is an implementation of a business rule. The business analysts who model an organization's business processes will design a set of rules for the organization's data. Examples of such rules might be that every employee must have a unique employee number, or that every employee must be assigned to a valid department. Creating constraints is described in Chapter 11—for now, remember that there is no way an INSERT command can insert a row that violates a constraint. So if you attempt to insert a row into EMPLOYEES with an EMPLOYEE_ID that already exists in another row, or with a DEPARTMENT_ID that does not match a row in the DEPARTMENTS table, the insert will fail. Constraints guarantee that the data in the database conforms to the rules that define the business procedures.

There are many possible sources for the row (or rows) inserted by an INSERT statement. A single row can be inserted by providing the values for the row's columns individually. Such a statement can be constructed by typing it into SQL*Plus or SQL Developer, or by a more sophisticated user process that presents a form that prompts for values. This is the technique used for generating the rows inserted interactively by end users. For inserts of multiple rows, the source of the rows can be a SELECT statement. The output of any and all of the SELECT statements discussed in the preceding eight chapters can be used as the input to an INSERT statement.

The end result of any SELECT statement can be thought of as a table: a two-dimensional set of rows. This "table" can be displayed to a user (perhaps in a simple tool like SQL*Plus), or it can be passed to an INSERT command for populating another table, defined within the database. Using a SELECT statement to construct rows for an INSERT statement is a very common technique. The SELECT can perform many tasks. These typically include joining tables and aggregations, so that the resulting rows inserted into the target table contain information that is much more immediately comprehensible to the end users than the raw data in the source tables.

exam

watch *An INSERT command can insert one row, with column values specified in the command, or a set of rows created by a SELECT statement.*

UPDATE

The UPDATE command is used to change rows that already exist—rows that have been created by an INSERT command, or possibly by a tool such as Datapump. As with any other SQL command, an UPDATE can affect one row or a set of rows. The size of the set affected by an UPDATE is determined by a WHERE clause, in exactly the same way that the set of rows retrieved by a SELECT statement is defined by a WHERE clause. The syntax is identical. All the rows updated will be in one table; it is not possible for a single update command to affect rows in multiple tables.

When updating a row or a set of rows, the UPDATE command specifies which columns of the row(s) to update. It is not necessary (or indeed common) to update every column of the row. If the column being updated already has a value, then this value is replaced with the new value specified by the UPDATE command. If the column was not previously populated—which is to say, its value was NULL—then it will be populated after the UPDATE with the new value.

A typical use of UPDATE is to retrieve one row and update one or more columns of the row. The retrieval will be done using a WHERE clause that selects a row by its primary key, the unique identifier that will ensure that only one row is retrieved. Then the columns that are updated will be any columns other than the primary key column. It is very unusual to change the value of the primary key. The lifetime of a row begins when it is inserted, then may continue through several updates, until it is deleted. Throughout this lifetime, it will not usually change its primary key.

One UPDATE statement can change rows in only one table, but it can change any number of rows in that table.

To update a set of rows, use a less restrictive WHERE clause than the primary key. To update every row in a table, do not use any WHERE clause at all. This set behavior can be disconcerting when it happens by accident. If you select the rows to be updated with any column other than the primary key, you may update several rows, not just one. If you omit the WHERE clause completely, you will update the whole table—perhaps millions of rows updated with just one statement—when you meant to change just one.

An UPDATE command must honor any constraints defined for the table, just as the original INSERT would have. For example, it will not be possible to update a column that has been marked as mandatory to a NULL value or to update a primary key column so that it will no longer be unique.

DELETE

Previously inserted rows can be removed from a table with the DELETE command. The command will remove one row or a set of rows from the table, depending on a WHERE clause. If there is no WHERE clause, every row in the table will be removed (which can be a little disconcerting if you left out the WHERE clause by mistake).

There are no "warning" prompts for any SQL commands. If you instruct the database to delete a million rows, it will do so. Immediately. There is none of that "Are you sure?" business that some environments offer.

A deletion is all or nothing. It is not possible to nominate columns. When rows are inserted, you can choose which columns to populate. When rows are updated, you can choose which columns to update. But a deletion applies to the whole row—the only choice is which rows in which table. This makes the DELETE command syntactically simpler than the other DML commands.

MERGE

Earlier versions of SQL did not have a MERGE command. MERGE was introduced with the SQL1999 standard, implemented by Oracle in database release 9i. Release 10g (conforming to the SQL2003 standard) provides some enhancements. Some proprietary SQL implementations had a command called UPSERT. This rather unpleasant sounding word describes the MERGE command rather well: it executes either an UPDATE or an INSERT, depending on some condition. But the term UPSERT is now definitely obsolete, because the current version of MERGE can, according to circumstances, do a DELETE as well.

There are many occasions where you want to take a set of data (the source) and integrate it into an existing table (the target). If a row in the source data already exists in the target table, you may want to update the target row, or you may want to replace it completely, or you may want to leave the target row unchanged. If a row in the source does not exist in the target, you will want to insert it. The MERGE command lets you do this. A MERGE passes through the source data, for each row attempting to locate a matching row in the target. If no match is found, a row can be inserted; if a match is found, the matching row can be updated. The release 10g enhancement means that the target row can even be deleted, after being matched and updated. The end result is a target table into which the data in the source has been merged.

A MERGE operation does nothing that could not be done with INSERT, UPDATE, and DELETE statements—but with one pass through the source data, it can do all three. Alternative code without a MERGE would require three passes through the data, one for each command.

MERGE may not be important for the OCP examinations, but it may be of vital importance for coding applications that perform well and use the database efficiently.

The source data for a MERGE statement can be a table or any subquery. The condition used for finding matching rows in the target is similar to a WHERE clause. The clauses that update or insert rows are as complex as an UPDATE or an INSERT command. It follows that MERGE is the most complicated of the DML commands, which is not unreasonable, as it is (arguably) the most powerful.

TRUNCATE

The TRUNCATE command is not a DML command; it is DDL command. The difference is enormous. When DML commands affect data, they insert, update, and delete rows as part of transactions. Transactions are defined later in this chapter in section 10.05, "Control Transactions." For now, let it be said that a transaction can be controlled, in the sense that the user has the choice of whether to make the work done in a transaction permanent, or whether to reverse it. This is very useful but forces the database to do additional work behind the scenes that the user is not aware of. DDL commands are not user transactions (though within the database, they are in fact implemented as transactions—but developers cannot control them), and there is no choice about whether to make them permanent or to reverse them. Once executed, they are done. However, in comparison to DML, they are very fast.

e x a m

w a t c h   Transactions, consisting of INSERT, UPDATE, and DELETE (or even MERGE) commands can be made permanent (with a COMMIT) or reversed (with a ROLLBACK). A TRUNCATE command, like any other DDL command, is immediately permanent: it can never be reversed.

From the user's point of view, a truncation of a table is equivalent to executing a DELETE of every row: a DELETE command without a WHERE clause. But whereas a deletion may take some time (possibly hours, if there are many rows in the table) a truncation will go through instantly. It makes no difference whether the table contains one row or billions; a TRUNCATE will be virtually instantaneous. The table will still exist, but it will be empty.

on the

job   DDL commands, such as TRUNCATE, will fail if there is any DML command active on the table. A transaction will block the DDL command until the DML command is terminated with a COMMIT or a ROLLBACK.

DML Statement Failures

Commands can fail for many reasons, including the following:

■ Syntax errors
■ References to nonexistent objects or columns

- Access permissions
- Constraint violations
- Space issues

As a SQL command can affect a set of rows, there is the complication that a command may partially succeed: the failure could occur only some way into the set. The preceding first three classes of error also apply to SELECT statements.

One purpose of reading this book is to prevent syntax errors. When they occur (and they will), they should be detected by the tool that is constructing the SQL to be sent to the database: SQL*Plus or SQL Developer if the SQL is being entered interactively, or whatever other tool is being used to generate a more sophisticated interface. There are any number of possible syntax errors, starting with simple spelling mistakes or transposition errors.

on the
()ob

People who type with only one finger do not make transposition errors.

Errors of this nature will not impact the database, because the database will never see them. The erroneous SQL is stopped at the source. The degree of assistance the tool provides for fixing such errors will depend on the effort the tool's developers take.

A SQL statement may be syntactically correct but refer to objects that do not exist. Typical problems are spelling mistakes, but there are more complex issues: a statement could refer to a column that existed at one time but has been dropped from the table or renamed. A statement of this nature will be sent to the database and will fail then, before the database attempts execution. This is worse for the database than a simple syntax error, but the statement is still stopped before it consumes any significant database resources.

A related error has to do with type casting. SQL is a strongly typed language: columns are defined as a certain data type, and an attempt to enter a value of a different data type will fail. However, you may get away with this because Oracle's implementation of SQL will, in some circumstances, do automatic type casting.

Figure 10-1 shows several attempted executions of a statement with SQL*Plus.

In Figure 10-1, a user connects as SUE (password, SUE—not an example of good security) and queries the EMPLOYEES table. The statement fails because of a simple syntax error, correctly identified by SQL*Plus. Note that SQL*Plus never attempts to correct such mistakes, even when it knows exactly what you meant to type. Some third-party tools may be more helpful, offering automatic error correction.

```
C:\WINDOWS\system32\cmd.exe - sqlplus hr/hr                          _□×
SQL> conn sue/sue
Connected.
SQL> select count(*) frm employees where hire_date='21-APR-00';
select count(*) frm employees where hire_date='21-APR-00'
                    *
ERROR at line 1:
ORA-00923: FROM keyword not found where expected

SQL> select count(*) from employees where hire_date='21-APR-00';
select count(*) from employees where hire_date='21-APR-00'
                     *
ERROR at line 1:
ORA-00942: table or view does not exist

SQL> select count(*) from hr.employees where hire_date='21-APR-00';

  COUNT(*)
----------
         2

SQL> select count(*) from hr.employees where hire_date='21/04/2000';
select count(*) from hr.employees where hire_date='21/04/2000'
                                                    *
ERROR at line 1:
ORA-01843: not a valid month

SQL>
```

The second attempt to run the statement fails with an error stating that the object does not exist. This is because it does not exist in the current user's schema; it exists in the HR schema. Having corrected that, the third run of the statement succeeds—but only just. The value passed in the WHERE clause is a string, '21-APR-00,' but the column HIRE_DATE is not defined in the table as a string, it is defined as a date. To execute the statement, the database had to work out what the user really meant and cast the string as a date. In the last example, the type casting fails. This is because the string passed is formatted as a European-style date, but the database has been set up as American: the attempt to match "21" to a month fails. The statement would have succeeded if the string had been '04/21/2007.'

Developers should never rely on automatic type casting. It is extremely lazy programming. They should always do whatever explicit type casting is necessary, using appropriate functions as discussed in previous chapters. If automatic type casting does work, at best there is a performance hit as the database has to do extra work. This may be substantial if the type casting prevents Oracle from using indexes. In this example, if there is an index on the HIRE_DATE column, it will be an index of dates; there is no way the database can use it when you pass a string. At worst, the result will be wrong. If the date string passed in were '04/05/2007,' this would succeed—but would it be the fourth of May or the fifth of April?

Oracle will attempt to correct data type mismatches in SQL statements (DML and SELECT) by automatic type casting, but the results are unpredictable and no programmer should ever rely on it.

If a statement is syntactically correct and has no errors with the objects to which it refers, it can still fail because of access permissions. If the user attempting to execute the statement does not have the relevant permissions on the tables to which it refers, the database will return an error identical to that which would be returned if the object did not exist. As far as the user is concerned, it does not exist.

Errors caused by access permissions are a case where SELECT and DML statements may return different results: it is possible for a user to have permission to see the rows in a table, but not to insert, update, or delete them. Such an arrangement is not uncommon; it often makes business sense. Perhaps more confusingly, permissions can be set up in such a manner that it is possible to insert rows that you are not allowed to see. And, perhaps worst of all, it is possible to delete rows that you can neither see nor update. However, such arrangements are not common.

A constraint is a business rule, implemented within the database. Typical constraints are that a table must have a primary key: a value of one column (or combination of columns) that can uniquely identify each row. An INSERT command can insert several rows into a table, and for every row the database will check whether a row already exists with the same primary key. This occurs as each row is inserted. It could be that the first few rows (or the first few million rows) go in without a problem, and then the statement hits a row with a duplicate value. At this point it will return an error, and the statement will fail. This failure will trigger a reversal of all the insertions that had already succeeded. This is part of the SQL standard: a statement must succeed in total, or not at all. The reversal of the work is a *rollback*. The mechanisms of a rollback are described in the section of this chapter titled "Controlling Transactions."

If a statement fails because of space problems, the effect is similar. A part of the statement may have succeeded before the database ran out of space. The part that did succeed will be automatically rolled back. Rollback of a statement is a serious matter. It forces the database to do a lot of extra work and will usually take at least as long as the statement has taken already (sometimes much longer).

CERTIFICATION OBJECTIVE 10.02

Insert Rows into a Table

The simplest form of the INSERT statement inserts one row into one table, using values provided in line as part of the command. The syntax is as follows:

INSERT INTO *table* [(*column* [,*column*...])] VALUES (*value* [,*value*...]);

For example:

```
insert into hr.regions values (10,'Great Britain');
insert into hr.regions (region_name, region_id) values
('Australasia',11);
insert into hr.regions (region_id) values (12);
insert into hr.regions values (13,null);
```

The first of the preceding commands provides values for both the columns of the REGIONS table. If the table had a third column, the statement would fail because it relies upon *positional notation*. The statement does not say which value should be inserted into which column; it relies on the position of the values: their ordering in the command. When the database receives a statement using positional notation, it will match the order of the values to the order in which the columns of the table are defined. The statement would also fail if the column order were wrong: the database would attempt the insertion but would fail because of data type mismatches.

The second command nominates the columns to be populated and the values with which to populate them. Note that the order in which columns are mentioned now becomes irrelevant—as long as the order of the columns is the same as the order of the values.

The third example lists one column, and therefore only one value. All other columns will be left null. This statement would fail if the REGION_NAME column were not nullable. The fourth example will produce the same result, but because there is no column list, a value of some sort must be provided for each column—at the least, a NULL.

on the Job   *It is often considered good practice not to rely on positional notation and instead always to list the columns. This is more work but makes the code self-documenting (always a good idea!) and also makes the code more resilient against table structure changes. For instance, if a column is added to a table, all the INSERT statements that rely on positional notation will fail until they are rewritten to include a NULL for the new column. INSERT code that names the columns will continue to run.*

Very often, an INSERT statement will include functions to do type casting or other editing work. Consider this statement:

```
insert into employees (employee_id, last_name, hire_date)
values (1000,'WATSON','03-Nov-07');
```

in contrast with this:

```
insert into employees (employee_id, last_name, hire_date)
values (1000,upper('Watson'),to_date('03-Nov-07','dd-mon-yy'));
```

The rows inserted with each statement would be identical. But the first will insert exactly the literals provided. It may well be that the application relies on employee surnames being in uppercase—without this, perhaps sort orders will be wrong and searches on surname will give unpredictable results. Also, the insertion of the date value relies on automatic type casting of a string to a date, which is always bad for performance and can result in incorrect values being entered. The second statement forces the surname into uppercase whether it was entered that way or not, and specifies exactly the format mask of the date string before explicitly converting it into a date. There is no question that the second statement is a better piece of code than the first.

The following is another example of using functions:

```
insert into employees (employee_id,last_name,hire_date)
values (1000 + 1,user,sysdate - 7);
```

In the preceding statement, the EMPLOYEE_ID column is populated with the result of some arithmetic, the LAST_NAME column is populated with the result of the function USER (which returns the database logon name of the user), and the HIRE_DATE column is populated with the result of a function and arithmetic: the date seven days before the current system date.

Figure 10-2 shows the execution of the previous three insertions, followed by a query showing the results.

Using functions to preprocess values before inserting rows can be particularly important when running scripts with substitution variables, as they will allow the code to correct many of the unwanted variations in data input that can occur when users enter values interactively.

To insert many rows with one INSERT command, the values for the rows must come from a query. The syntax is as follows:

INSERT INTO *table* [(*column* [, *column…*])] *subquery*;

Note that this syntax does not use the VALUES keyword. If the column list is omitted, then the subquery must provide values for every column in the table.

FIGURE 10-2

Using functions
with the INSERT
command

```
C:\WINDOWS\system32\cmd.exe - sqlplus hr/hr                              [_][□][x]
SQL> connect sue/sue;
Connected.
SQL> insert into employees (employee_id, last_name, hire_date)
  2  values (1000,'WATSON','03-Nov-07');

1 row created.

SQL> insert into employees (employee_id, last_name, hire_date)
  2  values (1000,upper('Watson'),to_date('03-Nov-07','dd-mon-yy'));

1 row created.

SQL> insert into employees (employee_id,last_name,hire_date)
  2  values (1000 + 1,user,sysdate - 7);

1 row created.

SQL> select employee_id,last_name,hire_date from employees;

EMPLOYEE_ID LAST_NAME  HIRE_DATE
----------- ---------- ---------
       1000 WATSON     03-NOV-07
       1000 WATSON     03-NOV-07
       1001 SUE        27-OCT-07

SQL> _
```

To copy every row from one table to another, if the tables have the same column
structure, a command such as this is all that is needed:

```
insert into regions_copy select * from regions;
```

This presupposes that the table REGIONS_COPY does exist (with or without
any rows). The SELECT subquery reads every row from the source table, which
is REGIONS, and the INSERT inserts them into the target table, which is
REGIONS_COPY.

There are no restrictions on the nature of the subquery. Any query returns
(eventually) a two-dimensional array of rows; if the target table (which is also a two-
dimensional array) has columns to receive them, the insertion will work. A common
requirement is to present data to end users in a form that will make it easy for them
to extract information and impossible for them to misinterpret it. This will usually
mean denormalizing relational tables, making aggregations, renaming columns, and
adjusting data that can distort results if not correctly processed.

Consider a simple case within the HR schema: a need to report on the salary bill
for each department. The query will need to perform a full outer join to ensure that
any employees without a department are not missed, and that all departments are
listed whether or not they have employees. It should also ensure that any null values
will not distort any arithmetic by substituting zeros or strings for nulls. This query is
perfectly straightforward for any SQL programmer, but when end users attempt to
run this sort of query they are all too likely to produce inaccurate results by omitting

the checks. A daily maintenance job in a data warehouse that would assemble the data in a suitable form could be a script such as this:

```
truncate table department_salaries;
insert into department_salaries (department,staff,salaries)
select
  coalesce(department_name,'Unassigned'),
  count(employee_id),
  sum(coalesce(salary,0))
from employees e full outer join departments d
on e.department_id = d.department_id
group by department_name
order by department_name;
```

The TRUNCATE command will empty the table, which is then repopulated from the subquery. The end users can be let loose on this table, and it should be impossible for them to misinterpret the contents—a simple natural join with no COALESCE functions, which might be all an end user would do, might be very misleading. By doing all the complex work in the INSERT statement, users can then run much simpler queries against the denormalized and aggregated data in the summary table. Their queries will be fast, too: all the hard work has been done already.

To conclude the description of the INSERT command, it should be mentioned that it is possible to insert rows into several tables with one statement. This is not part of the SQL OCP examination, but for completeness here is an example:

```
insert all
when 1=1 then
  into emp_no_name (department_id,job_id,salary,commission_pct,hire_date)
  values (department_id,job_id,salary,commission_pct,hire_date)
when department_id <> 80 then
  into emp_non_sales (employee_id,department_id,salary,hire_date)
  values (employee_id,department_id,salary,hire_date)
when department_id = 80 then
  into emp_sales (employee_id,salary,commission_pct,hire_date)
  values (employee_id,salary,commission_pct,hire_date)
select employee_id,department_id,job_id,salary,commission_pct,hire_date
from employees where hire_date > sysdate - 30;
```

To read this statement, start at the bottom. The subquery retrieves all employees recruited in the last 30 days. Then go to the top. The ALL keyword means that every row selected will be considered for insertion into all the tables following, not just into the first table for which the condition applies. The first condition is 1=1, which is always true, so every source row will create a row in EMP_NO_ NAME. This is a copy of the EMPLOYEES table with the personal identifiers removed, a common requirement in a data warehouse. The second condition is DEPARTMENT_ID <> 80, which will generate a row in EMP_NON_SALES for every employee who is not in the sales department; there is no need for this table to have the COMMISSION_PCT column. The third condition generates a row in EMP_SALES for all the salesmen; there is no need for the DEPARTMENT_ID column, because they will all be in department 80.

This is a simple example of a multitable insert, but it should be apparent that with one statement, and therefore only one pass through the source data, it is possible to populate many target tables. This can take an enormous amount of strain off the database.

EXERCISE 10-1

Use the INSERT Command

In this exercise, use various techniques to insert rows into a table.

1. Connect to the HR schema, with either SQL Developer or SQL*Plus.

2. Query the REGIONS table, to check what values are already in use for the REGION_ID column:

```
select * from regions;
```

This exercise assumes that values above 100 are not in use. If they are, adjust the values suggested below to avoid primary key conflicts.

3. Insert a row into the REGIONS table, providing the values in line:

```
insert into regions values (101,'Great Britain');
```

4. Insert a row into the REGIONS table, providing the values as substitution variables:

```
insert into regions values (&Region_number,'&Region_name');
```

When prompted, give the values 102 for the number, Australasia for the name. Note the use of quotes around the string.

5. Insert a row into the REGIONS table, calculating the REGION_ID to be one higher than the current high value. This will need a scalar subquery:

```
insert into regions values ((select max(region_id)+1
from regions), 'Oceania');
```

6. Confirm the insertion of the rows:

```
select * from regions;
```

7. Commit the insertions:

```
commit;
```

The following illustration shows the results of the exercise, using SQL*Plus:

```
C:\WINDOWS\system32\cmd.exe - sqlplus hr/hr
SQL> insert into regions values (101,'Great Britain');

1 row created.

SQL> insert into regions values (&Region_number,'&Region_name');
Enter value for region_number: 102
Enter value for region_name: Australasia
old   1: insert into regions values (&Region_number,'&Region_name')
new   1: insert into regions values (102,'Australasia')

1 row created.

SQL> insert into regions values
  2  ((select max(region_id)+1 from regions),'Oceania');

1 row created.

SQL> select * from regions;

 REGION_ID REGION_NAME
---------- -------------------------
       101 Great Britain
       102 Australasia
       103 Oceania
         1 Europe
         2 Americas
         3 Asia
         4 Middle East and Africa

7 rows selected.

SQL> commit;

Commit complete.

SQL>
```

CERTIFICATION OBJECTIVE 10.03

Update Rows in a Table

The UPDATE command changes column values in one or more existing rows in a single table. The basic syntax is the following:

UPDATE *table* SET *column=value* [,*column=value*…] [WHERE *condition*];

The more complex form of the command uses subqueries for one or more of the column values and for the WHERE condition. Figure 10-3 shows updates of varying complexity, executed from SQL*Plus.

The first example is the simplest. One column of one row is set to a literal value. Because the row is chosen with a WHERE clause that uses the equality predicate on the table's primary key, there is an absolute guarantee that at most only one row will be affected. No row will be changed if the WHERE clause fails to find any rows at all.

The second example shows use of arithmetic and an existing column to set the new value, and the row selection is not done on the primary key column. If the selection is not done on the primary key, or if a nonequality predicate (such as BETWEEN) is

FIGURE 10-3	
Examples of using the UPDATE statement	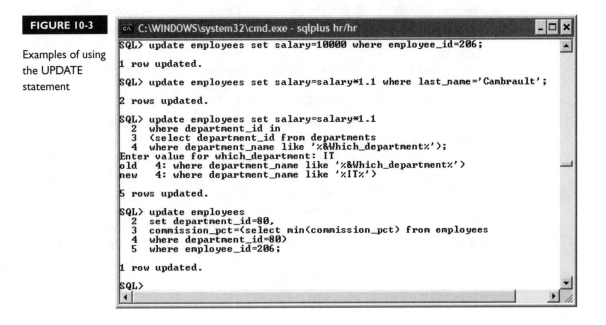

```
C:\WINDOWS\system32\cmd.exe - sqlplus hr/hr

SQL> update employees set salary=10000 where employee_id=206;

1 row updated.

SQL> update employees set salary=salary*1.1 where last_name='Cambrault';

2 rows updated.

SQL> update employees set salary=salary*1.1
  2  where department_id in
  3  (select department_id from departments
  4  where department_name like '%&Which_department%');
Enter value for which_department: IT
old   4: where department_name like '%&Which_department%')
new   4: where department_name like '%IT%')

5 rows updated.

SQL> update employees
  2  set department_id=80,
  3  commission_pct=(select min(commission_pct) from employees
  4  where department_id=80)
  5  where employee_id=206;

1 row updated.

SQL>
```

used, then the number of rows updated may be more than one. If the WHERE clause is omitted entirely, the update will be applied to every row in the table.

The third example in Figure 10-3 introduces the use of a subquery to define the set of rows to be updated. A minor additional complication is the use of a replacement variable to prompt the user for a value to use in the WHERE clause of the subquery. In this example, the subquery (lines 3 and 4) will select every employee who is in a department whose name includes the string 'IT' and increment their current salary by 10 percent (unlikely to happen in practice).

It is also possible to use subqueries to determine the value to which a column will be set, as in the fourth example. In this case, one employee (identified by primary key, in line 5) is transferred to department 80 (the sales department), and then the subquery in lines 3 and 4 set his commission rate to whatever the lowest commission rate in the department happens to be.

The syntax of an update that uses subqueries is as follows:

UPDATE *table*

SET *column*=[*subquery*] [,*column*=*subquery*…]

WHERE *column* = (*subquery*) [AND *column*=*subquery*…] ;

There is a rigid restriction on the subqueries using update columns in the SET clause: the subquery must return a *scalar* value. A scalar value is a single value of whatever data type is needed: the query must return one row, with one column. If the query returns several values, the UPDATE will fail. Consider these two examples:

```
update employees
set salary=(select salary from employees where employee_id=206);
update employees
set salary=(select salary from employees where last_name='Abel');
```

The first example, using an equality predicate on the primary key, will always succeed. Even if the subquery does not retrieve a row (as would be the case if there were no employee with EMPLOYEE_ID equal to 206), the query will still return a scalar value: a null. In that case, all the rows in EMPLOYEES would have their SALARY set to NULL—which might not be desired but is not an error as far as SQL is concerned. The second example uses an equality predicate on the LAST_NAME, which is not guaranteed to be unique. The statement will succeed if there is only one employee with that name, but if there were more than one it would fail with the error "ORA-01427: single-row subquery returns more than one row." For code that will work reliably, no matter what the state of the data, it is vital to ensure that the subqueries used for setting column values are scalar.

on the
Job

A common fix for making sure that queries are scalar is to use MAX or MIN. This version of the statement will always succeed:

```
update employees
set salary=(select max(salary) from employees where last_name='Abel');
```

However, just because it will work, doesn't necessarily mean that it does what is wanted.

The subqueries in the WHERE clause must also be scalar, if it is using the equality predicate (as in the preceding examples) or the greater/less than predicates. If it is using the IN predicate, then the query can return multiple rows, as in this example which uses IN:

```
update employees
set salary=10000
where department_id in (select department_id from departments
where department_name like '%IT%');
```

This will apply the update to all employees in a department whose name includes the string 'IT.' There are several of these. But even though the query can return several rows, it must still return only one column.

ex**a m**
watch
The subqueries used to SET column values must be scalar subqueries. The subqueries used to select the rows must also be scalar, unless they use the IN predicate.

EXERCISE 10-2

Use the UPDATE Command

In this exercise, use various techniques to update rows in a table. It is assumed that the HR.REGIONS table is as seen in the illustration at the end of Exercise 10-1. If not, adjust the values as necessary.

1. Connect to the HR schema using SQL Developer or SQL*Plus.

2. Update a single row, identified by primary key:

```
update regions set region_name='Scandinavia' where region_id=101;
```

This statement should return the message "1 row updated."

3. Update a set of rows, using a nonequality predicate:

```
update regions set region_name='Iberia' where region_id > 100;
```

This statement should return the message "3 rows updated."

4. Update a set of rows, using subqueries to select the rows and to provide values:

```
update regions
set region_id=(region_id+(select max(region_id) from regions))
where region_id in (select region_id from regions where
region_id > 100);
```

This statement should return the message "3 rows updated."

5. Confirm the state of the rows:

```
select * from regions;
```

6. Commit the changes made:

```
commit;
```

The following illustration shows the exercise, as done from SQL*Plus.

```
C:\WINDOWS\system32\cmd.exe - sqlplus hr/hr
SQL> update regions set region_name='Scandinavia' where region_id=101;

1 row updated.

SQL> update regions set region_name='Iberia' where region_id > 100;

3 rows updated.

SQL> update regions
  2  set region_id=(region_id+(select max(region_id) from regions))
  3  where region_id in (select region_id from regions where region_id > 100);

3 rows updated.

SQL> select * from regions;

 REGION_ID REGION_NAME
---------- --------------------------
       204 Iberia
       205 Iberia
       206 Iberia
         1 Europe
         2 Americas
         3 Asia
         4 Middle East and Africa

7 rows selected.

SQL> commit;

Commit complete.

SQL>
```

Delete Rows from a Table

To remove rows from a table, there are two options: the DELETE command and the TRUNCATE command. DELETE is less drastic, in that a deletion can be rolled back whereas a truncation cannot be. DELETE is also more controllable, in that it is possible to choose which rows to delete, whereas a truncation always affects the whole table. DELETE is, however, a lot slower and can place a lot of strain on the database. TRUNCATE is virtually instantaneous and effortless.

Removing Rows with DELETE

The DELETE commands removes rows from a single table. The syntax is as follows:

DELETE FROM *table* [WHERE *condition*];

This is the simplest of the DML commands, particularly if the condition is omitted. In that case, every row in the table will be removed with no prompt. The only complication is in the condition. This can be a simple match of a column to a literal:

```
delete from employees where employee_id=206;
delete from employees where last_name like 'S%';
delete from employees where department_id=&Which_department;
delete from employees where department_id is null;
```

The first statement identifies a row by primary key. One row only will be removed— or no row at all, if the value given does not find a match. The second statement uses a nonequality predicate that could result in the deletion of many rows: every employee whose surname begins with an uppercase "S." The third statement uses an equality predicate but not on the primary key. It prompts for a department number with a substitution variable, and all employees in that department will go. The final statement removes all employees who are not currently assigned to a department.

The condition can also be a subquery:

```
delete from employees where department_id in
(select department_id from departments where location_id in
  (select location_id from locations where country_id in
    (select country_id from countries where region_id in
      (select region_id from regions where region_name='Europe')
    )
  )
)
```

This example uses a subquery for row selection that navigates the HR geographical tree (with more subqueries) to delete every employee who works for any department that is based in Europe. The same rule for the number of values returned by the subquery applies as for an UPDATE command: if the row selection is based on an equality predicate (as in the preceding example) the subquery must be scalar, but if it uses IN the subquery can return several rows.

If the DELETE command finds no rows to delete, this is not an error. The command will return the message "0 rows deleted" rather than an error message because the statement did complete successfully—it just didn't find anything to do.

EXERCISE 10-3

Use the DELETE Command

In this exercise, use various techniques to delete rows in a table. It is assumed that the HR.REGIONS table is as seen in the illustration at the end of Exercise 10-2. If not, adjust the values as necessary.

1. Connect to the HR schema using SQL Developer or SQL*Plus.

2. Remove one row, using the equality predicate on the primary key:

   ```
   delete from regions where region_id=204;
   ```

   This should return the message "1 row deleted."

3. Attempt to remove every row in the table by omitting a WHERE clause:

   ```
   delete from regions;
   ```

   This will fail, due to a constraint violation.

4. Remove rows with the row selection based on a subquery:

   ```
   delete from regions where
   region_id in (select region_id from regions where region_
   name='Iberia');
   ```

   This will return the message "2 rows deleted."

5. Confirm that the REGIONS table now contains just the original four rows:

   ```
   select * from regions;
   ```

6. Commit the deletions:

   ```
   commit;
   ```

The following illustration shows the exercise, as done from SQL*Plus:

```
C:\WINDOWS\system32\cmd.exe - sqlplus hr/hr                              _ □ ×
SQL> delete from regions where region_id=204;

1 row deleted.

SQL> delete from regions;
delete from regions
*
ERROR at line 1:
ORA-02292: integrity constraint (HR.COUNTR_REG_FK) violated - child record
found

SQL> delete from regions where
  2   region_id in (select region_id from regions where region_name='Iberia');

2 rows deleted.

SQL> select * from regions;

 REGION_ID REGION_NAME
---------- -------------------------
         1 Europe
         2 Americas
         3 Asia
         4 Middle East and Africa

SQL> commit;

Commit complete.

SQL> _
```

Removing Rows with TRUNCATE

TRUNCATE is a DDL (Data Definition Language) command. It operates within the data dictionary and affects the structure of the table, not the contents of the table. However, the change it makes to the structure has the side effect of destroying all the rows in the table.

One part of the definition of a table as stored in the data dictionary is the table's physical location. When first created, a table is allocated a single area of space, of fixed size, in the database's data files. This is known as an *extent* and will be empty. Then, as rows are inserted, the extent fills up. Once it is full, more extents will be allocated to the table automatically.

A table therefore consists of one or more extents, which hold the rows. As well as tracking the extent allocation, the data dictionary also tracks how much of the space allocated to the table has been used. This is done with the *high water mark*. The high water mark is the last position in the last extent that has been used; all space below the high water mark has been used for rows at one time or another, and none of the space above the high water mark has been used yet.

Note that it is possible for there to be plenty of space below the high water mark that is not being used at the moment; this is because of rows having been removed with a DELETE command. Inserting rows into a table pushes the high water mark up. Deleting them leaves the high water mark where it is; the space they occupied remains assigned to the table but is freed up for inserting more rows.

Truncating a table resets the high water mark. Within the data dictionary, the recorded position of the high water mark is moved to the beginning of the table's first extent. As Oracle assumes that there can be no rows above the high water mark, this has the effect of removing every row from the table. The table is emptied and remains empty until subsequent insertions begin to push the high water mark back up again. In this manner, one DDL command, which does little more than make an update in the data dictionary, can annihilate billions of rows in a table.

on the
(j) o b

A truncation is fast: virtually instantaneous, irrespective of whether the table has many millions of rows or none. A deletion may take seconds, minutes, hours—and it places much more strain on the database than a truncation. But a truncation is all or nothing.

The syntax to truncate a table couldn't be simpler:

TRUNCATE TABLE *table*;

Figure 10-4 shows access to the TRUNCATE command through the SQL Developer navigation tree, but of course it can also be executed from SQL*Plus.

MERGE

The MERGE command is often ignored, because it does nothing that cannot be done with INSERT, UPDATE, and DELETE. It is, however, very powerful, in that with one pass through the data it can carry out all three operations. This can improve performance dramatically. Use of MERGE is not on the OCP syllabus, but for completeness here is a simple example:

```
merge into employees e using new_employees n
  on (e.employee_id = n.employee_id)
when matched then
  update set e.salary=n.salary
when not matched then
  insert (employee_id,last_name,salary)
  values (n.employee_id,n.last_name,n.salary);
```

FIGURE 10-4

The TRUNCATE
command in SQL
Developer, from
the command
line and from the
menus

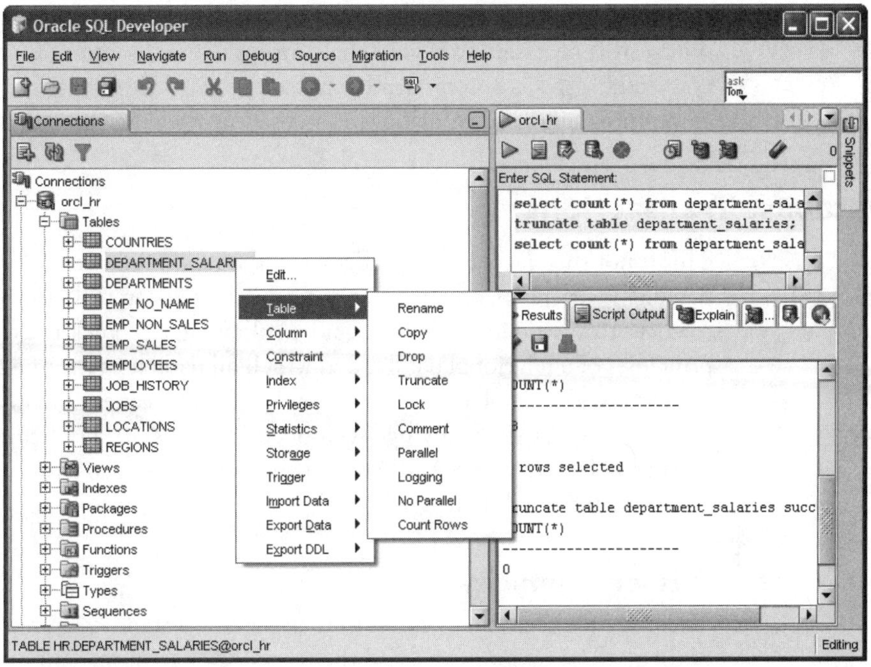

The preceding statement uses the contents of a table NEW_EMPLOYEES to
update or insert rows in EMPLOYEES. The situation could be that EMPLOYEES
is a table of all staff, and NEW_EMPLOYEES is a table with rows for new staff
and for salary changes for existing staff. The command will pass through NEW_
EMPLOYEES, and for each row, attempt to find a row in EMPLOYEES with the
same EMPLOYEE_ID. If there is a row found, its SALARY column will be updated
with the value of the row in NEW_EMPLOYEES. If there is not such a row, one will
be inserted. Variations on the syntax allow the use of a subquery to select the source
rows, and it is even possible to delete matching rows.

CERTIFICATION OBJECTIVE 10.05

Control Transactions

The concepts behind a *transaction* are a part of the relational database paradigm.
A transaction consists of one or more DML statements, followed by either a
ROLLBACK or a COMMIT command. It is possible use the SAVEPOINT

command to give a degree of control within the transaction. Before going into the syntax, it is necessary to review the concept of a transaction. Related topics are read consistency; this is automatically implemented by the Oracle server, but to a certain extent programmers can manage it by the way they use the SELECT statement.

Database Transactions

This is not the place to go into detail on the relational database transactional paradigm—there are any number of academic texts on this, and there is not space to cover this topic in a practical guide. Following is a quick review of some of the principles of a relational database to which all databases (not just Oracle's) must conform. Other database vendors comply with the same standards with their own mechanisms, but with varying levels of effectiveness. In brief, any relational database must be able to pass the ACID test: it must guarantee atomicity, consistency, isolation, and durability.

A is for Atomicity

The principle of *atomicity* states that all parts of a transaction must complete or none of them. (The reasoning behind the term is that an atom cannot be split—now well known to be a false assumption). For example, if your business analysts have said that every time you change an employee's salary you must also change the employee's grade, then the atomic transaction will consist of two updates. The database must guarantee that both go through or neither. If only one of the updates were to succeed, you would have an employee on a salary that was incompatible with his grade: a data corruption, in business terms. If anything (anything at all!) goes wrong before the transaction is complete, the database itself must guarantee that any parts that did go through are reversed; this must happen automatically. But although an atomic transaction sounds small (like an atom), it can be enormous. To take another example, it is logically impossible for an accounting suite nominal ledger to be half in August and half in September: the end-of-month rollover is therefore (in business terms) one atomic transaction, which may affect millions of rows in thousands of tables and take hours to complete (or to roll back, if anything goes wrong). The rollback of an incomplete transaction may be manual (as when you issue the ROLLBACK command), but it must be automatic and unstoppable in the case of an error.

C is for Consistency

The principle of *consistency* states that the results of a query must be consistent with the state of the database at the time the query started. Imagine a simple query that averages the value of a column of a table. If the table is large, it will take many minutes to pass through the table. If other users are updating the column while the query is in progress, should the query include the new or the old values? Should it include rows that were inserted or deleted after the query started? The principle of consistency requires that the database ensure that changed values are not seen by the query; it will give you an average of the column as it was when the query started, no matter how long the query takes or what other activity is occurring on the tables concerned. Oracle guarantees that if a query succeeds, the result will be consistent. However, if the database administrator has not configured the database appropriately, the query may not succeed: there is a famous Oracle error, "ORA-1555 snapshot too old," that is raised. This used to be an extremely difficult problem to fix with earlier releases of the database, but with recent versions the database administrator should always be able to prevent this.

I is for Isolation

The principle of *isolation* states that an incomplete (that is, uncommitted) transaction must be invisible to the rest of the world. While the transaction is in progress, only the one session that is executing the transaction is allowed to see the changes; all other sessions must see the unchanged data, not the new values. The logic behind this is first, that the full transaction might not go through (remember the principle of atomicity and automatic or manual rollback?) and that therefore no other users should be allowed to see changes that might be reversed. And second, during the progress of a transaction the data is (in business terms) incoherent: there is a short time when the employee has had his salary changed but not his grade. Transaction isolation requires that the database must conceal transactions in progress from other users: they will see the preupdate version of the data until the transaction completes, when they will see all the changes as a consistent set. Oracle guarantees transaction isolation: there is no way any session (other than that making the changes) can see uncommitted data. A read of uncommitted data is known as a *dirty read*, which Oracle does not permit (though some other databases do).

D is for Durable

The principle of *durability* states that once a transaction completes, it must be impossible for the database to lose it. During the time that the transaction is in progress, the principle of isolation requires that no one (other than the session concerned) can see the changes it has made so far. But the instant the transaction completes, it must be broadcast to the world, and the database must guarantee that the change is never lost; a relational database is not allowed to lose data. Oracle fulfills this requirement by writing out all change vectors that are applied to data to log files as the changes are done. By applying this log of changes to backups taken earlier, it is possible to repeat any work done in the event of the database being damaged. Of course, data can be lost through user error such as inappropriate DML, or dropping or truncating tables. But as far as Oracle and the DBA are concerned, such events are transactions like any other: according to the principle of durability, they are absolutely nonreversible.

The Start and End of a Transaction

A session begins a transaction the moment it issues any INSERT, UPDATE, or DELETE statement (but not a TRUNCATE—that is a DDL command, not DML). The transaction continues through any number of further DML commands until the session issues either a COMMIT or a ROLLBACK statement. Only then will the changes be made permanent and become visible to other sessions (if it is committed, rather than rolled back). It is impossible to nest transactions. The SQL standard does not allow a user to start one transaction and then start another before terminating the first. This can be done with PL/SQL (Oracle's proprietary third-generation language), but not with industry-standard SQL.

The explicit transaction control statements are COMMIT, ROLLBACK, and SAVEPOINT. There are also circumstances other than a user-issued COMMIT or ROLLBACK that will implicitly terminate a transaction:

- Issuing a DDL or DCL statement
- Exiting from the user tool (SQL*Plus or SQL Developer or anything else)
- If the client session dies
- If the system crashes

If a user issues a DDL (CREATE, ALTER, or DROP) or DCL (GRANT or REVOKE) command, the transaction he has in progress (if any) will be committed: it will be made permanent and become visible to all other users. This is because the DDL and DCL commands are themselves transactions. If it were possible to see the source code for these commands, it would be obvious. They adjust the data structures by performing DML commands against the tables that make up the data dictionary, and these commands are terminated with a COMMIT. If they were not, the changes made couldn't be guaranteed to be permanent. As it is not possible in SQL to nest transactions, if the user already has a transaction running, the statements the user has run will be committed along with the statements that make up the DDL or DCL command.

If a user starts a transaction by issuing a DML command and then exits from the tool he is using without explicitly issuing either a COMMIT or a ROLLBACK, the transaction will terminate—but whether it terminates with a COMMIT or a ROLLBACK is entirely dependent on how the tool is written. Many tools will have different behavior, depending on how the tool is exited. (For instance, in the Microsoft Windows environment, it is common to be able to terminate a program either by selecting the File | Exit options from a menu on the top left of the window, or by clicking an "X" in the top right corner. The programmers who wrote the tool may well have coded different logic into these functions.) In either case, it will be a controlled exit, so the programmers should issue either a COMMIT or a ROLLBACK, but the choice is up to them.

If a client's session fails for some reason, the database will always roll back the transaction. Such failure could be for a number of reasons: the user process can die or be killed at the operating system level, the network connection to the database server may go down, or the machine where the client tool is running can crash. In any of these cases, there is no orderly issue of a COMMIT or ROLLBACK statement, and it is up to the database to detect what has happened. The behavior is that the session is killed, and an active transaction is rolled back. The behavior is the same if the failure is on the server side. If the database server crashes for any reason, when it next starts up all transactions from any sessions that were in progress will be rolled back.

The Transaction Control Statements

A transaction begins implicitly with the first DML statement. There is no command to explicitly start a transaction. The transaction continues through all subsequent DML statements issued by the session. These statements can be against any number of tables: a transaction is not restricted to one table. It terminates (barring any of the events listed in the previous section) when the session issues a COMMIT or ROLLBACK command. The SAVEPOINT command can be used to set markers that will stage the action of a ROLLBACK, but the same transaction remains in progress irrespective of the use of SAVEPOINT.

COMMIT

Syntactically, COMMIT is the simplest SQL command. The syntax is as follows:

COMMIT;

This will end the current transaction, which has the dual effect of making the changes both permanent and visible to other sessions. Until a transaction is committed, it cannot be seen by any other sessions, even if they are logged on to the database with the same username as that of the session executing the transactions. Until a transaction is committed, it is invisible to other sessions and can be reversed. But once it is committed, it is absolutely nonreversible. The principle of durability applies. All database administrators dread a telephone call along these lines:

User: I've just deleted a million rows instead of one.

DBA: How?

User: Because I forgot to put a WHERE clause on my DELETE statement.

DBA: Did you say COMMIT?

User: Of course.

DBA: Um...

The state of the data before the COMMIT is that the changes have been made, but all sessions other than the one that made the changes are redirected to copies of the data in its prechanged form. So if the session has inserted rows, other sessions that SELECT from the table will not see them. If the transaction has deleted rows, other sessions selecting from the table will still see them. If the transaction has made updates, it will be the unupdated versions of the rows that are presented to other sessions. This is in accordance with the principle of isolation: no session can be in any way dependent on the state of an uncommitted transaction.

After the COMMIT, all sessions will immediately see the new data in any queries they issue: they will see the new rows, they will not see the deleted rows, they will see the new versions of the updated rows. In the case of the hypothetical conversation just discussed, one moment other sessions' queries will see millions of rows in the table; the next it will be empty. This is in accordance with the principle of durability.

ROLLBACK

While a transaction is in progress, Oracle keeps an image of the data as it was before the transaction. This image is presented to other sessions that query the data while the transaction is in progress. It is also used to roll back the transaction automatically if anything goes wrong, or deliberately if the session requests it. The syntax to request a rollback is as follows:

ROLLBACK [TO SAVEPOINT *savepoint*] ;

The optional use of savepoints is detailed in the section following.

The state of the data before the rollback is that the data has been changed, but the information needed to reverse the changes is available. This information is presented to all other sessions, in order to implement the principle of isolation. The rollback will discard all the changes by restoring the prechange image of the data; any rows the transaction inserted will be deleted, rows the transaction deleted will be inserted back into the table, and any rows that were updated will be returned to their original state. Other sessions will not be aware that anything has happened at all; they never saw the changes. The session that did the transaction will now see the data as it was before the transaction started.

on the **Job** *A COMMIT is instantaneous, because it doesn't really have to do anything. The work has already been done. A ROLLBACK can be very slow: it will usually take as long (if not longer) to reverse a transaction than it took to make the changes in the first place. Rollbacks are not good for database performance.*

EXERCISE 10-4

Use the COMMIT and ROLLBACK Commands

In this exercise, demonstrate the use of transaction control statements and transaction isolation. It is assumed that the HR.REGIONS table is as seen in the illustration at the end of Exercise 10-3. If not, adjust the values as necessary. Connect to the HR schema with two sessions concurrently. These can be two SQL*Plus sessions or two SQL Developer sessions or one of each. The following table lists steps to follow in each session.

Step	In your first session	In your second session
1	`select * from regions;`	`select * from regions;`
Both sessions see the same data.		
2	`insert into regions values(100,'UK');`	`insert into regions values(101,'GB');`
3	`select * from regions;`	`select * from regions;`
Both sessions see different results: the original data, plus their own change.		
4	`commit;`	
5	`select * from regions;`	`select * from regions;`
One transaction has been published to the world, the other is still visible to only one session.		
6	`rollback;`	`rollback;`
7	`select * from regions;`	`select * from regions;`
The committed transaction was not reversed because it has already been committed, but the uncommitted one is now completely gone, having been terminated by rolling back the change.		
8	`delete from regions where region_id=100;`	`delete from regions where region_id=101;`
9	`select * from regions;`	`select * from regions;`
Each deleted row is still visible in the session that did not delete it, until you do the following:		
10	`commit;`	`commit;`
11	`select * from regions;`	`select * from regions;`
With all transactions terminated, both sessions see a consistent view of the table.		

SAVEPOINT

The use of savepoints is to allow a programmer to set a marker in a transaction that can be used to control the effect of the ROLLBACK command. Rather than rolling back the whole transaction and terminating it, it becomes possible to reverse all changes made after a particular point but leave changes made before that point intact. The transaction itself remains in progress: still uncommitted, still rollbackable, and still invisible to other sessions.

The syntax is as follows:

SAVEPOINT *savepoint*;

This creates a named point in the transaction that can be used in a subsequent ROLLBACK command. The following table illustrates the number of rows in a table at various stages in a transaction. The table is a very simple table called TAB, with one column.

Command	Rows Visible to the User	Rows Visible to Others
truncate table tab;	0	0
insert into tab values ('one');	1	0
savepoint first;	1	0
insert into tab values ('two');	2	0
savepoint second;	2	0
insert into tab values ('three');	3	0
rollback to savepoint second;	2	0
rollback to savepoint first;	1	0
commit;	1	1
delete from tab;	0	1
rollback;	1	1

The example in the table shows two transactions: the first terminated with a COMMIT, the second with a ROLLBACK. It can be seen that the use of savepoints is visible only within the transaction: other sessions see nothing that is not committed.

on the **Ô**ob **The SAVEPOINT command is not (yet) part of the official SQL standard, so it may be considered good practice to avoid it in production systems. It can be very useful in development, though, when you are testing the effect of DML statements and walking through a complex transaction step by step.**

The AUTOCOMMIT in SQL*Plus and SQL Developer

The standard behavior of SQL*Plus and SQL Developer is to follow the SQL standard: a transaction begins implicitly with a DML statement and ends explicitly with a COMMIT or a ROLLBACK. It is possible to change this behavior in both tools so that every DML statement commits immediately, in its own transaction. If this is done, there is no need for any COMMIT statements, and the ROLLBACK statement can never have any effect: all DML statements become permanent and visible to others as soon as they execute.

In SQL*Plus, enable the autocommit mode with the command:

SET AUTOCOMMIT ON

To return to normal:

SET AUTOCOMMIT OFF

In SQL Developer, from the Tools menu, select Preferences. Then expand Database and Worksheet Parameters: you will see the Autocommit in SQL Worksheet check box.

on the
Ôob   *It may be hard to justify enabling the autocommit mode of the SQL*Plus and SQL Developer tools. Perhaps the only reason is for compatibility with some third-party products that do not follow the SQL standard. SQL scripts written for such products may not have any COMMIT statements.*

SELECT FOR UPDATE

One last transaction control statement is SELECT FOR UPDATE. Oracle, by default, provides the highest possible level of concurrency: readers do not block writers, and writers do not block readers. Or in plain language, there is no problem with one session querying data that another session is updating, or one session updating data that another session is querying. However, there are times when you may wish to change this behavior and prevent changes to data that is being queried.

It is not unusual for an application to retrieve a set of rows with a SELECT command, present them to a user for perusal, and prompt him for any changes. Because Oracle is a multiuser database, it is not impossible that another session has also retrieved the same rows. If both sessions attempt to make changes, there can be some rather odd effects. The following table depicts such a situation.

First User	Second User
select * from regions;	select * from regions;
	delete from regions where region_id=5;
	commit;
update regions set region_name='GB' where region_id=5;	

This is what the first user will see, from a SQL*Plus prompt:

```
SQL> select * from regions;
 REGION_ID REGION_NAME
---------- ------------------------
         5 UK
         1 Europe
         2 Americas
         3 Asia
         4 Middle East and Africa
SQL> update regions set region_name='GB' where region_id=5;
0 rows updated.
```

This is a bit disconcerting. One way around this problem is to lock the rows in which one is interested:

```
select * from regions for update;
```

INSIDE THE EXAM

Understanding Transaction Isolation

All DML statements are private to the session that makes them, until the transaction commits. The transaction is started implicitly with the first DML statement executed. Until it is committed, it can be reversed with a ROLLBACK. No other session will ever see changes that have not been committed, but the instant they are committed they will be visible to all other sessions.

Transaction structure is vital for good programming. A transaction is a logical unit of work: the changes made by the transaction, whether it is one statement affecting one row in one table, or many statements affecting any number of rows in many tables, should be self contained. It should not be in any way dependent on statements executed outside the transaction, and it should not be divisible into smaller, self-contained transactions. A transaction should be the right size; it should contain all the statements that cannot be separated in terms of business logic and no statements that can be.

The decisions on transaction structure may be complex, but with some thought and investigation, they can be made for any situation. Business and systems analysts can and should advise.

SCENARIO & SOLUTION

Transactions, like constraints, are business rules: a technique whereby the database can enforce rules developed by business analysts. If the "logical unit of work" is huge, such as an accounting suite period rollover, should this actually be implemented as one transaction?	Not necessarily. Such a transaction might take hours, occupying a vast amount of database resources. In such cases, you must discuss with your business analysts and DBA whether it is possible to break up the one business transaction into a number of database transactions. Of course, if something goes wrong partway through, you will have an accounting suite that is partly in one period and partly in another. This application will need to be able to sort out the mess.
Being able to do DML operations, look at the result, then roll back and try them again can be very useful. But is it really a good idea?	No, not really. If the application is designed so that end users can do this, the DBA will not be happy. He will see many transactions being rolled back, which stresses the database. It is much better for the application to do all such work on the client side and only submit the work to the database when it is ready and can be committed immediately.

The FOR UPDATE clause will place a lock on all the rows retrieved. No changes can be made to them by any session other than that which issued the command, and therefore the subsequent updates will succeed: it is not possible for the rows to have been changed. This means that one session will have a consistent view of the data (it won't change), but the price to be paid is that other sessions will hang if they try to update any of the locked rows (they can, of course, query them).

The locks placed by a FOR UPDATE clause will be held until the session issuing the command issues a COMMIT or ROLLBACK. This must be done to release the locks, even if no DML commands have been executed.

CERTIFICATION SUMMARY

There are four DML commands that affect data: INSERT, UPDATE, DELETE, and (the optional command) MERGE. TRUNCATE is a DDL command that is functionally equivalent to a DELETE command without a WHERE clause, but it is far faster. All DML commands can be rolled back, either automatically in the case of error, or manually with the ROLLBACK command—unless they have been committed with a COMMIT. Once committed, the changes can never be reversed. TRUNCATE, like all DDL commands, has a built-in COMMIT that is unstoppable.

✓ TWO-MINUTE DRILL

Describe Each Data Manipulation Language (DML) Statement

- ❑ INSERT enters rows into a table.
- ❑ UPDATE adjusts the values in existing rows.
- ❑ DELETE removes rows.
- ❑ MERGE can combine the functions of INSERT, UPDATE, and DELETE.
- ❑ Even though TRUNCATE is not DML, it does remove all rows in a table.

Insert Rows into a Table

- ❑ INSERT can enter one row or a set of rows.
- ❑ It is possible for an INSERT to enter rows into multiple tables.
- ❑ Subqueries can be used to generate the rows to be inserted.
- ❑ Subqueries and functions can be used to generate column values.
- ❑ An INSERT is not permanent until it is committed.

Update Rows in a Table

- ❑ UPDATE can affect one row or a set of rows in one table.
- ❑ Subqueries can be used to select the rows to be updated.
- ❑ Subqueries and functions can be used to generate column values.
- ❑ An UPDATE is not permanent until it is committed.

Delete Rows from a Table

- ❑ DELETE can remove one row or a set of rows from one table.
- ❑ A subquery can be used to select the rows to be deleted.
- ❑ A DELETE is not permanent until it is committed.
- ❑ TRUNCATE removes every row from a table.
- ❑ A TRUNCATE is immediately permanent: it cannot be rolled back.

Control Transactions

❑ A transaction is a logical unit of work, possibly several DML statements.

❑ Transactions are invisible to other sessions until committed.

❑ Until committed, transactions can be rolled back.

❑ Once committed, a transaction cannot be reversed.

❑ A SAVEPOINT lets a session roll back part of a transaction.

SELF TEST

The following questions will help you measure your understanding of the material presented in this chapter. Read all the choices carefully because there might be more than one correct answer. Choose all the correct answers for each question.

Describe Each Data Manipulation Language (DML) Statement

1. Which of the following commands can be rolled back?
- A. COMMIT
- B. DELETE
- C. INSERT
- D. MERGE
- E. TRUNCATE
- F. UPDATE

2. How can you change the primary key value of a row? (Choose the best answer.)
- A. You cannot change the primary key value.
- B. Change it with a simple UPDATE statement.
- C. The row must be removed with a DELETE and reentered with an INSERT.
- D. This is only possible if the row is first locked with a SELECT FOR UPDATE.

3. If an UPDATE or DELETE command has a WHERE clause that gives it a scope of several rows, what will happen if there is an error part way through execution? The command is one of several in a multistatement transaction. (Choose the best answer.)
- A. The command will skip the row that caused the error and continue.
- B. The command will stop at the error, and the rows that have been updated or deleted will remain updated or deleted.
- C. Whatever work the command had done before hitting the error will be rolled back, but work done already by the transaction will remain.
- D. The whole transaction will be rolled back.

Insert Rows into a Table

4. If a table T1 has four numeric columns, C1, C2, C3, and C4, which of these statements will succeed? (Choose the best answer.)
- A. insert into T1 values (1,2,3,null);
- B. insert into T1 values ('1','2','3','4');
- C. insert into T1 select * from T1;

D. All the statements (A, B, and C) will succeed.

E. None of the statements (A, B, or C) will succeed.

5. Study the result of this SELECT statement:

```
SQL> select * from t1;
         C1          C2          C3          C4
---------- ---------- ---------- ----------
          1           2           3           4
          5           6           7           8
```

If you issue this statement:

```
insert into t1 (c1,c2) values(select c1,c2 from t1);
```

why will it fail? (Choose the best answer.)

A. Because values are not provided for all the table's columns: there should be NULLs for C3 and C4.

B. Because the subquery returns multiple rows: it requires a WHERE clause to restrict the number of rows returned to one.

C. Because the subquery is not scalar: it should use MAX or MIN to generate scalar values.

D. Because the VALUES keyword is not used with a subquery.

E. It will succeed, inserting two rows with NULLs for C3 and C4.

6. Consider this statement:

```
insert into regions (region_id, region_name)
values ((select max(region_id)+1 from regions), 'Great Britain');
```

What will the result be? (Choose the best answer.)

A. The statement will not succeed if the value generated for REGION_ID is not unique, because REGION_ID is the primary key of the REGIONS table.

B. The statement has a syntax error because you cannot use the VALUES keyword with a subquery.

C. The statement will execute without error.

D. The statement will fail if the REGIONS table has a third column.

Update Rows in a Table

7. You want to insert a row and then update it. What sequence of steps should you follow? (Choose the best answer.)

A. INSERT, UPDATE, COMMIT

B. INSERT, COMMIT, UPDATE, COMMIT

C. INSERT, SELECT FOR UPDATE, UPDATE, COMMIT

D. INSERT, COMMIT, SELECT FOR UPDATE, UPDATE, COMMIT

8. If you issue this command:

```
update employees set salary=salary * 1.1;
```

what will be the result? (Choose the best answer.)

A. The statement will fail because there is no WHERE clause to restrict the rows affected.

B. The first row in the table will be updated.

C. There will be an error if any row has its SALARY column NULL.

D. Every row will have SALARY incremented by 10 percent, unless SALARY was NULL.

Delete Rows from a Table

9. How can you delete the values from one column of every row in a table? (Choose the best answer.)

A. Use the DELETE COLUMN command.

B. Use the TRUNCATE COLUMN command.

C. Use the UPDATE command.

D. Use the DROP COLUMN command.

10. Which of these commands will remove every row in a table? (Choose one or more correct answers.)

A. A DELETE command with no WHERE clause

B. A DROP TABLE command

C. A TRUNCATE command

D. An UPDATE command, setting every column to NULL and with no WHERE clause

Control Transactions

11. User JOHN updates some rows and asks user ROOPESH to log in and check the changes before he commits them. Which of the following statements is true? (Choose the best answer.)

A. ROOPESH can see the changes but cannot alter them because JOHN will have locked the rows.

B. ROOPESH will not be able to see the changes.

C. JOHN must commit the changes so that ROOPESH can see them and, if necessary, roll them back.

D. JOHN must commit the changes so that ROOPESH can see them, but only JOHN can roll them back.

12. User JOHN updates some rows but does not commit the changes. User ROOPESH queries the rows that JOHN updated. Which of the following statements is true? (Choose three correct answers.)

    A. ROOPESH will not be able to see the rows because they will be locked.

    B. ROOPESH will be able to see the new values, but only if he logs in as JOHN.

    C. ROOPESH will see the old versions of the rows.

    D. ROOPESH will see the state of the state of the data as it was when JOHN last created a SAVEPOINT.

13. Which of these commands will terminate a transaction? (Choose three correct answers.)

    A. COMMIT

    B. DELETE

    C. ROLLBACK

    D. ROLLBACK TO SAVEPOINT

    E. SAVEPOINT

    F. TRUNCATE

LAB QUESTION

Carry out this exercise in the OE schema.

    1. Insert a customer into CUSTOMERS, using a function to generate a unique customer number:

```
insert into customers
(customer_id,cust_first_name,cust_last_name)
values((select max(customer_id)+1 from customers),'John','Watson');
```

    2. Give him a credit limit equal to the average credit limit:

```
update customers set
credit_limit=(select avg(credit_limit) from customers)
where cust_last_name='Watson';
```

    3. Create another customer using the customer just created, but make sure the CUSTOMER_ID is unique:

```
insert into customers
(customer_id,cust_first_name,cust_last_name,credit_limit)
select customer_id+1,cust_first_name,cust_last_name,credit_limit
from customers
where cust_last_name='Watson';
```

4. Change the name of the second entered customer:

```
update customers
set cust_last_name='Ramklass',cust_first_name='Roopesh'
where customer_id=(select max(customer_id) from customers);
```

5. Commit this transaction:

```
commit;
```

6. Determine the CUSTOMER_IDs of the two new customers and lock the rows:

7. select customer_id,cust_last_name from customers
where cust_last_name in ('Watson','Ramklass') for update;
From another session connected to the OE schema, attempt to update one of the locked rows:

```
update customers set credit_limit=0 where cust_last_name='Ramklass';
```

8. This command will hang. In the first session, release the locks by issuing a commit:

```
commit;
```

9. The second session will now complete its update. In the second session, delete the two rows:

```
delete from customers where cust_last_name in ('Watson','Ramklass');
```

10. In the first session, attempt to truncate the CUSTOMERS table:

```
truncate table customers;
```

11. This will fail because there is a transaction in progress against the table, which will block all DDL commands. In the second session, commit the transaction:

```
commit;
```

12. The CUSTOMERS table will now be back in the state it was in at the start of the exercise. Confirm this by checking the value of the highest CUSTOMER_ID:

```
select max(customer_id) from customers;
```

SELF TEST ANSWERS

Describe Each Data Manipulation Language (DML) Statement

1. ☑ **B, C, D, F.** These are the DML commands: they can all be rolled back.

   ☒ **A, E.** COMMIT terminates a transaction, which can then never be rolled back. TRUNCATE is a DDL command and includes a built-in COMMIT.

2. ☑ **B.** Assuming no constraint violations, the primary key can updated like any other column.

   ☒ **A, C, D.** A is wrong because there is no restriction on updating primary keys (other than constraints). C is wrong because there is no need to do it in such a complex manner. D is wrong because the UPDATE will apply its own lock: you do not have to lock the row first.

3. ☑ **C.** This is the expected behavior: the statement is rolled back, and the rest of the transaction remains uncommitted.

   ☒ **A, B, D.** A is wrong because, while this behavior is in fact configurable, it is not enabled by default. B is wrong because, while this is in fact possible in the event of space errors, it is not enabled by default. D is wrong because only the one statement will be rolled back, not the whole transaction.

Insert Rows into a Table

4. ☑ **D.** A, B, and C will all succeed, even though B will force the database to do some automatic type casting.

   ☒ **A, B, C, E.** A, B, and C are wrong because each one will succeed. E is wrong because A, B, and C will all succeed.

5. ☑ **D.** The syntax is wrong: use either the VALUES keyword or a subquery, but not both. Remove the VALUES keyword, and it will run. C3 and C4 would be populated with NULLs.

   ☒ **A, B, C, E.** A is wrong because there is no need to provide values for columns not listed. B and C are wrong because an INSERT can insert a set of rows, so there is no need to restrict the number with a WHERE clause or by using MAX or MIN to return only one row. E is wrong because the statement is not syntactically correct.

6. ☑ **C.** The statement is syntactically correct, and the use of "MAX(REGION_ID) + 1" guarantees generating a unique number for the primary key column.

   ☒ **A, B, D.** A is wrong because the function will generate a unique value for the primary key. B is wrong because there is no problem using a scalar subquery to generate a value for a VALUES list. What cannot be done is to use the VALUES keyword and then a single nonscalar subquery to provide all the values. D is wrong because if there is a third column, it will be populated with a NULL value.

Update Rows in a Table

7. ☑ **A.** This is the simplest (and therefore the best) way.

    ☒ **B, C, D.** All these will work, but they are all needlessly complicated: no programmer should use unnecessary statements.

8. ☑ **D.** Any arithmetic operation on a NULL returns a NULL, but all other rows will be updated.

    ☒ **A, B, C. A** and **B** are wrong because the lack of a WHERE clause means that every row will be processed. **C** is wrong because trying to do arithmetic against a NULL is not an error (though it isn't very useful, either).

Delete Rows from a Table

9. ☑ **C.** An UPDATE, without a WHERE clause, is the only way.

    ☒ **A, B, D. A** is wrong because there is no such syntax: a DELETE affects the whole row. **B** is wrong because there is no such syntax: a TRUNCATE affects the whole table. **D** is wrong because, while this command does exist (it is part of the ALTER TABLE command), it will remove the column completely, not just clear the values out of it.

10. ☑ **A, C.** The TRUNCATE will be faster, but the DELETE will get there too.

    ☒ **B** is wrong because this will remove the table as well as the rows within it. **D** is wrong because the rows will still be there—even though they are populated with NULLs.

Control Transactions

11. ☑ **B.** The principle of isolation means that only JOHN can see his uncommitted transaction.

    ☒ **A, C, D. A** is wrong because transaction isolation means that no other session will be able to see the changes. **C** and **D** are wrong because a committed transaction can never be rolled back.

12. ☑ **C.** Transaction isolation means that no other session will be able to see the changes until they are committed.

    ☒ **A, B, D. A** is wrong because locking is not relevant; writers do not block readers. **B** is wrong because isolation restricts visibility of in-progress transactions to the session making the changes; the schema the users are connecting to does not matter. **D** is wrong because savepoints are only markers in a transaction; they do not affect publishing changes to other sessions.

13. ☑ **A, C, F.** COMMIT and ROLLBACK are the commands to terminate a transaction explicitly; TRUNCATE will do it implicitly.

    ☒ **B, D, E. B** is wrong because DELETE is a DML command that can be executed within a transaction. **D** and **E** are wrong because creating savepoints and rolling back to them leave the transaction in progress.

LAB ANSWER

Figure 10-5 shows the first five steps of the exercise.

Figure 10-6 shows the final seven steps of the exercise, as seen from the point of view of the first session.

```
C:\WINDOWS\system32\cmd.exe - sqlplus oe/oe
SQL> insert into customers
  2  (customer_id,cust_first_name,cust_last_name)
  3  values((select max(customer_id)+1 from customers),'John','Watson');

1 row created.

SQL> update customers set
  2  credit_limit=(select avg(credit_limit) from customers)
  3  where cust_last_name='Watson';

1 row updated.

SQL> insert into customers
  2  (customer_id,cust_first_name,cust_last_name,credit_limit)
  3  select customer_id+1,cust_first_name,cust_last_name,credit_limit
  4  from customers
  5  where cust_last_name='Watson';

1 row created.

SQL> update customers
  2  set cust_last_name='Ramklass',cust_first_name='Roopesh'
  3  where customer_id=(select max(customer_id) from customers);

1 row updated.

SQL> commit;

Commit complete.
```

```
C:\WINDOWS\system32\cmd.exe - sqlplus oe/oe
SQL> select customer_id,cust_last_name from customers
  2  where cust_last_name in ('Watson','Ramklass') for update;

CUSTOMER_ID CUST_LAST_NAME
----------- --------------
        983 Ramklass
        982 Watson

SQL> commit;

Commit complete.

SQL> truncate table customers;
truncate table customers
               *
ERROR at line 1:
ORA-00054: resource busy and acquire with NOWAIT specified or timeout expired

SQL> select max(customer_id) from customers;

MAX(CUSTOMER_ID)
----------------
             981

SQL>
```

11

Using DDL Statements to Create and Manage Tables

There are several types of data objects in a database that can be addressed by users with SQL. The most commonly used type of object is the table. Tables come in various forms, but SQL is not aware of this. A table may also be associated with other objects such as indexes or LOBs (a large object—a structure designed for storing big items of information, such as video recordings) that are addressed implicitly. The statement will address only the table with which the other objects are associated. This chapter details table creation; Chapter 12 will cover some other object types.

When creating a table, there are certain rules that must be followed regarding the table's structure: its columns may only be of certain data types. There are also rules that can be defined for the individual rows; these are known as *constraints*. The structural rules and the constraint rules together restrict the data that can be inserted into the table.

CERTIFICATION OBJECTIVE 11.01

Categorize the Main Database Objects

There are various types of objects that can exist within a database, many more with the current release than with earlier versions. All objects have a names, and all objects are owned by someone. The "someone" is a database user, such as HR. The objects the user owns are their *schema*. An object's name must conform to certain rules.

Object Types

This query lists the object types that happen to exist in this particular database, with a count of how many there are:

```
SQL> select object_type,count(object_type) from dba_objects

  2  group by object_type order by object_type;
OBJECT_TYPE          COUNT(OBJECT_TYPE)
------------------   ------------------
CLUSTER                             10
CONSUMER GROUP                      12
CONTEXT                              6
DIMENSION                            5
DIRECTORY                            9
```

```
EDITION                        1
EVALUATION CONTEXT            13
FUNCTION                     286
INDEX                       3023
INDEX PARTITION              342
INDEXTYPE                     12
JAVA CLASS                 22018
JAVA DATA                    322
JAVA RESOURCE                820
JOB                           11
JOB CLASS                     11
LIBRARY                      177
LOB                          769
LOB PARTITION                  7
MATERIALIZED VIEW              3
OPERATOR                      60
PACKAGE                     1240
PACKAGE BODY                1178
PROCEDURE                    118
PROGRAM                       17
QUEUE                         37
RESOURCE PLAN                  7
RULE                           1
RULE SET                      21
SCHEDULE                       2
SEQUENCE                     204
SYNONYM                    26493
TABLE                       2464
TABLE PARTITION              199
TRIGGER                      413
TYPE                        2630
TYPE BODY                    231
UNDEFINED                      6
VIEW                        4669
WINDOW                         9
WINDOW GROUP                   4
XML SCHEMA                    93
42 rows selected.
```

This query addresses the view DBA_OBJECTS, which has one row for every object in the database. The numbers are low, because the database is a very small one used only for teaching. A database used for a business application might have hundreds of thousands of objects. You may not be able to see the view DBA_OBJECTS, depending on what permissions your account has. Alternate views are USER_OBJECTS, which will show all the objects owned by you, and ALL_OBJECTS, which will show all the objects to which you have been granted access (including your own). All users have access to these.

The objects of greatest interest to a SQL programmer are those that contain, or give access to, data. These are

- Tables
- Views
- Synonyms
- Indexes
- Sequences

This chapter covers tables; the others are described in Chapter 12. Briefly, a view is a stored SELECT statement that can be addressed as though it were a table. It is nothing more than a SELECT statement but, rather than running the statement itself, the user issues a SELECT statement against the view instead. In effect, the user is selecting from the result of another selection. A synonym is an alias for a table (or a view). Users can execute SQL statements against the synonym, and the database will map them into statements against the object to which the synonym points. Indexes are a means of improving access times to rows in tables. If a query requires only one row, then rather than scanning the entire table to find the row, an index can give a pointer to the row's exact location. Of course, the index itself must be searched, but this is often faster than scanning the table. A sequence is a construct that generates unique numbers. There are many cases where unique numbers are needed. Sequences issue numbers in order, on demand: it is absolutely impossible for the same number to be issued twice.

The remaining object types are less commonly relevant to a SQL programmer. Their use falls more within the realm of PL/SQL programmers and database administrators.

Users and Schemas

Many people use the terms "user" and "schema" interchangeably. In the Oracle environment, you can get away with this (though not necessarily with other database management systems). A *user* is a person who can connect to the database. The user will have a username and a password. A *schema* is a container for the objects owned by a user. When a user is created, their schema is created too. A schema is the objects owned by a user; initially, it will be empty.

Some schemas will always be empty: the user will never create any objects, because they do not need to and (if the user is set up correctly) will not have the necessary privileges anyway. Users such as this will have been granted permissions, either through direct privileges or through roles, to use code and access data in other schemas, owned by other users. Other users may be the reverse of this: they will own many objects but will never actually log on to the database. They need not even have been granted the CREATE SESSION privilege, so the account is effectively disabled (or indeed it can be locked)—these schemas are used as repositories for code and data accessed by others.

Schema objects are objects with an owner. The unique identifier for an object of a particular type is not its name—it is its name, prefixed with the name of the schema to which it belongs. Thus the table HR.REGIONS is a table called REGIONS, which is owned by user HR. There could be another table SYSTEM.REGIONS that would be a completely different table (perhaps different in both structure and contents) owned by user SYSTEM and residing in his or her schema.

A number of users (and their associated schemas) are created automatically at database creation time. Principal among these are SYS and SYSTEM. User SYS owns the data dictionary: a set of tables (in the SYS schema) that define the database and its contents. SYS also owns several hundred PL/SQL packages: code that is provided for the use of database administrators and developers. Objects in the SYS schema should never be modified with DML commands. If you were to execute DML against the data dictionary tables, you would run the risk of corrupting the data dictionary, with disastrous results. You update the data dictionary by running DDL commands (such as CREATE TABLE), which provide a layer of abstraction between you and the data dictionary itself. The SYSTEM schema stores various additional objects used for administration and monitoring.

Depending on the options selected during database creation, there may be more users created—perhaps up to 30 in total. These others are used for storing the code and data required by various options. For example, the user MDSYS stores the objects used by Oracle Spatial, an option that extends the capabilities of the Oracle database to manage geographical information.

Naming Schema Objects

A schema object is an object that is owned by a user. All schema object names must conform to certain rules:

- The name may be from 1 to 30 characters long (with the exception of database link names that may be up to 128 characters long).
- Reserved words (such as SELECT) cannot be used as object names.
- All names must begin with a letter from "A" through "Z."
- The characters in a name can only be letters, numbers, an underscore (_), the dollar sign ($), or the hash symbol (#).
- Lowercase letters will be converted to uppercase.

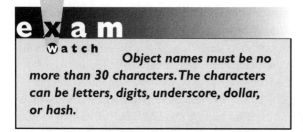

Object names must be no more than 30 characters. The characters can be letters, digits, underscore, dollar, or hash.

By enclosing the name within double quotes, all these rules (with the exception of the length) can be broken, but to get to the object, subsequently, it must always be specified with double quotes, as in the examples in Figure 11-1. Note that the same restrictions also apply to column names.

Although tools such as SQL*Plus and SQL Developer will automatically convert lowercase letters to uppercase unless the name is enclosed within double quotes; remember that object names are always case sensitive. In this example, the two tables are completely different:

```
SQL> create table lower(c1 date);
Table created.
SQL> create table "lower"(col1 varchar2(2));
Table created.
SQL> select table_name from dba_tables where
  2  lower(table_name) = 'lower';
TABLE_NAME
------------------------------
lower
LOWER
```

FIGURE 11-1

Using double quotes to use nonstandard names

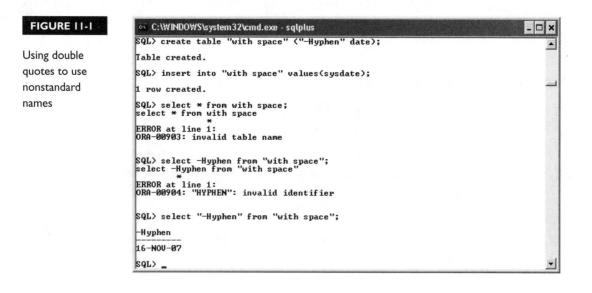

on the
!
ऀob

While it is possible to use lowercase names and nonstandard characters (even spaces), it is considered bad practice because of the confusion it can cause.

Object Namespaces

It is often said that the unique identifier for an object is the object name, prefixed with the schema name. While this is generally true, for a full understanding of naming, it is necessary to introduce the concept of a *namespace*. A namespace defines a group of object types, within which all names must be uniquely identified, by schema and name. Objects in different namespaces can share the same name.

These object types all share the same namespace:

■ Tables
■ Views
■ Sequences
■ Private synonyms

Thus it is impossible to create a view with the same name as a table—at least, it is impossible if they are in the same schema. And once created, SQL statements can address a view or a synonym as though it were a table. The fact that tables, views, and private synonyms share the same namespace means that you can set up several layers of abstraction between what the users see and the actual tables, which can be invaluable for both security and for simplifying application development. Indexes and constraints each have their own namespace. Thus it is possible for an index to have the same name as a table, even within the same schema.

EXERCISE 11-1

Determine What Objects Are Accessible to Your Session

In this exercise, query various data dictionary views as user HR to determine what objects are in the HR schema and what objects in other schemas HR has access to.

1. Connect to the database with SQL*Plus or SQL Developer as user HR.

2. Determine how many objects of each type are in the HR schema:

```
select object_type,count(*) from user_objects group by object_type;
```

The USER_OBJECTS view lists all objects owned by the schema to which the current session is connected, in this case HR.

3. Determine how many objects in total HR has permissions on:

```
select object_type,count(*) from all_objects group by object_type;
```

The ALL_OBJECTS view lists all objects to which the user has some sort of access.

4. Determine who owns the objects HR can see:

```
select distinct owner from all_objects;
```

Review the Table Structure

According to the relational database paradigm, a table is a two-dimensional structure storing rows. A row is one or more columns. Every row in the table has the same columns, as defined by the structure of the table. The Oracle database does permit variations on this two-dimensional model. Some columns can be defined as nested tables, which themselves have several columns. Other columns may be of an unbounded data type such as a binary large object, theoretically terabytes big. It is also possible to define columns as objects. The object will have an internal structure (possibly based on columns) that is not visible as part of the table.

The systems analysis phase of the system development lifecycle will have modeled the data structures needed to store the system's information into third normal form, as described in Chapter 1. The result is a set of two-dimensional tables, each with a primary key and linked to each other with foreign keys. The system design phase may have compromised this structure, perhaps by denormalizing the tables or by taking advantage of Oracle-specific capabilities such as nested tables. But the end result, as far as the SQL developer is concerned, is a set of tables.

Each table exists as a definition in the data dictionary. On creation, the table will have been assigned a limited amount of space (known as an *extent*) within the database. This may be small, perhaps only a few kilobytes or megabytes. As rows are inserted into the table, this extent will fill. When it is full, the database will (automatically) assign another extent to the table. As rows are deleted, space within the assigned extents becomes available for reuse. Even if every row is deleted, the extents remain allocated to the table. They will only be freed up and returned to the database for use elsewhere if the table is dropped or truncated (as described in Chapter 10).

EXERCISE 11-2

Investigate Table Structures

In this exercise, query various data dictionary views as user HR to determine the structure of a table.

1. Connect to the database with SQL*Plus or SQL Developer as user HR.

2. Determine the names and types of tables that exist in the HR schema:

```
select table_name,cluster_name,iot_type from user_tables;
```

Clustered tables and index organized tables (IOTs) are advanced table structures. In the HR schema, all tables are standard heap tables except for COUNTRIES which is an IOT.

3. Use the DESCRIBE command to display the structure of a table:

```
describe regions;
```

4. Retrieve similar information by querying a data dictionary view:

```
select column_name,data_type,nullable from user_tab_columns
where table_name='REGIONS';
```

CERTIFICATION OBJECTIVE 11.03

List the Data Types That Are Available for Columns

When creating tables, each column must be assigned a data type, which determines the nature of the values that can be inserted into the column. These data types are also used to specify the nature of the arguments for PL/SQL procedures and functions. When selecting a data type, you must consider the data that you need to store and the operations you will want to perform upon it. Space is also a consideration: some data types are fixed length, taking up the same number of bytes no matter what data is actually in it; others are variable. If a column is not populated, then Oracle will not give it any space at all. If you later update the row to populate the column, then the row will get bigger, no matter whether the data type is fixed length or variable.

The following are the data types for alphanumeric data:

- **VARCHAR2**   Variable-length character data, from 1 byte to 4KB. The data is stored in the database character set.
- **NVARCHAR2**   Like VARCHAR2, but the data is stored in the alternative national language character set, one of the permitted Unicode character sets.
- **CHAR**   Fixed-length character data, from 1 byte to 2KB, in the database character set. If the data is not the length of the column, then it will be padded with spaces.

on the
job

For ISO/ANSI compliance, you can specify a VARCHAR data type, but any columns of this type will be automatically converted to VARCHAR2.

The following is the data type for binary data:

- **RAW**   Variable-length binary data, from 1 byte to 4KB. Unlike the CHAR and VARCHAR2 data types, RAW data is not converted by Oracle Net from the database's character set to the user process's character set on SELECT or the other way on INSERT.

The following are the data types for numeric data, all variable length:

- **NUMBER**   Numeric data, for which you can specify precision and scale. The precision can range from to 1 to 38, the scale can range from −84 to 127.
- **FLOAT**   This is an ANSI data type, floating-point number with precision of 126 binary (or 38 decimal). Oracle also provides BINARY_FLOAT and BINARY_DOUBLE as alternatives.
- **INTEGER**   Equivalent to NUMBER, with scale zero.

The following are the data types for date and time data, all fixed length:

- **DATE**   This is either length zero, if the column is empty, or 7 bytes. All DATE data includes century, year, month, day, hour, minute, and second. The valid range is from January 1, 4712 BC to December 31, 9999 AD.
- **TIMESTAMP**   This is length zero if the column is empty, or up to 11 bytes, depending on the precision specified. Similar to DATE, but with precision of up to 9 decimal places for the seconds, 6 places by default.

- **TIMESTAMP WITH TIMEZONE** Like TIMESTAMP, but the data is stored with a record kept of the time zone to which it refers. The length may be up to 13 bytes, depending on precision. This data type lets Oracle determine the difference between two times by normalizing them to UTC, even if the times are for different time zones.

- **TIMESTAMP WITH LOCAL TIMEZONE** Like TIMESTAMP, but the data is normalized to the database time zone on saving. When retrieved, it is normalized to the time zone of the user process selecting it.

- **INTERVAL YEAR TO MONTH** Used for recording a period in years and months between two DATEs or TIMESTAMPs.

- **INTERVAL DAY TO SECOND** Used for recording a period in days and seconds between two DATEs or TIMESTAMPs.

The following are the large object data types:

- **CLOB** Character data stored in the database character set, size effectively unlimited: 4GB multiplied by the database block size.

- **NCLOB** Like CLOB, but the data is stored in the alternative national language character set, one of the permitted Unicode character sets.

- **BLOB** Like CLOB, but binary data that will not undergo character set conversion by Oracle Net.

- **BFILE** A locator pointing to a file stored on the operating system of the database server. The size of the files is limited to 4GB.

- **LONG** Character data in the database character set, up to 2GB. All the functionality of LONG (and more) is provided by CLOB; LONGs should not be used in a modern database, and if your database has any columns of this type they should be converted to CLOB. There can only be one LONG column in a table.

- **LONG RAW** Like LONG, but binary data that will not be converted by Oracle Net. Any LONG RAW columns should be converted to BLOBs.

The following is the ROWID data type:

- **ROWID** A value coded in base 64 that is the pointer to the location of a row in a table. Encrypted. Within it is the exact physical address. ROWID is an Oracle proprietary data type, not visible unless specifically selected.

The VARCHAR2 data type must be qualified with a number indicating the maximum length of the column. If a value is inserted into the column that is less than this, it is not a problem: the value will only take up as much space as it needs. If the value is longer than this maximum, the INSERT will fail with an error. If the value is updated to a longer or shorter value, the length of the column (and therefore the row itself) will change accordingly. If is not entered at all or is updated to NULL, then it will take up no space at all.

The NUMBER data type may optionally be qualified with a precision and a scale. The precision sets the maximum number of digits in the number, and the scale is how many of those digits are to the right of the decimal point. If the scale is negative, this has the effect of replacing the last digits of any number inserted with zeros, which do not count toward the number of digits specified for the precision. If the number of digits exceeds the precision, there will be an error; if it is within the precision but outside the scale, the number will be rounded (up or down) to the nearest value within the scale.

The DATE data type always includes century, year, month, day, hour, minute, and second—even if all these elements are not specified at insert time. Year, month, and date must be specified; if the hours, minutes, and seconds are omitted they will default to midnight. Using the TRUNC function on a date also has the effect of setting the hours, minutes, and seconds to midnight.

Oracle provides a range of type casting functions for converting between data types and in some circumstances will do automatic type casting. Figure 11-2 illustrates using both the manual and the automatic type casting techniques.

In the preceding example, the first INSERT uses type casting functions to convert the character data entered to the data types specified for the table columns. The second INSERT attempts to insert character strings into all three columns, but the insert still succeeds because Oracle can convert data types automatically if necessary—but only if the format of the data is suitable. Note that if the value for the date has been entered in any format other than DD-MM-YY, such as '18-Nov-07,' it would have failed.

on the
ⓙ o b   *Do not rely on automatic type casting. It can impact performance and may*
not always work. The Oracle environment is strongly typed, and programmers
should respect this.

FIGURE 11-2

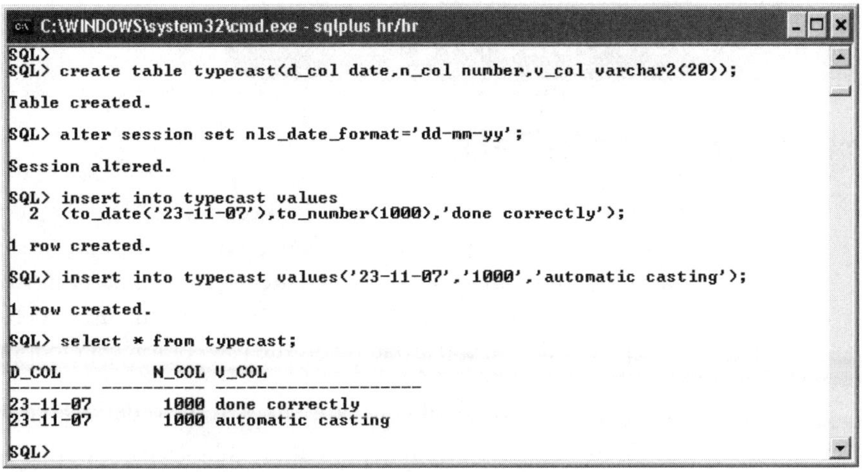

Use of type
casting functions
and automatic
type casting

```
SQL>
SQL> create table typecast(d_col date,n_col number,v_col varchar2(20));

Table created.

SQL> alter session set nls_date_format='dd-mm-yy';

Session altered.

SQL> insert into typecast values
  2  (to_date('23-11-07'),to_number(1000),'done correctly');

1 row created.

SQL> insert into typecast values('23-11-07','1000','automatic casting');

1 row created.

SQL> select * from typecast;

D_COL          N_COL V_COL
-------- ---------- --------------------
23-11-07        1000 done correctly
23-11-07        1000 automatic casting

SQL>
```

EXERCISE 11-3

Investigate the Data Types in the HR schema

In this exercise, find out what data types are used in the tables in the HR schema, using two techniques.

1. Connect to the database as user HR with SQL*Plus or SQL Developer.
2. Use the DESCRIBE command to show the data types in some tables:

```
describe employees;
describe departments;
```

3. Use a query against a data dictionary view to show what columns make up the EMPLOYEES table, as the DESCRIBE command would:

```
select column_name,data_type,nullable,data_length,data_
precision,data_scale from user_tab_columns where table_
name='EMPLOYEES';
```

The view USER_TAB_COLUMNS shows the detail of every column in every table in the current user's schema.

Create a Simple Table

Tables can be stored in the database in several ways. The simplest is the *heap* table. A heap is variable length rows in random order. There may be some correlation between the order in which rows are entered and the order in which they are stored, but this is a matter of luck. More advanced table structures, such as the following, may impose ordering and grouping on the rows or force a random distribution:

- **Index organized tables** Store rows in the order of an index key.
- **Index clusters** Can denormalize tables in parent-child relationships so that related rows from different table are stored together.
- **Hash clusters** Force a random distribution of rows, which will break down any ordering based on the entry sequence.
- **Partitioned tables** Store rows in separate physical structures, the partitions, allocating rows according to the value of a column.

Using the more advanced table structures has no effect whatsoever on SQL. Every SQL statement executed against tables defined with these options will return exactly the same results as though the tables were standard heap tables, so use of these features will not affect code. But while their use is transparent to programmers, they do give enormous benefits in performance.

Creating Tables with Column Specifications

To create a standard heap table, use this syntax:

```
CREATE TABLE [schema.]table [ORGANIZATION HEAP]
(column datatype [DEFAULT expression]
[,column datatype [DEFAULT expression]…);
```

As a minimum, specify the table name (it will be created in your own schema, if you don't specify someone else's) and at least one column with a data type. There are very few developers who ever specify ORGANIZATION HEAP, as this is the default and is industry standard SQL. The DEFAULT keyword in a column definition lets you provide an expression that will generate a value for the column when a row is inserted if a value is not provided by the INSERT statement.

Consider this statement:

```
CREATE TABLE SCOTT.EMP
(EMPNO NUMBER(4),
ENAME VARCHAR2(10),
HIREDATE DATE DEFAULT TRUNC(SYSDATE),
SAL NUMBER(7,2),
COMM NUMBER(7,2) DEFAULT 0.03);
```

This will create a table called EMP in the SCOTT schema. Either user SCOTT himself has to issue the statement (in which case nominating the schema would not actually be necessary), or another user could issue it if he has been granted permission to create tables in another user's schema. Taking the columns one by one:

- EMPNO can be 4 digits long, with no decimal places. If any decimals are included in an INSERT statement, they will be rounded (up or down) to the nearest integer.
- ENAME can store any characters at all, up to ten of them.
- HIREDATE will accept any date, optionally with the time, but if a value is not provided, today's date will be entered as at midnight.
- SAL, intended for the employee's salary, will accept numeric values with up to 7 digits. If any digits over 7 are to the right of the decimal point, they will be rounded off.
- COMM (for commission percentage) has a default value of 0.03, which will be entered if the INSERT statement does not include a value for this column.

Following creation of the table, these statements insert a row and select the result:

```
SQL> insert into scott.emp(empno,ename,sal) values(1000,'John',1000.789);
1 row created.
SQL> select * from emp;
     EMPNO ENAME      HIREDATE         SAL       COMM
---------- ---------- --------- ---------- ----------
      1000 John       19-NOV-07    1000.79        .03
```

Note that values for the columns not mentioned in the INSERT statement have been generated by the DEFAULT clauses. Had those clauses not been defined in the table definition, the columns would have been NULL. Also note the rounding of the value provided for SAL.

on the
Job

The DEFAULT clause can be useful, but it is of limited functionality. You cannot use a subquery to generate the default value: you can only specify literal values or functions.

Creating Tables from Subqueries

Rather than creating a table from nothing and then inserting rows into it (as in the previous section), tables can be created from other tables by using a subquery. This technique lets you create the table definition and populate the table with rows with just one statement. Any query at all can be used as the source of both the table structure and the rows. The syntax is as follows:

CREATE TABLE [*schema.*]*table* AS *subquery*;

All queries return a two-dimensional set of rows; this result is stored as the new table. A simple example of creating a table with a subquery is:

```
create table employees_copy as select * from employees;
```

This statement will create a table EMPLOYEES_COPY, which is an exact copy of the EMPLOYEES table, identical in both definition and the rows it contains. Any not null and check constraints on the columns will also be applied to the new table, but any primary-key, unique, or foreign-key constraints will not be. (Constraints are discussed in section 11.05, "Explain How Constraints Are Created at the Time of Table Creation.") This is because these three types of constraints require indexes that might not be available or desired.

The following is a more complex example:

```
create table emp_dept as select

last_name ename,department_name dname,round(sysdate - hire_date) service
from employees natural join departments order by dname,ename;
```

The rows in the new table will be the result of joining the two source tables, with two of the selected columns having their names changed. The new SERVICE column will be populated with the result of the arithmetic that computes the number of days since the employee was hired. The rows will be inserted in the order specified. This ordering will not be maintained by subsequent DML but, assuming the standard HR schema data, the new table will look like this:

```
SQL> select * from emp_dept where rownum < 10;
ENAME           DNAME              SERVICE
--------------- ---------------- ----------
Gietz           Accounting            4914
```

```
De Haan          Executive              5424
Kochhar          Executive              6634
Chen             Finance                3705
Faviet           Finance                4844
Popp             Finance                2905
Sciarra          Finance                3703
Urman            Finance                3545
Austin           IT                     3800
9 rows selected.
```

The subquery can of course include a WHERE clause to restrict the rows inserted into the new table. To create a table with no rows, use a WHERE clause that will exclude all rows:

```
create table no_emps as select * from employees where 1=2;
```

The WHERE clause 1=2 can never return TRUE, so the table structure will be created ready for use, but no rows will be inserted at creation time.

Altering Table Definitions after Creation

There are many alterations that can be made to a table after creation. Those that affect the physical storage fall into the domain of the database administrator, but many changes are purely logical and will be carried out by the SQL developers. The following are examples (for the most part self-explanatory):

- Adding columns:

  ```
  alter table emp add (job_id number);
  ```

- Modifying columns:

  ```
  alter table emp modify (comm number(4,2) default 0.05);
  ```

- Dropping columns:

  ```
  alter table emp drop column comm;
  ```

- Marking columns as unused:

  ```
  alter table emp set unused column job_id;
  ```

- Renaming columns:

  ```
  alter table emp rename column hiredate to recruited;
  ```

- Marking the table as read-only:

  ```
  alter table emp read only;
  ```

All of these changes are DDL commands with the built-in COMMIT. They are therefore nonreversible and will fail if there is an active transaction against the table. They are also virtually instantaneous with the exception of dropping a column. Dropping a column can be a time-consuming exercise because as each column is dropped, every row must be restructured to remove the column's data. The SET UNUSED command, which makes columns nonexistent as far as SQL is concerned, is often a better alternative, followed when convenient by

```
ALTER TABLE tablename DROP UNUSED COLUMNS;
```

which will drop all the unused columns in one pass through the table.

Marking a table as read-only will cause errors for any attempted DML commands. But the table can still be dropped. This can be disconcerting but is perfectly logical when you think it through. A DROP command doesn't actually affect the table: it affects the tables in the data dictionary that define the table, and these are not read-only.

Dropping and Truncating Tables

The TRUNCATE TABLE command was described in Chapter 10: it has the effect of removing every row from a table, while leaving the table definition intact. DROP TABLE is more drastic in that the table definition is removed as well. The syntax is as follows:

DROP TABLE [*schema.*]*tablename* ;

If *schema* is not specified, then the table called *tablename* in your currently logged on schema will be dropped.

As with a TRUNCATE, SQL will not produce a warning before the table is dropped, and furthermore, as with any DDL command, it includes a COMMIT. A DROP is therefore absolutely nonreversible. But there are some restrictions: if any session (even your own) has a transaction in progress that includes a row in the table, then the DROP will fail, and it is also impossible to drop a table that is referred to in a foreign key constraint defined for a another table. This table (or the constraint) must be dropped first.

EXERCISE 11-4

Create Tables

In this exercise, use SQL Developer to create a heap table, insert some rows with a subquery, and modify the table. Do some more modifications with SQL*Plus, then drop the table.

1. Connect to the database as user HR with SQL Developer.
2. Right-click the Tables branch of the navigation tree, and click New Table.
3. Name the new table EMPS, and use the Add Column button to set it up as in the following illustration:

4. Click the DDL tab to see if the statement that has been constructed. It should look like this:

```
CREATE TABLE EMPS
(
  EMPNO NUMBER,
  ENAME VARCHAR2(25),
```

```
SALARY NUMBER,
DEPTNO NUMBER(4, 0)
)
;
```

Return to the Table tab (as in the preceding illustration) and click OK to create the table.

5. Run this statement:

```
insert into emps select employee_id,last_name,salary,department_id
from employees;
```

and commit the insert:

```
commit;
```

6. Right-click the EMPS table in the SQL Developer navigator, click Column and Add.

7. Define a new column HIRED, type DATE, as in the following illustration below; and click Apply to create the column.

8. Connect to the database as HR with SQL*Plus.

9. Define a default for HIRED column in the EMPS table:

```
alter table emps modify (hired default sysdate);
```

10. Insert a row without specifying a value for HIRED and check that the new row does have a HIRED date but that the other rows do not:

```
insert into emps (empno,ename) values(99,'Newman');
select hired,count(1) from emps group by hired;
```

11. Tidy up by dropping the new table:

```
drop table emps;
```

CERTIFICATION OBJECTIVE 11.05

Explain How Constraints Are Created at the Time of Table Creation

Table constraints are a means by which the database can enforce business rules, and guarantee that the data conforms to the entity-relationship model determined by the systems analysis that defines the application data structures. For example, the business analysts of your organization may have decided that every customer and every invoice must be uniquely identifiable by number, that no invoices can be issued to a customer before that customer has been created, and that every invoice must have a valid date and a value greater than zero. These would implemented by creating primary-key constraints on the CUSTOMER_NUMBER column of the CUSTOMERS table and the INVOICE_NUMBER column of the INVOICES table, a foreign-key constraint on the INVOICES table referencing the CUSTOMERS table, a not-null constraint on the DATE column of the INVOICES table (the DATE data type will itself ensure that that any dates are valid automatically—it will not accept invalid dates), and a check constraint on the AMOUNT column on the INVOICES table.

When any DML is executed against a table with constraints defined, if the DML violates a constraint, then the whole statement will be rolled back automatically. Remember that a DML statement that affects many rows might partially succeed before it hits a constraint problem with a particular row. If the statement is part of a multistatement transaction, then the statements that have already succeeded will remain intact but uncommitted.

The Types of Constraints

The constraint types supported by the Oracle database are as follows:

UNIQUE

NOT NULL

PRIMARY KEY

FOREIGN KEY

CHECK

Constraints have names. It is good practice to specify the names with a standard naming convention, but if they are not explicitly named, Oracle will generate names.

Unique Constraints

A unique constraint nominates a column (or combination of columns) for which the value must be different for every row in the table. If based on a single column, this is known as the *key* column. If the constraint is composed of more than one column (known as a *composite key* unique constraint) the columns do not have to be the same data type or be adjacent in the table definition.

An oddity of unique constraints is that it is possible to enter a NULL value into the key column(s); it is indeed possible to have any number of rows with NULL values in their key column(s). So selecting rows on a key column will guarantee that only one row is returned—unless you search for NULL, in which case all the rows where the key columns are NULL will be returned.

Unique constraints are enforced by an index. When a unique constraint is defined, Oracle will look for an index on the key column(s), and if one does not exist it will be created. Then whenever a row is inserted, Oracle will search the index to see if the values of the key columns are already present: if they are, it will reject the insert. The structure of these indexes (known as B*Tree indexes) does not include NULL values, which is why many rows with NULL are permitted: they simply do not exist in the index. While the first purpose of the index is to enforce the constraint, it has a secondary effect: improving performance if the key columns are used in the WHERE clauses of SQL statements. However, selecting WHERE `key_column` IS NULL cannot use the index because it doesn't include the NULLs and will therefore always result in a scan of the entire table.

Not Null Constraints

The not null constraint forces values to be entered into the key column. Not null constraints are defined per column: if the business requirement is that a group of columns should all have values, you cannot define one not null constraint for the whole group, but instead must define a not null constraint for each column.

Any attempt to insert a row without specifying values for the not null constrained columns results in an error. It is possible to bypass the need to specify a value by including a DEFAULT clause on the column when creating the table, as discussed in the previous section on creating tables.

Primary Key Constraints

The primary key is the means of locating a single row in a table. The relational database paradigm includes a requirement that every table should have a primary key, a column (or combination of columns) that can be used to distinguish every row. The Oracle database deviates from the paradigm (as do some other RDBMS implementations) by permitting tables without primary keys.

on the **Job** *Tables without primary keys are possible but not a good idea. Even if the business rules do not require the ability to identify every row, primary keys are often needed for maintenance work.*

The implementation of a primary key constraint is, in effect, the union of a unique constraint and a not null constraint. The key columns must have unique values, and they may not be null. As with unique constraints, an index must exist on the constrained column(s). If one does not exist already, an index will be created when the constraint is defined. A table can have only one primary key. Try to create a second, and you will get an error. A table can, however, have any number of unique constraints and not null columns, so if there are several columns that the business analysts have decided must be unique and populated, one of these can be designated the primary key and the others made unique and not null. An example could be a table of employees, where e-mail address, social security number, and employee number should all be required and unique.

exam **Watch** *A primary key constraint is a unique constraint combined with a not null constraint.*

Foreign Key Constraints

A foreign key constraint is defined on the child table in a parent-child relationship. The constraint nominates a column (or columns) in the child table that corresponds to the primary key column(s) in the parent table. The columns do not have to have the same names, but they must be of the same data type. Foreign key constraints define the relational structure of the database: the many-to-one relationships that connect the table, in their third normal form.

If the parent table has unique constraints as well as (or instead of) a primary key constraint, these columns can be used as the basis of foreign key constraints, even if they are nullable.

Just as a unique constraint permits null values in the constrained column, so does a foreign key constraint. You can insert rows into the child table with null foreign key columns—even if there is not a row in the parent table with a null value. This creates *orphan* rows and can cause dreadful confusion. As a general rule, all the columns in a unique constraint and all the columns in a foreign key constraint are best defined with not null constraints as well; this will often be a business requirement.

Attempting to inset a row in the child table for which there is no matching row in the parent table will give an error. Similarly, deleting a row in the parent table will give an error if there are already rows referring to it in the child table. There are two techniques for changing this behavior. First, the constraint may be created as ON DELETE CASCADE. This means that if a row in the parent table is deleted, Oracle will search the child table for all the matching rows and delete them too. This will happen automatically. A less drastic technique is to create the constraint as ON DELETE SET NULL. In this case, if a row in the parent table is deleted, Oracle will search the child table for all the matching rows and set the foreign key columns to null. This means that the child rows will be orphaned, but will still exist. If the columns in the child table also have a not null constraint, then the deletion from the parent table will fail.

It is not possible to drop or truncate the parent table in a foreign key relationship, even if there are no rows in the child table. This still applies if the ON DELETE SET NULL or ON DELETE CASCADE clauses were used.

A variation on the foreign key constraint is the *self-referencing* foreign key constraint. This defines a condition where the parent and child rows exist in the same table. An example would be a table of employees, which includes a column for the employee's manager. The manager is himself an employee and must exist in the table. So if the primary key is the EMPLOYEE_NUMBER column, and the manager is identified by a column MANAGER_NUMBER, then the foreign key constraint will state that the value of the MANAGER_NUMBER column must refer back to a valid EMPLOYEE_NUMBER. If an employee is his own manager, then the row would refer to itself.

Check Constraints

A check constraint can be used to enforce simple rules, such as that the value entered in a column must be within a range of values. The rule must be an expression which will evaluate to TRUE or FALSE. The rules can refer to absolute values entered as literals or to other columns in the same row and may make use of some functions. As many check constraints as you want can be applied to one column, but it is not possible to use a subquery to evaluate whether a value is permissible or to use functions such as SYSDATE.

on the *!* o b *The not null constraint is in fact implemented as a preconfigured check constraint.*

Defining Constraints

Constraints can be defined when creating a table or added to the table later. When defining constraints at table creation time, the constraint can be defined in line with the column to which it refers or at the end of the table definition. There is more flexibility to using the latter technique. For example, it is impossible to define a foreign key constraint that refers to two columns, or a check constraint that refers to any column other than that being constrained if the constraint is defined in line, but both of these are possible if the constraint is defined at the end of the table.

SCENARIO & SOLUTION	
You are designing table structures for a human resources application. The business analysts have said that when an employee leaves the company, his employee record should be moved to an archive table. Can constraints help?	Probably not. Constraints are intended to enforce simple business rules: this may be too complicated. It may well be necessary to use a DML trigger on the live table, which will automatically insert a row into the archive table whenever an employee is deleted from the live table. Triggers can do much more complicated processing than a constraint.
Active transactions block some DDL statements against tables. If you want to add a constraint or rename a column in a busy table and find the statement always fails with "ORA-00054: resource busy and acquire with NOWAIT specified or timeout expired," what can you do?	Perhaps you shouldn't be doing this sort of thing when the database is in use, but should wait until the next period of scheduled downtime. However, if you really need to make the change in a hurry, ask the database administrator to quiesce the database: this is a process that will freeze all user sessions. If you are very quick, you can make the change then unquiesce the database before end users complain.

For the constraints that require an index (the unique and primary key constraints), the index will be created with the table if the constraint is defined at table creation time.

Consider these two table creation statements (to which line numbers have been added):

```
1   create table dept(
2   deptno number(2,0) constraint dept_deptno_pk primary key
3   constraint dept_deptno_ck check (deptno between 10 and 90),
4   dname varchar2(20) constraint dept_dname_nn not null);
5   create table emp(
6   empno number(4,0) constraint emp_empno_pk primary key,
7   ename varchar2(20) constraint emp_ename_nn not null,
8   mgr number (4,0) constraint emp_mgr_fk references emp (empno),
9   dob date,
10  hiredate date,
11  deptno number(2,0) constraint emp_deptno_fk references dept(deptno)
12  on delete set null,
13  email varchar2(30) constraint emp_email_uk unique,
14  constraint emp_hiredate_ck check (hiredate >= dob + 365*16),
15  constraint emp_email_ck
16  check ((instr(email,'@') > 0) and (instr(email,'.') > 0)));
```

Taking these statements line by line:

1. The first table created is DEPT, intended to have one row for each department.
2. DEPTNO is numeric, 2 digits, no decimals. This is the table's primary key. The constraint is named DEPT_DEPTNO_PK.
3. A second constraint applied to DEPTNO is a check limiting it to numbers in the range 10 to 90. The constraint is named DEPT_DEPTNO_CK.
4. The DNAME column is variable length characters, with a constraint DEPT_DNAME_NN making it not nullable.
5. The second table created is EMP, intended to have one row for every employee.
6. EMPNO is numeric, up to 4 digits with no decimals. Constraint EMP_EMPNO_PK marks this as the table's primary key.
7. ENAME is variable length characters, with a constraint EMP_ENAME_NN making it not nullable.
8. MGR is the employee's manager, who must himself be an employee. The column is defined in the same way as the table's primary key column of EMPNO. The constraint EMP_MGR_FK defines this column as a self-referencing

foreign key, so any value entered must refer to an already extant row in EMP (though it is not constrained to be not null, so can be left blank).

9. DOB, the employee's birthday, is a date and not constrained.

10. HIREDATE is the date the employee was hired and is not constrained. At least, not yet.

11. DEPTNO is the department with which the employee is associated. The column is defined in the same way as the DEPT table's primary key column of DEPTNO, and the constraint EMP_DEPTNO_FK enforces a foreign key relationship: it is not possible to assign an employee to a department that does not exist. Though this is nullable.

12. The EMP_DEPTO_FK constraint is further defined as ON DELETE SET NULL, so if the parent row in DEPT is deleted, all matching child rows in EMPNO will have DEPTNO set to NULL.

13. EMAIL is variable length character data, and must be unique if entered (though it can be left empty).

14. This defines an additional table level constraint EMP_HIREDATE_CK. The constraint checks for use of child labor by rejecting any rows where the date of hiring is not at least 16 years later than the birthday. This constraint could not be defined in line with HIREDATE, because the syntax does not allow references to other columns at that point.

15. An additional constraint EMP_EMAIL_CK is added to the EMAIL column, which makes two checks on the e-mail address. The INSTR functions search for the at symbol (@ and dot (.) characters (which will always be present in a valid e-mail address); if it can't find both of them, the check condition will return FALSE and the row will be rejected.

The preceding examples show several possibilities for defining constraints at table creation time. The following are further possibilities not covered:

- Controlling the index creation for the unique and primary key constraints
- Defining whether the constraint should be checked at insert time (which it is by default) or later on when the transaction is committed
- Stating whether the constraint is in fact being enforced at all (which is the default) or is disabled

It is possible to create tables with no constraints and then to add them later with an ALTER TABLE command. The end result will be the same, but this technique does make the code less self documenting, as the complete table definition will then be spread over several statements rather than being in one.

Work with Constraints

Use SQL*Plus or SQL Developer to create tables, add constraints, and demonstrate their use.

1. Connect to the database as user HR.
2. Create a table EMP as a copy of some columns from EMPLOYEES:

```
create table emp as

select employee_id empno, last_name ename, department_id deptno

from employees;
```

3. Create a table DEPT as a copy of some columns from DEPARTMENTS:

```
create table dept as

select department_id deptno, department_name dname from departments;
```

4. Use DESCRIBE to describe the structure of the new tables. Note that the not null constraint on ENAME and DNAME has been carried over from the source tables.

5. Add a primary key constraint to EMP and to DEPT and a foreign key constraint linking the tables:

```
alter table emp add constraint emp_pk primary key (empno);
alter table dept add constraint dept_pk primary key (deptno);
alter table emp add constraint

dept_fk foreign key (deptno) references dept on delete set null;
```

The preceding last constraint does not specify which column of DEPT to reference; this will default to the primary key column.

6. Demonstrate the effectiveness of the constraints by trying to insert data that will violate them:

```
insert into dept values(10,'New Department');
insert into emp values(9999,'New emp',99);
truncate table dept;
```

INSIDE THE EXAM

Using DDL Statements to Create and Manage Tables

The CREATE TABLE statement can be very complex indeed. The SQL Reference volume of the Oracle Database 11g documentation set devotes 69 pages to it, with another 85 pages for ALTER TABLE (by contrast, DROP TABLE takes only four pages). For examination purposes, only knowledge of the simplest table structure—the heap table—is required, with knowledge of the most basic data types. Understanding, defining, and using constraints is needed but not the methods for controlling when (or if) they are enforced.

7. Tidy up by dropping the tables. Note that this must be done in the correct order:

```
drop table emp;
drop table dept;
```

CERTIFICATION SUMMARY

Tables are two-dimensional structures consisting of rows of columns of defined data types. The Oracle database does permit user-defined data types, but for the most part you will be using the built-in data types.

Tables can be created from scratch: defining every column and then inserting rows. Alternatively, tables can be created using the output of a query. This latter technique can define the table and insert rows in one command, but there are limitations: it will be necessary to add primary key and unique constraints later, whereas they can be defined at table creation time using the former technique.

To assist with enforcing business rules, constraints can be defined for columns. These will maintain data integrity by making it absolutely impossible to insert data that breaks the rules.

✓ TWO-MINUTE DRILL

Categorize the Main Database Objects

- ❑ Some objects contain data, principally tables and indexes.
- ❑ Programmatic objects such as stored procedures and functions are executable code.
- ❑ Views and synonyms are objects that give access to other objects.

Review the Table Structure

- ❑ Tables are two-dimensional structures, storing rows defined with columns.
- ❑ Tables exist within a schema. The schema name with the table name make a unique identifier.

List the Data Types that Are Available for Columns

- ❑ The most common character data types are VARCHAR2, NUMBER, and DATE.
- ❑ There are many other data types.

Create a Simple Table

- ❑ Tables can be created from nothing or with a subquery.
- ❑ After creation, column definitions can be added, dropped, or modified.
- ❑ The table definition can include default values for columns.

Explain How Constraints Are Created at the Time of Table Creation

- ❑ Constraints can be defined at table creation time or added later.
- ❑ A constraint can be defined inline with its column or at the table level after the columns.
- ❑ Table-level constraints can be more complex than those defined inline.
- ❑ A table may only have one primary key but can have many unique keys.
- ❑ A primary key is functionally equivalent to unique plus not null.
- ❑ A unique constraint does not stop insertion of many null values.
- ❑ Foreign key constraints define the relationships between tables.

SELF TEST

The following questions will help you measure your understanding of the material presented in this chapter. Read all the choices carefully because there might be more than one correct answer. Choose all the correct answers for each question.

Categorize the Main Database Objects

1. If a table is created without specifying a schema, in which schema will it be? (Choose the best answer.)
   A. It will be an *orphaned* table, without a schema.
   B. The creation will fail.
   C. It will be in the SYS schema.
   D. It will be in the schema of the user creating it.
   E. It will be in the PUBLIC schema.

2. Several object types share the same namespace, and therefore cannot have the same name in the same schema. Which of the following object types is not in the same namespace as the others? (Choose the best answer.)
   A. Index
   B. PL/SQL stored procedure
   C. Synonym
   D. Table
   E. View

3. Which of these statements will fail because the table name is not legal? (Choose two answers.)
   A. create table "SELECT" (col1 date);
   B. create table "lowercase" (col1 date);
   C. create table number1 (col1 date);
   D. create table 1number (col1 date);
   E. create table update (col1 date);

Review the Table Structure

4. What are distinguishing characteristics of heap tables? (Choose two answers.)
   A. A heap can store variable length rows.
   B. More than one table can store rows in a single heap.
   C. Rows in a heap are in random order.

D. Heap tables cannot be indexed.

E. Tables in a heap do not have a primary key.

List the Data Types that Are Available for Columns

5. Which of the following data types are variable length? (Choose all correct answers.)

A. BLOB

B. CHAR

C. LONG

D. NUMBER

E. RAW

F. VARCHAR2

6. Study these statements:

```
create table tab1 (c1 number(1), c2 date);
alter session set nls_date_format='dd-mm-yy';
insert into tab1 values (1.1,'31-01-07');
```

Will the insert succeed? (Choose the best answer)

A. The insert will fail because the 1.1 is too long.

B. The insert will fail because the '31-01-07' is a string, not a date.

C. The insert will fail for both reasons A and B.

D. The insert will succeed.

7. Which of the following is not supported by Oracle as an internal data type? (Choose the best answer.)

A. CHAR

B. FLOAT

C. INTEGER

D. STRING

Create a Simple Table

8. Consider this statement:

```
create table t1 as select * from regions where 1=2;
```

What will be the result? (Choose the best answer.)

A. There will be an error because of the impossible condition.

B. No table will be created because the condition returns FALSE.

C. The table T1 will be created but no rows inserted because the condition returns FALSE.

D. The table T1 will be created and every row in REGIONS inserted because the condition returns a NULL as a row filter.

9. When a table is created with a statement such as the following:

```
create table newtab as select * from tab;
```

will there be any constraints on the new table? (Choose the best answer.)

A. The new table will have no constraints, because constraints are not copied when creating tables with a subquery.

B. All the constraints on TAB will be copied to NEWTAB.

C. Primary key and unique constraints will be copied but not check and not null constraints.

D. Check and not null constraints will be copied but not unique or primary key.

E. All constraints will be copied, except foreign key constraints.

Explain How Constraints Are Created at the Time of Table Creation

10. Which types of constraint require an index? (Choose all that apply.)

A. CHECK

B. NOT NULL

C. PRIMARY KEY

D. UNIQUE

11. A transaction consists of two statements. The first succeeds, but the second (which updates several rows) fails partway through because of a constraint violation. What will happen? (Choose the best answer.)

A. The whole transaction will be rolled back.

B. The second statement will be rolled back completely, and the first will be committed.

C. The second statement will be rolled back completely, and the first will remain uncommitted.

D. Only the one update that caused the violation will be rolled back; everything else will be committed.

E. Only the one update that caused the violation will be rolled back; everything else will remain uncommitted.

LAB QUESTION

Consider this simple analysis of a telephone billing system:

A subscriber is identified by a customer number and also has a name and possibly one or more telephones.

A telephone is identified by its number, which must be a 7-digit integer beginning with 2 or 3, and also has a make, an activation date, and a flag for whether it is active. Inactive telephones are not assigned to a subscriber; active telephones are.

For every call, it is necessary to record the time it started and the time it finished.

Create tables with constraints and defaults that can be used to implement this system.

SELF TEST ANSWERS

Categorize the Main Database Objects

1. ☑ **D.** The schema will default to the current user.
   ☒ **A, B, C, E. A** is wrong because all tables must be in a schema. **B** is wrong because the creation will succeed. **C** is wrong because the SYS schema is not a default schema. **E** is wrong because while there is a notional user PUBLIC, he does not have a schema at all.

2. ☑ **A.** Indexes have their own namespace.
   ☒ **B, C, D, E.** Stored procedures, synonyms, tables, and views exist in the same namespace.

3. ☑ **D, E. D** violates the rule that a table name must begin with a letter, and **E** violates the rule that a table name cannot be a reserved word. Both rules can be bypassed by using double quotes.
   ☒ **A, B, C.** These are wrong because all will succeed (though **A** and **B** are not exactly sensible).

Review the Table Structure

4. ☑ **A, C.** A heap is a table of variable length rows in random order.
   ☒ **B, D, E. B** is wrong because a heap table can only be one table. **D** and **E** are wrong because a heap table can (and usually will) have indexes and a primary key.

List the Data Types that Are Available for Columns

5. ☑ **A, C, D, E, F.** All these are variable length data types.
   ☒ **B.** CHAR columns are fixed length.

6. ☑ **D.** The number will be rounded to 1 digit, and the string will cast as a date.
   ☒ **A, B, C.** Automatic rounding and type casting will correct the "errors," though ideally they would not occur.

7. ☑ **D.** STRING is not an internal data type.
   ☒ **A, B, C.** CHAR, FLOAT, and INTEGER are all internal data types, though not as widely used as some others.

Create a Simple Table

8. ☑ **C.** The condition applies only to the rows selected for insert, not to the table creation.
   ☒ **A, B, D. A** is wrong because the statement is syntactically correct. **B** is wrong because the condition does not apply to the DDL, only to the DML. **D** is wrong because the condition will exclude all rows from selection.

9. ☑ **D.** Check and not null constraints are not dependent on any structures other than the table to which they apply and so can safely be copied to a new table.
☒ **A, B,C, E. A** is wrong because not null and check constraint will be applied to the new table. **B, C,** and **E** are wrong because these constraints need other objects (indexes or a parent table) and so are not copied.

Explain How Constraints Are Created at the Time of Table Creation

10. ☑ **C, D.** Unique and primary key constraints are enforced with indexes.
☒ **A, B.** Check and not null constraints do not rely on indexes.

11. ☑ **C.** A constraint violation will force a roll back of the current statement but nothing else.
☒ **A, B, D, E. A** is wrong because all statements that have succeeded remain intact. **B** and **D** are wrong because there is no commit of anything until it is specifically requested. **E** is wrong because the whole statement will be rolled back, not just the failed row.

LAB ANSWER

A possible solution:

■ The SUBSCRIBERS table:

```
create table subscribers
(id number(4,0) constraint sub_id_pk primary key,
name varchar2(20) constraint sub_name_nn not null);
```

■ The TELEPHONES table:

```
create table telephones
(telno number (7,0) constraint tel_telno_pk primary key
constraint tel_telno_ck check (telno between 1000000 and 9999999),
activated date default sysdate,
active varchar2(1) constraint tel_active_nn not null
constraint tel_active_ck check(active='Y' or active='N'),
subscriber number(4,0) constraint tel_sub_fk references subscribers,
constraint tel_active_yn check((active='Y' and subscriber is not null)
or (active='N' and subscriber is null))
);
```

This table has a constraint on the ACTIVE column that will permit only Y or N, depending on whether there is a value in the SUBSCRIBER column. This constraint is too complex to define in line with the column, because it references other columns. SUBSCRIBER, if not null, must match a row in SUBSCRIBERS.

■ The CALLS table:

```
create table calls
(telno number (7,0) constraint calls_telno_fk references telephones,
starttime date constraint calls_start_nn not null,
endtime date constraint calls_end_nn not null,
constraint calls_pk primary key(telno,starttime),
constraint calls_endtime_ck check(endtime > starttime));
```

Two constraints are defined at the table level, not the column level. The primary key cannot be defined in line with a column because it is based on two columns: one telephone can make many calls, but not two that begin at the same time (at least, not with current technology). The final constraint compares the start and end times of the call and so cannot be defined in line.

12
Creating Other Schema Objects

S
o far, most of the SQL statements used in this book have addressed tables. This seems reasonable: SQL commands interact with data, and data is stored in tables. In practice, most users never issue SQL that addresses tables: they issue SQL that addresses views or synonyms. Views and synonyms do not themselves store data; they provide a layer of abstraction between the users and the data. As tables, views, and synonyms share the same namespace, users need never be aware of which they are addressing.

Sequences are a mechanism for issuing unique numbers. In many databases, primary key values are defined as a unique number. A sequence can issue such numbers on demand, without programmers needing to worry about whether they really are unique. The structure of a sequence means that hundreds of numbers can, if necessary, be issued every second without any performance issues.

Index management is sometimes said to lie in the database administration domain, not the SQL developer's domain. For this reason, the treatment here is very brief. But whether or not index management is part of the developer's job, all developers must understand the purpose and design of indexes. In many cases the indexing strategy is crucial to adequate performance: get it right, and the benefits will be enormous; get it wrong, and the results may be disastrous. Use of indexes is transparent, but if the programmers are aware of them they can ensure that their code will be able to make the best use of what indexes are available and advise on what indexes should be created.

CERTIFICATION OBJECTIVE 12.01

Create Simple and Complex Views

To the user, a view looks like a table: a two-dimensional structure of rows of columns, against which the user can run SELECT and DML statements. The programmer knows the truth: a view is just a SELECT statement. Any SELECT statement returns a two-dimensional set of rows. If the SELECT statement is saved as a view, then whenever the users query or update rows in the view (under the impression that it is table), the statement runs, and the result is presented to users as though it were a table. The SELECT statement on which a view is based can be anything. It can join tables, perform aggregations, or do sorts; absolutely anything that is legal in the SELECT command can be used. However, if the view is *complex*, then only SELECT statements can be run against it. A *simple* view is one which can be addressed by DML statements as well as SELECT. As might be expected, simple views are based on relatively simple SELECT statements; complex views are based on more complicated statements.

Why Use Views at All?

It is usually not a good idea to let end users loose on tables. Possible reasons include:

- Security.
- Simplifying user SQL.
- Preventing error.
- Making data comprehensible. Table and column names are often long and pretty meaningless. The view and its columns can be much more obvious.
- Performance.

Examples of views for each of these purposes follow.

Views to Enforce Security

It may be that users should only see certain rows or columns of a table. There are several ways of enforcing this, but a view is often the simplest. Consider the HR.EMPLOYEES table. This includes personal details that should not be visible to staff outside the personnel department. But finance staff will need to be able to see the costing information. This view will depersonalize the data:

```
create view hr.emp_fin as select
hire_date,job_id,salary,commission_pct,department_id from hr.employees;
```

Note the use of schema qualifiers for the table as the source of the data (often referred to as either the *base* or the *detail* table) and the view: views are schema objects and can draw their data from tables in the same schema or in other schemas. If the schema is not specified, it will of course be in the current schema.

Finance staff can then be given permission to see the view but not the table and can issue statements such as this:

```
select * from emp_fin where department_id=50;
```

They will see only the five columns that make up the view, not the remaining columns of EMPLOYEES with the personal information. The view can be joined to other tables or aggregated as though it were a table:

```
select department_name, sum(salary) from departments natural join emp_fin
group by department_name;
```

A well constructed set of views can implement a whole security structure within the database, giving users access to data they need to see while concealing data they do not need to see.

Views to Simplify User SQL

It will be much easier for users to query data if the hard work (such as joins or aggregations) is done for them by the code that defines the view. In the last example, the user had to write code that joined the EMP_FIN view to the DEPARTMENTS table and summed the salaries per department. This could all be done in a view:

```
create view dept_sal as
select d.department_name, sum(e.salary) from
departments d left outer join employees e on d.department_
id=e.department_id
group by department_name order by department_name;
```

Then the users can select from DEPT_SAL without needing to know anything about joins, or even how to sort the results:

```
select * from dept_sal;
```

In particular, they do not need to know how to make sure that all departments are listed, even those with no employees. The example in the previous section would have missed these.

Views to Prevent Errors

It is impossible to prevent users making errors, but well constructed views can prevent some errors arising from a lack of understanding of how data should be interpreted. The previous section already introduced this concept by constructing a view that will list all departments, irrespective of whether they currently have staff assigned to them.

A view can help to present data in a way that is unambiguous. For example, many applications never actually delete rows. Consider this table:

```
create table emp(empno number constraint emp_empno_pk primary key,
ename varchar2(10),deptno number,active varchar2(1) default 'Y');
```

The column ACTIVE is a flag indicating that the employee is currently employed and will default to 'Y' when a row is inserted. When a user, through the user interface, "deletes" an employee, the underlying SQL statement will be an update that sets ACTIVE to 'N'. If users who are not aware of this query the table, they may severely misinterpret the results. It will often be better to give them access to a view:

```
create view current_staff as select * from emp where active='Y';
```

Queries addressed to this view cannot possibly see "deleted" staff members.

Views to Make Data Comprehensible

The data structures in a database will be normalized tables. It is not reasonable to expect users to understand normalized structures. To take an example from the Oracle E-Business suite, a "customer" in the Accounts Receivable module is in fact an entity consisting of information distributed across the tables HZ_PARTIES, HZ_PARTY_SITES, HZ_CUST_ACCTS_ALL, and many more. All these tables are linked by primary key–to–foreign key relationships, but these are not defined on any identifiers visible to users (such as a customer number): they are based on columns the users never see that have values generated internally from sequences. The forms and reports used to retrieve customer information never address these tables directly; they all work through views.

As well as presenting data to users in a comprehensible form, the use of views to provide a layer of abstraction between the objects seen by users and the objects stored within the database can be invaluable for maintenance work. It becomes possible to redesign the data structures without having to recode the application. If tables are changed, then adjusting the view definitions may make any changes to the SQL and PL/SQL code unnecessary. This can be a powerful technique for making applications portable across different databases.

Views for Performance

The SELECT statement behind a view can be optimized by programmers, so that users don't need to worry about tuning code. There may be many possibilities for getting the same result, but some techniques can be much slower than others. For example, when joining two tables there is usually a choice between the *nested loop* join and the *hash* join. A nested loop join uses an index to get to individual rows; a hash join reads the whole table into memory. The choice between the two will be dependent on the state of the data and the hardware resources available.

Theoretically, one can always rely on the Oracle optimizer to work out the best way to run a SQL statement, but there are cases where it gets it wrong. If the programmers know which technique is best, they can instruct the optimizer. This example forces use of the hash technique:

```
create view dept_emp as
select /*+USE_HASH (employees departments)*/ department_name, last_name
from departments natural join employees;
```

Whenever users query the DEPT_EMP view, the join will be performed by scanning the detail tables into memory. The users need not know the syntax for forcing use of this join method. You do not need to know it, either: this is beyond the scope of the OCP SQL examination, but the concept of tuning with view design should be known.

Simple and Complex Views

For practical purposes, classification of a view as *simple* or *complex* is related to whether DML statements can be executed against it: simple views can accept DML statements, complex views can't. The strict definitions are as follows:

- A simple view draws data from one detail table, uses no functions, and does no aggregation.
- A complex view can join detail tables, use functions, and perform aggregations.

Applying these definitions shows that of the four views used as examples in the previous section, the first and third are simple and the second and fourth are complex.

It is often not possible to execute INSERT, UPDATE, or DELETE commands against a complex view. The mapping of the rows in the view back to the rows in the detail table(s) cannot always be established on a one-to-one basis, which is necessary for DML operations. It is usually possible to execute DML against a simple view but not always. For example, if the view does not include a column that has a NOT NULL constraint, then an INSERT through the view cannot succeed (unless the column has a default value). This can produce a disconcerting effect because the error message will refer to a table and a column that are not mentioned in the statement, as demonstrated in the first example in Figure 12-1.

FIGURE 12-1

DML against
simple and
complex views

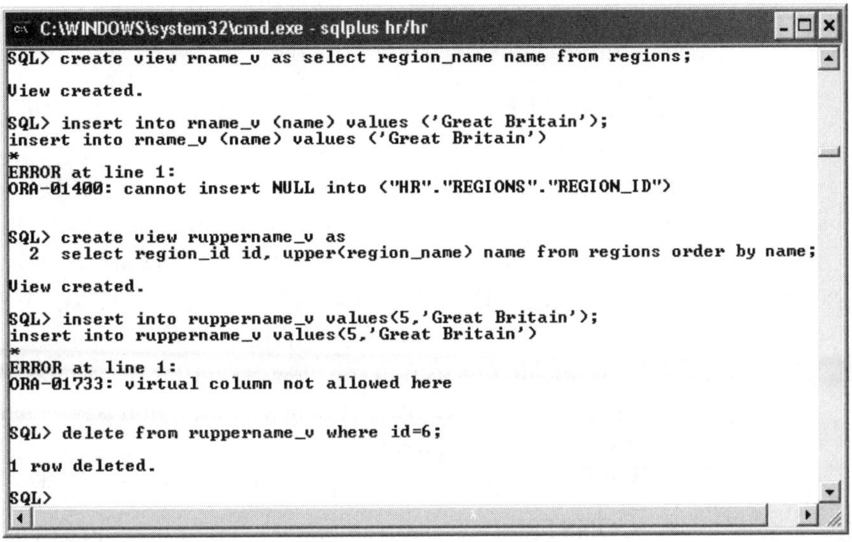

```
C:\WINDOWS\system32\cmd.exe - sqlplus hr/hr                              - □ x
SQL> create view rname_v as select region_name name from regions;
View created.

SQL> insert into rname_v (name) values ('Great Britain');
insert into rname_v (name) values ('Great Britain')
*
ERROR at line 1:
ORA-01400: cannot insert NULL into ("HR"."REGIONS"."REGION_ID")

SQL> create view ruppername_v as
  2   select region_id id, upper(region_name) name from regions order by name;
View created.

SQL> insert into ruppername_v values(5,'Great Britain');
insert into ruppername_v values(5,'Great Britain')
*
ERROR at line 1:
ORA-01733: virtual column not allowed here

SQL> delete from ruppername_v where id=6;
1 row deleted.

SQL>
```

The first view in the figure, RNAME_V, does conform to the definition of a
simple view, but an INSERT cannot be performed through it because it is missing a
mandatory column. The second view, RUPPERNAME_V, is a complex view because
it includes a function. This makes an INSERT impossible, because there is no way
the database can work out what should actually be inserted: it can't reverse engineer
the effect of the UPPER function in a deterministic fashion. But the DELETE
succeeds, because that is not dependent on the function.

on the job

*As a rule, simple views accept DML, complex views don't. But there are
exceptions.*

CREATE VIEW, ALTER VIEW, and DROP VIEW

The syntax to create a view is as follows:

CREATE [OR REPLACE] [FORCE | NOFORCE] VIEW

[*schema.*]*viewname* [(*alias* [,*alias*]…)]

AS *subquery*

[WITH CHECK OPTION [CONSTRAINT *constraintname*]]

[WITH READ ONLY [CONSTRAINT *constraintname*]] ;

Note that views are schema objects. There is no reason not to have a view owned
by one user referencing detail tables owned by another user. By default, the view will

be created in the current schema. The optional keywords, none of which have been used in the examples so far, are as follows:

- **OR REPLACE**   If the view already exists, it will be dropped before being created.
- **FORCE or NOFORCE**   The FORCE keyword will create the view even if the detail table(s) in the subquery does not exist. NOFORCE is the default and will cause an error if the detail table does not exist.
- **WITH CHECK OPTION**   This is to do with DML. If the subquery includes a WHERE clause, then this option will prevent insertion of rows that wouldn't be seen in the view or updates that would cause a row to disappear from the view. By default, this option is not enabled, which can give disconcerting results.
- **WITH READ ONLY**   Prevents any DML through the view.
- **CONSTRAINT** *constraintname*   This can be used to name the WITH CHECK OPTION and WITH READ ONLY restrictions so that error messages when the restrictions cause statements to fail, will be more comprehensible.

In addition, a set of alias names can be provided for the names of the view's columns. If not provided, the columns will be named after the table's columns or with aliases specified in the subquery.

Figure 12-2 first demonstrates the effect of creating a view, R1, which permits insertion of rows that cannot be seen. The second view, LOC1800, uses WITH CHECK OPTION to prevent this from happening.

FIGURE 12-2

Use of WITH CHECK OPTION to prevent seemingly anomalous behavior

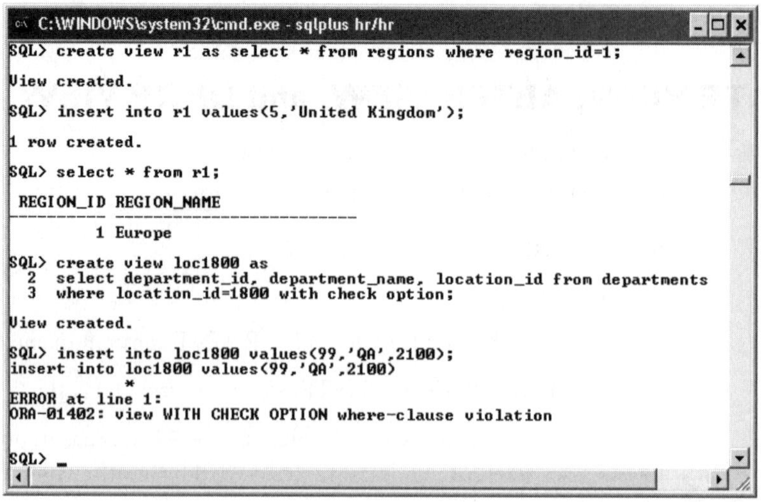

The main use of the ALTER VIEW command is to compile the view. A view must be compiled successfully before it can be used. When a view is created, Oracle will check that the detail tables and the necessary columns on which the view is based do exist. If they do not, the compilation fails and the view will not be created—unless you use the FORCE option. In that case, the view will be created but will be unusable until the tables or columns to which it refers are created and the view is successfully compiled. When an invalid view is queried, Oracle will attempt to compile it automatically. If the compilation succeeds because the problem has been fixed, the user won't know there was ever a problem—except that his query may take a little longer than usual. Generally speaking, you should manually compile views to make sure they do compile successfully, rather than having users discover errors.

Figure 12-3 shows the cycle of error and correction.

In the figure, the first statement creates a view EX_STAFF that references a column EMPLOYEES.LEFT_DATE, which does not exist. The statement does not fail because the creation is forced, but it does give a warning. An attempt to select from the view fails. After adding the necessary column to the detail table, the SELECT succeeds. This is because the view was compiled successfully automatically. Finally, there is a manual compilation of the view. It would have been better practice to do this immediately after adding the missing column.

It is not possible to adjust a view's column definitions after creation in the way that a table's columns can be changed. The view must be dropped and re-created. The DROP command is as follows:

DROP VIEW [*schema.*]*viewname* ;

By using the OR REPLACE keywords with the CREATE VIEW command, the view will be automatically dropped (if it exists at all) before being created.

FIGURE 12-3

How to correct errors and compile a view

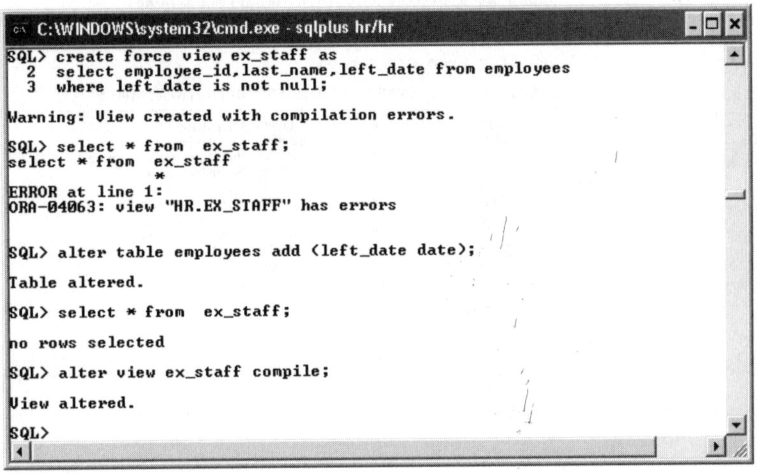

```
C:\WINDOWS\system32\cmd.exe - sqlplus hr/hr

SQL> create force view ex_staff as
  2   select employee_id,last_name,left_date from employees
  3   where left_date is not null;

Warning: View created with compilation errors.

SQL> select * from  ex_staff;
select * from  ex_staff
               *
ERROR at line 1:
ORA-04063: view "HR.EX_STAFF" has errors


SQL> alter table employees add (left_date date);

Table altered.

SQL> select * from  ex_staff;

no rows selected

SQL> alter view ex_staff compile;

View altered.

SQL>
```

EXERCISE 12-1

Create Views

In this exercise, you will create some simple and complex views, using data in the HR schema. Either SQL*Plus or SQL developer can be used.

1. Connect to your database as user HR.

2. Create views on the EMPLOYEES and DEPARTMENT tables that remove all personal information:

```
create view emp_anon_v as
select hire_date, job_id,salary,commission_pct,department_id from
employees;
create view dept_anon_v as
select department_id,department_name,location_id from departments;
```

3. Create a complex view that will join and aggregate the two simple views. Note that there is no reason not to have views of views.

```
create view dep_sum_v as
select e.department_id,count(1) staff, sum(e.salary) salaries,
d.department_name from emp_anon_v e join dept_anon_v d
on e.department_id=d.department_id
group by e.department_id,d.department_name;
```

4. Confirm that the view works by querying it, as in the following illustration:

CERTIFICATION OBJECTIVE 12.02

Retrieve Data from Views

Queries can be addressed to views exactly as though to tables. Views and tables share the same namespace, so syntactically there is absolutely no difference in the SELECT statements. The user need have no knowledge of which type of object he is addressing.

Consider this view:

```
create view dept_emp as
select department_name, last_name from
departments join employees using (department_id);
```

The following query:

```
select * from dept_emp where department_name='Marketing';
```

when parsed by Oracle for execution will become:

```
select * from
(select department_name, last_name
from departments join employees using (department_id))
where department_name='Marketing';
```

You rarely get anything for nothing (even when dealing with Oracle Corporation), and use of views certainly does not in any way reduce the work that the database has to do. Views can, however, reduce substantially the work that users have to do.

EXERCISE 12-2

Use Views

In this exercise, you will use the views created in Exercise 12-1 for SELECT and DML statements. Either SQL*Plus or SQL developer can be used.

1. Connect to your database as user HR.
2. Insert a new department through the DEPT_ANON_V view and attempt to insert an employee through EMP_ANON_V:

```
insert into DEPT_ANON_V values(99,'Temp Dept',1800);
insert into emp_anon_v values(sysdate,'AC_MGR',10000,0,99);
```

The insert into EMP_ANON_V will fail because of missing mandatory values. You will, however, be able to do this update through it:

```
update emp_anon_v set salary=salary*1.1;
```

Then roll back the changes:

```
rollback;
```

3. Find out the average salary of the department with the highest average salary, by querying the EMPLOYEES table:

```
select max(avg_sal) from
(select AVG(SALARY) avg_sal from employees group by department_id);
```

and find the same information from the DEP_SUM_V view, which is a much simpler query:

```
select max(salaries / staff) from dep_sum_v;
```

CERTIFICATION OBJECTIVE 12.03

Create Private and Public Synonyms

A synonym is an alternative name for an object. If synonyms exist for objects, then any SQL statement can address the object either by its actual name, or by its synonym. This may seem trivial. It isn't. Use of synonyms means that an application can function for any user, irrespective of which schema owns the views and tables or even in which database the tables reside. Consider this statement:

```
select * from hr.employees@prod;
```

The user issuing the statement must know that the employees table is owned by the HR schema in the database identified by the database link PROD (do not worry about database links—they are a means of accessing objects in a database other than that onto which you are logged). If a public synonym has been created with this statement:

```
create public synonym emp for hr.employees@prod;
```

then all the user (any user!) need enter is the following:

```
select * from emp;
```

This gives both data independence and location transparency. Tables and views can be renamed or relocated without ever having to change code; only the synonyms need to be adjusted.

As well as SELECT statements, DML statements can address synonyms as though they were the object to which they refer.

Private synonyms are schema objects. Either they must be in your own schema, or they must be qualified with the schema name. Public synonyms exist independently of a schema. A public synonym can be referred to by any user to whom permission has been granted to see it without the need to qualify it with a schema name. Private synonyms must be a unique name within their schema. Public synonyms can have the same name as schema objects. When executing statements that address objects without a schema qualifier, Oracle will first look for the object in the local schema, and only if it cannot be found will it look for a public synonym. Thus, in the preceding example, if the user happened to own a table called EMP it would be this that he would see—not the table pointed to by the public synonym.

The syntax to create a synonym is as follows:

CREATE [PUBLIC] SYNONYM *synonym* FOR *object* ;

A user will need to have been granted permission to create private synonyms and further permission to create public synonyms. Usually, only the database administrator can create (or drop) public synonyms. This is because their presence (or absence) will affect every user.

e x a m

ⓦ a t c h *The "public" in "public synonym" means that it is not a schema object and cannot therefore be prefixed* *with a schema name. It does not mean that everyone has permissions against it.*

To drop a synonym:

DROP [PUBLIC] SYNONYM *synonym* ;

If the object to which a synonym refers (the table or view) is dropped, the synonym continues to exist. Any attempt to use it will return an error. In this respect, synonyms behave in the same way as views. If the object is recreated, the synonym must be recompiled before use. As with views, this will happen automatically the next time the synonym is addressed, or it can be done explicitly with

ALTER SYNONYM *synonym* COMPILE;

EXERCISE 12-3

Create and Use Synonyms

In this exercise, you will create and use private synonyms, using objects in the HR schema. Either SQL*Plus or SQL developer can be used.

1. Connect to your database as user HR.

2. Create synonyms for the three views created in Exercise 12-1:

```
create synonym emp_s for emp_anon_v;
create synonym dept_s for dept_anon_v;
create synonym dsum_s for dep_sum_v;
```

3. Confirm that the synonyms are identical to the underlying object:

```
describe emp_s;
describe emp_anon_v;
```

4. Confirm that the synonyms work (even to the extent of producing the same errors) by running the statements in Exercises 12-1 and 12-2 against the synonyms instead of the views:

```
select * from dsum_s;
insert into dept_s values(99,'Temp Dept',1800);
insert into emp_s values(sysdate,'AC_MGR',10000,0,99);
update emp_s set salary=salary*1.1;
rollback;
select max(salaries / staff) from dsum_s;
```

5. Drop two of the views:

```
drop view emp_anon_v;
drop view dept_anon_v;
```

6. Query the complex view that is based on the dropped views:

```
select * from dep_sum_v;
```

Note that the query fails.

7. Attempt to recompile the broken view:

```
alter view dep_sum_v compile;
```

This will fail as well.

8. Drop the DEP_SUM_V view:

```
drop view dep_sum_v;
```

9. Query the synonym for a dropped view:

```
select * from emp_s;
```

This will fail.

10. Recompile the broken synonym:

```
alter synonym emp_s compile;
```

Note that this does not give an error, but rerun the query from step 9. It is definitely still broken.

11. Tidy up by dropping the synonyms:

```
drop synonym emp_s;
drop synonym dept_s;
drop synonym dsum_s;
```

CERTIFICATION OBJECTIVE 12.04

Create, Maintain, and Use Sequences

A sequence is a structure for generating unique integer values. Only one session can read the next value and thus force it to increment. This is a point of serialization, so each value generated will be unique.

Sequences are an invaluable tool for generating primary keys. Many applications will need automatically generated primary key values. Examples in everyday business data processing are invoice numbers or order numbers: the business analysts will have stated that every invoice and order must have a unique number, which should continually increment. Other applications may not have such a requirement in business terms, but it will be needed to enforce relational integrity. Consider a telephone billing system: in business terms the unique identifier of a telephone is the telephone number (which is a string) and that of a call will be the source telephone number and the time the call began (which is a timestamp). These data types are unnecessarily complex to use as primary keys for the high volumes that go through a telephone switching system. While this information will be recorded, it will be much faster to use simple numeric columns to define the primary and foreign keys. The values in these columns can be sequence based.

FIGURE 12-4

Use of a
sequence by
two sessions
concurrently

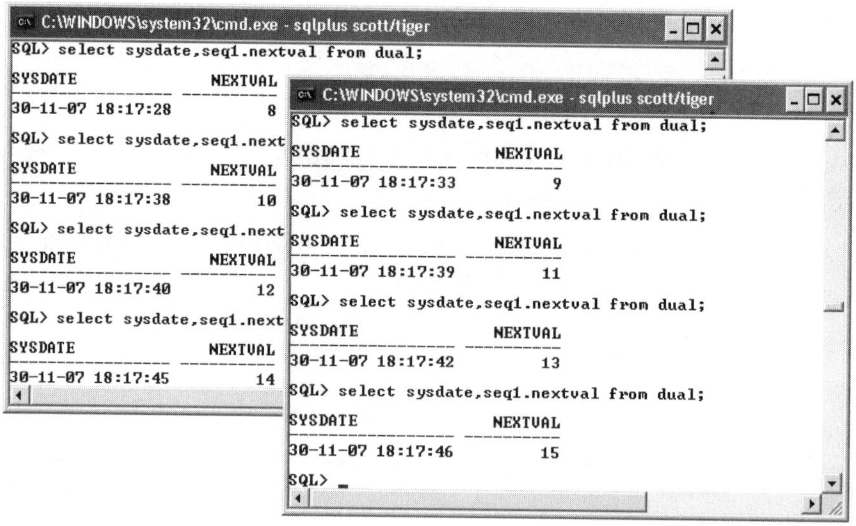

```
C:\WINDOWS\system32\cmd.exe - sqlplus scott/tiger
SQL> select sysdate,seq1.nextval from dual;

SYSDATE              NEXTVAL
-------------------- ----------
30-11-07 18:17:28             8

SQL> select sysdate,seq1.next

SYSDATE              NEXTVAL
-------------------- ----------
30-11-07 18:17:38            10

SQL> select sysdate,seq1.next

SYSDATE              NEXTVAL
-------------------- ----------
30-11-07 18:17:40            12

SQL> select sysdate,seq1.next

SYSDATE              NEXTVAL
-------------------- ----------
30-11-07 18:17:45            14
```

```
C:\WINDOWS\system32\cmd.exe - sqlplus scott/tiger
SQL> select sysdate,seq1.nextval from dual;

SYSDATE              NEXTVAL
-------------------- ----------
30-11-07 18:17:33             9

SQL> select sysdate,seq1.nextval from dual;

SYSDATE              NEXTVAL
-------------------- ----------
30-11-07 18:17:39            11

SQL> select sysdate,seq1.nextval from dual;

SYSDATE              NEXTVAL
-------------------- ----------
30-11-07 18:17:42            13

SQL> select sysdate,seq1.nextval from dual;

SYSDATE              NEXTVAL
-------------------- ----------
30-11-07 18:17:46            15

SQL> _
```

The sequence mechanism is independent of tables, the row locking mechanism, and commit or rollback processing. This means that a sequence can issue thousands of unique values a minute—far faster than any method involving selecting a column from a table, updating it, and committing the change.

Figure 12-4 shows two sessions selecting values from a sequence SEQ1.

Note that in the figure each selection of SEQ1.NEXTVAL generates a unique number. The numbers are issued consecutively in order of the time the selection was made, and the number increments globally, not just within one session.

Creating Sequences

The full syntax for creating a sequence is as follows:

CREATE SEQUENCE [*schema.*]*sequencename*

[INCREMENT BY *number*]

[START WITH *number*]

[MAXVALUE *number* | NOMAXVALUE]

[MINVALUE *number* | NOMINVALUE]

[CYCLE | NOCYCLE]

[CACHE *number* | NOCACHE]

[ORDER | NOORDER] ;

It can be seen that creating a sequence can be very simple. For example, the sequence used in Figure 12-4 was created with

```
create sequence seq1;
```

The options are shown in the following table.

INCREMENT BY	How much higher (or lower) than the last number issued should the next number be? Defaults to +1 but can be any positive number (or negative number for a descending sequence).
START WITH	The starting point for the sequence: the number issued by the first selection. Defaults to 1 but can be anything.
MAXVALUE	The highest number an ascending sequence can go to before generating an error or returning to its START WITH value. The default is no maximum.
MINVALUE	The lowest number a descending sequence can go to before generating an error or returning to its START WITH value. The default is no minimum.
CYCLE	Controls the behavior on reaching MAXVALUE or MINVALUE. The default behavior is to give an error, but if CYCLE is specified the sequence will return to its starting point and repeat.
CACHE	For performance, Oracle can preissue sequence values in batches and cache them for issuing to users. The default is to generate and cache the next 20 values.
ORDER	Only relevant for a clustered database: ORDER forces all instances in the cluster to coordinate incrementing the sequence, so that numbers issued are always in order even when issued to sessions against different instances.

Appropriate settings for INCREMENT BY, START WITH, and MAXVALUE or MINVALUE will come from your business analysts.

It is very rare for CYCLE to be used because it lets the sequence issue duplicate values. If the sequence is being used to generate primary key values, CYCLE only makes sense if there is a routine in the database that will delete old rows faster than the sequence will reissue numbers.

Caching sequence values is vital for performance. Selecting from a sequence is a point of serialization in the application code: only one session can do this at once. The mechanism is very efficient: it is much faster than locking a row, updating the row, and then unlocking it with a COMMIT. But even so, selecting from a sequence can be a cause of contention between sessions. The CACHE keyword instructs Oracle to pregenerate sequence numbers in batches. This means that they can be issued faster than if they had to be generated on demand.

The default number of values to cache is only 20. Experience shows that this is not enough. If your application selects from the sequence 10 times a second, then set the cache value to 50 thousand. Don't be shy about this.

Using Sequences

To use a sequence, a session can select either the next value with the NEXTVAL pseudo column, which forces the sequence to increment, or the last (or "current") value issued to that session with the CURRVAL pseudo column. The NEXTVAL will be globally unique: each session that selects it will get a different, incremented, value for each SELECT. The CURRVAL will be constant for one session until it selects NEXTVAL again. There is no way to find out what the last value issued by a sequence was: you can always obtain the next value by incrementing it with NEXTVAL, and you can always recall the last value issued to your session with CURRVAL, but you cannot find the last value issued.

exam
watch
The CURRVAL of a sequence is the last value issued to the current session, not necessarily the last value issued. You cannot select the CURRVAL until after selecting the NEXTVAL.

A typical use of sequences is for primary key values. This example uses a sequence ORDER_SEQ to generate unique order numbers and LINE_SEQ to generate unique line numbers for the line items of the order. First create the sequences, which is a one-off operation:

```
create sequence order_seq start with 10;
create sequence line_seq start with 10;
```

Then insert the orders with their lines as a single transaction:

```
insert into orders (order_number,order_date,customer_number)
values (order_seq.nextval,sysdate,'1000');
insert into order_lines (order_number,line_number,item_number,quantity)
values (order_seq.currval,line_seq.nextval,'A111',1);
insert into order_lines (order_number,line_number,item_number,quantity)
values (order_seq.currval,line_seq.nextval,'B111',1);
commit;
```

The first INSERT statement raises an order with a unique order number drawn from the sequence ORDER_SEQ for customer number 1000. The second and third statements insert the two lines of the order, using the previously issued order number from ORDER_SEQ as the foreign key to connect the lines to the order, and the next values from LINE_SEQ to generate a unique identifier for each line. Finally, the transaction is committed.

A sequence is not tied to any one table. In the preceding example, there would be no technical reason not to use one sequence to generate values for the primary keys of the order and of the lines.

A COMMIT is not necessary to make the increment of a sequence permanent: it is permanent and made visible to the rest of the world the moment it happens. It can't be rolled back, either. Figure 12-5 demonstrates this.

In the figure, the second insert is rolled back. But as the final query shows, the sequence was incremented in spite of this. Sequence updates occur independently of the transaction management system. For this reason, there will always be gaps in the series. The gaps will be larger if the database has been restarted and the CACHE clause was used. All numbers that have been generated and cached but not yet issued will be lost when the database is shut down. At the next restart, the current value of the sequence will be the last number generated, not the last issued. So, with the default CACHE of 20, every shutdown/startup will lose up to 20 numbers.

FIGURE 12-5

A sequence increment cannot be rolled back.

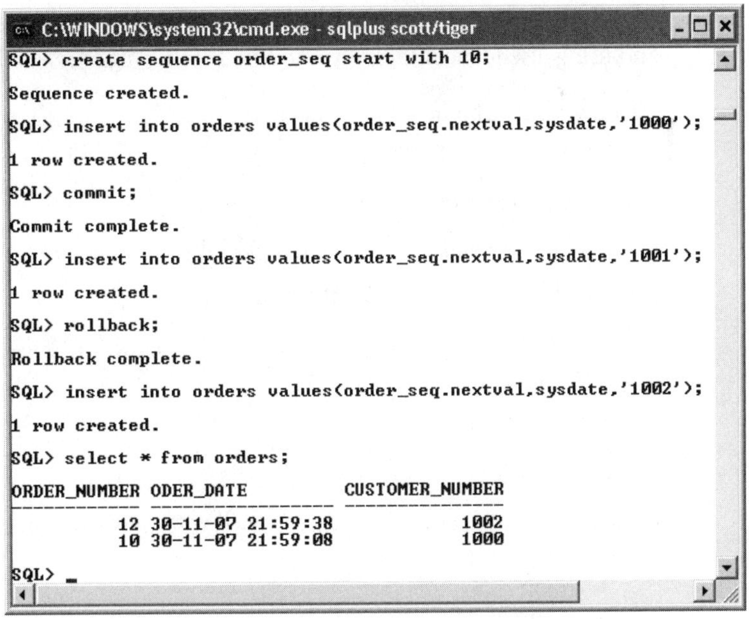

```
C:\WINDOWS\system32\cmd.exe - sqlplus scott/tiger

SQL> create sequence order_seq start with 10;

Sequence created.

SQL> insert into orders values(order_seq.nextval,sysdate,'1000');

1 row created.

SQL> commit;

Commit complete.

SQL> insert into orders values(order_seq.nextval,sysdate,'1001');

1 row created.

SQL> rollback;

Rollback complete.

SQL> insert into orders values(order_seq.nextval,sysdate,'1002');

1 row created.

SQL> select * from orders;

ORDER_NUMBER ODER_DATE            CUSTOMER_NUMBER
------------ -------------------- ---------------
          12 30-11-07 21:59:38               1002
          10 30-11-07 21:59:08               1000

SQL>
```

on the job *Some accountants get very upset at the idea of gaps in numbering. Ask them why it matters. It usually doesn't.*

If the business analysts have stated that there must be no gaps in a sequence, then another means of generating unique numbers must be used. For the preceding example of raising orders, the current order number could be stored in this table and initialized to 10:

```
create table current_on(order_number number);
insert into current_on values(10);
commit;
```

Then the code to create an order would have to become:

```
update current_on set order_number=order_number + 1;
insert into orders (order_number,order_date,customer_number)
values ((select order_number from current_on),sysdate,'1000');
commit;
```

This will certainly work as a means of generating unique order numbers, and because the increment of the order number is within the transaction that inserts the order, it can be rolled back with the insert if necessary: there will be no gaps in order numbers, unless an order is deliberately deleted. But it is far less efficient than using a sequence, and code like this is famous for causing dreadful contention problems. If many sessions try to lock and increment the one row containing the current number, the whole application will hang as they queue up to take their turn. After creating and using a sequence, it can be modified. The syntax is as follows:

ALTER SEQUENCE *sequencename*

[INCREMENT BY *number*]

[START WITH *number*]

[MAXVALUE *number* | NOMAXVALUE]

[MINVALUE *number* | NOMINVALUE]

[CYCLE | NOCYCLE]

[CACHE *number* | NOCACHE]

[ORDER | NOORDER] ;

This ALTER command is the same as the CREATE command, with one exception: there is no way to set the starting value. If you want to restart the sequence, the only

SCENARIO & SOLUTION

You are involved in designing a database to be used for online order entry and offline financial reporting. What should you consider with regard to views, synonyms, and indexes?	The data must be normalized for storage but should be denormalized into views for retrieval. The dual use of the database will be a problem: too many indexes will slow down the order entry, too few will impact adversely on reporting. An alternative approach would be create a separate set of tables (possibly denormalized and aggregated like the views) for reporting and update these with batch routines. Using synonyms at all times would make it easier to switch between implementations with and without separate reporting tables.
Should sequences always be used for primary keys?	In some cases, the business analysts may have defined a primary key based on attributes of the data. For example, a list of telephone subscribers could be keyed on telephone number: this is a formatted string that may have information such as geographical location (for a land line) or network operator (for a mobile) embedded within it. But usually a primary key does not have meaning, and in these cases a sequence is always the best way.

way is to drop it and re-create it. To adjust the cache value from default to improve performance of the preceding order entry example:

```
alter sequence order_seq cache 1000;
```

However, if you want to reset the sequence to its starting value, the only way is to drop it:

```
drop sequence order_seq;
```

and create it again.

EXERCISE 12-4

Create and Use Sequences

In this exercise, you will create some sequences and use them. You will need two concurrent sessions, either SQL Developer or SQL*Plus.

1. Log on to your database twice, as HR in separate sessions. Consider one to be your A session and the other to be your B session.

2. In your A session, create a sequence as follows:

```
create sequence seq1 start with 10 nocache maxvalue 15 cycle;
```

The use of NOCACHE is deleterious for performance. If MAXVALUE is specified, then CYCLE will be necessary to prevent errors when MAXVALUE is reached.

3. Execute the following commands in the appropriate session in the correct order to observe the use of NEXTVAL and CURRVAL and the cycling of the sequence:

	In Your A Session	In Your B Session
1st	select seq1.nextval from dual;	
2nd		select seq1.nextval from dual;
3rd	select seq1.nextval from dual;	
4th		select seq1.nextval from dual;
5th	select seq1.currval from dual;	
6th		select seq1.nextval from dual;
7th	select seq1.nextval from dual;	
8th		select seq1.currval from dual;
9th	select seq1.nextval from dual;	
10th		select seq1.nextval from dual;

4. Create a table with a primary key:

```
create table seqtest(c1 number,c2 varchar2(10));
alter table seqtest add constraint seqtest_pk primary key (c1);
```

5. Create a sequence to generate primary key values:

```
create sequence seqtest_pk_s;
```

6. In your A session, insert a row into the new table and commit:

```
insert into seqtest values(seqtest_pk_s.nextval,'first');
commit;
```

7. In your B session, insert a row into the new table and do not commit it:

```
insert into seqtest values(seqtest_pk_s.nextval,'second');
```

8. In your A session, insert a third row and commit:

```
insert into seqtest values(seqtest_pk_s.nextval,'third');
commit;
```

9. In your B session, roll back the second insertion:

```
rollback;
```

10. In your B session, see the contents of the table:

```
select * from seqtest;
```

This demonstrates that sequences are incremented and the next value published immediately, outside the transaction control mechanism.

11. Tidy up:

```
drop table seqtest;
drop sequence seqtest_pk_s;
drop sequence seq1;
```

CERTIFICATION OBJECTIVE 12.05

Create and Maintain Indexes

Indexes have two functions: to enforce primary key and unique constraints and to improve performance. An application's indexing strategy is critical for performance. Theoretically, the SQL developer does not need to be aware of the existence (or otherwise) of indexes, but if the developer does know what indexes exist and how they are structured, the developer can write code designed to exploit them.

There is no clear demarcation of whose domain index management lies within. When the business analysts specify business rules that will be implemented as constraints, they are in effect specifying indexes. The database administrators will be monitoring the execution of code running in the database and will make recommendations for indexes. The developer, who should have the best idea of what is going on in the code and the nature of the data, will also be involved in developing the indexing strategy.

What Indexes Are For

Indexes are part of the constraint mechanism. If a column (or a group of columns) is marked as a table's primary key, then every time a row is inserted into the table, Oracle must check that a row with the same value in the primary key does not already exist. If the table has no index on the column(s), the only way to do this is to scan right through the table, checking every row. While this might be acceptable for a table of only a few rows, for a table with thousands or millions (or billions) of rows, this is not feasible. An index gives (near) immediate access to key values, so the check for existence can be made virtually instantaneously. When a primary key constraint is defined, Oracle will automatically create an index on the primary key column(s), if one does not exist already.

A unique constraint also requires an index. The difference from a primary key constraint is that the column(s) of the unique constraint can be left null, perhaps in many rows. This does not affect the creation and use of the index: nulls do not go into the B*Tree indexes, as described in the next section, "Types of Index."

Foreign key constraints are enforced by indexes, but the index must exist on the parent table, not necessarily on the table for which the constraint is defined. A foreign key constraint relates a column in the child table to the primary key or to a unique key in the parent table. When a row is inserted in the child table, Oracle will do a lookup on the index on the parent table to confirm that there is a matching row before permitting the insert. However, you should always create indexes on the foreign key columns within the child table for performance reasons: a DELETE on the parent table will be much faster if Oracle can use an index to determine whether there are any rows in the child table referencing the row that is being deleted.

Indexes are critical for performance. When executing any SQL statement that includes a WHERE clause, Oracle has to identify which rows of the table are to be selected or modified. If there is no index on the column(s) referenced in the WHERE clause, the only way to do this is with a *full table scan*. A full table scan reads every row of the table, in order to find the relevant rows. If the table has billions of rows, this can take hours. If there is an index on the relevant column(s), Oracle can search the index instead. An index is a sorted list of key values, structured in a manner that makes the search very efficient. With each key value is a pointer to the row in the table. Locating relevant rows via an index lookup is far faster than using a full table scan, if the table is over a certain size and the proportion of the rows to be retrieved is below a certain value. For small tables, or for a WHERE clause that will retrieve a large fraction of the table's rows, a full table scan will be quicker: you can (usually) trust Oracle to make the correct decision, based on information the database gathers about the tables and the rows within them.

A second circumstance where indexes can be used is for sorting. A SELECT statement that includes the ORDER BY, GROUP BY, or UNION keywords (and a few others) must sort the rows into order—unless there is an index, which can return the rows in the correct order without needing to sort them first.

A third circumstance when indexes can improve performance is when tables are joined, but again Oracle has a choice: depending on the size of the tables and the memory resources available, it may be quicker to scan tables into memory and join them there, rather than use indexes. The *nested loop join* technique passes through one table using an index on the other table to locate the matching rows: this is usually a disk-intensive operation. A *hash join* technique reads the entire table into memory, converts it into a hash table, and uses a hashing algorithm to locate matching rows; this is more memory and CPU intensive. A *sort merge join* sorts the tables on the join column then merges them together: this is often a compromise between disk, memory, and CPU resources. If there are no indexes, then Oracle is severely limited in the join techniques available.

Types of Index

Oracle supports several types of index, which have several variations. The two index types of concern here are the B*Tree index, which is the default index type, and the bitmap index. The only variation worthy of consideration for examination purposes applies to B*Tree indexes: these can be either *unique* or *nonunique*. A unique index will not permit insertion of two rows with the same key values; a nonunique index will permit as many rows as you want with the same values. Nonunique is the default.

As a general rule, indexes will improve performance for data retrieval but reduce performance for DML operations. This is because indexes must be maintained. Every time a row is inserted into a table, a new key must be inserted into every index on the table, which places an additional strain on the database. For this reason, on transaction processing systems it is customary to keep the number of indexes as low as possible (perhaps no more than those needed for the constraints) and on a query-intensive system, such as a data warehouse, to create as many as might be helpful.

B*Tree Indexes

A B*Tree index (the "B" stands for "balanced") is a tree structure. The root node of the tree points to many nodes at the second level, which can point to many nodes at the third level, and so on. The necessary depth of the tree will be largely determined by the number of rows in the table and the length of the index key values.

on the

Job

The B*Tree structure is very efficient. If the depth is greater then three or four, than either the index keys are very long or the table has billions of rows. If neither if these is the case, then the index is in need of a rebuild.

The leaf nodes of the index tree store the rows' keys, in order, each with a pointer that identifies the physical location of the row. So to retrieve a row with an index lookup, if the WHERE clause is using an equality predicate on the primary key column, Oracle navigates down the tree to the leaf node containing the desired key value, then uses the pointer to find the row. If the WHERE clause is using a nonequality predicate (such as any of the operators LIKE, BETWEEN, >, or <) then Oracle can navigate down the tree to find the first matching key value and then navigate across the leaf nodes of the index to find all the other matching values. As it does so, it will retrieve the rows from the table, in order.

The pointer to the row is the *rowid*. The rowid is an Oracle proprietary pseudocolumn that every row in every table has. Encrypted within it is the physical address of the row. As rowids are not part of the SQL standard, they are never visible to a normal SQL statement, but you can see them and use them if you want. This is demonstrated in Figure 12-6.

A row's rowid is globally unique. Every row in every table in the whole database will have a different rowid. The rowid encryption gives the physical address of the row: from it, Oracle can calculate which operating system file and where in the file the row is, and go straight to it.

FIGURE 12-6

Displaying and using rowids

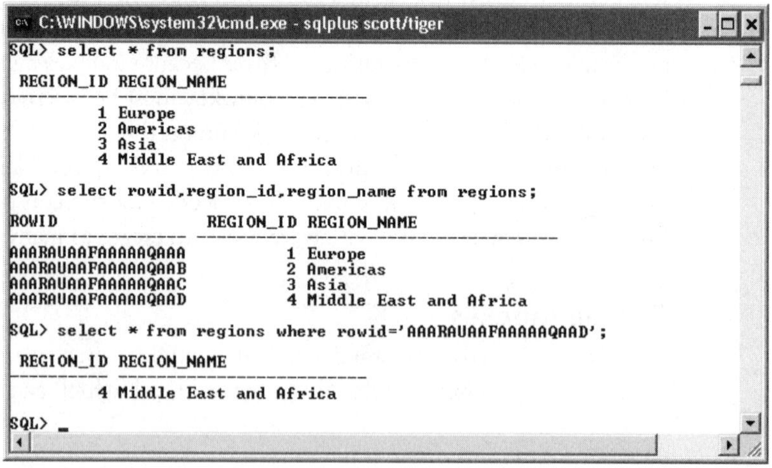

```
C:\WINDOWS\system32\cmd.exe - sqlplus scott/tiger

SQL> select * from regions;

 REGION_ID REGION_NAME
---------- -------------------------
         1 Europe
         2 Americas
         3 Asia
         4 Middle East and Africa

SQL> select rowid,region_id,region_name from regions;

ROWID               REGION_ID REGION_NAME
------------------ ---------- -------------------------
AAARAUAAFAAAAAQAAA          1 Europe
AAARAUAAFAAAAAQAAB          2 Americas
AAARAUAAFAAAAAQAAC          3 Asia
AAARAUAAFAAAAAQAAD          4 Middle East and Africa

SQL> select * from regions where rowid='AAARAUAAFAAAAAQAAD';

 REGION_ID REGION_NAME
---------- -------------------------
         4 Middle East and Africa

SQL> _
```

B*Tree indexes are a very efficient way of retrieving rows if the number of rows needed is low in proportion to the total number of rows in the table and if the table is large. Consider this statement:

```
select count(*) from employees where last_name between 'A%' and 'Z%';
```

This WHERE clause is sufficiently broad that it will include every row in the table. It would be much slower to such the index to find the rowids and then use the rowids to find the rows than to scan the whole table. After all, it is the whole table that is needed. Another example would be if the table were small enough that one disk read could scan it in its entirety: there would be no point in reading an index first.

It is often said that if the query is going to retrieve more than 2 to 4 percent of the rows, then a full table scan will be quicker. A major exception to this is if the value specified in the WHERE clause is NULL. NULLs do not go into B*Tree indexes, so a query such as this:

```
select * from employees where last_name is null;
```

will always result in a full table scan. There is little value in creating a B*Tree index on a column with few unique values, as it will not be selective: the proportion of the table that will be retrieved for each distinct key value will be too high. In general, B*Tree indexes should be used if:

- The cardinality (the number of distinct values) in the column is high, and
- The number of rows in the table is high, and
- The column is used in WHERE clauses or JOIN conditions

Bitmap Indexes

In many business applications, the nature of the data and the queries is such that B*Tree indexes are not of much use. Consider the table of sales for a chain of supermarkets, storing one year of historical data, which can be analyzed in several dimensions. Figure 12-7 shows a simple entity-relationship diagram, with just four of the dimensions.

The cardinality of each dimension could be quite low. Make these assumptions:

SHOP	There are four shops
PRODUCT	There are 200 products
DATE	There are 365 days
CHANNEL	There are two channels (walk-in and delivery)

FIGURE 12-7

A fact table with
four dimensions

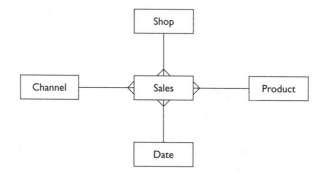

Assuming an even distribution of data, only two of the dimensions (PRODUCT and DATE) have a selectivity better than the commonly used criterion of 2 percent to 4 percent that makes an index worthwhile. But if queries use range predicates (such as counting sales in a month, or of a class of ten or more products) then not even these will qualify. This is a simple fact: B*Tree indexes are often useless in a data warehouse environment. A typical query might want to compare sales between two shops to walk-in customers of a certain class of product in a month. There may well be B*Tree indexes on the relevant columns, but Oracle will ignore them as being insufficiently selective. This is what bitmap indexes are designed for.

A bitmap index stores the rowids associated with each key value as a bitmap. The bitmaps for the CHANNEL index might look like this:

```
WALKIN      11010111000101011101011101.....
DELIVERY    00101000111010100010100010.....
```

This indicates that the first two rows were sales to walk-in customers, the third sale was a delivery, the fourth sale was a walk-in, and so on.

The bitmaps for the SHOP index might be:

```
LONDON      11001001001001101001010000.....
OXFORD      00100010011000010001001000.....
READING     00010001000100000100100010.....
GLASGOW     00000100100010000010000101.....
```

This indicates that the first two sales were in the London shop, the third was in Oxford, the fourth in Reading, and so on. Now if this query is received:

```
select count(*) from sales where channel='WALKIN' and shop='OXFORD';
```

Oracle can retrieve the two relevant bitmaps and add them together with a Boolean AND operation:

```
WALKIN              1101011100010101110101101.....
OXFORD              0010001001100001000100100.....
WALKIN & OXFORD     0000001000000001000000000.....
```

The result of the AND operation shows that only the seventh and sixteenth rows qualify for selection. This combining of bitmaps is very fast and can be used to implement complex Boolean algebra operations with many conditions on many columns using any combination of AND, OR, and NOT operators. A particular advantage that bitmap indexes have over B*Tree indexes is that they include NULLs. As far as the bitmap index is concerned, NULL is just another distinct value, which will have its own bitmap.

In general, bitmap indexes should be used if:

- The cardinality (the number of distinct values) in the column is low (such as male/female), and
- The number of rows in the table is high, and
- The column is used in Boolean algebra (AND/OR/NOT) operations

on the job *If you knew in advance what the queries would be then you could build B*Tree indexes that would work, such as a composite index on SHOP and CHANNEL. But usually you don't know, which is where the dynamic merging of bitmaps gives great flexibility.*

Creating and Using Indexes

Indexes are created implicitly when primary key and unique constraints are defined, if an index on the relevant column(s) does not already exist. The basic syntax for creating an index explicitly is as follows:

CREATE [UNIQUE | BITMAP] INDEX [*schema.*]*indexname*

ON [*schema.*]*tablename* (*column* [, *column...*]) ;

The default type of index is a nonunique B*Tree index. It is not possible to create a unique bitmap index (and you wouldn't want to if you could: think about the cardinality issue). Indexes are schema objects, and it is possible to create an index in one schema on a table in another, but most people would find this somewhat confusing. A *composite* index is an index on several columns. Composite indexes can be on columns of different data types, and the columns do not have to be adjacent in the table.

on the

Job

Many database administrators do not consider it good practice to rely on implicit index creation. If the indexes are created explicitly, the creator has full control over the characteristics of the index, which can make it easier for the DBA to manage subsequently.

Consider this example of creating tables and indexes and then defining constraints:

```
create table dept(deptno number,dname varchar2(10));
create table emp(empno number, surname varchar2(10), forename varchar2(10), dob
date, deptno number);
create unique index dept_i1 on dept(deptno);
create unique index emp_i1 on emp(empno);
create index emp_i2 on emp(surname,forename);
create bitmap index emp_i3 on emp(deptno);
alter table dept add constraint dept_pk primary key (deptno);
alter table emp add constraint emp_pk primary key (empno);
alter table emp add constraint emp_fk foreign key (deptno) references
dept(deptno);
```

The first two indexes created are flagged as UNIQUE, meaning that it will not be possible to insert duplicate values. This is not defined as a constraint at this point but is true nonetheless. The third index is not defined as UNIQUE and will therefore accept duplicate values; this is a composite index on two columns. The fourth index is defined as a bitmap index, because the cardinality of the column is likely to be low in proportion to the number of rows in the table.

When the two primary key constraints are defined, Oracle will detect the pre-created indexes and use them to enforce the constraints. Note that the index on DEPT.DEPTNO has no purpose for performance because the table will in all likelihood be so small that the index will never be used to retrieve rows (a scan will be quicker), but it is still essential to have an index to enforce the primary key constraint.

exam

Watch

A unique and primary key constraint can be enforced by indexes that are either unique or nonunique: in the latter case, it will be a nonunique index that happens to have only unique values.

Once created, use of indexes is completely transparent and automatic. Before executing a SQL statement, the Oracle server will evaluate all the possible ways of executing it. Some of these ways may involve using whatever indexes are available, others may not. Oracle will make use of the information it gathers on the tables and the environment to make an intelligent decision about which (if any) indexes to use.

on the
Ö o b

The Oracle server should make the best decision about index use, but if it gets it wrong it is possible for a programmer to embed instructions, known as optimizer hints, in code that will force the use (or not) of certain indexes.

Modifying and Dropping Indexes

There is a command, ALTER INDEX…but it cannot be used to change any of the characteristics described in this chapter: the type (B*Tree or bitmap) of the index, the columns, or whether it is unique or nonunique. The ALTER INDEX command lies in the database administration domain and would typically be used to adjust the physical properties of the index, not the logical properties that are of interest to developers. If it is necessary to change any of these properties, the index must be dropped and recreated. Continuing the example in the previous section, to change the index EMP_I2 to include the employees' birthdays:

```
drop index emp_i2;
create index emp_i2 on emp(surname,forename,dob);
```

This composite index now includes columns with different data types. The columns happen to be listed in the same order that they are defined in the table, but this is by no means necessary.

When a table is dropped, all the indexes and constraints defined for the table are dropped as well. If an index was created implicitly by creating a constraint, then dropping the constraint will also drop the index. If the index had been created explicitly and the constraint created later, then if the constraint is dropped the index will survive.

INSIDE THE EXAM

Creating Other Schema Objects

In many applications, users never see tables. The table data is abstracted into views, and the views further abstracted by synonyms. Use of views and synonyms is completely transparent to SQL: they all share the same namespace, and so code will run against any of them. Views can make complex relational structures much easier to use, and synonyms provide data ownership and location transparency.

Use of indexes is also transparent. They are required to enforce unique and primary key constraints (and strongly advised for foreign key constraints) and may optionally be created to enhance performance. Indexes come in two forms: B*Tree and bitmap. Arriving at an appropriate indexing strategy, which creates indexes of the right type on the right columns, is critical for performance.

B*Tree indexes are suitable for highly selective columns with a high cardinality; bitmap indexes are suitable for columns with only a few distinct values. The Oracle server will determine at statement execution time whether or not to use indexes, though programmers can control this by embedding hints in their code.

Sequences are a facility for generating unique numbers. It is absolutely impossible for two sessions to read the same value from a sequence. Sequences and their values exist outside the transaction processing structure. If a sequence is incremented, this increment cannot be rolled back and is immediately visible to all other sessions without any commit. Sequences bypass the mechanisms for atomic transactions and transaction isolation.

EXERCISE 12-5

Creating Indexes

In this exercise, create indexes on a copy of the EMPLOYEES table in the HR schema. Either SQL*Plus or SQL Developer can be used.

1. Connect to your database as user HR.

2. Create a table that is a copy of EMPLOYEES:

```
create table emps as select * from employees;
```

This table will have neither indexes nor primary, unique, or foreign key constraints, because these are not copied by a CREATE TABLE AS command. The NOT NULL constraints will have been copied. Confirm this by describing the table:

```
describe emps;
```

3. Create an index to be used for the primary key constraint:

```
create unique index emps_empid_i on emps(employee_id);
```

4. Demonstrate that a unique index cannot accept duplicates, even before a constraint is defined:

```
insert into emps(employee_id,last_name,email,hire_date,job_id)
values(198,'Watson','jw@bplc.co.za',sysdate,'IT_PROG');
```

This will return an error because the index cannot insert a second employee_id 198. Index uniqueness is an attribute of the index that can exist without a constraint but should not be relied upon to enforce data integrity.

5. Create additional indexes on columns that are likely to be used in WHERE clauses, using B*Tree for columns of high cardinality and bitmap for columns of low cardinality:

```
create index emps_name_i on emps(last_name,first_name);
create index emps_tel_i on emps(phone_number);
create bitmap index emps_mgr_i on emps(manage_id);
create bitmap index emps_dept_i on emps(department_id);
```

6. Define some constraints:

```
alter table emps add constraint emps_pk primary key (employee_id);
alter table emps add constraint emps_email_uk unique(email);
alter table emps add constraint emps_tel_uk unique(phone_number);
```

7. Display the index names and their type:

```
select index_name,index_type,uniqueness from user_indexes
where table_name='EMPS';
```

The view USER_INDEXES shows details of all indexes in your current schema. Note that in addition to the five indexes explicitly created in steps 3 and 5, there is also an index created implicitly with the name of the constraint defined on EMAIL. Note also that the unique constraint on PHONE_NUMBER is being enforced with a nonunique index; this is perfectly possible, because although the constraint mechanism uses indexes, it is independent of the structure of the index.

8. Tidy up by dropping the EMPS table, and confirm that all the indexes have also gone:

```
drop table emps;
select index_name from user_indexes where table_name='EMPS';
```

CERTIFICATION SUMMARY

Views are select statements, stored in the data dictionary. They can be queried as though they were tables, and in some cases they can be the object of DML statements. A simple view is columns from one table, with no aggregations or functions; a complex view can join tables, aggregate, and use functions. As a general rule, it is possible to do DML through a simple view but not through a complex view—but there are exceptions.

Synonyms are aliases that can be used to access views and tables. Synonyms can simplify code by making it unnecessary to specify schema qualifiers or database link names: they let code run without needing to know about data ownership or location. Tables, views, and synonyms share the name namespace: within a schema, they must all have different names and can be used interchangeably.

Sequences generate unique numbers, typically for use as primary key values.

Indexes have a dual purpose: enforcing constraints and enhancing performance. If an index is available when defining a constraint, Oracle will use it; otherwise, an index will be implicitly created. When creating indexes for performance, consider which columns are used for joining tables or in WHERE clauses and create B*Tree indexes on columns with high cardinality and bitmap indexes on columns with relatively few distinct values.

✓ TWO-MINUTE DRILL

Create Simple and Complex Views

❑ A simple view has one detail (or base) table and uses neither functions nor aggregation.

❑ A complex view can be based on any SELECT statement, no matter how complicated.

❑ Views are schema objects. To use a view in another schema, the view name must be qualified with the schema name.

Retrieve Data from Views

❑ A view can be queried exactly as though it were a table.

❑ Views can be joined to other views or to tables, they can be aggregated, and in some cases they can accept DML statements.

❑ Views exist only as data dictionary constructs. Whenever you query a view, the underlying SELECT statement must be run.

Create Private and Public Synonyms

❑ A synonym is an alternative name for a view or a table.

❑ Private synonyms are schema objects; public synonyms exist outside user schemas and can be used without specifying a schema name as a qualifier.

❑ Synonyms share the same namespace as views and tables and can therefore be used interchangeably with them.

Create, Maintain, and Use Sequences

❑ A sequence generates unique values—unless either MAXVALUE or MINVALUE and CYCLE have been specified.

❑ Incrementing a sequence need not be committed and cannot be rolled back.

❑ Any session can increment the sequence by reading its next value. It is possible to obtain the last value issued to your session but not the last value issued.

Create and Maintain Indexes

❑ Indexes are required for enforcing unique and primary key constraints.

❑ NULLs are not included in B*Tree indexes but are included in bitmap indexes.

❑ B*Tree indexes can be unique or nonunique, which determines whether they can accept duplicate key values.

❑ B*Tree indexes are suitable for high cardinality columns, bitmap indexes for low cardinality columns.

❑ Compound indexes have a key consisting of several columns, which can be of different data types.

SELF TEST

The following questions will help you measure your understanding of the material presented in this chapter. Read all the choices carefully because there might be more than one correct answer. Choose all the correct answers for each question.

Create Simple and Complex Views

1. Which of these is a defining characteristic of a complex view, rather than a simple view? (Choose one or more correct answers.)
   A. Restricting the projection by selecting only some of the table's columns
   B. Naming the view's columns with column aliases
   C. Restricting the selection of rows with a WHERE clause
   D. Performing an aggregation
   E. Joining two tables

2. Consider these three statements:

```
create view v1 as select department_id,department_name,last_name from
departments join employees using (department_id);
select department_name,last_name from v1 where department_id=20;
select d.department_name,e.last_name from departments d, employees e
where d.department_id=e.department_id and
d.department_id=20;
```

   The first query will be quicker than the second because (choose the best answer):
   A. The view has already done the work of joining the tables.
   B. The view uses ISO standard join syntax, which is faster than the Oracle join syntax used in the second query.
   C. The view is precompiled, so the first query requires less dynamic compilation than the second query.
   D. There is no reason for the first query to be quicker.

3. Study this view creation statement:

```
create view dept30 as
select department_id,employee_id,last_name from employees
where department_id=30 with check option;
```

What might make the following statement fail? (Choose the best answer.)

```
update dept30 set department_id=10 where employee_id=114;
```

A. Unless specified otherwise, views will be created as WITH READ ONLY.
B. The view is too complex to allow DML operations.
C. The WITH CHECK OPTION will reject any statement that changes the DEPARTMENT_ID.
D. The statement will succeed.

Retrieve Data from Views

4. There is a simple view SCOTT.DEPT_VIEW on the table SCOTT.DEPT. This insert fails with an error:

```
SQL> insert into dept_view values('SUPPORT','OXFORD');
insert into dept_view values('SUPPORT','OXFORD')
*
ERROR at line 1:
ORA-01400: cannot insert NULL into ("SCOTT"."DEPT"."DEPTNO")
```

What might be the problem? (Choose the best answer.)
A. The INSERT violates a constraint on the detail table.
B. The INSERT violates a constraint on the view.
C. The view was created as WITH READ ONLY.
D. The view was created as WITH CHECK OPTION.

Create Private and Public Synonyms

5. What are distinguishing characteristics of a public synonym rather than a private synonym? (Choose two correct answers.)
A. Public synonyms are always visible to all users.
B. Public synonyms can be accessed by name without a schema name qualifier.
C. Public synonyms can be selected from without needing any permissions.
D. Public synonyms can have the same names as tables or views.

6. Consider these three statements:

```
create synonym s1 for employees;
create public synonym s1 for departments;
select * from s1;
```

Which of the following statements is correct? (Choose the best answer.)

A. The second statement will fail because an object S1 already exists.

B. The third statement will show the contents of EMPLOYEES.

C. The third statement will show the contents of DEPARTMENTS.

D. The third statement will show the contents of the table S1, if such a table exists in the current schema.

7. A view and a synonym are created as follows:

```
create view dept_v as select * from dept;
create synonym dept_s for dept_v;
```

Subsequently the table DEPT is dropped. What will happen if you query the synonym DEPT_S ? (Choose the best answer.)

A. There will not be an error because the synonym addresses the view, which still exists, but there will be no rows returned.

B. There will not be an error if you first recompile the view with the command ALTER VIEW DEPT_V COMPILE FORCE;

C. There will be an error because the synonym will be invalid.

D. There will be an error because the view will be invalid.

E. There will be an error because the view will have been dropped implicitly when the table was dropped.

Create, Maintain, and Use Sequences

8. A sequence is created as follows:

```
create sequence seq1 maxvalue 50;
```

If the current value is already 50, when you attempt to select SEQ1.NEXTVAL what will happen? (Choose the best answer.)

A. The sequence will cycle and issue 0.

B. The sequence will cycle and issue 1.

C. The sequence will reissue 50.

D. There will be an error.

9. You create a sequence as follows:

```
create sequence seq1 start with 1;
```

After selecting from it a few times, you want to reinitialize it to reissue the numbers already generated. How can you do this? (Choose the best answer.)

A. You must drop and re-create the sequence.

B. You can't. Under no circumstances can numbers from a sequence be reissued once they have been used.

C. Use the command ALTER SEQUENCE SEQ1 START WITH 1; to reset the next value to 1.

D. Use the command ALTER SEQUENCE SEQ1 CYCLE; to reset the sequence to its starting value.

10. Study the following exhibit:

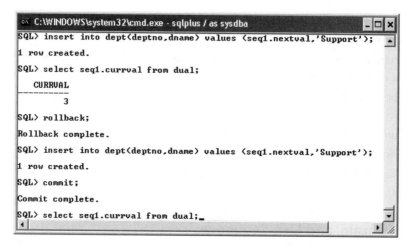

```
C:\WINDOWS\system32\cmd.exe - sqlplus / as sysdba
SQL> insert into dept(deptno,dname) values (seq1.nextval,'Support');

1 row created.

SQL> select seq1.currval from dual;

   CURRVAL
----------
        3

SQL> rollback;

Rollback complete.

SQL> insert into dept(deptno,dname) values (seq1.nextval,'Support');

1 row created.

SQL> commit;

Commit complete.

SQL> select seq1.currval from dual;_
```

Assuming that the sequence SEQ1 was created with the option ORDER and INCREMENT BY set to 1, what value will be returned by the final SELECT statement? (Choose the best answer.)

A. 2

B. 3

C. 4

D. It will depend on whether any other sessions are selecting from the sequence while the statements in the exhibit are being run.

Create and Maintain Indexes

11. A UNIQUE constraint on a column requires an index. Which of the following scenarios is correct? (Choose one or more correct answers.)

A. If a UNIQUE index already exists on the column, it will be used.

B. If a NONUNIQUE index already exists it will be used.

C. If a NONUNIQUE index already exists on the column, a UNIQUE index will be created implicitly.

D. If any index exists on the column, there will be an error as Oracle attempts to create another index implicitly.

12. This statement will fail:

```
create unique bitmap index on employees(department_id,hire_date);
```

Why? (Choose the best answer.)

A. Bitmap indexes cannot be unique.

B. The two columns are of different data types.

C. A bitmap index can be on only one column.

D. There is already a B*Tree index on DEPARTMENT_ID.

13. You have created an index with this statement:

```
create index ename_i on employees(last_name,first_name);
```

How can you adjust the index to include the employees' birthdays, which is a date type column called DOB? (Choose the best answer.)

A. Use ALTER INDEX ENAME_I ADD COLUMN DOB;.

B. You can't do this because of the data type mismatch.

C. You must drop the index and re-create it.

D. This can only be done if the column DOB is NULL in all existing rows.

LAB QUESTION

Figure 12-7 in this chapter shows an entity-relationship diagram for a simple system designed to store and analyze sales. The columns for the fact table SALES are as follows:

- **SALE_ID** System-generated primary key
- **CHANNEL_ID** Foreign key to CHANNELS
- **PRODUCT_ID** Foreign key to PRODUCTS
- **SHOP_ID** Foreign key to SHOPS
- **DAY_ID** Foreign key to DAYS
- **QUANTITY** The quantity of the product sold

It is expected that there will be several million SALES rows per year. The dimension tables are as follows:

PRODUCTS   A list of all products, including price. Cardinality of a few hundred

CHANNEL   Possible sales methods, such as walk-in, Internet, and telephone

SHOPS   Details of all the shops—no more that a couple of dozen

DAYS   Dates for which sales are being stored: 365, identified by day number

Write code to create the tables; create indexes; create constraints. Create sequences to be used for primary keys where necessary. Create some views that will present the data in an easy-to-understand fashion.

SELF TEST ANSWERS

Create Simple and Complex Views

1. ☑ **D, E.** Aggregations and joins make a view complex and make DML impossible.
   ☒ **A, B, C.** Selection and projection or renaming columns does not make the view complex.

2. ☑ **D.** Sad but true. Views do not help performance.
   ☒ **A** is wrong because a view is only a SELECT statement; it doesn't prerun the query. **B** is wrong because the Oracle optimizer will sort out any differences in syntax. **C** is wrong because, although views are precompiled, this doesn't affect the speed of compiling a user's statement.

3. ☑ **C.** The WITH CHECK OPTION will prevent DML that would cause a row to disappear from the view.
   ☒ **A, B, D. A** is wrong because views are by default created read/write. **B** is wrong because the view is a simple view. **D** is wrong because the statement cannot succeed because the check option will reject it.

Retrieve Data from Views

4. ☑ **A.** There is a NOT NULL or PRIMARY KEY constraint on DEPT.DEPTNO.
   ☒ **B, C, D. B** is wrong because constraints are enforced on detail tables, not on views. **C** and **D** are wrong because the error message would be different.

Create Private and Public Synonyms

5. ☑ **B, D.** Public synonyms are not schema objects and so can only be addressed directly. They can have the same names as schema objects.
   ☒ **A, C.** These are wrong because users must be granted privileges on a public synonym before they can see it or select from it.

6. ☑ **B.** The order of priority is to search the schema namespace before the public namespace, so it will be the private synonym (to EMPLOYEES) that will be found.
   ☒ **A, C, D. A** is wrong because a synonym can exist in both the public namespace and the schema namespace. **C** is wrong because the order of priority will find the private synonym first. **D** is wrong because it would not be possible to have a table and a private synonym in the same schema with the same name.

7. ☑ **D.** The synonym will be fine, but the view will be invalid. Oracle will attempt to recompile the view, but this will fail.

☒ **A, B, C, E. A** is wrong because the view will be invalid. **B** is wrong because the FORCE keyword can only be applied when creating a view (and it would still be invalid, even so). **C** is wrong because the synonym will be fine. **E** is wrong because views are not dropped implicitly (unlike indexes and constraints).

Create, Maintain, and Use Sequences

8. ☑ **D.** The default is NOCYCLE, and the sequence cannot advance further.

☒ **A, B, C. A** and **B** are wrong because CYCLE is disabled by default. If it were enabled, the next number issued would be 1 (not zero) because 1 is the default for START WITH. **C** is wrong because under no circumstances will a sequence issue repeating values.

9. ☑ **A.** It is not possible to change the next value of a sequence, so you must re-create it.

☒ **B, C, D. B** is wrong because, while a NOCYCLE sequence can never reissue numbers, there is no reason why a new sequence (with the same name) cannot do so. **C** is wrong because START WITH can only be specified at creation time. **D** is wrong because this will not force an instant cycle; it will only affect what happens when the sequence reaches its MAXVALUE or MINVALUE.

10. ☑ **D.** If the sequence is being used by other sessions, there is no knowing how many increments may have taken place between the first and the second INSERT statements.

☒ **A, B, C.** The answer would be 4, **C**, except that there could have been increments forced by other sessions. **A** and **B** are wrong because the ROLLBACK will not reverse the sequence increments.

Create and Maintain Indexes

11. ☑ **A, B.** Either a UNIQUE or a NONUNIQUE index can be used to enforce a UNIQUE constraint.

☒ **C, D. C** is wrong because there is no need to create another index (in fact, you can't index the same column twice even if you want to). **D** is wrong because if an index exists, Oracle won't attempt to create another.

12. ☑ **A.** The keywords BITMAP and UNIQUE are mutually exclusive. And you wouldn't want to do this, anyway.

☒ **B, C, D. B** and **C** are wrong because a bitmap index can be composite, with columns of different data types. **D** is wrong because the bitmap index is not on DEPARTMENT_ID alone, which would not be possible.

13. ☑ **C.** It is not possible to change an index's columns after creation.
☒ **A, B, D. B** is wrong because the data type is not the problem. **A** and **D** are wrong because an index's columns are fixed at creation time.

LAB ANSWER

This is a possible solution:

```
/*create the tables*/
create table sales (sale_id number, channel_id number, product_id number, shop_id number,
day_id number, quantity number);
create table products (product_id number, pname varchar2(20),price number);
create table channels (channel_id number, cname varchar2(20));
create table shops (shop_id number,address varchar2(20));
create table days (day_id number, day date);
/*pre-create indexes to be used for constraints*/
create unique index prod_pk on products(product_id);
create unique index chan_pk on channels(channel_id);
create unique index shop_pk on shops(shop_id);
create unique index day_id on days(day_id);
create unique index sales_pk on sales(sale_id);
/*create bitmap indexes on the dimension columns of the fact table*/
create bitmap index sales_chan on sales(channel_id);
create bitmap index sales_prod on sales(product_id);
create bitmap index sales_shop on sales(shop_id);
create bitmap index sales_date on sales(day_id);
/*add the primary key constraints/*
alter table products add constraint prod_pk primary key (product_id);
alter table channels add constraint chan_pk primary key (channel_id);
alter table shops add constraint shop_pk primary key (shop_id);
alter table days add constraint day_pk primary key (day_id);
alter table sales add constraint sales_pk primary key(sale_id);
/*add the foreign key constraints*/
alter table sales add constraint sales_prod_fk foreign key (product_id) references products;
alter table sales add constraint sales_chan_fk foreign key (channel_id) references channels;
alter table sales add constraint sales_shop_fk foreign key (shop_id) references shops;
alter table sales add constraint sales_day_fk foreign key (day_id) references days;
/*create the sequences for primary keys:
cache many values for the fact table, but don't pre-issue values for the largely static
```

```
dimension tables. This will save some memory*/
create sequence sales_seq cache 1000;
create sequence product_seq nocache;
create sequence channel_seq nocache;
create sequence shop_seq nocache;
create sequence day_seq nocache;
/*create a view to analyze sales in several dimensions*/
create view sales_analysis as
select cname,pname,address,day,sum(quantity) total
from sales,channels,products,shops,days
where sales.channel_id=channels.channel_id
and sales.product_id=products.product_id
and sales.shop_id=shops.shop_id
and sales.day_id=days.day_id
group by grouping sets(
(cname,pname,address,day),
(address,pname),
(pname,day));
```

A

About the CD

Thehe CD-ROM included with this book comes complete with MasterExam and an electronic version of the book. The software is easy to install on any Windows 98/NT/2000/XP/Vista computer and must be installed to access the MasterExam feature. You may, however, browse the electronic book directly from the CD without installation. To register for a second bonus MasterExam, simply click the Online Training link on the Main Page and follow the directions to the free online registration.

System Requirements

Software requires Windows 98 or higher and Internet Explorer 5.0 or above and 20MB of hard disk space for full installation. The electronic book requires Adobe Acrobat Reader.

Installing and Running MasterExam

If your computer CD-ROM drive is configured to auto run, the CD-ROM will automatically start up upon inserting the disk. From the opening screen you may install MasterExam by pressing the MasterExam button. This will begin the installation process and create a program group named "LearnKey." To run MasterExam, navigate to Start | Programs | LearnKey. If the auto run feature did not launch your CD, browse to the CD and click on the LaunchTraining.exe icon.

MasterExam

MasterExam provides you with a simulation of the actual exam. The number of questions, the type of questions, and the time allowed are intended to be an accurate representation of the exam environment. You have the option to take an open book exam, including hints, references, and answers; a closed book exam; or the timed MasterExam simulation.

When you launch MasterExam, a digital clock display will appear in the upper left-hand corner of your screen. The clock will continue to count down to zero unless you choose to end the exam before the time expires.

Electronic Book

The entire contents of the Study Guide are provided in PDF. Adobe's Acrobat Reader has been included on the CD.

Help

A help file is provided through the help button on the main page in the lower left-hand corner. An individual help feature is also available through MasterExam.

Removing Installation(s)

MasterExam is installed to your hard drive. For *best* results for removal of programs use the Start | Programs | LearnKey | Uninstall options to remove MasterExam.

Technical Support

For questions regarding the technical content of the electronic book or MasterExam, please visit www.osborne.com or e-mail customer.service@mcgraw-hill.com. For customers outside the 50 United States, e-mail international_cs@mcgraw-hill.com.

LearnKey Technical Support

For technical problems with the software (installation, operation, removing installations), please visit www.learnkey.com or e-mail techsupport@learnkey.com.

Glossary

A

ACID   Atomicity, consistency, isolation, and durability. Four characteristics that a relational database must be able to maintain for transactions.

ADDM   Automatic Database Diagnostic Monitor. A tool that generates performance tuning reports based on snapshots in the AWR.

AES   Advanced Encryption Standard. A widely used data encryption method.

AL16UTF16   A Unicode fixed-width 2-byte character set, commonly specified for the NLS character set used for NVARCHAR2, NCHAT, and NCLOB data types.

alias   In Oracle Net, a pointer to a connect string. An alias must be resolved into the address of a listener and the name of a service or instance.

ANSI   American National Standards Institute. A U.S. body that defines a number of standards relevant to computing.

API Application Programming Interface. A defined method for manipulating data, typically implemented as a set of PL/SQL procedures in a package.

ASCII American Standard Code for Information Interchange. A standard (with many variations) for coding letters and other characters as bytes.

ASM Automatic Storage Management. An LVM provided with the Oracle database.

attribute One element of a tuple (aka a column).

AVG A function that divides the sum of a column or expression by the number of nonnull rows in a group.

B

background process A process that is part of the instance: launched at startup.

BFILE A large object data type that is stored as an operating system file. The value in the table column is a pointer to the file.

bind variable A value passed from a user process to a SQL statement at statement execution time.

BLOB Binary Large Object. A LOB data type for binary data, such as photographs and video clips.

block The units of storage into which data files are formatted. The size can be 2KB, 4KB, 8KB, 16KB, 32KB, or 64KB. Some platforms will not permit all these sizes.

C

Cartesian product Sometimes called a cross join. A mathematical term that refers to the set of data created by merging the rows from two or more tables.

CET Central European Time. A time zone used in much of Europe (though not Great Britain) that is one hour ahead of UTC with daylight saving time in effect during the summer months.

character set   The encoding system for representing data within bytes. Different character sets can store different characters and may not be suitable for all languages. Unicode character sets can store any character.

check constraint   A simple rule enforced by the database that restricts the values that can be entered into a column.

client-server architecture   A processing paradigm where the application is divided into client software that interacts with the user and server software that interacts with the data.

CLOB   Character Large Object. A LOB data type for character data, such as text documents, stored in the database character set.

cluster   A hardware environment where more than one computer shares access to storage. A RAC database consists of several instances on several computers opening one database on the shared storage.

cluster segment   A segment that that can contain one or more tables, denormalized into a single structure.

COALESCE   A function that returns the first nonnull value from its parameter list. If all its parameters are null, then a null value is returned.

column   An element of a row: tables are two-dimensional structures, divided horizontally into rows and vertically into columns.

commit   To make permanent a change to data.

complete recovery   Following a restore of damaged database files, this applies each redo to bring the database up to date with no loss of data.

connect identifier   An Oracle Net alias.

connect string   The database connection details needed to establish a session: the address of the listener and the service or instance name.

consistent backup   A backup made while the database is closed.

constraint   A mechanism for enforcing rules on data: that a column value must be unique or may only contain certain values. A primary key constraint specifies that the column must be both unique and not null.

control file   The file containing pointers to the rest of the database, critical sequence information, and the RMAN repository.

CPU   Central Processing Unit. The chip that provides the processing capability of a computer, such as an Intel Pentium or a Sun SPARC.

D

data blocks   The units into which data files are formatted.

data dictionary   The tables owned by SYS in the SYSTEM tablespace that define the database and the objects within it.

data dictionary views   Views on the data dictionary tables that let the DBA investigate the state of the database.

data guard   A facility whereby a copy of the production database is created and updated (possibly in real time) with all changes applied to the production database.

data pump   A facility for transferring large amounts of data at high speed into, out of, or between databases.

database buffer cache   An area of memory in the SGA used for working on blocks copied from data files.

database link   A connection from one database to another, based on a username and password and a connect string.

data file   The disk-based structure for storing data.

DBA   Database Administrator. The person responsible for creating and managing Oracle databases—this could be you.

DBA role A preseeded role provided for backward compatibility that includes all the privileges needed to manage a database, except that needed to start up or shut down.

DBCA The Database Configuration Assistant. A GUI tool for creating, modifying, and dropping instances and databases.

DBMS Database Management System. Often used interchangeably with RDBMS.

DBWn or DBWR The Database Writer. The background process responsible for writing changed blocks from the database buffer cache to the data files. An instance may have up to 10 database writer processes, DBW0 through DBW9.

DDL Data Definition Language. The subset of SQL commands that change object definitions within the data dictionary: CREATE, ALTER, DROP, and TRUNCATE.

deadlock A situation where two sessions block each other, such that neither can do anything. Deadlocks are detected and resolved automatically by the database.

DECODE A function that implements if-then-else conditional logic by testing two terms for equality and returning the third term if they are equal or, optionally, returning some other term if they are not.

direct path A method of I/O on data files that bypasses the database buffer cache.

directory object An Oracle directory: an object within the database that points to an operating system directory.

DML Data Manipulation Language. The subset of SQL commands that change data within the database: INERT, UPDATE, DELETE, and MERGE.

DHCP Dynamic Host Configuration Protocol. The standard for configuring the network characteristics of a computer, such as its IP address, in a changing environment where computers may be moved from one location to another.

DNS Domain Name Service. The TCP mechanism for resolving network names into IP addresses.

domain   The set of values an attribute is allowed to take. Terminology: tables have rows; rows have columns with values. Or: relations have tuples; tuples have attributes with values taken from their domain.

DSS   Decision Support System. A database, such as a data warehouse, optimized for running queries as against OLTP work.

E

easy connect   A method of establishing a session against a database by specifying the address on the listener and the service name without using an Oracle Net alias.

EBCDIC   Extended Binary Coded Decimal Interchange Code. A standard developed by IBM for coding letters and other characters in bytes.

environment variable   A variable set in the operating system shell which can be used by application software and by shell scripts.

equijoin   A join condition using an equality operator.

F

fact table   The central table in a star schema, with columns for values relevant to the row and columns used as foreign keys to the dimension tables.

FGA   Fine Grained Auditing. A facility for tracking user access to data based on the rows that are seen or manipulated.

full backup   A backup containing all blocks of the files backed up, not only those blocks changed since the last backup.

G

GMT   Greenwich Mean Time. Now referred to as UTC, this is the time zone of the meridian through Greenwich Observatory in London.

grid computing   An architecture where the delivery of a service to end users is not tied to certain server resources but can be provided from anywhere in a pool of resources.

GROUP BY   A clause that specifies the grouping attribute rows must have in common for them to be clustered together.

GUI   Graphical User Interface. A layer of an application that lets users work with the application through a graphical terminal, such as a PC with a mouse.

H

HTTP   Hypertext Transfer Protocol. The protocol that enables the World Wide Web (both invented at the European Organization for Nuclear Research in 1989), this is a layered protocol that runs over TCP/IP.

HWM   High water mark. This is the last block of a segment that has ever been used—blocks above this are part of the segment but are not yet formatted for use.

I

I/O   Input/output. The activity of reading from or writing to disks—often the slowest point of a data processing operation.

IBM   International Business Machines. A well known computer hardware, software, and services company.

inconsistent backup   A backup made while the database was open.

INITCAP   A function that accepts a string of characters and returns each word in title case.

incremental backup   A backup containing only blocks that have been changed since the last backup was made.

inner join   When equijoins and nonequijoins are performed, rows from the source and target tables are matched. These are referred to as inner joins.

INSTR   A function that returns the positional location of the nth occurrence of a specified string of characters in a source string.

instance recovery   The automatic repair of damage caused by a disorderly shutdown of the database.

IOT   Index Organized Table. A table type where the rows are stored in the leaf blocks of an index segment.

IP   Internet Protocol. Together with the Transmission Control Protocol, TCP/IP: the de facto standard communication protocol used for client/server communication over a network.

IPC   Interprocess Communications Protocol. The platform-specific protocol, provided by your OS vendor, used for processes running on the same machine to communicate with each other.

ISO   International Organization for Standardization. A group that defines many standards, including SQL.

J

J2EE   Java 2 Enterprise Edition. The standard for developing Java applications.

JOIN...ON   A clause that allows the explicit specification of join columns regardless of their column names. This provides a flexible joining format.

JOIN...USING   A syntax that allows a natural join to be formed on specific columns with shared names.

joining   Involves linking two or more tables based on common attributes. Joining allows data to be stored in third normal form in discrete tables, instead of in one large table.

JVM Java Virtual Machine. The run-time environment needed for running code written in Java. Oracle provides a JVM within the database, and there will be one provided by your operating system.

L

LAST_DAY A function used to obtain the last day in a month given any valid date item.

LDAP Lightweight Directory Access Protocol. The TCP implementation of the X25 directory standard, used by the Oracle Internet Directory for name resolution, security, and authentication. LDAP is also used by other software vendors, including Microsoft and IBM.

LENGTH A function that computes the number of characters in a string including spaces and special characters.

LGWR Log writer. The background process responsible for flushing change vectors from the log buffer in memory to the online redo logfiles on disk.

library cache A memory structure within the shared pool, used for caching SQL statements parsed into their executable form.

listener The server-side process that listens for database connection requests from user processes and launches server processes to establish sessions.

LOB Large Object. A data structure that is too large to store within a table. LOBs (Oracle supports several types) are defined as columns of a table but are physically stored in a separate segment.

log switch The action of closing one online logfile group and opening another; triggered by the LGWR process filling the first group.

LVM Logical Volume Manager. A layer of software that abstracts the physical storage within your computer from the logical storage visible to an application.

M

MMON Manageability Monitor. The background process responsible for gathering performance monitoring information and raising alerts.

MOD The modulus operation, a function that returns the remainder of a division operation.

MONTHS_BETWEEN A function that computes the number of months between two given date parameters and is based on a 31-day month.

mounted database A situation where the instance has opened the database control file but not the online redo logfiles or the data files.

MTBF Mean time between failure. A measure of the average length of running time for a database between unplanned shutdowns.

MTTR Mean time to recover. The average time it takes to make the database available for normal use after a failure.

multiplexing To maintain multiple copies of files.

N

namespace A logical grouping of objects within which no two objects may have the same name.

natural join A join performed using the NATURAL JOIN syntax when the source and target tables are implicitly equijoined using all identically named columns.

NCLOB National Character Large Object. A LOB data type for character data, such as text documents, stored in the alternative national database character set.

NETBEUI NETBIOS Extended User Interface. An enhanced version of NETBIOS.

NETBIOS Network Basic Input Output System. The network communications protocol that was burnt onto the first network card that IBM ever produced.

NLS National Language Support. The capability of the Oracle database to support many linguistic, geographical, and cultural environments—now usually referred to as *globalization*.

node A computer attached to a network.

nonequijoin Performed when the values in the join columns fulfill the join condition based on an inequality expression.

null The absence of a value, indicating that the value is not known, missing, or inapplicable.

NULLIF A function that tests two terms for equality. If they are equal, the function returns null; else it returns the first of the two terms tested.

NVL A function that returns either the original item unchanged or an alternative item if the initial term is null.

NVL2 A function that returns a new if-null item if the original item is null or an alternative if-not-null item if the original term is not null.

O

OC4J Oracle Containers for J2EE. The control structure provided by the Oracle Application Server for running Java programs.

OCA
Oracle Certified Associate.

OCI Oracle Call Interface. An API, published as a set of C libraries, that programmers can use to write user processes that will use an Oracle database.

OCP Oracle Certified Professional. The qualification you are working toward.

ODBC Open Database Connectivity. A standard developed by Microsoft for communicating with relational databases. Oracle provides an ODBC driver that will allow clients running Microsoft products to connect to an Oracle database.

offline backup A backup made while the database is closed.

OLAP Online Analytical Processing. Select intensive work involving running queries against a (usually) large database. Oracle provides OLAP capabilities as an option, in addition to the standard query facilities.

OLTP Online Transaction Processing. A pattern of activity within a database typified by a large number of small, short, transactions.

online backup A backup made while the database is open.

online redo log The files to which change vectors are streamed by the LGWR.

OS Operating system. Typically, in the Oracle environment, this will be a version of Unix (perhaps Linux) or Microsoft Windows.

Oracle Net Oracle's proprietary communications protocol, layered on top of an industry standard protocol.

ORACLE_BASE The root directory into which Oracle products are installed.

ORACLE_HOME The root directory of any one Oracle product.

outer join A join performed when rows, which are not retrieved by an inner join, are included for retrieval.

P

parse An action that converts SQL statements into a form suitable for execution.

PGA Program Global Area. The variable sized block of memory used to maintain the state of a database session. PGAs are private to the session and controlled by the session's server process.

PL/SQL Procedural Language/Structured Query Language. Oracle's proprietary programming language, which combines procedural constructs, such as flow control, and user interface capabilities with SQL.

PMON Process Monitor. The background process responsible for monitoring the state of user's sessions against an instance.

primary key The column (or combination of columns) whose value(s) can be used to identify each row in a table.

projection The restriction of columns selected from a table. Using projection, you retrieve only the columns of interest and not every possible column.

R

RAC Real Application Clusters. Oracle's clustering technology, which allows several instances in different machines to open the same database for scalability, performance, and fault tolerance.

RAID Redundant Array of Inexpensive Disks. Techniques for enhancing performance and/or fault tolerance by using a volume manager to present a number of physical disks to the operating system as a single logical disk.

raw device An unformatted disk or disk partition.

RDBMS Relational Database Management System. Often used interchangeably with DBMS.

RAM Random Access Memory. The chips that make up the real memory in your computer hardware, as opposed to the virtual memory presented to software by the operating system.

referential integrity A rule defined on a table specifying that the values in a column (or columns) must map onto those of a row in another table.

relation A two-dimensional structure consisting of tuples with attributes (aka a table).

REPLACE A function that substitutes each occurrence of a search item in the source string with a replacement term and returns the modified source string.

RMAN   Recovery Manager. Oracle's backup and recovery tool.

rowid   The unique identifier of every row in the database, used as a pointer to the physical location of the row.

S

schema   The objects owned by a database user.

SCN   System Change Number. The continually incrementing number used to track the sequence and exact time of all events within a database.

segment   A database object, within a schema, that stores data.

selection   The extraction of rows from a table. Selection includes the further restriction of the extracted rows based on various criteria or conditions. This allows you to retrieve only the rows that are of interest and not every row in the table.

self-join   A join required when the join columns originate from the same table. Conceptually, the source table is duplicated and a target table is created. The self-join then works as a regular join between two discrete tables.

sequence   A database object, within a schema, that can generate consecutive numbers.

service name   A logical name registered by an instance with a listener, which can be specified by a user process when it issues a connect request.

session   A user process and a server process, connected to the instance.

SGA   System Global Area. The block of shared memory that contains the memory structures that make up an Oracle instance.

SID   (1) System Identifier. The name of an instance, which must be unique on the computer the instance is running on. (2) Session Identifier. The number used to identify uniquely a session logged on to an Oracle instance.

SMON   System Monitor. The background process responsible for opening a database and monitoring the instance.

spfile   Server parameter file. The file containing the parameters used to build an instance in memory.

SQL   Structured Query Language. An international standard language for extracting data from and manipulating data in relational databases.

SSL   Secure Sockets Layer. A standard for securing data transmission, using encryption, checksumming, and digital certificates.

SUBSTR   A function that extracts and returns a segment from a given source string.

SUM   A function that returns an aggregated total of all the nonnull numeric expression values in a group.

synonym   An alternative name for a database object.

sysdba   The privilege that lets a user connect with operating system or password file authentication and create, start up, and shut down a database.

sysoper   The privilege that lets a user connect with operating system or password file authentication and start up and shut down (but not create) a database.

system   A preseeded schema used for database administration purposes.

T

table   A logical two-dimensional data storage structure, consisting of rows and columns.

tablespace   The logical structure that abstracts logical data storage in tables from physical data storage in data files.

TCP   Transmission Control Protocol. Together with the Internet Protocol, TCP/IP: the de facto standard communication protocol used for client/server communication over a network.

TCPS   TCP with SSL. The secure sockets version of TCP.

tempfile   The physical storage that makes up a temporary tablespace, used for storing temporary segments.

TNS   Transparent Network Substrate. The heart of Oracle Net, a proprietary layered protocol running on top of whatever underlying network transport protocol you choose to use—probably TCP/IP.

TO_CHAR   A function that performs date-to-character and number-to-character data type conversions.

TO_DATE   A function that explicitly transforms character items into date values.

TO_NUMBER   A function that changes character items into number values.

transaction   A logical unit of work that will complete in total or not at all.

tuple   A one-dimensional structure consisting of attributes (aka a row).

U

UGA   User Global Area. That part of the PGA that is stored in the SGA for sessions running through shared servers.

UI   User interface. The layer of an application that communicates with end users—nowadays, frequently graphical: a GUI.

URL   Uniform Resource Locator. A standard for specifying the location of an object on the Internet consisting of a protocol, a host name and domain, an IP port number, a path and filename, and a series of parameters.

UTC   Coordinated Universal Time. Previously known as Greenwich Mean Time (GMT), UTC is the global standard time zone; all others relate to it as offsets, ahead or behind.

X

X-Windows   The standard GUI environment used on most computers, except those that run Microsoft Windows.

XML   Extensible Markup Language. A standard for data interchange using documents, where the format of the data is defined by tags within the document.

INDEX

D

U

What do *you* know?

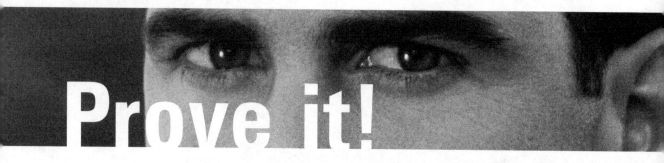

Prove it!

Use the Interactive Study Tools on the enclosed CD from LearnKey!

You will:

- Discover strengths and weaknesses in your comprehension of test objectives
- Build knowledge and confidence for optimal performance on test day
- Practice using the same types of questions and scenarios you'll see on the exam
- Focus your studies on critical topics
- Gauge your readiness to take certification exams

PLUS! ## Special LearnKey Training Discounts for Osborne Customers!

Because you purchased an Osborne Study Guide with an integrated testing CD, you are entitled to incredible savings on LearnKey training courses.

Save up to 60% on LearnKey multi-media Training!

- **Media-rich Courseware**
- **Motivating Instruction**
- **Challenging Labs**
- **Reference Material**
- **Practical & Proven**

Limited Time Offer - DON'T DELAY

Visit us at learnkey.com/osborne TODAY!

1.800.865.0165 • learnkey.com/osborne

 **LearnKey**

© 2006 LearnKey, Inc.   LK022102

GET YOUR FREE SUBSCRIPTION
TO ORACLE MAGAZINE

Oracle Magazine is essential gear for today's information technology professionals. Stay informed and increase your productivity with every issue of *Oracle Magazine*. Inside each free bimonthly issue you'll get:

- Up-to-date information on Oracle Database, Oracle Application Server, Web development, enterprise grid computing, database technology, and business trends
- Third-party vendor news and announcements
- Technical articles on Oracle and partner products, technologies, and operating environments
- Development and administration tips
- Real-world customer stories

IF THERE ARE OTHER ORACLE USERS AT YOUR LOCATION WHO WOULD LIKE TO RECEIVE THEIR OWN SUBSCRIPTION TO ORACLE MAGAZINE, PLEASE PHOTOCOPY THIS FORM AND PASS IT ALONG.

Three easy ways to subscribe:

① Web
Visit our Web site at otn.oracle.com/oraclemagazine. You'll find a subscription form there, plus much more!

② Fax
Complete the questionnaire on the back of this card and fax the questionnaire side only to +1.847.763.9638.

③ Mail
Complete the questionnaire on the back of this card and mail it to P.O. Box 1263, Skokie, IL 60076-8263

ORACLE®

FREE SUBSCRIPTION

○ **Yes, please send me a FREE subscription to *Oracle Magazine*.**   ○ **NO**

To receive a free subscription to *Oracle Magazine*, you must fill out the entire card, sign it, and date it (incomplete cards cannot be processed or acknowledged). You can also fax your application to +1.847.763.9638.
Or subscribe at our Web site at otn.oracle.com/oraclemagazine

○ From time to time, Oracle Publishing allows our partners exclusive access to our e-mail addresses for special promotions and announcements. To be included in this program, please check this circle.

○ Oracle Publishing allows sharing of our mailing list with selected third parties. If you prefer your mailing address not to be included in this program, please check here. If at any time you would like to be removed from this mailing list, please contact Customer Service at +1.847.647.9630 or send an e-mail to oracle@halldata.com.

signature (required)   date

X

name   title

company   e-mail address

street/p.o. box

city/state/zip or postal code   telephone

country   fax

YOU MUST ANSWER ALL TEN QUESTIONS BELOW.

① WHAT IS THE PRIMARY BUSINESS ACTIVITY OF YOUR FIRM AT THIS LOCATION? (check one only)
- ☐ 01 Aerospace and Defense Manufacturing
- ☐ 02 Application Service Provider
- ☐ 03 Automotive Manufacturing
- ☐ 04 Chemicals, Oil and Gas
- ☐ 05 Communications and Media
- ☐ 06 Construction/Engineering
- ☐ 07 Consumer Sector/Consumer Packaged Goods
- ☐ 08 Education
- ☐ 09 Financial Services/Insurance
- ☐ 10 Government (civil)
- ☐ 11 Government (military)
- ☐ 12 Healthcare
- ☐ 13 High Technology Manufacturing, OEM
- ☐ 14 Integrated Software Vendor
- ☐ 15 Life Sciences (Biotech, Pharmaceuticals)
- ☐ 16 Mining
- ☐ 17 Retail/Wholesale/Distribution
- ☐ 18 Systems Integrator, VAR/VAD
- ☐ 19 Telecommunications
- ☐ 20 Travel and Transportation
- ☐ 21 Utilities (electric, gas, sanitation, water)
- ☐ 98 Other Business and Services

② WHICH OF THE FOLLOWING BEST DESCRIBES YOUR PRIMARY JOB FUNCTION? (check one only)
Corporate Management/Staff
- ☐ 01 Executive Management (President, Chair, CEO, CFO, Owner, Partner, Principal)
- ☐ 02 Finance/Administrative Management (VP/Director/ Manager/Controller, Purchasing, Administration)
- ☐ 03 Sales/Marketing Management (VP/Director/Manager)
- ☐ 04 Computer Systems/Operations Management (CIO/VP/Director/ Manager MIS, Operations)
IS/IT Staff
- ☐ 05 Systems Development/ Programming Management
- ☐ 06 Systems Development/ Programming Staff
- ☐ 07 Consulting
- ☐ 08 DBA/Systems Administrator
- ☐ 09 Education/Training
- ☐ 10 Technical Support Director/Manager
- ☐ 11 Other Technical Management/Staff
- ☐ 98 Other

③ WHAT IS YOUR CURRENT PRIMARY OPERATING PLATFORM? (select all that apply)
- ☐ 01 Digital Equipment UNIX
- ☐ 02 Digital Equipment VAX VMS
- ☐ 03 HP UNIX
- ☐ 04 IBM AIX
- ☐ 05 IBM UNIX
- ☐ 06 Java
- ☐ 07 Linux
- ☐ 08 Macintosh
- ☐ 09 MS-DOS
- ☐ 10 MVS
- ☐ 11 NetWare
- ☐ 12 Network Computing
- ☐ 13 OpenVMS
- ☐ 14 SCO UNIX
- ☐ 15 Sequent DYNIX/ptx
- ☐ 16 Sun Solaris/SunOS
- ☐ 17 SVR4
- ☐ 18 UnixWare
- ☐ 19 Windows
- ☐ 20 Windows NT
- ☐ 21 Other UNIX
- ☐ 98 Other
- 99 ☐ None of the above

④ DO YOU EVALUATE, SPECIFY, RECOMMEND, OR AUTHORIZE THE PURCHASE OF ANY OF THE FOLLOWING? (check all that apply)
- ☐ 01 Hardware
- ☐ 02 Software
- ☐ 03 Application Development Tools
- ☐ 04 Database Products
- ☐ 05 Internet or Intranet Products
- 99 ☐ None of the above

⑤ IN YOUR JOB, DO YOU USE OR PLAN TO PURCHASE ANY OF THE FOLLOWING PRODUCTS? (check all that apply)
Software
- ☐ 01 Business Graphics
- ☐ 02 CAD/CAE/CAM
- ☐ 03 CASE
- ☐ 04 Communications
- ☐ 05 Database Management
- ☐ 06 File Management
- ☐ 07 Finance
- ☐ 08 Java
- ☐ 09 Materials Resource Planning
- ☐ 10 Multimedia Authoring
- ☐ 11 Networking
- ☐ 12 Office Automation
- ☐ 13 Order Entry/Inventory Control
- ☐ 14 Programming
- ☐ 15 Project Management
- ☐ 16 Scientific and Engineering
- ☐ 17 Spreadsheets
- ☐ 18 Systems Management
- ☐ 19 Workflow

Hardware
- ☐ 20 Macintosh
- ☐ 21 Mainframe
- ☐ 22 Massively Parallel Processing
- ☐ 23 Minicomputer
- ☐ 24 PC
- ☐ 25 Network Computer
- ☐ 26 Symmetric Multiprocessing
- ☐ 27 Workstation
Peripherals
- ☐ 28 Bridges/Routers/Hubs/Gateways
- ☐ 29 CD-ROM Drives
- ☐ 30 Disk Drives/Subsystems
- ☐ 31 Modems
- ☐ 32 Tape Drives/Subsystems
- ☐ 33 Video Boards/Multimedia
Services
- ☐ 34 Application Service Provider
- ☐ 35 Consulting
- ☐ 36 Education/Training
- ☐ 37 Maintenance
- ☐ 38 Online Database Services
- ☐ 39 Support
- ☐ 40 Technology-Based Training
- ☐ 98 Other
- 99 ☐ None of the above

⑥ WHAT ORACLE PRODUCTS ARE IN USE AT YOUR SITE? (check all that apply)
Oracle E-Business Suite
- ☐ 01 Oracle Marketing
- ☐ 02 Oracle Sales
- ☐ 03 Oracle Order Fulfillment
- ☐ 04 Oracle Supply Chain Management
- ☐ 05 Oracle Procurement
- ☐ 06 Oracle Manufacturing
- ☐ 07 Oracle Maintenance Management
- ☐ 08 Oracle Service
- ☐ 09 Oracle Contracts
- ☐ 10 Oracle Projects
- ☐ 11 Oracle Financials
- ☐ 12 Oracle Human Resources
- ☐ 13 Oracle Interaction Center
- ☐ 14 Oracle Communications/Utilities (modules)
- ☐ 15 Oracle Public Sector/University (modules)
- ☐ 16 Oracle Financial Services (modules)
Server/Software
- ☐ 17 Oracle9*i*
- ☐ 18 Oracle9*i* Lite
- ☐ 19 Oracle8*i*
- ☐ 20 Other Oracle database
- ☐ 21 Oracle9*i* Application Server
- ☐ 22 Oracle9*i* Application Server Wireless
- ☐ 23 Oracle Small Business Suite

Tools
- ☐ 24 Oracle Developer Suite
- ☐ 25 Oracle Discoverer
- ☐ 26 Oracle JDeveloper
- ☐ 27 Oracle Migration Workbench
- ☐ 28 Oracle9*i* AS Portal
- ☐ 29 Oracle Warehouse Builder
Oracle Services
- ☐ 30 Oracle Outsourcing
- ☐ 31 Oracle Consulting
- ☐ 32 Oracle Education
- ☐ 33 Oracle Support
- ☐ 98 Other
- 99 ☐ None of the above

⑦ WHAT OTHER DATABASE PRODUCTS ARE IN USE AT YOUR SITE? (check all that apply)
- ☐ 01 Access   ☐ 08 Microsoft Access
- ☐ 02 Baan   ☐ 09 Microsoft SQL Server
- ☐ 03 dbase   ☐ 10 PeopleSoft
- ☐ 04 Gupta   ☐ 11 Progress
- ☐ 05 IBM DB2   ☐ 12 SAP
- ☐ 06 Informix   ☐ 13 Sybase
- ☐ 07 Ingres   ☐ 14 VSAM
- ☐ 98 Other
- 99 ☐ None of the above

⑧ WHAT OTHER APPLICATION SERVER PRODUCTS ARE IN USE AT YOUR SITE? (check all that apply)
- ☐ 01 BEA
- ☐ 02 IBM
- ☐ 03 Sybase
- ☐ 04 Sun
- ☐ 05 Other

⑨ DURING THE NEXT 12 MONTHS, HOW MUCH DO YOU ANTICIPATE YOUR ORGANIZATION WILL SPEND ON COMPUTER HARDWARE, SOFTWARE, PERIPHERALS, AND SERVICES FOR YOUR LOCATION? (check only one)
- ☐ 01 Less than $10,000
- ☐ 02 $10,000 to $49,999
- ☐ 03 $50,000 to $99,999
- ☐ 04 $100,000 to $499,999
- ☐ 05 $500,000 to $999,999
- ☐ 06 $1,000,000 and over

⑩ WHAT IS YOUR COMPANY'S YEARLY SALES REVENUE? (please choose one)
- ☐ 01 $500, 000, 000 and above
- ☐ 02 $100, 000, 000 to $500, 000, 000
- ☐ 03 $50, 000, 000 to $100, 000, 000
- ☐ 04 $5, 000, 000 to $50, 000, 000
- ☐ 05 $1, 000, 000 to $5, 000, 000

100103